MINUTES

OF THE

PHILADELPHIA BAPTIST ASSOCIATION

A. D. GILLETTE
1807-1882

MINUTES

OF THE

PHILADELPHIA BAPTIST ASSOCIATION,

FROM

A. D. 1707, TO A. D. 1807;

BEING THE FIRST

ONE HUNDRED YEARS

OF ITS EXISTENCE.

EDITED BY A. D. GILLETTE, A. M.

PASTOR OF THE ELEVENTH BAPTIST CHURCH, PHILADELPHIA.

PHILADELPHIA:
AMERICAN BAPTIST PUBLICATION SOCIETY,
118 ARCH STREET.
1851.

he Baptist Standard Bearer, Inc.
NUMBER ONE IRON OAKS DRIVE • PARIS, ARKANSAS 72855

Thou hast given a *standard* to them that fear thee;
that it may be displayed because of the truth.
-- *Psalm 60:4*

Reprinted by

THE BAPTIST STANDARD BEARER, INC.
No. 1 Iron Oaks Drive
Paris, Arkansas 72855
(501) 963-3831

THE WALDENSIAN EMBLEM
lux lucet in tenebris
"The Light Shineth in the Darkness"

ISBN #1-57978-900-5

NOTICE.

At its 136th Anniversary, in 1843, the Philadelphia Baptist Association appointed a Committee to collect its early Minutes for publication. Efforts were immediately commenced, and have been sedulously followed up, till now, it is believed, we have all that can be procured.

At the meeting of the Association, in 1846, A. D. Gillette, Chairman of the Committee reported, "That through the kindness of Mrs. Harris, daughter of Samuel Jones, D. D.; Thomas Shields, since deceased, and others, we have obtained Minutes of various Sessions entire, as early as 1729. Deficiencies can be generally supplied of antecedent Sessions from the origin of the body, 1707, from a book kept with great care, by order of the Association. In 1777, there are no Minutes, the Association not having met that year, on account of the occupancy of Philadelphia by the British army.

"The Association ordered that the Minutes for the first Century, with Dr. S. Jones' Centennial Sermon, be published, believing that they contain matters of great value to the churches. The Circular Letters, especially, are a fund of rich theology."

At a meeting of the Committee, H. G. Jones, D. D., was requested to prepare a preface, and A. D. Gillette was appointed Editor, with instructions to preserve, as far as possible, the ancient style of composition, as found in the original Minutes.

HORATIO G. JONES,
HOWARD MALCOM,
A. D. GILLETTE,
WILSON JEWELL,
JOSEPH TAYLOR,
WM. SHADRACH,
} *Committee.*

Philadelphia, May, 1851.

Entered, according to Act of Congress, in the year 1851, by the
AMERICAN BAPTIST PUBLICATION SOCIETY,
In the Clerk's Office of the District Court of the United States, in and for the Eastern District of Pennsylvania.

STEREOTYPED BY GEORGE CHARLES.
PRINTED BY KING & BAIRD.

Sicut lilium inter spinas sic amica mea inter filias

On The Cover: We use the symbol of the "lily among the thorns" from Song of Solomon 2:2 to represent the Baptist History Series. The Latin, *Sicut lilium inter spinas sic amica mea inter filias*, translates, "As the lily among thorns, so is my love among the daughters."

Contents.

	PAGE
Early history of the Church at Lower Dublin,	11
the Church at Piscataqua,	13
the Church at Middletown,	13
the Church at Cohansie,	14
the Church at the Welsh Tract,	15
the Church at the Great Valley,	16
the Church at Cape May,	16
the Church at Hopewell,	17
the Church near Brandywine,	18
the Church at Montgomery,	19
the Church at Bethlehem,	20
the Church at Southampton,	20
the Church at Cranberry,	21
the Church at Philadelphia,	21
the Church at Morristown,	22
the Church at Scotch Plains,	22
the Church at Rocksberry,	23
the Church at Oyster Bay,	23
the Church at Tolpehokin,	23
First meeting of the Association, 1707,	25
Regulations for its government,	25
Arrival of Ministers in 1710,	25
Meeting of 1712,	26
Improper conduct of Thomas Selby,	26
Attention to the subject of the Ministry, 1722,	27
Query from Brandywine, and regulations on the Ministry, in 1723,	27
Queries on the Fourth Commandment on marriage, and on Church officers, 1724,	27
Proceedings of 1725—Query on divisions,	28
Meeting of 1727—Query on marriage,	28
Meeting of 1728—Query on Ruling Elders and on dismissions,	29
Meeting of 1729—first Circular Letter on Christian Duties—Query on laying on of hands,	29
Meeting of 1730—Query on Seventh-day Baptists—on spending the Sabbath, and on general meetings,	31
Meeting of 1731—Circular Letter on the State of Religion—Meeting house at Philadelphia,	31
Meeting of 1732—Query on Baptism—Great want of Ministers,	33
Meeting of 1733—Circular Letter—Prayer for an increase of Ministers,	33
Meeting of 1734—Circular Letter—Christian duties—Queries on Ministers of other denominations, on the proper conduct of meetings, and on worshiping with other bodies of Christians—Improper conduct of W. Davis,	34
Meeting of 1735—Circular Letter—State of Religion—Queries on contentious members, and on members uniting with distant Churches,	36
Meeting of 1736—Visiters appointed to Montgomery,	38
Meeting of 1737—Character of Letter,	38
Meeting of 1738—Circular Letter—Exhortation to Christian Duties—Query on laying on of hands—Supply of Catechisms,	39
Meeting of 1739—Circular Letter on Christian Duties—Queries on absence from communion, and on changes of the Association,	40

CONTENTS.

	PAGE
Meeting of 1740—Circular Letter—Christian exhortations—Queries on Baptism and Church fellowship,	42
Meeting of 1741—Circular Letter—Christian duties—Queries on Church duties,	44
Meeting of 1742—Circular Letter—State of the Churches—Reprinting Confession of Faith,	46
Meeting of 1743—Circular Letter on the State of Religion—Differences at Montgomery—Opposition to error—Confession of Faith,	47
Meeting of 1744—Query on Ordination—Visiters sent to Montgomery,	49
Meeting of 1745—Proceedings,	49
Meeting of 1746—Circular Letter on Christian Duties—Queries on preaching before ordination—on Ruling Elders—on women voting in the Church---on the communion of Churches, and on the character of members of the Association—Collection of Statistics,	49
Meeting of 1747—Circular Letter on Christian Duties—Query on preaching and communion—other proceedings,	55
Meeting of 1748—Circular Letter—Christian Exhortation—Queries on God's foreknowledge of evil—Censure of erroneous teachers, and on communion with polygamists,	57
Meeting of 1749—Circular Letter on the Duties of Christians—Queries on party-spirit in Churches, and on baptism by an unordained Minister—Essay on the Power and Duty of an Association, by Rev. Benjamin Griffith,	59
Meeting of 1750—Circular Letter on Christian Exhortation—Query on Church censure—Association fund,	64
Meeting of 1751—Circular Letter on Christian Duties,	66
Meeting of 1752—Circular Letter—State of the Churches—Query on the denial of the doctrine of Election, &c.,	67
Meeting of 1753—Circular Letter on Exhortation to Duties—Queries on the Assurance of Faith, and on Seventh-day Baptists,	70
Meeting of 1754—Circular Letter on Christian Duties—Day of humiliation and prayer,	70
Meeting of 1755—Circular Letter on Christian Exhortation—other proceedings,	71
Meeting of 1756—Circular Letter on Christian Duties—Query on marriage—Establishment of Grammar School—other proceedings,	73
Meeting of 1757—Circular Letter on the State of the Churches—other proceedings.	76
Meeting of 1758—Circular Letter—Exhortation to Christian Duties—Quarterly fasts—other proceedings,	76
Meeting of 1759—Circular Letter on Christian Duties—other proceedings,	78
Meeting of 1760—Circular Letter on Christian Duties and Privileges—other proceedings,	79
Meeting of 1761—Memorial from Dividing Creek—Queries on the Scriptures and Holy Spirit, and on God's pre-ordination—Pastoral Address by Rev. P. P. Vanhorne—Letter to Board in London—Statistics of the Churches,	81
Meeting of 1762—Proceedings—Pastoral Address, by Rev. S. Jones, A. B.—Statistics,	86
Meeting of 1763—Proceedings—Queries on the examination of candidates for baptism, and public excommunications—Pastoral Address, by Rev. Isaac Stelle—Statistics,	89
Meeting of 1764—Proceedings—Charter given to Rhode Island College—Pastoral Letter on Original State of the Churches—Statistics,	91
Meeting of 1765—Proceedings—Query on Baptism—Pastoral Address, by Rev. John Sutton—Statistics,	94
Meeting of 1766—Proceedings—Pastoral Address, by Rev. Abel Griffiths—Statistics,	98
Meeting of 1767—Proceedings—Queries on the right of excommunicated members—on dissatisfaction with a Minister—Marrying a first wife's sister—Pastoral Address, by Rev. Isaac Sutton—Statistics,	100
Meeting of 1768—Proceedings—Query on Baptism by an unordained Minister—Pastoral Address, by Rev. Isaac Stelle—Statistics,	104
Meeting of 1769—Proceedings—Rhode Island College—Query on family worship—Pastoral Address, by Rev. Abel Griffiths—Statistics,	107

CONTENTS.　　　　　　　　　　　　v

PAGE

Meeting of 1770—Proceedings—Pastoral Address by Rev. I. Stelle—Letters from New England—Statistics, ... 113
Meeting of 1771—Proceedings—Queries on members of disbanded Churches—Washing the Saint's feet—Pastoral Address, by Rev. Messrs. Griffiths, Blackwell and Vanhorne—Statistics, ... 118
Meeting of 1772—Proceedings—Ordination of Rev. I. Skillman—Pastoral Address—Statistics, ... 123
Meeting of 1773—Proceedings—Washing the Saint's feet—Pastoral Letter, by Messrs. Rogers and Vanhorne—Statistics, ... 128
Meeting of May, 1774, at New York—Proceedings—Circular Letter on the Holy Scriptures, by the Rev. Abel Morgan—Statistics, . . . 135
Meeting of October, 1774, at Philadelphia—Proceedings—Circular Letter on the Trinity, by Rev. Samuel Jones—Statistics, ... 140
Meeting of 1775—Proceedings—Circular Letter, by Rev. Abel Morgan, on the Divine Decrees—Statistics, ... 150
Meeting of 1776—Days of humiliation and prayer, on account of the state of the country—other proceedings—Circular Letter on Christian Duties, by Rev. Robert Kelsay—Statistics, ... 155
Meeting of 1778—Days of humiliation and prayer, on account of the state of the country—other proceedings—Circular Letter, by Rev. Samuel Jones—Duties of the Times, ... 159
Meeting of 1779—Proceedings—Circular Letter on Divine Providence, by Rev. Samuel Jones—and on Fasting and Prayer, by Rev. Abel Morgan, . 163
Meeting of 1780—Proceedings—Circular Letter on the Fall of Man, by Rev. Abel Morgan, ... 169
Meeting of 1781—Proceedings—Circular Letter on God's Covenant, by Rev. Samuel Jones—Statistics, ... 173
Meeting of 1782—Proceedings—Circular Letter on the Mediation of Christ, by Rev. Oliver Hart—Statistics, ... 180
Meeting of 1783—Proceedings—Query on laying hands on the baptized—Circular Letter on the Freedom of the Will, by Rev. Samuel Jones, A. M.—Statistics, ... 192
Meeting of 1784—Proceedings—Queries as to Christ being the object of prayer—Duty to a Church which receives unbaptized persons—Circular Letter on Effectual Calling, by Rev. John Gano—Statistics, . . . 199
Meeting of 1785—Proceedings—Circular Letter on Justification, by Rev. William Rogers—Statistics, ... 205
Meeting of 1786—Proceedings—Query on the administration of the Lord's Supper, by others than a Church—Circular Letter on Adoption, by Rev. Thomas Ustick—Statistics, ... 217
Meeting of 1787—Proceedings—Queries on a member declining communion—on baptism of a seperated husband and wife, and on regular baptisms—Circular Letter on Sanctification, by Rev. P. P Vanhorne—Statistics, . 227
Meeting of 1788—Proceedings—Queries on the belief of general redemption—Validity of regular baptisms—Circular Letter on Saving Faith, by Rev. David Jones—Statistics 236
Meeting of 1789—Proceedings—Circular Letter on Repentance unto Life, by Rev. Burgiss Allison—Statistics, ... 246
Meeting of 1790—Proceedings—Query on the preaching of a reclaimed Minister—Circular Letters on the Errors of Universal Salvation, by Rev. Samuel Jones, D. D., and on Good Works, by Rev. Benjamin Foster—Statistics—View of Baptist Associations in the United States, . . . 254
Meeting of 1791—Proceedings—Circular Letter on the Perseverance of the Saints, by Rev. William Vanhorne—Statistics, . . . 270
Meeting of 1792—Proceedings—Queries on marriage with a nephew—on the validity of irregular baptisms—on the words Bishop and Elder—on washing the saints' feet—on testimony of members' wives in disputed cases, and on the jurisdiction of councils—Circular Letter on Assurance, by Rev. Joshua Jones—Statistics, ... 281
Meeting of 1793—Proceedings—Circular Letter on Christian Duties, by Rev. Thomas Fleeson—Statistics, ... 292

CONTENTS.

	PAGE
Meeting of 1794—Proceedings—Queries on alteration of the Catechism—on the reception of dismissed members, and on the evidence of a non-member—Circular Letter on the Law of God, by Rev. Henry Smalley, A. M.—Statistics,	296
Meeting of 1795—Proceedings—Queries on a day of humiliation and prayer—General concert of prayer—the emigration of members—Re-printing an English Circular Letter—Amendments to the Catechism—Circular Letter on the Gospel, by Rev. Samuel Jones, D. D.—Statistics,	305
Meeting of 1796—Proceedings—Circular Letter on Fidelity, by Rev. W. Staughton—Statistics—Deaths,	316
Meeting of 1797—Proceedings—Circular Letter on Christian Liberty and Liberty of Conscience, by Rev. Thomas Memminger—Statistics—Addenda on Baptist Grammar School,	324
Meeting of 1798—Proceedings—Circular Letter on Religious Worship and the Sabbath Day, by Rev. David Jones, A. M.—Statistics,	333
Meeting of 1799—Proceedings—Circular Letter on General Christian Duties, by Rev. Samuel Jones, D. D.—Statistics,	341
Meeting of 1800—Proceedings—Query on establishing a Missionary Society—Circular Letter on the Divine Origin of the Gospel, by the Rev. W. Staughton—Statistics,	348
Meeting of 1801—Proceedings—Query on the independence of the Churches—Circular Letter on the Events of the last Century, by Rev. James Ewing—Statistics,	358
Meeting of 1802—Proceedings—Plan of a Committee of Correspondence—Circular Letter on the Baptism of the Holy Ghost, by Rev. T. B. Montanye—Statistics,	369
Meeting of 1803—Proceedings—Query on the choice of a Moderator—Circular Letter on the Work of the Holy Spirit, by Rev. William White—Statistics—Deaths,	379
Meeting of 1804—Proceedings—Query on Committee reporting to the body—Circular Letter on Prayer, by Rev. Burgiss Allison—Statistics—Deaths,	394
Meeting of 1805—Proceedings—Queries on the baptism of the Holy Ghost—Report of the Secretary—Circular Letter on Brotherly Love, by Rev. Silas Hough—Statistics,	409
Meeting of 1806—Proceedings—Queries on the Rules of Discipline—on the number of members necessary to form a Church, and on irregular baptisms—Report of Corresponding Committee—Circular Letter on Christian Missions, by Rev. W. Rogers—Death—Statistics,	421
Meeting of 1807—Proceedings—Queries on the revision of the Rules of Discipline—on the distribution of the Library, and on the celebration of marriage by an excommunicated Minister—Circular Letter on the Qualifications of a Gospel Minister, by Rev. W. Staughton—Statistics—Deaths,	437
CENTURY SERMON BY SAMUEL JONES, D. D.,	451

Preface.

The Philadelphia Association originated with churches planted by members from Wales. Attracted by the freedom of religious opinion established by Penn, they purchased and settled large tracts of land as early as 1683. Hence the Welsh names so common in Eastern Pennsylvania, such as Trediffrun, Uchland, Radnor, Merion, &c. Many of the descendants of these most excellent people remain in these parts to this day.

The first Baptist church in Pennsylvania, permanently planted, is believed to be that at Pennepek, a few miles north of the city. One had existed feebly at Coldspring, in Bucks County, for a short period, of which the father of the celebrated Dr. Benjamin Rush is supposed to have been a member. His remains, with a headstone, lie in the burial ground of this church, long since disused. The Welsh tract church, now in Delaware, was next founded. Soon after, churches arose at Middletown, Piscataqua and Cohansie, in New Jersey, and then followed the constitution of the Philadelphia Association, embracing the churches given in the following record:—

This Association has maintained, from its origin, a prominent and important standing in the denomination. It has been favored with the services of many distinguished ministers — men of eminent piety, solid judgment and finished education. Among these are found the names of Morgan Edwards, Abel Morgan, John Gano, Samuel Jones, David Jones, Keach, Griffith, Rogers, Ustic, Holcombe, Staughton, Brantly, and others, who have gloriously fought the good fight.

In every period of its existence the Association has firmly maintained the soundest form of Scripture doctrine; nor could any church have been admitted, at any period, which denied or concealed any of the doctrines of grace. The New Testament has always been its only rule of faith and practice, as with all Baptists. To let the world know how we understand the teachings of the Holy Ghost in these inspired books, the Association published, in 1742, its Confession of faith and discipline. This is in substance the same as that of the ancient Baptists in Poland and Bohemia; and of the Mennonites in Holland, and the early English and Welsh churches. This confession was published by ministers and brethren, representing about forty churches, met in London, in 1689. It was printed for the Philadelphia Association by Benjamin Franklin, and numerous editions have since been issued. Throughout the United States it is generally considered as the standard of orthodoxy among Baptists. It differs but slightly from the Westminster confession of faith published by "the Assembly of Divines."

By the formation of new churches, this Association extended over Virginia and New York, embracing a distance of about 400 miles, and including, on the North, the church at Amenia, Dutchess Co., N. Y., and Horseneck in Greenwich, Connecticut, on the East; and on the South, Ketockton in Virginia. The multiplication of churches caused the formation of the Ketockton, Baltimore, Salisbury and Delaware Associations, on the South; the Shaftesbury, Warren, Warwick, and New York Associations, on the North; the New Jersey, on the East; and Redstone and Monongahela, on the West. These have since been frequently divided, as the churches became too numerous to meet in one place.

The Philadelphia Association, from the first, has engaged earnestly in efforts for the proper education of its ministers and the spread of the gospel in the world. Rhode Island College, now Brown University, received its patronage and contributions from its origin, as the subsequent minutes show. It will be seen also that, from the first, it has been an effective missionary body. Hundreds of churches have been gathered by the able and self-denying men, sent out at its expense to regions where no religious privileges had before been enjoyed. The Aborigines were not overlooked in this labor of love. Among other efforts, the Rev. David Jones, before the American Revolution, made a missionary excursion, at his own expense, to the Indians of what was then the " Far West."

This was among the first, if not the very first, ecclesiastical body in America, it is believed, which took a stand on the subject of temperance. The following is copied from the Minutes of 1788:—" This Association, taking into consideration the ruinous effects of the great abuse of distilled liquors throughout this country, take this opportunity of expressing our hearty concurrence with our brethren of several other religious denominations, in discountenancing them in future, and earnestly entreat our brethren and friends to use all their influence, to that end, both in their own families and neighbourhood, except when used as a medicine."

This was the first Baptist Association formed in the United States. From its earliest history it has been forward in the work of Domestic Missions. The pastors were requested, and the churches urged, to be liberal in aiding them to visit destitute churches and settlements. Morgan Edwards, in 1771, and John Gano, afterwards, were appointed "EVANGELISTS," and sent into remote regions, especially South, to preach the gospel, and counsel the feeble churches, and instruct the scattered disciples of Christ. The design of founding Rhode Island College originated in this body. P. P. Vanhorn, Stephen Ustic, and Charles Thompson, were students in this institution; as were also William Rogers and Burges Allison, Doctors of Divinity.

As early as 1722, "it was proposed for the churches to make inquiry among themselves, if they have any young persons hopeful for the ministry, and inclinable for learning; and if they have, to give notice of it to Mr. Abel Morgan, before the first of November, that he might recommend such to the Academy, on Mr. Hollis, his account."

"1776. Concluded to raise a sum of money among our churches for the encouragement of a Latin grammar school, Mr. Isaac Eaton to be master thereof."

"1764. Agreed to inform the churches to which we respectively belong, that, inasmuch as a charter is obtained in Rhode Island government, toward erecting a Baptist college, the churches should be liberal in contributing towards carrying the same into execution."

"1776. Agreed to recommend warmly to our churches the interests of the college, for which a subscription is opened all over the Continent: this college hath been set on foot upwards of a year, and has now in it three promising youths, under the tuition of President Manning."

The publication of useful books, for general circulation, was suggested, in 1749, by the following:—

"Concluded, that every church belonging to this Association should consider that our principles are attacked anew, and monstrously represented; therefore, in order to our vindicating and justifying the same, money may be gathered in every congregation, in readiness against the next Association; and we hope timely notice shall be given both of the number of the books to be printed, and what the charge shall be to print them."

The reader of these minutes will see that the Divine blessing has rested on this band of disciples. At its commencement there were but about five hundred souls enrolled on its register. Now the denomination embraces nearly a million of communicants. At first, five churches constituted the body: now there are sixty-four, though a host of churches have been dismissed to form other Associations, and our geographical limits are scarcely more than the hundredth part of the first boundary.

With the growth of the body, evangelical efforts have correspondingly increased, till the world has become its field, and large sums are annually raised to send out missionaries, translate and distribute the Holy Scriptures, educate ministers, multiply books and tracts, and extend all other divinely appointed means of grace.

H. G. JONES.

AN ASSOCIATION BOOK,

CONTAINING

A BRIEF ACCOUNT

OF THE

BEGINNING AND PROGRESS OF THE CHURCHES HOLDING AND PRACTISING ADULT
BAPTISM, AND COMMONLY CALLED BAPTISTS, IN PENNSYLVANIA AND THE
JERSIES; NOW ANNUALLY ASSOCIATING AT PHILADELPHIA: WITH
THE TIME WHEN, AND THE PERSONS BY WHOM EACH
CHURCH WAS SETTLED, AND WHO WERE THE MIN-
ISTERS THAT LABORED AMONG THEM IN
EACH CHURCH.

TOGETHER ALSO

WITH AN ACCOUNT

OF THE

SEVERAL AFFAIRS THAT CAME TO BE CONSIDERED BY THE ASSOCIATION, SINCE IT
WAS SETTLED, AS FAR AS THE MINUTES OF THE SAME COULD BE FOUND.

COLLECTED PURSUANT TO AN ORDER OF THE ASSOCIATION,
CONVENED SEPTEMBER 19, ANNO DOMINI, 1749.

NOTE.—The above notice and the following records are gathered from minutes kept in compliance with an order of the Association, by Benjamin Griffith, down to 1760. After this, Morgan Edwards was probably the scribe, as the records are in his remarkably legible handwriting so late as 1799.—ED.

A BRIEF NARRATIVE

OF THE CHURCHES HOLDING BELIEVERS' BAPTISM,

IN PENNSYLVANIA AND THE JERSEYS.

THE CHURCH AT LOWER DUBLIN,
IN THE COUNTY OF PHILADELPHIA, PROVINCE OF PENNSYLVANIA.

By the providence of God, several persons from Radnorshire, in Wales, being baptized, upon profession of faith, members of a meeting, in the parish of Llanddowi, Henry Gregory, pastor, came over into this province and settled near Pennepek Creek. In the year of our Lord 1687, came Mr. Elias Keach, son of Mr. Benjamin Keach, of London, and preached unto the people there and at parts adjacent; at or about which time the above said persons, by name John Eaton, George Eaton, Samuel Jones, and John Watts, with others baptized by the said Elias Keach, agreed, by the advice of the said Mr. Keach, to set a day apart, and by fasting and prayer to settle themselves in a church state; which when they had solemnly accomplished, they made choice of the said Keach to be their pastor.

In the year 1692, Mr. Keach went home to England, and the church called the above named John Watts to be their minister. Samuel Jones and others were called to exercise their gifts, and to preach at home, while their minister went abroad. At this time, the church had several distant places to meet in by appointment, as at Philadelphia, Burlington, &c., where several persons that were members of the church resided, and they held their communion at the Lord's table at these several places; and by means of those gifted brethren their meeting at Pennepek was constantly supplied.

In the year 1702, Mr. Watts died; and the public work lay upon Samuel Jones, John Hart, and Evan Morgan, who, with the assistance of Thomas Griffith and others, carried on the work in town, and in the country, for a while.

In the year 1706, Samuel Jones and Evan Morgan were set apart to the work of the ministry by ordination, Messrs. Thomas Killingsworth, Thomas Griffith, and Elisha Thomas, assisting.

In the year 1708, Joseph Wood was ordained for the work of the ministry, with Samuel Jones and Evan Morgan. In the year 1709, on the 16th of February, Evan Morgan departed this life.

In the year 1710, in December, Mr. Nathaniel Jenkins, from Carmarthenshire, in South Wales, arrived at Philadelphia; he being an ordained minister, was received as such, and laboured in the exercise of his function, at Philadelphia and Pennepek, with the other brethren, till the summer following, when he removed to Cape May.

In the year 1711, in April, came Thomas Selby from Ireland, but was not ordained; and after causing a great deal of trouble by his ill behaviour, he went away to Carolina in 1712.

In 1711, came Mr. John Burrows, from Taunton in the West of England, and being an ordained minister, did exercise at Philadelphia, to the satisfaction of all well disposed Christians, till he removed to Middletown, 1713.

In the year 1712, about the middle of February, came, pursuant to letters of invitation from the Church of Philadelphia and Pennepek, Mr. Abel Morgan, being an ordained minister, and had the care of a church at Blaene Gwent, in South Wales, many years before he came over to this province, and was afterwards chosen pastor of the church; and so continued till he departed this life, which was on the 16th of December, 1722; Mr. Samuel Jones being departed in the year 1721, February 3. After the decease of the said pastor, this church at Philadelphia and Pennepek were destitute of an ordained minister, and had among themselves no ministerial supply but Mr. William Kinnersly, who was a gifted brother, and very useful, regular man; but being both aged and having several bodily infirmities, Mr. Jenkin Jones came from the church at Welsh Tract, in Newcastle county, to be their minister, which was in the year 1726; and after some time of continuance with the said church, Mr. Jones was unanimously chosen to be their pastor, and so continued until the year 1746, when the brethren residing in Philadelphia requested a dismission from the church at Pennepek, in order to incorporate a distinct church; which being granted, Mr. Jones was dismissed with the other city members; at and before which time, Mr. Peter Peterson Vanhorn and some others were upon trial for the ministry.

In the year of our Lord 1747, the church at Pennepek made choice of the above named Peter Peterson Vanhorn to officiate among them in the work of the ministry; and accordingly appointed a day of fasting and prayer, being the 18th of June, in the year aforesaid. After solemn prayers unto God, and a sermon suitable to the occasion, preached by Mr. Jenkin Jones, they proceeded to the ordination of the said person, having called to their assistance their former minister, Mr. Jenkin Jones, and Benjamin Griffith, John Davis, and Joshua Potts, who, by solemn prayer to God, laid their hands upon him, and afterwards gave him the right hand of fellowship as a minister of the gospel of Jesus Christ.

THE CHURCH AT PISCATAQUA.

IN NEW JERSEY.

About the year 1686, Mr. Thomas Killingsworth first planted or settled this church, and preached the gospel to them a considerable time. After his removal, the church had the ordinances of the gospel administered among them until the year 1715; about which time Mr. Drake was ordained, and he continued to preach and to administer the ordinances until about the year 1729; and then, by reason of his great age, he desisted preaching, but continued to administer the ordinances. About that time, Henry Lovall, from New England, came among them, who preached for the space of two years upon trial, and then was ordained, but never administered the ordinances; for, soon after his ordination, he behaved himself in so disorderly a manner that he was excommunicated from the church.

About which time, Mr. Benjamin Stelle was called to preach among them, and was approved and set apart by solemn ordination.

Their number, when first settled, was no more than six persons, and continued very small for the space of twenty years, and then began to increase, and came to be about twenty in number, and is since increased to upwards of one hundred.

The above account was sent by Mr. Stelle, 1746.

THE CHURCH AT MIDDLETOWN.

Though there is no particular record of the time when, nor the manner how, the baptized believers at Middletown did incorporate, yet it appears there were several Baptists in those parts from the first settling of the land; for in the year 1687, when the church of Lower Dublin did incorporate, it is recorded that the brethren there did advise the brethren at Middletown to incorporate likewise; and it is remembered that James Aston and James Brown were teaching elders among them, at first planting; and about the year 1690, Mr. Elias Keach lived one year amongst them, and preached to them: Mr. Thomas Killingsworth also visited them. In times following, there happened a grievous contention, and thereupon a division, among them of Middletown; and in the year 1712, other churches sent to assist them several ministers and messengers, viz.: Timothy Brooks, Abel Morgan, Joseph Wood, Elisha Thomas, Nicolas Johnson, Griffith Miles, James James, Edward Church, William Bettrig, and John Manners; who, being called by them, and sent by the other churches, being come among them, were desirous to undertake the deciding of matters of difference between them. Accordingly they did; and among other things it was judged, that to the intent to bring things into right order, they should subscribe to Elias Keach's

Confession of Faith, at least to the Covenant annexed to it; and in case that all could not find freedom to subscribe the said Confession and Covenant, that if such a number as might act as a church should do so, such should be deemed, and be really owned, the only regular Baptist Church in those parts; and the said persons advised further, that such as could not subscribe should be dealt *tenderly* with; and accordingly, Anno 1712, forty-two did subscribe, and twenty-six did not. Upon this Constitution, or Restoration, the Church at Middletown hitherto stands.

In the year 1713, Mr. John Burrows came to be their minister, and continued their minister during his life. Sometime after his death, George Eaglesfield preached among them till he died. In the year 1739, Mr. John Coward was called to exercise his gifts upon trial, who preached chiefly at Crosswicks, and still does among the brethren members of the church at Middletown. In the year 1739, Abel Morgan, from the Welsh Tract, at the request of the Church of Middletown, came to serve them in the gospel ministry, and is now living. As this church meets in two distant places, viz., at Middletown and Crosswicks, the Lord's Supper is observed in each place, once in two months alternately: one month in the one place, and the other month in the other place.

THE CHURCH AT COHANSIE.

The church of baptized believers at Cohansie was first planted and settled by Mr. Thomas Killingsworth, about the year 1690, (as may be gathered from a paragraph in Pennepek Church Book, page the 7th,) who laboured in the work of the ministry at Cohansie, Salem, and Penn's Neck, till he departed this life, which was in the year 1709; before which time, Mr. Timothy Brooks, from New England, being in those parts, and had kept a separate meeting, on account of some difference between them in some points. After Mr. Killingsworth's decease, they united, and Mr. Brooks became their minister, and continued several years with them, even till he was removed by death. After his decease, this church requested of the church at Cape May, and obtained assistance once a month for some time. About that time, William Butcher, a very hopeful young man, from Chester county, in Pennsylvania, married a wife, at Cohansie, and settled there, and preached among them, and was there ordained, and did officiate in the ministry, to their great satisfaction, for about two years, and then was removed by death; whereupon the church renewed their request to Cape May, and Mr. Nathaniel Jenkins supplied them again, as formerly, for several years; and Mr. Jenkins, finding great success, by the blessing of God on his monthly visits at Cohansie, and his people at the Cape declining, very many removed by death, in the great sickness that God visited those with, and many others removed to remote parts; and others some, to become careless and others disorderly; he thought his call to Cohansie to be clear, and therefore removed there; at the same time resolved to visit the people at the Cape as often as he could; and so continues, though now grown aged and his strength declining, yet expresses his thankfulness to God that he sees some growing gifts that are like to be useful when he is called home.

This account was sent by Mr. Nathaniel Jenkins, in 1746, and things remain in the same station in 1749.

THE CHURCH AT THE WELSH TRACT,

IN THE COUNTY OF NEWCASTLE UPON DELAWARE.

This church was constituted in Pembrokeshire, in South Wales, in the year 1701, at which time the first members of this church were about to come over into Pennsylvania; they then, by the advice and counsel of the churches they came from, in Pembrokeshire and Carmathenshire, entered into a church covenant, and state their number was sixteen persons; and among them was the Rev. Mr. Thomas Griffith, to be their minister. After their arrival in this country, they lived, near two years, near Pennepek and the parts adjacent; keeping together and meeting, as they were a distinct church, and had considerable addition to their number. In the year 1703, they removed and settled at the Welsh Tract aforesaid, and continued successful: and the said Mr. Griffith continued with them until he died, which was on the 25th of August, Anno Domini 1725: during which time, several able gifted ministers were raised, by the blessing of God, in the said church; they were Elisha Thomas and Enoch Morgan, both members when the said church was first constituted; the said Elisha Thomas was chosen pastor of the church, and after were Jenkin Jones, who removed to Philadelphia, and Owen Thomas. In the year 1730, Elisha Thomas died, and the said church continued under the ministry of the said Mr. Enoch Morgan and Mr. Owen Thomas; during which time, God raised up other two in the said church; viz., Mr. Abel Morgan, who since removed to Middletown, in East Jersey, and Mr. David Davis. On the 25th of March, 1740, died the said Enoch Morgan, and the church continues under the ministry of the said Owen Thomas and David Davis.

This narrative sent by the Rev. Owen Thomas, A. D. 1746, and they continue, as above last related, in the year 1749.

N. B. That this church appears to be very regular in its first settlement, and hath been the best supplied with ministers of any church belonging to this Association.

THE CHURCH AT THE GREAT VALLEY, OR TREDIFFRUN,
IN THE COUNTY OF CHESTER, PA.

In or about the years 1701 and 1702, some persons of our denomination came from South Wales, members at Rhydwillym, John Jenkins, pastor; settled in these parts, and being but few and destitute of ministerial helps, they made application to the church at the Welsh Tract; and as a branch of that church were supplied by their ministers, and being increased by some additions, by the blessing of God on means among them; in the year 1710, several persons that were members at Rhydwillym aforesaid, and other places, came into the province and settled in that neighbourhood. In the year 1711, they were advised to put themselves in church order by themselves, for they were far distant from other churches, and especially from the Welsh Tract, where hitherto they belonged as a branch of that church. Accordingly, in the month of April, 1711, a day was set apart, by fasting and prayer, to accomplish this solemn work, having for their assistance Mr. Elisha Thomas, and others from the Welsh Tract church, and after solemn prayers to God for his blessing, they gave themselves to God, and to one another in the Lord, according to 2 Cor. viii. 5, and had a right hand of fellowship as a sister church; and at the same time did unanimously choose Hugh Davis, an ordained minister, from South Wales, to be their minister, who is yet living, but past acting by reason of age. In the year 17—, John Davis, after due trial of his gifts, was called to the work of the ministry by solemn ordination, and is still their minister.

This church assembled chiefly, for many years, at the dwelling house of Richard Miles, in the township of Radnor, and afterward, for the convenience of the generality of the congregation, they built a meeting-house in the township of Trediffrun, in the said county of Chester.

THE CHURCH AT CAPE MAY.

There were some Baptists at that place almost as soon as that county was settled. Most knowing and noted was Mr. George Taylor, who used to exhort and pray with such as came to his house to him. In process of time, Mr. George Eaglesfield came there, and preached to them for some years; but he not endeavouring to gather a church, the few enlightened of their duty disliked him. Some of them went to Philadelphia and were baptized there, and got acquainted with the Rev. Thomas Griffith, an aged and first minister of the Baptist Church at Welsh Tract, and requested him to give them a visit, which he did, and tarried with them about half a year, and baptized several persons; and because he could not tarry longer, he departed, well respected. He directed them where and to whom to make application for a minister to settle amongst them, there being some from Wales arrived in Pennsylvania; and Nathaniel Jenkins, having left Philadelphia and moved to Pennepek, with an intent to settle, but had not, to him then and to the church they made their request, and he first gave them a visit early in the Spring, Anno Domini 1712; and they requested him to come and settle among them; which call he accepted, and in the month of May moved to the Cape. And towards the end of June, in the same year, 1712, the members, with the said minister, having sent for Mr. Brooks, of Cohansie, and some others, to assist them, they were settled and constituted a particular church of Jesus Christ, and owned as a sister church by those then present. The said Mr. Jenkins continued with them several years; but having little success, after a few years at first, Mr. Jenkins, for reasons mentioned at pages 14–15, removed to Cohansie, but continued visiting the Capes as often as he could; and about 1743, he, seeing some new life again stirring, encouraged some young ministers to visit them, and to see if they could reap any fruit of the seed formerly sown there. The first that he prevailed with to go was Mr. Abel Morgan. Mr. Jenkins acquainted him that there was a relick of a well founded church there; if he found lively stones to build upon it; and afterwards, Mr. Jenkin Jones, Mr. David Davis, Mr. Thomas Davis, besides Mr. Jenkins, visited and baptized many: so they are now a competent number of warm and loving disciples, and have one of themselves to be their minister, viz., Nathaniel Jenkins, eldest son of their former minister, to their good content and great satisfaction.

THE CHURCH AT HOPEWELL.

Several persons of the denomination of Baptists settled in and about Hopewell, in Jersey; some of them members of the Baptist church of Middletown, and others members at Philadelphia and Pennepek; and being remote from those churches, it was thought more for their benefit to be settled in a church-state by themselves, and accordingly they obtained dismissions from the said churches, and the assistance of their ministers and elders, by name Mr. Abel Morgan, Mr. John Burrows, Mr. Griffith Miles, Mr. Joseph Todd, and Mr. William Kinnersly; and on the 22d day of April, 1715, being a day appointed by fasting and prayer, they entered into a church covenant, and were owned a sister church, the number of persons being fifteen or sixteen, as appears by Pennepek Church Book, page 55. This church was afterwards visited chiefly by the said Abel Morgan, John Burrows, and Joseph Wood, until 1721, when Thomas Symmons came among them, and preached to them about two years, then removed to Carolina; and, after this, Mr. Eaglesfield preached there once a month, and others visited them at times. In the year 1727, they requested assistance from the church at Montgomery, and obtained Benjamin Griffith to visit them alternatively one month and Joseph Eaton another, for some time, and Joseph Eaton continued to supply them several years. About the year 1741, Thomas Davis, from the Great Valley, came, and settled with them about three years; and some time afterwards, James Carman and Benjamin Miller visited them. Malachia Bonham also preached among them in the year 1748. Isaac Eaton, from the church of Southampton, removed to the church at Hopewell, and being approved, was there ordained to be their minister; and their number is now esteemed one hundred and twelve.

This narrative dated December 26, 1749.

THE CHURCH NEAR BRANDYWINE.

There being divers persons in the townships of Providence, Burningham, and the parts adjacent that were baptized; some of them members of the church at Philadelphia, others elsewhere, and some of them were of the number that in the year 1690 had in some manner joined with those of Salem, &c., under the ministry of the Rev. Mr. Killingsworth; these, on the 14th day of June, Anno Domini 1715, at a meeting for that purpose appointed at the dwelling-house of John Powell, in Providence aforesaid, in the county of Chester, in the province of Pennsylvania, having for their assistance and direction the Rev. Mr. Abel Morgan, of Philadelphia, and some brethren from the church at the Welsh Tract, were constituted and settled in Gospel church, ordered, and owned, and declared as a sister church; and they, having no ministerial helps among themselves, depended altogether upon the assistance they could obtain from sister churches. In 1717, they concluded, for the better convenience of most of the members, to keep their meetings chiefly in the township of Burningham; and so continued till the year 1741; and then agreed to keep monthly meetings alternately; one month at Burningham, and the other month in the township of Newlin, in the same county, for the convenience of many of the members removed thither. About a year after, they thought proper to settle their monthly meetings altogether to the aforesaid township of Newlin. They have been, since their first settling at Burningham, in 1717, assisted with ministerial helps from the sister church at the Welsh Tract, and continue to be thence assisted hitherto.

Dated, 1749.

THE CHURCH AT MONTGOMERY,

IN THE COUNTY OF PHILADELPHIA.

In the year 1710, John Evans, and Sarah, his wife, from a church in Carmarthenshire, in South Wales, (James James, minister,) came over and settled in Montgomery aforesaid.. In 1711, came John James, and Elizabeth, his wife, from Pembrokeshire, members of the church at Rhydwillym, (John Jenkins, minister,) and settled in the same neighbourhood. After some time, Mr. Abel Morgan visited them, and preached to as many as came to hear, at the house of John Evans; and after his visiting for some time, as often as he could, several persons were proposed for baptism, which was administered by Mr. Morgan. In the year 1719, it was moved to them either to join with some neighbouring church, as that of Pennepek, being the nighest, or to be settled in gospel order as a distinct church by themselves. Upon which they consulted, and concluded, by reason of the distance of place and diversity of language, they understanding very little English, to be rather a church by themselves. Their conclusion being approved by Mr. Morgan, a day was set apart for the solemnizing of this great work, being the 20th day of June, 1719; and Mr. Abel Morgan, and Mr. Samuel Jones, being present to assist and direct in the work of the day, the first part being spent in fasting and prayer, with a sermon preached by Mr. Morgan, suitable to the occasion, they proceeded. Being asked whether they were desirous and freely willing to settle together as a church of Jesus Christ, they all answered in the affirmative; and being asked whether they were acquainted with one another's principles, and satisfied with one another's graces and conversation, it was also answered in the affirmative; and then for a demonstration of their giving of themselves up, severally and jointly, to the Lord, as a people of God and a church of Jesus Christ, they all lifted up their right hand. Then were they directed to take one another by the hand, in token of their union, declaring, at the same time, that as they had given themselves to God, so they did give themselves also to one another by the will of God, 2 Cor. viii. 5, to be a church according to the gospel; to worship God and maintain the doctrines of the gospel, according to their ability, and to edify one another. Then were they pronounced and declared to be a church of Jesus Christ; a right hand of fellowship was given to them as a sister church, with exhortations and instructions suitable to the station and relation they now stood in; and the whole was finished with solemn prayer to God for a blessing on the work of the day. Their number, nine or ten persons.

Mr. Morgan continued to visit them, and administer the ordinances among them; they were also supplied by Mr. Elisha Thomas, and other ministering brethren from the Welsh Tract. They soon had William Thomas, and John James, as gifted brethren to preach among them. In the year 1722, the church being considerably increased in number, they called the following persons to exercise their gifts upon trial:—John James, David Evans, Benjamin Griffith, and Joseph Eaton; and in the year 1725, the church unanimously agreed to call the said Benjamin Griffith to the work of the ministry by solemn ordination; which was accomplished on the 23d day of October, 1725: Mr. Elisha Thomas, and Mr. Jenkin Jones, acting and assisting by the call of the church.

The church, in the year 1727, called Joseph Eaton to the work of the ministry by ordination, which was accomplished on the 24th day of October; Mr. Elisha Thomas and their other minister, Benjamin Griffith, officiating at his ordination.

In the month of April, 1749, Joseph Eaton died, and Benjamin Griffith continued in the work, assisted by a hopeful young man, named John Thomas, not yet ordained.

February 1st, 1749.

THE CHURCH AT BETHLEHEM.

Several members of the Baptist church at Hopewell having removed and settled in and about Bethlehem, they the said members, and others added there, requested a dismission from the church at Hopewell; which, being obtained, they appointed the 31st day of July, Anno Domini 1742, to be constituted a distinct church of Jesus Christ, Mr. Joseph Eaton and others assisting. Thomas Curtis was called by them to preach upon trial. In the year 1745, on the 28th of October, Thomas Curtis was ordained to the work of the ministry, and continued to officiate among them till he departed this life, which was towards the latter end of April, 1749. In the year 174 , on the   day of   . Malachia Bonham was called to be their minister by solemn ordination.

THE CHURCH AT SOUTHAMPTON.

Some of the very early members of the church at Lower Dublin, commonly called Pennepek, were settled in and about Southampton; and in process of time the said church appointed a meeting to be kept, one Lord's day in the month, for the ease and benefit of their remote members; which meeting was for some time held at Peter Chamberlain's house, and after at the house of John Morris, who, being desirous to promote the glory of God and the interest of religion, did grant and confirm a small plantation for the use of the church, and another piece of land for a burying place and to build a meeting-house upon. The number of members, by the blessing of God on the means of grace, being increased in those parts, they requested the church of Pennepek to dismiss them, and to assist them to be a distinct church; which request was granted at a church meeting, held April the 5th, 1746, and on the 8th day of April, the dismissed members unanimously met at the meeting-house, built on the said piece of ground in Southampton. After some time spent in solemn prayers to God, they gave themselves to the Lord and to one another, by the will of God, to walk together in gospel fellowship, according to the rules of God's word. On the 29th day of May, 1746, Mr. Joshua Potts, a young man who had been a considerable time upon trial, was solemnly called to the work of the ministry by ordination, Mr. Jenkin Jones, their former pastor, and Mr. Abel Morgan, being present to act for and with the church. The number of members then was forty-six.

THE CHURCH AT CRANBRERY.

Most of the members of this church were heretofore members of the Baptist church meeting at Middletown and Crosswicks, and being far distant from that church, they requested dismission from that church, in order to settle by themselves. Their request being granted, they were settled and constituted a distinct church on the 1st day of November, Anno Domini 1745, the number of members then being seventeen. On the 3d day of the same month, Mr. James Carman, by unanimous choice and call of the church, was ordained to be their minister: Mr. Nathaniel Jenkins, and Mr. Abel Morgan assisting on both of those solemn occasions. There have been twenty-five persons added to them since.

August, 1750.

THE CHURCH AT PHILADELPHIA.

Philadelphia and Pennepek, or Lower Dublin, having continued one church from the first settlement thereof, though they had their respective places of meeting, they held their respective times of communion in the town and the country, their minister, Mr. Jenkin Jones, administering the ordinances of baptism and the Lord's supper, in both the city and the country, every month.

In April, Anno Domini 1746, the members residing in the city of Philadelphia did make their request to their brethren at Pennepek, as being of the two the elder branch, for a dismission, in order to be settled a distinct church by themselves; which was accordingly granted; and pursuant thereunto, the dismissed members did appoint the 15th day of May, in the said year of our Lord 1745, to meet and settle themselves in church order; and being accompanied by some brethren from Pennepek, they did in a solemn manner enter into church covenant, and united, as is usual on the like solemn occasions. Mr. Jenkin Jones being one of the number dismissed from Pennepek, and now a member of the church settled at Philadelphia, was called to exercise the ministerial functions among them.

THE CHURCH AT MORRISTOWN,

IN MORRIS COUNTY, NEW JERSEY.

Several of the members of the church of Piscataqua, living in Morris county, remote from that church, requested a dismission, to the end they might be constituted a distinct church by themselves; and accordingly they appointed to meet on the 11th day of August, 1752; and having Mr. Benjamin Miller, Mr. Isaac Stelle and Mr. Isaac Eaton for their assistance, and after having improved the fore part of this day in fasting and prayer, they were regularly incorporated in the usual manner, and the right hand of fellowship given to them as a sister church of Jesus Christ, and as such recommended to God by solemn prayer, and on the 4th day of October following, were admitted into the Association.

THE CHURCH AT SCOTCH PLAINS,

IN EAST JERSEY.

Several members of the church at Piscataqau, living at Scotch Plains, in the county of Essex, finding it difficult to travel to keep their places there, requested dismission from that church, in order to be incorporated a distinct church by themselves; and accordingly they of Piscataqua did grant it; and being dismissed thence, they appointed to come together on the 8th day of September, 1747, and having Abel Morgan and James Mott, from Middletown, for their assistance, they spent the fore part of the day in prayer and fasting, and afterwards they gave themselves in a solemn manner to the Lord, and to one another, by the will of God, and after the usual solemnity, were owned as a sister church; and on the 13th day of February following, Benjamin Miller was ordained to be their minister: Mr. Benjamin Stelle, of Piscataqua, and Mr. Abel Morgan, of Middletown, assisting at the ordination. Their number, when constituted, fourteen; their number, on the 10th of July, 1750, when the above narrative was dated, seventy-five.

THE CHURCH AT ROCKSBERRY,

IN MORRIS COUNTY, N. J.

A number of persons, baptized on profession of faith, residing at Rocksberry aforesaid, being desirous to put them in church order, for their better convenience, benefit, and edification; and being dismissed by the church they were related to, they appointed the 12th day of May, 1753; and having procured the Rev. brethren, Isaac Stelle, and Malachia Bonham, for their assistance, they were constituted after the same manner as other churches, the said ministers giving them a hand of fellowship as a sister church; and, at the Association in October following, were, upon their request, received into the number of our associating churches: their number then being fourteen persons.

THE CHURCH AT OYSTER BAY,

QUEEN'S COUNTY, LONG ISLAND.

Several persons baptized upon profession of their faith; some by ordained ministers from Rhode Island; some by Mr. Weeks, residing in the place, and some by Thomas Davis. In the year 1748, a considerable number of those baptized persons agreed and concluded to settle themselves in a regular church order, according to the rules and patterns of the New Testament. Accordingly they appointed the eleventh day of July, A. D. 1748, and then met; and with fasting and prayer, they were solemnly incorporated. A church covenant, in writing, was subscribed by men and women then present, to the number of twenty-eight; John Stephens and Thomas Davis being called to assist therein. In the year 1750, they, by their letter and messenger, Daniel Underhill, proposed to the Association of the baptized churches for admittance and union with the Association; which was, after inquiry, granted, and their said messenger received.

TULPOHOKIN.

This church takes the above name from a creek, near to which the meeting-house stands. It is situate in the township of Cymru, county of Berks, and province of Pennsylvania. It was constituted Aug. 19, 1738, and joined the Association September 23, of the same year. The original number was twenty-one. The first minister was Rev. Thomas Jones. What further concerns this church may be seen in the following memorial, sent me in the year 1761.

"We, whose names are underwritten, (some members of the Great

Valley church, some of the church of Montgomery,) being removed into another county, and so remote from the said churches, that we could not attend the means of grace, nor perform the duties of our membership as we could wish to do; being met together, according to appointment, on this 19th day of August, 1738; and having, by fasting and prayer, made our supplication to God, and a sermon preached on the occasion; and having unanimously owned the Confession of faith, set forth by the elders of baptized churches in England, and approved by the above named churches; and having showed our approbation of one another's principles and charitable judgment of each others' graces; and having mutually agreed to give ourselves to God, and to one another by the will of God; we covenant, as God shall help us, to maintain the worship of God and the truth of the gospel, to the edification of our own souls and the good of others; and to practice all gospel ordinances, according to the mind of God, revealed in his word; to admonish, exhort, and watch over one another in love, and also to reprove according to gospel rule; to keep our own secret matters to ourselves, according to the practice of the primitive gospel churches and the custom of our neighboring churches of the same order. In testimony whereof, we, in the sanctity of our hearts, and in the fear of God, desiring to wait upon, and trust in his faithful promises in our Lord and Redeemer Jesus Christ, for all blessings and graces, and the gifts of his Holy Spirit, to enable us to do our duties, for the honour of God and the ornament of the gospel of Jesus, have hereunto subscribed our names the day and year above named.

David Evan,	David Lewis,	Martha Jones,
James John,	George Rees,	Mary Loyd,
Thomas Jones,	John David,	Elizabeth Rees,
Evan Loyd,	Thomas Loyd,	Mary David,
Thomas Nicholas,	Rees Thomas,	Elenor Nicholas,
James Edwards,	Sarah Evans,	Margaret Edwards,
Henry Harry,	Elenor John,	Ann Rees.

⁎ As the churches that joined this Association since the year 1750 were erected and constituted after the same form and order of the Gospel with those whose constitutions are more at large herein before related, it is thought needless to give a copious account of every particular, and to relate the time of their admission to the Association only.

AN ACCOUNT

OF THE AFFAIRS THAT CAME TO BE CONSIDERED BY THE ASSOCIATION OF THE AFOREMENTIONED CHURCHES, SINCE THEY HELD AN ASSOCIATION, AS FAR AS ANY RECORDS OF THE SAME CAN BE FOUND.

1707.

THERE is no track or footsteps of any regular association, agreement, or confederation, between the first churches in these colonies of Pennsylvania and the Jerseys, that I can find, before the year 1707, when we have, in the records of the church of Pennepek, this account, viz:—Before our general meeting, held at Philadelphia, in the seventh month, 1707, it was concluded by the several congregations of our judgment, to make choice of some particular brethren, such as they thought most capable in every congregation, and those to meet at the yearly meeting to consult about such things as were wanting in the churches, and to set them in order; and these brethren meeting at the said yearly meeting, which began the 27th of the seventh month, on the seventh day of the week, agreed to continue the meeting till the third day following in the work of the public ministry. It was then agreed, that a person that is a stranger, that has neither letter of recommendation, nor is known to be a person gifted, and of a good conversation, shall not be admitted to preach, nor be entertained as a member in any of the baptized congregations in communion with each other.

It was also concluded, that if any difference shall happen between any member and the church he belongs unto, and they cannot agree, then the person so grieved may, at the general meeting, appeal to the brethren of the several congregations, and with such as they shall nominate, to decide the difference; that the church and the person so grieved do fully acquiesce in their determination.

1710.

In the year 1710, several able men, ministers and elders, and in the year following also, came over from South Wales and the West of England—as the Rev. Mr. Nathaniel Jenkins, Mr. John Burrows, Mr. Abel Morgan, and some that had been ruling elders in the churches they came from—all of them men long concerned in the affairs of churches and associations in their own countries.

1712.

One Thomas Selby made a disturbance and rupture in the church at Philadelphia and Pennepek; and application having been made to the Association, the Association did nominate persons from among themselves, to hear and determine of and concerning the said difference. And both parties consenting, the said nominated men proceeded to hear and determine of the same, and brought in their judgment and determination, confirmed under their hands, as followeth, (*vide* the afore mentioned book, page 47.)

"With respect to the difference between the members and others, some time belonging to the Baptist church at Philadelphia, as it hath been laid before us, persons chosen by both sides, they having referred the whole of their difference to our determination; we, doing what in us lies for the glory of God, and the peace of the whole church, in regard of the transactions past, and what may be best for the future, for the interest of the gospel, upon due consideration of what hath been laid before us, as followeth, viz:—We do find the way and manner of dealing and proceeding with each other hath been from the rule of the Gospel, and unbecoming Christians in many respects, and in some too shameful here to enumerate the particulars.

"And first, we judge it expedient in point of justice, that Mr. Thomas Selby be paid the money subscribed to him by the members of this church, and he discharged from any further service in the work of the ministry; he being a person, in our judgment, not likely for the promotion of the Gospel in these parts of the country; and considering his miscarriages, we judge he may not be allowed to communion.

"And secondly, as to the members of this congregation, we do apprehend the best way is, that each party offended do freely forgive each other all personal and other offences that may have risen on this occasion, and that they be buried in oblivion; and that those who shall for future mention or stir up any of the former differences, so as to tend to contention, shall be deemed disorderly persons, and be dealt with as such.

"And thirdly, that those that exempted themselves from their communion on this account, except as above, be allowed to take their places orderly without contention, and such as refuse to be deemed disorderly persons."

Subscribed—Timothy Brooks, Thomas Shepherd, Thomas Abbot, John Drake, Nicolas Jonson, Dickason Shepherd, Job Shepherd, James Bollen, Samuel Jones, John Hart, John Bray.

Let it be noted, that the said Thomas Selby, though he and his party referred as above said, yet he appeared afterwards very outrageous while he stayed in the province, and some of his adherents joined to other denominations, and never returned to seek their place in the church, and the church did accordingly exclude them. But the greatest part took their places personally.

1713.

From the year 1712 to the year 1720, though the churches continually maintained a yearly association, yet their minutes are not to be found, for aught I can hear. In the year 1720, nothing appeared before the Association. The minutes of 1721 are wanting.

1722.

At the Association, in the year 1722, it was proposed for the churches to make inquiry among themselves, if they have any young persons hopeful for the ministry, and inclinable for learning; and if they have, to give notice of it to Mr. Abel Morgan before the first of November, that he might recommend such to the acadamy on Mr. Hollis, his account.

1723.

At our Association, convened September 23, 1723, a query from the church at Brandywine came, viz., which way they might improve their vacant days of worship, when they have no minister among them to carry on the public work.

Solution. We conceive it expedient that the church do meet together as often as conveniency will admit; and when they have none to carry on the work of preaching, that they read a chapter, sing a psalm, and go to prayer and beg of God to increase their grace and comfort, and have due regard to order and decency in the exercise of those gifts at all times, and not to suffer any to exercise their gifts in a mixed multitude until tried and approved of first by the church.

Agreed, that the proposal drawn by the several ministers, and signed by many others, in reference to the examination of all gifted brethren and ministers that come in here from other places, be duly put in practice, we having found the evil of neglecting a true and previous scrutiny in those affairs.

1724.

In the year 1724, a query, concerning the fourth commandment, whether changed, altered, or diminished.

We refer to the Confession of faith, set forth by the elders and brethren met in London, 1689, and owned by us, chap. 22, sect. 7 and 8.

2d Query. Whether a believer may marry an unbeliever, without coming under church censure for it?

Answered in the negative.

3d Query. Whether an officer in the church, who forfeits his office, forfeits his membership? Answered in the negative. But if he forfeits his membership he forfeits his office. Whether he, if restored to his membership, must also be restored to office, is another case, not here considered.

4thly. Concluded and agreed, that a church ought to be unanimous in giving their voice in choosing and setting up, or deposing one set up, to act in any church office, or to act as an officer in the church. Any act of that nature, commenced without common consent, is void, and hath no power in it.

5thly. Concluded, that the letter from the churches to Association hereafter, may contain salutations, contemplations, congratulations, &c., in one page; and the complaints, queries, or grievances, &c., be written apart; for it is agreed that the former shall be read publicly the first day of the Association's meeting, and the latter, the church's doubts, fears, or disorders, &c., be opened and read to the Association only.

1725.

In the year 1725 nothing presented but what is common, and the Association concluded to send suitable exhortations especially answering the case of those that made their application for the time then being.

1726.

In the year 1726, the Association ordered that all the churches do observe a day of fasting and prayer, on account of several occurrences them then thereunto moving, and to be observed on the tenth day of November then next ensuing. And the said Association had a troublesome work about defraying the charges incurred by an unhappy youth, son to one of our ministering brethren in London, recommended to us here by our benefactors, Mr. Hollis and others, and ordered proper persons, viz., Mr. John Holme and Mr. Jenkin Jones, to write to Mr. Hollis, &c., and to carry on a correspondence with our friends in London.

One query from the church at Montgomery, viz:—In case there might be a division, and on the division a rent and separation follow in any church in Great Britain, and each party combining together in church form, each being sound in the faith, and during the separation both parties recommend members unto us here, as in full communion with them, how may the churches here proceed in such a case?

Answer. We do advise that the churches here may take no further notice of the letters by such persons brought here, than to satisfy themselves that such are baptized persons, and of a regular conversation, and to take such into church covenant as if they had not been members of any church before.

1727.

In the year 1727, it was agreed that the messengers of the churches, who usually met on the seventh day of the week, should, for the future, meet on the sixth day of the same week before the fourth Lord's day in September, at ten of the clock afore noon, in order to prepare for the affairs of the churches; and that the churches should endeavor to free their messengers from their businesses at home, and assist them with money to bear their expenses in that affair.

In answer to a query from the Great Valley, viz :—How far the liberty of marriage may be between a member and one that is not a member? Answered, by referring to our Confession of faith, chapter 26th in our last edition.

1728.

In the year 1728, the Association met the sixth day of the week.

1. Query from Hopewell: What course to take in choosing a ruling elder in the church? We answer, that a church wanting ruling elders or deacons, as in other cases, should set a day apart, and by fasting and prayer, seek the guidance and direction of God, and then unanimously pitch upon one or more of their brethren to act upon trial in the office of ruling elder or deacon; and our judgment is, that persons called upon trial in the said offices, may act by authority of the church, with as full power as if completely qualified; but not so teaching elders or ministers of the word and ordinances.

2. A query from the church at Montgomery: Whether a church is bound to grant a letter of dismission to any member to go to another church, while his residence is not removed?

Answered in the negative, we having neither precept nor precedent for such a practice in Scripture. See Discipline.

1729.

The elders and messengers of the baptized congregations, in Pennsylvania and the Jerseys, met at Philadelphia, September 27th and 28th, 1729, in a solemn Association. Sendeth greeting:—

Dearly beloved Brethren in the Lord Jesus Christ,—We heartily rejoice to see your care, diligence, requests, and desires, on our behalf, at the throne of grace; and also your care and diligence in maintaining our yearly correspondence and communion in the gospel. We, your representatives, met together in love, perused your letters and gladly received your messengers. We find cause to rejoice that God has crowned the labors of his ministers with such success. There have been considerable additions the past year in several churches, and some in most. Praise be rendered to our gracious God, we find the churches generally to be at peace and unity amongst themselves. We think it expedient to give you an account of our proceedings. We conferred together, without any jars or contentions in our debates; our souls have been refreshed, hearing of the welfare of the churches in general; also, in hearing the sweet and comfortable truths of the gospel declared among us, by the faithful labours of our ministering brethren, which we hope is to the glory of God and the good of souls. We earnestly desire you to walk worthy of your holy vocation, standing fast and striving together for the faith of the gospel. It is the general complaint of many, that there is much lukewarmness and deadness in matters of religion, which we hope is not a mere compliment, but rather the grief of the churches. In order to remedy this soul distemper, our advice and desire is, that you be diligent to keep your places in the house of God; be frequent and instant in prayer, both in secret and in public. Strive after the life and power of religion; make religion your earnest business. Keep your garments undefiled from the world; walk as becomes saints before God and men; improve your opportunities in all religious duties, both among your families and in the church. Stand fast for the defending and maintaining the ordinances of Christ; wait on God in them, that you may reap the benefits of Christ by them. Strive to keep together; maintaining the unity of the Spirit in the bond of peace; always resisting the assaults of Satan, who waiteth opportunities to disturb the peace of God's children. Be careful that you do nothing that may tend to breed disturbances in the church of God.

Query from the church at Philadelphia. Suppose a gifted brother, who is esteemed an orderly minister by or among those that are against the laying on of hands in any respect, should happen to come among our church; whether we may allow such an one to administer the ordinances of baptism and the Lord's supper or no?

Answered in the negative; because it is contrary to the rule of God's word: see Acts xiii. 2, 3; and xiv. 23: compared with Titus i. 5; 1 Tim. iv. 14; from which prescribed rules we dare not swerve. We also refer to the Confession of faith, chap. xxvii., sect. 9.

The messengers shall meet on the sixth day of the week, at the time before appointed, by 2 o'clock, P. M., to consider the affairs of the churches.

Agreed, that a sermon be preached on the seventh day, in the afternoon, as usual;—first day, a sermon to be preached in the morning, and another in the afternoon, with the administration of the Lord's supper;—on the second day of the week, a concluding sermon in the forenoon. Mr. Jones and Mr. Holmes shall send a letter to Mr. Walden and Mr. Hollis, in London, in order to maintain a christian correspondence.

Commending you to God and the word of his grace,

Your brethren, in the best of bonds,

Jno. David,	Ben. Stelle,	Owen Thomas,
Geo. Hugh,	Gershom Mott,	Joseph Eaton,
Jno. Devonald,	John Welledge,	Wm. Kinnersley,
Saml. Osgood,	John Clarkson,	John Holmes,
Jeremiah Kollet,	Jno. Bartholomew,	John Heart,
Robt. Chalfant,	Elisha Thomas,	George Eaton.
Dickison Shephard,	Jenkin Jones,	
Ebenezer Smith,	Simon Butler,	

1730.

In the year 1730, a query from Cohansie: In case a member of a regular church separate himself on the account of the seventh day, and join himself to those that hold the same for a Sabbath, when, at the same time, the church he was member of allowed, if it was to him a matter of conscience, he might observe it, and keep his place where he was a member, and that they would respect him as they used to do; yet, nevertheless, he goes away, and presumes to be a leader among the aforesaid seventh-day people. What must the church do in such a case in order to discharge their duty?

Resolved, That it is the duty of such a church, in as moderate a way and manner as they can, to disown such a member, so as he may not be looked upon to be a member any further with them on any account.

As to the application from Brandywine, it may be referred to the answer given in the same case to the same church, Anno Domini 1723; only here they were advised to read some sound, profitable, approved sermon books, in the absence of the ministers that visit them.

As to a request from the Great Valley, we would have them encourage the gifts they have among them, and send to their nearest neighbors' churches for helps and supplies as often as they and them can agree.

As to the request from Piscataqua, for the help of our ministering brethren at their general meeting, we judge it necessary that our ministering brethren do supply such general meetings; nevertheless, we not knowing who, nor how to bind any of them, we think it necessary that the church, where such are held, send to them, that, if possible, they may be certain of some help.

1731.

The elders, ministers, and messengers, of the baptized congregations in Pennsylvania and the Jerseys, met in Association at Philadelphia, September 24th, 1731. To the respective congregations we represent, send greeting:—

Dearly beloved and highly esteemed brethren, our joy and our crown, at the appearing of our Lord Jesus Christ, we cannot but rejoice to see your care and diligence, in maintaining this our annual communion, in sending your messengers to associate with us. We met together in love, admitted your messengers, perused your letters, and had cause to bless God that we find the churches in peace among themselves, without distraction, schism or division, or destructive errors, and that in most churches there hath been some addition this last year; for which we bless the great Husbandman, who gives success to the labours of his poor servants. Yet we find the old complaint of dullness, coldness, and indifference in the things of God; and we hope you do not rest in complaints, but that you endeavour to provoke one another to love and good works. Consider seriously, dearly beloved, that our Master will come the rounds, to view his servants, and woe then to the slothful and loitering. Therefore, bestir yourselves, be close and diligent, every one according to his work in the vineyard, lest ye be found unprofitable. Prize your privileges and admire your dignities; you are the redeemed of the Lord, therefore be not earthly minded; you are the children of the King of Zion, walk as such; ye are espoused to Christ, magnify your match; lean upon him, and duly prove the knowledge of your heavenly and best realities.

The harvest is great and the labourers are few; pray mightily for more, and treat honourably the few you have left. Your neglect of hearing them may provoke the Master of the vineyard to call home from you those labourers you have, as of late he hath many of our reverend brethren. See what gifts you have among you: if there be any hopeful youths, let them exercise themselves, and be kind to them and tender of them; take heed that you do not discourage them you have, lest you should be made to lament your imprudent and inconsiderate management.

We had a loving and comfortable conference together, in the public work we have had, both of ministers and hearers; also, necessary truths preached and plainly propounded according to the unerring rule of God's word.

Beloved of the Lord, we beseech you, add your hearty prayers to God, that our endeavours, both public and private, may be watered with blessings from on high. We commend you to the care of the Almighty and ever merciful God, who is able to do abundantly for us, beyond what we can ask or think.

We have appointed brother Enoch Morgan to preach the sermon next year; and, in case of failure, brother Owen Thomas.

Agreed to the request of the church of Philadelphia, setting forth that they have been at a great charge in building a meeting-house, which is to be very heavy, unless the rest of the churches of the same order will find in their hearts to contribute towards the defraying of the same.

The Association had neither queries nor requests from any of the churches; but the associated brethren, seeing no messengers from Piscataqua as usual, and hearing by some of our brethren of the sad and distracted condition of that congregation, they thought proper to write to them, and to appoint Mr. Jenkin Jones and Mr. Joseph Eaton to give them a visit before the winter, which, by the blessing of God, proved a means to reduce that church to peace and order.

Jenkin Jones,	Jno. Davis,	Wm. Hugh,
Enoch Morgan,	John Devonold,	George Eaton,
Nathaniel Jenkins,	Jno. Morgan,	Henry Oxly,
Benjamin Griffith,	Reynolds Howell,	Jno. Holmes,
Joseph Eaton,	Robert Chalfant,	Job Shepherd,
Owen Thomas,	Evan Mathias,	Jno. Coward,
William Kinnersly,	Jno. Heart,	Wm. Thomas.

1732.

In the year 1732, a question was moved: Whether a person, not being baptized himself, and presuming, in private, to baptize another; whether such pretended baptism be valid or no, or whether it might not be adjudged a nullity?

Resolved. We judge such baptism as invalid, and no better than if it had never been done.

Upon the consideration of the great want of ministerial helps, which some churches have moved, it is agreed by this Association, that a day of fasting and prayer be kept by all the churches in our communion, that the Lord may gift some among ourselves, such as may be serviceable; or order, in the course of his providence, some such to come among us from elsewhere; and we do fix upon the 26th day of October, next ensuing, for that purpose, humbly requesting the members of our churches conscientiously to observe the same.

1733.

The elders, ministers, and messengers, of the congregations holding believers' baptism, in Pennsylvania and the Jerseys, met in Association, at Philadelphia, the 22d day of September, 1733, to the several congregations we represent send Christian salutation:—

Dearly beloved in the bowels of Jesus Christ, and in the bonds of his gospel, whom we here represent, and whose interests we hope all of us have chiefly at heart; at the conclusion of our meeting, we think ourselves bound to give you an account of our affairs while together. We met, and had an Association sermon preached by Enoch Morgan; afterwards received and heard your letters; accepted your messengers; and are glad to see your care and diligence in sending them to maintain visible annual correspondence together. The letters show the churches to be at peace, and additions to most of them the last year. Blessed be God for it. At our public meeting we had many great and excellent truths of the gospel of Christ preached from divers texts by our ministering brethren, very edifying and comforting.

Dear brethren, our joy and crown at the appearing of our Lord Jesus Christ, the chief Shepherd, we beseech you to consider seriously your great privileges, as you are favored with those which belong to God's children, and have a nail in his holy place, and a name among the living in Jerusalem, and are called to glory and virtue. What obligations you are under to adorn your profession, to walk worthy of your vocation, and to make religion your main and most important business in life, that you may be found doing your Lord's will when he cometh.

We cannot but observe to you again the scarcity of ministerial supplies in many churches, and put you in mind of your duty to pray to the Lord of the harvest to send forth more men to the work of the harvest. Dear brethren, pray earnestly for a blessing on the labors of those you have, and let your frequent presence and walking with God in the use of means, be their encouragement. Most of the churches complain of much indifference and lukewarmness in the things of God: we hope it is not merely to complain, but out of experience. We advise you to keep close with God in every gospel duty, public and private; use all means to provoke one another to love and good works; pray fervently to God to give you more hearty affections and clearer sight of the excellency of Jesus Christ.

We conclude, commending you all to the care of God Almighty, in the name of the blessed Jesus. Amen.

Brother Jenkin Jones to preach the Association sermon the next year; in case of failure, brother Joseph Eaton.

Enoch Morgan,	Obadiah Holmes,	John Heart,
Ben. Griffiths,	John Garret,	Robert James,
John Davis,	Robert Chalffont,	Gershom Mott,
George Eaton,	—— Randolph,	Ben. Stelle,
John Davis,	Jenkin Jones,	John Evans,
John Holmes,	Joseph Eaton,	Richard Hall,
Ebenezer Smith,	Wm. Thomas,	Jer. Collett,
James Cox,	Simon Butler,	Joseph Fitz Randolph.
John Devonald,		

1734.

The elders, ministers, and messengers, of the congregations holding believers' baptism, in Pennsylvania and the Jerseys, met in Association at Philadelphia, on the 21st, 22d and 23d of September, A. D., 1734, to the several congregations we represent, send Christian salutation:—

Dearly beloved in our Lord and holy Redeemer Jesus Christ, and in the fellowship of the gospel of the Son of God, our joy and our crown of rejoicing in the day of his appearing, we have cause to bless God on your behalf, who is pleased to continue you as so many candlesticks to hold forth the glorious light of the gospel in these remote colonies. We return you our thanks for your care and diligence in sending your messengers to associate with us in this our yearly correspondence, and to assist in the work before us. We think it meet to give you an account of our affairs and procedure at this time. Beloved, we met in love at the time and place appointed, perused your Christian letters, accepted your messengers, and we find the churches we represent to be mostly in peace among themselves, though some of them are, at present, under disagreeable circumstances, which, we hope, God will remove in his mercy. Some additions have been made this last year in most of the churches, in some large additions, which is very comfortable to hear.

Our public opportunities have been so employed, that, by the blessing of Almighty God upon the labour of our ministering brethren, we hope all will be to his glory and the good of souls. Now, dearly beloved of us, and we hope also of the Lord Jesus Christ himself, the God of glory, who hath called you to glory and virtue, we exhort you, we beseech you, by the tender mercies of our gracious God, that you walk worthy of the vocation wherewith you are called; that your conversation may shine with gospel purity and holiness; that you behave yourselves as sons of God, without rebuke, in the midst of this crooked and perverse generation; that you make it your business to keep close with God, in gospel duties and the use of means; be instant in prayer for the prosperity of Zion; labour earnestly to keep the unity of the Spirit in the bond of peace; love one another from a pure heart, that so you prevent the great design of Satan, who endeavours to sow discord and animosities among God's people. We advise the churches that want ministerial helps to set a day apart, once a month, to implore the Lord of the harvest to thrust forth faithful labourers into his harvest; by fasting and prayer, continue in a faithful depending, waiting and heartily crying to God, until he be pleased to grant you the desirable blessing. Those that have such helps, we advise to beg a blessing thereupon, and successive continuation thereof.

Several queries from Middletown came to the Association, viz.—

1. Whether we may accept and take in a minister of a different persuasion at our appointed meetings.

Answered in the negative; unless the church see cause, upon some particular occasions.

2. Whether it may not be more convenient for us to keep up our meetings, as usual, by reading the Scriptures, singing of psalms, and prayer, than to admit men of different persuasions?

Answered in the affirmative.

3. Whether it be justifiable for our members to neglect our own appointed meetings, and at their pleasure go to hear those differing in judgment from us?

Answered in the negative. Heb. x. 25.

Brother Joseph Eaton to preach the Association sermon the next year; and in case of his failure, brother Benjamin Griffith to preach the same.

Minutes of the case between the Association and William Davis, considered September 30, 1734:—

Respecting the crimes alledged against him, of selling two books sent him, and of representing us in a wrong light to Mr. David Rees and Mr. Hollis. He, upon confession of his faults, was pardoned by the Association.

These advices and directions were given to the church of the Great Valley and William Davis:—

1. That William Davis should give himself a member of the church at the Great Valley, and those that were baptized by him shall be examined by the said church, or by a committee of the church appointed for that purpose; and if they be satisfied, then the persons may be received.

2. If they should unanimously agree to divide and constitute themselves in two separate churches, we advise that they be so divided

and ordered, as that there be *no picking and choosing in the case;* that is to say, that those who live in one place should not give themselves members to the church farthest off, for any reasons arising from biased ends or inclinations, or already received partialities.

3. That, on the proof that they happen to jar or disagree, or any person or persons be dissatisfied, whether it be in respect to their accommodating the present peace or agreement, or of hereafter dividing themselves, as above said, if they proceed—that in such cases they shall call for help from neighbouring churches.

We conclude, recommending you and the whole work into the hand of God, and remain,

    Yours, in gospel services and relations,

John Drake,	Samuel Jones,	John Donald,
Jenkin Jones,	John Garret,	George Eaton,
Benjn. Griffiths,	Abel Morgan,	Hr. Collett,
John Davis,	Enoch Morgan,	John Evans,
Simon Butler,	Owen Thomas,	Garret Wall,
John Dardis,	Joseph Eaton,	Robert Chalfant,
Samuel Osborne,	Jno. Holmes,	John Clarkson.
John Hart,		

1735.

The elders, ministers, and messengers of the baptized congregations in Pennsylvania and the Jerseys, met at Philadelphia, 27th, 28th, and 29th of September, A. D. 1735.

To the several congregations we are related unto, do send Christian salutation.

Dearly beloved in Christ Jesus our Lord, we rejoice to see your care and diligence in maintaining this annual Association. It is comfortable to us to see your zeal in the welfare of our Zion in general, and of the several little tabernacles we are related unto in particular, which our dear Lord hath placed in these remote parts. We have reason to praise God that you are preserved from the floods, delusions, errors, and other manifold temptations, which have hurled many away from the faith of God, and from holding fast their profession and duty to God and his people. Knowing that it is your expectation to hear of, and also our duty to acquaint you with, our affairs, we hereby give you an account of the same. We met at the time appointed, and perused your letters, whereby we find most of the churches to be at peace and unity, which we heartily pray God to preserve where it is, and to restore where it is not. To our great joy and comfort we find that large additions have been made this year to some churches, and some in every church belonging to this body; blessed be God for this refreshing news. Our ministering brethren have preached several of the important truths of the gospel, to our great comfort, which we hope Almighty God will water with his heavenly blessing. Dear brethren, as God, by his gospel, hath called you with an holy calling, we pray God that you may be fitted and furnished with all grace to adorn your profession, and make you fruitful vineyards unto himself, that your conversation may shine with gospel purity, to the praise and glory of his rich grace.

In the year 1735, upon a proposal made, that a book should be provided, and a scribe nominated to transcribe the minutes of the Association, and to insert therein all that may be of use and information to their successors;—it was agreed that Mr. Jenkin Jones be the scribe, and Mr. John Holme to be his assistant. But it failed then.

Query. If any member, or members, of a congregation grow scrupulous about matters merely indifferent in themselves, such as the mode of administration, as is usual in our churches, or the quality of the bread or wine, or the manner of serving, as the cup upon a plate, or without, making the same a matter of conscience, and thereupon totally refrain their communion. What is best to be done in such a case?

Solution. That such persons, contending, quarreling, and so refraining church communion upon such light grounds—since such things are left undetermined by our great Lawgiver—are much to be blamed; and a church is nowise obliged to yield to such vain humours, but may continue their order, according to the rules of expediency and harmless decency, and deal according to the word with such delinquents; for it is to be doubted that such person or persons have not a design to make a rupture, seeing the matter in debate is so trivial.

2. Upon a motion moved by some members of the Association: Whether a person that is a well-wisher to us, and desires to be admitted a member into a church far distant from the place of his abode; whereas a church of the same order is nearer to him than the church that he proposes to join with; whether it be orderly for the distant church to receive such an one? Yea or nay?

Resolved in the negative, there being substantial reasons to the contrary. Such practice is contrary to the intendment, in instituting particular churches.—*See Confession of Faith*, chap. xxvii. *See also our Treatise of Discipline*, 28, 29.

Brother Benjamin Griffith is to preach the Association sermon next year, and Brother John Davis alternate.

Recommending you to the blessing of heaven, we remain yours in the dearest of bonds.

Ebenezer Smith,	James Tapscot,	Jenkin Jones,
John Manners,	William Thomas,	Enoch Morgan,
Isaac Whitten,	Owen Thomas,	Nathaniel Jenkins,
Thomas Curtis,	Benjamin Griffith,	Hugh David,
George Eaton,	Joseph Eaton,	Jeremiah Collett,
Benjamin Stelle,	John Davis,	Joseph Powell,
John Clarkson,	John Holmes,	Griffith Evans,
Moses Martin,	John Hart,	Hugh Evans.
James Cox,	John Davis,	

1736.

In the year 1736, no queries appeared, nor any request made to this Association; nevertheless, the Association being informed of a discord and contention in the church at Montgomery, did nominate and appoint Mr. Jenkin Jones, and Mr. Owen Thomas, ministers, with any two other brethren that they might judge serviceable, to visit, and to endeavour to conciliate matters between them. And it was accordingly effected.

1737.

In the year 1737, there came no requests nor queries from the churches; and, consequently, no other from the Association, but a warm and loving exhortation to diligence and watchfulness in our religious duties, and to maintain the great and necessary doctrines of the Christian religion; and, in particular, to be steadfast against errors, and faithful in belief of the doctrine of the Holy Trinity, of man's creation, fall, restoration by grace through Christ, the real divine and human nature in union in the person of Christ.

1738.

The elders and messengers of the several congregations, holding believers' baptism in Pennsylvania and the Jerseys, met in Association at Philadelphia, the 23d day of September, and continued to 25th, 1738.

To the several congregations we represent, we wish grace and peace from God our Father, and our Lord Jesus Christ, may be multiplied.

"Dearly beloved in the faith and fellowship of the gospel, we are glad to see your care and diligence in sending your messengers to associate in this manner, hoping it proceeds from love to God, and due regard to the general interest of Jesus Christ, and the interest of the several little tabernacles in these provinces. At the close of our meeting, according to our practice and your expectation, we send you an account of our affairs; we perused your letters, received your messengers, and, by your letters, we have been informed that some have been added this year to most of the churches, and we rejoice to hear that the churches are in peace and unity. We have complaints of much coldness and indifference in the things of God and the concerns of religion, which, we hope, are not only by way of compliment, but from a sense of the growing evil. We beseech you, dear brethren, be earnest with God in prayer, for the increase of your graces; for, where these graces abound, they will make you that you shall be neither barren nor unfruitful in the things of God. Give all diligence to make your calling and election sure. Attend upon the means of grace. Keep close to your respective meetings. Exhort and admonish one another in love. Endeavor to provoke one another to love and good works. Have a special care to maintain a sure discipline, as well as doctrine. Let it be every one's endeavor to wait in the way of duty, for the coming of the Son of God from heaven; for he that cometh will come, and will not tarry, and will faithfully reward the labors of his faithful servants. In due time we shall reap, if we faint not. We recommend you to God, who is able to build you up in the holy faith which is in Christ Jesus; to make you abound in all the fruits of the Spirit, and, by his power, to keep you through faith unto salvation. We remain your brethren in the fellowship of the gospel."

John Davis,	David Davis,	Enoch Morgan,
James Cox,	John Manners,	Jenkin Jones,
James Mott,	John Holmes,	David Evans,
Joshua Martin,	Simon Butler,	Ebenezer Smith,
Joseph Powell,	John Heart,	Benjamin Griffith,
Stephen Shepherd,	John Coward,	George Eaton,
Abel Morgan,	Nath. Jenkins,	Thomas Davis.
Eben'r Kinnersly,	Joseph Eaton,	

Query. Whether a person, ordained by laying on hands, for a ruling elder, who should afterwards be called by the church, by reason of his gifts, to the word and doctrine, must be again ordained by imposition of hands? Resolved in the affirmative.

Agreed, that since the catechisms are expended, and few or none to be had, and our youth thereby not likely to be instructed in the fundaments of saving knowledge, that the several congregations we represent should consult amongst themselves what they can raise of money for so good a design, and send, against the 1st of May next, by their letters, to Mr. Jenkin Jones or John Holmes, in Philadelphia, that they may know what number to draw out of the press.

Ordered, that Mr. Enoch Morgan preach the Association sermon next year; in case of his failure, Mr. Jenkin Jones.

1739.

The elders and messengers of the congregations holding believers' baptism in Pennsylvania and the Jerseys, met in association at Philadelphia, 22d September, 1739.

To the congregations we represent, we send our Christian salutation.

Dearly beloved in our Lord and holy Redeemer, Jesus Christ, and in the fellowship of the gospel of the Son of God, our joy and crown of rejoicing in the day of his appearing, we have cause to bless God in your behalf, that our gracious God is pleased to continue us so many candlesticks to hold the glorious light of the gospel in these remote colonies; we also return thanks, brethren, for your care and diligence in sending your messengers to associate with us in this our yearly correspondence together, and to assist in the work before us. We think it meet, according to your desires, to give you an account of our affairs and proceedings at this time. We met in love, at the time and place appointed. After hearing a sermon, we perused your letters and received your messengers, and find the churches mostly in peace amongst themselves. Additions have been made in some churches. As we met in love, so we lovingly conferred together, and are now about to depart in peace. Our public opportunities have been so employed, that we hope, by the blessing of God upon the labors of our ministering brethren, it will be to the glory of God and the good of souls. Now, dearly beloved of us, we hope also by our Lord Jesus Christ himself, the Lord of glory, who hath called you with a holy calling, we exhort you, we beseech you by the tender mercies of our God, that you walk worthy of that vocation wherewith you are called, that your conversation may shine with gospel purity and holiness, that you behave yourselves as the sons of God, without rebuke, in the midst of this crooked and perverse generation with whom we live. Keep close with God, in all gospel duties. Be instant in prayer for the prosperity of Zion. Labor earnestly to keep the unity of the Spirit in the bond of peace; love one another with a pure heart; that so you prevent the great desire of Satan, who endeavors to sow discord and animosities among God's people. We further advise those churches that want ministerial help, to pray earnestly to the Lord of the harvest, to thrust forth faithful laborers into his harvest; and, as to those who have ministerial help, we exhort them, in the spirit of meekness and love, highly to prize such a mercy, and bless God for the same, and assist them, both by prayers and godly conferences, with other necessaries, according to the rule of God's word.

A query from the church at the Great Valley: In case that members will absent themselves from the communion of the church, and will give no reason for their so absenting, nor any account why they withdrew, notwithstanding messengers have been sent to such divers times, what ought the church to do further?

Solution. That the church shall send messengers once more to such, to inform them, that if they further absent themselves, without giving sufficient reason, the church may deal with such offenders as covenant breakers, and as despisers of the authority that is given to the church by Christ her head.

In answer to a proposal from Montgomery, concerning the keeping of the present Association, whether it be as usual, or altered?

Resolved, that it be continued as usual the present year, and other general meetings at the discretion of the churches where they are appointed; and if the churches desire the method of the Association altered, let them consult unanimously, and insert the same in next year's letters.

Upon a proposal made by a member of this Association, that some better method should be taken to keep up and maintain this present Association more regularly than it hath been heretofore.

Resolved, that a copy of the same be transmitted to every congregation relating to this body, that it may be concluded upon at the next meeting.

Agreed, that Brother Owen Thomas is to preach next year; in case of failure, Brother Jenkin Jones.

John Stelle,	John Davis,	Jenkin Jones,
Thomas Curtis,	Daniel Davis,	Joseph Eaton,
Richard Whiting,	John Bentle,	Hugh David,
George Eaton,	John Manners,	John Davis,
David Evans,	Enoch Morgan,	Thomas Jones,
John Wooledge,	Owen Thomas,	John Holme.
James Tapscott,		

1740.

The elders and messengers of the several congregations of the people owning believers' baptism in Pennsylvania and the Jerseys, meeting in Association at Philadelphia, September 27th, 1740:

To the churches we are related to in gospel order, we send our gospel salutation.

Dearly beloved and highly favored of the Lord Jesus, we wish increase of grace, that you may abound in all good works to the praise of him who hath called you from darkness into his marvellous light, that you may be owned and approved as so many delightful gardens or fruitful fields, receiving plentiful blessings from the God of heaven. Brethren, we hope your prayers for us have been accepted at the throne of Zion's King, and that we have experienced the fruits of them in the warm, affectionate love we saluted each other with, and the glorious truths of the gospel, held forth amongst us with all clearness and power, as also in the peace and harmony that appeared in our proceedings, wherein faith or discipline were concerned, though, perhaps, in some other things, we might have different apprehensions. We have great ground of rejoicing in the grace of God towards you, and of praising the Author and Giver, when we hear of your steadfast cleaving to the Lord in his ways and worship; that the power of hell hath not been able to blow you away, nor to hinder your growth and numbers, which we find to be very considerable the last year, God owning the labors of his poor instruments. This calls for our and your thanks abundantly. We beseech you, in the bowels of love, to go on in the strength of your God. Pray earnestly that he would stablish you and keep you from falling. You virgin professors, shake off sloth and slumber, the bridegroom is at the door! Search well your vessels; see that you have the true oil of the Spirit. Take heed of counterfeit grace. Rest not on the outside of the ark, but enter in at the right door; that you may be secured in the flood of great waters from being swallowed up and lost. It is an easy thing to profess Christ when the secular power draws not its sword against religion; but it is dangerous, nevertheless, for such to be asleep and careless, for the adversary hath golden baits; in days of peace, he glosses and beautifies errors and false doctrine, so that they are swallowed without chewing. It concerns all that would keep their garments undefiled, to try the spirits by the Scripture, and get the evidence of the Spirit of truth in your hearts, that you may not be cozened or cheated of true faith; that you may not take the apples of Sodom, instead of the saving fruits of the true tree of life, which is in the midst of the Paradise of God. Walk in love, peace, and holiness, adorning the doctrine of God our Saviour in all things.

Furthermore, we earnestly entreat you to approve, use, and exercise yourselves in all the duties enjoined on you in the charter of our salvation, and the institutions of worship, commanded by the Lord Jesus therein. Take heed of prejudice against any part of God's will recorded in the gospel. Be impartial and universal in your obedience to all. Keep constantly, as much as you may, your own meetings. Break not through nor step over the hedge of the gospel government. Have a tender regard for help, and encourage those that minister unto you in holy things, and if there be any promising gifts arising, nourish the same with love and acceptance. The harvest is great, but the laborers are few; pray that God would thrust out laborers into his vineyard.

Thus we commend you to God and the word of his grace, who is able to establish you to the end, and make you meet for the incorruptible inheritance: to whom be glory, now and for ever. Amen.

We are your brethren in Christ and the fellowship of the gospel.

Evan Loyd,	Job Shepherd,	James Jones,
Richard Whittan,	Jeremiah Collett,	John Remington,
John Watson,	Robert Chalfant,	Nathaniel Jenkins,
Evan James,	Thomas Edmunds,	Jenkin Jones,
John Manners,	Griffith Evans,	Owen Thomas,
Henry Hareys,	Benjamin Stelle,	Joseph Eaton,
James Mott,	William Thomas,	Benjamin Griffiths,
Joshua Martin,	Thomas Jones,	John Davis,
John Holmes,	George Eaton,	Abel Morgan,
Simon Butler,	John Coward,	David Davis.
John Davis,		

Brother Jenkin Jones is to preach the Association sermon next year; in case of failure, Brother Benjamin Griffith.

A query from Cohansie: Whether a pious person, of the number of Pedo-Baptists, who forbears to have his own children sprinkled, may be admitted in to our communion without being baptized? And doth not the refusing admittance to such an one, discover want of charity in a church so refusing?

Given to vote, and passed all in the negative. *Nemine contradicente.*

Reasons annexed. 1. It is not for want of charity that we thus answer. Our practice shows the contrary; for we baptize none but such as, in the judgment of charity, have grace, being unbaptized; but it is because we find, in the commission, that no unbaptized persons are to be admitted into church communion. Matt. xxviii. 19, 20; Mark xvi. 16. Compare Acts ii. 41; 1 Cor. xii. 13.

2. Because it is the church's duty to maintain the ordinances as they are delivered to us in Scripture: 2 Thess. ii. 15; 1 Cor. xi. 2; Isa. viii. 20.

3. Because we cannot see it agreeable, in any respect, for the procuring that unity, unfeigned love, and undisturbed peace, which is required, and ought to be in and among Christian communities. 1 Cor. i. 10; Eph. iv. 3.

Query 2, from Piscataqua: Whether it is regular to baptize persons proposing for baptism, upon the plea that they may be at liberty to communicate where they please?

Answered in the negative. *Nemine contra dicente*, for these reasons:—

1. Because, in the great commission, we are commanded to teach and observe all things which Christ hath enjoined upon us in the gospel. Matt. xxviii. 20.

2. Because it is not agreeable to the practice of the Apostles, who acted according to the said commission, as appears by Acts ii. 41, 42, compared with 2 Cor. viii. 5.

3. Because such a practice is directly destructive to all gospel rule, order, and discipline; for by such way all offences and irregularities, yea, even the most scandalous immoralities and fundamental errors must escape without proper censures, according to the gospel rule, Matt. xviii. 17; Rom. xvi. 17; Phil. iii. 16, 17; 1 Cor. v. 5; xi. 16, and xiv. 32, 33.

Added to the several churches belonging, in gospel love, to this Association, by baptism, the past year, one hundred and eleven souls.

1741.

The elders and messengers of the several churches holding believers' baptism in Pennsylvania and the Jerseys, met in Association at Philadelphia, September 26, 1741.

To the churches we represent, send greeting.

Dearly beloved in the most excellent relation in the gospel of Jesus Christ, our fellow soldiers in spiritual warfare, our fellow servants in the kingdom and patience of our dear Lord, our joy and crown of rejoicing at the day of his appearing. We met together at the time appointed, and, after a suitable sermon preached, we perused your letters and accepted your messengers. We found, by your letters, to our great comfort, that the churches in general are at peace: many have been added to their numbers. We have cause to hope our blessed God will yet dwell among his little tabernacles, which he hath erected in this wilderness. We are glad to hear of your unanimous reception of what we offered in answer to your queries last year. We desire the churches may often be reminded of such solutions, which greatly tend to preserving the gospel order among the churches. Dear brethren, we met and conferred together in love, concord, and harmonious unity among ourselves in our private meetings and prayers to God. Our ministering brethren have been enabled to preach upon important subjects, to our great satisfaction, and, we hope, to the benefit of many souls. We are now ready to part likewise in love. We hope our God will bring us to our respective homes again in safety, to the mutual comfort of both you and us; and we exhort you, with the bowels of Christian love, yea, we beseech you, in and by the tender mercies of our God, to remember you are called to glory and virtue. Endeavor to arise and set a due value on your privileges in the house of God. Remember, holiness becometh his house for ever. Endeavor to give all diligence to approve yourselves as sons of God without rebuke. Gird up the loins of your mind and be sober. Neglect not the assembling of yourselves together. Hold fast the form of sound words in faith and love which is in Christ Jesus. Hold the truths declared to you in the gospel. Keep close to sound doctrine. Adhere to gospel discipline and order, to the end that it may keep you pure. Shun all disorders and disorderly persons. Do all your things in love. Be affectionate one towards another. Keep continual correspondence with God in prayer, and promote religion in your families. The God of all consolation be with you, and bless you with all grace and gifts, sanctify you and fit you for a habitation unto himself, by his Spirit, while here, and make you meet partakers of the inheritance of the saints hereafter. We recommend you to God, who is able to make you persevere unto the end.

Joseph Stillwell,	John Davis,	Jenkin Jones,
John Manners,	Reynold Howell,	Joseph Eaton,
Hugh Evans,	John Beckingham,	Benjamin Griffith,
Joshua Potts,	Richard Hall,	John Davis,
David Evans,	John Garrett,	Abel Morgan,
George Eaton,	Owen Thomas,	David Davis.

Queries from the Great Valley:

1st Query. Suppose a difference happening between two of the brethren, and both refer their difference to the church to be determined; and the church take upon them to pass a judgment upon the matter in debate, according to the best of their understanding, and according to Scripture rule; yet one of the parties is dissatisfied with the judgment, though he cannot render any substantial reason for his so doing: what may be done with the brother so contending?

Solution. The Association having maturely considered the matter, according to the best light we could obtain, cannot help but to judge that the church acted rightly; and we judge the contending person worthy of reproof, because he, having submitted and preferred the matter to the church for final determination, yet, contrary to what might be expected from him as a man, much more as a Christian, refused to comply with the church's determination; (except the said person can give substantial and convincing reasons to make it appear that the church was not well informed of the matter;) as Matt. xviii. 17.

2d Query. Suppose a brother is put out of his full communion in the church, upon some dissatisfaction at his conduct, and afterwards shall give satisfaction to the majority of the church, by confession of his fault; but some are not satisfied, and have no substantial reason to render for the same, what may the church do in such a case?

Solution. We advise the church and the persons dissatisfied to use moderation for some time, and endeavor, by private means, to gain the dissatisfied party. If that fails, at your monthly meeting, urge such persons to produce sufficient reasons for their dissatisfaction; and for want of such reasons, or upon their refusing to produce such reasons, the church may deal with such as disorderly persons, according to Rom. xvi. 17, 18; 1 Cor. xi. 16, and xiv. 33.

Brother Benjamin Griffith is to preach the Association sermon next year; Brother Joseph Eaton in case of failure.

1742.

The elders and messengers of the baptized congregations in Pennsylvania and the Jerseys, met in Association at Philadelphia, September 25, 1742.

Send our Christian salutation.

Dearly beloved in the Lord Jesus,—We are heartily glad to hear how you have been preserved hitherto, as so many tabernacles upon which is the name of the Lord, notwithstanding the many enemies and oppositions you have to deal with. Surely it is an evident demonstration that you have the Lord on your side. We commend you, brethren, for your care and diligence to continue to walk with God, also your faithfulness in sending to maintain this our annual Association. We met in the love and unity of the gospel of Christ, and, after an Association sermon was preached, we perused your letters and received your messengers, as the lovely tokens of Christian friendship. Our consultations have been very agreeable to gospel fellowship. We trust we can say the Lord hath been amongst us powerfully, enabling our ministering brethren in the work of the gospel, so that several excellent truths of that gospel have been evidently displayed, such as had a direct tendency to the good of souls, both of saints and sinners. It rejoices us very much to hear that most of the churches have peace among themselves. Blessed be God, the additions this past year are sixty-seven. It seems plain that the Lord is yet visiting his churches with the manifestations of his mercy and grace. We entreat you, therefore, in the bowels of the gospel of Christ, to see your calling, brethren; to prize your places and stations in the house of God. Improve the privileges you enjoy by holy walking, as becometh saints; keep your places in the churches according to your covenant; take heed you do not neglect your own assemblies; be not carried away with every wind of doctrine, but walk steadily in all the ways of religion; keep close to God in family duties; make conscience of the life of religion between God and your souls in secret; take heed that your conversation be agreeable to your profession; endeavor always to carry a conscience void of offence before God and men; keep yourselves clean from the pollution of sin, and from the vain, wicked world. Now the God of peace be with you, to bless and sanctify you more and more, that you may abound in the work of the Lord, to the praise and glory of his rich grace, through Jesus; is the hearty desire of your beloved brethren in the gospel.

A motion was made in the Association for reprinting the Confession of faith, set forth by the elders of baptized congregations, met in London, A. D. 1689, with a short treatise of church discipline, to be annexed to the Confession of faith. Agreed, that the thing was needful and likely to be very useful; and in order to carry it on, it is ordered to send it to the several churches belonging to this Association; to make a trial of what sums of money can be raised, and to send an account to Mr. Jenkin Jones, to the intent, that when the several collections are computed, if it be found sufficient to defray the charges of the work, that then it shall go on; if not, then to drop it for this year; and if it be carried on, that then an addition of two articles be therein inserted: that is to say, concerning singing of psalms in the worship of God, and laying of hands upon baptized believers. Ordered, also, that the said Mr. Jones and Benjamin Griffith do prepare a short treatise of discipline, to be annexed to the said Confession of faith.

Thos. Curtis,	Abel Morgan,	Owen Thomas,
Job Warford,	John Davis,	Joseph Eaton,
Stephen Shepherd,	Wm. Marshall,	Ben. Stelle,
Joshua Potts,	Job Shepherd,	Thomas Jones,
Nath. Evans,	John Coward,	George Eaton,
John Bently,	Richd. Winter,	John Davis,
John Beckingham,	Robt. Chalfant,	Peter Nesherman.
James Mott,	Danl. Howell,	
David Davis,	Jenkin Jones,	

1743.

The elders, ministers, and messengers of the several congregations, baptized on profession of faith, meeting at Philadelphia, the 24th of September, 1743, and continued by adjournment to the 28th of the same month.

Unto the several churches, we send our loving and Christian salutation.

Dearly beloved in our glorious Redeemer,—We are very much refreshed in beholding your readiness in sending your messengers among us, and we bless God for the grace bestowed upon you, so as to unite you, as we hope, first to Christ, and then to one another in church relation, whereby you are capacitated, with united hearts, to send your comfortable letters, wherein we find our churches, in general, at peace and unity, and some increase in most of them.

We hope God has answered your prayers for us; for we met in love, had the necessary and precious truths of the gospel publicly dispensed with much warmth and clearness; continued in love and meekness in our debates and consultations; though we have been concerned in tedious and difficult business, which has not been the trouble of former Associations in these parts. Now we are to part from one another to our respective homes, after we have given you some necessary counsels.

Beloved brethren, we desire you in the bowels of love to stand fast in defence of the necessary truths of the gospel of Christ, concerning right faith and obedience; give up yourselves to the study of the word, and hold fast the profession of your faith without wavering, in these shaking and wavering days; neglect no duty that the gospel requires. We fear there are many among you who neglect prayer in and with your families. Oh sad! What life of religion can there be in such a Sardis-like state! having a name to live, and at the same time dead; without breath or panting after God. Keep up your stated meetings; worship the Lord on his day, and other appointed seasons; forsake not the assembling yourselves together; it is a dishonor to Christ, a discouragement to your ministers, and weakening the hands and grieving the hearts of your fellow-members, who have the credit of religion and the prosperity of Zion at heart. Bear one another's burdens; withdraw not your shoulders from helping one another; let not carnal interest, or a selfish, stiff, stubborn humor, prevent your kind and generous contribution to the necessity of the poor, or supporting your ministers, or the carrying on of any public work, which may be necessary to the decent and commodious worshiping of the Lord, who giveth all you enjoy. Let your light shine before men; walk in the paths of virtue, holiness, and pure conversation. Glorify God before the world:—it is pleasing unto him, and makes way, by growing and continuing therein, for your comfort and peace in this life, and will administer boldness, and an abundant entrance unto you, in the end, into that glorious kingdom prepared for the doers of God's will.

Tuesday, the house met according to appointment, at 8 o'clock, A.M., to consider further the affair begun yesterday, touching the differences at Montgomery. After some time spent in debate thereon, brother Joseph Eaton stood up, and freely, to our apprehension, recanted, renounced, and condemned all expressions, which he heretofore had used, whereby his brethren at Montgomery, or any persons elsewhere, were made to believe that he departed from the literal sense and meaning of that fundamental article in our Confession of faith, concerning the eternal generation and Sonship of Jesus Christ our Lord; he acknowledged with grief his misconduct therein, whether by word or deed. We desire that all our churches would take notice thereof, and have a tender regard for him in his weak and aged years, and in particular, of that great truth upon which the Christian religion depends; without which it must not only totter, but fall to the ground; which he confesses he was sometimes doubtful of. Our brother Butler, gave his acknowledgement, written in his own hand, in the following words:—" I freely confess that I have given too much cause for others to judge that I contradicted our Confession of faith, concerning the eternal generation of the Son of God, in some expressions contained in my paper, which I now with freedom condemn, and am sorry for my so doing, and for every other misconduct that I have been guilty of, from first to last, touching the said article, or any other matter."

Dear People: We pray God you would content yourselves and be satisfied with the revealed will of God, concerning the unutterable, as well as inconceivable, mysteries of Father, Son, and Holy Ghost, three in one, and one in three, the co-essentiality, the co-eternity, and co-equality, of the three glorious Persons in one eternal God; and that you suffer not a vain and over-curious search to be made thereinto by human reason and worldly wisdom. A number in one of our churches having suffered themselves to inquire therein, according to aforesaid rules of human reason and worldly wisdom, have been so entangled and confused, that they were carried so far as to question the Sonship of the second Person, as he is God, without having reference to his manhood and mediatory offices; which conception and supposition we not only disallow, but abhor and condemn, and are glad that God hath blessed means to convict the said parties of their sin and error; and herein we were *nemine contra dicente*, fully united to repel, and put a stop to, as far as we may, unto the Arian, Socinian, and Antitrinitarian systems; protesting unto the world our joint belief of, and our resolution to maintain, the eternal and inconceivable generation of the second Person in the ever adorable Trinity; and have, we hope, prevailed effectually, so as to bring the persons chiefly concerned, as questioning the same, to a free confession of their mistake therein.

And now, dear brethren, we conclude, praying God to bless you with increase of grace and numbers; and that you would not only read our advice over, and then put it by, but practice what, in love, we send unto you; that God may be glorified, love abound, the peace of the community continue and strengthen. May you be daily made meet for Christ's eternal embraces. Amen.

We had a copy of discipline designed to be annexed to our Confession of faith, by an order of a former Association, read and considered at this meeting, and approved by the whole house.

Brother David Davis to preach the next Association sermon; in case of failure, brother Abel Morgan.

Nathaniel Jenkins, Scribe.

Jno. Bently,	Jeremiah Hand,	John Davis,
Jno. Garrett,	Wm. Smith,	Job Shephard,
James Davis,	Wm. Fowler,	George Eaton,
Jeffrey Bently,	Jenkin Jones,	Moses Shephard,
Joshua Potts,	Owen Thomas,	Dano Evans,
Wm. Folwell,	Wm. Davies,	John Griffith,
James Mott,	Abel Morgan,	Reynold Howell.

1744.

The Association convened September 22d, 1744. Query from the church of Bethlehem: Suppose a person baptized by a man, who takes upon him to preach the gospel, and proceeds to administer the ordinances without a regular call or ordination from any church; whether the person so baptized may be admitted into any orderly church. Yea or nay?

Resolved: We cannot encourage such irregular proceedings; because it hath ill consequences every way attending it; it is also opposite to our discipline. We therefore give our sentiments that such administrations are irregular, invalid, and of no effect.

Agreed, that the messengers of the churches shall meet next year on Wednesday before the fourth Sunday in September.

Upon a request made to the Association by Simon Butler, it was agreed and appointed that our brethren, Nathaniel Jenkins, Owen Thomas, Benjamin Stelle, and Thomas Jones, visit the church of Montgomery on Wednesday after the first Sunday in November next, in order to try to accommodate the difference amongst them.

1745.

The Association convened on Wednesday, the 18th of September, 1745. Agreed and concluded, pursuant to requests made by the church of Bethlehem and brethren about Cranberry, that our reverend brethren, Nathaniel Jenkins and Jenkin Jones, be at Bethlehem the fourth Sunday in October, to assist at the ordination of Thomas Curtis; and the Friday after being the first day of November, they are to be at Cranberry, in order to settle the members there in church order.

The procedure of four messengers, sent by the Association the year before, was brought to the house by a report in writing, and read; and the question was put to the house, whether it was approved as reported.

Resolved in the affirmative. The report itself is not inserted, because Simon Butler and his party did not acquiesce with the determination.

A question being put to the house: Whether the messengers from the church of Montgomery be received as members of this Association?

Resolved in the affirmative. Accordingly, David Evans, Daniel Davis, and Daniel Griffith were received.

Concluded, that the Association continue as now kept, on Wednesday before the fourth Sunday in September, and the sermon begin at 10 o'clock, A. M.

1746.

The elders and messengers of the congregations baptized upon profession of faith, in Pennsylvania and the Jerseys, met at Philadelphia, the 24th day of September, 1746.

To the several churches we relate unto, sending Christian salutations.

Dearly beloved in the Lord Jesus, our joy and crown of rejoicing in the day of his appearing,—We rejoice to see your care and diligence in maintaining annual correspondence and Christian fellowship in the gospel of Christ. We, your representatives, being met together in love and gospel affection, having perused your letters, to the general comfort, find that our churches are at peace and unity, having had, in most of them, some additions, and, in some of them, a very considerable this last year. Blessed be the great God and Father of mercies for his goodness towards us on this behalf. Our consultations have been loving and unanimous, without any contradictions or heats in debate. We have had several things under consideration, a narrative of which we shall hereunto annex.

Now, dear brethren and fellow Christians, we exhort you to study and follow after those things that tend to peace and unity, provoking one another to love and good works, not neglecting the assembling yourselves together, as the manner of too many is, to the great loss and detriment of the whole body whereunto they belong, and showing a bad example to others.

Be diligent in reading the holy Scriptures, which are our only rule of faith and obedience, without which we can have no saving knowledge of God, or of Jesus Christ our Redeemer and hope. Put meditation also into practice, without which we cannot expect to profit. Pray without ceasing, in public and private, to the God of all grace, for the teaching and guidance of his Spirit, and his blessing to accompany your endeavors, and those of your ministers.

Brethren, we commend you to God and the word of his grace, praying that he would preserve you and us from enormities and immoralities in life, and make us meet to be partakers of the inheritance of the saints in light, through our Lord and Saviour Jesus Christ, to whom be glory everlasting.

Jenkin Jones,	John Davis,	Aaron Raily,
Owen Thomas,	John Griffith,	Henry Harris,
Benjamin Griffith,	John Watson,	Nathaniel Jenkins,
Benjamin Stelle,	John Stephenson,	John Manners,
John Davis,	John Garrat,	Robert Goeffry,
Abel Morgan,	Jephry Bentla,	Job Shepherd,
James Carman,	John Thomas,	Peter P. Vanhorn,
David Davis,	Daniel Griffith,	Stephen Watts,
Thomas Jones,	Benjamin Phillips,	Saml. Ashmead,
Joshua Potts,	John Vansand,	Wm. Ritenhouse.
William Marshall,		

1. Query from the church of Philadelphia: Whether it be lawful or regular for any person to preach the gospel publicly without ordination?

Answer: that which we have both rule and precedent for in the word of God, is, and must be, both lawful and regular, in 1 Tim. iii. We have a rule for proving such; for, having spoken concerning bishops, at the 10th verse the apostle speaks of deacons, saying, Let these also first be proved. The words have as immediate a reference to bishops as to deacons, else the word *also* would be superfluous. We may here argue from the less to the greater; for if the deacons, who are concerned but with the outward affairs of churches, must be proved, how much more ministers, who are to be stewards of the mysteries of God. 1 Tim. v. 22.

2. We have an undoubted instance in the case of Paul and Barnabas, who were teachers before their ordination. Acts xi. 25, 26. We have an account of Barnabas going to Tarsus to seek Saul; his finding him, his bringing him to Antioch, and of their assembling with that church, and of their teaching much people; at which time neither Paul nor Barnabas were ordained; and had it been either unlawful or irregular for men to preach without ordination, such a good man, full of the Holy Ghost as Barnabas was, would not surely be guilty of such a thing himself, nor promote Saul in doing so. But teach they did, and teachers they were called before ordination. Acts xiii. 3. But their ordination is expressed Acts xiii. 3, after they had been a long time teachers, and, with others, had taught much people, as Acts xi. 26. And it seems, by what Paul writes to the Galatians, chap. i. 18, and ii. 1, to be at least fourteen years, if not seventeen.

Seeing men are called teachers, as Paul and Barnabas are in Acts xiii. 1, and did undoubtedly teach profitably in the church of Antioch, before and without ordination, what reason can be given why there may not be in churches men of useful gifts, and profitable to teach all the days of their life without ordination? It is very probable that the Apostle Paul, seeing he occupied such a station himself a long time, speaks of such gifted brethren, Ephes. iv. 11, by the name of teachers. Seeing they are mentioned besides the pastors, or that such useful men may be the helps the same apostle mentions, 1 Cor. xii. 28, for helps cannot be more useful in any thing than in teaching. Our churches have had such teachers very frequently, as we might instance in many of them by name, if need were as well as the church of Antioch.

Here it will be proper to consider what time of trial or probation is, or ought to be taken, in proving church officers in general. We must note that the Holy Ghost hath no where limited or bounded the time that a church is to take for the trial of any of her officers; and therefore every particular church is at liberty to use her discretion in this matter; the call, choice, and ordination of her own officers being a special privilege that Christ hath given to his church under the gospel dispensation. See Davison's vindication of the Protestant ministers' mission. Since the Lord Jesus Christ hath left these important affairs to his church, and intrusted her to apply his directions, according to her circumstances, by the rules of prudence and discretion; therefore it must be an intrenchment upon her liberty and privilege, for any to use means to force or constrain a church, either to put a person on trial or to hasten his ordination; both of which ought to be the free, joyful, and unconstrained acts of a church. It is an indication of a heavy, self-willed, obstinate, and ungovernable temper in any gifted brother to refuse to exercise his gifts as the church shall be inclined to call him; and a specimen sufficient to foreshow what may be expected from such a one if preferred. It is therefore running an imprudent risk, to ordain to office in the church of God men of such fluctuating temper, who, if in any wise offended, will behave strangely, and leave the assemblings of the church, and frequent other assemblies. Though they may have some fine endowments, yet they can hardly be deemed faithful men. How the steady, sound, and orthodox principles and regular behaviour of men shall be found without considerable time of trial, none can tell.

Besides, is it not a great honor to a man, if God fits him with gifts to be helpful in the ministry of the word in any measure? But such as will not exercise their gifts upon trial, or without ordination, or as gifted brethren, seem to come near to what the apostle speaks of, 1 Cor. xii. 15; "If the foot say, because I am not a hand, I am not of the body." Such arguings plainly say, If I am not admitted to be bishop I will not be a helper; and such reasonings do cast a reflection on some worthy persons who have labored joyfully as helpers all their days, and whose memory is precious and honorable among the saints, when themselves are gone to rest.

2. Query: Whether it is regular for any to use the office of deacon, or to exercise the office of a ruling elder in a church, without ordination?

Solution. As touching ruling elders or deacons; if there had been no other rule but mere parity of reason, it would appear necessary to have a proof of the persons delegated to those offices by a trial in the office itself; for experience teacheth that some very regular members cannot become useful officers when tried, and if persons, likely to bear the ministerial function, may be found unfit for the office when tried, though sound in the faith, and of approved conversation, so may well minded and well respected persons be found, when tried, to be unfit for inferior offices. If it be objected that we have a precedent for choosing and ordaining deacons, without any proof or trial, it may be sufficient to answer, that the precedent in Acts vi. is very proper to inform us of the nature and property of the deacon's office; but cannot reasonably be pleaded to be imitable in future times, in that particular, in debate; because, 1, that was an extraordinary time, and done by extraordinary persons; and therefore not imitable in ordinary times nor ordinary persons, unless we could bring extraordinary times and persons to be alike, which we cannot. 2. Because the Holy Ghost, since that precedent, hath given us a positive rule to direct the church in ordinary times, which we are bound to follow, 1 Tim. iii. 10; from which the church in after ages ought not to deviate. Ordinarily it is improbable we should find the qualifications of a man for office without a trial; therefore, to ordain men to office in the church of God, without first being proved and approved, is against both rule and reason, and is therefore unlawful to be done by any church of Christ.

In ordinary, we see the churches of Christ inclined, and God's people are, by apparent motives, freely, lovingly, and affectionately moved, though not infallibly, to promote the ordination of such persons whose gifts, upon due exercise, they find to be useful by long experience, and whose apparent growth and proficiency, by long trial, is become manifest, and whose steady and circumspect behaviour in all things in doctrine and practice, are agreeable encouragements to intrust them, as men found faithful and fit for the office intended.

3. Query: Whether women may or ought to have their votes in the church, in such matters as the church shall agree to be decided by votes?

Solution. As that in 1 Cor. xiv. 34, 35, and other parallel texts, are urged against their votes, as a rule, and ought, therefore, to be maturely considered.

If, then, the silence enjoined on women be taken so absolute, as that they must keep entire silence in all respects whatever; yet, notwithstanding, it is to be hoped they may have, as members of the body of the church, liberty to give a mute voice, by standing or lifting up of the hands, or the contrary, to signify their assent or dissent to the thing proposed, and so augment the number on the one or both sides of the question. But, with the consent of authors and casuists, such absolute silence in all respects cannot be intended; for if so, how shall a woman make a confession of her faith to the satisfaction of the whole church? or how shall the church judge whether a woman be in the faith or no? How shall a woman offended, after regular private proceeding with an offending member, tell the church, as she is bound to do, if the offender be obstinate, according to the rule, Matt. xviii. 17? How shall a woman do, if she be an evidence to a matter of fact? Shall the church grope in the dark for want of her evidence to clear the doubt? Surely not. Again, how shall a woman defend herself if wrongfully accused, if she must not speak? This is a privilege of all human creatures by the laws of nature, not abrogated by the law of God.

Therefore there must be times and ways in and by which women, as members of the body, may discharge their conscience and duty towards God and men, as in the cases above said and the like. And a woman may, at least, make a brother a mouth to ask leave to speak, if not ask it herself; and a time of hearing is to be allowed, for that is not inconsistent with the silence and subjection enjoined on them by the law of God and nature, yet ought not they to open the floodgate of speech in an imperious, tumultuous, masterly manner. Hence the silence, with subjection, enjoined on all women in the church of God, is such a silence as excludes all women whomsoever from all degrees of teaching, ruling, governing, dictating, and leading in the church of God; yet may their voice be taken as above said. But if a woman's vote be singular, her reasons ought to be called for, heard, and maturely considered, without contempt.

4. Query: Whether churches may regularly associate with such other churches that will not admit their members into transient or occasional communion, and will not dismiss their members whose residences are removed; nor receive such whose residences are removed to them if dismissed? Or whether a church, by refusing transient communion to the members of another church, whose messengers are received in to associate with their own messengers, do not forfeit their own right in the Association, unless some new offence be given, or some undiscovered error be found in the church so refused?

We answer, that churches ought to unite in faith and practice, and to have and maintain communion together, as it is expressed in our abstract of church discipline, in order to associate regularly, because the latter is founded upon, and arises from the former; and we count that such a practice, for churches that cannot hold free communion together, to have their messengers, notwithstanding, admitted into the Association, to be inconsistent, and not to be continued in nor winked at; because it opens a door to greater and more dangerous confusions, and is in itself subversive of the being and end of an Association.

5. Query: Whether it is regular for an Association to receive in, and admit as members of the Association, such as at the same time they would not admit to the church communion, if opportunity offered?

We answer, no.

Concluded, that Brother Benjamin Griffith should collect and set in order the accounts of the several Baptist churches in these provinces, and keep a record of the proceedings of our denomination in these provinces; and that the several churches should draw out and send him, as soon as possible, what accounts they have on record in church books of their respective constitutions, and by whose ministry they have been supplied.

Also agreed, that Benjamin Griffith should have satisfaction for his trouble.

The Association agreed to make a subscription towards printing a treatise in vindication of believers' baptism. The members have made free to subscribe their sums for the purpose, and hope their brethren will cheerfully assist, and send their collections to Mr. Jones, at Philadelphia, against the 1st of March next.

Voted, that the letter from the society party came into the Association disorderly, and their messengers are not to be received as members in the house; which passed without any contrary votes.

The Association, next year, begins on Tuesday before the fourth Sunday in September. The sermon begins at 3 o'clock, P. M., by James Carman; in case of failure, by Joshua Potts.

1747.

The elders and messengers of the several congregations in Pennsylvania and New Jersey, baptized upon profession of faith, met at

Philadelphia, October 22d, 1747. Unto the churches of Christ, in gospel order, to whom we are related,

Send our loving salutation.

Dear and well beloved in Christ our hope,—We are much refreshed and comforted in our spirits by your diligent care and industry in sending your letters and messengers to this our meeting, which when we read revived our hearts, finding the churches generally in love, peace, and unity, and some additions in most, with considerable increase in some. Our numbers are multiplied by reason of divers young churches constituted of late, and in a thriving, prosperous appearance, which, put together, raises our hope that God is remembering the dust of Zion, and building anew his gospel Jerusalem. Your united and fervent prayers to God for us, we believe, were accepted in the court of our King above, by reason of your love, unity and concord. This breathes as a reviving wind in every member of this house, and as if so many hearts and souls were cast into one mould. Praise be to God. As to the sneers and reflections cast by some on our answers to questions sent us last year, we leave the authors to delight themselves in the product of their admiring fancies, seeing no cause to alter our apprehension, being persuaded that it is the duty of the churches to call and prove their candidates for the ministry, whom we judge ought to wait with self denying meekness, humbleness, and lowliness of mind to a further approbation from the churches of their ordination and investiture into the sacred functions, and not urge or hasten it themselves, contrary to the mind and judgment of the church which gave them a call to exercise their gifts. Contenting ourselves in the general satisfaction our churches have expressed in their letters of the comfort, edification, establishment, and consolation, they acknowledge to have received from our last letter, we desire and entreat you to weigh and deeply consider, that we are in the last days, the dregs and worst of times, of which we have been warned by the inspired writers, of scoffers, walking after their own lusts, 2 Peter iii. 3; of perilous days, 2 Tim. iii. 1. We are to mark those which cause divisions and offences, contrary to the doctrines we have received, and avoid them, who, by good words and fair speeches, deceive the hearts of the simple, Rom. xvi. 17, 18, that of your ownselves, should men arise, speaking perverse things to draw away disciples after them, Acts xx. Therefore, it concerns all who would be spiritually drest and beautifully adorned, to meet and be approved of the heavenly bridegroom; to be very careful how and with whom they walk; avoiding, both in principle and practice, in heart and life, in the church and in the world, in the family and in the field, whatever may cause us to contract filth or foulness on our beautiful garments; as Christ's virgins, look often in the glass of the gospel, espying and brushing away every spot of dust, keeping clean and neat for his everlasting embraces. Precious souls, suffer the word of exhortation, and be well established in gospel truths, in these shaking times. Look well that you be built upon the foundation of the apostles and prophets, Christ himself being your chief corner stone. Take heed that you build not on wood, hay, and stubble of men's inventions; be sure it be the gold, silver, and precious stones of the sanctuary, that you may not lose what you have wrought, but may receive a full reward, 2 John viii. Let it be your care to walk blameless and harmless, as the children of God, without rebuke, shining as lights in the world. Obey those who rule over you, and submit yourselves, for they watch for your souls. Grieve them not; provide for them as the word directs; neglect not meeting them in God's house at appointed times; avoid the spirit of contention, faction, and division; remember you are children of the same parents, God and his church; forget not your covenant relation one with the other.

"Finally, brethren, whatsoever things are honest, whatsover things are just, whatsoever things are lovely, whatsoever things are of good report, if there be any virtue, if there be any praise, think on these things." We commend you to God and the word of his grace; who is able to do exceeding, abundantly above all that we can ask or think, according to his power. Unto him be glory in the church by Christ Jesus, throughout all ages, world without end. Amen.

From your affectionate ministers and messengers,

Wm. Darby,	Wm. Coffin,	John Davis,
Recompese Standberry,	Jas. Tapscott,	Abel Morgan,
James Davis,	Stephen Watts,	Jas. Carman,
Joseph Weeks,	Richard Evans,	Joshua Potts,
Ben. Johnson,	John Manner,	Peter P. Vanhorn,
Thos. Huett,	Robert Chalfant,	John Stevenson,
Nathaniel Evans,	John Davis,	Ben. Miller,
Wm. Marshall,	Jeffrey Bently,	David Davis,
Augustine Stillman,	Nathl. Jenkins,	Enoch Morgan,
Job Shephard,	Jenkin Jones,	Thomas Jones.
Danl. Griffith,	Benj. Griffith,	

1. Query from Pennepek: Whether it is agreeable to gospel rule for a church to permit a gifted brother to preach the gospel, who refuses to communicate with them, unless they will comply with his own terms?

Answered in the negative.

2. Query: Whether such brother, by so refusing, does not forfeit his right not only to communion, but also to preach the gospel.

Answered in the affirmative.

Whereas the Association, having from time to time, for several years past, heard the allegations of the society party against the church of Montgomery, and all the endeavors used heretofore with said party not having had the desired effect:

Resolved: Not to enter upon their debates again, by receiving accusation or charges, either from the party themselves, or others espousing their cause, respecting the things that have been already heard and debated over and over, to little purpose.

The church lately constituted at Scotch Plains, in East Jersey, was received into the fellowship of this Association.

Likewise, the church lately settled at Horseneck, in the township of Greenwich, in New England, was received into the fellowship of this Association.

The members of the Association subscribed towards reprinting the catechism.

The Association sermon, next year, is to be on the Tuesday before the fourth Sunday in September, at 3 o'clock, P. M.

1748.

The elders, ministers, and messengers of the several congregations baptized upon profession of faith, in Pennsylvania and the Jerseys, met at Philadelphia, Sept. 20, 1748.

Send our loving salutation.

Dearly beloved brethren, who, we trust, will be our joy and crown of rejoicing in the day of the Lord Jesus, we cannot but express our great satisfaction, that you congratulate us with your letters, which much refresh our bowels, hearing that our churches, for the most part, are at peace and unity, and some of them having had considerable additions. Praised, magnified, and for ever adored be the riches of sovereign grace, that the labors of the poor servants of God in their ministerial office are not altogether lost and fruitless. The Lord has been watering his garden with the increase of God, which we pray may abound more and more.

The satisfaction you express to have received from our last year's narrative, encourages us to go on in the work of the Lord with cheerfulness. We trust, through your fervent prayers to God in our behalf, we met in love and gospel fellowship, and our debates and consultations were without heat and animosity; thanks be given to the most High for this valuable blessing. The doctrines of the glorious gospel have been held forth among us with power and clearness, under which we enjoy some comfortable measure of the divine presence. We are about to part from one another, not knowing whether we shall ever see each other in the flesh any more; therefore be exhorted to strive together with us, that we may be found worthy, in the worthiness of our exalted and glorious Redeemer, to meet in the celestial mansions above, forever to behold the reconciled face of our heavenly Father, in whose presence there is fulness of joy, and at whose right hand there are pleasures for evermore. To unwearied diligence in the use of all appointed means, read, hear, and meditate on the word; watch and pray without ceasing; give none offence, neither to the Jew nor to the Gentile, nor to the church of God; encourage and pray for your ministers, that God may furnish them with all necessary gifts and graces, for your edification and comfort, and that the word of the Lord may have free course in the hearts of poor sinners.

Finally, brethren, let your lights be shining, that you may be ready whenever the heavenly Bridegroom may call you to the marriage. To him be glory in the churches, both now and forever. Amen.

We, your brethren in the best of bonds,

Jenkin Jones,	Wm. Marshall,	Joseph Stout,
John Davis,	Wm. Chapman,	Edmund Drake,
Abel Morgan,	Wm. Derby,	Thos. Cocks,
Thos. Jones,	Thos. Worthington,	Wm. Buckingham,
James Carmel,	Jesse Bentley,	Edward Everey,
Josh. Botts,	Jno. Thomas,	Stephen Watts,
Thos. Curtis,	Jno. Marks,	Samuel Aschmead,
Peter Pet. Vanhorn,	Jph. Page,	Saml. Gui,
Jas. Stephens,	Andrew Brey,	Abraham Garison,
Benj. Miller,	Wm. Rees,	Jno. Levington.
Robert Kelsey,	Nathaniel Evans,	

Queries from the church at Horseneck, in New England:

1. Whether to deny the foreknowledge of the eternal God, concerning all future evil as well as good, be not a fundamental error?

Answer. We look upon such an opinion to be directly repugnant to Scripture; therefore exceeding erroneous and pernicious. First: Because it supposes God imperfect, and so no God, Psalm cxlvii. 5; Heb. iv. 13. Secondly: If so, there would be no room for the divine Being to make provision for the redemption of mankind before the fall of man, which is contrary to express Scripture testimony, Prov. viii. 28, 35; 2 Tim. i. 9. Thirdly: It is an error, which, in its nature and consequences, doth oppose and tend to overthrow the whole Christian religion, Acts ii. 23; iv. 28; Titus iii. 10.

2. Whether a member of the church holding such an opinion, endeavors to propagate it, and obstinately persists in it, is not worthy of the highest censure, notwithstanding he pleads matter of conscience?

Answer. We judge such worthy of the highest censure; because a church is to proceed against a person who is erroneous in judgment, as well as against one vicious in practice, notwithstanding they may plead conscience in the affair. Tit. iii. 10; 2 Thess. iii. 14.

A query from the church of Bethlehem: Whether a man who hath two wives living may be received into communion on his profession of faith. Answer. By no means. Matt. v. 32; xix. 9.

Concluded, that the churches in general be advised for the future not to send any queries to the Association before the matter has been well debated at home among themselves first.

Concluded, that it is most expedient for our ministers, when desired to preach among the society party, to exhort them to be first reconciled to Montgomery church, and then the way will be clear; for, otherwise, we think that for our ministers to preach among them, would tend to strengthen the party in their faction.

Concluded that the Association is to begin on Tuesday before the fourth Sunday in September, the next year, and the Association sermon to begin at three o'clock, P. M.

1749.

The elders and messengers of the churches of Christ, met in Association at Philadelphia, September 19th, 1749.

Dearly beloved brethren, who profess to be called out of darkness into light, adopted into the family of God, united to Christ by faith, and waiting for his second appearance from heaven, for the consummate happiness of all his redeemed people. Your affectionate letters were read, and your messengers received, whereby we find the churches are generally in peace, and there have been considerable additions this last year in some places. Blessed be the Lord, who succeedeth the labors of his servants in the gospel, for the edification of his saints and ingathering of sinners.

Your prayers for us, at this public season, we trust have been answered. We find from divers places requests for ministerial helps. Let all the churches who are supplied bless the Lord, duly improve the means they have, and with sympathising consideration pray the Lord of the harvest to send forth faithful laborers into his vineyard, for the supply of vacant places. We recommend to you the consideration of your great privileges. Walk worthy of them in all well pleasing; improve the means afforded you for your growth in grace; endeavor after a comfortable manifestation of your interest in the love of God in Christ Jesus; live on the Lord, and near him; beware of gradual inward backsliding from him, and an outward withdrawing from practical godliness; be much in secret prayer; regular and constant in morning and evening family worship; avoid all occasion of divisions; strengthen the hands of your ministry and one another; endeavor to fill up your place, in order to make your fellowship comfortable to yourselves; and recommend religion as desirable to others, that God may be glorified. That the God of mercy may fill your souls with grace and peace, and prepare you for every good word and work, and present you blameless and faultless, to his eternal glory, is the fervent desire of your brethren in the gospel of our salvation.

John Bartholomew,	John Watson,	John Davis,
Ashbury Smith,	Andrew Bray,	David Davis,
John Davis,	John Stout,	James Carman,
William Smith,	Saml. Ashmead,	Abel Morgan,
Thomas Smith,	James Davis,	Benj. Miller,
Thomas Cox,	Lewis Thomas,	Joshua Potts,
Crossen Collet,	Nathaniel Jenkins,	Isaac Eaton,
Robert Chalfant,	Jenkin Jones,	Malachia Bonham,
John Williams,	Owen Thomas,	Oliver Hart,
James Dorset,	Benj. Griffith,	William Marshall.

Two queries from the church at Pennepek: 1st. Whether persons that make themselves parties with dismembered ones, after due admonition given them, and they continue obstinate, do not expose themselves to the church's highest censure; and whether the church ought not to deal with them as such? Secondly, how often admonition ought to be repeated in such a case?

In answer to these queries, it is resolved, we entirely disapprove of such members continuing in their obstinacy, and condemn such a practice, and leave the church to their Christian prudence and discretion, to use all possible forbearance and lenity towards such members, if there is any probability of reclaiming them.

A query from the church at the Scotch Plains: Whether a person baptized by one that was not ordained, shall be received into the church, on the baptism already received; or whether he shall be baptized again, or shall such abide without the church's privileges all their days?

In answer, we refer to the solution of the like query, in the year 1744.

The Association unanimously approved and agreed to an essay of Benjamin Griffith, respecting the power and duty of an Association, to be inserted in the Association book.

The Association hath resolved to acquaint the several churches they relate unto, that some contribution may be made in every church, in order to defray the charges of a scribe, to write a journal of the beginning and proceedings of the Baptist societies in Pennsylvania and the Jerseys, and, as far as may be found, the proceedings of the Association, according to an order of this Association.

Concluded, also, that every church, belonging to this Association, should consider that our principles are attacked anew, and monstrously represented; that, therefore, in order to our vindicating and justifying the same, money may be gathered in every congregation, in readiness against the next Association at Philadelphia; and we hope timely notice shall be given, both of the number of books to be printed, and what the charge will be to print them.

Concluded, that the ensuing Association is to begin on the Tuesday after the third Sunday in September.

At our annual Association, met September the 19th, 1749, an essay on the power and duty of an Association of churches, was proposed, as above hinted, to the consideration of the Association; and the same, upon mature deliberation, was approved and subscribed by the whole house; and the contents of the same was ordered to be transcribed as the judgment of the Association, in order to be inserted in the Association book, to the end and purpose that it may appear what power an Association of churches hath, and what duty is incumbent on an Association; and prevent the contempt with which some are ready to treat such an assembly, and also to prevent any future generation from claiming more power than they ought—lording over the churches.

ESSAY.

That an Association is not a superior judicature, having such superior power over the churches concerned; but that each particular church hath a complete power and authority from Jesus Christ to administer all gospel ordinances, provided they have a sufficiency of officers duly qualified, or that they be supplied by the officers of another sister church or churches, as baptism, and the Lord's supper, &c.; and to receive in and cast out, and also to try and ordain their own officers, and to exercise every part of gospel discipline and church government, independent of any other church or assembly whatever.

And that several such independent churches, where Providence gives them their situation convenient, may, and ought, for their mutual strength, counsel, and other valuable advantages, by their voluntary and free consent, to enter into an agreement and confederation, as is hinted in our printed Narrative of discipline, page 59, 60, 61.

Such churches there must be agreeing in doctrine and practice, and independent in their authority and church power, before they can enter into a confederation, as aforesaid, and choose delegates or representatives, to associate together; and thus the several independent churches being the constituents, the association, council or assembly of their delegates, when assembled, is not to be deemed a superior judicature, as having a superintendency over the churches, but subservient to the churches, in what may concern all the churches in general, or any one church in particular; and, though no power can regularly arise above its fountain from where it rises, yet we are of opinion, that an Association of the delegates of associate churches have a very considerable power in their hands, respecting those churches in their confederation; for if the agreement of several distinct churches, in sound doctrine and regular practice, be the first motive, ground, and foundation or basis of their confederation, then it must naturally follow, that a defection in doctrine or practice in any church, in such confederation, or any party in any such church, is ground sufficient for an Association to withdraw from such a church or party so deviating or making defection, and to exclude such from them in some formal manner, and to advertise all the churches in confederation thereof, in order that every church in confederation may withdraw from such in all acts of church communion, to the end they may be ashamed, and that all the churches may discountenance such, and bear testimony against the defection.

Such withdrawing from a defective or disorderly church, or that ought to be towards a delinquent church, is such as ariseth from their voluntary confederation aforesaid, and not only from the general duty that is incumbent on all orthodox persons, and churches to do, where no such confederation is entered into, as 2 Cor. vi. 16, 17. Now, from that general duty to withdraw from defective persons or churches, there can no more be done, than to desist from such acts of fellowship as subsisted before the withdrawing, which is merely negative, and in no wise any thing positive. Churches, as they are pillars of truth, may, and ought to endeavor to promote truth among others also; which endeavors, if they prove fruitless, as they are but *mys-*

tico modo, they may be withdrawn; the withdrawing, therefore, must be accordingly; which is only to cease from future endeavors, leaving the objects as they were or are. But if there be a confederation and incorporation, by mutual and voluntary consent, as the Association of churches must and ought to be, then something positive may and ought to be done; and, though an Association ought not to assume a power to excommunicate or deliver a defective or disorderly church to Satan, as some do claim, yet it is a power sufficient to exclude the delegates of a defective or disorderly church from an Association, and to refuse their presence at their consultations, and to advise all the churches in confederation to do so too. A godly man may, and ought to withdraw, not only from a heathen, but from such as have the form of godliness, if they appear to want the power of it, 2 Tim. iii. 5, by the same parity of reason the saints, in what capacity soever they may be considered, may withdraw from defective or disorderly churches or persons; but excommunicate they cannot, there being no institution to authorize them so to do. But in the capacity of a congregational church, dealing with her own members, an Association, then, of the delegates of associate churches, may exclude and withdraw from defective and unsound or disorderly churches or persons, in manner abovesaid; and this will appear regular and justifiable by the light and law of nature, as is apparent in the conduct and practice of all regular civil and political corporations and confederations whatsoever; who all of them have certain rules to exclude delinquents from their societies, as well as for others to accede thereunto.

We judge those things in the 15th chapter of the Acts of the Apostles to be imitable by an Association, viz.: 1st, their disowning of the erroneous and judaising teachers, saying, to whom we gave no such commandment, verse 24; 2dly, the sending delegated persons of their own number, with Paul and Barnabas, to support their sentence in the place where the debate sprung up, verse 25; and a third thing followed in consequence thereof, viz., a delivering of the decrees to the other churches, to be observed, as well as the church of Antioch, chap. xvi. 4. Consistent therewith, the practice of after ages is found to be; when, because they had no council, synod, or association to convene, of course they called a council, in order to make head against any error or disorders, when in any particular church, such things grew too big for a particular church peaceably to determine, as the case about circumcision was at Antioch. In such cases all the churches were looked upon as one church, and all the bishops as universal, because of the unity of the faith and conformity of practice which ought to be in the churches of Christ; though in all other cases, the several distinct churches acted independent of each other, as Cyprian relates the practice of his time, viz.: That the bishops were so united in one body, that if any one of the body broached any heresy, or began to waste and tear the flock of Christ, all the rest came immediately to its rescue. Cyprian, cited by Bingham, book 2, page 101. And the same author observes, that they disowned the faulty, and advertised all the churches of the same. And Mr.

Crosby relates, that an Association in London did disown a certain disorderly church in London, and did caution all the churches they were related to, not to countenance them in any way, nor to suffer their members to frequent their meetings; and thus an Association may disown and withdraw from a defective or disorderly church, and advise the churches related to them to withdraw from, and to discountenance such as aforesaid, without exceeding the bounds of their power.

And further, that an Association of the delegates of confederate churches may doctrinally declare any person or party in a church, who are defective in principles or disorderly in practice, to be censurable, when the affair comes under their cognizance, and without exceeding the bounds of their power and duty, to advise the church that such belong unto, how to deal with such, according to the rule of gospel discipline; and also to strengthen such a church, and assist her, if need be, by sending able men of their own number to help the church in executing the power vested in her by the ordinance of Jesus Christ, and to stand by her, and to defend her against the insults of such offending persons or parties.

The above is a transcript of the said essay, according to the order given by the said Association, which was ordered to be taken without the then introduction and singularity. Taking the substance and contents thereof as the judgment of the Association, respecting their power and duty.

Consented to and transcribed by me, Benjamin Griffith.

Signed by the whole Association, whose names are—

Nathaniel Jenkins, Moderator,
Jenkin Jones,
Owen Thomas,
David Davis,
John Davis,
James Carman,
Abel Morgan, } Ministers.
Benj. Miller,
Joshua Potts,
Isaac Eaton,
Malachiah Bonham,
Oliver Hart,
William Marshall,
Jno. Bartholomew,
William Smith,

John Watson,
Thomas Smith,
Augsbury Smith,
Samuel Ashmead,
Lewis Thomas,
Thomas Coxs,
James Dorset,
John Davis,
Robert Chaffin,
John Williams,
James Davis,
Andrew Bray,
John Stout,
Crispin Collet.

On application made to the Association, to appoint proper persons to examine and approve the transcript of the above said essay, before it be inserted in the Association book, Mr. Jenkin Jones and Mr. Joshua Potts were named, and such others as could readiest be got; and accordingly Mr. Owen Thomas and those above named, did peruse and approve of the same as it is above inserted.

Brother Peter Peterson Vanhorn is to preach the Association sermon; and, in case of failure, Brother Isaac Eaton.

1750.

The ministers, elders, and messengers of the congregations owning the doctrine and practice of believers' baptism, in Pennsylvania and the Jerseys, met at Philadelphia, on the 18th, 19th, and 20th days of September, 1750.

Greeting:

Well beloved and longed for,—It is good refreshment to us, your servants, that our labors and endeavors at former Associations have been accepted and approved by you, our principals; which we gather from your pathetical acknowledgment in your letters, and your serious prayers for us, that we might be assisted from above with wisdom and strength to prosecute and press forward, to consider the things that are wanting, in order to the adorning and beautifying our little young Zion in this land, as we have heretofore made our efforts to defend and secure its foundations; and we confidently hope your prayers for us were accepted at the throne of grace, sweetened with the acceptable smell of the merits of our Lord and Redeemer. We met in love with God and thankful souls, that our blessed Lord has enabled the most of his servants in the ministry, at our small Zion, to be unanimous. Nothing has been presented from any of our churches whereby contentions or debates in the least might be moved. We hear from you of peace and agreement in the sound and wholesome principles of the gospel of our blessed Saviour. The old complaint is continued—deadness and indifference, coldness and decays of the first love; a sad distemper, but we hope not incurable, since our Mediator, after his ascension to the throne of his glory, has prescribed an infallible remedy, in the 2d and 3d of the Revelations, for inward and outward sores and maladies, which, if timely taken and rightly used, cannot fail of restoring you all to your former health, and warmth, and liveliness; yea, and make you stronger than ever you have been. Therefore, dear brethren and sisters, read and ponder the receipts of your soul's Physician; try and put in practice those wholesome directions, and you will never complain, for they are all peculiarly prepared by the most wise Artist, and suited for his spouse the church, of which you, in your small communions, up and down, are a part. Our dear flock and fellow members, we beseech and intreat you to improve the means of grace and your gospel privileges; prize your advantages, you that have pastors and teachers to break unto you the bread of life, and to direct you to the opened fountain, whereby, if you are well in the inner man, you may eat and drink that which is good, and cause your souls to delight themselves in fatness. Oh, if you had heard the mournful complaints and requests of souls destitute of the means of the courts of God and his ordinances, sent to us from remote places, it would cause melting compassions in your hearts, as it did in ours. Highly value, therefore, your prerogatives, and provoke not the Master to remove his candlestick from you. Consider, dear people, that you are God's building; and, if so, dishonor not the Master by being careless of your places and usefulness in the house of God; take heed that your communion be entire, at the call of your pastor, or according to your settled times. Beware of factions and rents in your churches; it is the old maxim of the enemy to divide and then to destroy. Keep together as an army with banners, terrible to those who would have you scattered from one another. Remember that you are God's husbandry. A barren field, after much labor and cost, is near the curse; but, if fruitful, receiveth blessing from God. Herein is the heavenly husbandman much glorified when you bring forth much fruit. To this ye were called at first, and now created in Christ the second time. Endeavor to answer both ends better from day to day, that you may be ripening for the garner of the glorious owner of the field. We conclude, with our hearty prayer for your establishment in every truth, your growth in grace, and a right and regular walking, as a peculiar people, prepared for every good work, vessels of honor, meet for the master's use. Amen.

Your messengers and servants in the house of our Lord Jesus.

Steven Watts,	Jos. Shepard,	Abel Morgan,
Rinold Howel,	Robert Chalfant,	Jas. Carman,
Wm. Marshel,	Robert Chalfant, Jr.,	Joshua Potts,
Thos. Edment,	Dan'l. Underhill,	Peter Vanhorn,
Thos. Coks,	Nath. Jenkins,	Benj. Miller,
Benj. Cheesman,	Jenkin Jones,	Malachiah Bonham,
Geo. George,	Benj. Griffith,	Thos. Davis,
Recompense Stanberry	Owen Thomas,	Thos. Jones,
Jos. Page,	Griffith Jones,	John Thomas.
Alex. Edwards,	John Davis,	

Query from Philadelphia: Whether a member in a church be censurable on the evidence of one accusing him of a fault, said to be committed for some length of time before, and nothing mentioned of it till it come out in anger arising on another occasion?

Answer: On the consideration of the circumstances of affairs, as represented to us, it is answered in the negative. 1st, because it appears to us it may be the effect of passion or discord; 2d, it does not appear likely that one should encourage what is charged, and afterwards use severity in correcting for the same.

Appointed Brethren Owen Thomas and Benjamin Griffith to write a letter to some people in Fairfax county, Virginia, in behalf of the Association.

The Association, taking into consideration the advantages and benefits that will arise to the interests of religion and the cause we profess, from a public fund or stock in bank, well regulated, have concluded to acquaint the several congregations we belong to with the proposal, that if it seem meet to them to further so good a purpose, by sending in yearly such sums as the Lord shall bless them with, and incline their hearts to contribute, that a beginning be made against next year.

Concluded to begin next year on Tuesday before the fourth Lord's day in September, and the sermon by Brother Isaac Eaton; in case of failure, by Brother Malachiah Bonham, at 3 o'clock, P. M.

1751.

The elders and messengers of the churches, baptized on profession of their faith, in Pennsylvania and the Jerseys, met at Philadelphia, 17th of September, 1751.

Greeting:

Brethren, well beloved in our Redeemer, it rejoiced us much when we perused your letters, and found your unity and fellowship in the gospel of Christ, except a few disorderly and disaffected persons in some of our societies, which is no new thing; for, in the primitive churches, gathered by the apostles, such uncomfortable members were found. We met together in gladness and gospel unanimity. We had no contentions, hates, or animosities. Your prayers for us we hope have been answered. We recommend to you the following counsels. Loving brethren, we have cause to be frequent in blessing the great Jehovah, the father of mercies, and the God of all comforts, for his distinguishing goodness in calling you from darkness to marvellous light, when you were in the snares of the worst of enemies. Praises are due to him who imparted the blessed eye-salve, and opened your souls to look upon the great object, Jesus, the Mediator of his covenant, who is able to save to the uttermost from all the powers that may oppose. Endeavor, brethren, to adorn the doctrine of the Lord Jesus in all things; for that will be evidence that you are Christians indeed, and not in name only. Let your conversations be as becometh the gospel, that, as you maintain sound and scriptural principles, and so shed forth their power and virtue in your behavior, you declare that you are seeking a better inheritance than can be found this side of heaven. Keep close and diligent to your stated time of public worship. Forsake not the assembling of yourselves together. It rejoices the heart of a Christian when his fellow servants say, Come, let us go up to the house of God. The contrary practice causes coldness, indifference, and gradual withering, and, at last, absolute dying, as Jude tells us, " twice dead, plucked up by the root;" from which fearful ruin, we pray God save you all, that you may not be a grief to those who labor among you in the word and doctrine, nor be barren and unfruitful in the knowledge of our Lord and Saviour Jesus Christ; nor want the comforts and hope of the glory that is to follow. You complain of deadness and lukewarmness in your souls; what can be the reason, but earthliness, or a careless, indolent, and unstable resolution to go forward? The Spirit is always ready, did we but attend and cherish his motions. By frequently meeting together, you might be strengthened with all might, according to his power, to run with patience the race that is set before you. Go on in the strength of your God, making mention of his righteousness, and his only. Shake off all sleepiness and sloth. The house above is prepared; the crown and seats are all ready; souls there wait for you, and wonder why the number is not yet completed. Long and pray for it. Be watchful unto death, and you shall enjoy a happy crown with them for ever. Seek for establishment in the ways of sincere piety, that you may grow like the palm tree in Lebanon. Keep the unity of the Spirit in the bond of peace. Obey them that rule over you in the Lord, that ye may be able to live in joy and not in sorrow, which will be unprofitable to you.

We recommend you to him who is able to do for you and ourselves far above what we are able to ask or think. To him be power and glory, dominion and thanks, for evermore.

From your fellow laborers in the mercy and grace of our exalted Saviour.

Robert Chalfant,	J. Williams,	Nath. Jenkins,
Job Sheppard,	John Thomas,	Jenkin Jones,
George George,	Malec. Bowen,	Abel Morgan,
Joshua Obdick,	Rees Jones,	John Davis,
David Sutton,	William Marshall,	David Davis,
John Stout,	William Darby,	Benjamin Griffith,
Nathan Evans,	Thomas Rees,	James Carman,
Robert Parsons,	William Taylor,	Peter P. Vanhorn,
Arnold Francis,	Wm. Cheesman, Jr.,	Joshua Potts,
Isaac Stelle,	B. Miller,	Isaac Eaton.

Brother M. Bowen is to preach the annual sermon next year; in case of failure, Brother I. Stelle. To begin two days before the fourth Lord's day in September, at 3 o'clock, P. M.

1752.

The elders and messengers of the several congregations in Pennsylvania and the Jerseys, baptized on profession of their faith, met in Association at Philadelphia, October 3d, 1752.

To the several congregations we represent, we send Christian salutation.

Dearly beloved in our Lord Jesus Christ, whose interest we hope all of us have chiefly at heart,—We met, and, after the Association sermon, received your letters, and, with great satisfaction, accepted your messengers, and rejoice to see your care and unwearied diligence in keeping up our annual correspondence; and so much the more our joy is increased in that we find our churches, for the most part, are at peace and unity among themselves, and have had considerable additions, the which valuable blessings we bespeak the great Master of assemblies to continue, and make more and more to abound to the glory of his great name, and the comfort of us who labor in the word and doctrine, and the mutual benefit of you all with whom we are concerned. And now, dear brethren, as our consultations have been loving and unanimous, so we are going in love to part, not knowing whether we shall ever see one anothers' faces in time any more. Therefore, we solemnly charge you, in the fear of God, that you labor constantly to walk answerable to your heavenly calling, and to any of you, among whom there may be discord, strife, and debates, we say, that as Satan hath made an inroad upon you, beware of giving a helping hand to so dangerous an enemy, but labor by all means to heal the breaches in Zion, that the church may still appear a company compact together, as an army with banners. And, if any of you are complaining of deadness, barrenness, and leanness, though in the present enjoyment of the precious means of grace, we say, see to it. No doubt carelessness, unwatchfulness, and worldly mindedness, are the causes hereof. Remember from whence you are fallen, and repent. What we say further, we say to all, watch, that at the heavenly bridegroom's coming, either by death or judgment, ye may be ready to meet him with joy, and not with grief. We commend you to God, and to the word of his grace, who is able to build you up, and to give you an inheritance among them that are sanctified. We rest your loving brethren in the faith and fellowship of the gospel. Amen.

Saml. Jones,	Ephraim Thomas,	Jas. Carman,
John Gano,	Jas. Mott,	Isaac Stelle,
John Stout,	Jenkin Jones,	Joshua Root,
David Goons,	Nathl. Jenkins,	Peter P. Vanhorn,
Wm. Juel,	Benj. Griffith,	Benj. Miller,
Icabud Thompson,	Abel Morgan,	Wm. Marshel,
Saml. Guy,	John Davis,	Augustus Stillman.
Jno. Thomas,		

Query from the church at Kingwood: Whether a person denying unconditional election, the doctrine of original sin, and the final perseverance of the saints, and striving to affect as many as he can, may have full communion with the church?

Answer: That the very consequence of it opposeth the absolute sovereignty of God over his own creatures contrary to express scriptures, which do declare and fully prove, the three parts denied by said questionist.

1st. That personal election is the truth of God, Eph. i. 5; Matt. xxiv. 24; and our infallible hope is proved by John, chap. x. 28; as also, the saints' perseverance, verse 29, John xvii. 6; they are the gift of the Father to his Son Christ, who will, and is able to keep them and secure their happiness, John xvii. 24.; Acts xiii. 48. The foundation of God standeth sure, whatever becomes of the presumptuous counsels of obstinate men. 2 Thess. ii. 13.; Titus i. 1.; 1 Peter i. 2-5.

2. That we are originally sinful or partakers of the first sin of human nature, being all included in Adam when he was created, and partakers of that happiness, with which he was indued, as his rightful heir; but he, forgetting that great favor bestowed freely upon him and his posterity, we, as well as himself, are justly shut out of

our native happiness, and have lost our right thereunto forever, unless our title be restored by the second Adam, the Lord from heaven, by being effectually called in time. Eph. ii. 12, 13; Rom. v. 12 to the end; Ecl. vii. 2. Upon which fundamental doctrines of Christianity, next to the belief of an eternal God, our faith must rest; and we adopt, and would that all the churches belonging to the Baptist Association be well grounded in accordance to our Confession of faith and catechism, and cannot allow that any are true members of our churches who deny the said principles, be their conversation outward what it will.

The Association, next year, is to begin on Tuesday after the second Lord's day, in October, at 3 o'clock, P. M. Brother Nathaniel Jenkins is to preach the sermon; in case of his failure, Brother Jenkin Jones.

1753.

The elders and messengers of the congregations baptized on profession of faith, in Pennsylvania and the Jerseys, met in Association at Philadelphia, the 16th of October, 1753.

To the several congregations we relate unto, send greeting:

Dearly beloved brethren in our Lord Jesus Christ,—We rejoice to hear that the most of our churches are at peace, and in divers places have had some addition, for which valuable blessing we pray that our God may perfect praise from us and you. We thank you for your constant diligence in endeavoring to keep up this annual correspondence, and it is with much satisfaction that we hear our past counsels and admonitions are solemnly regarded by you. We have to inform you that we met together in love and peace, and we trust, that through your prayers, and the abundant supply of the Spirit of grace, our consultations and debates have been attended with valuable blessing; and now as we are to part from each other, we tenderly counsel and advise you, in the fear of God, that ye labor to walk close with him in the several duties incumbent on you as Christians. Be not satisfied with generals, but labor in a constant, actual derivation from Christ, to perform each particular duty with life and power. For want of careful attendance and watchfulness hereunto, many have had their minds and consciences defiled by sin, to their great discomfort, to the dishonor of God, and grief of their brethren. Labor, dear souls, to keep the unity of the spirit in the bonds of peace. The want of diligence in the prosecution of the several duties hereunto tending, is one great reason why particular communities are sometimes distracted with dreadful disturbances, with Satan's inroad upon them; and therefore, beloved brethren, be exhorted to watch and pray lest ye enter into temptation, that at the heavenly bridegroom's coming you may be ready to meet him with exceeding joy. We commend you to God and to the word of his grace, who is able to preserve you to his heavenly kingdom through our Lord Jesus Christ, to whom, with the Father and the Holy Ghost, be glory forever. Amen.

Your brethren in the best of bonds.

Joseph Heart,	Jno. Stiles,	Jas. Carman,
Abel Griffith,	Wm. Cheesman,	Abel Morgan,
Icabed Tompkins,	Danl. Griffith,	Isaac Eaton,
Joshua Smaley,	Jas. Davis,	John Davis,
Samuel Morgan,	Geo. Drake,	Benj. Miller,
Jonathan Smith,	Jeffrey Bentley,	Malachia Bonham,
Wm. Marshal,	Geo. Bentley,	Isaac Still,
Henry Crosby,	Jenkin Jones,	Thos. Jones,
Benj. Stout,	Benj. Griffith,	Peter P. Vanhorn,
Stephen Watts.	Owen Thomas,	John Thomas.
David Lewis,		

1. Query from the Church at Kingwood: Whether the assurance of faith be absolutely necessary in order for admission to baptism?

The judgment of this Association is: It appears to us, both from scripture and experience, that true saving faith may subsist where there is not assurance of faith.—Therefore, in answer to the second query, That a person sound in judgment, professing his faith of reliance on Christ for mercy and salvation, accompanied with a gospel conversation, ought to be baptized.

Query from the church at the Scotch Plains: Whether a person, observing the seventh day as a Sabbath, and keeping the first day in condescension, may be received into membership?

Resolved, That such may, provided nothing else appear to the contrary.

Agreed to receive the church lately constituted at Rocksberry into fellowship with us.

Concluded, that any brother called by any of our churches to exercise his gift, when approved of at home, should, before his ordination, visit other churches, and preach among them, and obtain from those churches concurring evidence of their approbation, that it is proper and convenient that such may be ordained.

The Association is to begin next year, on Tuesday after the first Lord's day, in October. Brother Owen Thomas is to preach the sermon at 3 o'clock, P. M.; in case of failure, Brother Benjamin Griffith.

1754.

The elders and messengers met in Association at Philadelphia, October 8th, 1754. Greeting.

Dear brethren, our joy and crown in the day of the Lord,—We delight to inform you, that we met your messengers, and are thankful upon hearing, in your letters, of the general peace in the churches, with considerable increase in some of them. We trust your prayers for us have, in some measure, been answered, in that we have enjoyed sweet harmony in all our consultations to the great confirmation of one another. Being about to depart, suffer us to recommend to your consideration the following necessary things. Take heed, brethren, to maintain love and unity among yourselves. Beware of every thing that tends to schism. Exhort and provoke one another to love and good works, and the more as you see the day of deadness and lukewarmness approaching. Awake to repentance in the use of your temporal and spiritual privileges. Your professed and powerful enemy threatens and frowns; the obligations you are under, as followers of Jesus, are many and strong. Strive to uphold and strengthen your ministers. Omit not the duty of church relation one toward another; keep your place in the house of God. Be constant in family prayer, and frequent in secret; keep an hourly watch over your conduct in the world, lest you wound the precious cause of Christ.

Brethren, we commit you to the Lord and the word of his grace, praying for your establishment in the ways of Christ, the king of his church. Gird up the loins of your minds and be sober. Wait for the coming of the Lord from heaven with his mighty angels, to release his church from her militant state to glory and triumph.

Concluded, to receive the church of Ketockton, and the church of Opekon, in Virginia, into fellowship with this Association.

In consequence of the prevailing deadness that overspreads the land, and the imminent danger our continent seems actually to labor under, from the bold encroachments of our avowed enemies on our frontiers, concluded, that the second Thursday in November next, be observed as a day of humiliating, fasting, and prayer to God, that he may be mercifully pleased to remove the impending judgment.

Sermon next year is to be on Tuesday after the first Lord's day, in October, at 3 o'clock, P. M., by Brother Benjamin Griffiths; in case of failure, Brother Abel Morgan.

Benj. Stout,	Obah. Robbins,	Edwd. Lucas,
Wm. James,	Jon. Thomas,	Jenkin Jones,
Hen. Loyd,	Jon. Gano,	Benj. Griffiths,
Abm. Ashburn,	Jos. Davis,	Abel Morgan,
Dav. Sutton,	Saml. Watson,	Thos. Jones,
Reun. Wingate,	Wm. Marshall,	Isaac Eaton,
Ichad. Tompkins,	Saml. Ashmead,	Josa. Potts,
Owen Howell,	John Watson,	Peter P. Vanhorn,
Stn. Watts,	Josh. Sheppard,	John Davis,
Thos. Curtis,	Recompense Stansbury	Mal. Bonham.
Robt. Chalfant,	Isa. Mott,	

1755.

The elders and messengers of the several congregations of Christians baptized, upon profession of their faith, in Pennsylvania and the Jerseys, met at Philadelphia, October 7th, 1755.

To the several churches we respectively belong, send our loving salutation:

Dearly beloved brethren,—We, your delegates, having met in gospel affection, were refreshed in hearing your letters, and finding peace subsists throughout our churches, and some addition in several of them. We hope the public cause is in progressive circumstances. We had affectionate and pressing requests from many places for ministerial help. Our souls are concerned for those who are like to perish for lack of vision; therefore, we entreat you to be fervent and frequent at the throne of grace, that the Lord would send forth many faithful laborers into his vineyard. We earnestly recommend as necessary, that you might be free to spare your ministers some time to supply those who would otherwise be altogether destitute.

Be earnest and constant in attending on the duties of religion; neglect not secret prayer; pray for and with your families; labor for a general humiliation for your own sins and the sins of the land, seeing God, by his providence, calls loudly for it, and knowing that our civil and religious privileges are threatened. Improve the precious means of grace whilst you enjoy them. Strengthen and encourage your ministry; be careful to attend public worship; keep close to your communions; observe your place in all church meetings; and in all respects strive to walk worthy of the vocation wherewith you are called. Committing you to the Lord and the word of his grace, we subscribe ourselves your brethren in gospel relation.

Benj. Griffith, Moderator.

Samuel Borchilo,	Jesse Binely,	John Stiles,
Samuel Jones,	John Garet,	Joshua Obesick,
James Mott,	John Thomas,	George George,
Edward Keasly,	David Evans,	Jenkin Jones,
John Lonmay,	John Thomas,	John Davis,
Richard William,	James Carman,	Abel Morgan,
Peter Cochlan,	Job Sheperd,	Joshua Potts,
John Gare,	Isaac Eaton,	Peter P. Vanhorn,
Wm. Marshel,	Saml. Heaton,	John Gano,
John Hart,	Daniel Smith,	Isaac Still.
Jehobold Tompkin,		

Concluded, to receive the church lately constituted at Alloway's Creek, in Salem county; the church constituted in New Britain, in Bucks county, November 28, 1754; also, the church constituted in Baltimore county, Maryland, and two churches constituted in the province of Virginia, viz., one in Fairfax county, Oketon Tract; the other at Mill Creek, Frederick county.

Appointed, that one ministering brother from the Jerseys, and one from Pennsylvania, visit North Carolina: the several churches to contribute to bear their expense.

Brother Thomas Davis is to visit Cape May this fall, and stay with them a month. Brother Abel Morgan, the second Sabbath in

March. Our ministering brethren have unanimously agreed to visit several vacancies the ensuing year.

Concluded, that it be left to the discretion of the ministering brethren that travel to Carolina, to ordain Mr. Jaret, in Virginia.

Concluded to leave the ordination of W. Chrisley to the Jersey ministering brethren.

Our churches, in general, are advised to keep Thursday, the 23d of October, as a day of fasting and prayer, seeing our privileges, civil and religious, require it.

That Brother Abel Morgan is to preach the Associational sermon next year; in case of his failure, Brother David Davis, on Tuesday after the first Lord's Day, in October, at 3 o'clock, P. M.

The ministry that travel are to set out on Tuesday, the 28th of of October.

1756.

The elders and messengers of the several congregations, baptized on profession of faith, in Pennsylvania, New Jersey, and provinces adjacent, met in Association at Philadelphia, October 5th, 1756.

To the several churches we respectively relate unto, do send our loving salutation.

Dear brethren,—We your messengers and fellow members of the same mystical body, having met together in love and gospel unity, were refreshed by hearing your letters read, finding that our churches are generally at peace, and in divers parts have had considerable additions. Blessed be our God therefor. And now, dear brethren, as we are about to part from each other, suffer us to express our constant love and care for you, by recommending to you the following necessary duties, viz: Be constant at the throne of grace for the several purposes revealed to you in the holy scripture; not in a dead, lifeless, and formal manner; but labor after free access to God, in the blessed Mediator's name, that out of his fullness we may all receive, and grace for grace. Strive to excel in practical religion, and think that time lost wherein you do not make some advances in the Christian life. Be constant in reading, hearing, and meditating on the sacred word that you may profit thereby. Tremble at the thought of being found foolish virgins at last. Be careful of the instruction of youth, and those under your care, that when you come to give up your accounts to Him that is ready to judge the quick and dead, you may do it with joy and not with grief. Encourage and strengthen the hand of your ministers, and freely consent to their visiting of vacant places, that others may share the blessings of the gospel of peace with you.

Finally, brethren, fear God, and honor the king by every expression of duty and loyalty, seeing our nation and land are in danger by a potent enemy, preparing the worst of times, while you hope and pray for the best.

So we commend you to God, and to the word of his grace. Praying that you may be preserved safe to His heavenly kingdom, through Jesus Christ our Lord,

We rest your brethren in gospel relation,

Jenkin Jones, Moderator.

Wm. Buckingham,	John Clesy,	Isaac Eaton,
Jas. Davis,	Eleazer Evans,	Isaac Stelle,
Danl. Cornock,	John Stout,	Thos. Jones,
Abel Griffiths,	Robt. Chalfant,	Robt. Kelsy,
Geo. Eaton,	Jeremiah Collett,	John Davis,
Stephen Watts,	Benj. Griffiths,	Joseph Thomas,
Lewis Thomas,	Abel Morgan,	John Thomas.
Saml. Morgan,	John Davis,	

Query from the church at Morristown: Whether a woman may be received into the church that is married to her sister's husband, after her said sister's decease, said man having had children by both?

Resolved, that because such marriages are not tolerated by the laws of our land, we judge it unadvisable to receive such persons.

Concluded, to advise our several congregations to make some charitable contributions towards the relief of the present necessity of our brother, Mr. Samuel Heaton, who was driven from his possessions by the Indians.

Concluded, to appoint the last Thursday of this instant October, to be kept by our churches, by fasting and prayer, and so to be continued quarterly throughout the year, unless we shall have cause to turn our fasting into thanks and praise to God for deliverance granted.

Concluded, to publish in a public print, a certain William Leaton, for his irregular proceedings, in going about under the name of a Baptist minister, when he neither is, nor ever was, a member in any of our churches, if, upon warning given him, he does not desist.

Concluded, to raise a sum of money towards the encouragement of a Latin Grammar School for the promotion of learning amongst us, under the care of Brother Isaac Eaton, and the inspection of our brethren Abel Morgan, Isaac Stelle, Abel Griffith, and Peter Peterson Vanhorn.

Concluded, that Brother David Davis is to preach the Association sermon next year; and, in case of failure, Brother Isaac Stelle.

The Association to begin on Tuesday after the first Lord's day in October, at 3 o'clock, P. M.

1757.

The elders and messengers of the congregations in Pennsylvania, the Jerseys, and provinces adjacent, baptized on profession of their faith, met in annual Association in the city of Philadelphia, the fourth, fifth, and sixth days of October, 1757.

To the several congregations we respectively relate to, do send our loving salutation.

Dear brethren and fellow members of the mystical body of which Jesus Christ is the head, we, your delegates, have, according to appointment, met in gospel peace and unity, and conferred together, in our usual manner, about the affairs of the churches. Our consultations have been unanimous. The tidings from the churches considerably comfortable; they being generally at peace, and having some additions. Blessed be God for special favors in the worst of national calamities and distresses. We had many pressing calls from vacant places for ministerial helps, which we hope will be an inducement to all our churches to spare their ministers as much as possible to supply them. Dear brethren, as we with you, and you with us, remain the standing monuments of sparing goodness, in the midst of surrounding difficulties, be exhorted with us to double your diligence in the faithful discharge of every duty incumbent on you as Christians. Wrestle much with the Lord in prayer, in behalf of our bleeding land, still invaded and involved in ravage and bloodshed. Is it not affecting to think, that, though our last year's appointed fast days have been kept in our churches, so little of a real spirit of true humiliation appears. All our prayers, together with the prayers of Christians of other denominations, avail not as yet. National calamities still remain as sad tokens that the cause is not removed, or that the sin of our nation is very great. This is a loud alarm to us to awake from stupidity, and be earnest with the Lord. We commend you to the care and keeping of the great Shepherd, and Bishop of souls.

Lewis Thomas,	John Davis,	Benjamin Griffiths,
David Powell,	Saml. Hutton,	Jenkin Jones,
William Fobwell,	Henry Crosby,	Owen Thomas,
David Sutton,	William Marsh,	Abel Morgan,
Zebulon Stout,	Abel Griffith,	Benj. Miller
Isaac Wheaton,	Joshua Jones,	Robt. Celly,
Peter Rominee,	Saml. Morgan,	Joshua Potts,
Joseph Snether,	William Darly,	Peter. P. Vanhorn,
Timothy Parke,	James Mott,	Thomas Jones,
Sampson Davis,	Saftey Megee,	Isaac Eaton,
William Marshall,	Thos. Hart,	John Davis.
Isaac Evans,		

Agreed to receive the letter and messenger sent from the church recently constituted in Newtown, Sussex county, New Jersey, in union with this Association. William Marsh, their minister.

In answer to a request from a number of inhabitants in Bateman's precincts, Dutchess county, New York government, agreed that our brethren, Mr. Miller and Mr. William Marsh, visit them, and give the petitioners such directions and assistance as they shall judge convenient.

In answer to a request from Kingwood, for ministerial supplies, we advise them to apply to Montgomery, principally, and to others, as occasion requires.

Agreed, that our ministers visit Philadelphia as often as they conveniently can this year.

Concluded, that our churches shall continue the quarterly fasts by fervent prayer to God for our nation and kingdom, and for these American colonies, as was last year observed, unless God give us cause to turn our fasts to thanksgivings.

In consideration of the very great necessity for ministerial labor in many of the churches belonging to this Association, we request the church of Montgomery to send some of her young ministers to supply them as often as possible.

This Association having, in the year past, encouraged the Latin Grammar School to promote useful learning among us, have again resumed the consideration, and concluded to request the churches to contribute their mite towards its support.

The Association to begin next year on the Tuesday after the first Lord's day in October, at 3 o'clock, P. M. Sermon by Brother David Davis; in case of failure, Brother Isaac Stelle.

1758.

The elders and messengers of the congregations in Pennsylvania and the Jerseys, baptized, on profession of their faith, met in annual Association at Philadelphia, October 3d, 1758.

Send Christian salutation.

Dearly beloved brethren,—We, your messengers, met, according to appointment, and enjoyed the comfort of seeing each other once more; received good tidings from the churches in these parts of the world, of their peace and unity among themselves, and of more or less additions the last year, and of souls longing for the means of grace. Our ministering brothers preached among us the truth of the gospel. We have just cause to thank God for his desirable goodness bestowed on us. Your prayers for us, brethren, were not in vain. Experience of mercies ought to quicken us all in our future dependence, and continuance to call on his sacred name. We are now about to part with each other. Receive from us, holy brethren, a few words in faithfulness and love. Above all things bless the Lord for the riches of his grace, through Jesus Christ, for your souls. He hath raised you from the depths of sin and ruin, to life and salvation; to be the children of God and joint heirs with Christ. Praise him for the continuance of your precious enjoyments in the midst of threatening desolation. Improve the means of grace. Make a great account of the holy Scriptures. Encourage the gospel administrators among you, by prayers for them, and reducing their instruction to practice. Maintain a tender conscience. Be careful to abstain from all appearances of evil. Strive to make your church relation comfortable to each other. Watch over yourselves and over one another for good; walk with God. Desire nearness to him under affliction, deadness, and lukewarmness. Put in practice the doctrines Christ gives for its removal. Be much in prayer in your closets and families. Command your children and families to be present at these times. Afford them the opportunity of grace. Bear one another's burdens, and so fulfil the law of Christ, that the whole glory may be to God, in the church of Jesus Christ, throughout all ages, world without end. Amen.

Now, verily, beloved brethren, may grace make you perfect, establish, strengthen, and settle you in the faith and fellowship of the gospel.

Isaac Eaton,	John Davis,	Jeffry Bently,
Jenkin Jones,	Saml. Eaton,	Dav. Stout,
Benj. Griffith,	Wm. Marsh,	Jn. Stout,
David Davis,	Henry Crosby,	Jonas Grouble,
John Davis,	Saml. Watson,	Wm. Folwell,
Abel Morgan,	John Thomas,	Jonathan Bowen,
Ben. Miller,	Abel Griffis,	Hezekiah Smith.
Peter P. Vanhorn,	Eakeble Tompkins,	Able Davis,
John Garret,	Simon Butler,	Peter Copram,
Robt. Kilsey,	Jonas Shepperd,	Joseph Folwell,
George Eaton,	Jn. Stites,	Henry Woodrow.

Received into union with this Association the church of Christ, instituted in gospel order, November, 1757, Bateman's precincts, Dutchess county, in the province of New York; their letter was read, and their messenger, who is their minister, Samuel Walder, admitted.

Resolved to continue quarterly fasts. The first will be the fourth Thursday of October, to be kept by way of thanksgiving to God for our deliverance from he hand of our enemies and the success of his majesty's arms.

Resolved, to desire our churches to continue a contribution toward a Grammar School, under consideration that what has been done hitherto in that way, appears to have been well laid out, there being a number of well inclined youths applying themselves to learning therein.

TESTIMONIAL.

Ordered, that a testimonial be given and signed by the Rev. Jenkin Jones, minister of the Baptist meeting, or congregation, in Philadelphia, to the Rev. John Davis, late of Bucks county, in Pennsylvania, but now of Baltimore county, in the province of Maryland, certifying his regular ordination, according to the rites, ceremonies, and approved forms and usages of the Baptist church, and also his purity of life, manners, and conversation; and recommending him to the favor of all Christian people, where he now does, or may hereafter happen to dwell.

In pursuance of the above order, the following testimonial and certificate was given and signed by the Rev. Mr. Jones to the Rev. John Davis:

"To all Christian people to whom these presents shall come:

"I, Jenkin Jones, minister of the Baptist meeting or congregation of the city of Philadelphia, do send and certify, that the bearer hereof, Mr. John Davis, late of Buck's county, in the province of Pennsylvania, but now residing and dwelling in Baltimore county, in the province of Maryland, in the month of April, in the year of our Lord, one thousand seven hundred and fifty-six, was regularly admitted, ordained, and received holy order to preach the gospel of our Lord and Saviour Jesus Christ, to all people, according to the rites and ceremonies, and approved forms and usages of the Baptist church; and that at all times, before and since his ordination aforesaid, for any thing heard, known, or believed to the contrary, he lived a holy and unblemished life, as well in his conversation as in his actions. And I do humbly recommend him to the notice, esteem, and regard of all Christians, where he now does, or hereafter may, reside, or with whom he may have conversation or dealing.

"In testimony whereof, and by order of the general meeting or Association aforesaid, I have hereunto set my hand, at the city of Philadelphia, the sixth day of October, in the year of our Lord, One thousand seven hundred and fifty-eight.

JENKIN JONES.

The Association is to begin next year on Tuesday after the second Sunday in October, at 3 o'clock, P. M. Sermon by Brother Isaac Stelle; in case of failure, Brother Isaac Eaton.

1759.

The elders and messengers of the several congregations in Pennsylvania and the provinces adjacent, baptized on profession of their faith, met in annual Association, at Philadelphia, October the 16th, 1759.

To the several congregations we relate unto and represent, do send our Christian salutation.

Dearly beloved brethren,—We, your messengers, met according to appointment, and enjoyed the comfort of mutual conversation; received good tidings from the several churches in these parts of the world, of their unity in general among themselves, and of more or less increase in most of them, and of people seeking ministerial supplies, and longing for the means of grace.

Our consultations, while together, were without contention, and an agreeable harmony ran through the whole of our exercise. Your wishes and prayers, brethren, were not in vain, blessed be God for his peculiar favors bestowed on us. May a continued experience of His faithfulness excite us all to a constant dependence on Him for all future supplies.

And now, beloved brethren, receive in love the following counsels and advices on our parting from each other: Adore the Author of your restoration; remember the depth of that ruin and depravity from whence the gracious God hath raised you up to sit with Christ Jesus in heavenly places; make a profitable use of the means of grace; acquaint yourselves more abundantly with the holy scriptures;

let the doctrines of the gospel be reduced into proper actings of every grace in your souls, and holy practice in your conversation; endeavor always after heart religion; maintain and promote religion in your families; call them together to stated worship; read the word of God to them; instruct them; pray for them, and with them; use your counsels and authority to prevent them from evil customs, trifling or profaning the Lord's day; be patterns of godliness to them, patterns to all. Revive the things which are ready to die; and amongst other things revive Christian conversation; which is so profitable for mutual comfort, growth, and encouragement of religion. Labor to make your church fellowship every way useful to each other; watch over your own souls, and over one another for good; use the directions given by our Lord, in order to remove the plague of lukewarmness and indifference from you in the things of God, by prayer and holy practice. Encourage those who labor among you in the ministration of the gospel. Live in love and grow in grace, that in all God may be glorified in the churches every where, who is worthy of all praise and thanksgiving, world without end. Amen.

From your brethren in the household of faith,

Benjamin Griffith, Moderator.

Alexr. Edwards,	Saml. Morgan,	Henry Crosby,
Joseph Eldridge,	Benj. Miller,	Joseph Hart,
Josiah Jones,	George Eaton,	Owen Tomas,
Jno. Brown,	Abel Griffith,	Abel Morgan,
Peter Vanhorn,	John Davis,	Thos. Davis,
Wm. Davis,	Rob. Kelsy,	David Davis,
Daniel Griffith,	Isaac Eaton,	Isaac Stelle,
Rob. Chalfant,	Josiah Potts,	John Davis,
John Crow,	Saml. Heaton,	Samuel Burkalve.

Concluded, that the quarterly fast be observed the following year through our churches, as usual: only the first opportunity to be on Wednesday, the 31st October, and to be kept by way of thanksgiving for the peculiar mercies and favors granted to us, on the success of his majesty's arms, &c., &c.

Agreed and concluded upon, that one of our ministering brethren yearly, and from year to year, who is esteemed qualified in some competent measure, is to preach, at the opening of the Association, upon one of the fundamental articles of the Christian faith, and his subject to be given him by the Association the year before.

The subject next year to be concerning the Being and Attributes of God. Brother Isaac Taylor to preach the sermon, and in case of failure, Brother Abel Morgan to perform that office.

The Association to begin next year on the Tuesday after the second Lord's day in October, at 3 o'clock, P. M.

1760.

The elders and messengers met in Association at Philadelphia, October 14th, 1760.

To the several churches we represent send Christian salutation.

Beloved in our blessed Redeemer and glorious Lord,—We have renewed cause to adore our gracious God, that your united prayers for us have, in some good measure, we trust, been answered. We met according to appointment, and after a very agreeable discourse, find our churches are at peace, and have had several persons added to them this year. Glory be to God. We are now come to the close of our work, and are soon to part one from the other; looking upon it as our duty to endeavor to stir up your pure minds by way of remembrance, we entreat you to receive in love the following exhortations: First of all, adore the riches of divine love and grace that hath called you from darkness unto light, and from the kingdom of Satan unto God, which hath brought you from death to life, from being strangers and foreigners to be fellow citizens with the saints and of the household of God. Prize your privileges of being incorporated together in the relation you stand in to God and to one another. Remember that very solemn covenant you have entered into, on your admission, and see that you walk agreeable thereto, both before God and each other. Neglect not the assembling of yourselves together as the manner of some is. Use the means of grace with dilgence and zeal. Labor to believe the divine truths that you profess. Have the reality, preciousness, and purity of them deeply impressed upon your hearts. Labor to enjoy much of God through Christ, by the blessed Spirit. Let faith be in its proper exercise upon its glorious objects. Rely wholly upon the justifying righteousness of the Mediator for peace and acceptance, improving the promises of the gospel for your encouragement, establishment, and comfort.

Let your secret communion with God be witnessed by a holy conversation in the world. Let your moderation be known to all men. Be careful to perform all acts of Christian charity to the poor and needy. Sympathise with those who are in trouble. Pity and pray for those that are afflicted. Be diligent to maintain the worship of God in your families and in your closet. Be careful of the youth under you; instruct them in the principles of religion; encourage them in the practice of virtue; give them proper reproof when necessary. Such of you as are blessed with ministerial gifts, be careful to encourage and improve them. Those churches which are destitute of such precious mercies, let them improve the means they have; pray earnestly to God for further help, and use all proper means to improve the same. In a word, holy brethren, live in love, and may the God of all grace and love be with you, for Christ's sake.

Benj. Griffith, Moderator.

Willm. Japscott,	Philip Shepherd,	Thomas Davis,
John Chosey,	David Shepherd,	David Davis,
Saml. Brooks,	Edwd. Keasly,	Thomas Jones,
Amos Johnson,	Wm. Worth,	Josiah Potts,
Isaac Peet,	Sylvs. Townsend,	Benj. miller,
Hezekiah Smith,	Saml. Morgan,	P. P. Vanhorn,

Griffith Owen,	Josiah Jones,	Isaac Eaton,
And. Bray,	Danl. Griffith,	Geo. Eaton,
Saml. Burkalve,	Henry Woodro,	Robt. Kelsy,
Alex. Edwards,	Josiah Mure,	Willm. Marsh,
Robt. Chalfant,	John Davis,	Inchabod Tompkins.

In answer to a request from the church at Kingwood, respecting the difficulties about Mr. Bonham, who desires his place, and gives not satisfaction?

Concluded, to send, as messengers to assist them, Brothers Ben. Griffith, Benj. Miller, and Isaac Eaton, at their meeting house, first Tuesday in December, 10 o'clock, A. M.

Appointed Brothers S. Morgan and S. Burkalve to inquire after the books sent to our society by Mr. Hollis, and give the best account they can by next meeting.

Brother Abel Morgan is to preach the Association sermon next year; in case of failure, Brother B. Griffith. Subject, the Divinity and Authority of the Holy Scriptures.

The Association to meet, Tuesday after the second Lord's day, in October. Sermon to begin at 3 o'clock, P. M.

Continue our quarterly fasts, the one on Tuesday after the fourth Lord's day of this month to be regarded as a day of thanksgiving for mercies received; and the fast days to be quarterly thereafter.

1761.

This year, the Association met on Wednesday, October 14, 1761, at Philadelphia, when a sermon was preached by the Rev. Abel Morgan, on the Divine Origin and Authority of the Scriptures, from John xvii. 17. After sermon, the messengers of twenty-three congregations met to the number of forty-six, whereof nineteen were ministers, chose the Rev. Benjamin Miller, moderator, and the Rev. Abel Morgan, clerk.

After reading the following memorial from the church at Dividing Creek, constituted May 30, 1761, it was received into the Association.

MEMORIAL.

"Whereas, a number of persons resided near Dividing Creek, in the county of Cumberland, in the western division of the province of New Jersey; some of whom, members of Cohansie church, some of Cape May church, and some not of any particular church; and whereas these lived at a great distance from the said churches, and at the same time our Rev. brother Samuel Heaton providentially settled at the said creek; Therefore, the above said persons made applications to their respective churches for dismission, and leave to form themselves into a distinct church, both which they obtained. Accordingly, we whose names are under written, being sent by the church of Cohansie, did meet the said people at their meeting house on the day above mentioned; and after sermon, laid hands on such persons as had been baptized, but had not joined themselves to any church: then all gave themselves to the Lord and to each other by a solemn covenant which they signed; and were declared by us to be a regular gospel church; and as such we recommend them to our Association.

"Signed, at Dividing Creek, the day and the year above mentioned, by us,

"ROBERT KELSAY, Minister,
SETH BROOKS, Elder,
OBEDIAH ROBINS, Deacon."

The church constituted at the Dividing Creek, in Cumberland county, West Jersey, May 30th, 1761, was received into union with this Association.

Agreed, That our reverend brethren, Mr. Morgan Edwards and Mr. Peter Peterson Vanhorn, be appointed to take care of the Association book of records, and insert therein the minutes of our proceedings; the said book to be kept in the city of Philadelphia, and not to be removed thence without the order of the Association.

Reverend Mr. Morgan Edwards and Isaac Jones, Esq., are appointed librarians, to receive in the books that were some time since sent us by Mr. Thomas Hollis, and lend out the said books to such ministers as stand in need of them, for such length of time as the librarians shall judge proper and convenient; and that the minister or elder in every congregation should inquire for said books, and either transmit the books or receipts to the librarians at or before the next Association.

Query from Oyster Bay:

1. Whether it be entirely proper to call the Scriptures the rule, and the Spirit the guide?

Resolved: The Holy Scriptures we profess to be our full, sufficient, and only rule of faith and obedience, and caution all to beware of every impulse, revelation, or any other imagination whatever, inconsistent with, or contrary to, the holy Scriptures, under the pretence of being guided by the Spirit. The work of the Holy Spirit, illuminates the understanding to know the mind of God, contained in the Scriptures, and may properly be called a guide.

2. Whether it is right to alter the expression in the answer to the tenth question in our catechism, concerning God's fore-ordination, and read "whatsoever he *bringeth* to pass," instead of "whatsover *comes* to pass."

Resolved: God worketh all things after the council of his own will, Whatsoever comes to pass is either by his agency or permission; and, though he permit sin to be, is not, therefore, the author of it; neither is the said answer in the catechism expressive or productive of the inference and conclusions the adversaries of God's sovereignty would fain charge upon it.

Agreed, to continue our quarterly fast days, as usual, through our churches; the first to be on the Thursday after the fourth Lord's day in October, and so on Thursday after the fourth Lord's day every third month.

Agreed, that our Reverend brethren, Mr. Morgan Edwards and Mr. Peter Peterson Vanhorn, are appointed to revive and maintain an annual correspondence with the board of Baptist ministers at London, or elsewhere.—Every church should transmit an account of the number of members in each, to the above said brethren as soon as possible.

Agreed, that every church should send in an account to Mr. Edwards, at Philadelphia, what number of catechisms each are willing to take, in order to know whether there will be proper encouragement to have them reprinted.

Concluded, that Brother Benjamin Griffith is to preach the sermon next year; and, in case of failure, Brother Morgan Edwards; the subject—Doctrine of the Trinity. The Association to begin on Tuesday after the second Lord's day in October, at 3 o'clock, P. M.

The Association letter was written by the Rev. Peter Peterson Vanhorn, as follows:

PASTORAL ADDRESS.

"The elders and messengers of the several congregations in Pennsylvania, the Jerseys, and provinces adjacent, baptized on profession of faith, met in Association the 13th, 14th, and 15th days of October, 1761, at the city of Philadelphia.

"Send Christian salutation.

"Dearly beloved in our Lord Jesus, the great Shepherd of the sheep, your delegates met at the time appointed, and were agreeably entertained with a discourse, fixed upon last year, from John xvii. 17, "Sanctify them through thy truth, thy word is truth." We trust that your fervent prayers to God for us have prevailed, seeing we met in gospel fellowship, and have been enabled to preserve unanimity in all our consultations and conclusions. By letters from our churches, we had the pleasure and satisfaction to hear that peace and concord abounds, and considerable additions have been made in divers places. All glory to our God. And now, dear brethren, about to part from each other, we desire, in some measure, to answer your expectation. Suffer us to lay before you, for your observation, these few following necessary things.

"1st. Be much in the reading and study of the holy Scriptures, seeing the Apostle informs us they are able to make us wise to salvation, through faith in our Lord Jesus Christ.

"2d. Be much and often at the throne of grace, in prayer to God, seeing our blessed Lord has taught us that men ought always pray, and not faint, with this annexed encouragement, that he will avenge his own elect that cry day and night unto him.

"3d. Be careful of attending constantly with improvement upon the public worship of God, in the beauties of holiness.

"4th. Be careful of the instruction of youth, and those under your care; and ward against introducing such books among them as will have a tendency to corrupt their minds and have an evil influence on their manners.

"5th. For the cure of the common complaint of leanness, coldness, deadness in religion, make use of Christ in all his offices, titles, and relations, in whom are reposited all needful supplies. Strengthen and encourage the hands of your ministers, who watch for your souls as they that must give an account to God. Let your conversation be as becometh the gospel of Christ. And the very God of peace, who brought again our Lord Jesus Christ from the dead, comfort, strengthen, and establish you in all things. So pray your brethren in the faith and fellowship of the gospel. Amen.

"Benjamin Miller, Moderator.

"Abel Morgan,	John Thomas,	Wm. Marshall,
Morgan Edwards,	Joshua Jones,	Daniel Smith,
David Davis,	Robert Celsy,	Samuel Dodge,
John Davis,	Abel Griffith,	Benjamin Stelle,
Isaac Eaton,	Samuel Waldo,	Randel Drake,
Samuel Heaton,	Joseph Heart,	Jonas Goble,
Wm. Davis,	Steven Watts,	Wm. Folwell,
Thomas Davis,	Simon Butler,	Isaac James,
Thomas Jones,	John Stites,	Edmund Cosby,
Peter P. Vanhorn,	Isaac Jones,	Joshua More."
Henry Crosley,	Samuel Burcolo,	

COPY OF A LETTER SENT TO THE BOARD OF MINISTERS IN LONDON, BY ORDER OF THE ASSOCIATION.

"The Association of Particular Baptist Churches annually held at Philadelphia, to the Board of Particular Baptist Ministers in London:

"Reverend brethren,—We greet you well: and, as a part of that community, in the British dominions, (whereof you have in some sort the superintendence,) we offer you our acquaintance; and solicit a share of your public care and friendship. Our numbers in these parts multiply; for when we had the pleasure of writing to you, in 1734, there were but nine churches in our Association, yet now there are twenty-eight, all owning the Confession of faith put forth in London, in 1689. Some of the churches are now destitute; but we have a prospect of supplies, partly by means of a Baptist academy lately set up. This infant seminary of learning is yet weak, having no more than twenty-four pounds a year towards its support. Should it be in your power to favor this school any way, we presume you will be pleased to know how? A few books proper for such a school, or a small apparatus, or some pieces of apparatus, are more immediately wanted, and not to be had easily in these parts. We have also, of late, endeavored to form a library at Philadelphia, for the use of our brethren in the ministry, who are not able to purchase books. This design also wants the assistance of our brethren in England.

"However, our design in writing to you in this public manner is, to renew a correspondence which hath been dropped for some years past; and if you think well of it, we shall be glad to hear from you against our next Association in October. You may direct to our brother Morgan Edwards, at Philadelphia.

"We commend you to the grace of God, and desire your prayers for us, and remain your brethren in the faith.

"Signed, by order of the Association,
                        "PETER PETERSON VANHORN,
                         MORGAN EDWARDS."

Philadelphia, May 16, 1762.

THE STATE OF THE CHURCHES FOR THE YEAR.

[The Present State of the twenty-nine Churches, whose Messengers annually meet in Association, at Philadelphia, from the Provinces of Pennsylvania, Jersey, Virginia, Maryland, New England, and New York: collected partly from their Letters to the Association, and partly from private information in the year, 1761: By MORGAN EDWARDS.]

CHURCHES.	MINISTERS.	Baptized.	Excluded.	Dead.	Members.	Hearers.
Pennepek,	Peter Peterson Vanhorn,	3	0	3	50	300
Welsh Tract,	David Davies,	5	0	2	95	300
Great Valley,	John Davies,	7	0	0	110	200
Brandywine,	Abel Griffiths,	0	2	1	25	150
Montgomery,	Benjamin Griffiths,	3	0	1	90	150
Southampton,	Thomas Davies,	0	0	4	41	200
Philadelphia,	Morgan Edwards,	24	0	3	82	700
New Britain,	Joshua John,	1	0	1	50	200
Tulpohokin,	Thomas Jones,	1	0	0	27	100
Bethlehem,		0	0	0	0	0
Middletown,	Abel Morgan,	14	0	0	0	0
Piscataqua,	Isaac Stelle,	0	0	0	0	0
Cohansie,	Robert Kelsay,	5	0	2	104	600
Cape May,		0	0	3	60	300
Hopewell,	Isaac Eaton, A. M.,	0	0	0	94	400
Cranbury,		2	0	0	36	150
Scotch Plain,	Benjamin Miller,	14	2	4	134	800
Morristown,		1	0	3	22	0
Rocksberry,	Henry Crosley,	6	0	2	32	0
Kingwood,		1	0	0	0	0
Newtown,	William Marsh,	0	0	1	19	0
Salem,	John Sutton,	0	0	2	22	150
Dividing Creek,	Samuel Heaton,	12	0	0	20	100
Ketockton,	John Marks,	0	0	0	31	0
Opekon,	John Garret,	7	0	1	57	250
Oyster Bay,	David Sutton,	2	0	0	14	70
Bateman's Precincts,	Samuel Waldo,	18	0	0	52	400
Horse Neck,		0	0	0	7	150
Baltimore,	John Davies,	0	0	0	44	300
		126	4	33	4018	5970

1762.

The Association met this year, October 12th, and sat to the 14th. There were messengers or letters from eighteen churches. The other eleven we heard nothing of. Rev. Morgan Edwards was moderator, and Rev. Abel Morgan, clerk. They met at the Lutheran church, in Fifth street, between Arch street and Race street, where the sound of the organ was heard in the Baptist worship. The business done was as followeth:

1. A church constituted August 6, 1756, at Smith Creek, a branch of North Shannandoah, in the province of Virginia, was received into the Association the first day of meeting.

The first, and present minister of this church, is the Rev. John Alderson. The original constituents were but eleven, now they are thirty, including the eight that were baptized this year. One died since the constitution.

2. Certificates of the ordination and good morals of Rev. David Thomas and Rev. David Sutton, were drawn up by Rev. Samuel Jones and Isaac Jones, Esq., and the city seal affixed thereto by the Recorder, Benjamin Chew, Esq., for which he took no fees.

Here follows a copy thereof:

CERTIFICATE.

"The ministers and messengers of the several Baptist congregations in Pennsylvania and adjacent provinces, met in annual Association at the city of Philadelphia, October 12, 1762.

"To all Christian people, to whom these presents may come, send greeting.

"This certifies that the bearer hereof, Rev. David Thomas, late of Chester county, in the province of Pennsylvania, but now residing and dwelling in Farquair county, in the province of Virginia, was, (after due examination, whereby he appeared to have a competent share of learning and other prerequisites to the sacred office,) admitted into holy orders, according to the known and approved rites of the Baptist church, whereby he is authorized to preach the gospel, and administer the ordinances thereof. And also certifies, that at all times, before and after his ordination, (for any thing known, heard, or believed to the contrary,) he lived a holy and unblemished life. And we do hereby recommend him as such to the notice, esteem, and regard of all Christians where he now does, or hereafter may, reside.

"Signed by order of the Association, October 13, 1762, by their moderator,

"MORGAN EDWARDS, A. M."

"I, Benjamin Chew, Esq., Recorder of the city of Phildelphia, do hereby certify that the Rev. Morgan Edwards, A. M., who hath signed the above certificate is pastor of the Baptist church in this city of Philadelphia, and moderator of the above Association, and that he is a gentleman of most exemplary morals and piety.

In testimony of which I have hereunto caused the seal of this said city to be affixed this 15th day of October, A. D., 1762.

BENJAMIN CHEW, Recorder.

3. Agreed, to continue our quarterly fasts throughout our churches as heretofore on Thursday in each quarter month: the first to be on Thursday after the fourth Lord's day, in October.

4. Agreed, that the subject of the next Association sermon be the State of Man before and after the Fall: to be preached by Brother Morgan Edwards; in case of his failure, by Brother David Davis.

5. Agreed, that Brother Samuel Jones, A. B., should draw out the Association Letter to the churches. A copy of which here follows:

PASTORAL ADDRESS.

"The elders and messengers of the several baptized congregations in Pennsylvania and provinces adjacent, met in Association at Philadelphia, the 12th, 13th, and 14th of October, A. D. 1762.

"To the several churches we represent, do send our Christian salutation.

"Dearly beloved brethren,—We have the pleasure, at the close of this opportunity, of transmitting to you an account of our meeting together, according to appointment: a spirit of calmness and deliberation breathed in our consultations, and peaceful unanimity in our determinations. Glory be to God for this grace.

"Of twenty-nine churches belonging to this Association, eighteen met, by their delegates or letters, this year; and we hope, brethren, the same zeal which induced you to meet us at this time, will not suffer you ever to neglect corresponding with us in this manner; nor yet those who have been now wanting herein, to continue negligent of this invaluable privilege. By reading your letters, we learn that seventy-eight persons have been added to our number by baptism, this last year; sixteen have been removed by death and excommunication.

"And now, brethren, suffer the word of exhortation in love. Be desirous of excelling in vital piety, and labor to adorn the holy and great profession you have made, of being the disciples of Jesus and the adopted children of God. Neglect not the assembling yourselves together. Be doers as well as hearers of the word. Be mindful to maintain family worship, and to imbue the minds of those committed to your care with the savor of religion. Strengthen the hands of your ministers, and be liberal of your ministerial gifts to vacant places. Banish every thing low, and sordid conduct, the native product of grovelling minds, as being unworthy of the noble character of a Christian. Let a public spirit of benevolence and liberality be diffused among you. Be more ambitious of advancing the interest of the church of Christ, than of adding field to field, and becoming rich at the expense of religion.

"Finally, beloved brethren, we recommend you to the Lord, the adorable head of the church, who is able to perfect you in every grace and virtue, and to conduct you to his heavenly kingdom, where we hope to join with you and the thousands of his saints, to give blessing and honor, and glory and power unto him that sitteth on the throne, and the Lamb, for ever and ever. Amen.

"Morgan Edwards, Moderator.

Recompense Stanbury, William Connor, John Thomas,
William Marshall, Septimus Levering, Benj. Miller,
Alexander Edwards, John Garrett, Robert Kilsay,
J. J. Jones, Thos. Dungan, John Davis,
Barnaby Barnes, Walter Shewell, John Alderson,
Wm. Rigden, Benj. Griffith, Abel Griffith,
George George, John Davis, Joshua Jones,
David Cornogg, Abel Morgan, Samuel Jones.
H. Watts, Thos. Jones,

6. Agreed that the Association shall begin, next year, the Tuesday after the second Lord's day in October: the sermon to begin at 3 o'clock, P. M.

STATE OF THE CHURCHES DURING THE YEAR.

CHURCHES.	MINISTERS.	Baptized.	Dead.	Excom.	Members.
Pennepek,		0	0	0	52
Middletown,	Abel Morgan,	8	0	0	134
Piscataqua,	Isaac Stelle,	1	1	0	41
Cohansie,	Robert Kelsay,	2	2	0	104
Welsh Tract,	David Davis,	0	0	0	95
Great Valley,	John Davis,	1	0	1	110
Cape May,		0	4	0	56
Hopewell,	Isaac Eaton, A. M.,	1	0	0	95
Brandywine,	Abel Griffiths,	2	0	0	27
Montgomery,	Benjamin Griffiths,	4	1	1	92
Tulpehokin,	Thomas Jones,	3	1	0	29
Kingwood,		1	0	0	41
Cranberry,		0	0	0	41
Southampton,	Thomas Davis,	15	3	2	51
Philadelphia,	Morgan Edwards, A. M.,	17	2	1	116
Horseneck,		0	0	0	7
Scotch Plains,	Benjamin Miller,	0	0	2	144
Oyster Bay,		0	0	0	14
Morristown,		2	0	0	24
Rocksberry,	Henry Crosley,	6	2	0	32
Ketokton,	John Marks,	0	0	0	31
Opekon,	John Garret,	7	1	0	57
New Britain,	William Davis,	1	0	0	51
Salem,		0	0	0	22
Baltimore,	John Davis,	12	1	1	48
Newtown,	William Marsh,	0	1	0	0
Bateman's Precincts,	Samuel Waldo,	31	1	3	81
Smith's Creek,	John Alderson,	8	1	0	30
Dividing Creek,	Samuel Heaton,	3	0	0	23
New York,	John Gano,	7	0	0	27
		132	21	11	1585

1763.

The Association met this year, October 11th and sat till the 13th. Rev. Isaac Eaton, A. M., was chosen moderator; Rev. Isaac Stelle, clerk. After hearing a sermon on the State of Man before and after the fall, preached by Rev. Morgan Edwards, A. M., from Eccl. vii. 29, they proceeded to business.

There were present, messengers and letters from twenty churches; the other ten neglected both. The messengers' names follow:

Ministers,—Rev. Morgan Edwards, Peter Peterson Vanhorn, Samuel Jones, John Davis, Benjamin Griffith, John Thomas, Joshua Jones, Joseph Thomas, Benjamin Miller, Isaac Stelle, John Davis, David Sutton, David Jones, Isaac Eaton, Abel Griffith, Samuel Heaton, Robert Kelsay, John Gano, John Blackwell.

Laymen,—Messrs. Joshua Moore, Samuel Davis, Septimus Levering, George Westcott, Samuel Miles, Joseph Watkins, Henry Woodrow, Andrew Edge, William Mashal, Alexander Edwards, Isaac Lewis, William Buchamham, Joseph Hart, Samson Davis, Daniel Cornock, Thomas Sears, Daniel Drake, James Groven, Joseph Taylor, Richard Allison, John Manners, Jeffrey Bentley, Edward Busse, William Lock, David Shepherd, John Carman, Francis Van Dyke.

Adjourned till to-morow nine o'clock, A. M.

October 12. The Association met at the appointed time, and proceeded to business.

1. A church at New York, minister, Rev. John Gano, was received into the Association. This church was constituted June 19, 1762. The number of constituents were twenty-seven, and these chiefly members of the Scotch Plains. Now the number is forty-three.

2. At the request of the church of Salem, we have found them a supply for this year, who is the Rev. John Blackwell.

3. At a request of the church of Morristown, we appointed them a supply once a month the ensuing year.

4. A question was moved by the church of the Great Valley to this effect: Whether it be the prerogative of a church to receive applications for baptism, examine the candidates, and to judge of their qualifications for baptism? or whether these be the distinct and peculiar prerogatives of the ministers, exclusive of the laity?

The occasion of this question was the opinion and practice of the church of Philadelphia, who by a general vote have allowed the said prerogatives to belong to the minister, by the tenor of the commission relative to baptism, and the universal practice of the commissioners; and that there is neither precept nor precedent for the contrary in scripture. All allowed that this may be, and in some cases must be; but that the other practice was more expedient. However, none pretended to say it was warranted by scripture. The question was put,—Whether the point was a term of communion? and whether it should be debated, or dropped? None stood up for either. So that it was dropped.

5. In the letter of Cohansie it was queried: Whether it be best to

excommunicate delinquents before the church only, or publicly before the congregation?

Answered: If the offence be public, the cutting off should be so too; if private, it should be as private as may be.

6. Agreed, that the Association next year be held on the Tuesday after the second Lord's day in October. The sermon to be preached by Rev. John Gano; and in case of failure, by Rev. Samuel Jones. The subject to be, The Recovery of Man.

7. Rev. Isaac Stelle drew the Association letter, which is as follows:

PASTORAL ADDRESS.

The elders and messengers of the several Baptist congregations in Pennsylvania and provinces adjacent, now met in general Association at Philadelphia, the 11th, 12th, and 13th October, 1763.

To the several churches we represent, send Christian salutation.

Dearly beloved brethren,—We have the satisfaction to acquaint you of our meeting together, according to appointment. A good measure of brotherly love has subsisted among us, during the time of our consultation. Thanks be to the Lord, who is wisdom and council to his people.

We rejoice at the agreeable account from you; for we learn by the messengers and letters, that you are at peace and unanimity among yourselves. We find there is an addition to our churches of eighty-one members this year more than last; which is great cause of thankfulness to God, and encouragement to us all. May fervent zeal for the cause and interest of our dear Redeemer ever animate our souls.

And now, brethren, receive a word of exhortation in love. Strive to abound in vital piety; see that you walk worthy of the vocation wherewith you are called. Be careful to maintain a steady course of cheerful obedience to God all the days of your life. Neglect not prayer, neither family nor closet. Strengthen the hands of your ministers, and encourage their visits to vacant places. Delight yourselves in the word, worship and ordinances of God. Make the sacred oracles the rule of all your actions. Learn, by Christ's sermon on the mount, to forgive your enemies; strive to live peaceably with all men.

May you ever be able to walk together in the unity of the spirit and bond of peace, provoking one another to love and good works: and that being by promise united to an inheritance among them that are sanctified, you may at last hear the voice of the heavenly bridegroom say unto you, Come up hither; which, may God of his infinite mercy grant for Jesus sake. Amen.

ISAAC EATON, Moderator.

David Sutton,	Joseph Hart,	Isaac Stelle,
Samuel Jones,	James Grover,	Robert Kelsay,
Benjamin Miller,	Daniel Drake,	Samuel Heaton,
Joseph Thomas,	John Carman,	John Thomas,
John Blackwell,	Morgan Edwards,	John Gano,
Wm. Marshal,	Benjamin Griffith,	Abel Griffith.
John Manners,	John Davis,	

STATE OF THE CHURCHES DURING THE YEAR.

CHURCHES.	MINISTERS.	Baptized.	Dead.	Excom.	Members.
Pennepek,	Samuel Jones, A. B.,	6	0	0	58
Middletown,	Abel Morgan,	16	1	0	49
Piscataqua,	Isaac Stelle,	2	0	0	43
Cohansie,	Robert Kelsay,	0	1	1	102
Welsh Tract,	David Davis,	1	0	0	96
Great Valley,	John Davis,	1	2	0	109
Cape May,		1	0	0	57
Hopewell,	Isaac Eaton, A. M.,	1	1	0	96
Brandywine,	Abel Griffiths,	4	0	0	31
Montgomery,	Benjamin Griffiths,	4	3	0	93
Tulpehokin,	Thomas Jones,	0	0	0	29
Kingwood,	David Sutton,	5	0	0	48
Cranberry,		0	0	0	30
Southampton,	Samuel Jones, A. B.	3	1	1	52
Philadelphia,	Morgan Edwards, A. M.,	21	5	0	132
Scotch Plains,	Benjamin Miller,	12	1	2	144
Horse Neck,		0	0	0	7
Oyster Bay,		0	0	0	14
Ketokton,	John Marks,	0	0	1	30
Morristown,		0	2	0	22
Opekon,	John Garret,	0	0	0	63
Rocksberry,	Henry Crosley,	0	0	0	36
New Britain,	Joshua Jones,	4	1	0	54
Salem,	John Blackwell,	1	0	0	23
Baltimore,	John Davis,	6	1	0	56
Smith's Creek,	John Alderson,	0	0	0	30
Newtown,	William Marsh,	0	0	0	27
Bateman's Precincts,	Samuel Waldo,	2	0	1	84
Dividing Creek,	Samuel Heaton,	0	0	0	23
New York,	John Gano,	16	1	0	43
		96	20	6	1681

1764.

The Association met this year, on October 14th, and sat to October 16th.

The sermon was preached by Rev. John Gano, from Rom. xi. 7. The moderator was, Rev. Isaac Eaton. The clerk, Rev. Abel Morgan. There were present, messengers or letters from twenty-five churches. The chief business was as followeth:

1. A church constituted at New Mills, Northampton township, county of Burlington, and province of New Jersey, was received into the Association. This church was constituted June 23, 1764. The contituents were nine in number. The minister, Rev. Peter Peterson Vanhorn.

2. Agreed, to inform the churches to which we respectively belong, that, inasmuch as a charter is obtained in Rhode Island government, toward erecting a Baptist College, the churches should be liberal in contributing towards carrying the same into execution.

3. The subject for the next Association sermon to be Effectual Calling. The preacher, Samuel Jones; in case of failure, Isaac Stelle. The Association to meet next year, at 3 o'clock, P. M., on Tuesday after the second Sunday in October.

PASTORAL LETTER.

The elders and messengers of the several Baptist churches in Pennsylvania and provinces adjacent, met in general Association, at Philadelphia, October 16, 1764.

To the several congregations we represent, and stand related to in gospel bonds, grace, mercy, and peace, be multiplied through Jesus Christ our Lord.

Dear brethren,—As love enters deeply into the spirit and genius of our holy religion, so one very natural and important expression of it, is, the friendly association of churches for the great purposes of promoting the gospel of God, their own comfort and edification; being well persuaded that this was the principle, and these the views which gave rise to these annual meetings. And, as we trust, we are influenced by the same motives which inspired the breasts of our respected predecessors, so we are not without hopes, that the salutary ends proposed are, at least in some degree, answered. Our attempts, however, to serve the cause of our blessed Lord Jesus, and to assist your faith and joy, will, we doubt not, meet with your cordial acceptance. Suffer us, then, to inform you, that we met in love and peace, and were agreeably entertained with a discourse on the important subject of our recovery from ruin, by the mediation of the great High Priest of our profession, Christ Jesus. The letters from the several churches brought us the pleasing news, that the Lord is carrying on his work with power in sundry places; that peace and concord abound in our congregations, blessed be his holy name. Our consultations have been loving and unanimous through the whole. And now we are going to part, suffer the word of exhortation. Dear brethren, be careful to improve the favors you enjoy. Let the sacred oracles constantly be the man of your counsel. Make conscience of the duty of prayer in the family. Be careful of the education of youth. Bring up your children in the nurture and admonition of the Lord. Strengthen and encourage your ministers; be ready and willing to support them in visiting those churches that are destitute of the means of grace. So we commit you to God and the word of his grace, who is able to keep you from falling, and to present you faultless before the throne of his glory with exceeding joy. To Him be glory in the churches, now and forever. Amen. We rest your brethren in gospel relation.

Signed in behalf of the Association.

BENJAMIN MILLER, Moderator.

MINUTES OF THE PHILADELPHIA ASSOCIATION. 93

THE ORIGINAL STATE OF THIRTY-ONE BAPTIST CHURCHES WHOSE MESSENGERS ANNUALLY MEET IN ASSOCIATION AT PHILADELPHIA.

CHURCHES.	COUNTIES.	PROVINCES.	FIRST MINISTERS.	CONSTITUTED.	JOINED ASSOCIATION.	First Constituents.
Pennepek,	Philadelphia,	Penn'a.	Elias Keach,	November, 1687	These Churches first met in Association at Philadelphia, Sept. 27, 1707.	14
Middletown,	Monmouth,	N. Jersey.	Elias Keach,	1688		6
Piscataqua,	Middlesex,	N. Jersey.	Thos. Killingsworth,	1689		9
Cohansie,	Cumberland,	N. Jersey.	Thos. Killingsworth,	1690		16
Welsh Tract,	New Castle,	Penn'a.	Thomas Griffiths,	1701		15
Great Valley,	Chester,	Penn'a.	Hugh Davis,	April 22, 1711	September 20, 1711	37
Cape May,	Cape May county,	N. Jersey.	Nathaniel Jenkins,	June 24, 1712	September 20, 1712	16
Hopewell,	Hunterdon,	N. Jersey.	Isaac Eaton,	April 22, 1715	September 19, 1715	15
Brandywine,	Chester,	Penn'a.	William Boutcher,	June 14, 1715	September 19, 1715	10
Montgomery,	Philadelphia,	Penn'a.	Benjamin Griffith,	June 20, 1719	September 24, 1719	21
Tulpehokin,	Berks,	Penn'a.	Thomas Jones,	August 19, 1738	September 23, 1738	21
Kingwood,	Hunterdon,	N. Jersey.	Thomas Curtis,	May 23, 1742	September 25, 1742	17
Cranberry,	Middlesex,	N. Jersey.	James Carman,	November 1, 1745	September 24, 1746	48
Southampton,	Bucks,	Penn'a.	Joshua Potts,	April 8, 1746	September 24, 1746	56
Philadelphia,	Philadelphia,	Penn'a.	Jenkin Jones,	May 15, 1746	September 24, 1746	14
Scotch Plains,	Essex,	N. Jersey.	Benjamin Miller,	September 8, 1747	September 22, 1747	27
Horseneck,	Fairfield,	Connecticut.	John Stephens,	September 12, 1747	September 22, 1747	28
Oyster Bay,	Queen's county,	New York.	Thomas Davis,	July 11, 1748	September 18, 1750	11
Ketokton,	Loudon,	Virginia.	John Thomas,	October 8, 1751	October 8, 1752	16
Morristown,	Morris county,	N. Jersey.	Ichabod Tomkins,	August 11, 1752	October 4, 1752	3
Opekon,	Frederick county,	Virginia.	Samuel Heaton,	October 20, 1752	October 8, 1754	5
Rocksberry,	Morris county,	N. Jersey.	Henry Crosley,	May 12, 1753	October 16, 1753	22
Baltimore,	Baltimore,	Maryland.	John Davis,	November 1, 1754	October 7, 1755	19
New Britain,	Bucks,	Penn'a.	William Davis,	November 28, 1754	October 7, 1755	19
Salem,	Salem county,	N. Jersey.	Job Shepherd,	May 17, 1755	October 7, 1775	11
Smith's Creek,	Frederick county,	Virginia.	John Alderson,	August 16, 1756	October 12, 1762	8
Newtown,	Sussex,	N. Jersey.	William Marsh,	November 14, 1757	September 20, 1758	11
Bateman's Precincts,	Dutchess county,	New York.	Samuel Waldo,	November, 1758	September 20, 1758	12
Dividing Creek,	Cumberland,	N. Jersey.	Samuel Heaton,	May 30, 1761	October 14, 1761	27
New York,	New York,	New York.	John Gano,	June 19, 1762	October 11, 1763	9
New Mills,	Burlington,	N. Jersey.	Peter P. Vanhorn,	June 23, 1764	October 16, 1764	

STATE OF THE CHURCHES DURING THE YEAR.

CHURCHES.	MINISTERS.	Baptized.	Excom.	Died.	Members.
Pennepek,	Samuel Jones,	2	2	0	53
Middletown	Abel Morgan,	14	0	0	160
Piscataqua,	Isaac Stelle,	17	1	1	58
Cohansie,	Robert Kelsay,	0	2	2	100
Welsh Tract,	David Davis,	1	0	0	97
Great Valley,	John Davis,	5	8	0	106
Cape May,	John Sutton,	0	0	0	57
Hopewell,	Isaac Eaton,	13	1	0	108
Brandywine,	Abel Griffiths,	1	2	0	30
Montgomery,	Benjamin Griffiths,	0	0	0	93
Tulpehokin,	Thomas Jones,	0	1	0	28
Kingwood,	David Sutton,	5	0	0	55
Cranberry,		4	0	0	34
Southampton,	Samuel Jones,	5	1	0	56
Philadelphia,	Morgan Edwards,	6	3	0	135
Scotch Plains,	Benjamin Miller,	33	1	0	158
Horse Neck,		2	0	0	7
Oyster Bay,		2	0	0	14
Ketokton,	John Marks,	9	1	0	33
Morristown,		0	0	0	31
Opekon,	John Garret,	0	0	0	0
Rocksberry,	Henry Crosley,	9	0	0	45
Baltimore,	John Davis,	1	0	0	66
New Britain,	Joshua Jones,	0	1	0	53
Salem,		0	0	0	23
Smith's Creek,	John Alderson,	0	0	0	36
Newtown,		0	0	0	27
Bateman's Precincts,	Samuel Waldo,	2	0	0	88
Dividing Creek,	Samuel Heaton,	0	0	0	23
New York,	John Gano,	13	1	0	57
Newmills,	Peter Peterson Vanhorn,	10	0	0	19
		152	25	3	1650

Baptized this year 152, which is 40 more than were baptized last year.

1765.

The Association met at Philadelphia this year, October 15, and sat to October 17. Forty-four messengers present. Letters from the churches were read.

1. Received into the Association a church at Konoloway, in the township of Air, Cumberland county, Pennsylvania. It was constituted August 25, 1765. The number of constituents six.

2. Agreed, to have our Confession of faith reprinted by Morgan Edwards and Samuel Jones: the churches to send them money for the number they want before the first of December. The size and character to be left to the discretion of said persons.

3. Received, Rev. Noah Hammond, of Long Island, New York, in unity with the ministers, by giving him the right hand of fellowship in behalf of the Association. And ordered Mr. Gano and Mr.

Jones to be at Coram, township of Brookhaven, on Long Island, on November 1, to constitute twenty-three persons there into a church, and to acknowledge them as a sister church in behalf of the Association.

4. Agreed, that the minister of Philadelphia shall have the direction of the meetings at the Association, and the nomination of the preachers, that they may have proper notice of the same beforehand.

5. Query, from Smith's Creek: Whether it be proper to receive a person into communion who had been baptized by immersion by a minister of the church of England, if no other objection could be made? Answer: Yea, if he had been baptized on a profession of faith and repentance.

6. Agreed, that the churches in Virginia have our leave to form themselves into an Association, provided they go on the same plan, and hold union with us.

7. The Association next year to be held on Tuesday after the second Sunday in October. The sermon to be preached by Isaac Stelle; and in case of failure, by Peter Peterson Vanhorn. Subject, the Incarnation of the Son of God.

Here follows a copy of the Association letter to the churches, written by John Sutton:

PASTORAL ADDRESS.

"The elders and messengers of the several churches met, according to appointment, at Phildelphia, October 15, 16, 17, A. D., 1765.

"To the several churches to whom we respectively belong, send our Christian salutation.

"Dearly Beloved in our blessed Lord,—We rejoiced to hear from you, and the more so, when we perceived the Lord hath graciously visited a number of you with a day of his power, and brought many, first to give themselves to Him and to the churches according to his will, by which our number is increased by baptism three hundred and one, which exceeds the last year's increase by one hunred and forty-nine; blessed be God for his rich grace. We have had a good measure of peace, unity, and consolation in all our affairs. We hope the success of the gospel will raise in your hearts gratitude and thankfulness to God. And that you will strive with us in your prayers to God, that he will carry on his work with power, not only among his churches, but universally throughout the whole world. And to that end we exhort you, with ourselves, to walk worthy of that holy religion we profess. Encourage your ministers to visit the destitute churches. Give them all the assistance in so arduous a work that your circumstances will admit. In a word, as ye have received Christ Jesus the Lord, so walk ye in him: and his saving grace, and the love of God, and the influence of the Holy Ghost be with you, and rest upon you both now and forever. Amen.

"From your brethren in the faith and fellowship of the gospel.

"Signed by the moderator,

"BENJAMIN GRIFFITH."

STATE OF THE CHURCHES DURING THE YEAR.

CHURCHES.	MINISTERS.	Baptized.	Restored.	Died.	Excom.	Members.
Pennepek,	Samuel Jones,	2	0	1	0	54
Middletown,	Abel Morgan,	13	0	3	0	167
Piscataqua,	Isaac Stelle,	4	0	2	0	60
Cohansie,	Robert Kelsay,	21	0	2	0	119
Welsh Tract,	David Davis,	6	0	0	0	103
Great Valley,	John Davis,	1	0	2	0	103
Cape May,	John Sutton,	2	0	1	0	58
Hopewell,	Isaac Eaton,	86	1	0	0	196
Brandywine,	Abel Griffiths,	1	0	2	0	29
Montgomery,	Benjamin Griffiths,	2	0	3	2	90
Tulpehokin,	Thomas Jones,	0	0	0	0	28
Kingwood,	David Sutton,	17	0	2	0	69
Cranberry,		7	0	0	-0	41
Southampton,	Samuel Jones,	1	0	0	2	55
Philadelphia,	Morgan Edwards,	5	1	3	2	137
Scotch Plains,	Benjamin Miller,	25	0	2	0	149
Horseneck,		0	0	1	0	6
Oyster Bay,		0	1	0	0	15
Ketockton,	John Marks,	0	0	0	0	33
Morristown,		24	0	0	1	53
Opekon,	John Garret,	2	0	1	0	70
Rocksberry,	Henry Crosley,	5	0	0	0	50
Baltimore,	John Davis,	11	0	0	1	76
New Britain,	Joshua Jones,	1	0	1	0	53
Salem,		0	0	0	0	23
Smith's Creek,	John Alderson,	4	0	0	0	36
Newtown,		0	0	0	0	26
Bateman's Precincts,	Samuel Waldo,	19	1	0	0	108
Dividing Creek,	Samuel Heaton,	18	0	1	0	39
New York,	John Gano,	20	0	0	1	77
Newmills,	P. P. Vanhorn,	11	0	1	0	30
Kenoloway,	Joseph Powell,	0	0	0	0	6
Coram,	Noah Hammond,	0	0	0	0	23
		308	4	28	9	2234

1766.

The Association met at Philadelphia, on Tuesday, October 14th, A. D. 1766, at 3 o'clock, P. M., according to appointment, and opened with a sermon from John i. 14, preached by Rev. Isaac Stelle. After sermon the messengers came together. The moderator for last year resumed his seat; and, after prayer, moved for choosing a new moderator and clerk. The choice fell on Rev. Benjamin Miller and Rev. Samuel Jones. Adjourned to 9 o'clock next day. Divine service in the evening.

Wednesday, 15th. The Association met at nine in the morning. After prayer, the list of messengers was called over. Each answered to his name. They were—

Ministers,—Rev. Benjamin Miller, Abel Griffiths, Joseph Powell, Isaac Stelle, John Blackwell, David Jones, Joshuah Jones, John

Davis, Thomas Davis, John Waltam, Morgan Edwards, Samuel Heaton, Benjamin Griffiths, John Thomas, Samuel Jones, John Davis, Noah Hammond, David Thomas.

Laymen,—Messrs. David Powell, Joseph Merril, Samuel Dodge, Francis Vandike, Thomas Farr, Thomas Cox, David Thomas, John Crees, Walter Shewell, George George, Josiah Lewis, Joseph Griffiths, David Eaton, Isaac Jones, Samuel Davis, George Wescott, Joseph Shepherd, David Bowen, Samuel Meed, Alexander Edwards, John Wright, and Arthur Watts.

Moved and agreed to, for more order and expedition in despatching business: 1, That the moderator, shall, for the future, take his seat in the desk. 2, That every one who speaketh shall stand up, and address himself to the moderator. 3, That none shall interrupt the speaker till he hath done. 4, That no matter brought on shall be laid aside till finished, except postponing it be agreed to.

Adjourned to three.

The Association met again at three. After prayer, it was moved and agreed: That it is most necessary for the good of the Baptist interest, that the Association have at their disposal every year a sum of money. Accordingly it was further agreed: That the churches, henceforth, do make a collection every quarter, and send the same yearly to the Association, to be by them deposited in the hands of trustees; the interest whereof only to be by them laid out every year in support of ministers travelling on the errand of the churches, or otherwise, as the necessities of said churches shall require.

Pursuant to a petition from the church of Konoloway, it was agreed to desire the churches this year to collect money for their use, and send the same to the next Association, to be by them laid out so as to be of perpetual use to the said church.

Moved and agreed to: That a yearly intercourse between the Associations to the east and west of us be, by letters and messengers, now begun, and hereafter maintained. Accordingly, Rev. Samuel Jones was ordered to write to the Association to be held at Warren, the Tuesday before the second Sunday in September; and Rev. John Gano, Samuel Jones, and Morgan Edwards, appointed to meet them as delegates from us.

The Rev. M. Edwards was ordered to draw a letter to the Association, meeting at Mill Creek, in Virginia, the Saturday before the third Sunday in August; and Rev. Isaac Stelle, John Davis, and John Blackwell were delegated to meet them as our messengers.

As some tardiness hath been observed in sending messengers and letters to the Association, and in the attendance which the messengers give to the business of said Association, it was agreed to admonish the tardy churches, and hereby they are admonished; it was also agreed that those ministers who cannot return home in a day shall not appoint to be with their respective churches sooner than the second Sunday in October, and that they make no appointments in the way which will require them to leave Philadelphia sooner than is consistent with doing the business of the Association deliberately and wholly.

Received into the Association a church at Coram, in Long Island, constituted November 1, 1766; also the church of Croswicks, constituted May 13, 1766.

Ordered, That Abel Griffiths do draw up an Association letter to the churches.

PASTORAL ADDRESS.*

"The ministers and messengers of the several Baptist churches in Pennsylvania, the Jerseys, and provinces adjacent, met in Association at Philadelphia, the 14th, 15th, and 16th of October, A. D. 1766.

"To the several churches concerned, wish mercy and peace may be multiplied.

"Dear brethren, through the tender mercy of God, we have been preserved to see the time of our annual meetings, and, blessed be his name, we met in love, and preserved harmony and affection through the whole of our proceedings. We were agreeably entertained with a discourse on the Incarnation of the dear Redeemer, by Reverend Isaac Stelle. The discourse met with good acceptance. Much refreshed were we also by reading your letters; by which we find that our churches are generally at peace among themselves; and to our great joy, find the Lord is still giving us new manifestations of his walking in the midst of his golden candlesticks, and blessing the word by making it powerful to bring souls to the obedience of faith, and to enlist under the banner of the King of Zion, so that there have been added to our churches by baptism, since last Association, two hundred and forty-nine. There still remain complaints, from some of our churches, of deadness, which may the Lord remove, to his glory and the joy of his saints. Thirty of our members have been cut off by death, and nine excommunicated.

"Now, dear brethren, before we dissolve our Association, suffer a word of exhortation. Oh, endeavor to walk worthy of Christ, and to use all diligence to make your calling and election sure, that the joy thereof may excite in you a holy resignation to the will of God, and a holy resolution to forsake all and follow Christ. Be diligent in closet and family prayer. Be earnest for your households, and the land in general: especially for the welfare of Zion, that the Lord may make her a praise in the earth. O pray for your ministers, that the Lord will make them successful instruments in his hands for the comfort of saints and the conversion of sinners. Strengthen their hands, and be willing to spare them at seasons to supply the needs of destitute churches. Encourage men of promising

---

* NOTE.—The above is the earliest printed letter I have found, and was probably published by Rev. Morgan Edwards, at his own expense, and for his convenience; it being in folio size, about equal to the newspapers of the province of that early date.—*Ed.*

gifts among you. Neglect not the assembling of yourselves together, but value your place in the house of God. Endeavor to maintain gospel order in the churches. Strive against temptations and every lust, that you may keep your garments unspotted with the flesh. Give no occasion to the adversaries to blaspheme. Stir up every spark of grace in your souls to a lively exercise, that you may enjoy the comforts thereof while in the world. And contend earnestly for the faith once delivered to the saints. Finally, brethren, "whatsoever things are true, whatsoever things are honest, whatsoever things are pure, whatsoever things are lovely, whatsoever things are of good report, if there be any virtue, if there be any praise, think on these things."

"We conclude, with wishing you all grace to support you, and the Spirit of God to direct you safe through this vale of tears, and to bring you at last to the heavenly Canaan.

"BENJAMIN MILLER, Moderator.
"SAMUEL JONES, Clerk.

Philadelphia, October 16th, 1766.

Adjourned. Divine service in the evening.

Thursday 16th.—It was queried, Whether a complaint from any member of the associated churches, or from one excommunicated, might be received into the Association?

Resolved, That the query be considered, and determined next Association.

Agreed, to recommend warmly to our churches the interest of the College, for which a subscription is opened all over the continent. This college hath been set on foot upwards of a year, and has now in it three promising youths under the tuition of President Manning.

Agreed, that next Association be held on the Tuesday after the second Sunday in October, to begin at three o'clock, P. M. The sermon by Rev. P. P. Vanhorn; and, in case of his failure, by Rev. Benjamin Miller. The subject to be, "Final Perseverance."

The Association broke up. Divine service in the evening.

N. B. The reason why the number of members in every church in the following table, does not answer to the numbers received and lost is, that some transfer their memberships from one church to another.

MINUTES OF THE PHILADELPHIA ASSOCIATION.

STATE OF THE CHURCHES DURING THE YEAR.

CHURCHES.	PASTORS.	Baptized.	Restored.	Dead.	Excom.	Members.
Pennepek,	Samuel Jones,	0	0	1	1	52
Middletown,	Abel Morgan,	9	0	0	0	126
Piscataqua,	Isaac Stelle,	3	0	0	0	63
Cohansie,	Robert Kelsay,	13	0	5	0	131
Welsh Tract,	David Davis,	4	0	2	1	104
Great Valley,	John Davis,	0	0	2	0	101
Cape May,	John Sutton.	9	0	6	0	62
Hopewell,	Isaac Eaton,	20	0	2	1	211
Brandywine,	Abel Griffiths,	0	0	0	0	29
Montgomery,	Benjamin Griffiths,	0	0	2	0	88
Tulpehokin,	Thomas Jones,	0	0	0	0	28
Kingwood,	David Sutton,	5	0	0	0	75
Cranberry,		30	0	0	0	71
Southampton,	Samuel Jones,	3	0	1	0	56
Philadelphia,	Morgan Edwards,	8	0	4	0	137
Scots Plains,	Benjamin Miller,	10	0	1	2	156
Horseneck,		0	0	0	0	7
Oyster Bay,		0	0	0	0	15
Morristown,	John Waltam,	17	0	0	0	70
Rocksberry,	Henry Crosley,	0	0	0	0	50
Baltimore,	John Davis,	13	0	0	0	96
New Britain,	Joshua Jones,	0	0	0	0	53
Salem,		0	0	0	0	23
Newtown,		0	0	0	0	26
Bateman's Precincts,	Samuel Waldo,	0	0	0	0	118
Dividing Creek,	Samuel Heaton,	2	0	2	0	38
New York,	John Gano,	37	0	0	0	117
New Mills,	Peter Peterson Vanhorn,	8	0	0	0	38
Konoloway,	Joseph Powell,	11	0	0	0	20
Coram,	Noah Hammond,	21	0	0	0	44
Crosswicks,	David Jones,	5	0	0	0	48
		233	0	28	5	2253

Increase this year 199.

1767.

This year, the Association met at Philadelphia, on the 13th October. It was opened with prayers, and a sermon on Final Perseverance, preached by Rev. P. P. Vanhorn, from Heb. x. 14. After the sermon the messengers met, and when prayer was over, they chose Rev. Isaac Eaton to be moderator, and Rev. Samuel Jones, secretary, and read the letters. The messengers were:

Ministers,—Rev. Robert Kelsay, Samuel Heaton, John Blackwell, Isaac Stelle, P. P. Vanhorn, David Davis, David Sutton, Abel Griffiths, John Davis, Benjamin Griffiths, David Thomas, Joshua Jones, Benjamin Coles, Joseph Powell, David Jones, John Davis, John Walton, Samuel Jones, Abel Morgan, John Sutton, James Manning, Isaac Eaton.

Laymen,—Messrs. Philip Shepherd, David Bowen, Stephen Barton, Randal Drake, David Evans, Isaac Light, Jeffrey Bentley, Nicholas Haile, Arthur Chinworth, John Thomas, William Bennet, James Davis, Jacob Covenhoven, Walter Shewell, Thomas John, William Tapscott, Safely M'Gee, Samuel John, Alexander Edwards, James Dundan, Daniel Smith, David Dungan, Isaac Jones, George Westcott, Samuel Davis, Joseph Moulder.

The meeting concluded with prayer, and a sermon in the evening.

Wednesday morning, 14th. The Association met, according to adjournment, and after prayer, and calling the messengers' names, proceeded to business.

Received the contributions of the following churches towards an Association fund.

	£	s.	d.		£	s.	d.
Philadelphia,	16	10	4½	Hopewell,	1	13	0
Southampton,	4	4	4½	New York,	4	11	8
Pennepek,	2	11	10	Baltimore,	1	5	8
Great Valley,	5	0	0	Rev. John Sutton,	0	7	6
Welsh Tract,	3	0	4	Rev. Samuel Jones.	0	10	0
Cohansie,	1	0	0	Mr. Jeff. Benchley,	0	5	0
Kingwood,	0	12	0				

In all £41 10s. 8d., which was deposited in the hands of two brothers, viz., George Westcott and Alexander Edwards, Esqs.

Resolved, To continue a collection every quarter for the said fund.

Received contributions, for the use of the church of Konoloway, from the following churches:

	£	s.	d.		£	s.	d.
Montgomery,	2	10	0	Kingwood,	1	0	0
New York,	1	17	6½	Southampton,	1	12	0
New Britain,	2	5	9	Pennepek,	1	12	1½
Piscataqua,	1	8	8				

In all £12 6s. 1d., which was then delivered to the messengers of the church of Konoloway, they rendering the Association an account of the disposal thereof.

Agreed, That Rev. Isaac Eaton and John Hart, Esq., executors of Mrs. Hubs, will be allowed to pay £14 towards the education of Charles Thompson, out of the interest of the legacy left by said Mrs. Hubs for the use of the Association in Philadelphia.

Agreed, That the churches be requested to forward the subscription for Rhode Island College.

Agreed, That Philadelphia be supplied according to the course settled last year.

The following query was left on the book last year for consideration: Whether an appeal from any member of the associated churches, or from one excommunicated from any of said churches, may be made to the Association?

Resolved: That in some cases they may, as every church may

sometimes suspend their prerogatives, of which every church is to judge for itself.

Query from Hopewell: Whether a ruling elder is to be ordained by imposition of hands?

Resolved: To leave this matter to the discretion of the churches.

Query from Kingwood: Whether a church ought to suspend or excommunicate one for not keeping his place in the church, on account of his not approving the order of preaching used by the minister of the place?

Resolved: That the complaint is trivial, nevertheless that forbearance should be used, but how long, is left to the discretion of the church.

In answer to a request from Cohansie, it was agreed, that Rev. Messrs. Miller, Stelle, and Joshua Jones, do pay them a visit to settle their difference.

The query from Cohansie respected a person who had married his first wife's sister, and was answered thus: The case is doubtful.

Ordered, That Rev. Messrs. John Thomas, David Sutton, and Joseph Powell, do attend the new Association in Virginia, to be held on Saturday the third Sabbath in August, as messengers from us.

Agreed, That the Association to be held next year, at Warren, on Tuesday after the first Wednesday in September, be attended by Rev. Messrs. Benjamin Miller and Isaac Stelle, as our messengers.

Agreed, That the next Association be held on Tuesday after the second Sunday in October, and that Rev. Benjamin Miller do preach; and in case of his failure, Rev. John Davis. The subject to be Imputed Righteousness.

Rev. John Sutton to write to the Association in Virginia, and Rev. Samuel Jones to the Association in Warren; Rev. Isaac Sutton to write the circular letter, which was as follows:

PASTORAL ADDRESS.

"To the several churches, we send loving salutation.

"Dear Brethren,—As we are near parting, we have to inform you, that we met in love, and received your letters and messengers. We find, to our joy, that peace generally subsists in our churches, considerable increase in some of them. We received comfortable letters from the Associations in Virginia and Rhode Island. We have cause to bless God, that the religion of Jesus succeeds any where; and that it may increase and abound, permit us, to exhort and entreat you, to study more and more what shall be done to promote so valuable an interest. Endeavor to keep and maintain the unity of the Spirit in the bond of peace amongst yourselves. Attend diligently to all the ordinances of the gospel. Be conscientious in discharging all the positive and relative duties of Christianity. Beware of lukewarmness. Be diligent in a holy and humble walk with God in secret. Promote by word, action and communication, every thing that hath a tendency to advance the declarative glory of God, and the interest of his cause in the world, knowing that your fellowship of faith, and labor of love, will, through the exceeding riches of free grace, be rewarded by Jesus Christ at his coming.

"Brethren, we commit you to the Lord and the word of his grace, and remain yours in the faith and fellowship of the gospel.

"ISAAC EATON, Moderator.
"SAMUEL JONES, Clerk.

"Philadelphia, October 15, 1767."

STATE OF THE CHURCHES DURING THE YEAR.

CHURCHES.	MINISTERS.	Added by Letter.	Baptized.	Dead.	Dismiss'd.	Excom.	Members.
Pennepek,	Samuel Jones,	0	0	0	0	0	52
Middletown,	Abel Morgan,	0	13	1	0	0	138
Piscataqua,	Isaac Stelle,	0	0	0	0	0	63
Cohansie,	Robert Kelsay,	0	3	6	0	3	125
Welsh Tract,	David Davis,	0	4	0	0	0	106
Great Valley,	John Davis,	3	3	1	0	0	106
Cape May,	John Sutton,	0	6	2	0	0	66
Hopewell,	Isaac Eaton,	0	8	4	2	0	213
Brandywine,	Abel Griffith,	0	0	1	0	0	28
Montgomery,	Benjamin Griffith,	0	0	2	0	3	83
Tulpehokin,	Thomas Jones,	0	1	0	1	0	22
Kingwood,	David Sutton,	0	19	1	0	1	92
Cranberry,	Isaac Stelle,	0	5	1	0	0	76
Southampton,	Samuel Jones,	0	1	0	0	0	57
Philadelphia,	Morgan Edwards,	0	11	4	2	2	140
Scotch Plains,	Benjamin Miller,	0	8	1	21	0	142
Horse Neck,		0	0	0	0	0	7
Oyster Bay,	Benjamin Cole,	0	0	0	0	0	15
Morristown,	John Walton,	0	2	1	0	0	17
Rocksberry,	Henry Crosley,	0	0	0	0	0	50
Baltimore,	John Davis,	3	10	1	1	0	107
New Britain,	Joshua Jones,	0	0	1	3	0	49
Salem,		0	0	1	0	0	22
Newtown,		0	0	0	0	0	26
Bateman's Precincts,	Samuel Waldo,	0	0	0	0	0	118
Dividing Creek,	Samuel Heaton,	0	0	0	0	0	38
New York,	John Gano,	0	17	0	2	0	132
Northampton,	Peter P. Vanhorn,	0	5	1	0	0	42
Konolaway,	Joseph Powel,	4	1	0	0	0	25
Coram,	Noah Hammond,	0	4	1	0	0	47
Upper Freehold,	David Jones,	0	2	2	0	0	48
	Henry Crosley,	0	0	6	0	0	21
		10	123	31	32	9	2302

Increase this year, 49.

This year came a letter from the Association at Mill Creek, Virginia, whereby it appears that one church more hath joined them, and that the increase in that Association is thirty, viz., twenty-six by baptism, and four by letters dismissive and commendatory.

1768.

The Association met this year at Philadelphia, on the 11th, 12th, and 13th of October, A. D. 1768.

It was opened on Tuesday, at 3 P. M., with public service, and a sermon by Rev. Benjamin Miller, on "Imputed Righteousness," from Ps. lxxxix. 16. After sermon, they proceeded to the choice of a moderator and clerk, which fell on the Rev. Isaac Eaton, and Rev. Isaac Stelle. The letters were read, the names of the messengers taken. One to preach in the evening, and then adjourned to the next day.

Wednesday.—This day, at 9 A. M., the Association met. After prayer, they read a petition from the church constituted at Mount Bethel, which was received into the Association. This church was constituted, October 29th, 1767, by the Rev. Messrs. Miller, Crosley, and Walton. The number of constituents were thirteen from the Scotch Plains, to which were added from the same church five more, and afterwards six, and eleven by baptism; in all, thirty-five.

Agreed, That Philadelphia be supplied according to the first year's plan.

By order of the Association, the Rev. Isaac Eaton was ordered to give the sum of £14, out of the interest arising from Mrs. Hubs's legacy, for the use of Charles Thomson, a student in Rhode Island College.

Agreed, That the Association be held next year at New York, but ever after at Philadelphia; and then adjourned to 3 o'clock, P. M.

Met at 3. After prayer, proceeded to business. In answer to a query from New York, it was agreed that baptism, administered by a person not ordained, was invalid and disorderly.

Some of the New Mills people requested the help of this Association in a case of difficulty between them and their minister. Agreed, that Rev. Isaac Eaton, Samuel Jones, Mr. James Mott, and John Stout, do visit them on the fourth Lord's day in November, at 10 o'clock.

Rev. Isaac Stelle appointed to write the circular letter. Rev. J. Davis to write to the Association at Warren; and he and Rev. S. Jones to be messengers to meet them on the second Lord's day in September.

Rev. Samuel Jones to write to the Association in Virginia, to be held at Pignut Ridge, on Saturday before the third Lord's day in August; and Rev. John Davis, of Baltimore, to be our messenger.

At a request from some people in Sussex county, New Jersey, several of the ministers agreed to pay them a visit this year.

A letter from the church of Stratfield, in Connecticut, was received, intimating a separation, on account of washing feet, and the Lord's Supper administered every week.

Agreed, that Rev. John Gano, Isaac Stelle, and Benjamin Miller, do pay them a visit.

Adjourned to 9 o'clock to-morrow.

Thursday.—Met at 9 A. M. The Association advise the church of Warren to be cautious of one Henry Dawson, late from Dr. Gifford's church, in Eagle street, London.

Fourteen of our churches brought in their gatherings for the Association fund, amounting to £18, 17s. 11d., which was deposited in the hands of Mr. George Westcott, to be put out at interest. The churches that gave are the following:

	£.	s.	d.		£	s.	d.
Philadelphia,	5	0	0	Southampton,	2	2	4
Cohansie,	1	0	0	Piscataqua,	0	7	6
Pennepek,	2	1	4	Baltimore,	0	10	0
Welsh Tract,	2	6	9	Montgomery,	0	10	0
New York,	2	0	0	Salem,	0	10	0
Hopewell,	1	10	0	Cape May,	0	7	6
Kingwood,	0	5	0	Dividing Creek,	0	7	6

Some jealousy arising on account of an appeal to the Association, mentioned pages 100 and 101, it was agreed that the word *appeal* was not quite proper, as the Association claims no jurisdiction, nor a power to repeal any thing settled by any church; but if, before settlement, parties agree to refer matters to the Association, then to give their advice.

The Association to be held at New York on Tuesday after the second Sunday in October. Rev. John Davis to preach; and, in case of failure, Rev. Isaac Eaton, or Rev. David Jones.

Agreed, to request all the churches to lay themselves out to find any gifted brethren that may arise among them, and encourage them.

Rev. Isaac Stelle appointed to draw up the circular letter to the churches, a copy of which follows:

PASTORAL ADDRESS.

"Brethren,—We are happy now, at the close of our Association in having it in our power to say that we met in love, continued our business without discord and jarring, and parted in peace and friendship; that we are pleased with the accounts sent us from different churches, particularly the good news of the increase of Christ's kingdom on earth, for which we praise God, and pray for you that your faith fail not.

"And now, dearly beloved brethren in the bonds of Christian love, our request is, that as you have put on the Lord Jesus so walk ye in him, and that you may be enabled so to do, neglect not the assembling of yourselves together. Maintain the public worship of God, and keep yourselves unspotted from the world. Do all things whatsoever may tend to promote brotherly love and charity, always remembering that unity is the best security the church of Christ can have against attacks from every enemy; that if divided, you fall a more easy prey to your adversaries; that you cannot injure one another without injuring yourselves also; that by attending too much to distinctions and speculations, you rob your own souls of the real comfort of religion. And finally, brethren, "whatsoever things are true, whatsoever things are lovely, whatsoever things are of good report, if there be any virtue, and if there be any praise, think on these things." And may the God and Father of our Lord Jesus Christ bless you abundantly. Amen.

Signed, by order of the Association,

ISAAC EATON, Moderator,
ISAAC STELLE, Clerk.

STATE OF THE CHURCHES DURING THE YEAR.

CHURCHES.	MINISTERS.	Baptized.	Restored.	Dead.	Excom.	Members.
Pennepek,	Samuel Jones,	0	0	2	0	47
Middletown,	Abel Morgan,	5	0	4	0	138
Piscataqua,	Isaac Stelle,	4	0	2	0	64
Cohansie,	Robert Kelsay,	0	0	0	0	123
Welsh Tract,	David Davis,	2	0	1	0	109
Great Valley,	John Davis,	11	0	1	0	116
Cape May,		1	0	1	0	66
Hopewell,	Isaac Eaton,	3	0	5	2	217
Montgomery,		6	0	2	0	84
Tulpehokin,	Thomas Jones,	0	0	2	0	20
Kingwood,	David Sutton,	11	0	2	0	105
Southampton,	Samuel Jones,	0	0	1	0	55
Philadelphia,	Morgan Edwards,	6	0	3	1	146
Scotch Plains,	Benjamin Miller,	9	0	2	0	149
Morristown,	John Walton,	2	0	1	0	74
Baltimore,	John Davis,	7	0	2	0	112
New Britain,	Joshua Jones,	1	0	1	0	49
Salem,	Abel Griffiths,	0	0	0	0	22
Dividing Creek,	Samuel Heaton,	0	0	1	0	38
New York,	John Gano,	12	2	1	2	143
Croswicks,	David Jones,	3	0	1	0	50
Mount Bethel,	Henry Crosley,	11	0	0	0	35
Konoloway,	Joseph Powell,	0	0	0	0	25
Brandywine,		0	0	0	0	28
Cranberry,	Isaac Stelle,	0	0	0	0	76
Horse Neck,		0	0	0	0	7
Oyster Bay,	Benjamin Cole,	0	0	0	0	15
Rocksberry,	Henry Crosley,	0	0	0	0	50
Newtown,		0	0	0	0	26
Bateman's Precincts,	Samuel Waldo,	0	0	0	0	115
New Mills,		0	0	0	0	42
Coram,	Noah Hammond,	0	0	0	0	46
		94	2	35	5	3392

Increase this year, 81.

N. B. Nine churches have not sent to us this year—By a letter from the Association at Warren, it appears that the following churches were formed into an Association, September 9th, 1767, viz:—the church of Warren, Bellingham, Middleberry, Haverhill.

MINUTES

OF THE

PHILADELPHIA BAPTIST ASSOCIATION

HELD AT NEW YORK, OCTOBER 10TH, 11TH, AND 12TH,

1769.*

THE Association, this year, met at New York, on the afternoon of the 10th of October. Divine service being over, the Rev. Isaac Eaton was chosen moderator, and Rev. Morgan Edwards, clerk. Letters from twenty-six churches were read; also from the Warren Association, and that of Virginia. The names of the messengers were enrolled, who were,

Ministers,—Rev. Messrs. Isaac Eaton, Abel Morgan, Morgan Edwards, John Gano, Isaac Stelle, John Thomas, Samuel Jones, David Sutton, Joshua Jones, Samuel Waldo, John Waltam, John Sutton, Abel Griffiths, Noah Hammond, Robert Kelsay, David Jones, Henry Crossley, Benjamin Miller, Hezekiah Smith, James Benedict, John Lawrence, Simon Deacon, and Benjamin Coles.

Laymen,—Messrs. William Harper, Samuel Edmunds, William Bennet, William Lawson, Francis Van Dyke, Arthur Watts, Andrew Bray, Thomas Pollen, Jonathan Waldo, John Brookfield, Edward Kesby, James Grover, Richard Crosford, James Pew, John Stout, Henry Ludlem, Safety Maghee, Joseph Meeker, Timothy Hughes, Recompense Stanbury, John Stites.

Business done,—

1. A church, constituted April 16, 1769, at Lyon's Farms, in Newark township, Essex, New Jersey, was received into the Association; the number when constituted eleven.

2. Agreed, That any member of the associated churches, or of any other Baptist church, except he be under censure, may be present at the meeting of the Association. Adjourned to the morrow. A sermon in the evening.

October 11, eight o'clock.—The Association met, and after prayer and calling over the roll, proceeded to business.

[* NOTE.—The Minutes for this year, are the first that appear to have been issued by order of the Association. They were printed in small quarto form, on very good type and paper. In consequence of the above change, we give the full title to each of the succeeding Annual Minutes.—*Ed.*]

3. Henry Dawson appeared. Resolved, to dismiss his case, because we cannot judge between him and the parties in London, and to avoid him, because he stands excommunicated by two churches of the same faith and order. From the one justly, to our knowledge, and, for ought appears, justly, from Dr. Gifford's church, the preamble to his excommunication, observing that his breaking was "reproachful to religion."

4. A church, constituted November 7, 1764, in Goshen township, Orange county, New York, was received into the Association. This church began with three persons, and is increased to fifty-seven. The minister is the Rev. James Benedict.

5. Two churches in Philip's Patent, New York, sent their messengers with their church covenants and Confessions of faith in order to be first known to the Association, and the Association known to them, and then to join it, if mutual approbation should be obtained.

Agreed, That these churches are orthodox,—that they are rightly constituted,—their ministers regularly ordained,—and that letters be written to them to signify this our judgment, and to own them as sister churches.

Their messengers were allowed to sit in the Association. Their ministers are the Rev. John Lawrence, and the Rev. Simon Deacon. Adjourned.

The Association met again at half past two o'clock, and proceeded to business.

6. It was shown by some from Philadelphia, that they had obtained leave from the church they belonged to, to form themselves into a distinct society in the Northern Liberties of that city: and they were desirous to know the sense of the Association touching their design?

Voted, That if any of our ministers were free to constitute them into a church, in said Liberties, they might do it without offending the Association.

7. By letter and messengers from Warren, we were informed that they had petitioned the legislatures of Boston and Connecticut, in favor of their brethren who suffer for nonconformity to the religious establishments of those colonies; and, in case their petitions produced not a speedy or effectual redress of their grievances, requested that we would join with them in a petition to our gracious sovereign.

Voted, That this Association will not only join that of Warren, in seeking relief for our oppressed brethren, but will also solicit the concurrence of the Associations of Virginia and Carolina in the design, if need be.

Voted also, That letters and messengers be sent to signify this our resolution.

The letter to the Warren Association was drawn up by the Rev. Samuel Jones; the messengers, Rev. Samuel Waldo and Rev. Benjamin Coles. That to the Virginia Association, by Rev. Hezekiah Smith. The messenger, Rev. John Gano.

8. By a letter from the Virginia Association, we learn that two

MINUTES OF THE PHILADELPHIA ASSOCIATION.   109

churches have joined them, and that the increase this year is one hundred and sixty-seven. Adjourned.

October 12. The Association met at eight this morning.

9. A letter of thanks from the Rev. Peter P. Vanhorn was read.

10. Rev. Messieurs Robert Kelsay, John Walton, and David Jones were desired to attend at the Welsh Tract on the fourth Sunday in May, and at Cohansie the third.

11. In a letter from Bateman's Precincts, it was queried: How a church should proceed towards members who deny family worship to be a duty, and so disuse it?

Advice: Let the church bear with them, till it has used endeavors to convince them of their error, and reduce them to their duty by argument.

Ordered: That some thoughts on this subject be put together and printed.

12. The following churches and private persons contributed to the Association fund:

	£	s.	d.		£	s.	d.
Philadelphia,	1	10	0	Morristown,	0	7	10
York,	2	16	3	Cohansie,	0	7	6
Hopewell,	1	10	0	Philip's Patent,	0	7	6
Kingwood,	0	10	0	Salem,	0	7	6
Bateman's Precints,	0	9	4	New Britain,	0	7	6
Mount Bethel,	0	5	0	Coram,	0	7	6
Cape May,	0	7	6	Mr. Ward,	0	7	6
Warwick,	0	3	9	Mr. Willis,	1	10	0
Lyon's Farms,	0	5	6	Mr. Hall,	0	7	6

In all £12 8s. 6d., which sum was delivered to Rev. Samuel Jones, to be by him deposited in the hands of the treasurer, Mr. George Westcott, to be put to interest. This fund, in three years, has increased to £72 16s. 6d. The churches are desired to continue the collections.

13. We received pleasing accounts from Rhode Island College. Seven commenced this fall. The colony has raised £1200 towards the building, which will be begun early in the spring. About £1000, lawful currency of New England, have been sent us from home towards making up a salary for the president; and all the ministers of this Association have explicitly engaged to exert themselves in endeavoring to raise more for the same purpose.

Resolved, That the moneys, which may be raised in the provinces of New York, Jersey, and Pennsylvania, shall be put to interest in those provinces, and not be taken out of either; except the interest, which shall be subject to the order of the College to pay the president's salary, and for no other use. The persons appointed for receiving the donations are these:—In New York, the Rev. John Gano; in the Jerseys, John Stites, Esq.; in Pennsylvania, the Rev. Morgan Edwards. They are to see that the securities be sufficient, and that the bonds, mortgages, &c., be deposited with the treasurer of the College.

14. Voted, That £14, Jersey currency, be given Mr. Thomas

Eustick, towards defraying his expenses at College, out of the profits of the late Mrs. Hub's estate: he giving bond to return the money in case the Association should be disappointed in him. An order on Mrs. Hub's executors was drawn, and given to the Rev. John Gano, to be occupied.

15. Our number of ministers decreasing, and calls for them growing more numerous, it is earnestly requested that the churches will look among themselves for men of public gifts, and send them forth to preach the gospel.

16. The Association to be held at Philadelphia next year, to commence on the Tuesday after the second Sunday in October. The sermon to be preached by Rev. John Davis, of Baltimore; or, in case of failure, by Rev. Abel Morgan.

17. Rev. Abel Griffiths to draw a circular letter—the which follows:

PASTORAL ADDRESS.

"The ministers and other messengers of the congregations in Pennsylvania, the Jerseys, and provinces adjacent, met in annual Association, at New York, the 10th, 11th, and 12th of October, A. D. 1769.

"To the several churches we respectively relate unto, send greeting.

"Dearly beloved brethren in our Lord Jesus Christ,—Through the abounding goodness of Almighty God, in his providence, we have been favored with the high privilege of meeting in his name, according to appointment, in this city; and through divine goodness we met, and were preserved in love throughout all our consultations. For ever praised be the Lord for his goodness. We were agreeably entertained with a discourse upon the Union of Saints, by our brother, Rev. David Jones, from Gal. iii. 28; and much refreshed on hearing your letters read, by which we find that our churches are mostly at peace among themselves, and that the Lord's work is still carried on in some good measure among them; for there have been considerable additions to some churches. Sixty-eight have been baptized, thirty-six dead, and nine excommunicated. From the Warren Association, we find that four churches have been added to it, and an increase, by baptism, of fifty-five. To the Virginia Association, two churches have been added, with an increase, by baptism, of one hundred and sixty-seven. Two joined our Association, and two more became known to us, over which we have reason to rejoice.

"Now, dear brethren, suffer us, before we separate from each other, to lay before you these few necessary things. You profess to be followers of Christ: O strive to lay aside every weight and sin, and to walk as children of light in all holiness of conversation, that the ways of God be not reproached. Be diligent to keep your places in the house of God. Be careful to encourage men of useful gifts among you; for great is the want of ministerial helps at this time. Neglect not the worship of God in your families and closets. Pray for all men, especially for the household of faith. Finally, endeavor to live under the influence of the Spirit of God, and in the increase of every grace, that you may have the consolation thereof while here; and may be ready when the Great Bridegroom comes to open, and with him to enter into everlasting joy.

"ISAAC EATON, Moderator,
"M. EDWARDS, Clerk."

STATE OF THE CHURCHES DURING THE YEAR.

CHURCHES.	MINISTERS.	Baptized.	Restored.	Dead.	Excom.	Members.
Pennepek,	Samuel Jones,	0	0	0	0	49
Middletown,	Abel Morgan,	7	0	0	0	143
Piscataqua,	Isaac Stelle,	7	0	2	0	69
Cohansie,	Robert Kelsay,	0	0	7	1	115
Welsh Tract,		0	0	2	0	110
Great Valley,*	John Davis,	5	0	0	0	120
Cape May,		0	0	3	0	62
Hopewell,	Isaac Eaton,	4	0	4	1	208
Brandywine,		5	0	2	0	29
Montgomery,	John Thomas,	12	0	1	0	95
Tulpehokin,*	Thomas Jones,	2	0	0	0	16
Kingwood,	David Sutton,	3	0	0	1	75
Cranberry,*		0	0	2	0	76
Southampton,	Samuel Jones,	1	0	1	2	53
Philadelphia,	Morgan Edwards,	11	0	6	3	149
Scotch Plains,	Benjamin Miller,	1	0	3	0	133
Horse Neck,		0	0	0	0	7
Oyster Bay,		0	0	1	0	14
Morristown,	John Walton,	0	0	0	0	47
Knowlton,	Henry Crosley,	0	0	0	0	26
Baltimore,*	John Davis,	10	0	4	0	118
New Britain,	Joshua Jones,	7	0	0	0	56
Salem,	Abel Griffiths,	0	0	1	0	20
Newtown,		0	0	0	0	26
Bateman's Precincts,	Samuel Waldo,	0	0	0	1	113
Dividing Creek,*	Samuel Heaton,	1	0	0	0	38
New York,	John Gano,	1	0	2	0	140
New Mills,*		0	0	0	1	42
Konoloway,	Joseph Powell,	2	0	0	0	27
Coram,	Noah Hammond,	0	0	0	0	46
Croswicks,	David Jones,	2	0	0	0	53
Mount Bethel,		2	0	1	0	30
Goshen,	James Benedict,	0	0	0	0	57
Lyon's Farms,		3	0	0	0	15
		86	0	41	10	2379

N. B.—The churches marked thus * have sent neither letters nor messengers this year—their numbers stand as they were last Association. The increase in the rest is 15.

It is proposed to print the transactions of the Association in the same size every year, that the churches may in time bind them up. The tardy churches are again requested to send either letters or messengers every year, that those who are at the expense of printing may not be disappointed.

Our Confession of faith may be had at Philadelphia for 15 coppers, half bound. In sheets for 7 coppers. Catechisms, 4 coppers. Norcott, 5 coppers.

MINUTES

OF THE

PHILADELPHIA BAPTIST ASSOCIATION,

HELD AT PHILADELPHIA, OCTOBER 16TH, 17TH, AND 18TH,

1770.

October 16th. The Association met at 3 o'clock, P. M. Divine service being over, Rev. Samuel Jones was chosen moderator, and Rev. Morgan Edwards, clerk. Letters from thirty-four churches were read, also from the Warren Association, and that of Virginia. The names were enrolled, viz :

Ministers,—Rev. James Benedict, John Sutton, Robert Kelsay, Noah Hammond, Abel Griffiths, Isaac Stelle, John Davis, David Jones, Isaac Eaton, John Blackwell, Samuel Heaton, Peter Peterson Vanhorn, Joshua Jones, Joseph Powell, John Thomas, Samuel Jones, David Sutton, Benjamin Miller, Morgan Edwards, Simon Dakin, William Worth, Erasmus Kelly, and David Branson.

Laymen,—Messrs. David Lobdel, Dr. Ebenezer Blatchey, Hugh Glasford, Seth Bowen, Samuel Sims, Samuel Jones, John M'Kim, Robert M'Kim, Edmund Talbot, Griffith Jones, Daniel Cornog, Thomas Cox, Thomas Farr, Stephen Barton, Gideon Heaton, Peter Eaton, Joseph Hart, Joseph Griffiths, Henry Green, Andrew Bowen, Alexander Edwards, Andrew Bray, Recompence Stanbury, John Carman, George Wescott, Samuel Davis, Joseph Moulder, and Elisha Cole.

Adjourned. A sermon in the evening.

Oct. 17th. The Association met at 8 o'clock, A. M.; and after prayer and calling over the roll, proceeded to business. Agreed,

1. That messengers from other Associations are members of this.

2. A church in Courtland's Manor proposed to join us; but first desired satisfaction touching two questions. Ordered, that a letter be written to said church.

3. A church in Philip's Patent, whereof Rev. Simon Dakin is minister, was received into the Association. This church is in Dutchess county, New York government.

4. A letter from the people on Redstone creek, near Monongahela, was read. Ordered, that a letter be written to them, and Mr. James Sutton be recommended thither.

5. The church in the Northern Liberties of Philadelphia proposed to join the Association; but objections to it being made, the matter was referred to a committee, who brought in their report, and the junction was deferred.

Newtown to be supplied by the following ministers,—Mr. James Sutton, last Sunday in October; Rev. D. Sutton, last Sunday in November; Rev. Benjamin Miller, last Sunday in April; Mr. Worth, last Sunday in May; Rev. John Blackwell, last Sunday in June; Rev. Thomas Davis, last Sunday in July.

7. The Rev. Benjamin Miller and Isaac Stelle to assist at the yearly meeting in Cohansie.

8. Morristown to be supplied by Mr. James Sutton the first Sunday in November; by Rev. R. Kelsay, last Sunday in November; by Rev. Benjamin Miller, fourth Sunday in December; by Mr. Erasmus Kelly, fourth Sunday in March; by Rev. Isaac Stelle, fourth Sunday in April; by Rev. Joshua Jones, fourth Sunday in May; by Mr. Worth, first Sunday in June; by Rev. John Blackwell, first Sunday in July; by Rev. Samuel Jones, fourth Sunday in August.

9. Lyon's Farms to be supplied by Mr. James Sutton, second Sunday in November; by Rev. R. Kelsay, third Sunday in November; by Mr. Kelly, third Sunday in March; by Rev. J. Blackwell, second Sunday in April; by Rev. J. Jones, third Sunday in May; by Mr. Worth, second Sunday in June; by Mr. Ward, fourth Sunday in June; by Rev. J. Stelle, second Sunday in July; by Rev. S. Jones, third Sunday in August.

10. Manahawkin to be supplied by Mr. James Sutton, fourth Sunday in November; by Mr Branson, third Sunday in December; by Rev. J. Blackwell, fourth Sunday in April; by Mr. Worth, fourth Sunday in July.

11. Circular letter was drawn by Mr. Stelle. Letter to the Warren Association by Mr. Kelly, wherein he and Rev. Simon Dakin are messengers.

12. The contributors to the Association fund this year—

	£	s.	d.		£	s.	d.
Philadelphia,	5	0	0	Pennepek,	1	2	10
Hopewell,	1	0	0	Rev. Ebenezer Ward,	0	7	6
Welsh Tract,	2	18	0	Mr. Vandyke,	0	7	6
New York,	1	0	0	Kingwood,	0	10	0
New Mills,	0	5	0	Montgomery,	0	10	0
Coram,	0	7	6	Philip's Patent,	0	7	6
Baltimore,	0	10	0				

In all, £14 5s. 10d.; which sum was received by Rev. S. Jones, to be deposited in the treasurer's hands. This, added to £72 16s. 6d. upon interest, makes £87 2s. 4d. The last year's interest to be added to the principal for this year, because too inconsiderable to be otherwise employed.

13. The report of the abovesaid committee, and the vote of the Association, relative to last year's minute, to abide in Philadelphia.

14. By the letter from the Warren Association, it appears that our brethren in New England are sorely oppressed this year again, and no redress obtained, though diligently sought for; their case is to go home soon, to be laid at the feet of our gracious sovereign. Rev. Hezekiah Smith is appointed agent, who proposes to sail about the beginning of November. They request their brethren belonging to this Association, to help them to defray the expenses of the agent. The request was attended to with much sympathy. Collections to be made in all our churches immediately, and to be sent either to Mr. George Wescott, of Philadelphia, or Mr. Williams, of New York, to be by them remitted to London; and in case more be raised than will be spent, the remainder to be returned to the donors, or otherwise disposed of by their order. Also a committee was appointed to draw a memorial, addressed to Rev. Dr. Stennett, and others, in favor of our New England brethren's design.

15. Application was made to the Association in favor of Mr. Eustick and Mr. Vanhorn, Jr., for Mrs. Hubb's bounty towards educating youth for the ministry. It was granted to the latter, he to give a bond to return the money in case the Association should be disappointed in him. Agreed, also, that any person hereafter applying for said bounty, shall produce a recommendation from the church he belongs unto, relative to his ministerial gifts, upon such trials as they shall put him to.

16. Alexander Edwards, Esq., and Mr. George Wescott, are desired to treat with the trustees of the Grammar School, and urge that they will endeavor to promote the design of their trust.

17. Oct. 18th.—Collections for the Association fund to be continued.

18. The next Association to meet at Philadelphia, on Tuesday after the second Sunday in October. The sermon by Rev. Abel Morgan, or, in case of his absence, by Rev. Robert Kelsay.

PASTORAL ADDRESS.

The ministers and other messengers of the congregations in Pennsylvania, the Jerseys, and provinces adjacent, met in annual Association at Philadelphia, on the 16th, 17th, and 18th of October, A. D. 1770.

To the several churches we respectively relate unto, send greeting.

Dearly beloved brethren,—We, whom you in your letters are pleased to address as ministers and messengers of the churches of Christ, have again, through the protection and blessing of God, been permitted to assemble together according to our annual custom, professedly with views to the honor of God and the profit of men; and some good degree of love and union subsisted among us during our stay together. The sermon was preached by our much esteemed brother, Rev. John Davis, of Baltimore, from Heb. ii. 16. By your letters we find that our churches are mostly at peace, and some ingathering from the field of unregenerate men. From the Warren

Association we find that three churches joined them this year; and that the increase is fifty-six. Great additions have been made to the Virginia Association. We rejoice that the Lord Jesus doth still walk in the midst of his golden candlesticks. O, may he continue and increase his glorious work, so that the number of converts to him may be as the drops of morning dew! And while we hear good news from distant places, may it excite in us earnestness productive of fervent prayer to God for a revival of his work amongst us, which, of late, is rather decaying. We feel chastisement from heaven by the death of our beloved brother, Rev. John Walton; and pray that God will not suffer that church, with whom he resided, to be like sheep without a shepherd. Now, dear brethren, as we are about parting from each other, we would write to you as though we were writing our last; and this should induce you to attend as though you were never to hear from us again. We would attempt to stir you up to love and good works, though we have cause to be grieved for our own deadness. This we say to you all, strive to walk together in unity of the Spirit and bonds of peace. Neglect not the use of the Bible, nor public worship, nor private prayer. Set the best example before, and give good and wholesome advice to all under your care. Watch over all your thoughts, words, and ways, remembering that the glory of God and your present comfort much depend thereon. Be careful to encourage men of useful gifts among you, though they may not have the advantage of a liberal education. Let your moderation appear to all men, and let the world see by every part of your conduct that there is a divine reality in your religion. May the Lord open your ears to our words, and abundantly bless our advice to your hearts. So pray your brethren, who would serve you in the Lord.

Signed by the moderator and clerk,

SAMUEL JONES,
MORGAN EDWARDS.

CONTENTS OF LETTERS FROM NEW ENGLAND, RELATIVE TO THE SUFFERINGS OF OUR BRETHREN AT ASHFIELD, IN BOSTON.

"The laws of this province were never intended to exempt the Baptists from paying towards building and repairing Presbyterian meeting houses, and making up Presbyterian ministers' salaries; for, besides other insufficiencies, they are all limited both as to extent and duration. The first law extended only five miles round each Baptist meeting house; those without this circle had no relief, neither had they within: for, though it exempted their polls, it left their estates to the mercy of harpies, and their estates went to wreck. The Baptists sought a better law, and with great difficulty and waste of time and money, obtained it; but this was not universal. It extended not to any parish until a Presbyterian meeting house should be built, and a Presbyterian minister settled there; in consequence of which the Baptists have never been freed from the first and great expenses of their parishes, expenses equal to the current expenses of ten or twelve years. This is the present case of the people of Ashfield, which is a Baptist settlement. There were but five families of other denominations in the place when the Baptist church was constituted; but those five, and a few more, have lately built a Presbyterian meeting house there, and settled an orthodox minister, as they call him; which last cost them £200. To pay for both, they laid a tax on the land; and, as the Baptists are the most numerous, the greatest part fell to their share. The Presbyterians, in April last, demanded the money. The Baptists pleaded poverty, alleging that they had been twice driven from their plantations by the Indians last war; that they were but new settlers, and had cleared but a few spots of land, and had not been able to build commodious dwelling houses. Their tyrants would not hear. Then the Baptists pleaded the ingratitude of such conduct; for they had built a fort there at their own expense, and had maintained it for two years, and so had protected the interior Presbyterians, as well as their neighbors, who now rose up against them; that the Baptists to the westward had raised money to relieve Presbyterians who had like them suffered by the Indians; and that it was cruel to take from them what the Indians had left! But nothing touched the hearts of these cruel people. Then the Baptists urged the law of the province; but were soon told that that law extended to no new parish till the meeting house and minister were paid for. Then the Baptists petitioned the general court. Proceedings were stopped till further orders, and the poor people went home rejoicing, thinking their property safe; but had not all got home before said order came; and it was an order for the Presbyterians to proceed. Accordingly, in the month of April, they fell foul on their plantations; and not on skirts and corners, but on the cleared and improved spots; and so have mangled their estates and left them hardly any but a wilderness. They sold the house and garden of one man, and the young orchards, meadows, and corn-fields of others; nay, they sold their dead, for they sold their graveyard. The orthodox minister was one of the purchasers. These spots amounted to three hundred and ninety-five acres, and have since been valued at £363 8s., but were sold for £35 10s. This was the first payment. Two more are coming, which will not leave them an inch of land at this rate. The Baptists waited on the assembly five times this year for relief, but were not heard, under pretence they did no business; but their enemies were heard, and had their business done. At last the Baptists got together about a score of the members at Cambridge, and made their complaints known; but in general, they were treated very superciliously. One of them spoke to this effect,—'*The general assembly have a right to do what they did, and if you don't like it you may quit the place!*' But, alas, they must leave their all behind! These Presbyterians are not only supercilious in power, but mean and cruel in mastery. When they came together to mangle the estates of the Baptists, they diverted themselves with the tears and lamentations of the oppressed. One of them, whose name is Wells, stood up to preach a mock sermon on the occasion; and, among other things, used words to this effect: '*The Baptists, for refusing to pay an orthodox minister, shall be cut in pound pieces, and boiled for their fat to grease the devil's carriage, &c.*'"

STATE OF THE CHURCHES DURING THE YEAR.

CHURCHES.	MINISTERS.	Baptized.	Restored.	Dead.	Excom.	Members.
Pennepek,	Samuel Jones,	1	0	0	0	50
Middletown,	Abel Morgan,	2	0	0	0	144
Piscataqua,	Isaac Stelle,	8	0	2	0	73
Cohansie,	Robert Kelsay,	1	0	4	1	110
Welsh Tract,	John Sutton,	3	0	1	0	112
Great Valley,	John Davis,	2	0	3	1	115
Cape May,	Peter P. Vanhorn,	0	0	1	0	61
Hopewell,	Isaac Eaton,	2	0	5	0	202
Brandywine,		3	0	0	0	32
Montgomery,	John Thomas,	14	1	1	0	104
Tulpehokin,	Thomas Jones,	0	0	0	0	16
Kingwood,	David Sutton,	9	0	2	1	76
Mount Bethel,	Henry Crosley,	6	0	0	0	38
Southampton,	Erasmus Kelly,	0	0	0	1	52
Philadelphia,	Morgan Edwards,	6	0	3	2	150
Scotch Plains,	Benjamin Miller,	4	0	1	1	124
Horse Neck,		0	0	0	0	7
Oyster Bay,		1	0	0	0	15
Morristown,		3	0	2	0	46
Knowlton,		0	0	0	0	26
Baltimore,	John Davis,	14	0	1	1	131
New Britain,	Joshua Jones,	3	0	2	0	57
Salem,	Abel Griffiths,	3	0	1	0	22
Newtown,		2	0	0	0	27
Bateman's Precincts,	Samuel Waldo,	0	0	0	0	113
Dividing Creek,	Samuel Heaton,	7	0	1	0	44
New York,	John Gano,	9	0	5	0	129
New Mills,	David Branson,	3	0	0	0	45
Koholoway,	Joseph Powel,	0	0	0	0	29
Coram,	Noah Hammond,	4	0	1	0	30
Croswicks,	David Jones,	0	0	2	0	41
Goshen,	Sames Benedict,	5	0	1	2	61
Lyon's Farms,		5	0	0	0	20
Philip's Patent,	Simon Dakin,	1	0	0	0	65
		121	1	39	10	2367

N. B. Forty-five have been dismissed to churches belonging to other Associations; and 15 to constitute a new church which has not yet joined this Association. So that the increase in reality is 71, though it appears to be but 1, by comparing this year's number with the last.

MINUTES

OF THE

PHILADELPHIA BAPTIST ASSOCIATION,

HELD AT PHILADELPHIA, OCTOBER 15TH, 16TH, AND 17TH,

1771.

THE Association met at Philadelphia, October 15th, at three o'clock. Divine service being over, Rev. John Gano was chosen moderator, and Rev. Morgan Edwards, clerk. Letters from thirty-nine churches were read, also from the Virginia and Warren Associations. The messengers present were—

Ministers,—Rev. Samuel Jones, William Vanhorn, John Sutton, Robert Kelsay, John Davis, P. P. Vanhorn, Isaac Eaton, David Sutton, Morgan Edwards, Reune Runyon, John Davis, Joshua Jones, Abel Griffiths, Nicholas Cox, Samuel Heaton, John Gano, David Branson, David Jones, James Benedict, Benjamin Miller, John Blackwell, James Sutton.

Laymen,—Messrs. Alexander Edwards, James Mott, Joseph Stillwell, George Drake, Isaiah Lewis, Seth Bowen, David Bowen, John Davis, George George, John Jewell, Thomas Davis, Andrew Bray, Anthony Yerkes, Arthur Watts, Joseph Moulder, Thomas Shields, Joshua Moore, Samuel Mead, Thomas Francis, John Brookfield, David Evans, Edward Kesby, John Carman, Samuel Edmonds, John Briggs, Benjamin Truax, James Sexton, Philip Ketcham, Richard Jones, Lines Pangburn, John Mayhew, David Philips.

Adjourned. A sermon in the evening.

Oct. 16th. A church constituted at Manahawkin, August 25th, 1770, their number nine; another constituted at Pittsgrove, May 15th, 1771, their number seventeen; another at Vincent, constituted October 12th, 1771, their number fifty-two; another in the Northern Liberty, constituted October 29th, 1769, their number six, were all received into the Association.

2. By a letter from the Virginia Association, it appears that two churches joined them, with an increase of members, by baptism, to the number of two hundred and seventy-five. Their messenger was Rev. Richard Major. And by another from the Warren Association, that five churches joined them, with increase of members, one hundred and sixty-seven.

3. The church of Newtown desired the Association to appoint time and ministers to ordain Mr. Nicholas Cox; the Association reply, that the appointment of both properly belongs to his church.

4. It was queried in the letter from Goshen: What is to be done when a member of a church that is dissolved offers to become a member of another church?

Advised, That inquiry be made, whether he was a member at the time of said dissolution, and whether his faith and practice are agreeable to the gospel or not, and then proceed as the state of the case requires.

5. To a query from Dividing Creek, relative to washing the saints' feet, the following reply was made:

This query being founded on John xiii. 1-17, can no otherwise be determined than by fixing the genuine sense of that Scripture, which to do is earnestly recommended.

6. A motion being made in the Association, relative to the appointment of an Evangelist, it was universally agreed that such an appointment promised much advantage to the Baptist interests. Five ministers were put in nomination for the office, viz: Rev. Messrs. John Gano, Benjamin Miller, Samuel Jones, David Jones, Morgan Edwards. The choice fell on the last, which he accepted on the conditions then specified.

7. A motion being made for printing, in America, a book of Mr. Keach on the parables, it was advised, that endeavors should be used to see what number of subscribers can be obtained.

Adjourned. Sermon in the evening.

Oct. 17th. Appointed Rev. Messrs. Abel Griffiths, John Blackwell, and William Vanhorn, to write the circular letter and the letter to the Association of Virginia and Warren. The messengers to the former are Rev. John Davis and David Jones; the messengers to the other, Rev. John Gano and Morgan Edwards.

2. The following gentlemen were appointed trustees of Mrs. Hubb's donation, and to settle accounts with her executors, viz: Rev. Samuel Jones, of Pennepek, Rev. Isaac Eaton, John Stout, Esq., and John Jewell, of New Jersey.

3. The petition of Mr. Ebenezer David, student in Rhode Island College, was granted to the amount of £14, he giving a bond to the trustees to return the money in case their intention and the intention of the benefactor should not be answered.

4. The Association to be in New York next year; to begin the Tuesday after the second Sunday in October. Mr. Abel Morgan to preach; or, in case of his absence, Mr. Morgan Edwards.

5. Visiting Lyon's Farms is recommended to our ministers.

6. The pious design of Mr. Britton, of Shammony, was attended to; and the following persons have engaged to preach there this year, viz: Mr. Samuel Jones, the fourth Sunday in January, June, and September; Mr. John Thomas, the fourth Sunday in November, March, and July; Mr. William Vanhorn, the fourth Sunday in December, April, and August; Mr. John Blackwell, the fourth Sunday in May;

Mr. Joshua Jones, the fourth Sunday in February; Mr. David Branson, the fourth Sunday in this present month, October.

7. Manahawkin to be supplied by Mr. Branson, the third Sunday in December and May; Mr. David Jones, the third Sunday in November and March; Mr. Worth, the third Sunday in January and June; Mr. James Sutton, the third Sunday in February; Mr. Heaton, third Sunday in April; Mr. P. Vanhorn, the fourth Sunday in July; Mr. Runyon, the third Sunday in August; Mr. William Vanhorn, the third Sunday in September.

8. The Northern Liberty church to be supplied by Mr. Kelsay, the third Sunday in November; Mr. Worth, the third Sunday in February; Mr. Abel Griffiths, the second Sunday in January; Mr. Runyon, the third Sunday in June: Mr. Heaton, the third Sunday in March; Mr. D. Sutton, the third Sunday in April; Mr. Joshua Jones, the fourth Sunday in May; Mr. Runyon, the fourth Sunday in August.

9. The ministers expressed a readiness to supply Philadelphia, in case Mr. Edwards should proceed in the execution of his public office.

10. The contributors to the Association fund were—

	£	s.	d.		£	s.	d.
Church of Philadelphia,	2	12	0	Church of Hopewell,	1	0	0
Church of Cohansie,	0	15	0	Church of Kingwood,	0	5	0
Church of Southampton,	1	2	6	Church of New York,	3	0	0
Church of Baltimore,	0	10	0	Edward Kesby, Esq.,	0	7	6
Church of Pennepek,	1	0	0	Mr. Pangburn,	0	3	9
Church of Great Valley,	0	6	10½	Mr. John Briggs,	0	3	9

This, added to the former capital and interest, make £110 12s. 2½d.

A private letter from Rev. Samuel Harris, alias Col. Harris, of Pittsylvania, in Virginia, was read, to the great joy and entertainment of the Association; whereby it appears, that there are four Associations now in Carolina, and two in Virginia; that he hath planted seventeen churches lately; that two of our ministers are in Chesterfield gaol; that there is an unusual outpouring of the Spirit on all ranks of men in those parts; that many negroes endure scourgings for religion's sake; that two clergymen of the Church of England, preach Jesus Christ with unusal warmth.

PASTORAL ADDRESS.

The ministers and messengers of the several Baptist congregations in Pennsylvania, the Jerseys, and provinces adjacent, met in annual Association at Philadelphia, October 15th, 16th, 17th, 1771.

To the several churches we respectively relate unto, wish grace, mercy, and peace may be multiplied.

Dear brethren,—Through the good providence of God, we have been preserved to see one season more of our annual meeting; and, blessed be God, we met in love, and preserved love and harmony through the whole of our consultations. We were agreeably entertained with a discourse on the insufficiency of our own righteousness in point of justification, by our brother, Kelsay, from Phil. iii. 9; and much refreshed with your letters, by which we learn that our churches are mostly at peace among themselves; and that the Lord is still continuing his presence in the midst of his golden candlesticks, and blessing his word to the bringing of some to the obedience of faith. We also have good news from the eastern and western Associations, of seven churches joining them, and of increase, by baptism, to the number of four hundred and forty-two, which, with the increase in ours, make five hundred and twenty-four.

Now, beloved brethren, before we part from one another, we would remind you of these few necessary things, viz: That, as there be some complaints of deadness and coldness in religion, O be instant with the Lord in private and public prayers, wrestling with him for his blessing, and those measures of his Spirit and grace whereby your own souls may be quickened more and more, and you grow in grace and knowledge, and in the practice of every duty, and lay no stumbling block in the way of any. Be watchful against the temptations of Satan, the great enemy of the church. Be careful to keep your Christian graces in exercise, that you may be comfortable in the midst of difficulties. Be diligent in attending the means of grace. Neglect not the assembling of yourselves together as the manner of some is. Strengthen the hands of your ministers, and pray earnestly that God will bless their labors. Finally, brethren, be mindful of the exhortation, to keep your loins girt and your lamps burning, that, whenever the midnight cry be heard, you may be ready to go in with Christ to the marriage, which is the wish of your brethren.

Signed in our behalf,   JOHN GANO, Moderator,
MORGAN EDWARDS, Clerk.

Finding that the minutes of the Association do not fill the sheet as usual, I will, according to particular desire, add one agreement, that the Associating churches came to, dated the 27th of the seventh month, in the year 1707; and it is the first on record:

"Agreed, That no man shall be allowed to preach among the Associated churches, except he produce credentials of his being in communion with his church, and of his having been called and licensed to preach."

Before this, vain and insufficient men, who had set themselves up to be preachers, would stroll about the country under the name of Baptist ministers; also, ministers degraded and excommunicated, who, with their immorality, and the others, with their insufficiency and immorality too, brought disgrace on the very name of Baptists; which evil, the above agreement of the Association, if attended to, would in a great measure, remedy. Christ is the door to the ministry, and his church is the porter, for to it hath he given the keys; and whoever comes in at the door, to him the porter openeth, John x. 3; he that climbeth into the pulpit any other way, climbeth thither by an extraordinary call and mission, and must give an extraordinary proof thereof, as the Apostles did, or subject himself to a suspicion of iutrusion and imposture. And it has been found, that they who pretend to extraordinary calls and missions are such as could obtain no ordinary ones, because either their characters or gifts would not justify any church that should put them in the ministry. In truth, they are self-made preachers; and it has been said, that "a self-made preacher, a quack doctor, and a pettyfogging lawyer, are three animals that the world would do better without than with."

STATE OF THE CHURCHES DURING THE YEAR.

CHURCHES.	MINISTERS.	Baptized.	Added by Letter.	Restored.	Died.	Excom.	Members.
Pennepek,	Samuel Jones,	1	1	0	4	1	47
Middletown,	Abel Morgan,	2	0	0	3	0	142
Piscataqua,	Isaac Stelle,	1	0	0	1	0	72
Cohansie,	Robert Kelsay,	1	0	0	6	0	84
Welsh Tract,	John Sutton,	5	2	0	3	0	115
Great Valley,	John Davis,	13	0	0	4	1	72
Cape May,	Peter P. Vanhorn,	4	0	0	1	0	62
Hopewell,	Isaac Eaton,	0	0	0	0	1	199
Brandywine,		0	0	0	0	0	32
Montgomery,	John Thomas,	2	0	0	4	0	101
Tulpehokin,*	Thomas Jones,	0	0	0	0	0	16
Kingwood,	David Sutton,	4	0	1	0	0	79
Southampton,	William Vanhorn,	0	1	0	2	0	50
Philadelphia,	Morgan Edwards,	3	0	0	4	0	146
Scotch Plains,	Benjamin Miller,	4	0	0	1	1	126
Horse Neck,*		0	0	0	0	0	7
Oyster Bay,*		0	0	0	0	0	15
Morristown,	Reune Runyon,	0	1	0	0	0	40
Knowltown,*	Henry Crosley,	0	2	0	0	0	26
Baltimore,	John Davis,	16	0	0	5	2	132
New Britain,	Joshua Jones,	4	4	0	1	0	64
Salem,	Abel Griffiths,	1	0	0	0	0	23
Newtown,	Nicholas Cox,	0	2	0	0	0	29
Bateman's Precincts,	Samuel Waldo,	0	0	0	0	0	113
Dividing Creek,	Samuel Heaton,	0	0	0	2	0	41
New York,	John Gano,	4	1	0	1	0	147
New Mills,	David Branson,	10	0	0	0	0	55
Konoloway,	Joseph Powell,	8	2	0	0	0	39
Coram,	Noah Hammond,	1	0	0	0	0	31
Croswicks,	David Jones,	1	0	0	0	0	42
Mount Bethel,	Henry Crosley,	0	0	0	2	0	31
Goshen,	James Benedict,	6	1	0	0	2	66
Lyon's Farms,	Reune Runyon,	0	0	1	0	0	20
Philip's Patent,*	Simon Dakin,	0	0	0	0	0	65
Pittsgrove,	William Worth,	0	0	0	0	0	24
Manahawkin,		2	0	0	0	0	11
Vincent,	John Blackwell,	0	0	0	0	0	52
Tuckahoe,	James Sutton,	0	0	0	0	0	17
Northern Liberty,		0	0	0	0	0	16
		93	17	2	44	8	2449

N. B. The churches marked thus * sent no messengers; their numbers remain as they were last year. Increase this year, eighty-two.

MINUTES

OF THE

PHILADELPHIA BAPTIST ASSOCIATION,

MET AT NEW YORK, OCTOBER 13TH, 14TH, AND 15TH,

1772.

The Association sermon was preached by our respected brother in the ministry, Abel Morgan, from Eph. iii. 3. Brother Abel Morgan was chosen moderator, and James Manning, clerk. Letters were read from the following churches, and messengers came from the most of them, viz:

Pennepek, Samuel Jones; Middletown, Abel Morgan, James Grover, Richard Crawford, and Joseph Stillwell; Piscataqua, Isaac Stelle; Cohansie, Joseph Shepherd; Hopewell, John Stout and Stephen Barton; Brandywine and Kingwood, Andrew Bray; Southampton, William Vanhorn and Joseph Hart; Philadelphia, Ezekiel Robbins; Scotch Plains, Benjamin Miller and Abraham Hampton; Oyster Bay, Henry Ludlum; Morristown, Reune Runyon and John Brookfield; Baltimore, New Britain, and Salem, Abel Griffith; Newtown, Nicholas Cox and Hezekiah Smith; Bateman's Precincts, Samuel Waldo and Agrippa Martin; Dividing Creek and New York, John Gano, Isaac Skilman, Samuel Edmonds, and John Carman; Coram, Noah Hammond; Croswicks, David Jones and Thomas Farr; Mount Bethel, Henry Crosley; Goshen, James Benedict and Philip Ketcham; Lyon's Farms, Timothy Hughes and Ichabod Grummond; Philip's Patent, Simon Dakin; Pittsgrove and Manahawkin, Daniel Prine; Tuckahoe, and the second church in Philadelphia.

Letters were read from the Associations in Virginia, Warren, Newport, and South Carolina.

A letter from the second Baptist church in New York was read, requesting admission into the Association. Objections being made by the first church in the city against receiving it, on account of difficulties subsisting between the two churches, they were advised to call the aid of some sister churches to assist in settling them. Accordingly, they chose our brethren, Benjamin Miller, Gabriel Ogden, Isaac Stelle, Samuel Waldo, and Reune Runyon, who are to meet the Tuesday after the third Lord's day in November, to attend on that business.

A letter was read from the church at Philip's Patent, Cortland's

Manor, and Salem, under the pastoral care of Brother John Lawrence, which desired to be received into the Association. Their request was granted.

"We, the church of Christ at Tuckahoe, in the township of Great Egg Harbor, county of Gloucester, and province of New Jersey, holding believer's baptism by immersion only, the doctrine of election, laying on of hands, final perseverance of the saints in grace,—send greeting.

"To the annual Association met at New York, October 15th, 1772:—Wishing mercy, peace and a comfortable stay together, we would inform you as followeth. We are destitute, no minister being settled amongst us at present; but, through the goodness of God, we have had considerable supplies from the churches at Dividing Creek and Cape May. We consist of twenty-three members at the present. We have dismissed one this year by letter, and received one by letter. Four of the above-mentioned members were baptized and received in the present year. We are in sweet harmony amongst ourselves. We have not sent any messenger with our letter, by reason that the Association is at so great a distance from us.

"From yours, &c.,

"WILLIAM GOLDING, and others."

The relation of the conduct of the church at Bateman's Precincts, by Brother Waldo, respecting the excommunication of Henry Dawson, was heard and approved.

The thanks of the Association were returned to brother Morgan Edwards, for his services in travelling and visiting the churches to the southward; and the interest of the Association fund, for the last year, voted him, together with £6 more, made up by the brethren present, and sent him by Mr. Samuel Jones.

Thursday morning being appointed by the first Baptist church in this city for the ordination of Brother Isaac Skilman to the work of the gospel ministry, it was attended by fasting and prayer, and a sermon preached by Brother James Manning, on the Commission, from Matt. xxviii. 19, 20. Then the person was ordained by Messrs. John Gano, Abel Morgan, and Isaac Stelle; and the charge given by Mr. Miller.

The churches of New York and Philadelphia have collected, the last year, £3 proclamation, each, for the Association fund.

A certificate was given to Brother David Jones, who intends to visit the western tribes of Indians the next winter, to ascertain his good standing with us. Also, at his request, a motion was made to recommend his case to the respective churches, as he must be at the expense of paying his interpreter £5 per month; and the contribution made to be sent by their messengers to the next Association. If not wanted, the money will be returned to the donors.

The people at Woolwich, in Gloucester, requesting to be constituted into a church, and the ordination of Mr. Locke, were advised from the smallness of their number, as appears by their letter, to join themselves as a branch to a neighboring church, until it shall please the Lord to add to their number.

The next Association to be held at Philadelphia, the Tuesday after the second Lord's day, in October. The Sermon to be preached by Brother Morgan Edwards; or, in case of failure, by Brother Samuel Jones.

Supplies were requested for the church under the care of brother David Jones, and the following agreed upon:—Samuel Jones, second Lord's day in November, at Upper Freehold; Nicholas Cox, third at Upper, and fourth at Lower Freehold; Abel Morgan, the second in December, and second in February, at Upper Freehold; Abel Griffith, first in January, at Upper, and second at Lower Freehold; Robert Kelsay, second in March, at Upper, Benjamin Miller, fourth of March, at Lower Freehold.

The following are the supplies for Hopewell:—November, the fourth Lord's day, Mr. Gano; March, second, Mr. Griffith; February, third, Mr. Vanhorn; December, fourth, Mr. Crosly; March, fourth, Mr. Miller; June, fourth, David Jones; last in May, Mr. Runyon; July, second, Mr. Kelsay; April, fourth, Mr. Ward; July, fourth, Messrs. Samuel Jones and Gano.

For Manahawkin:—January, first and second Lord's day, Mr. Crosly; May, fourth, Mr. Miller; July, third, Mr. Kelsay; August, fourth, David Jones.

For Lyon's Farms:—December, the second Lord's day, Mr. Miller; February, the first, Mr. Crosly; last in March, Mr. Stelle; April, first, and August, first, Mr. Runyon; Mr. Ward, May, first, and second in August.

For Oyster Bay:—Mr. Hammond; June, second, Mr. Lawrence; March, fourth, Mr. Gano; May, third, Mr. Stelle; August, fourth, Mr. Ward; November, third, Mr. Runyon.

The following supplies, in consequence of a request, for Neshamony:—Mr. John Thomas, June, the fourth Lord's day, and September, fourth; Mr. Samuel Jones, November, fourth, and July, fourth; Mr. Joshua Jones, March, fourth, and August, fourth; Mr. Vanhorn, October, fourth, and April, fourth; January, fourth, Mr. Blackwell.

Letters were sent to the Associations of Warren, Virginia, South Carolina, and Newport, Rhode Island.

PASTORAL ADDRESS.

The elders and messengers of the Baptist churches in Pennsylvania, the Jerseys, and provinces adjacent, met in annual Association in the city of New York, October 13, 14, and 15, 1772.

To the several churches we respectively relate unto, send our Christian salutation.

Dear Brethren,—Through divine favor, we had the happiness to meet together, according to appointment, and enjoy this annual interview with much love. The solemnity was opened by a sermon from

Eph. iii. 8, preached by our worthy Brother Abel Morgan, wherein the unsearchable riches of grace in a glorious Redeemer, the gospel minister's directory in the discharge of his office; together with the glory and excellency of the New Testament dispensation, were opened and enforced with much clearness and fervor.

By the letters and messengers, we find that a comfortable degree of unity subsists in the several churches; and that additions have been made to the most of them, of such as we hope shall be saved; for which we desire to join with you in giving glory to the head of the church, who still continues to walk among the golden candlesticks. Nevertheless, too evident it is, that lukewarmness and indifference too much abound, while the love of many waxeth cold, whereby our divine Redeemer is wounded in the house of his friends. For this, beloved, we have reason to be humbled before God, and to weep between the porch and the altar.

Our consultations have been in much love and unity, while many particulars of weight and general concern have been duly attended to; now, at the close, we have reason to bless God, in humble confidence, that our meeting together has been for the better, and not for the worse.

Before we part, you will suffer us to address you in the spirit of meekness, while we remind you of these few necessary things. Neglect not the assembling of yourselves together, as the manner of too many is; see that your conversation be as becometh the gospel of Christ; maintain the unity of the Spirit in the bond of peace; labor ever to live under the inflence of the love of God shed abroad in your hearts; neglect not family worship and closet devotion; give diligence to make your calling and election sure; let it be your greatest care to grow in grace and abound in every good word and work; endeavor to walk exemplary before all men; do all that in you lieth to suppress the growth of vice and immorality, and in particular, we earnestly recommend it to you to keep a watchful eye over the morals of the youth committed to your care, that they may be brought up in the nurture and fear of the Lord; be zealous for the truth, strict in discipline, and careful of admitting members into your churches; strengthen the hands, and encourage the hearts of your ministers, and promote their visiting destitute places. If there be the appearance of promising gifts among you, let such be forwarded, and pray to the Lord of the harvest, that he would send forth many faithful laborers into the vineyard, for truly the harvest is great, while the laborers are but few. Finally, brethren, add to your faith, virtue; and to virtue, knowledge; and to knowledge, temperance; and to temperance, patience; and to patience, godliness; and to godliness, brotherly kindness; and to brotherly kindness, charity; that so you may be fruitful, and abound to the glory of God: to whom, and to the word of his grace, we commend you. Amen.

ABEL MORGAN, Moderator.
JAMES MANNING, Clerk.

STATE OF THE CHURCHES DURING THE YEAR.

CHURCHES.	MINISTERS.	Baptized.	Added by Letter.	Restored.	Dead.	Excom.	Members.
Pennepek,	Samuel Jones,	5	4	0	0	0	54
Middletown,	Abel Morgan,	0	0	0	2	0	140
Piscataqua,	Isaac Stelle,	1	0	0	0	0	73
Cohansie,	Robert Kelsay,	0	0	0	1	0	83
Welsh Tract,*	John Sutton,	0	0	0	0	0	115
Great Valley,*	John Davis,	0	0	0	0	0	72
Cape May,*	P. P. Vanhorn,	0	0	0	0	0	62
Hopewell,		0	0	0	6	0	192
Brandywine,		1	0	0	2	0	29
Montgomery,*	John Thomas,	0	0	0	0	0	101
Tulpehokin,*	Thomas Jones,	0	0	0	0	0	16
Kingwood,	David Sutton,	3	0	0	0	1	79
Southampton,	William Vanhorn,	5	1	0	0	0	55
Philadelphia,	William Rogers,	23	1	0	3	0	164
Scotch Plains,	Benjamin Miller,	1	1	0	1	0	127
Horse Neck,*		0	0	0	0	0	7
Oyster Bay,		0	0	0	0	0	15
Morristown,	Reune Runyon,	1	0	0	0	0	41
Knowltown,*		0	0	0	0	0	26
Baltimore,	John Davis,	9	4	0	0	2	140
New Britain,*	Joshua Jones,	0	0	0	0	0	64
Salem,	Abel Griffiths,	0	2	0	2	0	23
Newtown,	Nicholas Cox,	10	1	0	1	0	37
Bateman's Precincts,	Samuel Waldo,	0	0	0	1	2	110
Dividing Creek,	Samuel Heaton,	0	0	0	1	1	39
New York,	John Gano,	20	0	0	3	0	164
New Mills,*	David Branson,	2	0	0	0	0	57
Konoloway,*	Joseph Powell,	0	0	0	0	0	39
Coram,	Noah Hammond,	0	0	0	0	0	31
Croswicks,	David Jones,	3	0	0	1	0	42
Mount Bethel,	Henry Crosly,	0	1	0	0	0	32
Goshen,	James Benedict,	3	1	0	0	0	70
Lyon's Farms,		0	0	0	0	0	20
Philip's Patent,	Simon Dakin,	8	0	0	0	1	72
Pittsgrove,	William Worth,	6	0	0	0	1	29
Manahawkin,		1	0	0	0	0	12
Vincent,*		0	0	0	0	0	52
Tuckahoe,		0	1	0	0	0	17
Northern Liberty,		0	0	0	0	1	15
Cortland's Manor and Salem,	John Lawrence,	0	0	0	0	0	72
		102	17	0	24	9	2588

Increase this year, 139.

N. B. The churches marked thus * sent no messengers; their numbers remain as they were last year.

MINUTES

OF THE

PHILADELPHIA BAPTIST ASSOCIATION,

HELD AT PHILADELPHIA, OCTOBER 12TH, 13TH, AND 14TH.

1773.

THIS year the Association met at Philadelphia, October 12th, and began at 3 o'clock, P. M., as usual, with divine service. The sermon by our brother, Rev. Morgan Edwards, from Num. xxiii. 9; who, after observing, that "standing alone and unreckoned among the nations" meant a religious "singularity;" and comparing his text with the king of Moab's sense of it, chap. xxiv. 10, advanced this doctrinal point, and exemplified it in the case of the Baptists from the beginning of Christianity to the present time. "Standing alone and unnumbered with any religious society, is, in some supposable cases, a commendable and blessed thing." Those who have solicited a copy of the sermon for the press, will be gratified when all the Association sermons come to be printed.

2. After divine service, Brother John Gano was chosen moderator, and Brother Morgan Edwards, clerk. Letters from forty-two churches were read, and the names of the messengers enrolled.

3. A letter from the Warren Association was read, whereby it appears that three churches joined them, with an increase of one hundred and four members; that the oppression of the Baptists in Massachusetts continues; the paragraph relating to this follows: "Our sufferings in Boston government on religious accounts still continue in several places; a particular narrative of which is to be printed, with a fair representation of the treatment which the Baptists have met with in said government in time past."

4. A letter from the Congaree Association, in South Carolina, was read, soliciting the continuance of our correspondence, and exhibiting the state of their churches, whereby it appears that there was a great increase among them; but the number is not specified. Next year they promise to be more exact.

5. Also a letter from Quekuky Association, in North Carolina, thanking us for our care in sending messengers among them; exhibiting the state of their churches, and soliciting the continuance of

correspondence and MISSIONS. The increase of members this year among them is two hundred and seventy-five.

6. No letter from Sandy Creek Association, in the same province, nor from the Rapidanne Association, in Virginia. A letter was prepared by the Ketokton Association, and Rev. Richard Major appointed messenger. By some means the letter came not to hand; but the messenger informs us of a very great increase among them, with the addition of three churches to their Association. No letter from the Charleston Association, in South Carolina. But as letters and a messenger are sent to each, we hope to have it in our power next year to gratify the churches with the state of their brethren to the southward.

7. The second church of New York applying for admission, and some obstacles appearing in the way, a committee was appointed to meet at New York, November 8th, to inspect into the matter; and, if the obstacles could be removed, to receive said church into union, in the name and behalf of the Association. The persons appointed are Rev. Messrs. Benjamin Miller, Isaac Stelle, and Alderman Stites.

8. The case of Mr. Henry Dawson, late of London, but now of Newport, Rhode Island, came before the Association.

Agreed, That Messrs. Samuel Jones, David Jones, David Sutton, Henry Williams, and Joseph Hart, be a committee to consider the matter, and make their report.

They met, and reported as follows: "As it doth appear to us that the said Henry Dawson hath deposited all his substance in a safe hand for the benefit of his creditors, and otherwise manifested a suitable inclination, and endeavors, to the utmost of his abilities, to pay and discharge his debts, we are of opinion that any minute or record, formerly made by this Association respecting him, should and ought to become null and void, as if the same had not been made.

The Association agreed thereto, and the records were made void.

N. B. The reason of our having to do with Mr. Dawson was that, till of late, he professed himself to be a First-day Baptist, but now is in the observance of the Seventh day.

9. A letter from a company of people at Oyster Bay, on Long Island, was read, requesting help in their present difficulties.

Resolved, That Messrs. Benjamin Miller, John Lawrence, John Gano, Isaac Stelle, Ebenezer Ward, Henry Williams, and John Stites, do meet at said Oyster Bay, the 10th of November, to give them the help they requested, and also to provide supplies for them this year.

10. A petition from a certain number of well disposed persons at Cowmarsh, in Kent, was attended to, and the following supplies provided for them:—Fourth Sunday in November, Rev. John Blackwell; second in April, Rev. William Worth; last in May, Rev. P. Peterson Vanhorn.; last in July, Rev. Morgan Edwards; the fourth in September, Rev. Robert Kelsay.

11. An answer to a query from the Great Valley, to be sent with their letter.

12. The money brought in by the church of Cape May, Salem, and Croswick, for the use of our suffering brethren being remanded: ordered, that Treasurer Wescott deliver said money to their messengers, and the rest to the other churches, if demanded by their messengers.

13. Agreed, that Messrs. Rogers and Vanhorn shall write the circular letter; and Messrs. Jones and Edwards write to the Associations corresponding or to correspond with us. Also, that Brother Abel Morgan do, against next Association, consider a plan, and present a specimen of a circular letter to be addressed to the churches.

Agreeable to a request in the letter from New York, our ministers were pressed to visit the brethren at Pigskill, in New York government; and at Stamford, in Connecticut.

14. The usefulness of a travelling minister on this continent appearing more manifest by trials, and Brother Morgan Edwards declining the office, it was agreed, that Brother John Gano be a messenger of the churches for this year; and that the treasurer do pay him the interest of the Association fund, to help defraying his expenses.

15. Agreeable to a petition from the church of Newmills, the following supplies were provided for them, as they are destitute, occasioned by the excommunication of their late minister, Mr. David Branson, of whom the churches should be aware:—Fourth Sunday in December, Rev. Samuel Jones; second in February, Rev. William Worth; fourth in March, Rev. David Jones; first in April, Rev. P. Peterson Vanhorn; fourth in June, Rev. Robert Kelsay; third in August, Rev. Ebenezer Ward; fourth in September, Rev. Samuel Jones; fourth in October, Rev. William Vanhorn.

16. The following supplies are provided for Hopewell church:—Fourth Sunday in October, Rev. John Blackwell; fourth in November, Rev. Nicholas Cox; first in February, Rev. Morgan Edwards; third and fourth in February, Rev. William Worth; second in April, P. Peterson Vanhorn; fourth in May, Rev. Samuel Jones; fourth in June, Rev. William Rogers; fourth in July, Rev. David Jones; second in August, Rev. Ebenezer Ward; fourth in October, Rev. John Blackwell.

17. Agreeable to a petition from the church of Kingwood, their case was considered; and Brother Abel Morgan appointed to write to them. The letter is as follows:

"Beloved brethren,—Whereas you have, in your letter, informed the Association that you are not agreed among yourselves about the genuine sense of that place of Scripture, John xiii., relative to washing the saints' feet; and also request the Association to give you their opinion of it. The Association, taking the same into consideration, are not so happy as to be universally agreed themselves in the point, so as to give you the fixed determined sense of the words; and not choosing at present to enter into disputes upon the subject, they thought proper to choose I should write you a line upon the occasion, desiring (which is also my earnest desire) you to avoid all unbecoming heats, perverse disputings, contentions, hard thoughts, and evil speaking among yourselves on this account; but rather to forbear with one another in love, that though you cannot see alike in all things, yet you would still follow the things that make for peace; for hereunto were ye called. Endeavor to keep the unity of the Spirit in the bond of peace. Let not those who are bound in conscience to practice it, condemn those who are not convinced it is a duty; nor those who cannot see it a duty, despise those who are for practising it. Let all things, brethren, be done among you to edification. Unity is the great design God hath in view to accomplish, Eph. i. 10. Unity among God's people is that which the devil hates, and labors to destroy, who is the sower of discord among brethren.

"With my hearty desire for your prosperity, I am yours,
"ABEL MORGAN.

" Philadelphia, October 14, 1773."

18. Agreed, that by reason of the distances of several of our sister churches to the eastward, the Association should meet twice in the year; once at New York, on the Wednesday after the fourth Lord's day in May, at 3 o'clock, for the conveniency of said eastern churches; and at Philadelphia, on Wednesday after the second Lord's day in October. The sermon to be preached, at New York, by Rev. Samuel Jones, or, in case of failure, by Rev. Abel Morgan; that at Philadelpha by Rev. Isaac Stelle, or, in case of failure, by Rev. William Rogers.

19. Pursuant to a petition from Lyon's Farms, the following supplies were obtained for them:—Third Sunday in November, Rev. Nicholas Cox; last Sunday in December, Rev. Morgan Edwards, who is to be at Piscataqua the Friday before, at 12 o'clock; fourth in May, Rev. Ebenezer Ward.

20. The Association fund being again recommended, the following donations were added this year:

	£	s.	d.		£	s.	d.
Church of Philadelphia,	4	0	0	Church of Montgomery,	0	7	9
Church of York,	2	0	0	Rev. David Jones,	0	7	6
Church of New Britain,	0	7	6	Mr. Hugh Glasford,	0	8	0
Church of Pennepek,	0	12	9				

In all, £8 3s. 3d., which increased the capital to £118 14s. 5d.

21. Voted, That £18 arising from Mrs. Hubb's donation, be equally divided between Messrs. Peter Smith and Thomas Gier; they giving the usual obligations to the trustees.

22. Voted, that Messrs. John Gano and William Vanhorn be our messengers to the Warren Association; and to the southern Associations Mr. Gano only.

PASTORAL LETTER.

The ministers and messengers of the several Baptist congregations in Pennsylvania, the Jerseys, and provinces adjacent, met in annual Association at Philadelphia, October 12th, 13th, and 14th, 1773.

To the several churches we respectively relate unto, send Christian salutation.

Much esteemed brethren,—Almighty God, in his kind providence, having favored us with another anniversary Association, for which it surely behoveth us to call upon our souls and all that is within us to bless and praise his holy and reverend name.

Through divine goodness we met in peace, and preserved love and harmony. We have (as by our minutes appears) endeavored so to act, that the great Head of the church may be glorified, and much benefit redound to the several branches we stand respectively related unto. The particular accounts transmitted in many of your letters, together with those of other Associations, are truly very refreshing. Oh, help us to magnify the Lord for his rich favors and tender mercies, which are over all his works!

But, alas, that usual complaint of deadness and lukewarmness in the things of religion, still prevails. It is much to be lamented that vital piety, in many places, decays, for the revival of which we have thought meet to appoint four days in the year ensuing as days of fasting and united prayer and supplication at the throne of grace, viz: the Fridays after the fourth Lord's days in November, February, May, and August. Prayer, you are sensible, has done wonders; it is the very breath of the new creature; yea, it is a command from Christ himself, "Ask, and it shall be given you, &c." Matt. vii. 7, 8. Moreover, for our encouragement, let us remember, that if any two or three of us shall agree to petition for any thing in the name of Jesus, it shall be granted unto us.

We entreat you, therefore, unitedly to assemble together, and to be instant with the Lord in prayer, wrestling with him for his blessing, and those measures of his Spirit and grace, whereby our souls may be quickened, and religion more and more revived in our land.

JOHN GANO, Moderator,
MORGAN EDWARDS, Secretary.

⁎ The following books may be had of Mr. Samuel Davis, Hatter, at the corner of Christ Church Alley, in Third street, viz: "Baptist Confessions of Faith," 1s. 1d.; "Norcott on Baptism," 4d.; "Catechisms," 3d.; "Materials towards a history of the Baptists, 4s., unbound, 3s. "Customs of Primitive Churches," 3s. 9d.; Stennett's Sermons," 20s.

THE MINISTERS AND MESSENGERS AT THE ASSOCIATION, AND THE STATE OF THE CHURCHES FOR THE YEAR.

CHURCHES.	MINISTERS AND MESSENGERS.	Baptized.	Received by Letter.	Dismis'd.	Dead.	Excom.	Members.
Pennepek,	Samuel Jones, A. M. Alexander Edwards, Esq.,	6	4	1	0	0	63
Middletown,	Abel Morgan, A. M.,	2	0	0	0	0	142
Piscataqua,	Isaac Stelle,	2	1	0	2	2	72
Cohansie,	Robert Kelsay, Philip Shepherd, David Bowen,	0	2	2	4	0	79
Welsh Tract,	John Sutton, Hugh Glasford,	22	1	2	4	3	129
Great Valley,	John Davis, Thomas Jones, James Davis,	0	6	2	2	2	72
Cape May,	Peter P. Vanhorn,	0	0	0	0	1	61
Hopewell,	John Stout, David Stout,	0	0	0	3	0	191
Brandywine,	Robert M'Kim, James Shields,	0	0	0	0	0	29
Montgomery,	John Thomas, Elijah Davis, James Morgan,	6	2	1	1	0	103
Tulpehokin,†	Thomas Jones,	0	0	0	0	0	16
Kingwood,	David Suttor, Andrew Bray, Esq., Elcana Holmes,	3	1	0	1	0	80
Southampton,	William Vanhorn, Joseph Hart, Esq.,	11	0	1	2	0	63
Philadelphia,	William Rogers, A. M., George Wescott, Samuel Davis,	15	3	3	4	3	172
Cranberry,	—— ——	0	0	0	1	0	24
Scotch Plains,	Benjamin Miller,	2	0	5	2	0	122
Horse Neck,†	—— ——	0	0	0	0	0	7
Oyster Bay,	William Roe,	6	0	0	1	0	20
Morristown,	Renue Runyon,*	4	6	2	0	0	49
Knowlton,†	—— ——	0	0	0	0	0	41
Baltimore,	John Davis, David Lane,	12	1	1	6	0	146
New Britain,	Joshua Jones, David Evans,	1	0	5	4	0	56
Salem,	Abel Griffiths,* John Holmes, Esq., Edward Keasby, Esq.,	1	0	0	0	0	24

CHURCHES.	MINISTERS AND MESSENGERS.	Baptized.	Received by Letter.	Dismis'd.	Dead.	Excom.	Members.
Newtown,	Nicholas Cox, Peter Smith, Evy Adams,	49	0	1	0	0	67
Bateman's Precincts,	Samuel Waldo,*	2	0	0	3	1	108
Dividing Creek,	Samuel Heaton,* David Shepherd, William Newcomb,	0	0	0	0	0	39
New York,	John Gano, Henry Williams,	13	0	5	1	0	171
New Mills,	Samuel Gaskill, Peter Lane,	0	0	0	2	1	55
Konoloway,	Joseph Powell,	5	2	3	0	0	39
Coram,†	Noah Hammond,*	0	0	0	0	0	31
Croswicks,	David Jones, Caleb Carman,	4	0	0	2	0	44
Mount Bethel,	Abner Sutton,	0	2	6	0	0	28
Goshen,	James Benedict,* Philip Ketcham,	0	0	0	0	0	0
Lyon's Farms,	Ichabod Grummon,	2	0	0	0	0	22
Philip's Patent,	Simon Dawkin,* Ebenezer Ward, John Lawrence,	10	0	0	0	1	81
Pittsgrove,	Wildiam Worth, David Elwell,	7	3	0	1	0	38
Manahawkin,†		0	0	0	0	0	12
Vincent,	David Thomas, John Griffiths,	5	0	0	0	0	57
Tuckahoe,†	William Lock,*	0	0	0	0	0	17
Northern Liberty,	Joseph Bull,	0	0	0	0	0	15
		190	35	40	46	14	2585

Note.—The ministers' names in small capitals. Those marked thus * not present. The Churches marked thus † sent neither letters nor messengers, and their numbers remain as last year. A dash ——— denotes no minister.

MINUTES

OF THE

PHILADELPHIA BAPTIST ASSOCIATION,

HELD AT NEW YORK, MAY 25TH.

1774.

New York, May 25.—At 3 o'clock, the Association began, as usual, with Divine service. The sermon was preached by our brother, Rev. Samuel Jones, from Matth. v. 16.

2. After Divine service, Brother Samuel Jones was chosen moderator, and Brother William Rogers, clerk. Letters from several churches were read, and the names of the messengers enrolled.

3. Adjourned.—Sermon in the evening by our brother, Rev. Abel Morgan.

4. Thursday, May 26. Met at 8 o'clock, and after prayer proceeded to business.

5. A letter from Stanford church was read, desiring admittance among, and union with us; received accordingly.

6. The minutes and letters from Charleston Association, South Carolina, were read. The plan adopted by them respecting Rhode Island College recommended to us. Agreed to recommend the same to the churches we stand respectively related unto; and whoever shall see good to contribute, the money so gathered, agreeable to the plan, to be remitted to Colonel Job Bennet, in New Port, Rhode Island, or brought unto the next Association.

7. A letter from the Association at Little River and Broad River, South Carolina, was read, by which it appears that sixty-six joined them by baptism the year past; their number of members six hundred and ninety-two. Good news from a far country.

8. A motion being made, that Brother John Gano should give an account of his travels to the southward: he accordingly did, by which it appears he has been indefatigable in his labors, and that a minister, travelling annually, according to the plan proposed, may answer very valuable purposes.

9. The second church in New York having been received into the Association by the committee appointed last Association, they presented their letters and messengers, who took their seats.

10. The Association of ministers and elders, from the several Bap-

tist churches, met at Philadelphia, October 12th, 1773, thought it expedient that some plan of the general letter to the churches, somewhat different from the usual mode of addressing them, should be considered and fixed upon, and nominated Brother Abel Morgan to present a specimen at the next Association; who, considering the case, proposes as follows:—

I. That the contents of the general letter shall consist of observations and improvements of some particular article of faith, contained in our Confession, beginning with the first, and so on in order, unless occasion require the contrary; the manner and improvement, whether explanatory, confirmatory, consolatory, or by questions and answers, to be concluded by the writer. Also, that a brother be nominated beforehand, to prepare against the next meeting.

II. Let diligent care be used to caution the churches against innovation in doctrine and practice, and to watch against errors, and avoid them wherever they rise, and by whomsoever they may be propagated.

III. That suitable endeavors be made as heretofore, to resolve cases and questions proposed by the churches, to the best of our knowledge, according to the scripture.

IV. That all seasonable counsel and advice be given to the churches; and, as occasion may require, let them be pressed with fervency and convincing arguments.

V. That records be kept of all the copies of letters sent from, and received by, the Association.

11. Agreeable to a petition from the church at Lyon's Farms, supplies were provided.

12. Supplies were also provided for Oyster Bay.

13. Agreed, That Brother Samuel Jones prepare the general letter against next Association.

CIRCULAR LETTER.
BY REV. ABEL MORGAN.

The Association of elders and messengers of the several Baptist congregations in Pennsylvania, and the neighboring colonies, met at New York, May 25th, 1774.

Send our Christian salutation.

Beloved Brethren,—Whereas, unity in judgment (Eph. iv. 12, 13; 1 Cor. i. 10), and growth in every grace (Eph. iv. 15; 1 Thes. iv. 9. 10), are the two principal ends of all ministerial means and institutions; whatever, therefore, directly or natively tends to promote those valuable purposes, is hereby manifested to be good and right. The meeting of churches by their messengers at stated seasons, is esteemed to have this useful tendency. Such meetings ought then, not only to be continued, but also improved to the utmost for obtaining those desirable aforesaid designs. And that they may be more so, it is thought expedient, that henceforth the contents of the general letters to the churches consist of an improvement of some article of our Confession of faith, following the order therein observed, unless some particular requires otherwise, beginning with the first, viz., Of the Holy Scriptures; which are contained in the books of the Old and New Testament, as in our said adopted Confession.—These holy writings are of God, divinely inspired, 2 Tim. iii. 16; the word of God, John x. 36; 1 Cor. xiv. 36, 37; the mind of Christ, 1 Cor. ii. 26; of Divine authority, Isa. xl. 8; the infallible ground of faith and certain rule of obedience, Isa. viii. 20; full and complete in all its parts, historical, doctrinal, and prophetical; every way useful and profitable: e. gr. to obtain the saving knowledge of the one only living and true God, Father, Son, and Holy Ghost, 2 Tim. iii. 15; the knowledge of his essential attributes and immutable counsels, Heb. vi. 17; also of his works, of creation, providence, and particularly of redemption by Jesus Christ, the eternal Son of God, the one Mediator, God-Man. In the Scriptures we are clearly informed of the offices which he executes; of his unparalleled condescension and glorious exaltation, his approbation with the Father; and of his grace, love, merits, titles, and benefits.

The Scriptures are likewise useful, to give us the knowledge of man's ruin by sin; his misery, guilt, and condemnation; the consequences of his transgression; of the ever wonderful way of recovery by Christ, together with the certain characters of those who are restored; the change produced in them, and their obligations to new obedience; the blessedness of the godly, and the misery of the wicked and unbelievers; and also, the final state of both, after this life. Hence, be exhorted, brethren, to consider what a special privilege God has granted you, and continued with you. The Bible in your hands! Let this word of God dwell richly in your hearts also, in its doctrines, promises, commands, cautions, and threatenings; for your enlightening, your acting of every grace, your avoiding every sin, and for your perfecting holiness in the fear of God, 2 Cor. vii. 1. Some are forbid the use of the Bible, others are taught and persuaded to slight the Scriptures, while others again corrupt the word of God, 2 Cor. ii. 17. All those come short of receiving the full benefit thereof. Beware ye, dear brethren, lest your adversary, the devil, render it useless to you, by your neglecting of it. Frequently read the Scriptures in your retirements, read them in your families; make conscience of giving opportunities to all your households, of hearing what God says of them and to them. Speak of God's word, meditate upon it, and according to it, Psalm l. 23. Especially, look that you have an experimental acquaintance with the operation of Divine truth upon your hearts, 1 Thes. ii. 13. Pray God for a blessing to accompany it wherever it is preached; and always admire God, and praise him for his special kindness in giving you the holy Bible.

Samuel Jones, Moderator,
William Rogers, Clerk.

THE MINISTERS AND MESSENGERS AT THE ASSOCIATION, AND STATE OF THE CHURCHES DURING THE YEAR.

CHURCHES.	MINISTERS AND MESSENGERS.	Baptized.	Received by Letter	Dismiss'd	Dead.	Excom.	Members.
Pennepek,	Samuel Jones,	1	1	1	0	0	65
Middletown,	Abel Morgan, James Grover, William Bown,	0	0	0	1	0	141
Piscataqua,†	Isaac Stelle,*	0	0	0	0	0	72
Cohansie,	Robert Kelsay,*	0	2	0	0	0	81
Welsh Tract,†	John Sutton,*	0	0	0	0	0	129
Great Valley,†	John Davis,*	0	0	0	0	0	72
Cape May,	Peter P. Vanhorn,*	0	0	0	2	0	59
Hopewell,†	——— ———	0	0	0	0	0	191
Brandywine,†	——— ———	0	0	0	0	0	29
Montgomery,	John Thomas,*	0	0	1	0	0	102
Tulpehokin,†	Thomas Jones,*	0	0	0	0	0	16
Kingwood,	David Satton,*	0	0	0	0	0	80
Southampton,	William Vanhorn,*	1	0	0	0	0	64
Philadelphia,	William Rogers,	2	2	0	2	5	169
Cranberry,†	——— ———	0	0	0	0	0	24
Scotch Plains,	Benjamin Miller, John Stites, Esq., Abraham Hompton,	1	0	0	0	0	121
Oyster Bay,	Elijah Wheeler, Albert Alberson, Henry Ludlam,	2	0	1	0	0	22
Morristown,	Reune Runyon, Ebenezer Blackley,	3	2	0	1	0	54
Knowlton,†	——— ———	0	0	0	0	0	41
Baltimore,†	John Davis,*	0	0	0	0	0	146
New Britain,†	Joshua Jones,*	0	0	0	0	0	56
Salem,	Abel Griffiths, Edward Keasby, Esq.,	0	0	0	1	0	23
Newtown,	Nicholas Cox,	3	0	1	0	0	69
Bateman's Precincts,†	Samuel Waldo,*	0	0	0	0	0	108
Dividing Creek,	Samuel Heaton,*	0	0	0	0	0	39
1. New York,	John Gano, Henry Williams, Samuel Edmonds, Thomas Ustick, John Carman,	1	1	33	1	0	139
New Mills,†	——— ———	0	0	0	0	0	55
Conoloway,	Joseph Powell,*	0	0	0	0	0	39
Coram,	Noah Hammond,*	1	0	0	0	1	30

MINUTES OF THE PHILADELPHIA ASSOCIATION.

CHURCHES.	MINISTERS AND MESSENGERS.	Baptized.	Received by Letter.	Dismis'd.	Dead.	Excom.	Members.
Upper Freehold,	DAVID JONES,	2	2	0	0	0	48
Mount Bethel,†	ABNER SUTTON,*	0	0	0	0	0	28
Goshen,	{ JAMES BENEDICT, Samuel Robert,	10	0	0	2	0	96
Lyon's Farms,	Timothy Hughes,	0	0	0	0	0	22
Philip's Patent,	{ JOHN LAWRENCE,* Ebenezer Ward,	7	4	0	0	0	92
Pittsgrove,	WILLIAM WORTH,	0	2	0	0	1	40
Manahawkin,†	—— ——	0	0	0	0	0	12
Vincent,†	—— ——	0	0	0	0	0	57
Tuckahoe,†	WILLIAM LOCK,*	0	0	0	0	0	17
Northern Liberty,†	—— ——	0	0	0	0	0	15
2. New York,	{ JOHN DODGE, Francis Vandyke,	0	0	0	0	0	14
Stanford,	{ Ebenezer Ferris, Nehemiah Brown,	0	0	0	0	0	25
		34	16	37	13	6	2709

NOTE.—The Ministers' names are in SMALL CAPITALS. Those marked thus * were not present. The Churches marked thus † sent neither letters nor messengers, and their numbers remain as last year. A dash ——— denotes no settled minister.

MINUTES

OF THE

PHILADELPHIA BAPTIST ASSOCIATION,

HELD IN PHILADELPHIA, OCTOBER 12TH, 13TH, AND 14TH,

1774.

October 12th.—At 3 o'clock, P. M., the Association was opened with a suitable discourse, from Jer. xxiii. 28, "The prophet that hath a dream, let him tell a dream; and he that hath my word, let him speak my word faithfully: what is the chaff to the wheat? saith the Lord;" by our beloved Brother Isaac Stelle.

2. After Divine service, Brother Benjamin Miller was chosen moderator, and Brother William Vanhorn, clerk. Letters from thirty-nine churches were read.

3. October 13th.—President Manning, of Rhode Island, Benjamin Coles, of Connecticut, and John Corbley, of Virginia, ministering brethren, being present, their company and assistance were desired.

4. A letter and minutes from the Baptist Association, held at Medfield, in the Massachusetts Bay, September 13th and 14th, 1774, were read, which informs us, that they had a very comfortable interview; that 146 had joined their churches by baptism, and that three churches more were received, which increases their number to twenty-seven. Our much esteemed brother in the ministry, Isaac Backus, was their messenger to us.

5. A letter and minutes from the Ketockton Association, held at Brenton, Virginia, August 17th–19th, 1774, were read, by which it appears that the brethren there are walking in truth, and increasing in number daily; 217 have been added by baptism, and three churches were received. Their messengers to us were our esteemed brethren, David Thomas and Daniel Fristoe.

6. A letter and minutes from the Association held at Charleston, in South Carolina, were read. The plan adopted by them respecting Rhode Island College, recommended to us.

Agreed, To recommend the same to the churches we stand respectively related unto; and that our Brethren John Gano and William Rogers receive the monies so raised, and remit the same to Colonel Job Bennet, treasurer.

7. A letter from the Baptist church, at King's street, in Fair-

field, Connecticut, constituted November 3d, 1773, was read, requesting to join this Association; which was granted, after satisfaction given of their faith and practice, and their messenger, William Brundage, received.

8. Letters from well disposed people in different places, requesting supplies, were read, viz: Mudderkill Forrest, in Kent county, Carnarven, in Berks, and Tolbert, in Northumberland, in the province of Pennsylvania; also, from Baltimore Town, in Maryland.

9. A Letter from our Brother James Sutton, setting forth the loss of his papers and effects by fire, was read:

Agreed, That this minute certify his regular standing in the ministry; and, in lieu of the interest of the Association fund, which he requested, agreed, rather to recommend to the churches to contribute to his necessities.

10. After deliberations on some queries from the church at the Welsh Tract, it was finally agreed, that our Brethren Abel Morgan, Isaac Backus, Isaac Stelle, and Samuel Jones, form a minute in answer to them, which being done and approved, is here inserted:

"Whereas, a book was published, entitled, 'The Customs of the Primitive Churches,' which the author proposed should be altered, amended, and corrected, by his ministering brethren, and then re-printed for the use of the churches, which was never done; and whereas, we have reason to think, that it is understood by many abroad to have been adopted by us in its present form, as our custom and mode of church discipline and practice; it is therefore thought meet, that we should thus publicly testify to the contrary, as it is not, nor ever has been adopted by us, or by any of the churches belonging to the Assocation."

11. The Association considering that the catechising or instructing youth in the principles of the Christian religion, though so plain and important a duty, is yet too generally neglected, have thought it expedient to recommend to the churches, seriously to consider and promote the same.

12. The general letter formed by Brother Samuel Jones, being read and considered, was approved.

13. The case of our brethren suffering under ecclesiastical oppressions in New England, being taken into consideration, it was agreed to recommend to our churches to contribute to their necessities, agreeable to the pattern of the primitive churches, who contributed to the relief of the distressed brethren in Judea. And that the money raised for them be remitted to Mr. Backus, to be by him, in conjunction with the committee of advice in said colony, distributed to the brethren.

14. The case of our brethren above considered, induced us to appoint a committee of grievances, who may from time to time receive accounts of the sufferings and difficulties of our friends and brethren in the neighboring colonies; and meet as often as shall appear needful in the city of Philadelphia, to consult upon and prosecute such

measures for their relief, as they shall judge most expedient; and may correspond with the Baptist committee in the Massachusetts Bay, or elsewhere. Accordingly, the following gentlemen were appointed, viz.,

Robert Strettle Jones, Esq., Mr. Samuel Davis, Mr. Stephen Shewel, Mr. Thomas Shields, Mr. George Wescott, Alexander Edwards, Esq., Benjamin Bartholemew, Esq., Rev. William Rogers, A. M., John Evans, Esq., John Mayhew, Esq., Edward Keasby, Esq., Rev. Samuel Jones, A. M., Rev. Morgan Edwards, A. M., Rev. William Vanhorn, A. M., Mr. Abraham Beakly, Abel Evans, Esq., Samuel Miles, Esq., Mr. James Morgan, and Mr. John Jarman.

Any five of them to be a quorum.

15. Agreeable to a proposal made in the last Association, held at New York, Brother William Rogers was requested to copy off, into the Association book, all the letters from all the Associations corresponding, or to correspond, with this; and the letters from this Association to them, together with the letters from this Association to particular persons.

16. Voted, That £18, arising from Mrs. Hubb's donation, be given to Mr. Burgess Alison, he to give the usual obligations to the trustees.

17. Voted, That Brother Gano be paid by the treasurer the interest due on the Association fund, towards defraying his expenses in travelling the last year: accordingly he received £12.

18. Recommended to our churches to continue four days of fasting and prayer in the year ensuing, viz., the Friday before the last Lord's day in November, February, May, and August, to humble ourselves before Almighty God, implore his blessing on the means of his grace, and the interposition of Divine Providence in this day of public calamity.

19. The money raised for increasing the fund of Rhode Island College, is as follows:

The church at New York raised above what was proposed by the plan adopted.

	£	s.	d.		£	s.	d.
Church of Cohansie,	0	15	0	Hugh Glassford,	0	7	0
Church at Salem,	0	4	6	Andrew Bray,	0	5	0

The four last sums above mentioned were received by Brother William Rogers.

20. The collections for the Association fund are as follows:

	£	s.	d.		£	s.	d.
Philadelphia,	3	0	0	New Mills,	0	12	6
New York,	2	0	0	Newtown,	0	10	0
Southampton,	1	0	0	Hugh Glassford,	0	5	0

The above sum of £7 7s. 6d. was paid to George Wescott, treasurer.

21. Supplies were granted to the following destitute places: Hope-

well, Oyster Bay, New Mills, Lyon's Farms, Vincent, King Street, Mudderkill, Peak's Kiln, Baltimore town.

Brother David Sutton, William Worth, and Elkana Holmes are to visit the inhabitants of Tolbert township, at times to be fixed upon by themselves.

22. Brother Peter Peterson Vanhorne was requested to write a letter to the Associations of Warren, Rhode Island, Ketockton and Rappidanne, in Virginia; also, to that of Sandy Creek, and Quekuky, in North Carolina, and to the Congaree and Charleston Association, in South Carolina.

23. Brother John Gano and Brother William Rogers were appointed messengers to the Warren and Rhode Island Associations, and Brother Isaac Stelle and William Worth to the Ketockton Associations, in Virginia.

24. A motion being made and the question put:—Whether this Association divide, and another be held annually at New York?

After deliberation, it was voted, not to divide.

25. The Association meeting twice in the year, not answering so well as was expected;

Agreed, To meet annually; and that it be held next year at Philadelphia.

26. Voted, That the Association begin on Tuesday after the second Lord's day in October, at three o'clock, P. M.; and that Brother William Rogers preach the introductory sermon; or, in case of failure, Brother William Vanhorne.

27. Agreed, That Brother Abel Morgan prepare a general letter against the next Association.

N. B. The printing of the memorial, drawn up by the committee of grievances, and read before the Association, is, for special reasons, deferred.

CIRCULAR LETTER.
BY REV. SAMUEL JONES.

The Association of elders and brethren of the several Baptist churches in Pennsylvania and the colonies adjacent, held at Philadelphia, October 12th, 13th, and 14th, 1774.

Send our Christian salutation.

Beloved brethren,—Agreeable to the plan adopted at our last Association, for the general letter to the churches, we come now to address you on the next article contained in our Confession of faith, which treats of the being and perfections of God, and includes the doctrine of the Trinity.

This is an important article; a foundation, a corner stone in the Christian faith. Remove this, and the whole superstructure will fall. Material then it is that we clearly conceive of, firmly believe, and without wavering, hold the same agreeable to the form of sound words, wherein it is held forth in divine revelation.

First. That there is an only living and true God, the supreme and eternal Jehovah, is manifest.

1. From the reason of things. Since there cannot be an effect without cause, there must be a first cause, self existent and independent.

2. From the works of creation, all marvellous and astonishing from the least to the greatest. As also,

3. From those of Providence, in sustaining and well ordering the whole universe, through all the successive periods of time. And especially,

4. From the consciousness of a Supreme Being impressed on every rational soul. Above all,

5. From the holy Scriptures. Deut. vi. 4; xxiii. 39; iv. 35; Psalm lxxxvi. 10; Isa. xlv. 5.

Secondly. The perfections of God may be easily deduced from the same sources, especially his wisdom, power, and goodness infinite. And though his mercy, justice, truth, and holiness be not so clear from the works of creation and providence, yet there is a strong consciousness of these, as well as of his omniscience, omnipresence, &c., while they are also abundantly manifested by his word and Spirit.

Thirdly. Now, in this Divine and Infinite Being, there are three subsistences, the Father, the Son, and the Holy Ghost. The Father, neither begotten nor proceeding; the Son, or Word, eternally begotten of the Father, John i. 14, 18; iii. 16; 1 John iv. 9; and the Holy Ghost proceeding from the Father and the Son, John v. 26, constituting, in the undivided essence of the Godhead, a trinity of persons, each of them possessed of all divine perfections, and every way co-equal, and these three are one, the One God. 1 John v. 7.

That there are three appears through all the sacred writings, in reference to the works of creation, providence and grace, 1 Pet. i. 2; in whose name baptism is administered, Matt. xxviii. 19; and to whom divine worship and adoration are addressed, 2 Cor. xiii. 14; and that these Three are One, or that there is One, and but one God, is no less clear as above.

Now, that we may further explain this doctrine, and remove some difficulties attending it, so far as the mysteriousness of the subject will admit, we shall endeavor to resolve the following queries.

Question 1. How can Three be One, and One Three?

Answer. Three are not said to be One, and One Three, in the same respect strictly. We do not say that there are Three persons in One person, nor that there are Three Gods in One God; but three persons or subsistences in the undivided essence of the One God.

Question 2. Why are these three subsistences called persons?

Answer 1. Because they are distinguished by personal relative properties; the Father begetting, the Son begotten, and the Holy Ghost proceeding.

2. They are styled I, Thou, and He. They speak, are spoken to, and spoken of.

3. They have each of them understanding and will. And besides,

4. They have personal characters, as Creator, Redeemer, Judge, Comforter, Intercessor, &c., and are covenanted with, sent, &c. Ps. cx. 1, 3, 6, 7; John viii. 16; xiv. 16, 17, 26.

In one word they have attributed to them and spoken of them every thing essential to and descriptive of personality.

Question 3. In what respect is Christ the only begotten Son of God?

Answer 1. Not with respect to his human nature; for he was the only begotten Son of God before. In that case the Spirit would have been the Father. And in his human nature he was manifested to be what he was before, namely, the only begotten of the Father.

2. Nor with respect to his resurrection; for he was so before he rose by his own power. And by his resurrection from the dead, he was manifested to be what he was before. Rom. i. 4.

3. Nor yet with respect to his mediatorial office; for it is his sonship that adds lustre to this office, Heb. iv. 14, as well as efficacy. 1 John i. 7. Neither is there any thing in that office that should give rise to the title Son, only Son, only begotten. Further, this did not make the Son a son, but a priest. Heb. i. 8; vii. 28. And his priesthood and sonship are distinctly spoken of, Acts viii. 37; ix. 20; while also in the capacity of a Mediator he was a servant.

4. It remains, then, that he was the only begotten Son of God by eternal generation, inconceivable and mysterious. He was his Son, John v. 18; 1 John v. 5; his own Son, Rom. viii. 3, 32; his only begotten Son, John i. 14, 18; iii. 16; 1 John iv. 9; was with him in the beginning, John i. 1; before his works of old, even from everlasting, Mic. v. 2; Prov. viii. 22, 23.

Question 4. If he was the Son of God by generation as to his divine nature, how could he be co-equal and co-eternal with the Father?

Answer. When we conceive of the Father and the Son, there is a priority in the order of nature, but not in the order of time. As God's eternal decrees, the mind and thought, the sun and light; though these be prior and successive among themselves in the order of nature, yet not in point of time. The instant the sun existed, light did exist also, proceeding from it, or, as it were, generated by it. So the instant there is a Father, there must be a Son; and as the Father exists a Father from eternity, so does the Son a Son.

Thus, dearly beloved, we have endeavored to set before you this essential article of our faith in as clear a manner as the narrowness of our limits, and the mysteriousness of the subject, would permit. But let no one presume to think that he can, by searching, find out the Almighty to perfection, nor vainly inquire where the Lord has not revealed. Let us rather be humbly thankful, that the Divine Majesty has condescended to make such wondrous discoveries of his being and perfections.

Let us set the Triune God before us in all our ways and enjoyments, and rejoice in him, who is worthy of our highest confidence and purest affection, worthy of all divine worship and adoration. Finally, brethren, let us be established in the present truth, nor suffer any to remove us from the firm basis of divine revelation. Now to the King eternal, immortal, invisible, the only wise God, Father, Son, and Holy Spirit, be all honor, glory, divine worship, praise, power and dominion, both now and evermore. Amen.

BENJAMIN MILLER, Moderator.
WILLIAM VANHORN, Clerk.

THE MINISTERS AND MESSENGERS AT THE ASSOCIATION, AND STATE OF THE CHURCHES DURING THE YEAR.

CHURCHES.	MINISTERS AND MESSENGERS.	Baptized.	Added by Letter.	Restored.	Dead.	Dismis'd.	Excom.	Members.
Pennepek,	Samuel Jones, Alexander Edwards, Peter Smith,	0	0	0	0	0	0	65
Middletown,	Abel Morgan, James Mott, William Bown,	1	0	0	1	0	0	141
Piscataqua,	Isaac Stelle,	0	0	0	0	0	0	72
Cohansie,	Robert Kelsay, Isaac Mulford,	4	0	0	1	0	0	84
Welsh Tract,	John Sutton, John Bowen, Hugh Glassford,	1	0	0	5	1	0	124
Great Valley,	John Davis,* Samuel Jones, Griffith Jones, John Davies,	0	0	0	1	0	1	70
Cape May,	Peter P. Vanhorn,	0	0	0	2	0	0	57
Hopewell,	Nathaniel Stout, William Parks,	0	0	0	1	3	4	155
Brandywine,	John Baldwin,	1	0	0	0	1	0	29
Montgomery,	John Thomas,	4	0	0	0	2	0	104
Kingwood,	David Sutton, Elkana Holmes, Andrew Bray,	7	0	0	0	1	0	86
Southampton,	William Vanhorn, John Blackwell, Arthur Watts,	1	0	0	0	0	1	64
Philadelphia,	William Rogers, Morgan Edwards, Samuel Davies, Joshua Moore, John Brown, Ezekiel Letts, George Bright,	7	1	0	4	0	0	173
Cranberry,	———— ————	1	2	0	0	0	0	27
Scotch Plains,	Benjamin Miller,	4	0	0	5	0	0	122

MINUTES OF THE PHILADELPHIA ASSOCIATION. 147

CHURCHES.	MINISTERS AND MESSENGERS.	Baptized.	Added by Letter.	Restored.	Dead.	Dismis'd.	Excom.	Members.
Oyster Bay,	—— ——	4	0	0	0	0	0	26
Morristown,	Reune Runyon, John Brookfield,	10	0	0	0	0	0	64
Knowlton,†	—— ——	0	0	0	0	0	0	41
Baltimore, (now Harford)	John Davies,*	6	4	0	3	6	3	144
New Britain,	Joshua Jones,	1	0	0	0	3	1	53
Salem,	Abel Griffiths, Abner Long,	1	2	0	3	0	0	23
Newtown,	Nicholas Cox, Hezekiah Smith, jr.,	9	1	0	0	0	1	78
Bateman's Precincts,	Samuel Waldo,*	0	0	0	0	0	1	107
Dividing Creek,	Samuel Heaton, Jonadab Shepherd,	3	0	0	0	0	0	34
1. New York,	John Gano, Abraham Cannon,	2	0	0	0	0	0	139
New Mills,	Samuel Gaskill,	2	0	0	0	6	0	51
Kolonoway,	Joseph Powell,*	16	2	0	0	0	0	57
Coram,	Noah Hammond,	3	0	0		0	0	33
Upper Freehold,	David Jones,* Thomas Farr, Peter Sexton, Burgess Alison,	1	1	0	0	0	0	50
Mount Bethel,	Abner Sutton,	0	0	0	0	6	0	22
Goshen,	James Benedict,*	10	8	0	0	0	0	113
Lyon's Farms,	—— ——	0	0	0	0	0	0	22
Oblong,	Simon Dawkin,*	17	0	0	0	13	0	76
Philip's Patent,	John Lawrence,*	6	0	0	0	0	0	98
Pittsgrove,	William Worth, Joseph Champness,	0	0	0	0	0	0	40
Manahawkin, (now Stafford)	Henry Crosly,	1	4	1	1	0		15
Vincent,	William Wells, David Phillips,	0	0	0	0	0	0	57
Tuckahoe,	William Lock,	0	0	0		1	0	24
Northern Liberty,†	—— ——	0	0	0	0	0	0	15
2. New York,†	John Dodge,*	0	0	0	0	0	0	14
Stamford,	—— ——	6	1	0	0	0	0	32
King Street,	William Brundage,	0	0	0	0	0	0	13
		129	26	1	27	43	15	2804

Note.—The ministers' names are in SMALL CAPITALS. Those marked thus * were not present. The churches marked thus † sent neither letters nor messengers, and their numbers remain as last year. A dash —— denotes no settled minister.

MINUTES

OF THE

PHILADELPHIA BAPTIST ASSOCIATION,

HELD AT PHILADELPHIA, OCTOBER, 10TH, 11TH, AND 12TH,

1775.

Tuesday, October 10.—At three o'clock, P. M., the Association was opened with a suitable discourse, from Mark xvi. 15, "And he said unto them, Go ye into all the world, and preach the gospel to every creature," by our brother, Rev. William Rogers.

2. After sermon, Brother John Gano was chosen moderator, and Brother William Rogers, clerk. Letters from thirty-two churches were read.

3. The Rev. Messrs. James Manning, Morgan Edwards, and Peter Peterson Vanhorne being present, their company and assistance were desired.

4. Wednesday, October 11.—A letter from Warren Association was read, which informed us, that during the last year, many were added to their several churches by baptism, but the number is not specified—hope to receive their minutes if printed. Their messenger to us, was the Rev. William Williams.

5. A letter from Quekuky Association, in North Carolina, was read; it appears that it was their last year's letter, but did not come to hand until several weeks after our Association was held. When they wrote they were in a very comfortable state; their increase two hundred and seventy; two churches constituted, and two ministers were ordained; the number of members then appertaining to their thirteen churches was fourteen hundred and fifty-eight.

6. A letter and minutes from Charleston Association, in South Carolina, were read: we are pleased to hear of their happy interview together. Brother Elhanan Winchester, their messenger to us, not present. Our other sister Associations did not write to us—should be glad to hear from them all at our next annual meeting.

7. In consequence of two letters received from the church at Coram; the first lamenting their loss of a worthy pastor, Rev. Noah Hammond, requested our assistance and prayers: the second was expressive of their great satisfaction in Brother Ebenezer Ward's visits, and edification under his ministry, which concludes by desiring this Association to ordain him as an itinerant.

Agreed, That this Association claim no such right, and, therefore, resolved to encourage Mr. Ward to assist said church in all that he consistently can, until either the church, whereof he is a member, chooses to have him ordained, or he first becoming a member at Coram, and they should continue in the same mind, which, if they do, and write for assistance, we make no doubt our brethren will duly attend to it.

8. Recommended to our churches to continue the four quarterly days of fasting and prayer, as the troubles of the nation increase, and too much deadness among Christians still prevalent. The days to be observed are the Thursday before the last Lord's days in November, February, May, and August.

9. The Rev. Samuel Stillman was desired to draw up a letter for the several Associations corresponding with this.

10. The collections are as follow:

FOR THE ASSOCIATION FUND.				FOR THE COLLEGE.			
Philadelphia church,	£2	0	0	Pennepek church,	£0	17	6
New York, "		1	2	6	Delivered to Mr. Rogers.	—	—	—
Pennepek, "		1	0	0				
Delivered to Mr. Westcott.	£4	2	6	FOR BROTHER JAMES SUTTON.			
				Southampton church,	£2	6	2
FOR OUR SUFFERING BRETHREN IN NEW ENGLAND.				Cohansie, "	2	0	0
				Philadelphia, "	3	12	0
Philadelphia church,	£8	14	6	Morristown, "	0	15	0
Cohansie, "	2	0	0	Newtown, "	0	7	6
Rev. David Sutton,	0	1	0	Mr. Joseph Chambloss,	0	4	0
Deliv'd to Mr. Stillman,	£10	15	6	Deliv'd to Mr. Jno. Sutton,	£9	4	8

11. Voted, That £18, arising from Mrs. Hubb's donation, be equally divided between Messrs. Enoch Morgan and Burgess Allison, they giving the usual obligations to the trustees.

12. The general letter to the churches, drawn up by the Rev. Abel Morgan, being read, was unanimously approved of, and the Rev. John Gano appointed to write one for next year.

13. The Rev. Abel Morgan was requested to copy off into the Association book, all the letters from the Associations corresponding, or to correspond with this; also the letters from this Association to them, together with the letters from this Association to particular persons.

14. Supplies granted to the following destitute places:—Upper Freehold, Oyster Bay, Lyon's Farms, New Mills, Cow Marsh, Baltimore town, Talbort township, and Peakskiln.

15. Requested, That the Rev. Messrs. John Gano and Samuel Jones be our messengers to Warren and Rhode Island Associations; to that of Ketockton, in Virginia, Rev. John Sutton; and to all the southern Associations, Rev. Messrs. Morgan Edwards and Peter Peterson Vanhorn.

16. Voted, That the next Association be held at New York, to begin on Tuesday after the second Lord's day in October, at three

o'clock, P. M., and that Rev. Samuel Stillman preach the introductory sermon; or, in case of failure, Rev. William Vanhorne.

CIRCULAR LETTER.
BY REV. ABEL MORGAN.

The Association of elders and brethren of the several Baptist churches in Pennsylvania, and the colonies adjacent, held at Philadelphia, October 10th, 11th, and 12th, 1775.

To the several churches we are in connection with, send our Christian salutation.

Beloved Brethren,—In the primitive times, when people were converted by the ministry of the gospel, and united together in church relation and fellowship, it was the practice of the Apostles to establish them in the truths which they had believed and professed, Acts xv. 41, for their edification and comfort, Acts ix. 31. We now, according to our measure, would endeavor to follow this worthy pattern, for the like excellent design. The subject, which next in order comes to be considered, is the doctrine of God's decree. Confession of faith, chap. III. Whereon we observe,

1. That God, the supreme, who is self-existent, and every way an independent sovereign, the creator of all things, hath an absolute right to dispose of all his creatures; and before his works of old, to appoint and determine all things to a certain end. This article of our belief, both scripture and reason do jointly and sufficiently confirm, Isa. xlvi. 10; Psalm xxxiii. 11; Prov. xix. 21.

2. The rule of his fore-appointment, of what shall come to pass in time, is the wise counsel of his most holy will and pleasure. Eph. i. 11.

3. In accomplishing his purpose, no violence is offered to the will of the creature, good, Psalm cx. 3; or bad, James i. 13, 14; nor the use of means taken away, Ezek. xxxvi. 37; neither is God, in anywise, the author of sin, though he decreed to permit it to be, Acts xiv. 16; Gen. xlv. 5; Acts ii. 23.

4. The special objects of God's decree are angels and men.

5. When all the human race, by the sin of the first man, were involved in guilt, Rom. v. 12, and fallen under condemnation, and all become the children of wrath; it would manifestly be doing them no injustice, if they were, to every individual, left in that state, and eternally punished for their sins: this would have been their proper desert, their just reward. But God, out of his mere free grace and love, without any moving cause in the parties chosen, hath predestinated some unto life, through a Mediator, Eph. i. 4; Rom. xi. 5, 6, (without any wrong done to others) together with all the means subservient to this end, viz., their redemption by the blood of Christ, and renovation by the Spirit of holiness, to the praise of his glorious grace; the other left to act in sin, to their final destruction, to the glory of divine justice, Rom. ix. 22, 23.

The bounds of a letter will not permit us to enter on the discussion of the several objections, and remove out of the way the many cavils, which are raised by men of different principles, in opposition to this scripture doctrine; that has been repeatedly well done heretofore by others; but only add a word, with a view to relieve and support those distressed souls, whoever and wherever they be, whilst they acknowledge this awful truth, but at the same time are greatly exercised about it; frequently raising objections against themselves, fearing they are not of the elect of God: and, should this be the case, they infer, that all their endeavors must be in vain, their acts of worship unacceptable. The consolations and promises of the gospel are proposed to them to little purpose. Their souls refuse to be comforted; their hope flags, their expectation fails; they are greatly disheartened; yea, the very duties of religion become to them difficult, and oftentimes burthensome; briefly, they are ready to halt, and to sink down in the gulf of despair, believing the decree of God to be immutable. So that this solemn truth, instead of administering joy to their souls, and exciting in them adoration and praise to God, becomes to them an occasion of terror, discouragement, and great depression of spirit. The topics, whence they generally derive these gloomy apprehensions are such as follow, viz., the gross darkness of mind under which they are shut up; no signs of election; extreme ignorance of God and of Christ; find no returns of prayer; so full of sin; manifold afflictions; cannot act faith; backslidings, unprofitableness, heart rising against God, and such like.

To remove these difficulties: 1. Let the parties consider that there may be very great and just reasons for the ground of these complaints, without calling in question their election.

2. Let them seriously observe the frame and temper of their soul under all or any of these defects, whether a sense of their case excites in them more humiliation and sorrow for sin, Psalm xxxviii. 17, 18; and more vehement cries and ardent wishes for seasonable help, Ps. xxxviii. 4, 5, 21, 22. If so, the evidence is in their favor.

3. Let such know and learn, that the way for their relief is not by laboring to pry into the secret purpose of God, or in their thoughts to dwell upon it, to their own discouragement, but abide by, and cleave to, his revealed will, which directs all indigent ones to Christ the Mediator for supply, and to the use of those means prescribed for the satisfaction and peace of laboring souls: "Make your calling sure." 2 Pet. i. 10. In so doing shall the fearful be able to look back, and know their election before time, and forward, and view their salvation to come, when time shall be no more. This glorious truth is not designed to deter troubled souls from coming to Jesus Christ.

4. It directly tends to administer support to the laboring soul, when we find those very springs of complaints, doubts, and fears, from which they argue to their disadvantage, are no other than what the Scripture declares to have been the case with the very elect of God; for instance, these complain of darkness, so did they, "Why hidest thou thyself?" Psalm x. 1. Job emphatically, xxiii. 8, 9. See Isa. l. 10. Do these sorrowful ones lack tokens of their election? But hath not God in special mercy hedged up their way, to keep them from sin, and made it bitter to their souls? Hos. ii. 6, 7; Lam. iii. 19, 20. Do they not find thirstings after Christ? Psalm xlii. 1–3. Do they

not groan earnestly, and are burdened, because of their depravity, &c.? 2 Cor. v. 2. These are encouraging tokens, the very characters of the elect; who also in their day bewailed their ignorance of God. Prov. xxx. 2, 3. The exhortation "to grow in the knowledge of Christ," intimates their deficiency therein. How pathetically did they expostulate with God about his deferring to answer their prayers. "Will the Lord cast off forever? Hath God forgotten to be gracious?" Psalm lxxvii. 7–3. "O Lord, how long shall I cry, and thou wilt not hear?" Hab. i. 2. How feelingly did they acknowledge themselves full of sin; "Mine iniquities are gone over my head." Psal. xxxviii. 3–8. "Wretched man that I am." Rom. vii. 18, 24. Do these fear because they cannot put forth acts of faith? Consider the case of the godly; "I am shut up, and I cannot come forth." Psalm lxxxviii. 8. Christ would have men to know their own insufficiency, John xv. 5; vi. 44; who himself is the author and finisher of faith. Hence, Song i. 4, "draw me." Sore afflictions are the very portion of the dear chosen ones of God in the world. Psalm lxxiii. 10, 14; xxxiv. 19; 1 Cor. xi. 32; Heb. xii. 6–8. Let these languishing souls hear the gracious word of promise to backsliders, Hos. xiv. 4. Christ teaches all the elect to esteem themselves unprofitable. Luke xvii. 10. Do these perplexed ones faint, because they find in themselves heart-risings against God? This indeed is very alarming and dreadful in its consequences; but there is on record an instance of this sad case, in one that was undoubtedly a chosen vessel, an elect of God. Jonah iv. 3, 4, 9, whose heart not only rose up against God, but also in his reply vindicated himself therein. "I do well to be angry." 'Tis probable this by far is an higher degree than any of these dejected ones are got to. Hence we observe, that not one distressed soul hath ground to argue against himself from any of the above-mentioned cases, or the like, that he is passed by, and, without hope, left to perish in his sins. None can conclude his preterition but from final impenitence, and the sin against the Holy Ghost. From the former he cannot, because he is yet in life; nor from the latter, because final impenitence is an inseparable ingredient of that sin.

5. Guard against every device of Satan, who aims to prevent people profiting by the gospel of Jesus Christ. 1 Pet. v. 8.

6. Inasmuch as we are authorized to encourage the weak, the feeble, and fearful to be strong. Isa. xxxv. 3, 4, We therefore exhort and charge all those into whose hands this may come, who are, and have been, sorely afflicted on the aforesaid account, that they would press forward in the ways of godliness, seek the Lord Jesus unfeignedly, pray without ceasing, and faint not, Luke xviii. 1, 7, endeavor for satisfactory experience of grace in their own souls; that hereafter they may rejoice in this, and every other truth of God.

Lastly, We would earnestly caution all persons, on the other hand, who confidently conclude themselves to be of the elect of God, to beware at all times of living a dissolute, vain, irreligious life, or giving themselves liberty to continue in sin, because election is unalterable; pleading or thinking they shall be saved, let them live and act as they will (this truth hath been thus horribly abused.) Such corrupt principles, wicked practices, and black characters, are inconsistent with the pure doctrines of the gospel. Remember that holiness becometh the house and people of the Lord forever, and is indispensably enjoined on every one that nameth the name of Christ. 2 Tim. ii. 19 : 2 Thess. ii. 13 : 1 Pet. i. 14, 16.

Now unto him that is able to keep you from falling, and to present you faultless before the presence of his glory, with exceeding joy, to the only wise God our Saviour, be glory and majesty, dominion and power, both now and ever. Amen.

JOHN GANO, Moderator.
WIILLAM ROGERS, Clerk.

THE MINISTERS AND MESSENGERS AT THE ASSOCIATION, AND STATE OF THE CHURCHES DURING THE YEAR.

CHURCHES.	MINISTERS AMD MESSENGERS.	Baptized.	Added by Letter.	Restored.	Dismis'd.	Excom.	Dead.	Members.
Pennepek,	Samuel Jones, A M., Alexander Edwards, Peter Smith,	5	0	0	0	0	1	69
Middletown,	Abel Morgan, A. M., James Mott,	2	0	0	0	0	4	139
Piscataqua,	Isaac Stelle,	3	0	0	0	0	0	75
Cohansie,	Robert Kelsay, Providence Ludlam, David Bowen,	1	0	0	0	0	5	80
Welsh Tract,	John Sutton, Enoch Morgan,	2	0	0	4	0	2	120
Great Valley,	David Jones, A. M., Thomas Jones, Griffith Jones,	1	0	0	0	0	1	70
Cape May,	—— ——	0	0	0	0	1	4	52
Hopewell,	Benjamin Coles, John Blackwell, Zebulon Stout, jr.,	0	2	0	1	0	1	155
Brandywine,	Abel Griffiths,* Thomas Davis,	0	0	0	0	0	0	29
Montgomery,	John Thomas, Isaac James,	2	0	0	0	0	3	103
Kingwood,	David Sutton, Elkana Holmes,	2	0	0	0	2	2	84
Southampton,	William Vanhorn, A. M., John Gilbert, Joseph Hart,	0	0	0	0	0	1	63
Philadelphia,	Samuel Stillman, A. M., William Rogers, A. M., Joshua Moore, George Bright, Benjamin Thaw,	2	0	0	0	0	1	174
Cranberry,†	—— ——	0	0	0	0	0	0	27

CHURCHES.	MINISTERS AND MESSENGERS.	Baptized.	Added by Letter.	Restored.	Dismis'd.	Excom.	Dead.	Members.
Scotch Plains,	BENJAMIN MILLER,*	12	0	0	0	0	5	129
Oyster Bay,	Elijah Wheeler,	2	0	0	0	0	1	27
Morristown,	REUNE RUNYON, Isaac Brookfield,	12	4	0	0	0	0	80
Knowlton,	—— ——	5	0	0	0	0	0	14
Harford, (Maryland)	JOHN DAVIS,* Abraham Britton,	5	1	0	6	0	2	142
New Britain,	JOSHUA JONES,	0	0	0	0	0	3	50
Salem,†	—— ——	3	0	0	0	0	0	26
Newtown,	NICHOLAS COX, Hezekiah Smith,	4	0	0	1	1	1	79
Bateman's Precincts,	SAMUEL WALDO,*	47	0	0	0	0	3	152
Dividing Creek,	SAMUEL HEATON,	0	0	0	0	0	2	32
1. New York,	JOHN GANO, James Stiles,	1	2	0	0	1	2	139
New Mills,	Samuel Gaskill, Jacob Woolston,	4	0	0	0	0	2	53
Kolonoway,	JOSEPH POWELL,*	3	0	0	0	0	0	60
Coram,	—— ——	0	0	0	0	0	0	34
Upper Freehold,	Thomas Farr, Thomas Cox, jr., Jonathan Holmes, Edward Taylor,	1	0	0	1	0	0	50
Mount Bethel,†	—— ——	0	0	0	0	0	0	22
Goshen,†	JAMES BENEDICT,*	0	0	0	0	0	0	113
Lyon's Farms,	—— ——	0	0	0	0	0	0	22
Oblong,	SIMON DAWKIN,*	13	5	0	0	2	0	92
Philip's Patent,†	JOHN LAWRENCE,* Ebenezer Ward,	0	0	0	0	0	0	98
Pittsgrove,	WILLIAM WORTH, Cornelius Austin,	0	0	0	0	0	0	40
Manahawkin,†	HENRY CROSLY,*	0	0	0	0	0	0	15
Vincent,†	—— ——	0	0	0	0	0	0	57
Tuckahoe,	WILLIAM LOCK,*	0	0	0	0	0	0	24
Northern Liberty,†	—— ——	0	0	0	0	0	0	15
2. New York,†	JOHN DODGE,*	0	0	0	0	0	0	14
Stamford,	—— ——	1	0	0	0	0	2	31
King Street,†	—— ——	0	0	0	0	0	0	13
		133	14	1	13	7	48	2863

NOTE.—The ministers' names are in SMALL CAPITALS. Those marked thus * were not present. The churches marked thus † sent neither letters nor messengers, and their numbers remain as last year. A dash ——— denotes no settled minister. Increase this year, 59.

MINUTES

OF THE

PHILADELPHIA BAPTIST ASSOCIATION,

HELD AT THE SCOTCH PLAINS, IN THE STATE OF NEW JERSEY,
OCTOBER 15TH AND 16TH,

1776.

October 15—At three o'clock, P. M., the Association was opened with a discourse from Col. i. 28: "Whom we preach, warning every man, and teaching every man in all wisdom, that we may present every man perfect in Christ Jesus," by our brother, William Vanhorne.

2. After divine service, Brother Isaac Stelle was chosen moderator, and Brother William Vanhorne, clerk.

3. Proceeded to read the letters from the churches.

Adjourned to nine o'clock to-morrow morning.

October 16—Association met, pursuant to adjournment.

4. A letter was read from the Association held at the High Hills of Santee, dated May 16th, 1773.

5. This Association, taking into consideration the awful impending calamities of these times, and deeply impressed with a sense of our duty to humble ourselves before God, by acknowledging our manifold sins, and imploring his pardon and interposition in favor of our distressed country; and also to beseech him to grant, that such blessings may accompany the means of his grace that a revival of pure and undefiled religion may universally prevail;

Resolved, That it be and it is hereby recommended to our churches, to observe four days of humiliation in the year ensuing, by prayer, abstinence from food, and labor, and recreations, lawful on other days. The days proposed for humiliation are the Friday before the last Lord's day in November, February, May, and August.

6. Application being made to the Association for the benefit of Mrs. Hubb's donation by Messrs. Enoch Morgan, Burgess Alison, and James Darrah;

Resolved, That it be equally divided between the latter, they giving the usual security.

7. Agreed, That Brother Samuel Jones be requested to write the circular letter for next year.

8. On motion, Resolved, That Brother Abel Morgan be desired

to compose a letter on the subject of humiliation, fasting, and prayer, against the next Association.

9. Brother John Sutton being requested to bring in a draught of a letter to the Associations corresponding with us; and having brought in the same, and it being read, was approved.

10. Agreed, That Brother Ward be our messenger to Warren Association.

11. Brother James Benedict was requested to preach the Association sermon next year; and, in case of failure, Brother John Sutton was desired to be prepared.

12. Voted, That the Association meet next year in Philadelphia, on the Tuesday after the second Lord's day in October, at three o'clock, P. M.

Supplies granted to the following destitute places:—New Mills, Upper Freehold, Mount Bethel, Lyon's Farms, and Cow Marsh.

13. The circular letter appointed to be drawn up the last year for this Association not coming to hand, Brother Robert Kelsay was desired to prepare one to the churches; and having brought in the same, it was read, approved, and is as follows:

CIRCULAR LETTER.
BY REV. ROBERT KELSAY.

The elders and messengers of the several churches met at Scotch Plains, New Jersey.

Send our Christian salutation.

Beloved Brethren,—Through the sparing mercies of God, we have been permitted to see the revolution of another year, and to meet together, although not at the place appointed by our last Association. Nevertheless, we have abundant cause to admire the goodness of God, that we have a being, and are not driven fron our habitations as many of our brethren have been. Dark and gloomy are the clouds which hang over us; therefore, brethren, since the Lord seems to be contending with our guilty land, both by sword and epidemical diseases, his judgments being so evidently amongst us, there is a loud call to the inhabitants in general, and especially to his professing people, to learn lessons of righteousness. Suffer us, therefore, your friends, brethren and ministers, to recommend these few things in love to your serious consideration.

First. We exhort you in the words of our Lord, to watch against a drowsy disposition, and remissness in fulfilling the solemn obligations incumbent upon us, to the glory of him that called us out of darkness into his marvellous light.

Secondly. Take special heed to maintain peace amongst yourselves, in these days of confusion. And, let every one be honestly engaged to fill up their proper stations as creatures bound to eternity, not knowing how long we may enjoy those privileges which we have abused. Let it never be said of one professing to be born from above, that such a one is careless in prayer; reading the scriptures;

attending worship and maintaining discipline, seeing we must all be accountable to God for our stewardship at last.

Thus, brethren, in a few words, we commend you to God and the word of his grace. Subscribing ourselves yours in gospel relations.

Isaac Stelle, Moderator.
William Van Horne, Clerk.

THE MINISTERS AND MESSENGERS AT THE ASSOCIATION, AND STATE OF THE CHURCHES DURING THE YEAR.

CHURCHES.	MINISTERS AND MESSENGERS.	Baptized.	Added by Letter.	Dismis'd.	Dead.	Excom.	Members.
Pennepek,	Samuel Jones,* Peter Smith,	4	3	2	1	0	73
Middletown,	Abel Morgan,* James Mott,	5	0	0	3	0	141
Piscataqua,	Isaac Stelle, Moses Martin, Randolph Drake,	2	0	0	2	0	75
Cohansie,	Robert Kelsay, Philip Shepherd, David Elwell,	0	0	1	3	0	76
Welsh Tract,	John Sutton,	2	0	0	2	0	120
Great Valley,	John Davies,*	0	0	0	2	0	68
Cape May,†	David Smith,*	0	0	0	0	0	52
Hopewell,	Benjamin Coles, Nathaniel Stout, James Darrah,	101	0	1	7	1	247
Brandywine,	Abel Griffiths,*	0	0	0	0	0	29
Montgomery,	John Thomas,	0	0	0	2	0	101
Kingwood,	David Sutton, Andrew Bray,	1	2	5	0	0	82
Southampton,	William Vanhorne, John Blackwell,*	0	0	0	2	0	61
Philadelphia,	Joshua Moore, Thomas Fleeson, George Bright,	3	0	3	1	1	172
Cranberry,†		0	0	0	0	0	27
Scotch Plains,	Benjamin Miller,* John Stites, Recompence Stanbury,	1	0	2	2	0	126
Oyster Bay,†		0	0	0	0	0	27
Morristown,	Reune Runyan. John Brookfield,	4	2	2	3	0	81
Knowlton,	John Honeywell,	11	3	0	0	1	27
Harford,	John Davies,*	2	0	0	2	0	142
New Britain, †	Joshua John,*	0	0	0	0	0	50
Salem,†		0	0	0	0	0	26

CHURCHES.	MINISTERS AND MESSENGERS.	Baptized.	Received by Letter.	Dismiss'd.	Dead.	Excom.	Members.
Newtown,	{ NICHOLAS COX, Hezekiah Smith, sr.,	2	0	0	1	0	80
Bateman's Precincts,	SAMUEL WALDO,*	0	0	0	0	0	152
Dividing Creek,	SAMUEL HEATON,	0	0	0	0	0	32
1. New York,†	JOHN GANO,*	0	0	0	0	0	139
New Mills,	{ ——— ——— Samuel Gaskill,	0	0	0	0	0	53
Konoloway,†	JOSEPH POWEEL,*	0	0	0	0	0	60
Coram,†	——— ———	0	0	0	0	0	34
Upper Freehold,	{ Thomas Cox, jr., Edward Taylor,	13	0	1	1	0	61
Mount Bethel,	John Worth,	5	0	0	1	0	27
Goshen,	{ JAMES BENEDICT, William Howard,	27	1	0	0	0	141
Lyon's Farms,	{ Ichabod Grummon,	0	0	0	0	0	22
Oblong,†	SIMON DAWKIN,*	0	0	0	0	0	92
Philip's Patent,	{ JOHN LAWRENCE,* Ebenezer Ward,	7	4	0	1	0	108
Pittsgrove,†	William Worth,	0	0	0	0	0	40
Manahawkin,†	HENRY CROSSLY,*	0	0	0	0	0	15
Vincent,†	——— ———	0	0	0		0	57
Tuckahoe,†	WILLIAM LOCK,*	0	0	0	0	0	24
Northern Liberty,†	——— ———	0	0	0	0	0	15
2. New York,†	JOHN DODGE,*	0	0	0	0	0	14
Stamford,	——— ———	0	0	0	0	0	31
King Street,†	——— ———	0	0	0	0	0	13
		188	15	17	35	3	3013

NOTE.—The ministers' names are in SMALL CAPITALS. Those marked thus * not present. The churches marked thus † sent neither letters nor messengers, and their numbers remain as last year. A dash ——— denotes no settled minister.

1777.

[In consequence of the ravages of war, and Philadelphia being occupied by the British army, the Association held no meeting this year.—*Ed.*]

MINUTES

OF THE

PHILADELPHIA BAPTIST ASSOCIATION,

HELD AT HOPEWELL, NEW JERSEY, OCTOBER 13TH AND 14TH,

1778.

---

1. October 13—The Association being met at three o'clock, P. M., according to appointment, it was opened with a suitable discourse, from Matt. xxii. 4, by Brother Abel Morgan.

2. After service, proceeded to make choice of a moderator and clerk. To the former appointed Benjamin Miller, and to the latter Samuel Jones, and then adjourned to nine o'clock, next morning.

3. October 14th, nine o'clock.—After prayer, proceeded to read the letters from the churches.

4. The Association, deeply impressed with a sense of the calamities of the times, the prevalence of vice and profanity, and the declension of vital piety:
Resolved, To recommend to the churches to observe four days, the ensuing year, of humiliation, fasting, and prayer, and abstinence from labor and recreations; viz., the second Thursday in November, February, May, and August; and they entreat the same may be religiously observed in a solemn and devout manner.

5. Mr. George Wescott requesting to be released from being treasurer to the Association;
Agreed, That Samuel Jones render the thanks of the Association to Mr. Wescott for his past services, and be appointed to that trust in his stead, receive the money in said Wescott's hands, and put the same in the continental fund.

6. A motion being made for raising a fund, the interest of which to be appropriated to the particular and express purpose of preaching the gospel in destitute places, among the back settlements, at the discretion of the Association;
Agreed to recommend the same to the churches, and that the interest of whatever may be raised for that purpose, shall be strictly appropriated to that use only.

7. Brother John Blackwell appointed to write a letter to the Association in Virginia. The messengers, Brother Thomas Fleeson, and Brother John Pittman.

8. Brother Benjamin Cole appointed to write a letter to the Association in Rhode Island government. The messengers, Brother Ebenezer Ward, and Brother Elkanah Holmes.

9. The circular letter was read, and approved of.

10. Brother Samuel Jones appointed to write the circular letter for next year. The subject, Divine Providence.

11. The Association to meet next year at Philadelphia, on Tuesday after the second Lord's day in October, at three o'clock, P. M.

12. Brother Benjamin Cole to preach the Association sermon; in case of failure, Brother Nicholas Cox.

CIRCULAR LETTER.
BY REV. SAMUEL JONES.

The elders and messengers of the several Baptist churches, meeting at Pennepek, Middletown, Piscataqua, Cohansie, Hopewell, Kingwood, Southampton, Philadelphia, Scotch Plains, Morristown, Knowlton, Newtown, Upper Freehold, Mount Bethel, and Pittsgrove, being met in Association at Hopewell, New Jersey, October 13th and 14th, 1778.

The said churches send greeting.

Dear Brethren,—You must be sensible that we live in a day of very general calamity and distress; a day of lukewarmness and hardness of heart; a day of great corruption, both as to doctrine and manners: We, therefore, earnestly beseech you in the bowels of compassion and Christian love, that you consider the rod and him that has appointed it; that you humble yourselves under the mighty hand of God; that you remember from whence you have fallen, and repent, and do your first works; and that you hold fast that form of sound words that was once delivered to the saints. Do not give up or slight any of the glorious doctrines of the gospel; they are all excellent, and worthy of your highest regard. It is with real concern we perceive that real religion is so much on the decline; and therefore, we beg you would take care, that you do not rest in mere notions. Notional religion may carry a person far in a Christian profession; but experimental knowledge of Christ can only bring us to heaven. We know it will be in vain to plead "we have eat and drank in thy presence," and altogether as vain it will be to plead, "we have assented to the doctrines of the gospel," unless we feel their sanctifying influence on our hearts.

Professors of religion are too ready to join with the men of the world, in the useless, vain, and sinful customs of it; and it is to be feared, that the honors, pleasures, and especially the profits of the world, are too eagerly pursued by many amongst us, who name the name of Christ. Holy brethren, partakers of the heavenly calling, abstain from this fleshly lust, which warreth against the soul. Remember that we are not to love the world, nor the things of the world. We are strangers and pilgrims on earth, and therefore we should set our affections, not on things below, but on things above. The woman clothed with the sun, had the moon under her feet. Had we a proper estimation of heavenly things, we should not be so fond of earthly enjoyments.

Consider, dear brethren, whose you are, and whom you ought to serve. You profess to be the people of the Lord; you have declared your attachment to Jesus Christ: consider, then, the great High Priest of your profession, who was holy, harmless, undefiled, and separate from sinners; who went about continually doing good. So tread in his steps, and imitate his example, that you may be able to say to others, "be ye followers of us, as we are also of Christ."

Moreover, brethren, we exhort you to pay a due regard to the public worship of God, and carefully attend the means of grace. The Lord loveth the gates of Zion more than all the dwellings of Jacob. Forsake not, therefore, the assembling of yourselves together. Wait on the Lord, and he shall strengthen your hearts. Shall the Lord rain manna round about our tents, and we not go out to gather it? Shall we starve our souls by such cruel negligence?

Remember, dear brethren, that attendance on the worship of God, in all the branches of it, in the sanctuary, in the family, and in the closet, is necessary to a growth in grace, and a delightful intercourse with God. And whether in the church, in the family, or in the world, let it be your care to honor the gospel. Many professors give themselves too much liberty, and walk not so circumspect as they ought. By this means the gospel is sometimes reproached, the doctrine of grace, and the good ways of God brought into contempt. If we were to adorn our profession with a holy life, the truths of our holy religion would be had in greater esteem. For nothing makes religion appear so amiable in the eyes of the world, or sets the gospel in so respectable a point of view, as a holy life in those that profess it. A Christian should remember that he has always something to do. The duty incumbent on him is very extensive. Be desirous, therefore, to know the extent of your duty, and when you know, be careful to put it in practice. Then shall we not be ashamed, when we have respect to all his commandments, and in keeping of them there is great reward.

We would likewise entreat you, as brethren, to dwell together in unity. Stifle the first risings of animosity. Be ashamed of being contentious. Let the disciples of the Prince of peace seek after and follow the things that make for peace. And while we exhort you to these necessary duties, we cannot but put you in mind, that all must be done in the name and strength of Christ. Without him we can do nothing. In ourselves we cannot discharge one duty, resist one temptation, or subdue one corruption. Let all, therefore, be done in the name, and with a dependence on the grace of Christ.

Motives to excite and stir you up to these things are at hand. Let us, in this view, remind you of the free love of God, by which you were chosen to salvation through sanctification of the Spirit and belief of the truth. Remember the love of Christ, who redeemed you by his blood, and the great things the Spirit of God has done for your souls, in the application of that precious blood to purge your consciences from dead works. And may you not only think on these things, but by the grace of God feel the power of them on your hearts continually.

And now, dear brethren, what shall we say more to you. Our hearts are enlarged. We seek not yours but you. Above all things we desire your spiritual welfare. For this we meet together, for this we pray, for this we preach, for this we give our advice, and wish we could do more. Dearly beloved, follow that which is good, forsake that which is evil, "be steadfast, unmoveable, always abounding in the work of the Lord." Amen.

BENJAMIN MILLER, Moderator.
SAMUEL JONES, Clerk.

MINUTES

OF THE

PHILADELPHIA BAPTIST ASSOCIATION,

HELD AT PHILADELPHIA, OCTOBER 12TH AND 13TH,

1779.

The Association being met according to appointment, it was opened with a suitable discourse from 2 Cor. v. 20, by Brother Benjamin Miller.

2. After service proceeded to make choice of a moderator and clerk. To the former appointed Benjamin Miller, and to the latter Samuel Jones.

3. After reading a few of the letters from the churches, adjourned to nine o'clock next morning.

4. October 13th, 9 o'clock.—After prayer, proceeded to read the remainder of the letters.

5. The circular letter read and approved of.

6. Mr. Samuel Jones reported that on settling with Mr. Wescott, it appeared there was a balance of one hundred and nine pounds, nineteen shillings, and one penny in said Wescott's hands, which he put in the continental fund.

7. Also, that he had received of the money of Mrs. Hubb's donation, two hundred and twenty-eight pounds, fifteen shillings, and two pence. Agreed the same be put in the continental fund.

8. The piece written by Mr. Morgan on fasting and prayer being read and much approved of, agreed the same be printed with our letter.

9. Concluded to continue the days of fasting and prayer as in the year past, viz: the second Thursday in November, February, May, and August.

10. Brother James Benedict having lately suffered by the Indians, agreed to recommend his case to the churches, and desire them to make collections for his relief, and convey the same as soon as may be to Mr. Coles, at Hopewell.

11. There being a call for the catechisms from divers places, agreed that the churches inquire among themselves, and see how many they will take of them, at seven shillings and sixpence apiece, and make a return of the same to the next Association.

12. Brother Thomas Fleeson to write to the Association of Virginia, and be a messenger to them.

13. Brother John Blackwell to write to the Warren Association, and Brother Elcanah Holmes to be messenger.

14. Brother Abel Morgan to prepare the Association letter for next year.

15. The Association next year to be held at Philadelphia, on Tuesday after the third Sunday in October, at 3 o'clock.

16. Brother Samuel Jones to preach the Association sermon, and in case of failure, Brother John Blackwell.

CIRCULAR LETTER.

BY REV. SAMUEL JONES.

The elders and messengers of the several Baptist churches meeting at Pennepek, Middletown, Piscataqua, Cohansie, Hopewell, Montgomery, Kingwood, Southampton, Philadelphia, Scotch Plains, Morristown, New Britain, Pitsgrove, Newtown, Dividing Creek, New Mills, Upper Freehold, Lyon's Farms, and Oblong, being met in Association at Philadelphia, October 12th and 13th, 1779.

To the said churches send greeting.

Dearly beloved brethren,—Seventy-two years have now elapsed since the first Association that was held in this place; during which period, but more especially of late, we have been led to note many remarkable displays of Divine Providence, which, by appointment, is to be the subject of our present address. Confession of faith, chap. V.

When we admit the divine authority of the holy Scripture, and by the light thereof, together with that of nature, we discover the being and perfections of God, we are next led to consider his purposes and decrees, and the execution of these in the works of creation and providence. These are all material objects of faith, and main pillars, as well as essential parts of true religion.

That the all-wise and omnipotent Jehovah is the Creator and disposer of all things is a matter of general consent, discoverable by the light of nature; insomuch that creation and providence may be said to be the two testaments out of which natural religion is deduced; but still much more manifest by the sure testimony of the Scripture of truth. See Ps. civ.; Acts xvii. 25, 28, &c.

Creation is the effect of Almighty power and wisdom, whereby the eternal God created all things, visible and invisible, even the whole universe, out of nothing. Col. i. 16. But chiefly man, the glory of this lower creation, being made after his own image, in knowledge, righteousness, and true holiness. Gen. i. 27.

By Divine Providence is meant the superintendence of the Deity over all his works and all possible events. Whereby,

1. He upholds and sustains all things, animate and inanimate. Heb. i. 3; Acts xvii. 28.

2. Provides for all living. Acts xvii. 25; Ps. civ. 21; cxxxvi. 25.

3. And governs the whole universe. Ps. ciii. 19. Providence is,

1. General, Acts xvii. 25, or particular, Matt. x. 29.
2. Mediate, by second causes, 1 Kings, xiii. 24; xxii. 22, and the fixed laws of nature. Or immediate by his will and appointment.
3. Ordinary, in the common course of things, or extraordinary. 1 Kings xvii. 4; Dan. vi. 22; iii. 27.

In this view we are led to conceive of the Divine Being as the head of a vast family, extending his care and beneficence to every individual of it; or as a great monarch, who has his eye not only on those near his throne, but extends the benefits of his benign influence to the remotest parts of his vast dominions. For as we would not expect the greatest to be above, so neither are the least below his notice; insomuch that a sparrow does not fall to the ground without him, and the very hairs of our heads are all numbered. Matt. x. 29, 30.

O how august and stupendous this work of God! It is a most rich display of all the divine perfections; especially of wisdom, goodness, and power; and it excites and improves all the powers, best faculties and affections of the soul, as well as every grace and virtue; as love, reverence, admiration, gratitude and the like. For who can contemplate such manifestation of power as we see in the ways of Providence, and not feel a reverential awe of him, who controls and sustains all creation? Who can view that infinite wisdom manifest in the whole, and not be filled with wonder and astonishment? Or who can trace the footsteps of goodness and mercy visible every where, but especially in the recovery of man, which is a particular dispensation of Providence, and not feel the springs of love, gratitude, and praise excited in him? Surely one would think it must be impossible; but we shall grow wiser and better while we read in the book of Providence that lies continually open before us. Yet, after all, we must remember that in our present state we can comprehend but a very small part of this vast whole, as it is mentioned in the book of Job. "Lo, these are parts of his ways, but how little a portion is heard of him." Job xxvi. 14.

But as all the ways of God are mysterious to us in this imperfect state, while we are so prone to judge of the whole from seeing a part, so there lies one objection against the doctrine we are speaking of. Not such as has been made by those who are fond of caviling, but which has been a difficulty to the godly. To the Psalmist, Ps. lxxiii. 2, 5. To Jeremiah, Jer. xii. 1; Heb. i. 13; and to Job, x. 3, and many others since: namely, that it is not just and equal, the wicked being often prosperous and the righteous afflicted. To which it might be sufficient to say with the Apostle, "Who art thou that repliest against God?" Rom. ix. 20.

But we would further observe,
1. Inequality is necessary in all governments, and the beauty of them, as there must be different members in a body.
2. Wicked men may have some virtues, which cannot be rewarded but in this life.
3. All do not prosper.

4. The prosperous wicked are not so happy as they are thought to be. Prov. xiv. 13, 14.

5. Their prosperity will have an end; while, on the other hand,

6. The righteous have imperfections.

7. And afflictions are necessary to perfect them in grace and holiness.

8. Lastly, their reward will be hereafter, when the equality will be made. Ps. lxxxiii. 17.

In regard of the question, how Providence can be versant about evil actions without destroying the liberty of the will, but that man may still remain a free agent, we have but room to suggest, that what is natural in the act is of God, what is sinful of man, like the ascending of vapors and exhalations from all bodies is owing to the sun; but that stench should arise from any, is owing to their being corrupted in themselves. So, also, speaking is from God; but speaking wickedly from man.

As for the concerns of Providence with good actions, there is but little danger of our erring by ascribing too much to it.

Finally, brethren, the well ordering, sustaining, and overruling all things and all possible events, in the whole universe, and through all ages, is the object of Providence, under the direction of him, whose kingdom ruleth over all. Ps. ciii. 19.

Two or three things we would now point out by way of improvement, and so conclude.

First. We ought to accustom ourselves to see and acknowledge our God, and set him before us, in all these his ways, wherein his wisdom, power, mercy, and goodness shine.

1. That such a display of divine perfections may not pass unheeded.

2. That so much goodness may not be lost on us, and rise up in judgment against us.

3. That we may not miss of means so powerful to promote virtue and vital piety.

4. Wherein if we fail we must be stupid and ungrateful to a degree not only unworthy of the Christian, and the means we enjoy, but also of the powers we are endowed with. Dan. v. 23.

Second. When chastised, we ought to "hear the rod and him that has appointed it." Mich. vi. 9. This is and has been our case for some years past, which we have not room now to enlarge upon.

Third. When the profusion of a kind Providence is showered on our heads, it becomes us to be taught humility, dependence, love, and gratitude. Rom. ii. 4. And this has always been our case, though more remarkably of late, when the Lord remembered mercy in the midst of deserved judgment. For if you consider the steps whereby divine Providence interposed in our favor during the present contest with Great Britain, you must see and know that the most high God ruleth in the kingdom of men, and that he appointed over it whomsoever he will. Dan. v. 21.

Thus, dear brethren, we have just entered on the subject, and, as it were, traced some of its outlines, than which our limits would allow us little more. We shall now conclude in the words of the Apostle to the Romans, chap. xi. 33, 36. " O the depth of the riches, both of the wisdom and knowledge of God! How unsearchable are his judgments, and his ways past finding out! For of him, and through him, and to him, are all things, to whom be glory for ever. Amen."

BENJAMIN MILLER, Moderator.
SAMUEL JONES, Clerk.

ON FASTING AND PRAYER.
BY REV. AEEL MORGAN.

In compliance with the request of a former Association, here follow some brief remarks concerning fasting. That it is the duty of Christians, on certain occasions, to fast or to abstain from their usual refreshment, at the stated times, cannot with any just reason be once called into question; forasmuch as Christ himself takes it for granted, " when thou fastest," and proceeds to give necessary directions how to act therein. Matt. vi. 16. Of the various kinds or diversities of fasts, our concern at present is only about a religious fast, which is either private or public; private, when one alone sets himself by fasting and prayer to seek the Lord, as David did, who fasted, lying all night upon the earth, 2 Sam. xii. 16. Daniel, who sought by prayer and fasting, ix. 3. Anna, a prophetess, who served God with fastings and prayers, Luke ii. 37. Public fasting, appointed either by the civil power, as Jehosaphat proclaimed a fast throughout all Judah, 2 Chron. xx. 3; also Ezra, vii. 14; viii. 21. The king of Ninevah, Jonah iii. 5. Or by mutual agreement of the members of churches; for instance, in that famous Christian church at Antioch, when Barnabas and Saul, by the command of the Holy Ghost, were separated to the work appointed them, Acts xiii. 2, 3.

The concomitants, or what should accompany religious fastings, are: 1, unfeigned confession of our sins, Dan. ix. 5, with a sense of the evil of them, and turning from them to God; otherwise, it appears so much like hypocrisy and lying to God with our tongues. Also 2, with prayer, Joel i. 14; emphatically expressed by " crying unto the Lord." 3, undissembled humiliation, intimated by outward tokens, as being clothed with sackcloth and laying in ashes, Dan. ix. 3; Jonah iii. 8. And 4, to avoid all acts of oppression, and to show kindness to the needy. The fast which the Lord has chosen, and which he approves of, is to loose the bands of wickedness, to undo the heavy burdens, and to let the oppressed go free, to break every yoke, to deal your bread to the hungry, to relieve the poor, to cover the naked, Isaiah lviii. 6, 7. Alas, how far are our fasts from being accompanied with those things which the Lord requires!

The occasions of fasting and prayer are such as: 1. To deprecate lawful judgments felt or feared; as sword, famine, pestilence, or other sore afflictions. 2. To intreat for the revival of religion, the coming and spread of the Mediator's kingdom, success of the gospel, unity of Christians, and the like desirable blessings. 3. Occasion on some weighty, important undertakings, as the constitution of churches, ordination of church officers, Acts xiv. 23. Preparation for the reception of the Lord's supper, protection from imminent danger, Ezra viii. 21.

The length of time to be observed in fasting is not determined; it must be regulated by agreement, prudence, or public order; at least it ought to be so long till public worship is over.

When our continent is filled with tears and blood, ravages and desolation abound, perpetrated by English troops, and, if possible by the more wicked combinations of base traitors among ourselves, as now it is, when religion declines, and iniquity triumphs, it is a time which calls aloud for humiliation before God, fasting and prayer, with a steadfast endeavor for a reformation through our sinful afflicted land.

MINUTES

OF THE

PHILADELPHIA BAPTIST ASSOCIATION,

HELD AT PHILADELPHIA, OCTOBER 17TH AND 18TH,

1780.

Tuesday, October 17—At 3 o'clock, P. M., Rev. Samuel Jones, pursuant to appointment, preached the introductory sermon, from Matt. xvi. 18, "And I say also unto thee, That thou art Peter, and upon this rock I will build my church; and the gates of hell shall not prevail against it."

2. After divine service, Rev. Isaac Stelle was elected moderator, and Rev. William Rogers, clerk.

3. Letters from twenty-one churches were read, complaining in general of great declension in religion and vital piety; also, of amazing prevailing stupidity, which are such tokens of the divine displeasure as do loudly call for deep humiliation of spirit.

The Association ardently wish to hear from all the other churches in the Union, who have, at this our annual meeting, neglected writing to us; likewise request an exact return of their full number in communion, to be forwarded to the next Association, in order that the state of our churches may be published as formerly.

4. Rev. Oliver Hart, of Charleston, South Carolina, and Rev. William Rogers, of this city, being present—also, our brethren Thomas Fleeson, and John Pitman, they were admitted by the Association to the full privilege of members.

5. A letter from the Warren Association, held the 12th ult., brought by their messenger, Rev. Elhanan Winchester, was read, giving a most pleasing account of the work of God's Spirit in many parts of New England. Seven hundred and sixty-five members were added to their last Association, and upwards of one thousand had, within one year, been baptized in Massachusett's State only, who had not then joined that body.

6. The minutes of the Charleston Association, held in November, 1779, were read. Near three hundred were baptized among them that year; two hundred and thirty-nine in three months, at Pedee, by one minister. God grant, that the several churches of this our sister Association may be speedily delivered from British oppression!

Adjourned to nine o'clock to-morrow morning.

Wednesday, October 18—Met agreeably to adjournment.

7. A letter from Cowmarsh, Kent county, on Delaware, was read, desiring supplies, as they are destitute of a stated ministry. The Association approve the request, and purpose helping them as much as possible.

8. The circular letter prepared by the Rev. Abel Morgan was read, and unanimously adopted. Rev. Samuel Jones was appointed to compose one for the next year. Subject—God's Covenant.

9. Rev. William Vanhorne, who was requested to write to the Warren Association, and Rev. John Blackwell, to that of Virginia, brought in their letters respectively, which, after examination, were approved.

The messengers appointed to visit the former, at their next annual meeting, are Rev. Messrs. William Rogers and Elhanan Winchester, with Mr. John Pitman. To the latter, Mr. Thomas Fleeson.

10. The members of this Association, on consideration of the awful declension of religion in these middle States, and our national distresses, recommend to all our churches to continue the observation of the second Thursday in November, February, May, and August, as days of fasting, humiliation, and prayer.

11. After some conversation on the state of the Association library, it was thought proper to nominate a librarian. Accordingly having made choice of Rev. William Vanhorne, he accepted: and full power is hereby given him to collect all the books now out, and distribute them with those now on hand, as he sees proper, and render an account thereof at our next meeting.

12. Resolved, That our next Association be held in Philadelphia, the Tuesday after the third Lord's day in October.

Sermon, at usual time, by Rev. John Blackwell; or, on failure, by Rev. Nicholas Cox.

13. Rev. Oliver Hart was unanimously requested to preach this evening.

Thus having, through Divine favor, enjoyed a comfortable interview together, upon finishing our business, we closed at one o'clock, in Christian love and fellowship.

CIRCULAR LETTER.
BY REV. ABEL MORGAN.

The elders and messengers of the several Baptist churches, meeting at Pennepek, Middletown, Piscataqua, Cohansie, Tredyffrin, Cape May, Hopewell, Brandywine, Montgomery, Southampton, Philadelphia, Cranberry, Scotch Plains, New Britain, Salem, Newtown, Dividing Creek, New Mills, Upper Freehold, Lyon's Farms, and Pittsgrove.

To the said churches send our Christian salutation.

Beloved Brethren,—At the close of our annual Association, we now address you on the solemn subject of the sixth chapter of our Confession of faith, which treats of the Fall of Man.

Such is the excellency and usefulness of divine revelation contained in that sadly neglected book, the Bible, that it affords us an infallible certainty respecting things past, present, and to come, which do so nearly concern us to know; among other articles, man's creation, who was made upright, righteous and holy, after the likeness, or image of God, happy in the favor of God, and communion with him, endued with power to fulfil the law, given him for the rule of his obedience to his Creator, in that perfect state.

Moreover, by the same word of truth, we are assured of the sorrowful change which befel our first parents, by their acting contrary to the command of God; beguiled by Satan, the father of lies, man fell, lost his creation excellencies, his honor, his God,—his favor, knowledge of him, communion with him, fitness for his service, and ability to perform it; lost his life, his life to God, even his natural or animal life being forfeited, he became subject to death, the sanction of the law, the penalty denounced in case of disobedience; then the consequents of his evil deed immediately took place, which are guilt and depravity, with all the miseries which do accompany the same, both present and future. Thus man became separated from God, an enemy unto him, to his glory and government, from the first sin, even until now—obnoxious to the curse of a just law violated, and under the wrath of God due to transgressors; also, wofully polluted throughout soul and body, "We are all as an unclean thing," Isa. lxiv. 6.

Man, by his departure from God, is become idolatrous, turned from the only true God unto self, which is the grand idol of the whole world ever since Adam's revolt. Self was the very alluring bait, wrapped up in the first temptation, "Ye shall be as gods." Now it cannot be otherwise, but that He who will not give his glory to another, should always abhor and detest any one, and every one, that sets up another god in the room of the true God, and lives to him as man doth to self.

Again, what further aggravates the evil of the first sin of man, is the capacity which Adam stood in, viz., as the public head and representative of all his posterity,—that in him, and with him, all have sinned, and fell from happiness in his first transgression, "All have sinned," Rom. v. 12; which is evident not only by divine testimony, but is also universally manifested by the aversion to good,— the ignorance, stupidity, selfishness, and propensity to evil apparent in every one by nature, Eph. ii. 3.

May we all, therefore, brethren, not only assent to the truth of the historical narration of these things, but also know the absolute necessity of a real, abiding convincing sense of our case, thus ruined, guilty, and depraved. In order,

1, To suppress all pride, and high conceits of ourselves, our supposed excellency and goodness;

2, Truly to acknowledge whatever favors mankind receive, that they are every way gratuitous, and wholly undeserved;

3, For our humiliation before God, confession of our sins, and deep distress of soul;

4, To raise in our minds a becoming admiration of God's patience and forbearance with a sinful world, in that vindictive justice is not immediately executed on transgressors;

5, To learn the true and proper cause of his forbearance,—viz., the interposition of the Mediator, Christ Jesus, between the execution of the penalty and man's desert;

6, To give us enlarged views of rich mercy and grace with God, in constituting a way whereby to restore creatures so unworthy from present ruin and future misery, even by his own beloved Son;

7, To teach us the necessity we are under of a renovation;

Again, an abiding sense of our case is necessary, in order to make us all anxiously inquisitive about our acquaintance with, and an interest in, Christ the Mediator; and to excite all believers in him to continued thanksgiving and praise, that they should not henceforth live to themselves, but unto him that died for them, and rose again.

God, who is wise in counsel, and excellent in working, suffered or permitted man to fall, and thence took occasion to bring the greatest good out of the worst of evils, or overruled the fall of man, to the more abundant display of his divine perfections—to the everlasting disappointment and confusion of his enemies, the security of his elect, and the endless praise of his glorious name.

By order,

ISAAC STELLE, Moderator.
WILLIAM ROGERS, Clerk.

MINUTES

OF THE

PHILADELPHIA BAPTIST ASSOCIATION,

HELD AT PHILADELPHIA, OCTOBER 12TH, 13TH, AND 14TH,

1781.

Tuesday, October 23d.—At three o'clock, P. M., the Association was opened with a suitable discourse, from 2 Cor. xi. 22–28, by Brother John Blackwell.

2. After sermon, Brother Samuel Jones was elected moderator, and Brother Thomas Fleeson, clerk. Letters from twenty-six churches were read.

3. A letter and minutes from the Warren Association, which met at South Brimfield in September last, were read. Their messengers to us were President Manning and Brother William Rogers.

4. Wednesday, October 24th.—Met, pursuant to adjournment, at nine o'clock, A. M. A special report in writing, relative to the Association library, was presented by Brother William Vanhorn. Ordered, that this be left among our papers. Our brethren, Samuel Jones and Joshua Jones, with the librarian, are requested to examine all the books, distinguish, by some mark, those appertaining to the library, take into consideration the expediency of repairing the bindings, and make their report at our next annual meeting.

5. Our brethren, Samuel Jones, Oliver Hart, Abel Morgan, and James Manning, were appointed a committee to take into consideration the proposals and queries offered by Pennepek, Hopewell, and Philadelphia churches, and report thereon in the afternoon.

6. The church at Stamford having excommunicated Robert Morris, their late preacher, for gross immoralities, and departure from the faith as held by us, we think proper to notify the churches, that they may beware of him.

7. Brother Blackwell was requested to draw up an advertisement informing the public that David Branson, who imposes on them under the character of a Baptist preacher, is an excommunicated person, and ought not, by any means, to be countenanced. The advertisement being brought in, was read, and, after some amendment, approved of. Ordered to be inserted in one of the Philadelphia newspapers.

8. Half past two o'clock, P. M. The committee appointed to con-

sider the proposals and queries from Pennepek, Hopewell, and Philadelphia churches, respecting the doctrine of "universal restoration," and the proceedings of the Philadelphia church on that affair, do report:

First. That the proceedings of the protesters in that business were regular and fair.

Secondly. That the declaration of the ministers who were called to their assistance, respecting the protesters, was weighty, full, and decisive.

Thirdly. That although the non signers are already virtually excluded, yet, in order to their more formal excommunication, the Philadelphia church be advised to appoint at their meeting of business, two of their regular male members to go with the protest to the non protesters, one by one, in order to their signing it, and warn them, that in case they refuse to sign, they should openly and formally, by name, be excommunicated.

SAMUEL JONES,
OLIVER HART,
ABEL MORGAN,
JAMES MANNING.

Resolved unanimously, That the above report of the committee is approved; and that this Association advise all the churches to beware of Elhanan Winchester, and not admit him, or any who advocate "universal salvation," to the office of public teaching, or suffer any who avow the same to continue in their communion.

9. Brother Oliver Hart was appointed to write a letter, in order to be forwarded to the next Warren Association; and our brethren, Abel Griffith, William Rogers, Elkanah Holmes, and Nicholas Cox, were chosen messengers.

10. Brother William Rogers was requested to write to the next Virginia Association; and our brethren, Thomas Fleeson and Philip Hughes were appointed messengers.

11. Thursday, October 25th.—Met at sunrise. The general letter to the churches, drawn by Brother Samuel Jones, being read, was approved of; and Brother Oliver Hart was nominated to write one for next year. Subject—"Christ the Mediator."

12. Supplies were granted to the following destitute churches:— Knowlton, Tuckahoe, Cowmarsh, and Upper Freehold.

13. Voted, That the next Association be held at Philadelphia, to begin on Tuesday after the third Lord's day in October, at three o'clock, P. M. Introductory sermon by Brother Nicholas Cox; in case of failure, by Brother Abel Morgan.

14. And now, dear brethren, having come to a close of our annual meeting, before we address you by our circular letter, we feel ourselves constrained to acknowledge the great goodness of God towards us, and to call on you to join with us in thankfulness and praise, as well for the unanimity and brotherly love which prevailed throughout our meeting, as for the recent signal success granted to the

American arms, in the surrender of the whole British army, under the command of Lord Cornwallis, with the effusion of so little blood.

CIRCULAR LETTER,
BY REV. SAMUEL JONES.

The elders and messengers of the several churches met in Association at Philadelphia, October 23d, 1781.

To the several churches in union with this Association, send greeting.

Dearly beloved in the Lord,—In the connection of divine truth, and progress of our order, we come to write to you, in the next place, of what, in our Confession of faith, Chap. VII., is called God's Covenant; by which is meant the transactions of God with and towards man, respecting his duty and happiness; more especially the exertions of infinite wisdom and mercy, in the contrivance and establishment of the scheme of redemption, for the recovery and salvation of lost man, through a precious and blessed Mediator.

Passing over the prohibition to Adam, respecting the forbidden fruit, which is commonly called the covenant of works, his being the public head and representative of his posterity, as he certainly was, Rom. v. 12, we come to the intimation made to him immediately after the fall, respecting the seed of the woman, that it should bruise the serpent's head; upon which is founded the notion of the covenant of grace made with Adam, which was nothing else than a bare discovery, revelation, and manifestation of the eternal counsel of God, respecting man's recovery, carrying in it a promise of eternal life. No stipulations and re-stipulations, no conditions whatever; nothing more nor less to be performed on Adam's part; nothing but a glorious manifestation, as was said before, of the rich grace and mercy of God in Christ. And the farther discovery of this rich grace, that was made to the patriarchs, Abraham, Isaac, and Jacob, was exactly of the same tenor; a promise, that in their seed all the nations of the earth should be blessed, Gen. xii. 3; xxvi. 4; xxviii. 14. Not a word of a covenant, or any conditions. Hence, in the New Testament, where reference is had thereunto, the same language is constantly used; as for instance: "For the promise is unto you and your children," Acts ii. 39. "Of this man's seed has God, according to his promise," Acts xiii. 23. "For the hope of the promise made of God unto our fathers," Acts xxvi. 6. "Heirs according to the promise," Gal. iii. 21, 22, 29. "The promise of eternal inheritance," Heb. ix. 19. "To perform the mercy promised," Luke i. 72. "And this is the promise that he has promised us, even eternal life," 1 John ii. 29. For all the promises of God in him, are not yea and nay, if you will, and if not, in the strain of a covenant, but yea and amen, 2 Cor. i. 20. In like manner, we read of gifts: "If thou knewest the gift of God," John. iv. 10. "Free gift," Rom. v. 15–18. "Unspeakable gift," 2 Cor. ix. 15. "Gave gifts unto men," Eph. iv. 8. Hence, also, the administrations of grace are called the

Old and New Testament, because a testament contains free gifts and legacies made over, and insured to the heirs. It is true we read in Isa. lix. 21, "As for me, this is my covenant with them." And in Jer. xxxi. 31–34, "I will make a new covenant with the house of Israel, after those days, saith the Lord," speaking of the gospel day. With respect to which we observe, First. That in these places you see nothing that looks like a covenant. Secondly. That the word covenant, in the Old Testament, sometimes means a statute, ordinance, establishment, appointment and decree, as in Jer. xxxiii. 2; Gen. ix. 9–11; Numb. xviii. 19. Thirdly. That the use of the word covenant might be more consonant with that legal dispensation, than that of a testament. Fourthly and lastly. That it might seem odd to speak of a testament, while the testator was yet living, as the Apostle hints, Heb. ix. 15, 16. But when our Saviour was about to lay down his life, and considered himself as already dead, he lays aside the use of the word covenant, and takes up the more proper word testament, saying, "This is the new testament in my blood," Matt. xxvi. 28. And ever afterward, the word testament was constantly used, when reference is had to the dispensations of grace, as you may see in the margin of your Bibles. And besides, when we consider the nature of a covenant, we clearly see there could be no possible room for such a thing ever to exist between God and man, respecting spiritual things; for the idea of a covenant necessarily includes these things following: 1, Mutual wants in the parties covenanting. 2, Mutual benefits enjoyed by them. 3, Power in each party to perform the conditions of the covenant. 4, Each party is brought under obligations to the other, by the performance of those conditions. 5, Merit on both sides. 6, and lastly, Neither party ought to be under prior obligations to the other, respecting the conditions of the covenant; of which particulars not one can be admitted in the present case.

As for the Abrahamic covenant, as some call it, it only respected temporal things, and the externals of religion, though it had the promise of the Messiah tacked to it, and was therefore called the covenant of promise, Eph. ii. 12. It was with regard to selecting Abraham and his descendants from the other nations of the earth to a national church state, and the enjoyment of the land of Canaan, the peaceable and quiet possession of which they were to enjoy, upon condition of their observing the external rituals of that dispensation, and being obedient, which they promised, and had in their power to do. And this was the covenant of which they received circumcision, an external mark or token, as a seal to confirm it, Gen. xii. 18; xvii. 7, 8; xxvi. 4; xxviii. 14; Exod. xix. 3–9; xxiv. 3–8; Lev. xxvi. 3, 40; Deut. v. 29. The word covenant seems to have been introduced into the Christian system of religion, because it favored of a legal strain, so acceptable to those who are fond of terms and conditions to be performed by man; while others that do not favor legalism, yet too incautiously make use of the word covenant, in bare compliance with custom; though these are generally careful to inform us, that it means a testamentary covenant, a free, absolute, unconditional covenant, which is much the same thing as to say that it is no covenant at all.

The sum, then, is this, that the glorious dispensations and manifestations of the rich grace and mercy of God in Christ, contain free, absolute, and unconditional promises of the free, rich, and unmerited gifts of God, conveyed to the heirs as legacies, in a testamentary way.

Having thus shown you, dear brethren, that there can be no such thing as a covenant between God and man, respecting spiritual blessings and service, we come now to consider what foundation there is to style the glorious transactions between the persons of the ever blessed Trinity, respecting man's recovery, a covenant; and here, undoubtedly, there is some appearance of that kind. If ever there was a covenant of grace, this is it. If ever there was a covenant of redemption, here you will find it. And, on the part of Christ, a covenant of works too; forasmuch as the great work of redemption, the fulfilling of the law of God, in behalf of his people, for whom he undertook as their surety, was performed by him, Psalm cxix. 122; Isa. xxxviii. 14.

The passages of Scripture that speak of this glorious transaction as a covenant, are these following: "And my covenant shall stand fast with him," Ps. lxxxix. 28: "And give thee for a covenant of the people," Isa. xlii. 6; xlix. 8; "Neither shall the covenant of my peace be removed," Isa. lvi. 4, 6; "As for thee also, by the blood of thy covenant," Zech. ix. 11; "Even the messenger of the covenant," Mal. iii. 1. But then it is spoken of under other views, in these that follow: "According to the eternal purpose, which he purposed in Christ Jesus our Lord," Eph. iii. 11; "And the counsel of peace shall be between them both," Zech. vi. 13; "For I have not shunned to declare unto you the whole counsel of God," Acts xx. 27; "The immutability of his counsel," Heb. vi. 17; "Being delivered by the determinate counsel and foreknowledge of God," Acts ii. 23. And besides, Christ is said to be foreordained to that work, 1 Pet. i. 20; sent, John x. 35; to have received a commandment, John x. 18; was therefore a servant, Isa. xlii. 1; cheerfully obeyed, Ps. xl. 7, 8; and was rewarded, Ps. ii. 8; Phil. ii. 9. From the whole, then, we see, that there was a counsel held in eternity, even from everlasting, respecting the recovery of man; that the Triune God did then contrive, find out, adjust and settle, speaking after the manner of men, the whole plan and scheme of that great and glorious work, who should be saved, by what means, and after what manner; that the Son of God, the second person in the Trinity, should be a Mediator, should undertake for his chosen ones as their surety, and should assume human nature, that he might make satisfaction to divine justice in their behalf; that all the gifts and graces necessary for the purpose should be treasured in him, Col. i. 19. That the blessed Spirit should co-operate in manifesting the whole to the world, and applying the same to the chosen ones, namely, by enlightening their darkened understandings, working in them faith and repentance, changing their vile affections, converting them from the service of sin and Satan, to the service of the living God, carrying on the work of grace begun, and keeping them by the power of God, unto salvation; by every means making them meet for the inheritance of the saints in light, and finally bringing them to the full possession of it.

Thus, dear brethren, we have briefly laid before you the plan of our redemption, as concerted in eternity, and brought into effect in time. You see the glorious covenant of grace, which was well ordered in all things, and sure. You see the Son of God appointed to the mediatorial work, and all grace treasured up in him for that purpose. You see him undertake, go through with it, and the Spirit co-operate to accomplish the whole. You see the dispensations of grace to man are free, absolute, and unconditional; the gifts of God dispersed in a testamentary way, free and firm. Nothing of works, but all of grace. Nothing of the will of man, but all of the will of God; that we might all, and at all times, cry grace, grace, and whosoever glorieth, might glory in the Lord.

O blessed and glorious scheme! What a rich display have we here of the wisdom, justice, holiness, truth, mercy, pity, compassion, and condescension of God! See the harmony of the divine attributes in this stupendous plan, that is every way worthy of a God! What shall we render unto him for such rich, unmerited grace! Never to the endless ages of eternity, never shall we be able to render adequate compensation. O that the love of God were abundantly shed abroad in each of our hearts, that we might for ever admire, with astonishment admire, his rich grace; that we might for ever love, fear, honor, reverence, and serve him, with all our hearts unfeignedly.

"Now, the God of peace, that brought again from the dead our Lord Jesus, that great Shepherd of the sheep, through the blood of the everlasting covenant, make you perfect in every good work to do his will, working in you that which is well pleasing in his sight, through Jesus Christ, to whom be glory for ever and ever. Amen."

By order of the Association,

SAMUEL JONES, Moderator,
THOMAS FLEESON, Clerk.

THE MINISTERS AND MESSENGERS AT THE ASSOCIATION, AND THE STATE OF THE CHURCHES FOR THE YEAR.

CHURCHES.	MINISTERS.	Baptized.	Received by Letter.	Restored.	Dismiss'd.	Excom.	Died.	Members.
Pennepek,	Samuel Jones,	2	2	0	0	0	1	58
Middletown,	Abel Morgan,	1	0	0	0	0	0	95
Cohansie,	Robert Kelsay,*	25	1	0	0	0	3	81
Great Valley,	Thomas Jones,	0	0	0	0	0	1	35
Cape May,	David Smith,	13	0	0	0	0	0	58
Hopewell,	Oliver Hart,	0	0	0	2	1	3	213
Brandywine,	Abel Griffiths,	0	0	0	0	0	0	19
Kingwood,	David Sutton,	1	1	0	1	0	1	69
Southampton,	William Vanhorn,	1	0	0	0	1	2	56
Philadelphia,	—— ——	7	0	0	0	0	0	86
Cranberry,	Peter Wilson,	3	0	0	0	0	0	37
Knowlton,	—— ——	0	0	0	0	0	0	16
New Britain,	Joshua Jones,	2	0	0	0	0	0	30
Salem,	—— ——	18	0	0	0	0	1	34
Newtown,	Nicholas Cox,	2	0	1	0	1	0	68
Dividing Creek,	Peter P. Vanhorn,	37	0	1	2	0	2	65
New Mills,	David Loofborrow,	0	0	0	0	0	0	56
Konoloway,	Joseph Powell,*	4	0	0	0	0	0	42
Upper Freehold,	—— ——	2	1	0	1	0	0	66
Mount Bethel,	Abner Sutton,	0	0	0	3	0	1	22
Pittsgrove,	William Worth,	34	0	0	0	0	4	70
Tuckahoe,	—— ——	11	0	0	0	0	0	34
Stamford,	—— ——	16	3	0	4	2	5	39
Amenia Precinct,	Elkana Holmes,	0	0	0	0	0	0	35
London Tract,	Thomas Fleeson,	0	0	0	0	0	0	28
Cow Marsh,	—— ——	0	0	0	0	0	0	23
		179	8	2	13	5	24	1435

Note.—The ministers whose names are marked thus * were not present. A dash —— denotes churches destitute of a settled minister.

⁂ The three last mentioned churches having been lately constituted, were, at their request, received into fellowship.

As no letters came to hand from Piscataqua, Welsh Tract, Montgomery, Scotch Plains, and several other churches belonging to this Association, we are unable to give any just account of their present number of members; a satisfaction we hope to enjoy another season.

MINUTES

OF THE

PHILADELPHIA BAPTIST ASSOCIATION,

HELD AT PHILADELPHIA, OCTOBER 22D AND 23D,

1782.

Tuesday, October 22.—At three o'clock, P. M., a sermon was preached, from Acts xvi. 17, "These men are the servants of the Most High God, which show unto us the way of salvation," by Brother Nicholas Cox.

2. After sermon, Brother Oliver Hart was chosen moderator, and Brother William Vanhorn, clerk. Letters from thirty churches were read.

3. A letter and minutes from the Warren Association were read. Their messengers, Elders James Manning, William Rogers, and William Williams.

4. A letter from the Ketockton Association was read.

5. A late branch of the church at Montgomery being constituted a church at Hill Town, were, at their request, received into this Association.

6. Adjourned till to-morrow morning, nine o'clock.

7. Wednesday, October 23d.—Met pursuant to adjournment.

The committee appointed last year to examine the books in the hands of the librarian, report, That they have proceeded in that business, and conclude, that about three pounds ten shillings would repair them.

Agreed to collect the above sum immediately; which was done, and put into the hands of the librarian.

8. This Association being informed of some difficulties subsisting in the church at Goshen, recommended to our brethren, Samuel Jones, Nicholas Cox, and William Vanhorn to visit them.

9. A letter from Mr. Aitkin, printer in this city, was read, setting forth, that he had, with great pains and much expense, just completed the first English edition of the Bible in America, together with Watt's Psalms, and requesting this Association to make the undertaking as universally known as we can.

Voted, That this Association, on the recommendation of Congress of said impression, present their thanks to Mr. Aitkin, for his faithful execution of this laborious and important undertaking, and most heartily recommend to all the churches with which we are connected, to encourage the sale thereof.

Adjourned to half after two o'clock, P. M.

10. Met pursuant to adjournment.

Voted, That the seventh article of the Warren Association minutes be adopted by us, which is as follows: "The Association, from a representation made to them by the corporation of the College in Providence, of the low state of the funds of said College, and the urgent necessity of increasing them, in order to support suitable instructors therein, and from an idea of the great importance of good education, have taken into consideration, as the most probable method to accomplish this valuable end, the recommendation of a subscription throughout all the Baptist societies on this continent, as well as to all the friends of literature of every denomination, on the following conditions:

"We the subscribers promise and engage to pay the several sums affixed to our names, to ⸺⸺, to be by him paid to John Brown, Esq., of Providence, treasurer of the corporation, or his successor in said office, or order; to be placed at interest, and the interest only to be applied for the above purpose.

"N. B. The several churches are desired to insert in the above blank the name of the most suitable person in the society for this service."

11. Brother Thomas Ustick was appointed to write a letter to the Warren Association, and Brother Samuel Jones to the Ketockon, in answer to their request on the subject of last year's letter. Messengers to the former, Brother Nicholas Cox, and to the latter, William Worth, Thomas Fleeson, and Abner Sutton.

12. As we have received information, that a legacy has been left to this Association, in the last will and testament of John Honeywell, of Knowlton, in Sussex county, New Jersey, deceased,

Resolved, That our treasurer, Rev. Samuel Jones, who is also in said will constituted a trustee of the same, proceed immediately to make use of all due and necessary measures to recover said legacy for and in our behalf, and at our expense.

13. Supplies were granted to the following destitute churches:—Piscataqua and Knowlton.

14. Next Association to be held at Philadelphia, to begin on Tuesday after the third Lord's day in October, at three o'clock, P. M. Sermon by Brother Abel Morgan; and, in case of failure, by Brother Oliver Hart.

CIRCULAR LETTER.
BY REV. OLIVER HART.

The ministers and messengers of the several Baptist churches, met in Association, at Philadelphia, October 22d, 1782.

Send Christian salutation to the churches with whom we are in union.

Well beloved in our dear Redeemer,—We are now, in course, to address you on the subject contained in the eighth chapter of our Confession of faith, which treats of Christ the Mediator.

A mediator is concerned with parties at variance, betwixt whom he stands as a middle person, and his business is to bring them together and make peace between them. Christ acts in the capacity of a Mediator between God and men, 1 Tim. ii. 5. "There is one God, and one Mediator between God and men, the man Christ Jesus." For the elucidation of this point, we may,

I. Consider what a Mediator between God and men supposes.
II. Take a view of the appointment of Christ to that office.
III. Consider his ability, suitableness, and qualifications for the great work.
IV. How he hath effected it, or what he hath done for that purpose.
V. Point out some of the blessed effects of Christ's mediatorship.

I. A Mediator between God and men supposes—

First. A difference subsisting between them. This commenced upon Adam's eating the forbidden fruit; prior to which the most cordial amity and friendship subsisted between God and man. But this first act of disobedience broke the tender ties of love and esteem. Adam flew from, as dreading the divine presence; and soon contracted a contrariety of soul to the perfections of the Deity, and a horrid enmity against God. Thus the staff of friendship was broken, and the quarrel commenced, entirely on the part of man. On the other hand, God, whose law had been violated, and whose goodness and friendship had been abused, appeared in the disagreeable light of an enemy to man; and, in fact, he was an injured sovereign, insisting that reparation should be made for the dishonor done him, by this violation of faith and breach of friendship.

Second. A Mediator between God and men, supposes inability on man's part to repair the injuries done by sin, or to restore himself to the divine favor. Could he have done this, there would have been no need of the interposition of a Mediator; but the divine law was to be punctually observed, and satisfaction was to be made for the breach of it; which were impossible terms to man in his fallen state.

Third. A Mediator between God and men seems to suppose, that God could not, consistent with the honor due to his law, and the glory of his divine perfections, pardon man and receive him into favor, merely as a simple act of mercy. Had he done so, his justice must have bled, his holiness would have been tarnished, his truth shaken, and the rights of his throne and government infringed. Consequences, which it would be horrid and blasphemous to attribute to any of the proceedings of the Almighty; for the Judge of all the earth will do right. Hence appears the necessity of a Mediator. And this leads us,

II. To take a view of the designation or appointment of Christ to that office.

In order to which, we must look into the transactions of the Deity from eternity, before his works of old, Prov. viii. 22; for thus early was Christ appointed to the mediatorial office, in the counsel, decree, and purpose of Jehovah. The Apostle Peter confirms this truth with a strong note of asseveration, 1 Per. i. 20, where, after having spoke of redemption by the precious blood of Christ, he says, "Who verily was foreordained before the foundation of the world." And our Lord himself fully establishes this point, Prov. viii. 23, "I was set up from everlasting, from the beginning, or ever the earth was," —set up, constituted, or appointed Mediator. God, from eternity, foresaw that Adam would fall from his allegiance, integrity, and fidelity; and that the whole human race would be involved in guilt, and must inevitably perish, unless a medium were provided for their recovery, in a way consistent with the glory of the divine perfections. To effect which, the Three Persons in the Godhead, the Father, the Son, and the Holy Ghost, formed a council, and entered into a covenant of grace, in order to lay the plan on which the salvation and happiness of fallen man should proceed; and to determine which of those divine persons should engage in the arduous work, Jehovah, the Father, in his manifold wisdom, having predestinated a select number of the fallen race to the adoption of children, by Jesus Christ, according to the eternal purpose which he purposed in Christ Jesus our Lord, (Eph i. 5; iii. 10, 11,) now proposed the business, or work of saving the elect, to Jehovah the Son; as well knowing the love he bare to them, as also with what alacrity he would comply with his will, proposing to furnish him with a body, and every way equip him for the discharge of his trust. The Son, whose will was the same with that of the Father, readily consented to engage in the work, and did in effect, say, "Father, thy will is that rebellious man should obtain favor, the means therefore of his restoration shall not be wanting; here am I, send me on that important design. Man shall be saved, in a way that will secure the honors of divine government; and by means through which the glory of the divine perfections will shine forth with the brightest effulgence." The cheerfulness with which Christ then complied with the requisition of the eternal Father, is pointed out by the Psalmist, Psalm xl. 7, 8, "Then said I, lo, I come; in the volume of the book it is written of me, I delight to do thy will, O my God: yea, thy law is within my heart." And Christ himself is represented as speaking of his being appointed to the mediatorial office, by the eternal Father, in Psalm lxxxix. 19, 20, "Then thou spakest in vision to the holy One, and saidst, I have laid help upon One that is mighty; I have exalted One chosen out of the people; I have found David my servant, with my holy oil have I anointed him." Thus it appears that God was in Christ, even from everlasting, reconciling the elect world unto himself, not imputing their trespasses unto them, 2 Cor. v. 19; and that Christ was thus early chosen and appointed to the mediatorial office, in the counsel of peace, which was between them both, namely, the Father and the Son; and in the covenant of grace, of which Christ is the Mediator, Heb. xii. 24.

III. We pass on to consider the ability, suitableness, and qualifications of Christ for the great work.

Had not Christ been able, fit and every way qualified for the discharge of the mediatorial office, the work might have been marred in his hands; God might have been frustrated in his designs of mercy to his creatures, and all mankind might have perished in their sins. Events which cannot be admitted, even in idea; for God laid help upon One that is mighty, and exalted One chosen out of the people; every way able to save, even to the uttermost, Psalm lxxxix. 19; Heb. vii. 25.

First. The ability of Christ to execute the office of a Mediator will appear, when we consider who and what he was. He was no other than the eternal Son of God, of the same nature and essence with Jehovah the Father; for he and the Father were one; of one nature or essence, equal in power and glory; equally possessed of divine attributes and godhead characters, and alike objects of divine worship and adoration. He was the brightness of his Father's glory, and the express image of his person; who upheld all things by the word of his power; superior even to angels, and the object of their religious adoration and worship, Heb. i. 3, 6. And even as Mediator, all power in heaven and earth was given unto him. Thus powerful, thus able, was the divine person chosen and appointed to the office of a Mediator between God and men. We will proceed,

Second. To consider his suitableness or fitness for the discharge of that office. Power, simply considered, did not render him eligible. No, not even his eternal power and godhead. But what principally fits Christ for the execution of his mediatorial office, is the union of the divine and human natures in his one person. Hereby he is Immanuel, God with us; and being partaker of both natures, he must have an interest in, and a concern for both; therefore, while he mediates for man, he must still have a view to the glory of God.

Not to take any notice of his suitableness as the Son of God, and middle person of the Trinity, which yet seems to have some weight, it was necessary that the Mediator should be man, possessed of a human body and a reasonable soul, and so in all points be made like to his brethren, in whose cause he engaged; that he might appear to be their brother and near kinsman, after the flesh; which must afford them the greatest encouragement, when they fly for refuge to lay hold on the hope set before them. Nothing could affect—nothing could encourage the distressed sons of Jacob more than those tender—those moving words, "I am Joseph, your brother." And nothing can more encourage the spiritual Israel, than to know that their Mediator and days-man is their brother, kinsman, and friend. Again, it was necessary that satisfaction and atonement for sin should be made in the same nature that had sinned; therefore, the Mediator must be man. The apostle confirms this observation when he says, "For verily he took not on him the nature of angels, but he took on him the seed of Abraham," Heb. ii. 16; intimating that the nature of angels would not have been eligible to have made conciliation for the sins of human nature. Moreover, it was needful that the Mediator should be man, that he might be capable of obeying the law, given to man and broken by him. Therefore, "he was made of a woman, and made under the law, that he might redeem them that were under the law," Gal. iv. 4, 5. "For as by one man's disobedience many were made sinners, so by the obedience of one shall many be made righteous." Further, it was necessary that the Mediator should be man, that he might be capable of dying, to make an atonement for the sins of men. As God, he could not die. And "without shedding of blood there could be no remission." Therefore, a body was prepared for him, that he might die, the just for the unjust, to bring us unto God, 1 Pet. iii. 18. In fine, it was needful the Mediator should be man, "that he might be a merciful and faithful high priest;" have a fellow-feeling with his people under their infirmities—sympathise with them under their afflictions, and succor them under their temptations. Heb. ii. 17; iv. 15.

But then, the Mediator must not only be man, he must be more than man; he must be a divine person; otherwise he would not be able to draw nigh unto God, and treat with him about the terms on which peace was to be restored to guilty man; and enter into a covenant with him to perform those conditions. "For, who is this that engaged his heart to approach unto me, saith the Lord?" Jer. xxx. 21. Could men or angels have done this? No. None but Jehovah's fellow was equal to this arduous task. Moreover, had the Mediator been only man, he could never have supported under the amazing load of sufferings he had to endure; therefore, he must be God as well as man. All the sins of an elect world were imputed to him, and all the ponderous weight of divine wrath, demerited by those sins, was to fall on his devoted head. "Surely," saith the prophet, "he hath borne our griefs, and carried our sorrows," Isa. liii. 4. A load which would not only have borne down an individual of the human race, but even crushed, as it were, to atoms, all created intelligences, angels as well as men. None could have sustained the stroke of that flaming sword, divine justice, but that wonderful Man, even the God-Man, who was Jehovah's Fellow, Zech. xiii. 7. In fine, it was necessary that Christ should be God, to raise himself from the dead; for had he remained in the grave, we must have perished in our sins, 1 Cor. xv. 17, 18. And to have raised himself, had he been only man, he could not; therefore, he must be God.

Now this Mediator was not only God and man, but he was the God-man; God and man in one person. The human nature was taken into union with, and subsisted in the person of the Son of God. And this personal union was necessary in order to give efficacy, dignity, and merit to his obedience and sufferings. Had he been a mere man, his obedience and righteousness could have been beneficial only to himself; nor could his sufferings and death have atoned for the sins of others; but being God and man, in one person, his mediatorial righteousness is the righteousness of God, and therefore all-sufficient to justify men; and his blood is the blood of the Son of God, and so cleanses from all sin, and is a proper atonement for it.

And in this view, God is said to have purchased the church "with his own blood," Acts xx. 28. Thus having taken a view of the ability and suitableness of Christ for the office of Mediator, we shall,

Third. Consider his qualification for the great work. Although the ability and suitableness of Christ, involve the idea of qualifications for the execution of his mediatorial office, yet those spoken of are purely personal, or such as relate to his person as the God-man; besides which, he sustains various relative characters and offices, which qualify him for his work, as,

1. That of a covenant head to the elect. As such, God chose him from all eternity, and chose all his people in him, as members of his mystical body, Isa. xlii. 1; Eph. i. 4. As such, God made a covenant with him of life and peace, respecting the salvation and happiness of his people. This covenant was confirmed of God, in Christ, i. e., made sure with his covenant-people, in Christ, their head and representative. All the promises and blessings of the covenant are secured to the elect in Christ, their federal head. All that Christ did and suffered, was in their room and stead. They were crucified with Christ, arose from the dead, ascended up into heaven, and sat down at the right hand of God with him; or in him representatively, as their covenant head, Gal. ii. 20; Col. iii. 1; Eph. ii. 6.

2. Christ is the surety of his people. As such, he drew nigh to God, in covenant, and engaged to do and suffer all that the law and justice of God required, to make satisfaction for their sins. He put himself in their law place, took the whole debt of his people upon himself, and became reponsible for it. They owed a debt of obedience to the law, and a debt of punishment for the violation of it; this double debt he assumed payment of, and did pay: in consequence of which, the elect, who were the principal debtors, were set free; and Jehovah, the Father, said, "Deliver them from going down to the pit; I have found a ransom," Job xxxiii. 24. Although the ransom price was not actually paid until the death of the surety; yet he being the Lamb slain from the foundation of the world, in the decrees and purposes of God, who had accepted of his suretyship-engagements, the virtue and efficacy of his obedience, sufferings and death was applied to all the Old Testament saints; and they were justified, pardoned, and saved thereby, as fully and amply as those under the New, 2 Cor. v. 19; Acts xv. 11; Heb. xi. 13.

3. The Mediator is an advocate for all the chosen people of God, 1 John ii. 1. In his character he drew nigh unto God, in the eternal council and covenant of grace, "and made intercession for the transgressors," Isa. liii. 12. This he did, not by laboring to extenuate their crimes, but by offering himself as their sponsor, to stand in their room and stead; bear their sins; make an atonement for their guilt; restore to the law its honors, and answer all the demands of justice, Isa. liii. 4–6; Rom. v. 11; Isa. xlii. 1. And the advocacy of the Mediator proved efficacious to the pardoning, justifying, and glorifying an elect world, Rom. viii. 33, 34.

4. Another office which Christ sustains, is that of a prophet,

Acts iii. 22. Under this character he was expected by the Jews, John vi. 14, and in this capacity he acted as Mediator. As a prophet, he not only foretold future events, as the destruction of Jerusalem, the calamities that should befall the Jews, the end of the world, &c.; but he taught, and does teach his people, so as never man taught. He teaches the knowledge of God, even the saving knowledge of the Most High, as a God of grace and mercy, as a God in covenant, pacified towards poor sinners, notwithstanding all that they have done, John xvii. 3; Ezek. xvi. 63. He teaches the knowledge of himself, as the only and alone Mediator, the Redeemer and Saviour of lost sinners, Matt. xi. 28. He teaches man to know himself, that he is a sinner, lost and undone, without power to help or deliver himself, and the necessity of a better righteousness than that of his own, Phil. iii. 8, 9. He teaches the necessity of holiness in order to happiness, Heb. xii. 14. All which, this great Prophet teaches powerfully and efficaciously, by his word and Spirit.

5. Again, the Mediator is a priest, Psalm cx. 4. He is "an High Priest over the house of God," Heb. x. 21. The business of a priest was to minister at the sanctuary, and offer up gifts and sacrifices for the sins of the people, Heb. viii. 3. "For every high priest is ordained to offer gifts and sacrifices: wherefore it is necessary that this man should have somewhat also to offer;" and for this purpose a body was prepared him: a true body and a reasonable soul, even the whole of human nature; which being united to the person of the Son of God, was offered up a sacrifice, to satisfy divine justice for the sins of an elect world. And by this oblation a true and proper atonement was made for sin, satisfaction to divine justice was given, the wrath of an offended Deity was appeased, and sinners have free access unto God, as a God in covenant, a Father and Friend. Amazing scheme of salvation! Astonishing to men and angels! 1 Pet. x. 12. Intercession was another branch of the priestly office. Christ ever lives to make intercession for his people, Heb. vii. 25. He prays for them that they may be pardoned, justified, sanctified, and saved; yea, he prays that where he is, there they may be also, that they may behold his glory, John xvii. 24. But,

6. The Mediator is also a king, Psalm ii. 6. Saints are the subjects of his mediatorial kingdom; whom he rules by the most wholesome laws; and unto whom he hath given a most glorious charter of privileges, contained in the covenant of grace; which is ordered in all things and sure, 2 Sam. xxiii. 5. He rules in his people by the power of divine grace, and he rules for them, conquering and subduing all his and their enemies; and "he must reign till he has put all enemies under his feet," 1 Cor. xv. 25. These are some of Christ's qualifications for his work as Mediator.

IV. We are now to consider how he hath effected it, or what he hath done for that purpose.

Besides those eternal transactions and covenant engagements, already taken notice of, and in consequence thereof, the eternal Son of God did, in time, take upon him human nature, with all its sinless infirmities. According to ancient predictions he was to be made of the woman's seed, and born of a virgin; therefore he was conceived by the power of the Holy Ghost, in the womb of the virgin Mary; of whom he was born, free from sin. Thus "the Word was made flesh," and dwelt with men on earth; some of whom "beheld his glory, the glory as of the only begotten of the Father, full of grace and truth," John i. 14. The grand design of his incarnation was to save an elect world: in order to which, as he was made of a woman, so he was made under the law. He was born under obligations to keep the law, as the surety of his people. The law must be kept, or man could not be saved. It is holy, just, and good, righteous in all its demands. Perfect obedience it positively requires; a single deviation therefrom exposes to the curse, Gal. iii. 10. Had Christ failed only in one point, his mediation would have been of no avail. But his obedience was complete. Divine justice could not charge it with the least flaw. "Such an High Priest became us, who is holy, harmless, undefiled, and separate from sinners," Heb. vii. 26. And such an one was Jesus Christ: "who did no sin, neither was guile found in his mouth," 1 Pet. ii. 22.

Again, Christ, as Mediator, not only kept the law inviolable, but he died the cursed death of the cross, to atone for the sins of his people. Without shedding of blood there could be no remission. And as the blood of slain beasts was insufficent to cleanse from sin, Christ offered his own, Heb. ix. 19. "Neither by the blood of goats and calves, but by his own blood, he entered once into the holy place: having obtained eternal redemption for us." "The blood of Jesus Christ," being the blood of the Son of God, hath a divine efficacy, and "cleanseth from all sin," 1 John i. 7. But, not only did Jesus suffer in his body, he endured infinitely greater torture in his soul. His bodily sufferings were indeed great, beyond compare. In this view, he was emphatically "a man of sorrows, and acquainted with grief," Isa. liii. 3. His wounded, mangled, bruised body, was so changed from what it had been, as to excite astonishment in the beholders. "As many were astonished at thee. His visage was so marred more than any man, and his form more than the sons men," Isa. lii. 14. So distorted were his limbs, as to extract from him this grievous complaint; "My bones are all out of joint. I may tell all my bones, they look and stare upon me," Psalm xxii. 14–17. Let imagination paint to faith's view the innocent Jesus, clothed in a robe of mock majesty, enveloped round with invidious foes taunting and jeering at him, spitting on his face, smiting it with their hands, piercing his head with a crown of thorns, plowing furrows, long and deep, on his back, with a whip of wires; driving iron spikes through his hands and feet, nailing them to the cross, and thus suspending him between heaven and earth, exposed naked to the inclement rays of a burning sun, a spectacle to men and angels. Thus behold the agonizing Jesus, and judge whether there were ever any sorrows like unto his sorrows, or pains comparable to those he endured. But, after all, the sufferings of his soul were infinitely superior to these.

These he bore—those he deprecated. Apprehensions of the divine wrath, which was to fall on his soul, caused his human nature to shrink, and drew from him these mournful accents, "Now is my soul troubled, and what shall I say? Father save me from this hour," John xii. 27. And when the vials of wrath began to be poured out upon him, he was in an agony—sweat great drops of blood, and said, "My soul is exceeding sorrowful, even unto death." "O my Father, if it be possible, let this cup pass from me; nevertheless not as I will, but as thou wilt," Luke xxii. 44; Matt. xxvi. 38, 39. And when his soul was made an offering for sin, and divine wrath was poured out upon him to the uttermost, he cried out, "My God! my God! why hast thou forsaken me?" Matt. xxvii. 46. Thus Jesus, the Mediator, suffered for us men, and for our salvation. Thus he died, commending his spirit into the hands of his heavenly Father, Heb. ii. 10. And that his humiliation might be reduced to the lowest degree, he was laid in the grave, where he continued three days and three nights, but his body "saw no corruption." On the third day he arose from the dead; for it was not in the power of the grave to hold him. Though he had been put to death in the flesh, he was quickened by the Spirit, Heb. iii. 18. The resurrection of Christ from the dead is an essential part of his mediatorial work; for had he not been raised out of the grave, all that he had done would have been ineffectual to the salvation of sinners. Hence saith the apostle, "If Christ be not raised, your faith is vain, you are yet in your sins," 1 Cor. xv. 17. If the Head had continued under the power of death, the members must have remained there also. "But now is Christ risen from the dead, and become the first fruits of them that slept," 1 Cor. xv. 20. After his resurrection he continued many days on earth, showing himself to his disciples; comforting, encouraging, and confirming them; and then "ascended up on high, leading captivity captive;" when the everlasting doors were opened to receive the King of glory; and the heavenly arches rang with joyful acclamations; shouting, The Redeemer! God the Father manifested his approbation of all that he had done, and the high esteem he had for him as Mediator, by placing him at his right hand, "Far above all principality, and power, and might, and dominion, and every name that is named," Eph. ii. 21. There the Mediator now sits, pleading the value of his merits on behalf of his chosen people; and we may be sure that "he is able to save them to the uttermost, that come unto God by him, seeing he ever liveth to make intercession for them," Heb. vii. 25.

V. We proceed to point out some of the effects of his mediatorship.

First. With regard to God. Hereby God is glorified, more than he would have been if Adam had never fallen, or if all mankind had perished under the ruins of sin, John xvii. 4. All the moral perfections of the Deity are illustriously displayed and glorified in the salvation of sinners, through Jesus Christ. His wisdom appears conspicuous in contriving the plan; his power, in effecting it; his love, in giving his own Son; his justice, in punishing him; his mercy, in pardoning sinners; and his holiness in cleansing them from sin in his Son's blood. The angels, at the Redeemer's birth, sang, "Glory to God in the highest, and on earth peace, good will towards men." And all the ransomed of the Lord will praise God for this wonderful scheme of salvation, to all eternity.

Second. With regard to the law of God. The mediatorship of Christ hath restored to the law all its rights and honors; for he hath magnified the law and made it honorable, by yielding a perfect obedience to it, and dying to make satisfaction for the breach of it.

Third. With regard to man, the blessed effects of Christ's mediatorship are scarce to be enumerated.

1. Hereby that desirable blessing peace, lost by sin, is restored to all the people of God. Christ is "the Prince of peace," Isa. ix. 6. His covenant is a covenant of peace, Isa. liv. 10. His gospel is the gospel of peace, Rom. x. 15. And this blessing he bequeathed to his people as a legacy, John xiv. 27. 1. Through him they have peace with God, Rom. v. 1. Of him it is said, "This man shall be the peace," i. e. the peace-maker, Micha. v. 5; and "he hath made peace by the blood of his cross," Col. i. 20. 2. They have peace of conscience, "joy and peace in believing," Rom. xv. 13. Their hearts being sprinkled from an evil or guilty conscience, they enjoy great peace within. 3. They have peace one with another, Mark ix. 50. Being all one in Christ, their hearts are knit together in love, Gal. iii. 28; Col. ii. 2. The enmity betwixt Jews and Gentiles is removed, and they are united together in one body; "For he is our peace, who hath made both one, and hath broken down the middle wall of partition between us," Eph. ii. 13.

2. Pardon of sin is another effect of Christ's mediatorship. God, for Christ's sake, forgives his people, Eph. iv. 32. The blood of Christ was shed to make an atonement for, and obtain the remission of our sins; and God "is faithful and just to forgiving us our sins, and cleanse us from all unrighteousness," 1 John i. 9.

3. Justification is also through the mediatorship of Christ, "In the Lord shall all the seed of Israel be justified, and shall glory." Isa. xlv. 35. The righteousness of Christ, as mediator, is the sole matter and cause of a sinner's justification before God, Rom. v. 17, 18. This righteousness Christ wrought out by his active and passive obedience to the law; and by it, "all that believe are justified from all things, from which they could not be justified by the law of Moses," Acts xiii. 39.

4. Adoption is likewise through the mediation of Christ, and on account of what he hath done and suffered for us. He was "made of a woman, made under the law, to redeem them that were under the law; that we might receive the adoption of sons," Gal. iv. 4, 5. By this act of divine grace, we are received into the family of God, as his dear children; and are favored with the grace and "spirit of adoption, whereby we cry, Abba, Father;" being "heirs of God and joint heirs with Christ," and so entitled to all the blessings and privileges of the sons of God, Rom. viii. 15–17.

5. Through the mediation of Christ we enjoy the renewing, comforting, and sanctifying influences of the Holy Spirit. He was a party concerned in the covenant of grace, of which Christ is the Mediator: and he is sent by Christ to convince the world of sin, renew the soul, comfort the people of God, sanctify and make them meet for heaven, John xvi. 8; Tit. iii. 5; Heb. xii. 14.

6. All the blessings and privileges of the gospel come flowing to us through the mediation of Christ. The gospel itself is his gospel, Rom. xv. 20. The doctrines of it are his doctrines; they treat of his person, offices, grace, blood, and righteousness. The promises, which are exceeding great and precious, "are all yea and amen, in Christ," 2 Pet. i. 4; 2 Cor. i. 20. Gospel ordinances were instituted by Christ, and represent, the one, his death, burial, and resurrection; the other, his body broken, and blood shed, for our salvation, Rom. vi. 3, 4; 1 Cor. xxiv. 25. In a word, the laws, rules, and discipline of his house, are all good and wholesome, having a tendency to assimilate us to Christ and prepare us for glory.

7. Once more: through the mediation of Christ, we have liberty of access unto God, and are invited to "come boldly to the throne of grace, that we may obtain mercy, and find grace to help us in time of need," Heb. iv. 16.

8. In fine, eternal life is enjoyed through the mediation of Christ; for, although heaven is no where said to be purchased by Christ, yet sinners are redeemed in order that they may enjoy it. They are "vessels of mercy prepared unto glory," Rom. ix. 23. And it is the will of Christ, that all those whom the Father hath given unto him, should be with him, where he is, that they may behold his glory, John xvii. 27.

Thus, dear brethren, have we endeavored to treat of Christ the Mediator, and we trust that his fulness and suitableness have, in some measure, been made to appear. That you may live to, for, and upon him, and at last live and reign with him, is the prayer of yours in the faith and fellowship of the gospel.

Signed by order of the Association,

OLIVER HART, Moderator.
WM. VANHORN, Clerk.

THE MINISTERS AND MESSENGERS AT THE ASSOCIATION, AND STATE OF THE CHURCHES DURING THE YEAR.

CHURCHES.	MINISTERS AND MESSENGERS.	Baptized.	Received by Letter.	Dismis'd.	Excom.	Dead.	Members
Pennepek,	SAMUEL JONES,	3	0	0	0	2	59
Middletown,	ABEL MORGAN,*	0	0	0	0	0	95
Piscataqua,	———	0	0	0	0	1	0
Cohansie,	ROBERT KELSAY,*	43	1	0	0	6	120
Great Valley,	THOMAS JONES,	0	0	0	0	0	35
Cape May,	DAVID SMITH,*	9	0	0	0	0	67
Hopewell,	OLIVER HART,	2	0	5	1	4	205
Brandywine,	ABEL GRIFFITH,	0	0	0	0	0	19
Montgomery,	DAVID LOOFBOUGHROW,	0	1	54	0	0	27
Kingwood,	DAVID SUTTON,	0	1	0	0	0	70
Southampton,	WILLIAM VANHORN,	0	0	0	0	1	55
Philadelphia,	THOMAS USTICK,	3	0	0	46	2	87
Cranberry,	PETER WILSON,	3	0	0	0	1	39
Scotch Plains,	BENJAMIN COLE,	2	0	1	0	6	101
Harford, Maryland,	JOHN DAVIS,*	10	0	0	0	0	0
New Britain,	JOSHUA JONES,	3	0	0	0	1	32
Salem,	———	8	0	0	0	3	39
Newtown,	NICHOLAS COX,	3	0	0	0	1	70
Bateman's Precincts,	SAMUEL WALDO,*	1	0	0	0	1	0
Dividing Creek,	PETER P. VANHORN,	2	1	5	1	1	61
New Mills,	———	2	1	1	0	1	57
Upper Freehold,	JOHN BLACKWELL,	4	2	0	0	2	70
Mount Bethel,	ABNER SUTTON,	1	0	0	0	0	23
Pittsgrove,	WILLIAM WORTH,	20	0	1	0	0	89
Vincent,	———	0	0	0	0	0	35
Stamford,	———	4	0	0	0	1	42
Amenia Precincts,	ELKANA HOLMES,	3	0	0	0	0	38
London Tract,	THOMAS FLEESON,	1	0	0	0	1	28
Cow Marsh,	———	13	0	0	0	0	35
Hilltown,	JOHN THOMAS,	0	0	0	0	0	61
		140	7	65	48	31	1659

NOTE.—Ministers marked thus * were absent. A dash ——— denotes churches destitute of a settled minister.

MINUTES

OF THE

PHILADELPHIA BAPTIST ASSOCIATION,

HELD AT PHILADELPHIA, OCTOBER 21ST, 22D, AND 23D,

1783.

Tuesday, October 21st.—At three o'clock, P. M., Rev. Oliver Hart delivered a very suitable discourse, according to appointment, from Haggai ii. 4; "Yet now be strong, O Zerubbabel, saith the Lord, and be strong, O Joshua, son of Josedech, the high priest, and be strong all ye people of the land, saith the Lord, and work; for I am with you, saith the Lord of hosts."

2. After sermon, Brother John Gano, being first received as a member, was chosen moderator, and Brother Thomas Ustick, clerk.

3. Letters from twenty-seven churches were read.

Adjourned till to-morrow morning, nine o'clock.

4. Wednesday, October 22d.—Met pursuant to adjournment. As several letters from our churches take notice of the happy event of the present peace, so far as it has been effected; and intimate the propriety of acknowledging the same by a day of public thanksgiving,

Resolved, That although the event be glorious, and the prospect promising, calling for our humble and sincere acknowledgments, yet we think it most expedient to defer the observation of a day on the occasion, that, after recommendation of Congress, we may unite with the continent in so desirable a work.

5. The subject of the introductory sermon being very important, and treated much to our satisfaction, Brother Hart is requested to prepare the same for immediate publication; and the churches are requested to forward their subscriptions to Brother Ustick without delay.

6. The church at Welsh Tract having requested that we would consider the expediency of reprinting a pamphlet, entitled "A Scripture Manual," by T. Craner; Resolved, As we have agreed to publish the introductory sermon on the same subject, and our ports are now open, the churches disposed may furnish themselves from abroad; but should it appear that they are out of print, our brethren, Samuel Jones, William Vanhorn, and Thomas Ustick, are re-

quested to examine said piece, and consider the propriety of its republication.

7. In answer to the query from Newtown church: Whether laying on of hands be an ordinance of the gospel to be administered to all baptized persons, or only in particular cases? we observe, that imposition of hands on baptized persons has been the general practice of the churches in union with this Association, and is still used by most of them; but it was never considered by the Association as a bar of communion. Resolved, That any person scrupling to submit thereto, may be admitted to the fellowship of the church without it.

Brother Gano is requested to preach this evening.

Adjourned till to-morrow morning, nine o'clock.

8. Thursday, October 23d.—Met pursuant to adjournment. By request, Rev. Jacob Hutton, from Broughton, in England, presented his letter of recommendation, which being satisfactory, the members of the Association thereupon gave him a cordial reception.

9. Brother William Vanhorn was appointed to write to the Warren, Brother Oliver Hart to Charleston, and Brother John Pitman to the Ketockton Association. Our messengers to the first, Rev. John Gano, Burgess Allison, and William Vanhorn; to the last, Rev. William Worth and Thomas Fleeson.

10. Supplies were granted to the following destitute churches:— Lyon's Farms, Morristown, and Kingwood.

11. The circular letter for the present year was prepared by Brother Samuel Jones; appointed Brother Abel Morgan and John Gano to write for next year.

12. Resolved, That our next Association be at New York, on the first Tuesday in October, at three o'clock, P. M. The introductory sermon by Brother Abel Morgan; and, in case of failure, by Brother Thomas Ustick.

CIRCULAR LETTER.

BY REV. SAMUEL JONES, A. M.

The elders and brethren of the several churches, met in Association at Philadelphia, October 21st, 1783.

To the several churches to which we relate, send greeting.

Dearly beloved,—Through the kind indulgence of a gracious God, we met according to appointment. We have been favored, as usual, with peace and harmony, during the whole of our consultations, for which we call on you to join us in giving glory to the Head of the church.

For the result of our deliberations, together with the good tidings we received from different parts, we refer you to the minutes of our proceedings, which we herewith send you.

The point of doctrine, which, according to our order, comes next under consideration, is, the freedom of man's will. Confession of faith, Chap. IX.

The inquiry concerning the liberty of the will is, whether man, as a moral agent, acts freely, without any restraint or constraint. That he should act thus freely, without any coercive force on the will, is necessary, in order to his being a free agent, or the subject of moral government. For if he acted under constraint, as his actions would not be free, they could not be charged to him, as virtuous or vicious, but must be placed to the account of that being, under whose influence he acted. So essential is it to the cause of morality to support the liberty of the will.

How it can be that the decrees of God, and the superintendence of Providence, do not interfere with this freedom and liberty of the will, is what renders the subject difficult; and it will, perhaps, remain in some measure inexplicable, until we arrive to a state of a more free and clear exercise of our mental powers, and a greater perfection in knowledge.

That there is a Divine Providence is as certain and necessary, as that there is a God : and that the Divine Being governs and sustains the universe, as that he made it.

Nor is there much difficulty in admitting and conceiving this precedence of the Deity among the orders of inanimate nature ; nor yet with regard to moral agents, so far as respects good actions; but how far the divine agency is versant about evil actions, is one of the most perplexing inquiries in the whole compass of theology.

Nevertheless, that the providence of God has a concern in evil actions is clear, not only from what we have suggested above, but also from those Scriptures following, on which no consistent meaning can be put, without admitting that superintendence of the divine Being, of which we are speaking.

Joseph, addressing his brethren concerning their selling him into Egypt, tells them, that it was not they that sent him thither, but God. Gen. xiv. 8. And God is said to harden Pharaoh's heart. Exod. iv. 21. The same is also said of Sihon, king of Hesbon. Deut. ii. 30. And David, speaking of Shimei's cursing him, says, that God had bid him. 2 Sam. xvi. 10.

By these, and such like passages, it is clear that the providence of God is some how conversant even about evil actions ; but we know it must be in such a way as that he is neither the author nor approver of sin ; and it may be in these ways following :

1. By causing the object to be presented, which, through the corruptions of our nature, may be the occasion of sin ; as in the case of Joseph and his brethren, David and Shimei. Now all this may be, and yet the Supreme Disposer of all things perfectly clear; for the presentation of the object does not lay a necessity of sinning, nor is the object presented with a view to occasion the sin. Thus our blessed Lord, a little before his crucifixion, knew that his going to Jerusalem at that time would prove the occasion, by presenting the object, of his being apprehended and crucified. But he did not go thither with that view ; nor did his going, or his knowing what they would do, lay them under a necessity of doing it.

2. It may be in suffering and permitting sin, not in suggesting it,

or influencing to it, as the Apostle James, speaks: "Let no man say, when he is tempted, that he is tempted of God; for God cannot be tempted with evil, neither tempteth he any man. But every man is tempted when he is drawn away of his own lusts and enticed." Jam. i. 13, 14,

3. The providence of God is conversant about evil actions, in overruling them to his own glory, as in the case of Joseph, just now mentioned; but especially the fall of man, and the sufferings of our Redeemer.

It may further be of use, in considering this subject, to distinguish between what is natural and what is sinful in an action; the former being from God, but the latter from ourselves. Thus the power of speech, and the faculties of the mind are from God, but the misuse and abuse of those powers and faculties to the purposes of blasphemy, and the like, must be from the corruptions of our own hearts. This is illustrated by an apt similitude, taken from the sun's drawing forth vapors from the earth, by that heat, which has a tendency to exhale them; but the stench that attends what is exhaled from a dunghill, or any putrid substance, is not owing to the sun, but the nature of the substance from whence it is drawn.

In the chapter referred to above, the free agency of man is applied to his fourfold state.

1. The state of innocence; concerning which there is no difficulty except the decree, which affects all states and actions alike.

2. His fallen state; wherein man is naturally inclined and prone to that which is evil, but averse to that which is good. Now, in conversion, the operations of grace do not offer violence to the will; but the understanding is enlightened, and a discovery is made to the creature of his awful situation in a state of sin and guilt, in consequence of which, sin is embittered, the attention is turned to the spiritual concern of the soul, the desire is excited after pardon, and thus is wrought in him to will and to do, and he is made willing in the day of God's power.

3. The state of man after conversion, wherein he is actuated by a two-fold principle; the remains of nature, and the principle of grace: as the apostle speaks, Rom. vii. 15, 24. Concerning the first there is no difficulty, and the other operates much after the same manner as in conversion, explained above.

4. And lastly, the state of glory, wherein the inclination will only be to that which is good, which, however, is not inconsistent with freedom, but is the perfection of it, as in the Divine Being himself, since liberty consists in freedom to follow the desire, while it is confined within the limits of the agent's power.

As for the inference of the decree with the liberty of which we are speaking, if it be hard to conceive how it should not, so, let it be remembered, it is as hard to conceive how it should. The blessed Jesus, for instance, is said to be delivered by the determinate counsel and fore-knowledge of God, Acts ii. 23. But what influence could this fore-knowledge have on the Jews, who were not conscious of it, and never adverted to it in all their proceedings, but acted freely, according to the natural course of their wicked inclinations, even those vile affections of malice, hatred, selfishness, envy, and the like, they were actuated by.

Thus, dear brethren, we have brought to your view, and briefly explained this abstruse subject, so far as the nature of it, and the narrowness of our limits would admit. You see three things are certain: 1st, The decrees and providence of God: 2dly, That he is neither the author nor approver of sin: yet, 3dly, That man is a free agent. And if there be any difficulty in perceiving the agreement between the first and the last, yet not near so great as to reject all three, or either of them. It is not necessary we should know every thing. There are mysteries in nature as well as in providence and grace. We should beware of picking the lock, as one expresses it, of which the key is not in our keeping. It becomes us rather humbly to adore that God, who does all things well, Mark vii. 37; but gives account of his matters to none, Job xxxiii. 13; and be thankful for that wonderful and all-sufficient discovery of divine truth, that has been made. Let us use diligence in improving those discoveries to the glory of God, and our own advancement in grace, that we may be built up in faith and holiness. Now unto the King eternal, immortal, invisible, the only wise God, be honor and glory, for ever and ever. Amen.

JOHN GANO, Moderator.
THOMAS USTICK, Clerk.

THE MINISTERS AND MESSENGERS AT THE ASSOCIATION, AND STATE OF THE CHURCHES DURING THE YEAR.

CHURCHES.	MINISTERS AND MESSENGERS.	Baptized.	Received by Letter.	Dismiss'd.	Dead.	Excom.	Members.
Pennepek,	Samuel Jones, A. M., John Pitman, John Stancliff, Jesse Dungan,	5	1	0	1	0	64
Middletown,	Abel Morgan, A. M., Samuel Morgan, John Cook,	2	1	0	0	0	98
Piscataqua,†	—						
Cohansie,	Robert Kelsay,* Philip Shepherd, David Elwell,	6	6	0	3	0	129
Great Valley,	Nicholas Cox, Thomas Jones,	0	2	0	1	0	38
Cape May,	David Smith,* Thomas Yates,	8	0	0	5	0	70
Hopewell,	Oliver Hart, Nathaniel Stout,	4	1	2	1	3	204
Brandywine,†	Abel Griffith, John Garrett,	0	0	1	0	0	18

CHURCHES.	MINISTERS AND MESSENGERS.	Baptized.	Received by Letter.	Dismis'd.	Dead.	Excom.	Members.
Montgomery,	David Loughborough,	9	1	0	0	3	34
Kingwood,	Andrew Bray,	11	0	6	1	0	75
Southampton,	Wm. Vanhorn, A. M., Isaac Hough,	2	0	0	2	0	55
Philadelphia,	Thomas Ustick, A. M., Benjamin Thaw, George Ingols, David Bowen, Thomas Shields, John M'Kim,	6	1	0	1	10	99
Cranberry,†	Peter Wilson,	5	0	0	1	0	43
Scotch Plains,	Benjamin Cole,*	3	0	0	1	0	103
Hartford, Maryland,	John Davis,*	0	0	0	0	0	0
New Britain,	Joshua Jones, Benjamin Matthew,	5	0	0	1	0	36
Salem,	Thomas Sayer,	8	0	0	1	0	46
Newtown,	James Finn,	7	1	4	0	0	75
Bateman's Precincts,†	Samuel Waldo,*	0	0	0	0	0	0
Dividing Creek,	Peter P. Vanhorn,	4	0	6	1	1	57
New Mills,	Samuel Gaskill,	12	0	0	1	0	68
Upper Freehold,	John Blackwell, Samuel Cox, Samuel Sexton,	12	1	0	2	0	81
Mount Bethel,†	Abner Sutton,*	0	0	0	0	0	23
Pittsgrove,	William Worth, Artist Seagraves, Cornelius Austin,	5	0	1	2	0	91
Vincent,†		0	0	0	0	0	35
Stamford,	Elkanah Holmes,*	17	2	0	2	0	60
Amenia Precincts,†		0	0	0	0	0	38
London Tract,	Thomas Fleeson, John Evans,	0	0	0	0	0	27
Cow Marsh,		0	0	0	0	0	35
Hilltown,	John Thomas, Nathan Evans, Elijah Davis,	35	0	0	2	0	94
Welsh Tract,	John Boggs,* Isaiah Lewis,	0	0	0	0	0	52
Tuckahoe,	William Lock,*	22	1	1	1	0	56
Lyon's Farms,	Jacob Hutton,	0	0	0	0	0	10
Morristown,		6	0	0	0	0	50
		194	18	21	34	14	1964

Note.—The ministers' names are in SMALL CAPITALS. Those marked thus * were not present. The churches marked thus † sent neither letters nor messengers, and their numbers remain as last year. A dash denotes no settled minister.

MINUTES

OF THE

PHILADELPHIA BAPTIST ASSOCIATION,

HELD AT NEW YORK, OCTOBER 5TH, 6TH, AND 7TH,

1784.

Tuesday, October 5th.—At three o'clock, P. M., Brother Thomas Ustick delivered a suitable discourse, from 1 Phil. i. 27, "That ye stand fast in one Spirit, with one mind, striving together for the faith of the Gospel."

2. Brother Samuel Waldo was chosen moderator, and Brother William Vanhorn, clerk.

3. Letters from the churches were read.

Adjourned till to-morrow morning, nine o'clock.

4. October 6th.—Met pursuant to adjournment. A letter and minutes from the Warren Association were read; whereby it appears that they are, in general, at peace amongst themselves. The additions to their churches this year are fifty-eight; their whole number three thousand five hundred and sixty-one. That, besides this Association, they correspond with four others in New England, viz., one in Vermont, one in New Hampshire Grants, one in Stonington, in Connecticut, and another in the State of New Hampshire, consisting of six churches and four hundred members, which opened a communication with them this present year.

5. A letter from the Ketockton Association was read, informing us that they enjoy peace among themselves; that the additions to their churches this year were thirty-four; and that two churches joined them at their last meeting.

6. Our ministering brethren, William Rogers, Burgess Allison, Ebenezer Ward, and Nicholas Cox, being present, their company and assistance were desired.

7. A letter from a church constituted the last year in Lower Smithfield, Northampton county, State of Pennsylvania, under the care of Elder David Jane, was read, requesting admission to the Association. Upon a particular and satisfactory relation of their faith and practice, by Brother Cox, who assisted at their constitution, we are free to receive them into union with us, when they shall appear by their messengers.

8. Brother William Rogers was requested to prepare a letter to the Warren Association; Brother Nicholas Cox, one to that of Ketockton, in Virginia; and Brother Ezekiel Robins, one to that in South Carolina.

Adjourned to three o'clock, P. M.

9. Met pursuant to adjournment.—To a query: Whether Jesus Christ was an object of prayer? we answer: We are surprised that one of our sister churches, or any of the members thereof, should be in doubt of an article of faith so plainly revealed in the word of God. The instance of the penitent thief on the cross; of Stephen when stoned, praying to the Lord Jesus; and the injunction to honor the Son as we honor the Father, are sufficiently plain on this point.

Upon inquiry of the messenger from the church who sent the query, and by information of others present, we found that something had been delivered amongst them, and elsewhere, by one in the ministry; which, in our opinion, favors of that deistical error that we discard and abhor as heresy. We therefore seriously recommend it to all our churches, and those who compose them, to try the spirits, whether they be of God, and if they do not maintain the divinity of Jesus Christ, neither to receive them into their houses, nor to bid them God speed.

10. In answer to a query from one of our churches: What measures ought to be taken with a sister church who holds and actually admits unbaptized persons to the Lord's supper? we observe, That such a church may and ought, in the first instance, to be written to by a sister church, exhorting them to desist from such a practice, and to keep the ordinances as they were delivered to them in the word of God.

11. The letters prepared for the different Associations being presented and read, were approved.

12. The circular letter, written by Brother John Gano, was presented and read.

Adjourned till to-morrow morning, nine o'clock.

13. October 7th.—Met pursuant to adjournment. With respect to the request from the church at Kingwood for supplies, we answer, That from the representation made to us, we are in hope transient visits will not be wanted, as, in our opinion, Providence points out clearly the propriety of Brother Cox's settlement with them.

14. From a statement of the circumstances of a bequest of Mr. Honeywell to this Association, which was laid before us by Brother Elkana Holmes, we are induced to appoint our brethren, Elkana Holmes, Dr. John Dodge, Ebenezer Ferris, together with Brother Samuel Jones, or any two of them, a committee to treat with any person or persons concerning the same.

15. Brother Vanhorn reported that he got the binding of the books of the Association library repaired; and from the vouchers he produced, it appears there was a balance of cash in his hands of 16s. 6d.; 4s. of which he is ordered to pay for the postage on the Ke-

tockton Association letter, the residue is granted to him for his superintendence of said business.

16. Whereas, there has been much inattention in some of our churches to a communication with this Association by letters and messengers; and the same being in our opinion of importance to the interest of the churches, we recommend to our Brethren John Gano and Samuel Jones, the former to write to those in the eastern parts, and the latter to those in the western parts of this Association, and press them to a due regard to that connection and correspondence of the churches, which experience has proved to be both comfortable and in many instances advantageous.

17. Met pursuant to adjournment, at three o'clock, P. M. The circular letter being again read and considered, was approved.

18. Our Brethren John Gano and William Rogers, are appointed messengers to the Warren Association; Brother Thomas Fleeson and Brother Elkana Holmes, to that of Virginia. Our Brethren Gano, Rogers, and Vanhorn, jun., or either of them, to that of Charleston, South Carolina.

19. Brother William Rogers is appointed to write the circular letter for the next year.

20. Supplies granted to the following destitute churches:—Scotch Plains, Morristown, Lyon's Farms, and Dividing Creek.

21. Brother William Rogers is appointed to superintend the printing of the minutes of this Association.

22. Resolved, That our next Association be held at Philadelphia, the first Tuesday in October, at three o'clock, P. M. Brother John Dodge is appointed to preach the introductory sermon; or, in case of failure, Brother Elkana Holmes.

CIRCULAR LETTER.

BY REV. JOHN GANO.

The elders and brethren of the several churches, met in Association at New York, October 5th, 6th, and 7th, 1784.

To the churches with whom we are connected, send greeting:

Dearly beloved—The preceding minutes will give you every necessary information relative to our meeting, the state of our churches, and our endeavors for their prosperity. We trust, you will unite your efforts with ours, to the same good purpose; and that our thanksgivings for the present peace, harmony, and increase of our churches, our prayers for their further growth, with a more powerful effusion of the Divine Spirit and grace upon them, will be mutually offered up. May the consideration of our effectual calling prove an incentive thereunto! Which is the subject now to be considered, as in the tenth chapter of our Confession of faith.

That we may investigate this subject as fully as the limits of a letter will allow, we will consider, first, the call; secondly, the Author of the call; thirdly, the called; and fourthly, its efficacy.

I. The call. This is an act of sovereign grace, which flows from the everlasting love of God, and is such an irresistible impression made by the Holy Spirit upon the human soul, as to effect a blessed change. This impression or call is sometimes immediate, as in the instance of Paul and others; though more ordinarily through the instrumentality of the word and providence of God. Though in both the impression or power upon the soul or rational principle of operation must be the same. This may be considered as one power capable of exerting itself in various modes; as in perceiving, choosing, refusing, loving, hating, &c. Likewise the impression before mentioned may be viewed as one spiritual principle of operation in the soul, exerting itself in divers ways, rather than as different principles of grace.

II. We are to consider the Author of the call. The Author is God, the Father, Son, and Spirit. As in 1 Thess. ii. 12, "That ye walk worthy of God, who hath called you unto his kingdom and glory." Also, in 2 Tim. i. 9, "Who hath saved us, and called us with an holy calling, not according to our works, but according to his own purpose and grace," &c. In others it more directly applies to the Father, who is said to call them unto the fellowship of his Son. Sometimes it is ascribed to the Son, as in Proverbs i. 20, viii., where saints are said to be called of Jesus Christ. Lastly, it is ascribed to the Holy Ghost, as in Phil. i. 6; "Being confident of this very thing, that he who hath begun a good work in you will perform it until the day of Jesus Christ." Upon the whole this call is heard as it is in deed and in truth, the call of God, and not the voice of man.

III. We are to consider who are the called. They are such as God hath chosen and predestinated both to grace and glory, elected and set apart in Christ, as redeemed by his blood, although by nature children of wrath even as others; not of the Jews only, but also of the Gentiles. This is an holy, heavenly, and, consequently, an high calling.

IV. Its efficacy. It is effectual to bring the subjects of it to a piercing sense of their guilt and impurity. The mind is deeply convicted, that the fountain is in his very heart or nature, from which all its criminal actions have sprung; and that the lust within disposes us to violate the laws of God in as great a variety of ways as nature is capable of exerting itself, agreeable to Paul's expression, "Sin revived and I died." The soul is affected with a view of its sinfulness and the malignity of sin in its nature, as entirely opposed to the holy law of God; hence arises an abhorrence of sin, as vile and odious, and a sense of its demerit as deserving eternal death. This call produces a consciousness of the absolute impossibility of our contributing in the least degree towards a recovery from this wretched condition, and destroys all confidence of help in the flesh. It is a call to Christ, and gives a view of him in his suitableness and ability as a Saviour; the merit of his obedience and sacrifice, and the treasures of his grace are all brought into view, which creates desires of an interest in him, and resolutions of looking unto and relying wholly upon him for salvation; at the same time cordially acknowledging desert of rejection from him, and yet strengthened to rely entirely upon and surrender all unto the disposal of Christ; setting to our seals that God is true; believing the record he has given of his Son, which is eternal life, and that this life is in his Son. The changes produced are from darkness to light, from bondage to liberty, from alienation and estrangedness to Christ to a state of nearness and fellowship with him and his saints. This call administers peace of conscience towards God, and disposes its subjects to peace with mankind, so far as is consistent with righteousness.

This is an holy calling, and is effectual to produce the exercise of holiness in the heart, even as the saints are created in Christ Jesus unto good works. God having called us, not to uncleanness, but to holiness, yea, even to glory and virtue, and "to live holily, righteously, and godly in this present evil world;" and to conform us, both as men and as Christians, to the pure dictates of nature and the authority of revelation, in all virtuous actions. To believe what is divinely revealed, and to obey what is divinely enjoined; in which the saints are required to persevere unto "an inheritance incorruptible and undefiled, and that fadeth not away, which is reserved in heaven for them," and unto which this effectual vocation ultimately tends. From all which considerations, we learn what it is to be both good and great, and that the way to advance in durable riches and righteousness; to live on high; live above the vanities and pomp of this trifling world, and to shame those who walk unworthily, is to retain a sense of our heavenly vocation. Thus will the hearts and hands of all God's people, and especially his ministers, be supported and strengthened; thus will the religion of our adorable Redeemer be honored in the world; thus shall we glorify God in life and enjoy his peace in death, and leave behind a finished testimony that our calling was effectual and our profession sincere.

Signed by order of the Association,

SAMUEL WALDO, Moderator.
WILLIAM VANHORN, Clerk.

THE MINISTERS AND MESSENGERS AT THE ASSOCIATION, AND STATE OF THE CHURCHES DURING THE YEAR.

CHURCHES.	MINISTERS AND MESSENGERS.	Baptized.	Added by Letter.	Dsmiiss'd.	Excom.	Dead.	Members.
Pennepek,	SAMUEL JONES,*	4	2	2	0	1	67
Middletown,	ABEL MORGAN,* Richard Crawford, William Bown,	0	0	1	0	1	95
Piscataqua,	REUNE RUNYAN, John Runyan,	2	0	0	0	2	40
Cohansie,	ROBERT KELSAY,* David Elwell, Nathan Shepherd,	1	3	1	2	8	121
Welsh Tract,†	JOHN BOGGS,*	0	0	0	0	0	52
Great Valley,†	—— ——	0	0	0	0	0	38

CHURCHES.	MINISTERS AND MESSENGERS.	Baptized.	Added by Letter.	Dismis'd.	Excom.	Dead.	Members.
Cape May,†		0	0	0	0	0	70
Hopewell,	Oliver Hart,* Nathaniel Stout, Stephen Barton,	0	0	3	0	2	199
Brandywine,	Abel Griffiths,*	0	0	0	1	1	16
Montgomery,	David Loofborrow,	4	2	1	0	2	37
Kingwood,	Thomas Runyan,	0	0	1	0	1	73
Southampton,	William Vanhorn,	0	0	1	0	0	54
Philadelphia,	Thomas Ustick, Thomas White,	3	12	6	0	1	107
Cranberry,	Peter Wilson, William Tindel,	9	0	3	0	0	49
Scotch Plains,	David Morris,	0	0	0	0	5	98
Morristown,	Ezekiel Gobel,	0	0	0	0	1	50
New Britain,†	Joshua Jones,*	0	0	0	0	0	36
Salem,	Peter P. Vanhorn,*	0	0	0	0	1	45
Newtown,	James Finn,*	2	0	0	2	1	74
Pawling's Precincts,	Samuel Waldo,	5	1	1	2	0	53
Dividing Creek,		0	2	1	0	2	49
New York,	John Gano, Samuel Dodge, Ezekiel Robbins, Zebulon Barton,	0	0	0	0	0	61
New Mills,		7	1	2	0	0	73
Upper Freehold,	John Blackwell,* James Cox,	5	0	0	0	1	84
Mount Bethel,	Abner Sutton,*	0	0	0	0	0	23
Lyon's Farms,	Ichabod Grummon,	0	0	0	0	0	12
Pittsgrove,†	William Worth,*	0	0	0	0	0	91
Tuckahoe,†	William Lock,*	0	0	0	0	0	56
Stamford,	Elkana Holmes, Sylvenus Reynolds, Elijah Hunt,	19	0	0	2	0	77
King Street,	John Dodge, William Brundage,	0	0	0	0	0	17
Cow Marsh,		0	0	0	0	0	35
London Tract,	Thomas Fleeson,	1	0	0	0	1	27
Hilltown,	John Thomas, Moses Aaron,	4	0	0	0	0	98
		166	23	21	9	33	2077

Note.—The ministers' names are in SMALL CAPITALS. Those marked thus * not present. The churches marked thus † sent neither letters nor messengers. A dash ——— denotes no settled minister.

MINUTES

OF THE

PHILADELPHIA BAPTIST ASSOCIATION,

HELD AT PHILADELPHIA, OCTOBER 4TH, 5TH, AND 6TH,

1785.

Tuesday, P. M., October 4th.—The Association was opened with a suitable discourse from John xvi. 8, by Brother Samuel Jones.

2. Brother Oliver Hart was chosen moderator, and Brother William Rogers, clerk. Letters from thirty churches were read.

3. Brother James Manning, president of Rhode Island College, being present, his company and assistance were desired.

Adjourned till to-morrow morning, half past eight o'clock.

Wednesday, October 5.—Met pursuant to adjournment.

1. The minutes of our last year's Association were read.

2. A letter and minutes from Charleston Association, held at the High Hills of Santee, October 27th, 1783, were received from their annual committee and read.

3. A letter from the Warren Association, held at Wrentham, State of Massachusetts, September 14th, 1785, was delivered by their messenger, Brother Hezekiah Smith, and read, whereby it appears that in the neighborhood of Boston, several persons of unblemished reputation were imprisoned the winter past, by reason of their refusing to support a way of worship repugnant to the dictates of their own minds. Though the constitution under which they live, equally secures their privileges with those who, repugnant to all sound policy, continue to persecute them.

4. A letter from Ketockton Association, Virginia, held August 19th, 1785, was read. Their messenger, Brother Elijah Craig, took his seat among us.

5. Brother Peter P. Vanhorn was requested to prepare a letter for Charleston Association; Brother Thomas Ustick, for the Warren, and Brother Thomas Fleeson, for Ketockton. Messengers to Charleston Association, Brother John Gano; to the Warren, Brother William Rogers; to that of Ketockton, Brother Eliphaz Dazey.

6. The church of Philadelphia, having represented that a number of books lately taken from the city and committed to the care of the Association librarian, belonged to said church.

Agreed, That in order to bring the matter to an issue, our brethren, S. Jones, W. Vanhorn, and Joshua Jones, be a committee on behalf of the Association, to meet a committee of Philadelphia church, that the right of said property may be adjusted.

Adjourned to three o'clock, P. M.

1. Met pursuant to adjournment.—Our brethren, Samuel Jones and Hezekiah Smith, having in the morning been appointed to consider upon that part of the letter from Great Valley church, which requests information relative to a minute of last year, concerning "Jesus Christ as an object of prayer," reported, "that the person, of whom the churches were then cautioned to beware, and the cause whereon their procedure was founded, be all referred for further investigation and settlement to the church at Upper Freehold, whereof he is a member, though not their present minister." Agreed, that said report be adopted.

2. The query from Philadelphia church, relative to the "administration of the Lord's supper, among any of our brethren and sisters, however numerous they may be in any one place, during the period of their remaining unorganized, or unconstituted as a distinct, regular church by themselves," requiring mature deliberation, it is thought best to postpone our final conclusion thereon until next Association.

3. Brother Samuel Jones is appointed to copy into the Association book, all such minutes, as by him may be judged of real utility and future advantage.

Adjourned until to-morrow morning, half past eight o'clock.

Sermon in the evening by Brother Smith, from 1 John v. 3.

Thursday, October 6.—Met pursuant to adjournment.

1. The circular letter composed, according to appointment, by Brother William Rogers, having been the day past presented and read, was again taken under consideration and approved. Brother Thomas Ustick is appointed to write one for the ensuing year.

2. The letters to the different Associations, corresponding with this, were brought in, read and adopted.

3. Resolved, That the thanks of this Association be given to Brother Isaac Backus, of Middleborough, Massachusetts, for his unwearied pains and great labor, in collecting and compiling the history of the Baptists in New England, consisting of two volumes large octavo, a work highly esteemed by this Association.

4. Agreed to recommend to the several churches, to make enquiry among themselves in the course of the year, what number they will respectively take, of an intended publication of materials towards a history of the Baptists in New Jersey, and transmit an account thereof to our next general meeting.

5. Supplies were granted for the destitute church at Scotch Plains.

6. Voted, That our next Association be held in Philadelphia, on the first Tuesday in October, 1786. Introductory sermon to be preached at three o'clock, P. M., by Brother John Gano; in case of failure, by Brother William Vanhorn.

7. Brother William Rogers, is requested to superintend the printing of the minutes and circular letter of the Association, and to forward the same to the churches.

Business closed. Sermon in the evening by Brother Manning, from John i. 29.

CIRCULAR LETTER.
BY REV. WILLIAM ROGERS.

The ministers and messengers of the several Baptist churches, convened in Association, at Philadelphia, October 4, 1785.

To the respective churches, with whom we are connected, send Christian salutation.

Dearly beloved in our Lord Jesus Christ,—The subject, which we are to address you upon, is contained in Chapter XI. of our Confession of faith, which treats of Justification. A subject truly important! One of the fundamental articles of our holy religion! As such, demands our very particular attention. Therefore, wherein we are obliged, owing to the confined limits of our annual epistle, to study brevity, our hope and expectation is, that you will individually make up such deficiency by serious meditation.

Perspicuity being our aim, we shall,
I. Explain the term.
II. Consider the Author.
III. The objects interested.
IV. The blessings resulting.

We are, I. To explain the term. Justification, spiritually or evangelically considered, is a complete acquittal from imputed and contracted guilt; a deliverance from the condemning power of sin; an act of free grace flowing from Jehovah's sovereign good will and pleasure. By many eminent divines this leading doctrine of our creed is viewed as twofold—eternal and declarative. By the former, we understand that which existed in the divine mind from everlasting, respecting the chosen seed, united with Christ their head, "who hath saved us, according to his own purpose and grace, which was given us in Christ Jesus, before the world began," 2 Tim. i. 9. By the latter, viz., declarative justification, is designed that which, in time, takes place in or on the conscience of a believer, commonly styled justification by or through faith. It is upon this, dear brethren, we now address you, this is the light wherein our Confession treats upon it, agreeing herewith, our catechism tells us that "justification is an act of God's free grace, wherein he pardoneth all our sins, and accepteth us as righteous in his sight, only for the righteousness of Christ imputed to us, and received by faith alone." To be thus fully absolved from all sin and guilt, by virtue of Christ's plenary satisfaction, and pronounced "heirs of eternal life." Oh how enlivening the thought! how animating the reflection! "Bless the Lord, O our souls, and all that is within us, bless his holy name!"

"We come, II. To consider the Author of our justification. In other words from whom it proceeds. Blended with which we must just hint at some of the causes hereof.

Educated in the school of Jesus, and instructed by the unerring Spirit of the Most High, you are ready, dearly beloved, to anticipate us under this head, by exclaiming with an inspired apostle, "It is God who justifieth," Rom. viii. 33. A Triune God, Father, Son, and Holy Ghost. A truth this, when viewed in all its parts, calculated to excite not only within us, but amid the angelic choir the highest wonder. "Which things the angels desire to look into," 1 Pet. i. 12. "Whom God hath set forth to be a propitiation, through faith in his blood, to declare his righteousness for the remission of sins that are past, through the forbearance of God; to declare, I say, at this time his righteousness, that he might be just, and the justifier of him who believeth in Jesus," Rom. iii. 25, 26. "Be it known unto you, therefore, men and brethren, that through this man is preached unto you the forgiveness of sins: and by him all that believe are justified from all things, from which ye could not be justified by the law of Moses," Acts xiii. 38, 39. "And such were some of you; but ye are washed, but ye are sanctified, but ye are justified in the name of the Lord Jesus, and by the Spirit of our God," 1 Cor. vi. 11. Many other texts might be quoted, did we not believe you to be already well established in this peculiar excellency of gospel revelation! Nevertheless for our mutual edification, permit us, previous to our dismission of this head, to mention, with all due conciseness, a few of the causes of our being thus justified or pronounced righteous. "The works of the Lord are great, sought out of all them who have pleasure therein," is of equal force now as when penned by Israel's king. Thus supported, we will not be backward in asserting—

1. That from this main pillar, this sublime characteristic of gospel truth, man's obedience to a law of works is to be utterly excluded. Paul peremptorily says, "By the deeds of the law no flesh shall be justified in his sight," Rom. iii. 20. This single declaration, confirmed by repeated equal testimony, condemns at once every idea of justification by virtue of our own doings. Those who harbor a sentiment so opposed to Jehovah's revealed will, vainly imagine, consistent with themselves, to bring the Supreme Governor of universal nature under obligation to do them good. But, beloved, we have not so learned Christ; we do not wish to rob the blessed Redeemer of the highest diadem in his mediatorial crown; we do not intend thus basely to detract from that glory which peculiarly belongs to the sacred Three-One. "For there is not a just man upon earth, who doeth good and sinneth not," Ecc. vii. 20. "But we are all as an unclean thing, and all our righteousnesses are as filthy rags," Isa. lxiv. 6.

2. What is by too many denominated, compliance with gospel terms, we do not admit as having any claim hereunto. Those who cherish this opinion are grossly mistaken. The gospel of our salvation is unconditional: it knows no terms on our part as leading to a justifying righteousness. Faith and repentance are graces bestowed by the Spirit of God, they are blessings flowing from the covenant

which is ordered in all things and sure. In fine, regeneration of soul, sanctification of heart, sincerity of disposition, holiness of life, persevering fidelity, undeviating acquiescence in Jehovah's government, steady zeal for Imanuel's interest, all our own pious frames of mind, comfortable feelings, and approving testimonies of conscience, are, with respect to this all-essential doctrine, to be kept totally out of view. To what then is our justification to be ascribed?

We reply, first. To the mere grace or favor of God as the moving cause, "being justified freely by his grace," Rom. iii. 24. "But after that the kindness and love of God our Saviour toward man appeared; not by works of righteousness, which we have done, but according to his mercy he saved us," Tit. iii. 4, 5. That, which never could have been found out by men or angels, the wisdom of Jehovah contrived and his love hath made known. This is the original source. Here is the fountain from whence all doth spring.

Second. To the life and passion of Jesus as the procuring cause. "But God commendeth his love towards us, in that while we were yet sinners, Christ died for us. Much more then, being now justified by his blood, we shall be saved from wrath through him," Rom. v. 8, 9. He fulfilled every precept, bore the whole penalty of the law in the room and stead of his people. Thus was the law magnified and rendered honorable, an end made of sin, and everlasting righteousness brought in. "And this is his name whereby he shall be called, THE LORD OUR RIGHTEOUSNESS," Jeremiah xxiii. 6. Oh glorious name! predicted long before his incarnation. Unto whom should we go, but unto our once bleeding but now risen Saviour, for acceptance? For us he drank the bitter cup. It will not do to substitute any thing in the place of this noble sacrifice; it is now a righteous thing with God, freely to justify and abundantly to pardon: "In the Lord shall all the seed of Israel be justified, and shall glory," Isa. xlv. 25. The robe of Christ's righteousness is a garment down to the foot, wherewith every member of the mystical body is amply covered, "for he hath made him to be sin for us, who knew no sin; that we might be made the righteousness of God in him," 2 Cor. v. 21. "Such a High Priest became us, who is holy, harmless, undefiled, and separate from sinners," Heb. vii. 26. Should any question, how doth Christ's righteousness, thus consisting of the holiness of his nature, his active and passive obedience, become ours in such wise that we are necessarily deemed righteous too?

We readily Answer—By imputation; by making it over unto us; reckoning it ours, or placing it to our account, being wrought out by our elder brother on behalf of the whole ransomed flock. "David describeth the blessedness of the man, unto whom God imputeth righteousness without works," Rom. iv. 6. Pursuant, therefore, to the unalterable purpose of heaven; agreeable to the economy of man's redemption; this righteousness of the precious Jesus, whereof so many glorious things are spoken, is as much ours as though wrought out by ourselves in our own proper persons; Rom. v. 18, 19; Phil. iii. 8, 9. Thus clothed upon with raiment of needlework—thus united with the head, how can the members be viewed by God the judge of all but as perfectly and completely justified. "And ye are complete in him, who is the head of all principality and power," Col. ii. 10.

Third. Our justification is by some ascribed to faith as an instrumental cause. Strictly speaking, we apprehend faith as no cause at all in this momentous procedure, but rather as an effect. It is true, the scriptures frequently mention a justification by faith. By such expressions it is evident the object, and not the act, of faith is designed; the object of faith is Christ and his righteousness; this the believing soul lays fast hold on. Faith is the eye which discovers, the hand which receives; espying a Saviour's worth, charmed with his merit, the believer is so enraptured as to cast away all his heavy burden, falls at Messiah's feet, confides in the promise, and pleads atoning blood: "With the heart man believeth unto righteousness," Rom. x. 10. It is beautifully noticed by one of our very first and most orthodox writers. "The reason why any are justified is not because they have faith; but the reason why they have faith is because they are justified." If justified faith as a work performed by us or a grace wrought within us; where would have been the necessity of the death and resurrection of Jesus? Faith is that precious grace, by which we do in a certain manner put on the righteousness of the Lord's anointed, and receive the greatest of all blessings from the God of our salvation. "It is grace (saith one) which quarrels much with human pride and makes its only boast of Sharon's rose; and never was meant to be our justifying righteousness in the sight of God, else it would learn to boast." Faith says, "In the Lord have I righteousness;" and tells a sinner, "I cannot save thee; thou art saved by grace through faith." The grace of Jesus, and that alone brings salvation; and the sinner, through faith as an instrument, puts in his hand, is enabled to reach the rich donation; just as a beggar, by his empty cap stretched forth, receives an alms. We proceed,

III. To mention the objects interested. In the examination of this particular, what abundant reason have we to adopt the prophetic language, "To the law and to the testimony: if they speak not according to this word, it is because there is no light in them." Isa. viii. 20. The persons justified through rich and sovereign grace are, in the living oracles, declared to be "ungodly," Rom. iv. 5; also, "sinners," Gal. ii. 17. Was it not for declarations like these, where could be our comfort? We are all sinners; we are all ungodly; does it from hence follow, that all who are sinners, all who are ungodly, are without exception justified? By no means! The whole canon of scripture combine with the dictates of sound experience to render every such idea inadmissible! It is true, we read "that by the righteousness of one, the free gift came upon all men unto justification of life," Rom. v. 18. By a careful revision of what goes before, and follows after, we shall find the apostle did not mean all men absolutely, but all the chosen, all believers; his epistle was directed to "all that be in Rome, beloved of God, called to be saints." Moreover, the justified are represented as a peculiar people, and have such characters ascribed to them, as cannot, without the greatest inconsistency and abuse of language, be ascribed to all the progeny of fallen Adam. They are spoken of as those who are predestinated, redeemed, pardoned, effectually called, sanctified, regenerated, &c. That these things are not true, with respect to all the lapsed family, every unprejudiced mind must acknowledge. Upon the whole, those who are unworthy and guilty in themselves, but in the everlasting covenant elected and beloved, have the righteousness whereon their justification is founded, not only exhibited to them by the gospel, but brought nigh by the Holy Ghost; these are the "purchased possession," this is the "bride, the Lamb's wife;" between whom and the Lord Jesus, an union not only now exists but hath existed, ancient as eternity itself. "I have loved thee with an everlasting love; therefore, with loving kindness have I drawn thee," Jer. xxxi. 3. A multitude which no man can number.

IV. The last thing proposed for investigation, we now hasten to unfold; viz: the blessings resulting herefrom.

Where, dear brethren, shall we begin, and how shall we end; blessings great indeed crowd in upon us! blessings beyond compare are consequential on our being thus freely justified! a doctrine pregnant with comfort inexpressible; a foundation is hereby laid not simply for fluctuating hope, but for the full assurance of present and of future bliss. By virtue hereof, we experience: 1. A freedom or deliverance from sin and condemnation. From all sin, as to its guilt, from its reigning power and dominion, and by and by from its in-being: "The blood of Jesus Christ his Son, cleanseth us from all sin," 1 John i. 7; Heb. x. 12–14. Our sins are covered and hid from the all penetrating eye of divine justice, and when sought for hereafter shall not be found. "There is, therefore, now no condemnation to them who are in Christ Jesus," Rom. viii. 1; Gal. iii. 13. When seriously reflecting on our happy rescue from the hands of Satan, our accusing foe; also from death and the grave, as penal evils: but more especially from the pains of hell and the wrath to come, and all as the effect of love divine! what heart among us can remain cold and lifeless? what tongue among us can cease to praise? 2. As justified, we enjoy peace with God. "Therefore, being justified by faith, we have peace with God through our Lord Jesus Christ," Rom. v. 1; connected herewith is real peace of mind! Oh, happy souls! brought fully to behold a crucified Redeemer making peace by the blood of his cross: "The chastisement of our peace was upon him," Isa. lii. v. Knowing this to be the case, well may we, "on the dove-like wings of faith, fly far away from the storms and tempests of an opposing conscience, and find in the Rock of Ages a quiet sanctuary and safe retreat."

3. The acceptance of our persons and services is another blessing resulting herefrom. The Father is well pleased with both for the alone sake of Christ his Son, "to the praise of the glory of his grace, wherein he hath made us accepted in the beloved," Eph. i. 6. Christ's

garments smell of myrrh, aloes, and cassia, wherewith his people being clad, the Lord smells a sweet smell in them also. A view of this emboldens us to draw near to the King of kings, Heb. x. 19–22. The person, the blood, the righteousness, the mediation of Jesus are the only foundation of all our pleas at the celestial throne.

4. As justified we are blessed through life, shall be so at death, yea, throughout eternity. While on earth, we are expressly assured that " all things work together for our good ;" when summoned to die, we need not fear the grim messenger. The property of temporal death with respect to God's people is greatly changed; it puts an end to all their sorrows, hath its sting taken away, and will prove to be our very great gain. In honor and triumph are such conveyed to the mansions above, and oh ! with what joy are the everlasting doors expanded wide for their reception. Our bodies, though mouldered to dust, will nevertheless enjoy a glorious resurrection—our persons, at the last day, an honorable distinction and gracious approbation from the Judge supreme; never ceasing felicity, consummate happiness, and perpetual glory will be our portion. " Eye hath not seen, nor ear heard, neither have entered into the heart of man, the things which God hath prepared for them who love him," 1 Cor. ii. 9. We shall then, oh joyful period ! live and reign with Christ for ever and ever, and our song will uninterruptedly be, " Unto him who loved us, and washed us from our sins in his own blood, and hath made us priests and kings unto God and his Father, to him be glory and dominion for ever and ever," Rev. i. 5, 6. Justification and glorification are closely connected; they go, as it were, hand in hand, Rom. v. 8, 10; viii. 30.

Having thus endeavored to explain this leading article of the Christian faith, we shall now close our address with such inferences as appear easily deducible therefrom.

1. Hereby we are taught the futility of opinions which, however remotely, lead to self dependence. Justification either by our own external performances or any inherent holiness whatever, are sentiments fully exploded by all who are acquainted with the truth as it is in Jesus: we are justified in such a way as excludes, in every sense, all boasting in ourselves. " Where is boasting, then ? It is excluded. By what law ? Of works ? Nay; but by the law of faith," Rom. iii. 27.

2. The necessity of highly prizing that righteousness which is revealed in the gospel, as the only foundation of genuine hope and solid joy. This righteousness as hath been proved, is the alone matter of our justification in Jehovah's sight; a righteousness which was devised and provided for us by the Father; wrought out for us by the Son, and now made over unto us by the Holy Ghost; a righteousness perfect and divine, wherewith justice is satisfied, the law magnified, the Triune glorified, and grace, superabounding grace displayed. To exhibit this righteousness, to elucidate its worth, to inform us of the peculiar happiness of those to whom it is imputed, is the main design both of the Old and New Testaments. May we,

therefore, "search the Scriptures, for they are they which testify of Immanuel, God with us." We also—

3. From hence, learn that the standing of all who are justified is secure indeed. To fall therefrom is utterly impossible. How can such come into condemnation, or be made partakers of the second death? They cannot; the righteousness of the Mediator is an everlasting righteousness. This being the sole ground of our confidence, it evidently follows that our abiding is safe; the believer can never lose his interest therein; the act which justifies is in itself unalterable; it is coeval with the eternal covenant; the benefit thereof is insured, and will for ever be enjoyed by us. "No weapon that is formed against thee shall prosper; and every tongue that shall rise against thee in judgment thou shalt condemn. This is the heritage of the servants of the Lord, and their righteousness is of me, saith the Lord," Isa. liv. 17. The love wherewith we are loved, the grace wherewith we are visited, will endure unto the end.

> "For Christ in every age has prov'd,
> His purchase firm and true;
> If this foundation be removed,
> What shall the righteous do?"

Is it then, dearly beloved brethren, as hath been represented? Supported by the unerring volume, we think this question may be fully answered in the affirmative. What improvement, then, ought we to make of so essential a part of truth divine? Examine yourselves. Have you any solid reason whereon to ground your belief that you are the objects interested? Admire then the grace of God, in imputing to you righteousness so complete; rejoice therein, and have no confidence in the flesh; ascribe the whole of your finished salvation to Jehovah's boundless love; sing, in humble notes, the church's song, "Not unto us, O Lord, not unto us, but unto thy name give glory, for thy mercy, and for thy truth's sake," Ps. cxv. 1. Live near to God, to whose unmerited favor alone you are indebted for a translation from surrounding darkness into marvellous and stupendous light. The doctrine of justification, when rightly viewed, unavoidably leads to strict holiness both in life and conversation. Evidence, then, by your constant fruit, that you are the called of God in Christ Jesus; persevere in the discharge of every duty. "Do we then make void the law through faith? God forbid. Yea, we establish the law," Rom. iii. 31. "For we are his workmanship, created in Christ Jesus unto good works, which God hath before ordained, that we should walk in them," Eph. ii. 10. Be not discouraged, though you have foes without and foes within. Greater is he who is for us, than all those who are against us. Owing to indwelling corruption and pride of heart, we too often offend the best of Beings; for our consolation it is recorded, "If we forsake his law, and walk not in his judgments; if we break his statutes, and keep not his commandments, then will he visit our transgressions with a rod, and our iniquities with stripes. Nevertheless, his loving kindness will he not utterly take from us, nor suffer his faithfulness to fail," Ps. lxxxix. 30–33. See also Isa. liv. 7, 8. Chastised we may be with the rod of a father, but not with the wounds of an enemy. "What though your afflictions are great? there is no wrath in the portion of your cup; though men should condemn you, God will not; though devils accuse you, they shall not prevail."

How honored are the subjects of Jehovah's grace! By far more dignified than the angels who never sinned! Frequently call to mind that celestial anthem, which, through eternity, will be chaunted on the highest key by all the redeemed throng; "Worthy is the Lamb that was slain to receive power, and riches, and wisdom, and strength, and honor, and glory, and blessing," Rev. v. 12. You can never think enough of Christ and his righteousness; let this then be your constant theme.

> "Some this, some that good virtue teach,
> To rectify the soul;
> But we first after Jesus reach,
> And richly grasp the whole."

To conclude. The doctrine of justification, the subject treated upon in this letter, being a doctrine so infinitely momentous, we do, with all Christian affection, as members of the same body with you, recommend it to the serious and candid perusal of all. A doctrine, we trust, wherein our associated churches are firmly established; for wherever the gospel is purely preached, this doctrine must necessarily not only make a part, but a distinguished part thereof. That the light of divine truth may emit its rays in such wise, as to dispel every gloom and all the mists of error; that soundness in every article of our orthodox faith may be restored among, and contended for, by all God's children, wherever dispersed; that the good word of the kingdom may run to and fro and be abundantly glorified, even from the rising to the setting sun; that whenever it is dispensed it may be accompanied with the demonstration of the Spirit and of power; finally, that the peace of God, which passeth all understanding, may visit all our borders, is, dear brethren, the unfeigned wish and cordial prayer of yours, in the best of bonds.

By order of the Association,

OLIVER HART, Moderator.
WILLIAM ROGERS, Clerk.

THE MINISTERS AND MESSENGERS AT THE ASSOCIATION, AND STATE OF THE CHURCHES DURING THE YEAR.

CHURCHES.	MINISTERS AND MESSENGERS.	Baptized.	Received by Letter.	Dismis'd.	Excom.	Dead.	Members.
Pennepek,	Samuel Jones, John Holmes, Jesse Dungan, Benjamin Dungan, Isaac Hough,	4	0	2	0	0	69
Middletown,†	Abel Morgan,*	0	0	0	0	0	95
Piscataqua,	Reune Runyan, Abraham Munday,	0	0	0	0	1	39
Cohansie,	Robert Kelsay,* Nathan Shepherd, Joel Shepherd,	1	1	2	2	3	116
Welsh Tract,	John Boggs, Andrew Edge, Thomas Ainger,	10	2	3	0	2	60
Great Valley,	James Davis, Daniel Cornog,	1	0	2	0	1	30
Cape May,	Artis Seagraves,* Jonathan Hildreth,	13	2	2	0	6	72
Hopewell,	Oliver Hart, John Jewell, Nathaniel Stout,	1	0	1	4	5	190
Brandywine,	Abel Griffiths,	2	0	2	0	0	16
Montgomery,	David Loofborrow,	0	0	0	0	0	37
Kingwood,	Nicholas Cox,	6	4	0	0	0	83
Southampton,	William Vanhorn, Joseph Hart, Arthur Watts,	0	0	0	0	4	50
Philadelphia,	Thomas Ustick, William Rogers, Joseph Watkins, Samuel Davis, jr., Elisha Gordon,	3	5	1	1	2	111
Cranberry,	Peter Wilson, Samuel Minor, John Hull,	23	0	0	0	1	71
Scotch Plains,	Joseph Manning,	0	0	0	1	1	96
Morristown,	—— ——	3	0	1	0	0	52
Knowlton,	—— ——	10	1	0	0	0	35
New Britain,	Joshua Jones, Edward Mathew,	1	0	0	0	0	37
Salem,	Peter P. Vanhorn, John Briggs,	3	0	1	0	3	44
Newtown,†		0	0	0	0	0	74
Pawling's Precincts,†	Samuel Waldo,*	0	0	0	0	0	53

MINUTES OF THE PHILADELPHIA ASSOCIATION.

CHURCHES.	MINISTERS AND MESSENGERS.	Baptized.	Received by Letter.	Dismiss'd.	Excom.	Dead.	Members.
Dividing Creek,	— —	4	2	0	1	3	51
New York,	John Gano,* Stephen Gano,	55	1	1	2	1	136
New Mills,	— — Samuel Jones,	2	1	0	0	0	76
Upper Freehold,	John Blackwell, James Tapscott, Christopher Morris,	5	0	2	0	1	86
Mount Bethel,	Abner Sutton,*	7	0	0	0	0	30
Lyon's Farms,	— —	7	0	0	0	0	20
Pittsgrove,	William Worth,* David Elwell,	1	2	0	0	4	86
Tuckahoe,†	— —	0	0	0	0	0	56
Stamford,†	— —	0	0	0	0	0	77
King Street,	John Dodge,*	0	0	0	0	0	17
Cow Marsh,†	— —	0	0	0	0	0	31
London Tract,	Thomas Fleeson,	3	0	0	0	0	30
Hilltown,	John Thomas,* Nathan Evans,	2	0	1	0	3	96
Lower Smithfield,¶	David Jayne,	0	0	0	0	0	33
Mispilion,¶ (Del.)	Eliphaz Dazey,	6	0	0	0	0	16
		167	21	21	11	41	2271

Note.—The ministers' names are in SMALL CAPITALS. Those marked thus * not present. The churches marked thus † sent neither letters nor messengers, and their numbers remain as last year. A dash ——— denotes no settled minister.

⁂ The two last mentioned churches marked thus ¶ were, after giving full satisfaction as to their faith and order, received among us at this annual meeting, and the names of their messengers enrolled accordingly.

MINUTES

OF THE

PHILADELPHIA BAPTIST ASSOCIATION,

HELD IN PHILADELPHIA, OCTOBER 3D, 4TH, AND 5TH,

1786.

October 3d, three o'clock, P. M.—According to appointment, Brother John Gano opened the Association with a very suitable discourse, from 1 Tim. iv. 1: "Now, the Spirit speaketh expressly, that in the latter times some shall depart from the faith, giving heed to seducing spirits, and the doctrines of devils."

2. Brother Samuel Jones was chosen moderator, and Brother Thomas Ustick, clerk. Letters from thirty-five churches were read.

October 4, nine o'clock.—Met pursuant to adjournment.

3. Doctor Manning, president of the University at Providence, Rhode Island, being present, his company and assistance were desired.

4. The letters and minutes of the Association at Warren, Charleston, Ketockton, and Georgia, containing agreeable accounts, were read. Their numbers are,

Warren,	3,451	Ketockton,	935
Charleston,	966	Georgia,	223

5. Unanimously agreed, that in future no person be permitted to speak in this Association more than twice upon the same subject, without special permission.

Adjoured till half past two, P. M.

6. Met pursuant to adjournment.—Inasmuch as the difficulty mentioned in our last year's minutes, and occasioned by conversation, &c., of Brother David Jones, which led some of our brethren to suppose that he denied "our Lord Jesus Christ to be the object of prayer," has not been settled according to the recommendation of last year; wherefore

This Association, after having the whole matter again discussed, concludes,

First. That our brethren, Oliver Hart and William Vanhorn, had reason to understand Brother Jones according to their respective declarations. Nevertheless,

Second. Upon Brother Jones' free acknowledgment of his full belief in the Deity of our Lord Jesus Christ, and that he is the object of prayer, this Association is willing to continue Brother Jones in fellowship.

Adjourned till to-morrow, nine o'clock, A. M.

Sermon in the evening by Brother Hart, from Isa. xxxv. 10.

October 5.—Met pursuant to adjournment.

7. Whereas, the consideration of a query from the Philadelphia church, relative to "the administration of the Lord's supper among any of our brethren and sisters, however numerous they may be in any one place, during the period of their remaining unorganized or unconstituted as a distinct, regular church by themselves," was postponed to the present year. We answer,

First. That the Lord's supper ought not to be administered to persons who are not members of any church, though baptized.

Second. That this ordinance should not be administered to members of churches in a scattered situation, without the consent of one or more of those churches; but permission being first obtained, they may proceed.

8. The churches are desired, within six months, to transmit to the care of Brother Ustick, such moneys as they are inclined to appropriate to the purpose of printing the materials of the history of the Baptists in the State of New Jersey, reckoning at the rate of three shillings per volume.

9. The letter to the Charleston Association, prepared by Brother Fleeson; that to the Ketockton Association, by Brother Vanhorn; and that to the Warren Association, by Brother Rogers; were read and approved.

Our brethren, Nicholas Cox and Lewis Richards, are appointed messengers to the Ketockton, and brothers William Rogers and William Vanhorn, to the Warren Association.

10. The circular letter prepared by Brother Thomas Ustick, was read and approved. Brother Peter P. Vanhorn is appointed to write one for the ensuing year.

11. Supplies were granted for the following destitute places:— Morristown and Great Valley.

12. Voted, That our next Association be held at New York, on the first Tuesday in October, 1787. Introductory sermon to be preached at three o'clock, P. M., by Brother William Vanhorn; in case of failure, by Brother John Bogs.

13. Brother Ustick is requested to superintend the printing of the minutes, and forward them to the churches.

Sermon in the evening by Brother Lewis Richards, from Matt. x. 16.

CIRCULAR LETTER.
BY REV. THOMAS USTICK.

The elders and brethren of the several Baptist churches, convened in Association, at Philadelphia, October 3d, 1786.

Send Christian salutation to the churches with whom we are united.

Dearly beloved,—The present meeting has afforded us an opportunity of hearing the most agreeable tidings from some of our churches, which convince us, that "God is waiting to be gracious" and "ever mindful of his covenant." Jer. xxxi. 33, "I will put my law in their inward parts, and write it in their hearts; and will be their God, and they shall be my people." And again, 2 Cor. vi. 18, "I will be a father unto you, and ye shall be my sons and daughters, saith the Lord Almighty." We are daily realizing the accomplishment of these divine promises. It is, therefore, with peculiar pleasure, that we now address you on the interesting and glorious subject of Adoption. See Confession of faith, Chap. XII.

The adoption of a person into a family imports, that previous to that transaction he did not bear the relation of a child in that family; and therefore could have no claim to the distinguishing name, peculiar titles, proper estates, or special interests of the family. He may, indeed, be an alien, or an enemy, and yet become an adopted son. Because the act, which constitutes him a son in a law sense, entirely depends upon the will of the adopter. Spiritual adoption may be defined, as the sovereign or authoritative act of God's grace, by which persons are translated from the family of Satan into the family of God: and being put among the children are justly entitled to all the privileges of a divine and everlasting inheritance.

When we consider that it is said of God, "that he calleth those things which be not as though they were," we shall readily perceive that the decree of adoption has its date in eternity; but the manifestation or execution of the decree in time, at different periods, with respect to individuals, by the spirit of adoption; and at the consummation of time, with respect to the collective mystical body of Christ, by the resurrection. This distinction is purely scriptural. The decree, moving cause, and end, are all comprehended in Eph. i. 5, "Having predestinated us unto the adoption of children by Jesus Christ to himself, according to the good pleasure of his will, to the praise of the glory of his grace, wherein he hath made us accepted in the beloved." For as persons may be elected to offices, before they are qualified or invested with power to execute the office; so in the family of God persons are really elected to the state and privilege of sons from eternity. Hence for the accomplishment of this decree we read, Gal. iv. 4, 5, "But when the fulness of the time was come, God sent forth his Son, made of a woman, made under the law, to redeem them that were under the law, that we might receive the adoption of sons." Accordingly, in their conversion they are recognized by Jehovah as sons and daughters, John i. 12, "But as many as received him, to them gave he power to become the sons of God, even to them that believe on his name." Lastly, the perfect manifestation or consummation of this glorious grace is mentioned, Rom. viii. 23, "Waiting for the adoption, to wit, the redemption of our body."

Justification and adoption are law phrases. They both have reference to our former condition; and are each in different respects expressive of the important blessings of salvation. No single term could answer the end of fully expressing the nature of our salvation. Different phrases therefore are used to help our conceptions of those blessings, which are ineffable; and for the perfect knowledge of which we must wait, until their consummation in glory.

Justification is a great blessing; but adoption is greater. Justification is the constituting or making a person righteous in the eye of the law; delivering him from every charge of guilt, or obnoxiousness to punishment, and furnishing him with an active righteousness, commensurate to its utmost demands. A justified person then is no longer under condemnation; no longer liable to endure the curse of the law, or the wrath of God. "For we are justified freely by his grace, through the redemption that is in Christ." Thus our progenitors, whilst innocent, were free from every charge of guilt. Wherefore simply to be justified, would be only recovering us from the ruins of the apostacy, and reinstating man in his former dominion, holiness and happiness. This would be grace. It would be free, unmerited grace; and, admitting it to be confirmed, would be infinitely valuable. But who does not see, that the price of our redemption is too precious to be expended in this way, and for no greater end? Here then comes in the necessity of the superlative grace of adoption; which is necessary to render our state better than it was before—necessary to raise us above the condition of servants; and to enlarge the expressions of the infinite kindness of God towards the elect; and especially necessary to reward, in an ample and satisfactory manner, the beloved Son of God for the arduous work of our redemption. The persons for whom Christ died, were the objects of his delight from eternity. He could not therefore have been satisfied, that they should be eternally removed from his presence. Observe his own declaration, John xvii. 24, "Father, I will that they also whom thou hast given me be with me where I am, that they may behold my glory." Since, then, by justification we can look back with joy upon the dangers of sin, death, and hell, from which we have escaped; so by adoption we are permitted to look upwards to a state of exalted, permanent, and unalloyed bliss, to which we have an indefeasible right as the sons of God and the bride of Christ.

Adoption may be distinguished likewise from regeneration. By the former we are brought into the relation of children to God; and by the latter we receive the nature, likeness, and image of God. Besides, as we can have no idea of regeneration in a subject, who has not received the filial nature; so we can have no finished idea of adoption in one who has not received the filial spirit. There is that temper or spirit in true believers, which leads them to think and act agreeable to the holy nature of God, and correspondent to the exalted character and dignified relation which they sustain as the children of God. This principle is not natural to man, but is the fruit of the Spirit of God. It is said of the wicked, "that the spirit of disobedience worketh in their hearts." Their condition is servile. The spirit of bondage exercises their minds and governs their conduct. On the other hand, the sons of God are led to action by the spirit of adoption; who moulds and tempers their minds after a divine manner into the image of Christ, 2 Cor. iii. 18. Hence they are not impelled by the fears of a slave, but are drawn by the cords of love. "For ye have not received the spirit of bondage again to fear; but ye have received the spirit of adoption, whereby we cry, Abba, Father," Rom. viii. 15. The Spirit of God, as a spirit of love and obedience to the Father, engaged the immaculate Redeemer, in the actions of his life and sufferings of death, to fulfil all righteousness. This Spirit God giveth not unto him by measure, John iii. 34. And we, agreeably to his promise, receive the same holy unction in our measure. "And because ye are sons, God hath sent forth the Spirit of his Son into your hearts, crying, Abba, Father," Gal. iv. 6. This Spirit is in all the regenerate sons of God. "For as many as are led by the Spirit of God, they are the sons of God," Rom. viii. 14. It is also a Spirit of love. "For every one that loveth is born of God," 1 John iv. 7. This love appears to be genuine, when its operations are unconfined and universally extended to all the members of the family of God. "By this shall all men know that ye are my disciples, if ye have love one to another," John xiii. 35. Having this Spirit in measure, we shall be able to support the relations which we sustain in the heavenly family; as the sons of God, brethren of Christ, and joint-heirs of the same eternal inheritance, with dignity and delight, in this present life. But when all the sons and daughters of Jehovah have their adoption consummated in a glorious resurrection, they shall then enjoy this Spirit in perfection, as one glorious bride adorned for her husband.

When persons are removed from one family to another by this act of liberality, it is generally supposed, that they make a gainful exchange. Without this prospect, no one would consent to this translation. And, although the consent of the person cannot be obtained, because of non-age or some other impediment; yet the Author of adoption always concludes, that he confers an obligation. And in spiritual adoption the subjects are invariably convinced, that the grace is unspeakably great. Wherefore they can never return to the family of Satan, or heartily espouse the interests of sin. For these realize the truth of that divine declaration, 1 Tim. iv. 8. "Godliness is profitable unto all things, having promise of the life that now is, and of that which is to come."

Many would esteem it a great privilege to be translated from a poor family into one that is rich; but to be saved by this means from impending ruin, from immediate death, must inexpressibly enhance the value of the blessing. Though some might be inclined to despise the idea of dependence, which a change of family implies; yet we conclude, that none would refuse the favor, if death must inevitably follow their refusal. Such was the situation of Moses, according to the narration in chapter second of Exodus. His life was most imminently exposed to destruction, and he must have perished, had not God interposed by his providence for his deliverance. Happy for Moses! happy for the tribes of Israel! that by the disposal of Providence, he fell into the hands of one whose heart was made susceptible of the tender feelings of humanity; and who had it in her power to spare his life, notwithstanding the cruel edict of the Egyptian king. The adoption of Moses into the royal family, and the preservation of his life, were closely connected. For by this act she not only gave him a new name—Moses; because, says she, "I drew him out of the water;" and made ample provision for his support and royal education: but she also gave him his life; she rescued him from a double death: from perishing in the waters, and from the sword of barbarous jealousy.

How exactly parallel does this history run with the adoption of sinners into the family of God, who were justly exposed to both the first and second death. He, who is author of all compassion, stretched out his omnipotent arm for their deliverance; and with infinite benevolence says of every subject of redemption, "Deliver him from going down to the pit, I have found a ransom," Job xxxiii. 24. Thus sparing them as his own children, and even delivering to justice, in the sinners' room, his only begotten Son, that he might place them in the condition of children, and bring them to the inheritance of everlasting glory. "For God so loved the world, that he gave his only begotten Son; that whosoever believeth in him should not perish, but have everlasting life," John iii. 16.

In this glorious grace, God appears as our father, and we as his children. Respecting this relation we can have no knowledge, until we are the "children of God by faith in Christ Jesus." Then we are made to see, "what is the fellowship of the mystery, which from the beginning of the world hath been hid in God," Eph. iii. 9. By this powerful grace we, who are sinners of the gentiles, are authorised to claim all the privileges of the sons of God; being no longer considered as "strangers and foreigners, but fellow-citizens with the saints, and of the household of God; and are built upon the foundation of the apostles and prophets, Jesus Christ himself being the chief corner stone," Eph. ii. 19, 20, upon whom the weight of the building rests, and in whom both bodies are united. If therefore we are Christ's, then are we Abraham's seed and heirs according to the promise. Although the author of the Romans remarks, that "to the Isralites pertaineth the adoption;" yet he quickly subjoins, "They which are the children of the flesh, these are not the children of God; but the children of the promise are counted for the seed." Surely this privilege is beyond comparison glorious; that we, who formerly were not considered the Lord's people, should now be called the children of the living God. Not by any alteration of Jehovah's plan; but "according to the eternal purpose which he purposed in Christ Jesus our Lord." For our regeneration, knowledge of the gospel, faith and repentance, are not only the effects of a prior, but of an everlasting cause, viz., the love of God. "I have loved thee with an everlasting love; therefore, with loving kindness have I drawn thee." Behold and be astonished, brethren, at this stupendous grace. "Behold what manner of love the Father hath bestowed upon us, that we should be called the sons of God." We miserable sinners! we presumptuous rebels! we profligate prodigals! we, the avowed enemies of God and godliness, are, by this inestimable grace, denominated "the sons of God." Let the sons of earth boast in their line of famous ancestors; in their near alliance to the great and renowned; yet the pedigree of believers in Jesus is unspeakably more illustrious. Seeing they are born not of blood, nor of the will of the flesh, nor of the will of man, but of God. Believers are privileged with peculiar titles and distinguishing names or characters throughout the volume of inspiration; concerning which, we cannot now treat particularly, but would rather refer you to that gracious declaration of him that is holy, of him that is true, in Rev. iii. 12, "Him that overcometh will I make a pillar in the temple of my God, and he shall go no more out: and I will write upon him the name of my God, and the name of the city of my God, which is New Jerusalem, which cometh down out of heaven from my God: and I will write upon him my new name."

The privileges which believers enjoy in the militant state of the church are many. If depressed with trials and infirmities, they have a compassionate and almighty Parent to pity and succor them. If, through the remaining power of sin they wantonly transgress, he can and will chastise them: "For whom the Lord loveth he chasteneth, and scourgeth every son whom he receiveth," Heb. xii. 6. Wherefore, "O Lord, correct me, but with judgment; not in thine anger, lest thou bring me to nothing," Jer. x. 24. Should the triple host of darkness, the world, the flesh, and the devil, violently attack the souls of believers, almighty power is engaged for their protection. Whilst, therefore, the ears of our omnipotent and gracious Parent are indulgent to our petitions, and whilst "the Spirit itself maketh intercession for us with groanings which cannot be uttered," we may rest assured, that all things will co-operate for the security of our temporal, spiritual, and eternal interests.

"The precious sons of Zion comparable to fine gold," in the present state, are generally "esteemed as earthen pitchers, which men dash in pieces without any regret." The world knoweth us not. Though persecuted with a flood of reproaches and contumely from the mouth of the serpent, the righteous is still more excellent than his neighbor. God delights to honor him. He is, even in this world, indulged with the best company; regaled with the most delicious entertainments; invested with the highest honors, and adorned with a robe of righteousness, beautiful beyond description. They are honored with His gracious visits, "of whom the whole family in heaven and earth is named." The dear Redeemer is ever with his church. The holy angels minister to the saints; and their mutual society and conversation is heavenly and spiritual. They unitedly feast upon the emblems of Jesus' body and blood at the table of the Lord, where God manifests his love to their souls. All the special ordinances of the house, all the privileges of the church, which Christ has purchased with his blood, are appropriated to the use of believers. The Christian's inventory is most glorious; and comprehensive of all substantial blessings. "For all things are yours; whether Paul, or Apollos, or Cephas, or the world, or life, or death, or things present, or things to come; all are yours; and ye are Christ's; and Christ is God's," 1 Cor. iii. 21. Thus, believers are "heirs of God and joint heirs with Christ." A few more revolving seasons will translate you, the suffering heirs of glory, "to an inheritance incorruptible, undefiled, and that fadeth not away, reserved in heaven for you."

The relative duties incumbent upon us as members of this family, towards God and each other, are many, and cannot now be particularized. In general, let us regard the apostolic exhortation, Eph. v. 1, "Be ye, therefore, followers of God, as dear children; and walk in love, as Christ also hath loved us." Let us constantly approach the throne of grace with humble confidence, and implore divine assistance, that we may be able to support the profession we have made, with that dignity of conduct, and holiness of conversation, which becomes those who are called to glory and virtue.

Meditate often, brethren, upon that state of permanent bliss which you shall possess in the kingdom of your heavenly Father. Happiness which cannot be perceived by sense nor described by language. See 1 Cor. ii. 9. Let us realize, therefore, the obligations conferred upon us in this ineffable blessing of adoption; and acknowledge, for ever acknowledge, with unfeigned gratitude, the riches of his goodness.

> O goodness infinite! goodness immense!
> And love that passeth knowledge! Words are vain;
> Language is lost in wonders so divine;
> Come, then, expressive silence, muse his praise."

Signed, by order of the Association

SAMUEL JONES, Moderator.
THOMAS USTICK, Clerk.

THE MINISTERS AND MESSENGERS AT THE ASSOCIATION, AND STATE OF THE CHURCHES DURING THE YEAR.

CHURCHES.	MINISTERS AND MESSENGERS.	Restored.	Baptized.	Received by Letter.	Dismis'd.	Excom.	Deceased.	Members.
Pennepek,	Samuel Jones, John Stancliff, George Guthrie, John Wright, George Edwards, Isaac Hough, John Holmes,	0	1	1	1	0	2	68
Middletown,	Samuel Morgan,* John Cook,	0	22	2	4	0	4	107
Piscataqua,	Reune Runyan, Ephraim Pyatt,	0	78	3	0	0	0	121

CHURCHES.	MINISTERS AND MESSENGERS.	Restored.	Baptized.	Received by Letter.	Dismis'd.	Excom.	Deceased.	Members.
Cohansie,	Robert Kelsay,* Providence Ludlam, Nathan Shepherd,	0	0	2	8	3	6	100
Welsh Tract,	John Boggs,	0	12	0	12	0	3	57
Great Valley,	Daniel Cornog, Abner Davis,	0	0	1	1	0	0	30
Cape May,	Artis Seagraves,	0	0	2	0	0	2	72
Hopewell,	Oliver Hart, Nathaniel Stout, William Park,	0	3	0	1	0	1	191
Brandywine,	Abel Griffiths, John Kimbler,	0	1	0	0	0	0	17
Montgomery,	David Loofborrow,	0	0	1	0	0	1	37
Tulpehokin,†								
Kingwood,	Nicholas Cox,	2	10	2	1	0	0	96
Southampton,	David Jones, Arthur Watts, Elias Yerkes,	0	0	0	1	0	1	48
Philadelphia,	Thomas Ustick, William Rogers, Samuel Davis, sr., Joseph Watkins, Richard Reily, Samuel Davis, jr., Elisha Gordon,	0	6	1	2	6	4	105
Haight's Town,	Peter Wilson, John Tyndall, William Cubberly,	0	66	1	5	2	0	131
Scotch Plains,	William Vanhorn,	0	47	2	2	0	5	138
Horse Neck,†								
Oyster Bay,†								
Morristown,	Ebenezer Blachly,	1	27	0	2	0	1	77
Knowlton,†		0	0	0	0	0	0	35
Harford (Maryland),	John Davis,							
New Britain,	Joshua Jones, Edward Mathew,	0	0	0	0	0	0	37
Salem,†	Peter P. Vanhorn, Samuel Vance,	0	7	3	1	0	0	54
Newtown,†	James Finn,*	0	0	0	0	0	0	74
Pawling's Precincts,	Samuel Waldo,* John Waldo,	0	0	1	0	0	0	54
Dividing Creek,	Jonadab Shepherd,	0	0	0	2	0	1	44
New York,	John Gano, Thomas Slow,	0	41	0	2	0	1	170
New Mills,	Beriah Taylor,	0	10	0	2	0	3	81

CHURCHES.	MINISTERS AND MESSENGERS.	Restored.	Baptized.	Received by Letter.	Dismis'd.	Excom.	Deceased.	Members.
Konoloway,†	JOSEPH POWELL,							
Upper Freehold,	{ JOHN BLACKWELL, Edward Taylor,	3	11	3	35	0	3	60
Mount Bethel,	{ ABNER SUTTON, Samuel Vail,	1	76	1	2	0	0	106
Goshen,†								
Lyon's Farms,	—— ——	0	5	0	11	0	0	13
Philip's Patent,†								
Pittsgrove,	{ WILLIAM WORTH, David Elwell,	0	6	1	0	1	3	89
Manahawkin,†								
Vincent,†								
Tuckahoe,	ISAAC BUNNELL,	0	8	0	0	0	0	63
Cortland's Manor,†								
Stamford,†	EBENEZER FERRIS,*	0	0	0	0	0	0	77
King Street,†	JOHN DODGE,*	0	0	0	0	0	0	17
Cow Marsh,	—— ——	0	0	0	1	0	2	28
London Tract,	THOMAS FLEESON,	0	2	0	2	1	1	28
Hilltown,	{ JOHN THOMAS, Elijah Britton,	0	6	0	2	0	0	99
Lower Smithfield,†	DAVID JAYNE,*	0	0	0	0	0	0	38
Mispilion, (Del.)	—— ——	0	1	0	1	0	0	16
Baltimore,¶	LEWIS RICHARDS,	0	0	0	0	0	0	25
Duck Creek,¶	ELIPHAZ DAZEY,	0	0	0	0	0	0	51
Wilmington,¶	{ John Stow, Thomas Ainger,	0	0	0	0	0	0	34
Canoe Brook,¶	{ Obed Denham,	0	0	0	0	0	0	28
Jacobs Town,¶	{ Peter Sexton, William Snowdon,	0	0	0	0	0	0	44
		7	446	27	102	13	44	2755

NOTE.—The ministers' names are in SMALL CAPITALS. Those marked thus * were not present. From the churches marked thus † we received no intelligence. A —— dash denotes no settled minister.

⁎ The churches marked thus ¶ being sound in faith, and regular in practice, were freely received into union with this Association.

MINUTES

OF THE

PHILADELPHIA BAPTIST ASSOCIATION,

HELD AT NEW YORK, OCTOBER 2D, 3D, 4TH, AND 5TH,

1787.

October 2d.—At three o'clock, P. M., sermon by Brother William Vanhorn, from Isa. liii. ii., "He shall see of the travel of his soul, and shall be satisfied."

2. Brother James Manning was chosen moderator, and Brother William Vanhorn, clerk.

3. Proceeded to read the letters from the churches.

Adjourned till half past eight o'clock to-morrow morning.

Sermon this evening, by Brother William Fristoe, from 2 Cor. vi. 10 : "As poor, yet making many rich."

October 3d.—Met pursuant to adjournment.

2. Voted, That the brethren in the ministry, from distant parts, be requested to take a seat amongst us, and give us their assistance.

3. Received a very agreeable letter from the Virginia Association, by their messenger, our esteemed Brother William Fristoe, in which we note two things particularly :

First, That a happy union has taken place between the Regular and Separate Baptists in Virginia ;* of which we also had information by a letter from our Brother John Leland, by order of the committee of Regular and Separate Baptists. In this union we sincerely rejoice.

Secondly, They warn us to beware of a certain Duncan M'Clean, late one of their ministers, who has embraced the doctrine of universal salvation.

In a postscript, Brother Leland informs us, that about twelve hundred persons have been baptized, and added to their churches, within about two years.

4. A letter from the Charleston Association was received, with their minutes, containing very agreeable information of the state of religion in some of their churches.

5. A letter from the Warren Association was read, and their messenger, Brother Manning, entered into a particular detail of the progress of the gospel in various parts of New England. Brother William Wood, of Kentucky, did the same with respect to the

---

* See page 233, for "Plan of Union."

interest of religion in that place: and some of the brethren present gave us the like intelligence from Redstone and Georgia. By all which, we were made to rejoice in the prosperity of Zion throughout this continent: and encouraged to believe that the purity of the doctrines and ordinances of the gospel of Christ, are prevailing more and more.

6. A church on Staten Island, constituted 30th of December, 1785, was received.

7. A church at Pittstown, county of Luzerne, in the State of Pennsylvania, constituted 7th of August, 1786, was received.

8. Query, from the church at Lower Dublin: Whether a person declining communion with the church, be it for what cause it may, ought to be excluded, while his moral and religious character in other respects is unexceptionable?

Voted in the affirmative.

Adjourned to three o'clock, P. M.

1. Met pursuant to adjournment.—The circular letter being read, it was moved, that a committee be appointed to revise it. Brethren Joshua Jones, David Jones, and Elkana Holmes, are hereby appointed; to report thereon to-morrow.

2. Brother Samuel Jones represented, that a real estate in New Castle county, in the State of Delaware, had been demised by Reese Jones, to the ministers of this Association, for the education of young men.

Resolved, That this Association will engage in the recovery of said estate, and become amenable for the expenses arising.

Voted, That our brethren, Samuel Jones, Colonel Samuel Miles, Samuel Davies, sr., David Jones, and William Rogers, or any three of them, be, and they are hereby appointed and authorised, by every eligible method, to recover said estate for the intention of the testator; and to proceed therein with all convenient speed.

Adjourned to nine o'clock, to-morrow morning.

Sermon this evening by Brother John Stanford, from Psalm l. 2, "Out of Zion the perfection of beauty, God hath shined."

1. October 4th.—Met pursuant to adjournment.—Agreeable to appointment yesterday, Brother Samuel Jones produced a letter, addressed to the committee of the District Association, in Virginia, which, being read and amended, was approved.

2. Pursuant to a request yesterday, Brethren Oliver Hart, William Vanhorn, and Stephen Gano, brought in a draft of a letter addressed to the Associations throughout America, which being read, was approved.

Ordered, That ten copies be brought in this afternoon.

3. Brother S. Jones, and Brother John Stanford, are requested to form proposals for printing an abridgment of Doctor Gill's Exposition of the Bible.

Adjourned to three o'clock, P. M.

1. Met pursuant to adjournment.—In answer to the query from the church at Goshen, we reply: If a man and wife should separate,

be it for what cause it may, if either of the parties be innocent in the matter, and should apply for baptism, such may be admitted; but may not marry to another without a legal divorce.

2. The first church in New York queried: Whether a person applying to one of our churches for admission as a member, and satisfies the church that he has been previously baptized by immersion, on a profession of his faith in Christ; but at the same time confesses, the person who administered the ordinance was, at the time, neither ordained to the work of the ministry, nor baptized himself by immersion, but only chosen and called by a religious society to officiate as their teacher or minister, should be received.

3. Resolved, That the above query be held over on consideration till next Association, and that our brethren Holmes, Ferris, S. Jones, D. Jones, or any of the brethren, who choose to engage in it, be requested to deliver their thoughts in writing, upon the subject at the next Association.

4. Brother Samuel Jones informed the Association, that a manuscript of the history of the Baptists, in the State of New Jersey, was lost by the depredations of the enemy in the late war, and that those who had advanced cash for putting it to the press, might call upon Brother Ustick, of Philadelphia, who will refund the same.

Adjourned to six o'clock to-morrow morning.

Sermon this evening by Doctor Manning, from John xvii. 21. "That they all may be one, as thou, Father, art in me, and I in thee, that they also may be one in us: that the world may believe thou hast sent me."

October 5th.—Met pursuant to adjournment.

1. On application from Shelburne, in Nova Scotia, after consideration, it was agreed that their request ought to be attended to. Several of our ministers being in nomination, Brother William Van Horn finally concluded to go and pay them a visit, on condition the church at the Scotch Plains could be supplied during his absence; which was agreed to.

2. Agreed to the report brought in this morning by the committee appointed yesterday, viz: that our honored brother, Dr. Samuel Jones, prepare for the press an abridgment of Dr. Gill's Exposition of the Bible, desiring our brethren in the ministry to give him all the assistance they can in the work. That subscription papers, with the proposals and conditions of printing said work be prepared immediately, to forward with our minutes, and that it be recommended to all our churches to promote said subscriptions.

3. The committee on the circular letter having presented the same, with some alterations, it was read and adopted.

4. Supplies for destitute places.

N. B. As the supply for Nova Scotia is, on further consideration, postponed till next summer, on account of the short time before winter will set in at that place, the supplies for Scotch Plains this fall are also postponed.

5. Brother David Jones to write the circular letter for next year.

6. Messengers to the Associations are as follows: To New Hampshire, Brother James Manning; to Warren and Stonington, Brother William Vanhorne; to Woodstock, Brother Ebenezer Ferris; to Vermont, Brother Elkana Holmes; to Shaftsbury, Brother Stephen Gano; to Redstone, Brother David Jones; to Virginia, Brother David Loofborrow; to South Carolina and Georgia, Brother Oliver Hart.

7. Agreed, That Brother Rogers be requested to write a letter to the Kentucky Association at his leisure, reserving a copy to be presented to the next Association.

8. Voted, unanimously, That the Association be held next year at Philadelphia, on the first Tuesday in October, 1788. Introductory sermon to be preached at three o'clock, P. M., by Brother John Dodge, and, in case of failure, by Brother Elkana Holmes.

9. Brother Stanford and Brother Samuel Dodge are requested to superintend the printing of the minutes, and forwarding them to the churches and Associations.

CIRCULAR LETTER.
BY REV. P. P. VANHORN.

The messengers of the several Baptist churches, belonging to the Philadelphia Association, met in the city of New York, October 2d, 3d, 4th, and 5th, 1787.

To the churches to which they are respectively related, greeting.

Dear brethren,—We beg leave to introduce our circular letter by informing you, that our souls have been refreshed at this meeting, by the glorious tidings brought from different parts, of the advancement of our Redeemer's cause. We congratulate you on this joyful event, portentous, we hope, of the speedy accomplishment of the promises made by the Father to Christ, the King of Zion. As also, on the kind interposition of Divine Providence, visible in that happy union which obtained among the members of the late federal convention, to agree upon and report to the States in this Union, a form of a Federal Government; which promises, on its adoption, to rescue our dear country from that national dishonor, injustice, anarchy, confusion and bloodshed, which have already resulted from the weakness and inefficiency of the present form; and which we have the greatest reason to fear is but the beginning of sorrows, unless the people lay hold on this favorable opportunity offered to establish an efficient government, which, we hope, may, under God, secure our invaluable rights, both civil and religious; which it will be in the power of the great body of the people, if hereafter found necessary, to control and amend.

As we wish you to grow in grace, and in the knowledge of our Lord and Saviour Jesus Christ, we shall address you on the important subject of Sanctification. We are exhorted to contend earnestly for the faith, once delivered to the saints; and as there are some who deny the work of sanctification, and too many who are little acquainted with it, we shall therefore consider the subject in the following order—

I. We shall explain the term sanctification.
II. Give some reasons why sanctification is necessary.
III. The happy effects in the subjects of it.

I. In a performance of this nature, brevity must be expected; yet enough may be said to display our sentiments on the subject. By searching the Scriptures, you will find the term hath various significations.

1. It is used to signify the setting apart a person or thing to the peculiar service of God. This is the general use of the word in the Old Testament, and in this sense God is said to sanctify the Sabbath, Gen. ii. 3; and to the same purpose it is applied to the first born, Exod. xiii. 2. Thus the temple, the priests, the altar and sacrifices, were sanctified under the law.

2. It is used for that holiness and purity of nature, which gives us a meetness for the inheritance of the saints in light; and, in some respects, may be distinguished from regeneration, though it is radically connected with it. The Apostle, speaking of our salvation, said, "It was not by works of righteousness which we have done, but according to his mercy, he saved us by the washing of regeneration and renewing of the Holy Ghost," Tit. iii. 5.

By washing of regeneration, we understand that great change, which is instantaneously made in us by the power of the Holy Ghost, when we are first made alive in Christ Jesus; and from that period we are new creatures, created in Christ Jesus unto good works. The word is used in the same sense in 1 Cor. vi. 11, where the Apostle says, "But ye are washed, but ye are sanctified." In regeneration, the divine nature is begun in us by the power of the Holy Ghost, and without this work, there can be no growth in grace. From these passages of Scripture, we see that the Holy Ghost makes a distinction between regeneration and sanctification; in regeneration we receive a new nature or principle, and sanctification is the growing of that new nature to the stature of a man in Christ Jesus. The washing of regeneration is never repeated, but the renewing of the Holy Ghost is carried on through the whole life of a Christian, till he ascends to be with Jesus, Phil. i. 6. It is the Holy Ghost which begins it, and it is his work to finish it; for in the great plan of salvation, the Holy Spirit is as firmly engaged to begin and finish this work, as the Son of God was to finish the work of redemption assigned him to do. The council of God has ordained this way to make us meet for that state of glory, to which we have a right by the adorable Redeemer's righteousness; and therefore we are said to be "chosen unto salvation, through sanctification of the Spirit," 2 Thess. ii. 13.

II. We now proceed to demonstrate the necessity of sanctification.

1. We premise, that the necessity of sanctification and regeneration arise from the same cause, the fall of man. This has incapacitated us for communion with God; therefore, notwithstanding all our blessed Redeemer has done, we are represented to be in a lost state till this good work is begun. As sanctification is a progressive work, the necessity of it arises from the consideration that we are at first

only babes in Christ, and not complete in holiness; for the best men have a body of sin and death. Every renewed soul must feel this to be his case. The great Apostle groaned under it, and the beloved disciple said, "If we say we have no sin, we deceive ourselves," 1 John i. 8. The Holy Ghost is promised to dwell with us and remain in us as his temple, and ye know the temple of the Lord must be holy." "Without holiness, no man shall see the Lord."

2. Sanctification is necessary, because without it we cannot honor and glorify God. For this our blessed Lord prayed, and for this we should daily apply to the throne of grace, that we may understand the mysteries of his kingdom, and the glory of his grace; that we copy after his great example, and honor him in every dispensation of his providence.

3. It was the great design of Christ's coming into the world; therefore his name is called Jesus, because he saves his people from the demerit and the pollution of sin; purifying a peculiar people unto himself, zealous of good works. This great end of the Redeemer's coming shall be fully accomplished in all God's elect by the effectual operations of his Holy Spirit; whose work it is to glorify the Son of God, in applying his benefits to the heirs of glory, and give them a meetness to that inheritance that fadeth not away.

III. We shall now attempt to consider the effects of sanctification.

1. The effects of it appear immediately after regeneration, in a sincere and hearty detestation of sin. The prophet having spoken of a new heart and a new spirit, adds, "Then shall ye remember your own evil ways and your doings that were not good, and shall loathe yourselves in your own sight," Ezek. xxxvi. 31. No man can loathe himself till he is born of God, because the new man only sees the deformity of sin. After he is turned he truly repents after a godly sort, and is humbled in dust and ashes before God; firmly believing that nothing can deliver him from guilt, but the precious blood of the dear Redeemer.

2. Another effect is, we see more clearly our divorcement from the law, by the satisfaction of Christ, as the way by which life is to be obtained by the believing soul, who, at the same time, honors the law, by acknowledging that it is good, just, and holy. It is the fatal mistake of all in a state of nature, to expect acceptance with God, by the deeds of the law; but the renewed man knows that Christ is the end of the law for righteousness to every one that believeth. The great Apostle says, "I, through the law, am dead to the law, that I might live unto God." What a display of infinite wisdom in the plan of salvation! Here we see the sinner saved by grace, flowing consistent with all the perfections of God, and, at the same time, maintaining the honor of the divine law. Vain are the expectations of all who separate what God has joined together. Preserve divine truth in its own order, and it is glorious and harmonious. In the great plan of salvation, God joined together justification by the righteousness of Christ, imputed unto us by an act of grace, by which we have a right to eternal life, and sanctification, which gives us a meetness for the

inheritance of the saints in light. One great error in religion is, separating what God has joined together, and joining together what God has separated. Beware of all who applaud the imputed righteousness of Christ, and, at the same time, either deny the work of the Holy Spirit in sanctification, or speak lightly or reproachfully of it. He, therefore, who would either verbally or doctrinally exclude the imputed righteousness of Christ, and, at the same time, make great professions of holiness and zeal for religion, ought to be considered as an inveterate enemy to the blessed Redeemer and his truth.

Now, dear brethren, we take our leave of you, by entreating you to walk worthy of the vocation wherewith you are called. Watch over one another in love; in humility, seek spiritual growth to glorify your heavenly Father, and appear as lights in the world. May the God of all grace sanctify you wholly, and preserve you blameless unto the coming of our Lord Jesus Christ. Amen.

JAMES MANNING, Moderator.
WILLIAM VANHORN, Clerk.

THE PLAN OF UNION.

AFTER a long debate about the utility of adopting a Confession of faith, agreed to receive the Regular Baptists. But to prevent its usurping a tyrannical power over the consciences of any, we do not mean that every person is to be bound to the strict observance of every thing therein contained: yet that it holds forth the essential truths of the gospel, and that the doctrine of salvation by Christ, and free unmerited grace alone, ought to be believed by every Christian, and maintained by every minister of the gospel. And that the terms, *Regular* and *Separate* shall be buried in oblivion; and that from henceforth, we shall be known by the name of the United Baptist Church of Christ in Virginia.

COPY TEST.

N. B. This union respects all the Baptists below the Alleghany, and does not affect those on the Western waters.

THE MINISTERS AND MESSENGERS AT THE ASSOCIATION, AND THE STATE OF THE CHURCHES FOR THE YEAR.

CHURCHES.	MINISTERS AND MESSENGERS.	Baptized.	Received by Letter.	Dismis'd.	Excom.	Dead.	Members.
Lower Dublin, Pennepek,	Samuel Jones, Thomas Webster, John Holmes,	2	1	0	0	0	69
Middletown,	Samuel Morgan, John Cook, John Stillwell,	1	0	0	0	4	104
Piscataqua,	Reune Runyan, Jeremiah Manning, Abraham Monday, Hezekiah Smith, jr. George Drake,	22	0	0	1	2	140
Cohansie,	Robert Kelsay,*	0	0	1	4	0	95
Welsh Tract,	John Boggs,*	15	1	0	3	0	70
Great Valley,	—— ——	27	1	2	2	0	54
Cape May,†	Artist Seagraves,*	0	0	0	0	0	72
Hopewell,	Oliver Hart, David Snowden,	0	3	2	1	2	185
Brandywine,	Abel Griffith,*	0	0	2	0	0	15
Tolpehokin,†	—— ——	0	0	0	0	0	0
Montgomery,		0	0	2	0	5	30
Kingwood,	Nicholas Cox, John Robinson,	18	2	2	0	1	112
Southampton,	David Jones, William Watts,	3	1	0	0	1	53
Philadelphia,	Thomas Ustick,* William Rogers,	7	3	2	0	2	111
Haightstown,	Peter Wilson, John Morford, Abraham Freeling,	48	1	4	0	1	175
Scotch Plains,	William Vanhorn, Joseph Manning, Jacob Fitz Randolph, Joseph Fitz Randolph,	19	1	5	1	0	152
Horse Neck,	—— ——	0	0	2	0	1	14
Oyster Bay,	Benjamin Coles, Albert Albertson,	0	0	0	0	0	9
1. Morristown,	David Loofborrow, John Brookfield,	8	2	1	0	1	85
Knowlton,	David Finn,	30	0	23	1	1	42
Hartford,†	John Davies,*	0	0	0	0	0	0
New Britain,	Joshua Jones, Benjamin Mathews,	0	0	0	1	0	20
Salem,	Peter P. Vanhorn,*	0	1	1	0	1	36
Newtown,	Silas Southward,*	0	0	0	0	0	74
Pawling's Precincts,	Samuel Waldo,*	0	0	0	0	0	0
Dividing Creek,	John Garrison,*	0	0	0	1	0	43

CHURCHES.	MINISTERS AND MESSENGERS.	Baptized.	Received by Letter.	Dismis'd.	Excom.	Deceased.	Members.
1. New York,	John Gano, Stephen Gano, Samuel Dodge, Thomas Longly, Thomas Slow,	29	2	4	5	1	192
New Mills,	—— ——	0	0	1	1	4	84
Konoloway,†	—— ——	0	0	0	0	0	0
Coram,†	—— ——	0	0	0	0	0	0
Upper Freehold,	John Blackwell,*	2	1	1	1	0	61
Mount Bethel,	Abner Sutton, John Manning,	13	0	3	0	3	113
Goshen, or Warwick,	Thomas Jones, Jonathan Sylsby,	4	0	0	0	0	32
Lyon's Farms,	Ichabod Grummon,	0	0	0	0	0	13
Philip's Patent,	—— ——	0	0	0	0	0	0
Pittsgrove,	William Worth,* David Elwell,	0	0	1	0	2	86
Manahawkin,†	—— ——	0	0	0	0	0	0
Vincent,†	—— ——	0	0	0	0	0	0
Tuckahoe,†	Isaac Bunnel,*	0	0	0	0	0	63
Cortland's Manor,	—— ——	0	0	0	0	0	0
2. New York,	John Dodge, Francis Vandyke,	0	0	0	0	0	10
Stamford,	Ebenezer Ferris, Elijah Hunter	24	6	20	2	0	64
Cow Marsh,†	—— ——	0	0	0	0	0	28
London Tract,	Thomas Fleeson,	0	1	0	0	1	28
Hilltown,	John Thomas,* Enoch Thomas,	0	2	1	0	0	100
Lower Smithfield,	David Jayne,	3	0	0	3	1	29
Mispilion,†	—— ——	0	0	0	0	0	16
Baltimore,	Lewis Richards,*	1	2	1	0	0	28
Duck Creek,	Eliphaz Dazey,*	5	0	0	0	1	55
Wilmington,	—— ——	21	0	0	0	0	55
Canoe Brook,	—— —— Isaac Price,	7	1	1	0	0	35
Jacobstown,	Burgiss Allison,* James Cox, William Snowden,	0	0	1	0	0	43
Staten Island,	Elkana Holmes, Anthony Fountain, Nicholas Cox,	0	0	0	0	0	26
Pittstown,	James Finn,	0	0	0	0	0	32
		309	32	83	27	35	2953

Note.—The ministers' names are in SMALL CAPITALS. Those marked thus * not present. The churches marked thus † sent neither letters nor messengers. A dash —— denotes no settled minister.

MINUTES

OF THE

PHILADELPHIA BAPTIST ASSOCIATION,

HELD AT PHILADELPHIA, OCTOBER 7TH, 8TH, AND 9TH,

1788.

October 7th, three o'clock, P. M.—Brother Elkanah Holmes preached, by appointment, from 2 Cor. iv. 5, "For we preach not ourselves, but Christ Jesus the Lord; and ourselves your servants for Jesus' sake."

2. Brother Samuel Jones was chosen moderator, and Brother Thomas Ustick, clerk. Letters from thirty-four churches were read.

October 8th, 8½ o'clock, A. M.—Met according to adjournment.

3. Proceeded to read the letters from the respective corresponding Associations. Doctor Manning presented a letter from the Warren Association as their messenger, which, with their minutes, contained agreeable intelligence. Brother Stephen Gano, as messenger from Shaftsbury Association, gave in their letter and minutes, which contain comfortable tidings. The Charleston minutes, and a letter also from that Association, came to hand, by which it appears that their circumstances are prosperous and their numbers increasing. A letter was likewise received from the Ketockton Association, giving accounts of a marvellous revival; that in one particular church three hundred had been added. They further add, that the harmony of their assembly was such, that there did not appear to be among the watchmen, as they beautifully express it, "one discordant note."

4. A letter and minutes, which contain the sentiments and plan of the Stonington Association, were received. From which it appears, that they have adopted the same printed Confession which this Association has heretofore approved. We shall therefore cheerfully concur with them in maintaining a mutual correspondence.

5. A letter from the Salisbury Association was presented by our brethren, Philip Hughes and Jonathan Gibbons; and, as their sentiments and plan are conformable to ours, their messengers were unanimously accepted. Agreeable accounts were likewise received from the New Hampshire Association.

6. Letters from three of our Associations in England, both for 1786 and 1787, forwarded by Brother John Rippon, of Southwark, London, to Brother Ustick, were delivered and received with pleasure.

Agreed, That Brother Ustick remit at least fifty copies of our minutes for the different Associations in England.

7. By a letter from the church at the Great Valley, we were informed that the Divine Providence has removed, in the year past, that ancient and beloved servant of Christ, Thomas Jones, as we trust, to the church triumphant. The translation of the righteous is their gain, but our loss. Let us, therefore, lay it to heart, and earnestly pray the Lord of the harvest, to raise up faithful laborers to succeed them, whom he is pleased to take home to himself. They subjoin, that there was a mistake in the last year's minutes, and that there have not been, for a number of years past, any persons excluded from that church.

8. Having received information from the church at Pawling's Town, that it is more convenient for them to meet with the Shaftsbury Association, and that they desire our concurrence in removing their membership;

We agree, That hereafter the church at Pawling's Town, be considered as belonging to the Shaftsbury Association.

Adjourned till half past two, P. M.

9. Met according to adjournment.—Whereas, the church at Jacob's Town, after acknowledging the unspeakable mercies of God to our nation and churches, have taken notice of the army of God—the Hessian Fly—as a judgment; and propose to the Association, the propriety of appointing days of fasting and prayer on this account.

Concluded, after considering the matter, that the Association, upon this occasion, rather refer the propriety of conforming to this motion, to the decision of each particular church, who can determine what days may best suit their convenience.

10. Our brethren, Abel Griffith, Thomas Fleeson, Nicholas Cox, Joshua Jones, and David Jones, were desired to examine the circular letter, and to propose the amendments, which they may think necessary, to-morrow morning.

11. The church at Cape May query: "Whether a member, who professes that Christ died for all mankind, and that every individual of the human race will finally be saved, ought to be excommunicated?"

Agreed, That every such person, upon conviction, and after proper steps have been taken, ought to be excluded.

12. Agreed, That Brother William Vanhorn prepare a letter for the Warren Association; Brother Philip Hughes, for Shaftsbury; Brother Stephen Gano, for Charleston; Brother Montanye, for Ketockton; Brother Richards, for Stonington; Brother James Jones, for Salisbury; and Brother Joseph Stevens, for New Hampshire.

Adjourned till to-morrow half after eight, A. M.

Our aged and venerable Brother Kelsay preached in the evening, from Acts viii. 35. His address to the young ministers gave them great pleasure. He advised them, First. To study, with earnest prayer, as if all depended on their own endeavors; but, in preaching, to depend upon Divine assistance, as though they had not studied at all. Second. To be concise in preaching, and to conclude when done. Third. To pray for a blessing on their labors immediately after preaching: and Fourth. To embrace every seasonable opportunity of conversing with precious souls, and not to forget such as were in menial circumstances.

13. Met according to adjournment.—Appointed our Brethren Nicholas Cox, William Vanhorn, and Thomas Montanye, messengers to Shaftsbury Association; Brother Burgis Alison, to Warren; Brother Dazey, to Ketockton; and Brethren Samuel Jones, John Boggs, Thomas Fleeson, and Eliphaz Dazey, to that at Salisbury.

14. As the church at Wilmington are in debt, and fear that they shall lose their meeting house unless assisted: and as the church at Staten Island is desirous of building a house for the worship of God, we recommend it to the churches to make separate contributions, at such times and ways as is most agreeable to themselves, and forward the same to the aforesaid churches.

15. In answer to a query from the first church in New York, of last year, held over to this time, respecting the validity of baptism, administered by a person who had never been baptized himself, nor yet ordained; we reply, that we deem such baptism null and void:

First. Because a person that has not been baptized must be disqualified to administer baptism to others, and especially if he be also unordained.

Second. Because to admit such baptism as valid, would make void the ordinances of Christ, throw contempt on his authority, and tend to confusion: for if baptism be not necessary for an administrator of it, neither can it be for church communion, which is an inferior act: and if such baptism be valid, then ordination is unnecessary, contrary to Acts xiv. 23; 1 Tim. iv. 14; Tit. i. 5, and our Confession of faith, Chap. XXVII.

Third. Of this opinion we find were our Associations in times past; who put a negative on such baptisms in 1729, 1732, 1744, 1749, and 1768.

Fourth. Because such administrator has no commission to baptize, for the words of the commission were addressed to the apostles, and their successors in the ministry, to the end of the world, and these are such, whom the church of Christ appoint to the whole work of the ministry.

16. The report of the committee appointed to examine and correct the circular letter not being satisfactory, a new committee was nominated; viz., brethren Manning, Vanhorn, Boggs and Hughes, who were desired to report in the afternoon.

17. This Association, receiving information from Dr. Manning, that Mr. Dobson, printer in this city, has now published Mr. Booth's Apology for the Baptists, and likewise proposes to publish Booth's Pædobaptism examined and refuted, upon the principles and concessions of Pædobaptist writers, do recommend both these pieces as worthy the perusal of all enquirers after truth, as affording the most convincing and demonstrable evidence in favor of the principles and

practice of our churches. As such we recommend them to all our churches and sister Associations.

Adjourned till half after two, P. M.

18. Met according to adjournment.—In the course of the day the letters for the respective Associations with whom we correspond, were produced and approved.

19. Our Brother Allison is appointed to prepare the circular letter against next Association.

20. Brother John Dodge is requested to preach the introductory sermon; in case of failure, Brother Lewis Richards.

21. Voted, That this Association consider themselves amenable for, and promise to defray the expenses accruing from the proceedings of the ministers of the Association, in attempting to recover the estate demised by Reese Jones to the ministers of the Association, for the education of young men.

22. The amendments proposed by the committee appointed this morning to revise the circular letter, were accepted; and, with those amendments, the circular letter prepared by Brother David Jones, was approved.

23. Supplies for Hilltown.

24. This Association, taking into consideration the ruinous effects of the great abuse of distilled liquors throughout this country, take this opportunity of expressing our hearty concurrence with our brethren of several other religious societies, in discountenancing the use of them in future; and earnestly entreat our brethren and friends to use all their influence to that end, both in their own families and neighborhood, except when used as medicine.

25. Our Brethren Samuel Jones, David Jones, and Burgiss Allison, are appointed a committee to prepare a collection of Psalms and Hymns for the use of the associated churches; and the churches of this and of our sister Associations are requested to conclude how many of said collection they will take, sending information to Brother Ustick with all convenient dispatch.

26. Voted, That our next Association be held at Philadelphia, on the first Tuesday in October, 1789.

27. Brother Ustick is requested to superintend the printing of these minutes, and forward them to the churches and Associations.

Brother Stephen Gano preached in the evening, from 1 Tim. iv. 8.

CIRCULAR LETTER.

BY REV. DAVID JONES.

The messengers of the Baptist churches, belonging to the Philadelphia Association, met in the city of Philadelphia, October 7th, 1788.

To the churches with whom they are connected, greeting.

Beloved brethren,—The great design of our annual meeting is to promote the welfare of the church of Christ, by giving our advice in difficult cases, and by the use of every other means, to preserve the unity of the spirit in the bond of peace. To accomplish this end, it has been thought expedient to select a chapter of our Confession of faith annually, to be the foundation of our circular letter. That which comes under consideration this year, is the doctrine of Saving Faith, contained in the fourteenth chapter.

By such, as have wished to suit their definitions to carnal minds, the subject has been rendered very abstruse; but divine truth is plain and easy to them who are taught of God, and have learned of Christ to be meek and lowly in heart, believing all things contained in the holy scriptures.

The method in which we propose to treat the subject shall be,

First. To explain what we mean by saving faith.

Second. To give some distinguishing properties, or marks, of this precious grace.

I. It has been the custom of divines, in ages past, to use the word saving, when treating of this grace; hence it is probable, some have been led to suppose that this grace had something in it so meritorious as to justify the subject before God, at least in a conditional sense; but who ever reads our Confession of faith, will find that we exclude any such meaning, and only use the word to distinguish true faith from that kind, which is found in unregenerate men and devils. Saving faith may be thus defined, "That grace whereby the elect are enabled to believe to the saving of their souls, which is the work of the Spirit of Christ in their hearts, and is ordinarily wrought by the ministry of the word." By this grace the person is enabled to believe all divine truths revealed in the holy scriptures; and in particular to apprehend the Lord Jesus Christ, and to rely alone on his atoning blood for acceptance in the sight of God. The apostle, speaking of salvation, said, "By grace ye are saved through faith; and that not of yourselves, it is the gift of God," Eph. ii. 8. The same apostle informs us that the Ephesians were dead in trespasses and sins, and were by nature the children of wrath even as others; but when the gospel of Christ was preached, the Holy Ghost working with the word, opened their hearts to receive it, and by his powerful operations implanted this grace, by which they were enabled to believe the record that God has given of his Son. The precious grace of faith is a free and sovereign gift of God, conveyed through the power of the Holy Ghost, and the instrumentality of the word; and is co-existent with regeneration, if not an essential part of it; and as it is not of ourselves, we see that all boasting is excluded, so that we may all say, "by the grace of God, we are what we are." When the apostle was enumerating the fruits of the Spirit, he mentions faith as one, Gal. v. 22. This is a truth which every one, who is born of God, knows, and in substance will acknowledge. We know that this doctrine is too humiliating to carnal hearts, but it is as true as if they believed it; and if it was not so, there would be no true Christians on earth. Blessed be God, he has not left himself without many witnesses in our days, who are willing to confess that they were as unable to believe on the Lord Jesus, as to keep the law of Moses, till God gave them a new heart and a new spirit, through the powerful operations of the Holy Ghost. We will freely acknowledge, therefore, that our faith is through the operation of God, to the praise and glory of his free grace; and in the Psalmist's words, conclude, "Not unto us, O Lord! not unto us, but unto thy name give glory, for thy mercy and for thy truth's sake."

II. We now give some distinguishing properties, or marks, of this precious grace.

1. This faith receives the whole mind of God, and has a due respect to every part of his counsel, when made known to the subject. The language of this grace is, Lord, what wilt thou have me to do? It never selects some and rejects other parts of God's will. This grace never wishes any doctrines expressly contained in the Bible, to have been left out. No; as far as it knows the mind of God, so far it obeys. It is a truth to be lamented, that education directs too much the practice of many in the world; but where the voice of this grace is attended to, the person receives the truth in the love of it. The apostle had no exception to any part of the revealed will of God. When he was before Felix, he said, "But this I confess unto thee, that after the way, which they call heresy, so worship I the God of my fathers, believing all things, which are written in the law and the prophets, and have hope towards God—that there shall be a resurrection, both of the just and unjust," Acts xxiv. 14, 15. Here is the distinguishing property of this grace, "believing all things." Whether acceptable or not to the Jews or Gentiles, yet his faith believed all things written in the law or prophets, and his hope was according to his faith. The Psalmist could say, "Then shall I not be ashamed, when I have respect unto all thy commandments," Psalm cxix. 6. Has the Lord requested us to take up our cross and follow him; then, says faith, I will confess him before men. The true Christian is pleased with the whole counsel of God; the way in which he walks is a straight and narrow way, but it is as wide as faith wishes it. Christ is to the unbeliever, a stone of stumbling and rock of offence; but to the believing soul, he is altogether lovely and precious.

2. This faith is not dead and fruitless, it will not allow men to live in sinful ways. The doctrines of grace may be abused to lasciviousness and all manner of ungodliness; but the work of God in the soul, cannot produce such effects. There are many vain talkers in the world, who walk after their own lusts, and speak much of salvation by Christ, and walk according to the course of this world; but where this precious grace is communicated, it is as fire in the soul, which will produce works meet to repentance; hence says the apostle, "In Christ Jesus neither circumcision availeth any thing, nor uncircumcision: but faith which worketh by love," Gal. v. 6. There is a faith which works not at all, or it works either out of fear of punishment, or with a view of reward; but this divine grace, which is peculiar to the regenerate, obeys out of love. If there was neither heaven nor hell, the true believer would wish to live soberly, righteously, and godly in this present world. We are taught to pray that the will of God may be done on earth as it is done in heaven, and this is the case when all our obedience flows from love. It is then we serve the

Lord our God as the angels in heaven, when all our works originate from love, and our souls are humbled in us, because we serve him no better; we find that when we would do good, evil is present with us, but this leads us to make Christ our all in all.

3. Another distinguishing property, or mark of this grace, is to be dead to the law with respect to our dependence on works for justification before God: we see that all our righteousnesses are as filthy rags after regeneration, as well as before. The apostle said, "Yea, doubtless, I count all things but loss for the excellency of the knowledge of Christ Jesus my Lord," Phil. iii. 8. Faith can bear no other recommendation to God, but the atoning blood of the blessed Jesus: it can admit of no other righteousness, but that which God imputes unto us without works, even the righteousness of the Lamb of God, which can justify us from all things, from which we never could be justified by the law of Moses. Hence we may see that all legal, conditional preaching, is wounding to the souls of true believers, and can answer no other purpose than to support the hope of hypocrites; but when Jesus is represented as bleeding and dying on the cross, to atone for our sins, our languishing hope is quickened, and the soul says, "The life that I now live, I live by the faith of the Son of God, who loved me," and, O amazing to express! "gave himself for me." The language of faith is, now I can venture into the eternal world, when I behold my bleeding Lord, as the way of acceptance into divine favor. "Whom have I in heaven but thee, and there is none on earth that I desire besides thee!"

Dearly beloved, we have briefly endeavored to explain what we mean by saving faith, and have given some of the distinguishing properties or marks of it; and it has been with this view, to alarm the formalist, and refresh the soul of the sincere, humble Christian, as well as to detect all vain talkers, whose faith is not productive of works agreeable to the gospel of Christ. If you can say, "Lord, I believe, help thou my unbelief;" remember that full assurance is not essential to the being of this grace; and little faith is always attended with fear and doubting. Let the disciple's prayer be yours, "Lord, increase our faith." By it the elders obtained a good report; and as you are partakers of like precious faith, endeavor to walk worthy of the vocation wherewith you are called, and "add to your faith virtue, and to virtue knowledge, and to knowledge temperance, and to temperance patience, and to patience godliness, and to godliness brotherly kindness, and to brotherly kindness love; for if these things be in you, and abound, they will make you to be neither barren, nor unfruitful in the knowledge of our Lord and Saviour Jesus Christ: to whom be glory in the church throughout all ages." Amen.

We remain your brethren in the fellowship of the gospel.

Signed, by order of the Association,

SAMUEL JONES, Moderator.
THOMAS USTICK, Clerk.

THE MINISTERS AND MESSENGERS AT THE ASSOCIATION, AND STATE OF THE CHURCHES DURING THE YEAR.

CHURCHES.	MINISTERS AND MESSENGERS.	Baptized.	Received by Letter.	Dismis'd.	Excom.	Deceased.	Members.
Lower Dublin, Pennepek,	Samuel Jones, Benjamin Dungan, Thomas Holmes, Jesse Dungan,	1	0	2	1	0	67
Middletown,	Samuel Morgan, William Blair,	8	0	1	2	0	131
Piscataqua,	Reune Runyan, Jeremiah Manning, Esq.,	8	0	2	0	1	145
Cohansie,	Robert Kelsay, Providence Ludam, Jonathan Bowen,	0	0	0	0	3	93
Welsh Tract,	John Boggs,	23	0	1	0	2	90
Great Valley,	Daniel Cornog, William George, Jonathan Philips, Michael M'Cees,	36	0	0	0	1	89
Cape May,	Amos Cresse,	3	0	0	0	7	63
Hopewell,	Oliver Hart,* David Stout, jr., Jediah Stout,	2	0	17	1	5	164
Brandywine,	Abel Griffiths, Joshua Vaughan, John Powel,	5	4	0	0	0	24
Montgomery,	Charles Humphrey,	0	0	0	0	0	28
Tulpehokin,†		0	0	0	0	0	0
Kingwood,	Nicholas Cox, Joshua Opdyek, Jonathan Welverton,	54	0	6	0	0	160
Southampton,	David Jones, Arthur Watts, Elias Yerkes, Elias Dungan,	1	0	0	0	3	51
Philadelphia,	Thomas Ustick, Morgan Edwards, William Rogers,* Samuel Miles, Esq., Joseph Watkins, George Ingolls, Benjamin Thaw,	1	3	1	2	2	111
Haight's Town,	Peter Wilson, William Covenhoven, Alexander M'Gowan,	45	2	1	1	0	221
Scotch Plains,	William Vanhorn, Robert Fitz Randolph,	12	0	15	1	2	146

CHURCHES.	MINISTERS AND MESSENGERS.	Baptized.	Received by Letter.	Dismis'd.	Excom.	Deceased.	Members.
Horse Neck,†	—— ——	0	0	0	0	0	14
Oyster Bay,†	BENJAMIN COLES,*	0	0	0	0	0	9
Morristown,	{ DAVID LOOFBORROW,* John Brookfield,	3	0	1	0	0	87
Knowlton,†	DAVID FINN,*	0	0	0	0	0	42
Hartford,†	JOHN DAVIS,*	0	0	0	0	0	0
New Britain,	{ JOSHUA JONES, Edward Matthew, Benjamin Matthew,	0	0	0	0	1	19
Salem,	{ PETER P. VANHORN,* John Briggs, John Walker,	0	0	0	0	4	32
Newtown,†	SILAS SOUTHWORTH,*	0	0	0	0	0	74
Pawling's Town,	SAMUEL WALDO,*	13	0	0	0	3	67
Dividing Creek,	JOHN GARRISON,*	0	0	0	0	0	43
1. New York,	{ BENJAMIN FOSTER,* Thomas Montanye, John Bedint,	14	1	15	2	3	187
New Mills,	Samuel Jones,	13	0	0	0	0	95
Konoloway,†	JOSEPH POWELL,*	0	0	0	0	0	0
Coram,†	—— ——	0	0	0	0	0	0
Upper Freehold,	Edward Taylor,	0	0	2	1	1	45
Mount Bethel,	ABNER SUTTON,*	2	0	4	0	0	111
Goshen or Warwick,	THOMAS JONES,*	0	0	0	0	0	32
Lyon's Farms,	JOSEPH STEVENS,	3	0	0	0	1	15
Philip's Patent,†		0	0	0	0	0	0
Pittsgrove,	{ WILLIAM WORTH, Hosea Snethen,	0	1	0	3	2	82
Manahawkin,†	—— ——	0	0	0	0	0	0
Vincent,†	—— ——	0	0	0	0	0	0
Tuckahoe,†	ISAAC BUNNELL,*	0	0	0	0	0	63
Cortland's Manor,†	—— ——	0	0	0	0	0	0
2. New York,†	JOHN DODGE,*	0	0	0	0	0	10
Stamford,	EBENEZER FERRIS,*	38	0	9	1	1	89
Cow Marsh,†	—— ——	0	0	0	0	0	28
London Tract,	THOMAS FLEESON,	9	0	0	0	0	37
Hilltown,	{ JOHN THOMAS,* Elijah Britton, Jonathan Jones, Robert Shannon,	0	0	0	0	1	99
Lower Smithfield,†	DAVID JAYNE,*	0	0	0	0	0	29
Mispilion,†	JOSHUA DEWEES,*	0	0	0	0	0	16
Baltimore,	LEWIS RICHARDS,	8	0	0	1	0	35
Duck Creek,	{ ELIPHAZ DAZEY, James Jones,	12	0	0	1	2	64

CHURCHES.	MINISTERS AND MESSENGERS.	Baptized.	Received by Letter.	Dismis'd.	Excom.	Deceased.	Members.
Wilmington,	Thomas Ainger, Caleb Way, John Redman,	2	0	2	1	2	49
Canoe Brook,	—— ——	6	0	4	1	1	35
Jacob's Town,	BURGISS ALLISON, Ashur Cox,	1	3	0	0	0	47
Staten Island,	Elkana Holmes,	3	0	0	1	0	28
Pittstown,	James Finn,	0	0	0	0	0	32
		326	14	83	20	48	3198

NOTE.—The ministers' names are in SMALL CAPITALS. Those marked thus * not present. From the churches marked thus † we received no intelligence. A dash —— denotes no settled minister.

MINUTES

OF THE

PHILADELPHIA BAPTIST ASSOCIATION,

HELD AT PHILADELPHIA, OCTOBER 6TH, 7TH, 8TH, AND 9TH,

1789.

October 6th, 3 o'clock, P. M.—Sermon by Brother Lewis Richards, from John viii. 36, "If the Son, therefore, shall make you free, ye shall be free indeed."

2. Brother Oliver Hart was chosen moderator, and Brother William Vanhorn, clerk.

3. Letters from thirty-nine churches were read.

4. Three churches constituted within the last year; one at Marcus Hook, in May; another at the Ridge, August 23; and the last on September 26; desiring to join this Association, were admitted.

Adjourned to nine o'clock to-morrow morning.

Agreed to meet at six o'clock to-morrow morning for prayer.

October 7th.—Met pursuant to appointment.

1. Very agreeable letters were received from the Charleston, Warren, Ketockton, and Shaftsbury Associations. Brother Stephen Gano, messenger from the Shaftsbury Association, present.

2. The ministering brethren providentially present, not messengers from the churches, are invited to take a seat amongst us.

3. After conferring upon the necessity and importance of raising a fund for the education of pious and promising young men for the ministry,—we, the members present, do engage to promote subscriptions in our respective churches and congregations, for said purpose; and to bring in the moneys raised, with the subscription papers to the next Association, to be at their disposal.

Agreed, That our Brother Samuel Jones, shall take young Mr. Silas Walton under his care, for instruction, for one year, at £25 for his accommodations, including the use of necessary books, on our account, if he should judge it expedient; upon this condition, nevertheless, that the said Walton give his obligation to refund the money within seven years, if he should not become a minister of our order within that time, and continue therein.

Met pursuant to adjournment.—The church at North-East Town, formerly called Cortland's Manor, in the State of New York, being situated nearer the Shaftsbury Association, requested to be dismissed from this to the said Association.

Agreed, That their request be granted; and when they shall be received by them, they will be fully dismissed from us.

2. As we had reason to fear, at the last Association, that Mr. Worth, of Pittsgrove, was far gone in the doctrine of universal salvation, we are well certified, by undoubted authority, that he is now fully in that belief. We, therefore, to show our abhorrence of that doctrine, and of his disingenuous conduct for a long time past, caution our churches to beware of him, and of Artist Seagreaves, of the same place also, who has espoused the same doctrine.

3. Agreeably to a recommendation in the letter from the church at Baltimore, this Association declare their high approbation of the several societies formed in the United States and Europe, for the gradual abolition of the slavery of the Africans, and for guarding against their being detained or sent off as slaves, after having obtained their liberty; and do hereby recommend to the churches we represent to form similar societies, to become members thereof, and exert themselves to obtain this important object.

4. The circular letter was presented, read, and ordered to lie on the table.

5. Our Brethren, Messrs. Ustick, Wilson, Richards, and M'Laughlin, are appointed to prepare letters to the Associations corresponding with us, and bring them in to-morrow morning.

Adjourned to eight o'clock to-morrow.

Sermon in the evening by Brother Foster.

October 8.—Met pursuant to adjournment.

1. The church at Mispilion having signified it was more convenient for them to meet with the Salisbury Association, and that they request our concurrence therein.

Agreed, That the church at Mispilion be hereafter considered as belonging to the Salisbury Association.

2. The circular letter was again read and approved.

Adjourned to three o'clock, P. M.

Met pursuant to adjournment.—The letter to the Warren Association, written by Brother Wilson, was approved, and Dr. Manning appointed messenger. The letter to the Shaftsbury Association, by Brother Ustick, was approved, and our Brethren Nicholas Cox and Thomas Montanye were appointed messengers. Also, the letter to the Charleston Association, and that to Salisbury, were presented, read, and approved.

2. Dr. Jones is appointed to write a letter to the church at Pittsgrove.

Adjourned to six o'clock, to-morrow morning.

Sermon in the evening by Dr. Manning.

October 9.—Met pursuant to adjournment.

1. This Association taking under consideration the proposals of Mr. Isaac Collins, of Trenton, in New Jersey, to print an edition of the Holy Bible, in quarto, after the Oxford edition; and his request

to this Association to patronize the work. Being desirous to encourage so laudable a design, we appoint our brethren, the Rev. Oliver Hart, Dr. Samuel Jones, Rev. Benjamin Foster, and Rev. Burgiss Allison, to concur with any committee appointed by any other denomination to revise and correct the proof sheets, and, if necessary, to fix upon the most correct edition of the scriptures to be recommended to the printer, from which to make his impression. And that the same committee be ordered to use their influence to prevent the Apocrypha, or any notes of any kind, being printed and included in said edition, as having a dangerous tendency to corrupt the simplicity and truth of the sacred scriptures, by being thus intimately associated with them; and, particularly, as being incompatible with the union of people of different religious sentiments in promoting the work. And, moreover, the Association recommend to all the churches and congregations in their bounds, to encourage the undertaking.

2. Supplies were granted to the following destitute churches:—Salem, Morristown, Cohansie, and Great Valley.

3. On motion, unanimously agreed, That, as our churches in the middle States have greatly increased, a history of the same appears to be eligible and useful: And, as Brother Morgan Edwards has commenced a collection of materials for such a history in the state of New Jersey, he be requested to proceed as it may be convenient for him, and that any of our brethren, so laudably disposed, be entreated either to collect materials or assist therein.

4. Voted, That the Association be held at New York, the first Tuesday in October next.

We take this opportunity to observe, that, for the encouragement of the churches in the State of New York and adjacent places, we have met at New York a few times; but with much inconvenience to the western churches of our Association: and now recommend it to the churches to give their opinion the next Association on the expediency of the eastern churches forming a new Association at New York, if they request them.

5. Doctor Jones is appointed to preach the Association sermon next year; and, in case of failure, Brother Hart is requested to be prepared.

6. Brother Benjamin Foster is appointed to write the circular letter for next year.

7. Brother Ustick is requested to superintend the printing of the minutes, and forwarding them to the churches and Associations.

Sermon in the evening by Brother S. Gano.

CIRCULAR LETTER.
BY REV. BURGISS ALLISON.

The elders and messengers of the several churches met in Association at Philadelphia, October 6th, 1789.

To the several churches in union with this Association, send greeting.

Dearly beloved,—Inasmuch as our divine Lord and Master has been pleased, in his infinite mercy, to furnish us with the means of grace, for our furtherance and growth therein; and for the declarative glory of his great and holy name; and as one of these means is the assembling of ourselves together, our predecessors have wisely instituted this annual Association of the churches; that by hearing of the welfare of each other, conferring together upon difficult matters, admonishing and exhorting to steadfastness in the faith, and addressing each other upon the important doctrines of grace; the Redeemer's cause and interest might be promoted in the world, and Zion built up upon the foundation laid in the gospel. In pursuance of this, in our circular letters, we have addressed you upon those essential doctrines of divine truth; and, for connection sake, have followed the order in which they are treated in our Confession of faith: That which comes next in succession, is Repentance unto life and salvation.

1. By repentance, in general, we understand, sorrow or pain arising from a retrospective view of any action or circumstance, in which we have been agents, which is contrary to, either the dictates of conscience, the word of God; that from whence we see any evil consequences accruing to ourselves, or that which is evil in its own nature, and which is increased in proportion to the light and evidence we have thereof. This repentance may be considered in a two-fold point of view, generally known by the appellations of evangelical and legal. This distinction the apostle seems to have had an eye to, in 2 Cor. vii. 10, where he tells us, "That godly sorrow worketh repentance unto salvation not to be repented of; but the sorrow of the world worketh death." This is indeed implied when we speak of repentance unto salvation, since its distinguishing characteristic, presupposes that there is a repentance which is not unto salvation.

2. The repentance which is not unto life and salvation, or, what is generally denominated, mere legal repentance, originates in self-love, terminates in the fear of future punishment, or penal evil; and is but a transient view of that legal condemnation which is the consequence of sin: but never leads the soul to the gospel refuge. Hence, if any reformation is effected, it finally terminates in apostacy: Agreeable to the apostle's assertion, 2 Pet. ii. 22; "But it hath happened unto them, according to the true proverb, The dog is turned to his own vomit again; and the sow that was washed, to her wallowing in the mire."

3. Repentance, which is unto life and salvation, has God for its Author; and does not arise from the power of free-will, or the dictates of a natural conscience; but from the grace of God as the efficient, and operation of the divine Spirit as the impulsive cause; without which no means, as judgments, mercies, or the most powerful ministry, of themselves can effect. It is produced in the soul by divine illumination, through which we are led to see something of the nature and perfections of God, the holiness of the divine law, and the strictness of justice. Rom. vii. 9, "But when the commandment came, sin revived, and I died." Hence a discovery of the evil

and accursed nature of sin, the pollution and defilement of nature, and the state of condemnation into which the soul is involved. The person is now filled with shame and confusion of face; with sorrow and contrition of soul. He views his heart as a cage of unclean birds, as a nest of pollution and sink of iniquity: and conceives himself to be the most hell-deserving, as well as undeserving of God's creatures, and is made to adopt that lamentable complaint, "The whole head is sick, and the whole heart is faint." This godly sorrow and repentance for sin, is not excited merely from a view of the demerits of sin, of its evil consequences to the soul, or a fear of hell and damnation: but on account of the evil that is in sin; its contrariety to a holy God. He mourns that he has offended God, wounded Christ, and grieved the holy Spirit. It farther produces an ingenuous confession of sin, and forsaking it, in bringing forth fruits meet for repentance in life and conversation.

This is not called repentance unto salvation, as being the cause of salvation, or condition of it; for Christ alone is the fulfiller of the conditions: and, therefore to fit his people for the enjoyment of it, he hath sent forth his Spirit into their hearts, to convince "of sin, of righteousness, and of judgment;" to beget evangelical repentance in them; a hatred to sin, and a turning from it to God. Agreeably to which, it is said, Matt. i. 21, "Thou shalt call his name Jesus, for he shall save his people from their sins." But it is said to be unto salvation, as itself is a blessing of salvation and a part of it; an evidence of an interest in it, and terminates in the full enjoyment of it.

This repentance is wrought in the hearts of God's people, as above, in order to their sanctification, that they may be qualified to enjoy the heavenly inheritance.

4. Again, as the Christian experiences the inherence of sin as long as he lives, "for there is none that liveth and sinneth not," though freed from the reigning power and dominion of sin; so he has continued reason to exercise the grace of repentance, and humble himself under every transgression in particular, as well as the remains of corruption in general. Such was the exercise of the apostle, Rom. vii. 24, "O wretched man that I am, who shall deliver me from the body of this death." Thus is the Christian continually, while in the exercise of grace, aspiring after holiness, and mourning over his depravity. His sanctification is carried on, and will finally be accomplished, when he shall be admitted into the mansions of eternal blessedness and ineffable glory; "where all sorrow and sighing shall flee away;"—where there shall be no more sin, and consequently no need of repentance or sorrow, for the Lord our God "shall wipe away all tears from our eyes."

Thus, dearly beloved, have we endeavored to consider repentance unto life and salvation, according to the gospel sense of the doctrine. May the great Head of his church, through the influence of the divine Spirit, give us a humbling view of all our imperfections, that we may live to the honor of his great name, and ascribe all the glory of our salvation to the riches of his grace, through our Lord Jesus Christ. Amen.

OLIVER HART, Moderator.
WILLIAM VANHORN, Clerk.

THE MINISTERS AND MESSENGERS AT THE ASSOCIATION, AND STATE OF THE CHURCHES DURING THE YEAR.

CHURCHES.	MINISTERS AND MESSENGERS.	Baptized.	Received by Letter.	Dismis'd.	Excom.	Deceased.	Members.
Lower Dublin,	Samuel Jones, John Wright, William Rooper, Benjamin Dungan,	1	0	2	0	0	66
Middletown,	Samuel Morgan, Jacob Covenhoven,	6	1	0	1	3	134
Piscataqua,	Reune Runyan, Henry Smalley,	4	2	2	2	0	147
Cohansie,	Nathan Shepherd, David Shepherd,	0	3	0	0	6	90
Welsh Tract,	John Boggs, James Griffith,	12	5	3	0	0	104
Great Valley,	Daniel Cornog, Michael McKees, John Davies, Jonathan Philips, Owen Thomas, Abner Davies,	8	1	0	2	2	91
Cape May,†		0	0	0	0	0	63
Hopewell,	Oliver Hart, John Jewel, James Ewen,	8	5	8	1	4	164
Brandywine,	Abel Griffith, Joshua Vaughan, Thomas Davies,	9	5	1	0	0	37
Montgomery,	Edmund Pennington,	0	0	0	0	0	28
Tulpehokin,†		0	0	0	0	0	0
Kingwood,	Nicholas Cox, Richard Carter, John Koughler, James Drake,	37	2	9	2	4	186
Haight's Town,	Peter Wilson, Alexander M'Gowan, Samuel Minor,	26	3	5	5	0	240
Southampton,	David Jones, Thomas Folwell, Benjamin Bennet, William Watts,	3	0	0	0	1	53

CHURCHES.	MINISTERS AND MESSENGERS.	Baptized.	Received by Letter.	Dismiss'd.	Excom.	Deceased.	Members.
Philadelphia,	Thomas Ustick, William Rogers, John Stancliff, George Ingolls, John McLeod,	21	0	28	0	0	104
Scotch Plains,	William Vanhorn, Jacob Fitz Randolph,	1	0	4	5	1	137
Horse Neck,†	——— ———	0	0	0	0	0	14
Oyster Bay,†	Benjamin Coles,*	0	0	0	0	0	9
Morristown,	——— ———	0	0	4	0	0	83
Knowlton,†	——— ———	0	0	0	0	0	42
Harford,†	John Davies,	0	0	0	0	0	0
New Britain,	Joshua Jones, Benjamin Matthew, Edward Matthew,	2	0	0	0	0	21
Salem,	John Holmes, John Walker,	0	0	0	0	1	31
Newtown,†	Silas Southworth,*	0	0	0	0	0	74
Dividing Creek,	John Garrison,*	3	0	0	0	5	41
1. New York,	Benjamin Foster, William Thomson, William Durel,	19	2	4	13	2	196
New Mills,	David Gaskil, Benjamin Hedger,	7	0	0	0	2	100
Konoloway,†	Joseph Powell,*	0	0	0	0	0	0
Coram,	——— ———	0	0	0	0	0	0
Upper Freehold,	Joseph Stephen, Edward Taylor,	11	1	0	1	0	56
Mount Bethel,	Abner Sutton,*	0	0	10	0	0	101
Warwick,	Thomas Montanye, Amos Park,	142	7	3	4	1	192
Lyon's Farms,	——— ———	0	0	0	0	0	15
Philip's Patent,†	——— ———	0	0	0	0	0	0
Pittsgrove,	John Kelly, Armenius Snethen,	0	0	0	0	0	0
Manahawkin,†	——— ———	0	0	0	0	0	0
Vincent,	——— ———	0	0	0	0	0	22
Tuckahoe,†	Isaac Bunnel,*	0	0	0	0	0	0
Northeast Town,	Simon Dakin,*	0	0	0	0	0	54
2. New York,†	John Dodge,*	0	0	0	0	0	10
Stamford,†	Ebenezer Ferris,	0	0	0	0	0	89
Cow Marsh,	——— ———	1	0	4	0	2	23
London Tract,	Thomas Fleeson,* George Evans,	3	0	2	0	3	35

MINUTES OF THE PHILADELPHIA ASSOCIATION. 253

CHURCHES.	MINISTERS AND MESSENGERS.	Baptized.	Received by Letter.	Dismis'd.	Excom.	Deceased.	Members.
Hilltown,	{ John Thomas, James M'Laughlin, Nathan Evans, John Davies, jr.,	3	0	1	0	3	98
Lower Smithfield,†	David Jayne,*	0	0	0	0	0	29
Mispilion,	Joshua Dewees,*	1	0	0	1	0	16
Baltimore,	{ Lewis Richards, George Prestman, William Taggart,	10	2	0	0	0	48
Duck Creek,	{ James Jones,* John Patton,	1	2	5	0	0	63
Wilmington,	{ Thomas Ainger, Thomas Brooks, Andrew Hawke,	14	0	11	1	2	49
Canoe Brook,	Isaac Price,	2	1	2	0	0	35
Jacob's Town,	{ Burgiss Allison, James Cox, Samuel Sexton,	18	0	1	1	1	52
Staten Island,†	—— ——	0	0	0	0	0	28
Pittstown,†	James Finn,*	0	0	0	0	0	32
Marcus Hook,	{ Eliphaz Dazey, Richard Riley,	0	0	0	0	0	18
Rocksberry,	{ Abraham Levering, Charles Nice, John Levering,	0	0	0	0	0	36
Falls township, Bucks county,	} Joseph Richardson,	0	0	0	0	0	13
		373	42	109	39	43	3369

Note.—The ministers' names are in SMALL CAPITALS. Those marked thus * were not present. From the churches marked thus † we received no intelligence. A dash —— denotes no settled minister

MINUTES

OF THE

PHILADELPHIA BAPTIST ASSOCIATION,

HELD AT NEW YORK, OCTOBER 5TH, 6TH, AND 7TH,

1790.

Tuesday, October 5th.—At three o'clock, P. M., Dr. Samuel Jones delivered the introductory sermon, from John vii. 17: "If any man will do his will, he shall know of the doctrine, whether it be of God."

2. After worship, proceeded to business. Dr James Manning was chosen moderator, and Brother William Vanhorn, clerk.

3. Letters from the churches were read.

4. Letters from corresponding Associations were read, viz., Charleston, Warren, Ketockton, Shaftsbury, and Vermont; also a letter from an Association lately formed at Danbury, in the State of Connecticut, desiring union and correspondence with us, was read. After the usual inquiries respecting their doctrine and practice, their request was agreed to, and their messenger, Elder Adam Hamilton, received.

Adjourned to nine o'clock to-morrow morning.

Wednesday, October 6th.—Met pursuant to adjournment. In answer to the query from the church at the Scotch Plains: Whether a minister who has been excommunicated, and in process of time is restored again, has a right, on said restoration, to preach the gospel? We advise, that with his restoration to membership, before he exercises the functions of the ministry, he be expressly approbated therein by the church, and we think it expedient that it be with the advice of sister churches.

Resolved, That in answer to requests from the churches at Cape May and Pittsgrove, Brethren Samuel Jones, Samuel Morgan, William Vanhorn, and Ezekiel Robins, be a committee to prepare a letter to them on the subject of their difficulties.

Adjourned to three o'clock, P. M.

Met pursuant to adjournment.—As it appears expedient that Mr. Silas Walton should continue another year under the tuition of Dr. Jones, and as Mr. Carter, of Virginia, has generously engaged five pounds towards his assistance, it is agreed that we will be accountable for twenty pounds in addition thereto, said Walton giving a bond for refunding said twenty pounds in seven years, without interest; and it is recommended to the churches to promote subscriptions or collections the ensuing year, to raise said sum, and make additions to our fund, and transmit the same to our next Association.

Voted, That Brother S. Jones, Brother Hart, and Brother Allison be, and they are hereby appointed a committee to revise the materials for a history of the Baptist churches in the State of New Jersey, collected by Brother Morgan Edwards.

Letters to the corresponding Associations, ordered to be prepared by to-morrow afternoon, as follows; Brother Earl, to that of the Warren, Brother Ustick, to the Charleston, Brother D. Jones, to Ketockton, Brother Fleeson, to Shaftsbury, Brother Runyan, to Vermont, and Brother Smalley to that of Danbury.

Adjourned to nine o'clock to-morrow morning.

Sermon this evening by Elder Adam Hamilton, from Heb. xii. 1, 2. "Wherefore, seeing we also are compassed about with so great a cloud of witnesses," &c., &c.

Thursday, October 7th.—Met pursuant to adjournment. A letter written by Dr. Jones, opposed to universal salvation, being read, and esteemed very seasonable at this juncture, it was adopted as the circular letter for the present year, in lieu of that prepared by Brother Foster, agreeably to appointment, which was also read, generally approved, and though not revised, was nevertheless agreed to be printed.

Resolved, That it be a standing rule of this Association, that the circular letter be produced early in the session, and being read, a committee shall be appointed to examine, and, if necessary, correct it.

On the receipt of a letter from Mr. Isaac Collins, printer, of Trenton, respecting subscriptions for his Bible, we earnestly recommend to our churches, to promote the subscriptions, which are amongst them. Our committee, appointed last year to inspect this work, inform us, that it is executed as far as the book of Job, and with the greatest accuracy. Returns of the subscriptions, and the money paid on subscribing, may be made to the Rev. Mr. Foster, of New York, Rev. Mr. Allison, of Bordentown, and the Rev. Mr. Ustick, of Philadelphia.

Cash paid, agreeably to the recommendation of last Association, for a fund, &c., is as follows:

	£	s.	d.		£	s.	d.
Lower Dublin,	4	7	9	Haight's Town,	3	0	0
Piscataqua,	1	2	6	Philadelphia,	3	1	3
Cohansie,	1	2	6	Scotch Plains,	2	15	0
Hopewell,	2	11	0	New York,	8	1	8
Brandywine,	0	9	4	Baltimore,	9	7	6

In all £35 18s 7d., Pennsylvania currency.

Adjourned to three o'clock, P. M.

Met, pursuant to adjournment.—The subject of forming a new Association, to be held at New York, being considered, it did not appear there were a sufficient number of churches desired dismission for that purpose.

In answer to a query from the church at Stamford, accompanied with a number of quotations from certain authors, holding what is called the new system of divinity: Whether we hold them as Scripture truths, and whether such persons as hold them, and endeavor to promote them, are to be held in fellowship in a gospel church? We reply, that we apprehend danger, lest by these fine spun theories, and the consequences which are drawn from them by some, the great doctrines of the imputation of Adam's sin, Christ's proper atonement, imputed righteousness, &c., should be totally set aside, or, at least, the glory of them sullied. We therefore advise, that great care should be taken to guard against innovations not calculated to edify the body of Christ. But that the individual churches must judge for themselves, when any of their members so far deviate from that system of doctrine held by the churches of this Association, as to require their exclusion.

This Association lament they have occasion again to call the attention of that part of Zion we represent, to another awful instance of departure from the faith once delivered unto the saints. Mr. Nicholas Cox, late a brother in the ministry, having espoused, and artfully, as well as strenuously endeavored, to propagate the fatal notion of the universal restoration of bad men and devils from hell. As such, we caution our churches, those of our sister Associations, and Christian brethren of every denomination, to be aware of him.

The request of the churches at Stamford, Warwick, first and second of New York, King Street, and Staten Island, for permission to join other Associations, if it should be found more convenient, was granted.

Supplies for destitute churches at Salem, Pittsgrove, Lyon's Farms, 2d New York, and Staten Island.

Letters to the corresponding Associations, according to order of yesterday, were brought in, read, and approved. Dr. Manning appointed messenger to the Warren Association. Elder Hamilton to Shaftsbury, and Elder Ferres to Danbury.

This Association sincerely regret the failure of an appointment, the last year, to address the President of the United States; but deem it at present out of season.

Association to be held, first Tuesday in October, next in Philadelphia.

Brother William Vanhorn is appointed to write the circular letter for next year.

Brother Oliver Hart is appointed to preach the Association sermon next year, and, in case of failure, Brother William Vanhorn is requested to be prepared.

Brother William Vanhorn is requested to superintend the printing of the minutes, and forward them to the churches and Associations.

Sermon this evening by Brother Thomas Fleeson, from Rev. iii. 4: "Thou hast a few names even in Sardis, which have not defiled their garments; and they shall walk with me in white, for they are worthy."

CIRCULAR LETTER.
BY REV. SAMUEL JONES, D. D.

The elders and messengers of the several churches met in Association, in the city of New York, October 5th, 1790.

To the several churches in union with this Association, send greeting.

Dearly beloved,—We are happy, at the close of our annual meeting, that we can say, it was agreeable and comfortable through the whole. We had refreshing news from several churches in our connection, as well as from the Associations that correspond with us. It is matter of joy, and calls for acknowledgment and giving of thanks, that peace and good order so generally prevail, and that the work of the Lord is carried on with power in many places. We have, however, to lament, that there are some appearances, in two or three of our churches, of the leprosy of universal salvation, which, perhaps, the Lord may permit to spread, that they which are approved may be made manifest. But, when we see such an Achan, such a troubler of Israel, in the camp, we may well suspect the Lord has a controversy with us. It behoves us, then, to humble ourselves, to implore the divine mercy, and to do our endeavor to prevent the spreading of so dangerous a plague. To this end we have concluded to address you at this time on the aforesaid subject.

The notion of universal salvation, as now propagated, is explained two ways. Some of them say that there is no hell, or, if there be, that there shall not any of the human race be sent there, but that all, good and bad, shall be taken to heaven together. Others say, that though there be a place of future punishment, and though some of the human race are sent thither for a time, yet that they all finally shall be released, and brought safe to heaven.

We doubt not, dear brethren, but it will seem strange to such of you as may not have heard these things before, that any who pretend to be the ministers of Christ, should advance such dangerous notions. Yet so it is. He who, in the beginning, gave divine revelation the lie, when he said to the woman, "Ye shall not surely die," has ever since been going about, like a roaring lion, seeking whom he may devour; and endeavoring, by various means, to deceive and lull asleep, and among others, by endeavoring to evade the force of divine truth.

As for the first of these notions, namely, that not any of the human race are ever sent to a place of future punishment, but that all, good and bad, are taken to heaven, we shall say but little to it; not only because we have no room, but also because we deem it unnecessary. The Scripture, on the one hand, is so express, particular, and positive, and, on the other, the methods they take to evade these Scriptures are so disingenuous, and their endeavors to accommodate other Scriptures to their own views so trifling, that it is hard for any one to believe that they believe themselves, or that they can be serious and in earnest, when the Scriptures positively and without equivocation say, "the wicked shall be turned into hell, and all the nations that forget God," Ps. ix. 17. " That the whole body should be cast into hell," Matt. v. 29. " To be cast into hell fire," Matt. xviii. 9. " How can ye escape the damnation of hell," Matt. xxiii. 33. " To be cast into hell," Mark ix. 45, 47. " And in hell he lift up his eyes, being in torment," Luke xvi. 23 ; besides a number of other places. What need we more, not to mention the dissolute manners which might be expected to attend, and which actually have been the consequences of so licentious a tenet, as that of which we are speaking.

The other way of explaining this notion, namely, that, though some of the human race are sent to a place of future punishment for a time, yet that they shall all finally be released, and brought safe to heaven; this merits more attention, because it is more plausible, though not more true.

Here we shall consider,

I. That the Scripture is express against it.

II. That there are no Scriptures for it.

III. That there can be none, since it would be likely to do much hurt, but could do no good.

IV. And lastly, that if the notion was in some degree likely to be true, yet that it would be safest to reject it.

I. The Scripture expressly says that future punishment will be for ever, 2 Pet. ii. 17 ; Jude, verse 13 ; for ever and ever, Rev. xx. 10 ; xiv. 11 ; xix. 3.

And we read of "eternal damnation," Mark iii. 29 ; "eternal judgment," Heb. vi. 2 ; "eternal fire," Jude, verse 7 ; "everlasting fire," Matt. xxv. 41 ; xviii. 8 ; "everlasting punishment," Matt. xxv. 26 ; and of one sin that " it shall not be forgiven, neither in this world, neither in the world to come," Matt. xii. 32. In this absolute manner is expressed the endless duration of the awful denunciations of the wrath of God; and to cut off all pretence of every possible evasion, there are three things remarkable :

1. That the eternal duration of the punishment of the wicked, is expressed in the very same words as eternal duration in general, Dan. ii. 20.

2. In the very same words also, whereby the eternal duration of the happiness of the righteous is expressed, Dan. xii. 2; Rev. xxii. 5; John iii. 16; Matt. xxv. 26.

3. Nay, in the very same words whereby the eternal duration of God himself is expressed, Gen. xxi. 33 ; Psalm xc. 2 ; Dan. vii. 27 ; Lam. v. 19 ; Deut. xxxii. 40.

II. Since the awful subject before us is so clearly revealed in the word of God, it may seem trifling to undertake to show that there is no Scripture in favor of a release from future punishment, as if it might be possible for Scripture to say and unsay, to speak for and against the same thing. Nevertheless, it may be of use to mention the principle Scriptures that are pretended to hold forth a redemption from hell, in order to show, that beside the foregoing reason, there are generally reasons sufficient, arising out of the texts themselves and contexts, to show that they mean no such thing as they are brought to prove.

Thus, for instance, the "all men" in 1 Tim. ii. 4, can never mean every individual of the human race, for there are some "who were before ordained unto condemnation," and are "vessels of wrath fitted for destruction," (Jude 4; Rom. ix. 22;) but rather all sorts of men, as ver. 1, kings and peasants, rich and poor, bond and free, male and female, young and old; and who are therefore to be prayed for: nor can 2 Pet. iii. 9, admit of such an interpretation; for this means, not any of the *us* mentioned before, or the *beloved* in the first verse; nor 1 John ii. 2, which means that the benefits of Christ were not to be confined to the Jews only, but to be extended to the Gentiles also; nor Rom. v. 18, for here the first and second Adams, and their respective offspring are put in opposition, showing that as the offspring of the one was lost by his sin, the offspring of the other shall be saved by his grace; the one offspring condemned for one offence, the other saved from many; nor Col. i. 20, for *all* here must be understood in a limited sense; for it cannot include angels in heaven, who could not be reconciled to God, since they never had been in a state of irreconciliation: all the elect of God then are meant, who are spoken of as reconciled by the blood of the cross. Nor Eph. i. 10, which only says, that all *in* Christ shall be brought together, but not those who never were in him, and die in their sins; nor 1 Cor. xv. 22; for this speaks of the resurrection of the body from natural death, not of a resurrection from spiritual death. Nor Rom. xi. 32, which speaks of having mercy on all, that is, on all that believe, as in the parallel place, Gal. iii. 22. Nor Zech. ix. 11, for these are the words of Christ to the Jewish church, comforting them in the prospect of the favor that should be shown them by Cyrus, and comparing their distressed situation in the Babylonish captivity, to the situation of one in a pit, wherein was no water: and it is said this deliverance should be wrought in virtue of the covenant made in their behalf, which is therefore called *their* covenant. Nor Rev. xx. 13; for this speaks of gathering them from all quarters to the general judgment, who in the next verse are said to be cast into the lake of fire. Nor Heb. xii. 23; for here all the saved are said to be the *first born*, to denote their excellency, high privileges, right of priesthood, and large inheritance. Nor James i. 18; for the *first fruits* here means all the saved, as in the last, who are separated and distinguished by grace from others, as the first fruit was wont to be from the crop, and consecrated to God as that was. Nor 1 Cor. xv. 25, 28, and Phil. ii. 10; Rev. v. 13; for these are only expressive of the universal dominion of Christ, and of homage and adoration paid him on that account. Nor Ezek. xvi. 53, 55; for, if Sodom was to be restored, it must be to its former state, which was a very bad one. If restored should be understood in an improper sense, then by Sodom may be understood the Gentile nations, who were like unto Sodom in practice, Deut. xxxii. 32; Isa. i. 10; Jer. xxiii. 14; Rev. xi. 8; and Israel, by Samaria, who shall be restored when all the Jews, with the fulness of the Gentiles, shall be brought in at the time of the latter day glory. Or that when Sodom and Samaria should return to their former state, then the Jews should to theirs: as much as to say, they never should, as they never were. For, though many of them returned from the Babylonish captivity, yet they were never restored to their former state and glory. And besides, it is expressly said, with respect to "Sodom and Gomorrah, and the cities about them," that they "are set forth for an example, suffering the vengeance of eternal fire," Jude, verse 7.

Thus, brethren, we have cited the principal passages brought in support of this wild notion of universal salvation, and you see how little they are to the purpose. Thus it is that people in a strait will catch at any thing.

III. Further, it is not only manifest that there is no text to support such a notion, but that there cannot be such a text. It cannot be that the Divine being has published any thing that would be, not only contrary to those plain texts, that speak positively of the eternal duration of future punishment, but that it would also be perfectly useless, and at the same time dangerous. If the wicked were ever to be released from hell, time enough to let them know it after they get there, and not before, to encourage them in sin. To give them so much as a hint of it in this life, would be exactly the same as if the Divine Being, when he prohibited the use of the forbidden tree, had told Adam, that if he should eat of that tree, he would contrive a way for his escape, of which we know that not the least item was given before the fall, and indeed than which nothing could be more unworthy the Divine Being. So that if there was any passage within the lids of the Bible that gave information of a release from hell, we might be sure, such a text could never be the word of God.

IV. We only add, that if the notion of restoration from hell was in some degree probable, which it is not, yet it would be much safest to reject it altogether; for if those who place dependence on it should at last find themselves mistaken, awful will be the disappointment. On the other hand, those who place no dependence on it, but seek to avoid future punishment, by placing their dependence on a better hope, if they should be mistaken, they will nevertheless share equal benefit with others.

Let us, therefore, carefully avoid a notion so unscriptural, so useless, and at the same time so dangerous. But, beloved, of you we hope better things, though we thus speak. We do not apprehend much danger, but judge it seasonable, and that it might be of use to give a word of caution.

"Now unto him that is able to keep you from falling, and to present you faultless before the presence of his glory, with exceeding joy, to the only wise God our Saviour, be glory and majesty, dominion and power, both now and ever. Amen."

JAMES MANNING, Moderator.
WILLIAM VANHORN, Clerk.

N. B. The clerk takes the liberty of informing those who wish to see the subject discussed more at large, that they will find their attention amply rewarded by reading Edwards against Chauncey.

CIRCULAR LETTER.
BY REV. BENJAMIN FOSTER.

The messengers, to the churches of the Philadelphia Baptist Association, send Christian salutation.

Beloved Brethren,—We rejoice that the Father of mercies has permitted us once more to meet, in order that we might unitedly pursue the promotion of that cause which we believe is unspeakably precious to the dear churches we have the honor to represent. But the success of our feeble efforts to advance the important object in view depends wholly on the blessing of Him "who worketh all things after the counsel of his own will." To Him, therefore, we humbly commit the concerns of Zion in general, and the transactions of this our meeting in particular; fervently beseeching Him that of his abundant grace and mercy he would grant our labor may not be in vain in the Lord!

Notwithstanding the darkness and delusions of a sinful world, and the various imperfections of God's people in the present state, blessed be God! we are united in the leading and essential truths of divine revelation. And, therefore, on these important and glorious subjects, we can address you with greater freedom and pleasure. You will permit us, this year, to call your attention to the subject of Good works, treated of in the sixteenth chapter of our excellent Confession of faith.

Works may be said to be good either in a natural, or in a moral or spiritual sense. The action or influence of the sun on the earth is good, as a useful and an important natural blessing. The movements of a machine may be denominated such on account of the purposes of convenience and profit answered by them. But the actions which are under consideration are good, not merely on account of natural advantages in their tendency, or of which they may be the occasion, but on account of their being right in a spiritual sense, and proper to be performed by creatures possessed of rational and immortal souls; and who are the subjects of obligations to God, and created intelligences in the moral world which can never be dissolved; and who enjoy the means of information respecting their duty and their everlasting welfare; and who must give an account of the deeds done in the body, whether they be good or whether they be evil.

Actions which are good in this sense are such as are agreeable to the will of God revealed in his word. The action performed, the temper exercised, and the motives by which men are actuated in conduct of this nature are required by God in the holy scriptures.

The thing done may answer to the letter of the requisition, or be what is expressed in the command; but the action may not be pleasing in the sight of God on account of a deficiency in temper, motive or design. The action as good must be intended, the authority of him who enjoins the action must be respected, and the end proposed by Infinite Wisdom and Goodness must be presumed, or there will not be a compliance with the spirit of the command.

An intelligent creature may not only comply with a divine precept so far as it respects what is external, but do that which is highly beneficial, and yet there may be a material deficiency in the action. Good may be done in a natural respect, and the action notwithstanding may not be good in a spiritual respect, though performed by one possessed of rational powers of mind. "Though I bestow all my goods to feed the poor; and though I give my body to be burned, and have not charity, (that is true love to God and man,) it profiteth me nothing," 1 Cor. xiii. 3.

Good works are the performances of those who are good. Goodness must first exist, in some measure, in the state of the soul before it can be expressed in life and conversation. Persons wholly under the dominion of sin, as is the case with all the unconverted, are totally incapacitated on account of the fixed opposition of their minds to the truth, to perform actions right and pleasing in the sight of God. As the tree must be made good before the fruit will be good: so the nature of man must be renewed by divine grace, in order that the fruit may be unto holiness, and the end everlasting life. To suppose that one under the influence of a carnal mind, and in a state of unbelief, may, while he continues in this state, perform actions truly good, is to suppose what is unreasonable in itself, and expressly contradicted by the word of truth, which informs us, that they who are in the flesh cannot please God; and that without faith it is impossible to please him.

Jehovah is the great and all-important object in the performance of good works. The Christian directs and finishes his course under the influence of an approving and pleasing belief of what God is, and what he has done. The high estimation that his soul possesses of the excellencies and glories of the Deity, in his attributes, works, and designs, is expressed in every work of faith, and in all his labor of love. The life that he lives of the flesh, he lives by faith in the Son of God; by whose gospel he is effectually taught to deny ungodliness and every worldly lust, and to live soberly, righteously, and godly in this present world. The beauties of the divine character exhibited in the great atonement, and impressed on the believer's mind, lay him under a willing constraint to shun the paths of vice, and to be found in the ways of justice, mercy, and truth. Though in the performance of good works, he is not wholly divested of a regard to self, yet he is not merely influenced by a selfish gratitude arising from reflections on the reception of past favors, by fond expectations of future enjoyments, or by a slavish fear of approaching wrath: but mainly by the noble principle of love to the blessed God on account of his spotless purity, and the unchanging holiness of his nature. Is the Christian attending to the civil affairs of life, engaged in the sacred duties of devotion, or employed in acts of beneficence and compassion, he does all to the glory of God. The believer, as far as his actions answer to the will of heaven, directs his attention to the greatest possible good, as he pursues the divine glory, and in subordination to this, his own happiness in connection with the good of others. But alas! when we review the best actions of our lives, we find a sad deficiency in these respects, in the performance: and after attending to the most unspotted characters in the Christian world, we must undoubtedly conclude, that there is none doeth good and sinneth not.

Good works are by no means the foundation of our acceptance or justification in the sight of God. Nothing that we ever have done, and nothing possible for us ever to perform, will have the least concern or weight in the important affair of our acquittal from guilt, and acceptance as righteous before the tribunal of a holy God. Nothing on earth or in heaven can be found to answer this glorious purpose but the finished righteousness, and the atoning death of the great Immanuel, God with us.

It is equally true, and may as evidently be deduced from the word of truth, that foreseen good works are not the cause of our election to salvation. One end of our election was to bring us to the love and practice of holiness: and, therefore, good works, or holiness of life, could not have been the reason of the eternal purpose to recover us to the divine image and favor. The purpose of election stands "not of works, but of him who calleth," Rom. ix. 11. All the graces of the Spirit, and all our acts of true religion and virtue, are to be considered as effects of the unconditional and eternal counsel of God in Christ.

And, permit us, dear brethren, further to add, that the same reasons, in effect, forbid us to suppose that good works are the condition of our regeneration or of our being called out of darkness into marvellous light. If we are so happy as to be the subject of this glorious change, not a tribute of praise is to be ascribed to ourselves; but all the glory is to be given to God, "who hath saved us, and called us with an holy calling, not according to our works, but according to his own purpose and grace, which was given us in Christ Jesus before the world began," 2 Tim. i. 9.

Notwithstanding our salvation is not by works of righteousness which we have done, nor our regeneration and effectual calling on account of any previous goodness of temper or conduct in us; yet we are to consider that those who are renewed are the subjects of an alteration in the state of their minds from sin to holiness: and that this moral change will be attended, as opportunity may be given for action, with holiness of life and conversation. A renewed mind includes a temper of love to the moral character of Jehovah. And as the divine law, or the moral rule given by God to his creature man, is with propriety considered as a transcript of this character, there will be the same freedom in the Christian to yield subjection to this holy law, in its sacred and various injunctions, as to love the divine image, or to be truly pleased with the beauties of holiness in the face of Jesus Christ. Those who, by divine grace, imbibe the genuine spirit of Christianity, will pay a sacred respect to all God's holy commands.

It becomes the disciples of Jesus not merely to avoid the neglect of the express precepts of their divine Lord; but to be ready to every good work. Though they cannot be profitable to their Maker, or add to his essential glories; yet they may and ought to be profitable to themselves, and a blessing to their fellow creatures. He who, regardless of his own improvements in the divine life, and unconcerned about the good of others, seeks only to shun the reproofs of conscience, gives us reason to doubt his acquaintance with true religion.

We are not only to engage, but to persevere in the performance of good works. Those who have never experienced a real and genuine work of God upon their souls, may, from selfish motives, perform the externals of duty for a while: but when the floods come, and the winds of temptation blow and beat on the house, then it appears to have had its foundation in the sand. But as true believers have the seed of God abiding in them, they are those who, by perseverance in the ways of righteousness and truth, will renew their strength, brave every storm, and baffle every hostile attempt, till they finish their heavenly course with complete and eternal joy.

Dearly beloved, let us urge the importance of good works, and endeavor to excite you to a faithful and diligent performance of them, from the following considerations.

Remember, they are the duties you owe to God—to that Being who is infinitely great and infinitely good; the creator and preserver of all things, the former of your bodies, and the Father of your spirits; and who stands in a relation to you which no alteration of circumstances, in time or through eternity, can possibly dissolve.

Consider that in this way you will be the followers of God as dear children. Your heavenly Father is universal, unremitted, and eternal in the operations of his goodness. He acts for the noblest end, as he has made all things for himself. His works are done in righteousness and truth. Without upbraiding, and in a rich profusion he bestows the blessings of his providence, and gives the enjoyments of his grace. And you are directed by the great Head of the church to abound in works of goodness and love, "that ye may be the children of your Father who is in heaven: for he maketh his sun to rise on the evil and on the good, and sendeth rain on the just and on the unjust," Matt. v. 45.

What a powerful motive to excite you to the performance of good works, is the conduct of Him who was made flesh and dwelt among us! He went about doing good, attending to the business of his Father, and improving in the best manner the golden moments of time. "I must work," says he, "the works of him that sent me while it is day: the night cometh when no man can work," John ix. 4. And is it possible that those who love his person, possess his temper, feel the power of his divine religion, and have enlisted under him as the Captain of their salvation, should ever live uninfluenced by so bright and perfect an example, or fail to follow him wheresoever he goeth!

How much to induce us to works of virtue, piety, and mercy, from reflections on the unmerited and unbounded goodness of God towards us! How great the designs of God's love in the covenant of redemption, made by the eternal Three-in-One before the foundation of the world! How wonderful is his mercy in the gift of his dear Son as the infinite price of our release from eternal ruin. How astonishing his compassion in saving us from sin and hell, and giving us a title to a crown of immortal glory! And can the objects of eternal love, and the subjects of such marvellous grace be indifferent to the service of the great Benefactor of their perishing and sinful souls! Has God done such great things for us, and shall we fail to do the little we can for him? Has he in fact done all things for us, and is not something to be done by us, in a way in which he will consider it as done unto himself? Would not a thousand lives spent in his service, and a thousand deaths suffered in his cause, be but a small testimony of gratitude and love for his undeserved and matchless grace in the eternal salvation of one poor sinner, bound to unutterable woe?

Is it not the habitual desire, and the fervent wish of your souls to recommend the religion of Jesus, and to promote the declarative glory of God? In this way they will be effected; by such a line of conduct you will find an answer to the devout exercises of your own minds. "Let your light so shine before men, that they may see your good works and glorify your Father who is in heaven," Matt. v. 16.

To these things, dear brethren, you will attend if you are in the pursuit of real advantage, of substantial good to yourselves. For in keeping God's commands there is great reward. A cheerful compliance with the divine will, a tender regard to the dictates of conscience and the voice of reason, and the performance of whatever may promote and honor religion, and conduce to make ourselves and others happy, in time and through eternity, will be attended with that peace and comfort which the world never did, and never can give. As you would wish to enjoy the blessings of God's kingdom, seek ever to be found in these paths of wisdom. For her ways are ways of pleasantness, and all her paths are peace. He who walketh uprightly walketh safely. The more diligent you are in works of piety and mercy, the greater reason you have to expect that God will confirm your minds in the truth, support you in the day of trial, increase your graces, establish your hopes, and in the end render your conquest and triumph complete over all your spiritual and powerful enemies. Then on the brink of death, and the invisible world brought near to view, in the exulting language of a Paul, each one of you may say, "I have fought a good fight, I have finished my course, I have kept the faith: henceforth there is laid up for me a crown of righteousness which the Lord, the righteous Judge, shall give me at that day," 2 Tim. iv. 7, 8.

When addressing the churches of Jesus Christ on the duties of their holy profession, we trust, beloved, you will not be offended if we conclude the subject by exhorting you to the performance of them in a few particulars. If the works of Christian churches be not found perfect before God, but be attended to with partiality and sloth, how does the enemy blaspheme, and how deeply wounded is the blessed Jesus in the house of his friends! You expect that your ministers,—and undoubtedly you may with propriety,—will be diligent in every good work which belongs to their pastoral office, and concerns your spiritual and eternal welfare. If they should be found negligent and unfaithful, how great their guilt, and how dreadful their doom when the blood of immortal souls shall be required of them by their angry Judge! It certainly much concerns them well to improve their time, to study to show themselves approved workmen, who need not to be ashamed before God, angels, and men, when the books shall be opened, and the judgment fixed. They are to watch for souls as those who must give an account. But in return, you must consider it as your incumbent duty to strengthen their hands for this good work, by affording them a competent supply of the necessaries and conveniences of life. For if they have sown unto you spiritual things, is it a great thing if they should reap your carnal things? And has not your dear Lord ordained, that they who preach the gospel should live of the gospel? And can it be said that you have diligently followed every good work, if you suffer your ministers to live in indigence, and their minds to be perplexed, for want of those enjoyments of which God has granted you a rich supply? Provide houses decent and convenient for the public worship of God. Is it fit for the servants of the most High to dwell in their ceiled houses, and to let the house where his honor dwells, and where his adorable Majesty is addressed, to lie waste? Pay proper attention to the poor; but especially endeavor to relieve the wants of your needy brethren and sisters. It is more blessed to give than to receive; for they who give to the poor, lend unto the Lord. Encourage family order and government, and make your habitations houses of prayer. Let not the duties of the closet be neglected: but in those places of retirement be statedly found, in order to pray to your heavenly Father in secret; and your Father, who seeth in secret, will reward you openly. Forsake not the assembling of yourselves together, as the manner of some is: but continue in the apostles' doctrine, in fellowship, in breaking of bread and in prayers. Let proper discipline be attended to, and supported: let the respective members keep their places, and highly respect the authority of Christ in the churches. Be at peace among yourselves; warn them that are unruly; comfort the feeble minded; support the weak; and be patient to all men. And blessed indeed is that servant whom his Lord, when he cometh, shall find so doing!

MINUTES OF THE PHILADELPHIA ASSOCIATION.

THE MINISTERS AND MESSENGERS AT THE ASSOCIATION, AND THE STATE OF THE CHURCHES FOR THE YEAR.

CHURCHES.	MINISTERS AND MESSENGERS.	Baptized.	Received by Letter.	Dismis'd.	Restored.	Excom.	Deceased.	Members.
Lower Dublin,	SAMUEL JONES,	1	1	0	1	2	0	67
Middletown,	SAMUEL MORGAN,	8	1	0	0	0	3	140
Piscataqua,	{ REUNE RUNYAN, Henry Smalley,	1	1	0	0	0	1	148
Cohansie,	{ ——— Providence Ludlam,	23	0	0	0	0	4	109
Welsh Tract,†	JOHN BOGGS,*	0	0	0	0	0	0	104
Great Valley	———	0	0	1	0	0	4	86
Cape May,	JOHN STANCLIFF,*	4	1	0	0	5	2	61
Hopewell,	{ OLIVER HART, James Ewen, James Hunt,	3	4	5	0	0	1	165
Brandywine,	ABEL GRIFFITHS,	7	1	2	0	0	0	43
Montgomery,	———	0	0	3	0	0	0	25
Tulpehokin,†	———	0	0	0	0	0	0	0
Kingwood,†	———	0	0	0	0	0	0	180
Haight's Town,	{ PETER WILSON, Alexander McGowan, Peter Jobs,	18	3	7	0	1	5	248
Southampton,	{ DAVID JONES, Benjamin Bennet,	1	0	1	0	0	0	53
Philadelphia,	{ THOMAS USTICK, Samuel Davies, jr.,*	5	2	6	1	1	0	105
Scotch Plains,	{ WILLIAM VANHORN, Jacob Fitz Randolph, Marmaduke Earle, Joseph Drake,	4	2	4	0	1	2	136
Oyster Bay,	———	0	0	0	0	0	0	25
Morristown,	{ ——— Michael Parce,	10	0	2	0	0	0	91
Knowlton,	DANIEL VAUGHAN,*	2	0	0	0	2	0	43
Hartford,†	JOHN DAVIES,*	0	0	0	0	0	0	120
New Britain,†	JOSHUA JONES,*	0	0	0	0	0	0	21
Salem,	———	28	0	0	0	0	0	59
Wantage, late Newtown,	} SILAS SOUTHWORTH,*	8	1	12	0	2	1	66
Dividing Creek,†	———	0	0	0	0	0	0	41
1. New York,	{ BENJAMIN FOSTER, Samuel Dodge, Abraham Cannon, William Norris, Ezekiel Robins, John Bedient,	22	0	21	0	2	3	192
New Mills,	———	5	0	14	0	0	2	89
Konoloway,†	JOSEPH POWEL,*	0	0	0	0	0	0	0

CHURCHES.	MINISTERS AND MESSENGERS.	Baptized.	Received by Letter.	Dismis'd.	Restored.	Excom.	Deceased.	Members.
Coram,	—— ——	0	0	0	0	0	0	30
Upper Freehold,	{ Joseph Stephens, Edward Taylor,	17	2	1	0	0	1	74
Mount Bethel,†	Abner Sutton,*	0	0	0	0	0	1	101
Warwick,	{ Thomas Montanye, John M. Foght, Abijah Whitney, Thomas D. Madam,	8	3	3	1	5	2	194
Lyon's Farms,	{ Aaron Ball, Michael Law,	0	1	0	0	0	0	16
Philip's Patent,†	—— ——	0	0	0	0	0	0	0
Pittsgrove,	—— ——	0	0	0	0	0	0	0
Manahawkin,†	—— ——	0	0	0	0	0	0	0
Vincent,	—— ——	1	0	0	0	0	2	22
Tuckahoe,†	Isaac Bunnel,*	0	0	0	0	0	0	0
2. New York,	{ Francis Vandyke, Joseph Stout,	3	18	0	0	0	0	32
Stamford,	{ Ebenezer Ferris, Elijah Hunter,	5	0	2	0	0	1	72
King Street,	{ Benjamin Sutton,	33	5	16	0	3	2	36
Cow Marsh,†	—— ——	0	0	0	0	0	0	23
London Tract,	Thomas Fleeson,	1	0	0	0	0	1	34
Hilltown,	J. M'Laughlin,	12	1	10	0	0	2	99
Lower Smithfield,	David Jayne,	0	2	2	0	1	2	26
Baltimore,	Lewis Richards,*	3	4	0	0	1	1	53
Duck Creek,†	John Patton,*	0	0	0	0	0	0	63
Wilmington,	Thomas Ainger,	0	0	2	0	1	1	45
Canoe Brook,	—— ——	27	1	1	0	1	0	62
Jacob's Town,	{ Burgiss Allison, William Snowden,	1	0	3	0	0	0	60
Staten Island,	{ Elkana Holmes, Anthony Fountain, Nicholas Cox,	0	0	0	0	0	0	28
Pittstown,†	James Finn,*	0	0	0	0	0	0	28
Marcus Hook,	Eliphaz Dazey,*	0	0	0	0	0	0	18
Roxbury,	*Curtis Gilbert,*	4	2	1	0	0	0	39
Falls Township,	—— ——	4	0	0	0	0	0	17
		264	56	117	3	28	42	3587

Note.—The ministers' names are in SMALL CAPITALS. Licensed preachers in *italic.* Those marked thus * were not present. From churches marked thus † we received no letter. A dash —— denotes no settled minister.

A VIEW OF THE BAPTIST ASSOCIATIONS, &c., IN THE UNITED STATES OF AMERICA, AND VERMONT.

	ASSOCIATIONS.	STATES IN WHICH THEY MEET.	TIMES OF MEETING.	MINISTERS.	CHURCHES.	MEMBERS.
1	Bowdoinham,	Massachusetts,	September,	8	8	500
2	New Hampshire,	New Hampshire,	2d Wednesday in June,	7	8	500
3	Woodstock,	New Hampshire and Vermont,	4th Wednesday in September,	14	24	950
4	Vermont,	Vermont,	1st Wednesday in October,	6	11	500
5	Warren,	Massachusetts,	Tuesday after 1st Wednesday in September	25	41	3400
6	Rhode Island,	Rhode Island and Massachusetts,	3d Friday in September,	15	12	500
7	Groton,	Connecticut,	3d Friday in June,	8	11	1500
8	Stonington,	Rhode Island and Connecticut,	3d Tuesday in October,	10	13	1000
9	Danbury,	Connecticut,	4th Wednesday in September,	14	15	870
10	Shaftsbury,	Massachusetts and New York,	1st Wednesday in June,	10	22	1500
11	Philadelphia,	Pennsylvania,	1st Tuesday in October,	49	56	4100
12	Redstone,	Pennsylvania,	3d Saturday in October,	9	11	600
13	Salisbury,	Maryland and Virginia,	3d Saturday in August and October,	6	14	1400
14	Ketockton,	Virginia,	3d Friday in August,	10	12	650
15	Chappawamsick,	do.	2d Wednesday in September,	7	14	850
16	Orange District,	do.	2d Friday in October,	22	32	4600
17	Dover do.	do.	1st Friday in May and October,	36	26	5100
18	Lower do. and Kehukey,	do. and N. C.	4th Saturday in May and 2d in October,	45	51	5500
19	Middle do.	do.	1st Saturday in May and October,	24	25	2000
20	Upper do.	do.	4th Saturday in May and 1st in October,	11	18	1200
21	Roanoke do.	do. and N. C.	2d Saturday in June and 4th in October,	18	18	2700
22	S. Kentucky,	do.	4th Friday in May and October,	15	14	1200
23	N. Kentucky,	do.	May and October,	10	12	1100
24	Ohio,	do.		4	5	300
25	Holston,	North Carolina,	1st Saturday in June and 2d in October,	10	17	1200
26	Sandy Creek,	do.	4th Saturday in October,	10	13	1200
27	Yadkin,	do.	4th Saturday in April and September,	11	14	800
28	Charleston,	South Carolina,	4th Saturday in October,	16	19	1850
29	Bethel,	do.	2d Saturday in August,	9	16	1200
30	Georgia,	Georgia,	2d Saturday in May and October,	22	31	2700
				452	533	50970
			Churches not belonging to Associations,	100	150	8000
				552	733	58970
			Seventh Day Baptists,	12	15	2000
			Sum Total,	564	748	60970

Note (associations 15–23): These nine Associations meet in a general committee by their representatives, at Richmond, in the month of May, annually.

MINUTES

OF THE

PHILADELPHIA BAPTIST ASSOCIATION,

HELD IN PHILADELPHIA, OCTOBER 4TH, 5TH, AND 6TH,

1791.

October 4th.—At 3 o'clock, P. M., Rev. Oliver Hart delivered the introductory sermon, from 2 Chron. xxix. 35, "So the service of the house of the Lord was set in order."

2. After worship, proceeded to business. Rev. Dr. Samuel Jones was chosen moderator, and Rev. John Stancliff, clerk.

3. Letters from thirty-three churches were read.

Adjourned to half past eight to-morrow morning.

October 5th.—Met pursuant to adjournment.

1. Whereas a difficulty respecting the second church in New York was brought before us, we wish a mutual council may be called to settle the matter.

2. The new constituted church at Sideling Hill, Belfast township, Bedford county, made application for admittance into this Association; but an objection arising, in consequence of a letter sent by Brother Powell, their admission was postponed until next meeting of Association, when the objectors will have opportunity to show their reasons, why the request of said church should not be granted.

3. Letters from the corresponding Association of Stonington, Shaftsbury, and Danbury, were received and read. Brother Vanhorn was appointed to write to the Stonington; Brother Bryant, to the Shaftsbury; and Brother Allison, to the Danbury Association.

4. A copy of a neat quarto Bible, of Mr. Collin's impression, was laid before the Association by Dr. Rogers, which was highly approved of; and as the subscriptions for the same will continue open till the 1st of January next, at four dollars each, it is hereby recommended to the several churches and individuals of our body to patronize so laudable an undertaking.

5. Query from the church at Great Valley: What steps ought a church to take in respect of a member, who hath married the son of a former husband's sister?

Referred to the next Association.

6. Doctor Rogers read a paragraph of a letter from the Rev. Abraham Booth, of London, directed to himself, in which was intimated the expediency of our reconsidering the decision of this Asso-

ciation, in 1788, respecting "the invalidity of Baptism when administered by an unbaptized person."
Agreed to refer it to the next meeting of the Association.

7. The circular letter was read. Our Brethren Ustick and Allison were desired to revise the same, in conjunction with the author, Brother Vanhorn.

Adjourned to three o'clock, P. M.

1. Met according to adjournment.—The churches at Scotch Plains, Canoe Brook, Piscataqua, and Morristown, requested liberty to join an Association at New York, should they think proper. Their request was granted; and they will be considered as dismissed from us, when received by them.

2. Supplies were granted to the following destitute churches:— At Great Valley, Dividing Creek, and Kingwood.

3. The collections, agreeably to last year's recommendation, were as follows:

	£	s.	d.		£	s	d.
Lower Dublin,	1	19	1	Haight's Town,	2	0	0
Cohansie,	1	2	6	Scotch Plains,	1	0	0
Philadelphia,	3	5	5	Morristown,	0	15	0

In all £10 3s. 0d.

Agreed to return this sum to those churches, as the necessity for the same has ceased.

4. Doctor Samuel Jones, our treasurer, stated, that he had funded the two small certificates belonging to the Association, with his own, and meant to be accountable for their value;—six per cents, at 20s. and 6d.; three per cents, at 11s. 4d.; deferred, 12s. 2d. The reason for his conduct was approved.

5. Resolved, That the Rev. Samuel Jones, the Rev. Morgan Edwards, Samuel Miles, Esq., Thomas Shields, Esq., Rev. Dr. William Rogers, Rev. Burgiss Allison, and Rev. Thomas Ustick, be a committee to effectuate the incorporation of the Association by charter.

6. Agreeably to the report of the committee, the circular letter, composed by Brother Vanhorn, was approved.

7. Voted, That the money raised last year, remaining in the treasurer's hands, be allowed, on the usual terms, to Brother David Stout, who is a candidate for the ministry, and a member of the church at Kingwood.

Adjourned to nine o'clock to-morrow morning.

Rev. Reune Runyan preached in the evening, from Rom. iii. 24.

October 6th.—Met pursuant to adjourment.

1. The letters to the Stonington, Shaftsbury, and Danbury Associations, were read and approved.

2. Doctor Rogers is desired to write to Ketockton, Brother Vanhorn, to Warren, and Brother Hart, to Charleston Association.

3. During the past year two of our brethren in the ministry were removed by death, viz., Rev. John Thomas, of Hilltown, Bucks county, aged seventy-nine years, and Rev. Abner Sutton, of Mount Bethel, New Jersey, aged forty-six years.

4. Doctor Jones is requested to prepare an abstract, from the proceedings of this Association, of those particulars which are most material and important, against next meeting of the Association.

5. The Association to be held next year at Philadelphia, on the first Tuesday in October. Rev. William Vanhorn is appointed to preach the introductory sermon; and in case of failure, Rev. Dr. William Rogers.

6. Rev. Joshua Jones is appointed to write the circular letter for next year.

7. Brother Ustic is requested to superintend the printing of the minutes, and to forward them to the several churches and Associations.

Sermon in the evening, by Rev. John Boggs, from Matt. xxii. 29.

CIRCULAR LETTER.

BY REV. WILLIAM VANHORN.

THE elders and messengers of the several churches met in Association in the city of Philadelphia, October 4th, 1791.

To the churches in union with this Association, send greeting.

Beloved brethren,—We are happy at the close of this anniversary meeting, to inform you, we have enjoyed an agreeable interview. By communications from the churches, we rejoice to hear that peace is enjoyed so generally, and that to many of them considerable additions have been made. It is matter of much satisfaction, that, in this day of prevailing error, there appears amongst you so general a concern for the preservation of divine truth. From corresponding Associations we have received very agreeable intelligence. On the whole, we have been called upon to very grateful acknowledgments for the goodness and grace of God manifested the year past. But our joys abate, while we reflect on the heavy tidings so generally mentioned in your letters, of the death of our highly esteemed and dearly beloved Brother, DR. MANNING; who, engaged in the dearest interests of religion, of science, and the prosperity of his country, fell from the zenith of glory and usefulness. In the general loss we sustain an important part. No longer shall we enjoy his able counsels, his divine and persuasive eloquence, nor his personal friendship. But while we trust he fell, to rise to higher, to celestial glories, and joys unspeakable, resignation becomes us. May the Lord sanctify to the churches and ministers of Christ, the awful stroke; enable us to feel, and faithfully discharge, the duties devolving on us, and imitate his amiable example.

The subject on which we are now to address you, brethren, is, the Perseverance of the saints in grace, till it shall be consummated in glory. Confession of faith, Chap. XVII.

A doctrine which forms an important article in the system of divine truth, and of which Revelation abounds with evidence; a sentiment calculated to administer the truest spiritual support to the real Christian, to influence him to the warmest zeal for God, and holiness of life.

In treating on this subject, in an epistolary way, it will not be expected to enter at large on what might be said on it, nor formally to encounter all the unreasonable objections which have been raised against it. To convince you of this truth, we trust, dear brethren, there is no necessity. To quicken your graces, and awaken your gratitude, for so divine a support in your Christian race, is chiefly intended.

By asserting the perseverance of the saints in grace, we do not mean to convey an idea, that through the various and powerful oppositions, with which they are beset in this state of spiritual warfare, none of them may fall into sin, be overtaken in transgression, to the wounding of their own souls, the tenderest feelings of their brethren, the churches of Christ, the interests of religion in general, and the displeasure of God,—but, that through this unspeakable grace and mercy he will not suffer them so to fall, and continue therein, as totally and finally to perish. He will, by sore chastisements, or such other means as, in his wisdom shall seem best, bring them to an affecting sense of their sins, to genuine repentance for them, and deep humiliation before him,—as in the instances of Peter, David, and others,—and restore them. "If his children forsake my law, and walk not in my judgments; if they break my statutes, and keep not my commandments; then will I visit their transgression with the rod, and their iniquity with stripes. Nevertheless, my loving kindness will I not utterly take from him, nor suffer my faithfulness to fail. My covenant will I not break, nor alter the thing that is gone out of my lips." Psalm lxxxix. 30–34.

We exclude, in the consideration of this subject, all false professors of religion, of every description, whatever may be their attainments, as in the grace of knowledge, talents, or tongues, and power of working miracles, who, nevertheless, are, and continue destitute of the renewing grace of God. Hence, those who have made a fair show in religion for a time, as the foolish virgins, Matt. xxv. The branches who were in the true vine, either by profession only, or in relation to Abraham, John xv. Those, who in a sense may have tasted of the good word of God, as the stony ground hearers, Matt. xiii.; or, as Herod, who heard John gladly, Matt. vi. 20. Those who may have embraced the doctrine of the gospel, frequently styled "The Faith," in the New Testament, Acts xxiv. 24; 1 Tim. i. 21; 2 Tim. iii. 8; as Hymeneus and Alexander, who in time made shipwreck thereof, 1 Tim. i. 20. Those who have been enlightened, and had the gift of prophecy, as Balaam, 1 Cor. xiii. 2; or who had the gift of tongues—power to work miracles, and, as such, tasted of the powers of the world to come, or of the gospel dispensation, as Judas, Heb. vi. 5,—all such we exclude,—of all such there is no sufficient evidence, that any of them were renewed by the grace of God, but of many of them the fullest testimony they were not. We, therefore, cannot plead their perseverance in grace, which they never had; nor can such instances of defection, with any propriety, be produced as objections to the doctrine in contemplation.

We assert, that those only will persevere in the way of eterna life, and attain unto it, in whom the regenerating grace of God has, or will take place. That this will be the happy event with all such, through the riches of sovereign mercy and goodness, the following considerations evince.

The everlasting love of God to his people, manifested in Christ Jesus, tends to establish the truth.

Of his church of old, God says, "I have loved thee with an everlasting love, therefore, with loving kindness have I drawn thee," Jer. xxxi. 3. This is the true origin of the stupendous plan laid by God the Father, for the salvation of his people. The true source of the execution of this plan is by the mediation of Christ the Son. From hence proceeds the execution of the gracious offices of the Holy Ghost, in the conversion of sinners, as a necessary preparation for the enjoyment of heaven. It is he who draws and leads them from death to life—from sin to holiness—from enmity to God to the love of him. Agreeably to this, divine testimony says, "We love him, because he first loved us," 1 John iv. 19. "Having loved his own, he loveth them to the end," John xiii. 1,—even to everlasting.

That the love of God, in its manifestations and influences, would issue in the perseverance of the saints, and bring them to glory, Paul had the fullest assurance, when he asks with an air of triumph, "Who shall separate us from the love of Christ? Shall tribulation, or distress, or persecution, or famine, or nakedness, or peril, or sword? Nay, in all these things we are more than conquerors through him that loved us. For I am persuaded, that neither death, nor life, nor angels, nor principalities, nor powers, nor things present, nor things to come,—nor height, nor depth, nor any other creature, shall be able to separate us from the love of God which is in Christ Jesus our Lord," Rom. viii. 35, 37–39.

This sentiment receives strength from the connection which subsists between the grace given to sinners, and God's eternal decrees; when the good work is begun, it is the gracious accomplishment of his purposes to them from everlasting. "Who hath called us with an holy calling, according to his own purpose and grace, which was given us in Christ Jesus before the world began." On this foundation, then, the purpose of God, his word proceeds. The gospel is preached wherever it comes. "As many as were ordained to eternal life, believed," Acts xiii. 48. "He that believeth on the Son, hath everlasting life," John iii. 36. "He that believeth, shall be saved," Mark xvi. 16,—shall not perish. "The Lord added to the church daily such as should be saved," Acts ii. 47,—should not be lost. Such is the inseparable connection between election—grace communicated, and the contemplation of it in glory. "For whom he did predestinate, them he also called; and whom he called, them he also justified; and whom he justified, them he also glorified," Rom. viii. 30.

The possession Christ has taken of the believer, by his grace, deserves notice. Formerly Satan had dominion; kept his goods in peace; reigned and ruled in them in the state of their unbelief and disobedience. But when the King of Zion arrests the sinner; casts out the strong man armed; takes the empire of the soul to himself, and establishes the kingdom of his grace, who shall dispossess him? Can it be supposed, that he who is conquered, dethroned, routed, and enfeebled, shall regain what he was unable to hold? Does Christ take possession, but to keep it! Shall any power subdue Omnipotence, recaptivate a new born heir of eternal life? No, none shall be able to pluck them out of his hand; nor out of his Father's hand, who is greater than all, John x. 25–29.

The nature of this divine life merits our attention. The soul of man being immortal; eternal in its future existence; that which is necessary to its happiness ought to be of the like nature and duration. That principle of divine life by which the soul is quickened in regeneration, is such; "I give unto them eternal life, and they shall never perish," John x. 28. Its source is the eternal Jehovah; its communication free; its continuance durable as the immortal Spirit. It is assimilated to a seed that remaineth—to a well of water springing up unto everlasting life, which the scorching heat of persecution, fiery trials, and darts of the devil, shall not dry up, but the riches of grace will replenish; to the smoking flax which shall not be quenched —a spark of life which the many waters of affliction cannot quench, nor floods of temptation drown; which will not expire amidst the dashing of the most boisterous waves of trouble and distress; but nourished by him that gave it—will live and glow, till it shall blaze in eternal day.

All obstructions to the saints' perseverance and salvation are removed. The demands of the law of God against them are fully answered by Christ their surety. There is no condemnation to such, Rom. viii. 1. The awful separation between God and them, made by sin, is healed; peace and reconciliation is made by the blood of the cross, Col. i. 20; Rom. v. 1. The way of communication with God is open; on God's part, to confer all spiritual blessings upon them; on their part, that they may have free access to God, through the mediation of Christ, Eph. ii. 18. Their enemies are conquered, Ps. lxxxix. 23. The "works of the devil" destroyed, 1 John iii. 8. Sin is dethroned, and "shall not have dominion over them," Rom. vi. 14. The world is overcome. And, though imperfections cleave to them, and trials surround them, they have a prevailing advocate with the Father, Jesus Christ, "who ever liveth to make intercession for them," Rom. viii. 33, 34.

It is a pleasure to observe, that the means for the promoting and effecting the perseverance of the saints are well established. Gifts for men, for the perfecting of the saints, the work of the ministry, the edifying of the body of Christ, Eph. iv. 12. The divine word, rich in all important truth, tending to establish the soul in righteousness; the rich and precious promises of the gospel for encouragement and comfort; the most suitable instructions in every state of the spiritual warfare; faithful warnings against sin; the glorious examples of the saints, who have gone before us, to engage us to emulate their conduct; the falls and transgressions of others, held up as beacons, to warn all the camp of Israel against iniquity; the ministrations of the word, also, opening, illustrating, and enforcing the above; the ordinances of the gospel; prayer, Christian fellowship; together with the laws and discipline of the house of God; all tending, under a divine influence, to accomplish their final perseverance.

The Lord Jesus, overruling all things together for good to them who love God, is a further confirmation of this truth, Rom. viii. 28. The gospel shall work effectually in them who believe, 1 Thess. ii. 13. The various dispensations of Providence shall concur to this end. Prosperity sanctified, shall promote gratitude, obedience, and humility; adversity shall correct us; afflictions teach the vanity of worldly enjoyments; bereavements, their uncertainty, and the necessity of a better hope. These will cause the children of God to cleave to him. Tribulation shall work patience, and patience experience, and experience hope, that maketh not ashamed; and he that hath this hope in him purifieth himself.

But, brethren, the time would fail us to dwell on the considerations arising from the covenant of grace, ordered in all things, and sure; redemption by Jesus Christ; the charge he has taken of his people; the promises of the gospel, all tending to establish this doctrine. As also from the perfections of God, his immutability, justice, power, wisdom, faithfulness, and truth, all engaged to bring the heirs of grace, through perseverance therein, to glory.

A popular objection made to this doctrine is, that it tends to licentiousness; that if the perseverance of the saints is sure, they may be as wicked as any—all will be well.

Strange, that proving the perseverance of saints in grace should be a license for them to be devils in wickedness! That advancing in holiness should be a reason for abounding in sin! It is fatal to this objection, that it bears the strongest features of that raised against the doctrines of grace of old: "Let us continue in sin, that grace may abound;" and may be well answered in like manner: "God forbid. How shall we, who are dead to sin, live any longer therein," Rom. vi. 1, 2. The objection is founded on the perverse disposition, not of a renewed, but of an unrenewed heart, which the love of God does not constrain; which does not love God for his holiness, nor delights in his law; nor has seen his ways,—ways of pleasantness, and paths of peace; but is in love with sin, and rejoices in an excuse or opportunity to indulge it. As such, it is inapplicable to the real saint, who delights in the law of God after the inward man. The objection, therefore, ought to fall, and men of grace be ashamed to raise it again.

Another objection is, that the certainty of the saints' perseverance in grace leads to negligence and inattention to the duties of religion. We are ready to compare notes, not for a transient flight of zeal, but through the whole lives of those real professors of religion who hold, and those who oppose, this doctrine. This objection rests on the same foundation with the other, and as liable to the same fate. It cannot be proved that this sentiment had this effect on the immediate real disciples of Christ; but it is abundantly evident it had the reverse tendency. Paul, who had the highest confidence that he who had begun a good work in the saints at Philippi, would perform it till the day of Jesus Christ, and represents them as faithful and zealous brethren, says of himself, "I press forward toward the mark for the prize of the high calling of God in Christ Jesus," Phil. iii. 14. His brethren he exhorts, "Having these promises, dearly beloved, let us cleanse ourselves from all filthiness of the flesh and of the spirit, perfecting holiness in the fear of God," 2 Cor. vii. 1.

To indulge a licentious spirit, or indifference to the duties of religion, on the ground of these objections, would be a most flagrant violation of the laws of reason, gratitude, and love.

May you, dear brethren, continue persuaded of this truth, and partake of the support to be derived from it. How uncertain are all temporal enjoyments and prospects! How happy for the people of God, that in the most important of all concerns, those of religion, there is a stability! That the foundation standeth sure,—the Lord knoweth them that are his! Having begun a good work in you, he will perform it. That the perseverance of the saints in grace to the consummation of it in glory is sure! How supporting the reflection! how animating the prospect!

Shall not the stupendous plan of sovereign grace and love, by which the sinner's salvation will be so surely and fully completed, for ever command the admiration of angels and men!

Will not the warmest gratitude glow in every heart on the remembrance of it? Shall not the most cheerful obedience be rendered? the most ardent affection arise to God? the most devout adoration ascend from every soul? Surely these are the genuine offspring of grace, so great, so sure, so rich, so free.

Is there a professor amongst us to whom these emotions are not more common than the rising sun! Be alarmed, oh man! Has the law of sin gained the ascendancy over the law of thy mind? or hath the law of the spirit of life in Christ Jesus never made thee free from the law of sin and death? Examine thyself.

Are any fallen into sin, how great their ingratitude! How aggravated their transgressions, to sin against such amazing love, unspeakable goodness, and rich grace! to offend against so many and great obligations to obedience. What pungent distress, what shame, what sorrow, must ensue! How light my affliction compared with my sin! says the offender; surely he has not visited me according to my sin, nor rewarded me according to my transgression. And oh! will he not take his loving kindness from me, nor suffer his faithfulness to fail? Is there yet hope? Oh, grace beyond degree!

With this prospect before us in prosperity, with this support in affliction, trial, and darkness, to which we are liable in this pilgrimage state, let us press forward in the way of truth and holiness.

Now, unto God the Father be glory in the church, through Jesus Christ, world without end. Amen.

SAMUEL JONES, Moderator.
JOHN STANCLIFF, Clerk.

THE MINISTERS AND MESSENGERS AT THE ASSOCIATION, AND STATE OF THE CHURCHES DURING THE YEAR.

CHURCHES.	MINISTERS AND MESSENGERS.	Baptized.	Received by Letter.	Dismiss'd.	Restored.	Excom.	Deceased.	Members.
Lower Dublin,	Samuel Jones, D. D., John Wright, Benjamin Dungan,	0	0	4	0	0	0	63
Middletown,	Samuel Morgan,* William Blair,	17	0	0	0	0	5	152
Piscataqua,	Reune Runyan, *Peter Bryant,*	1	1	4	0	2	3	141
Cohansie,	Henry Smalley,* Jonathan Bowen, David Shepherd, John Siffin,	13	1	0	0	0	2	121
Welsh Tract,	John Boggs, Andrew Molton,	14	5	5	0	1	3	114
Great Valley,	John Beauly, Isaac Abraham, Daniel Cornog, Nathaniel Davis, Andrew Garden,	0	1	2	0	0	3	82
Cape May,	John Stancliff,	2	0	1	0	4	5	53
Hopewell,	Oliver Hart,	6	0	3	0	0	0	168
Brandywine,	Joshua Vaughan, William Simonson, Thomas Davis,	8	0	2	0	0	0	49
Montgomery,	Isaac Johnson, Edmond Pennington,	1	0	2	0	0	1	23
Tulpehokin,†		0	0	0	0	0	0	0
Kingwood,	*James Drake, David Stout,*	0	0	0	9	0	0	80
Haight's Town,	Peter Wilson, Nehemiah Dye, Lloyd Holmes,	22	0	5	1	4	3	259
Philadelphia,	Thomas Ustick, William Rogers, D. D., Morgan Edwards, Thomas Shields, George Ingolls, John M'Leod, Hugh Gorley,	6	10	6	0	0	4	111
Southampton,	David Jones, *Benjamin Bennet,* Elias Yerkes, jr., Arthur Watts,	6	0	2	2	0	2	57
Scotch Plains,	William Vanhorn,	1	1	0	0	0	2	136
Oyster Bay,†		0	0	0	0	0	0	25
Morristown,		5	0	0	0	0	2	94

MINUTES OF THE PHILADELPHIA ASSOCIATION. 279

CHURCHES.	MINISTERS AND MESSENGERS.	Baptized.	Received by Letter.	Dismis'd.	Restored.	Excom.	Deceased.	Members.
Knowlton,†	DANIEL VAUGHAN,*	0	0	0	0	0	0	43
Hartford,†	JOHN DAVIES,*	0	0	0	0	0	0	120
New Britain,†	JOSHUA JONES,	0	0	0	0	0	0	21
Salem,	{ Ephraim Lloyd, Abraham Harris, }	12	0	0	0	2	3	66
Wantage,†	SILAS SOUTHWORTH,*	0	0	0	0	0	0	0
Dividing Creek,	—— ——	2	0	0	0	0	3	40
1. New York,	BENJAMIN FOSTER,*	9	1	5	3	2	0	198
New Mills,	{ David Gaskill, Richard Watkin, }	2	4	2	0	0	1	86
Konoloway,†	JOSEPH POWELL,*	0	0	0	0	0	0	0
Coram,†	—— ——	0	0	0	0	0	0	30
Upper Freehold,	{ JOSEPH STEPHENS,* Edward Taylor, }	7	1	2	0	1	0	78
Mount Bethel,†	—— ——	0	0	0	0	0	0	101
Lyon's Farms,†	—— ——	0	0	0	0	0	0	16
Philip's Patent,†	—— ——	0	0	0	0	0	0	0
Pittsgrove,†	—— ——	0	0	0	0	0	0	0
Manahawkin,†	—— ——	0	0	0	0	0	0	0
Vincent,†	—— ——	0	0	0	0	0	0	22
Tuckahoe,†	ISAAC BUNNELL,*	0	0	0	0	0	0	0
2. New York,	Joseph Stout,	0	0	0	0	0	0	0
King Street,†	—— ——	0	0	0	0	0	0	36
Cow Marsh,	Job Meredith,	8	2	1	0	0	0	30
London Tract,	THOMAS FLEESON,	0	4	0	0	0	0	38
Hilltown,	{ JAMES M'LAUGHLIN, Robert Shannon, John Pugh, }	4	0	1	0	0	1	102
Lower Smithfield,	DAVID JAYNE,*	0	0	0	0	0	0	26
Baltimore,	{ LEWIS RICHARDS,* George Prestman, }	5	5	0	0	0	0	63
Byrn Sion, Duck Creek,	{ JAMES JONES,* JOHN PATTON, GIDEON FERRELL, John Crawford, Hugh Durburrow, Gasper Harwood, }	32	3	0	1	3	12	83
Wilmington,	{ THOMAS AINGER, Thomas Brooks, Jesse Walraven, }	12	0	3	1	3	0	53
Canoe Brook,	—— ——	14	0	2	0	0	1	73
Jacob's Town,	{ BURGISS ALLISON, James Cox, }	2	1	1	0	0	3	59
Staten Island,	ELKANA HOLMES,*	0	0	0	0	0	0	28
Pittstown,†	JAMES FINN,*	0	0	0	0	0	0	28
Marcus Hook,	ELIPHAZ DAZEY,	1	0	2	0	0	1	16

CHURCHES.	MINISTERS AND MESSENGERS.	Baptized.	Received by Letter.	Dismis'd.	Restored.	Excom.	Deceased.	Members.
Rocksberry,	{ Curtis Gilbert, Michael Conrad, Cornelius Holdgate,	5	0	0	0	0	0	44
Falls Township,	{ Alexander M'Gowan, Joseph Richardson, jr., Jeremiah Ward,	7	1	0	0	0	0	25
		224	41	55	8	22	60	3253

NOTE.—The ministers' names are in SMALL CAPITALS. Licenced preachers in *italics*. Those marked thus * were not present. From the churches marked thus † received no intelligence. A dash —— denotes no settled minister.

MINUTES

OF THE

PHILADELPHIA BAPTIST ASSOCIATION,

HELD AT PHILADELPHIA, OCTOBER 2D, 3D, 4TH, AND 5TH,

1792.

October 2.—At three o clock, P. M., Rev. Doctor William Rogers delivered the introductory sermon, from Phil. iii. 8, "Yea, doubtless, and I count all things but loss for the excellency of the knowledge of Christ Jesus my Lord.

2. After worship, proceeded to business. Rev. Isaac Skillman was chosen moderator, and the Rev. Burgiss Allison, clerk.

3. Letters from thirty-six churches were read.

Adjourned to nine o'clock to-morrow morning.

October 3.—Met agreeably to adjournment.

1. Two letters were read from the Warwick Association, for the years 1791 and 1792; the former not having come forward last year. This Association, according to their request, was received by their messengers, Rev. Thomas Montanye and Benjamin Pelton, as a corresponding Association.

2. A letter was also read from the New York Association, requesting union and correspondence with us, which was unanimously agreed to.

3. The Rev. Messrs. William Augustus Clarke, from London, Hunt and German, from New Jersey, and David Sutton, being present, were invited to sit with us.

4. An application was again made by the newly constituted church at Sideling Hill to be admitted into connection with this Association. After examining the objections which had been made, and not thinking them sufficient to ground a rejection upon, the said church was admitted. Nevertheless the Association disapprove of multiplying churches by dividing those already established, without evident necessity; and also, of any one minister by himself undertaking to constitute a church.

5. An application was also made by the church at West Creek, New Jersey, lately constituted, desiring to be admitted. It was accordingly received.

6. Letters were received, and read, from the Associations of Charleston, Shaftsbury, Warren, and Danbury; and printed minutes

from those of Warwick, New York, Warren, Charleston, Kehukee, Bethel, and Portsmouth, Virginia.

7. The following brethren to write to the corresponding Associations, viz., Dr. Samuel Jones, to that of New York; Mr. Smalley, to Warwick; Mr. Blackwell, to Warren; Mr. Stevens, to Shaftsbury; Mr. Stancliff, to Danbury; and Mr. Ustick, to Charleston.

8. The circular letter was read, and Messrs. Samuel Jones, David Jones, and James M'Laughlin appointed a committee to revise the same.

9. Three o'clock, P. M.—Mr. Smalley appointed to write the circular letter for the ensuing year.

10. A query from the Church at Great Valley, referred from last Association: Whether the degree of affinity there mentioned, viz., between a widow and her first husband's nephew, is sufficient to exclude them from church communion, in case of their marriage?

Determined in the negative.

11. Resolved, That a certain lot of ground, the bequest of Mrs. Hubbs, in Hopewell township, Hunterdon county, New Jersey, be sold by the trustees, and the money added to the Association funds, after the expense of erecting a head-stone for Mr. and Mrs. Hubbs, each, shall be deducted.

Adjourned until nine o'clock to-morrow morning.

Rev. Mr. Clarke preached this evening, from Acts xv. 36.

October 4.—Met pursuant to adjournment.

12. This Association, taking into consideration the difficulty subsisting in the second church at New York, do profess, that by any transaction of either last Association, or this, they do not pretend to decide which party is in the wrong, or to have received either of them in particular, but recommend the calling a council to have all differences amicably settled among themselves.

13. A query respecting the validity of baptism by an unordained and unbaptized administrator, referred in the sixth section of October 5, in our minutes of last year, was taken up, and determined in the negative.

14. Three o'clock, P. M.—The committee appointed to revise the circular letter written by Brother Joshua Jones, approved the same, and made their report.

15. A query from the church at Marcus Hook: Would it not be expedient for this Association to republish Dr. Gill's Nature, Order, and Discipline of a Gospel Church, or some other equally good, and recommend the same to the churches?

In answer, That, whereas most of the churches are unacquainted with Dr. Gill's piece referred to, the Association recommend that they make themselves acquainted therewith against next annual Association, by which means they will be prepared to determine upon the expediency thereof.

16. Queries from the church at Great Valley: Are the words bishop and elder of the same meaning in the writings of the apostles?

Yes. This Association, therefore, recommend that the terms

pastors, bishops and elders, as used in our Confession of faith, be adopted.

17. Query from the church at West Creek: Is the washing of feet a gospel ordinance?

This Association consider the washing of feet, as mentioned in the New Testament, only as a pattern of humility; nevertheless have no objection to those practising it who think it a duty.

18. The churches of Mount Bethel and Lyon's Farms request a dismission from this Association to join that of New York, as being more convenient.

19. Whereas, there is or ought to be a considerable sum of money in the hands of the heirs, executors, or administrators of the late Isaac Jones, Esq., belonging to the funds of the grammar school under the direction of this Association, the amount of which is at present uncertain; therefore,

Resolved, That Dr. Samuel Jones, Dr. William Rogers, and Samuel Miles, Esq., be a committee to ascertain the amount and situation of this money, with full power to use such means (whether in conjunction with the trustees, or separate from them,) as may be best calculated to recover the said money; and, if need be, to employ council learned in the law for the above purpose.

20. Letters written to the Shaftsbury, Warren, Danbury, Charleston, Warwick, and New York Associations were read and approved; and the following brethren appointed as messengers:—To Warren, Dr. Samuel Jones and Rev. William Augustus Clarke; to Danbury, Mr. Benjamin Pelton; to Charleston, Rev. Peter Philanthropos Roots; to Warwick and New York, Rev. Dr. Samuel Jones, Rev. Joseph Stephens, and Rev. Peter Wilson.

21. Elders Patten, Clingan, and Vaughan, agree to travel for three months in the ensuing year, about Juniata and the West Branch of Susquehanna, to preach the gospel to the destitute; and this Association recommend that a sufficient sum be subscribed by the churches, and paid immediately into the hands of Col. Samuel Miles, to bear their expenses.

22. In answer to a letter received from some destitute persons at Niagara, it is recommended to such of the ministering brethren as have it in their power to pay them a visit.

Adjourned until to-morrow morning at nine o'clock.

This evening Brother Roots preached from Heb. ii. 3.

October 5, nine o'clock, A. M.—Met according to adjournment.

23. Some difficulties subsisting in the Pittstown church, the Association appoint Dr. Samuel Jones, David Jones, and Thomas Fleeson, as a committee to enquire into the matter this afternoon, and, in conjunction with those of the parties present, endeavor to remove them.

24. Two queries from the Pittstown church.

First query: Where there is a positive contradiction between two men, both members of the church, is the testimony of either of their wives to be received, supposing her also a member. Yes.

Second query: Where a council is called to settle a difficulty between two churches, ought that council to give judgment, or to propose measures of reconciliation?

It is our judgment that the council should both give their opinion, and likewise advise to measures of reconciliation.

25. Supplies were granted to the following destitute churches:—Kingwood, Dividing Creek, and Pittsgrove.

26. Three o'clock, P. M.—The committee appointed last year to effectuate the incorporation of this Association, by charter, are continued the ensuing year.

27. Dr. Jones, agreeably to a resolve of last year, brought in an abstract from the minutes of the preceding years.

28. The next Association to meet in Philadelphia, on the first Tuesday in October, 1793.

29. Brother Skillman to preach the introductory sermon; and, in case of failure, Brother David Jones.

30 Brother Ustick is requested to superintend the printing of the minutes, and forward them to the churches.

Rev. Mr. Montanye preached in the evening.

CIRCULAR LETTER.
BY REV. JOSHUA JONES.

The elders and messengers of the several churches met in Association, in the city of Philadelphia, October 2d, 1792.

To the churches in union with this Association, send greeting.

Dearly beloved brethren,—According to the course of our order, the subject of our circular letter, this year, is the assurance of grace and salvation. Confession of faith, Chap. XVIII.

This is a subject of very great importance, with which all true Christians are concerned, and, perhaps, for the most part, make the matter of their most serious inquiry. It is, therefore, very obvious that it requires to be discussed with the greatest care, whereby it may tend to minister some revival of hope to the doubting Christian, and that the joy of faith may be increased in those that are of a higher attainment; while, at the same time, the nominal professor may be detected and convinced of his delusion.

In order to attempt something for the illustration of this very important article, several particulars are to be considered; as

First. That there are degrees in this grace of assurance, as well as in other graces of the Spirit. Divine revelation, and the experience of all ages, make it abundantly manifest, that there are some, who from a deep sense of their own sinfulness, together with the weak exercise of their graces, cannot help hesitating respecting their own interest in the great salvation that is in Christ; but yet they have such expectation of obtaining salvation by him, as bears them up from falling into despair. The true Christian views his own sins in their own colors, and they appear, attended with their several aggravations, horrid and detestable in his view; and he finds, by sad experience, that there is a body of sin and pollution in his nature, so that he cannot well tell how a gracious change in his heart can consist with so much sin and defilement; yet he would endeavor to conclude with the Psalmist, lxv. 4, "iniquities prevail against me: as for our transgressions thou shalt purge them away." The believer has a view, though it be weak, to the fountain opened for sin and for uncleanness; and it is from this source he draws all his comforts, that his sins are pardoned; and this confidence, though weak, enables him to look unto Jesus, whom he hath pierced with his sins, and hope that there is healing virtue in his blood; so that he rests his soul upon it, as that alone that can cleanse him from all sin. Though all this may not amount to a full assurance, that his state god-ward is good, yet he would not exchange it for all that the world could give him in lieu thereof.

Second. We are to consider that this grace of assurance is attainable in this life, not only in extraordinary cases, such as martyrdom, and under some other very difficult cases that some may be called to; but also in the common course of the dispensation of grace; for it may be justly observed, that every true Christian may and has a just right to conclude that his state God-ward is a state of peace, were it not for the remainder of unbelief that cleaves unto him; but this is what prevents it: and where this is done away and overcome, the Christian may say with holy Job, "I know that my Redeemer liveth;" and with the apostle, "I am crucified with Christ; nevertheless I live; yet not I, but Christ liveth in me; and the life which I now live in the flesh, I live by the faith of the Son of God, who loved me, and gave himself for me," Gal. ii. 29. And again, "For me to live is Christ, and to die is gain," Phil. i. 21. It is abundantly evident from divine revelation, that the grace of assurance in this life is attainable.

1. Because that it appears to be the privilege of believers in common; for this see 1 Cor. ii. 12, "For we have not received the spirit of the world, but the Spirit which is of God, that we may know the things that are freely given us of God." Here we see the apostle addresses these Corinthian believers, that they were interested in the same grace of assurance in common with himself; and in the first Epistle of John v. 20, "And we know that the Son of God is come, and hath given us an understanding, that we may know him that is true; and we are in him that is true; even in his Son Jesus Christ. This is the true God and eternal life." There is such provision made for it, so that the heirs of glory might have an undoubted hope of enjoying it. For this see Heb. vi. 17, 18, 19, "Wherein God willing more abundantly to show unto the heirs of promise, the immutability of his counsel, confirmed it by an oath: that by two immutable things, in which it was impossible for God to lie, we might have a strong consolation, who have fled for refuge to lay hold on the hope set before us. Which hope we have as an anchor to the soul, both sure and steadfast, which entereth into that within the veil." And moreover, it is spoken of as something blamable in Christians, that they do not know their union with Christ, 2 Cor. xiii. 5, "Know ye

not your ownselves, how that Jesus Christ is in you, except ye be reprobates?"

2. It appears that assurance is attainable in the present state of things, because it is inculcated upon us, to use diligence to make our calling and election sure. And were it not attainable, we conclude that so interesting a point would not be enjoined us; but it appears that is not the case. And it appears that those that live in a nearness to God in their affection of love, incline to keep his word practically, and the more we are in this salutary employment, there is a motive annexed, that is infinitely beyond the merit of our doing; for there is a promise to the disciples of Christ, to such as love him, and keep his word, that the Father and the Son will come and make their abode with them, by which we are to understand, that it means a manifestation of his fatherly love, and receive more of the Spirit of adoption, whereby they are, enabled to cry, Abba, Father. From hence it appears that those Christians that live in a nearness to God in their love and affections, have, for the most part, the clearest discovery of his love. But yet—

Thirdly. There is another particular to be inquired into; that is, the source and efficient cause from whence this full assurance of hope doth proceed, and that is the Spirit of God. Hence it is said, "that the Spirit itself beareth witness with our spirit, that we are the children of God," Rom. viii. 16. It is said "the Spirit itself." Now when it is said, that a person doth something himself, it is to be understood, that he doth it not by another, or by a deputy; so that we are to understand, that it is the Holy Spirit that is the sole efficient cause of a Christian's having a clear manifestation of his interest in Christ; and this cannot be attained unto, without the witness of the Spirit. Here it may be inquired, how the Spirit doth witness? In answer to this, we are to consider what our Lord says concerning the Spirit, as we read in John xvi. 14. Our Lord, speaking there of the Spirit, says, "He shall glorify me, for he shall receive of mine, and shall show it unto you." By which we are to understand, that it is owing to the influence of the Holy Spirit, that any Christian is enabled to behold the sufficiency that is in the blood of Christ to cleanse from all sins, and make an appropriation of it to himself; and the Holy Spirit is called the Comforter, which is very comprehensive, and includes in it not only comfort, but strength, light, and joy; because his assurance of hope is upon the blood and righteousness of Jesus Christ, and to behold that there is forgiveness of sins through his blood, and that now all are "justified from all things, from which they could not be justified by the law of Moses." It must be observed, that the Spirit witnessing by the word of grace, enables the soul to appropriate those great and precious promises to himself, by virtue of the witness of the Spirit itself, with our spirit, that we are the children of God. But here may arise a very serious inquiry, how may a believer know that it is the Spirit of God and not the spirit of delusion? We shall say no more, in answer to this, than that the Spirit itself can and will resolve it to his own children by his own powerful efficacy. Much might be said on this head, but brevity forbids us to enlarge.

Fourthly. We are to consider that the faith of assurance is not the essence of the faith of reliance, for the lowest degree must be attained before the highest, for the sealing of the Spirit comes after believing, and not always upon believing, for there are little children in this grace as well as strong men; for in our regeneration, we are to conclude that every grace of the Spirit, that is inseparably connected with salvation, is implanted in the heart of every true believer, though they may be weakly exercised by the sincere Christian. The conversion of some is more obvious than of some others, both to themselves and to their fellow Christians, and the Spirit may sweetly breathe on them his own impression, and the comforts derived therefrom; so that he that has only the faith of reliance, has some degree of appropriation; and yet not being clear of being beclouded, and of uncomfortable doubts prevailing in his breast,—so as yet he loves, and wonders at the stupendous love, wisdom, and faithfulness of God, in laying "help on One who is mighty to save," and therefore he leans upon him for life and salvation,—and yet those that have the faith of reliance, it is of that nature that it tends to purify the heart, and overcome the world; so that the soul is brought to an humble submission to the will of God, and beholds that there is no salvation in any other, and is enabled to rejoice that it is even so, and concludes, that this is all his hope. Although his sins appear to him of the deepest dye, yet he hopes to find mercy through the atoning blood of Jesus, because that it is revealed in the word of grace that it was to this end Jesus Christ came into the world to save sinners, the chief of sinners. Let it be observed, that if a Christian, whose faith amounts to no higher than that of affiance—if he discovers in himself one link of the precious chain of salvation, he upon the best grounds may conclude, that he has the whole; for there is not one soul, that shall perish, that has one of the saving graces of the Spirit, but then one is never alone; and that the Spirit of God may withhold the shinings of his face upon the operation that he hath wrought upon the heart of the believer, that relies on the merits of Christ for salvation—and the believer may walk in darkness, as to the comfortable manifestation of everlasting love; for we find that this has been the case with some of God's dear children: and hence it is that such go mourning all the day; and this has been the case with some that had great nearness to God, and intimacy with him, as we may see in the 51st Psalm. It comes to pass commonly in consequence of their departing from God by sin, which was the case with the Psalmist, and in consequence of it their faith is shaken, and their assurance intermitted, and yet in regard of their secret state Godward, it is a state of peace—it is immovable and immutable, and the union subsisting, never can be dissolved. But,

Fifthly. We are to consider that there is such a thing as false hope, and counterfeit assurance; and this we are to guard against as one of the most pernicious evils that may befall the human mind.

But by thus observing, we do not mean to discourage you, dear brethren, from appropriating to yourselves the riches of divine grace, and an assurance of an eternal weight of glory. But there is such a similarity between a sincere Christian and a nominal one, as there is between wheat and tares in the blade, which teaches us that a close inspection ought to be exercised by every one of us, whether we have in possession a vital principle of true religion. For the holy Scriptures hold forth unto us that many will be deceived at last, and meet a dreadful overthrow, by reason of building on a false foundation—as we may see in Matt. vii. 22, 23. So that it is not every one that says he has an assurance of faith, who really hath it. And the apostle saith, "If a man thinketh himself to be something, when he is nothing, he deceiveth himself," Gal. vi. 3; and a great many passages of holy writ might be adduced to prove this awful truth. But we proceed finally, to point out the great utility of the grace of assurance of hope, to those that have it, during their pilgrimage here on earth.

1. It enables them to submit, with cheerfulness, to adverse dispensations, upon the account that they are enabled to believe that their heavenly Father does every thing for good to them that love him.

2. Full assurance of hope enables them to believe whatever God is pleased to reveal concerning himself, because that there is now a greater nearness to God than heretofore, and the more knowledge the believer has of God, the more acquaintance he has with himself, whereby he is made to behold his own impotence and ignorance; for until such time as the believer attains to some degree of assurance, carnal reason will retard his progress in the exercise of faith, particularly in some points that are beyond his rational comprehension. For the more assurance the believer attains unto, the more carnal reason is overcome; and therefore forms a just idea of the infinite disproportion that is between him and that Infinite Being in whom he confides. Believing that God's proceedings with all his creatures, are in infinite wisdom, justice and holiness; and that the Judge of the whole earth will do right; and this is one great means whereby the children of God are kept from apostatizing from the great fundamental articles of the Christian faith; and for want of which many in the present day run into such extremes of error, in turning the true meaning of the sacred Scriptures, in those very essential articles of the Christian faith, contrary to the very literal meaning of them. This comes to pass by leaning too much on their own carnal wisdom and judgment—so they conclude that God has a different meaning from what his word conveys, and that impenitent sinners shall pass with impunity. From such errors as drown the wicked in perdition, those that have a well founded hope are finally preserved.

3. The grace of assurance will be of the greatest use in our last conflict with death, knowing that Christ has taken away the sting of death, and that death itself will be destroyed; so that the assured Christian is made to rejoice, that he has no cause to fear that any

ill consequence will attend his exit out of time into eternity; and it enables him not only to submit to, but also to obey, with cheerfulness, the messenger his heavenly Father sends; being confident, upon good grounds, that he will be admitted into the society of "the spirits of just men made perfect," and so ever be with the Lord; where the weary are at perfect rest, and the wicked forever cease from troubling. The assurance of this is a prelibation or a foretaste of that heavenly glory that awaits all the children of God in a coming world.

Dear brethren, let these things sink deep into your hearts, whereby ye may be found in the lively exercise of every grace, and in the faithful discharge of every duty; and be enabled, with patience, to run the race that is set before you, "still looking to Jesus who is the author and finisher of our faith."

Now, unto him who is able to keep you from falling, and present you faultless before the presence of his glory, with exceeding joy. To the only wise God, our Saviour, be glory and majesty, dominion and power, both now and forever." *Amen.*

Signed by order of the Association,

ISAAC SKILLMAN, Moderator.
BURGISS ALLISON, Clerk.

Rev. CURTIS GILBERT, of Rocksberry, died in the year past.

THE MINISTERS AND MESSENGERS AT THE ASSOCIATION, AND STATE OF THE CHURCHES DURING THE YEAR.

CHURCHES.	MINISTERS AND MESSENGERS.	Baptized.	Received by Letter.	Dismis'd.	Restored.	Excom.	Deceased.	Members.
Pennepek,	SAMUEL JONES, D. D., John Wright,	0	0	0	0	0	1	63
Middletown,	William Blair, John Smock,	2	0	4	0	0	2	123
Piscataqua,†	—— ——	0	0	0	0	0	0	141
Cohansie,	HENRY SMALLEY, A. M., David Bowen, Daniel Harris, Howell Watson,	15	0	1	0	1	7	127
Welsh Tract,†	JOHN BOGGS,*	0	0	0	0	0	0	114
Great Valley,	DAVID JONES, A. M., Daniel Cornog, Isaac Abrams,	0	3	6	0	0	2	77
Cape May,	JOHN STANCLIFF,	0	0	2	0	0	2	49
Hopewell,	OLIVER HART, A. M.,* JOHN BLACKWELL, Daniel Drake, James Ross,	4	0	1	2	0	2	171

CHURCHES.	MINISTERS AND MESSENGERS.	Baptized.	Received by Letter.	Dismis'd.	Restored.	Excom.	Deceased.	Members.
Brandywine,	Joshua Vaughan, James Shields, William Simpson, John Garrett, William Griffith,	17	2	0	0	0	3	66
Montgomery,	Peter Evans, Charles Humphries, Edmond Pennington,	0	0	0	0	0	0	23
Tulpehokin,†	—— ——	0	0	0	0	0	0	0
Kingwood,	James Drake, David Stout,	0	0	2	0	0	2	76
Haight's Town,	Peter Wilson, A. M.,	20	0	6	1	0	3	271
Philadelphia,	Thomas Ustick, A. M., William Rogers, D. D., Morgan Edwards, A. M. Samuel Miles, Esq., Thomas Shields, Esq., John M'Leod, George Ingolls, Aaron Vanhorn,	6	7	1	3	1	1	124
Southampton,	Benjamin Bennett, Thomas Folwell, Elias Yerkes, jr., William Watts,	2	0	3	0	0	1	55
Knowlton,†	Daniel Vaughan,*	0	0	0	0	0	0	43
Hartford,†	John Davies,*	0	0	0	0	0	0	120
New Britain,	Joshua Jones, James Dungan,	4	0	0	0	0	2	27
Salem,	Isaac Skillman, A. M., Ephraim Lloyd, John Walker,	2	2	0	0	3	5	62
Dividing Creek,	Jonadab Shepherd,	15	0	0	0	4	2	50
New Mills,	Isaac Carlisle, David Gaskill, Joseph Barber,	3	2	0	0	0	3	88
Konoloway,†	Joseph Powell,*	0	0	0	0	0	0	0
Coram,†	—— ——	0	0	0	0	0	0	30
Upper Freehold,	John Stephens, Edward Taylor,	3	0	4	0	0	2	75
Philip's Patent,	—— ——	0	0	0	0	0	0	0
Pittsgrove,†	—— ——	0	0	0	0	0	0	0
Manahawkin,	—— ——	0	0	0	0	0	0	0
Vincent,	John Gwin,	2	2	2	0	0	1	24

MINUTES OF THE PHILADELPHIA ASSOCIATION.

CHURCHES.	MINISTERS AND MESSENGERS.	Baptized.	Received by Letter.	Dismis'd.	Restored.	Excom.	Deceased.	Members.
Tuckahoe,	Isaac Bunnel,	36	4	26	1	3	14	46
Cow Marsh,	Joseph Flood, John Gruwell,	6	0	1	0	2	1	33
London Tract,	Thomas Fleeson, John Whitting,	1	0	1	0	1	0	37
Hilltown,	James M'Laughlin, Enoch Thomas, Isaac Morris, Robert Shannon,	2	0	0	0	0	0	104
Lower Smithfield,†	David Jayne,*	0	0	0	0	0	0	26
Baltimore,	Lewis Richards,* William Clingan, Charles P. Polk,	4	3	0	0	1	2	65
Bryn Sion, Duck Creek,	James Jones, John Patton, Gideon Ferrol, Samuel Davis,	3	0	1	0	0	4	81
Wilmington,	Thomas Ainger,* Thomas Brooks, Abram Simson,	1	1	1	0	2	0	52
Jacob's Town,	Burgiss Allison, A. M. James Cox,	0	0	0	0	0	0	59
Pittstown,	James Finn,	0	0	0	0	0	0	134
Marcus Hook,	Eliphaz Dazey, Richard Riley, George White,	2	0	0	0	0	0	18
Rocksberry,	John Levering, Anthony Levering, Wickard Jacoby,	2	0	0	0	0	1	46
Falls Township,	Alexander M'Gowan, Malachi Richardson, George White,	8	4	2	0	0	0	35
Sideling Hill,	Thomas Runyan,	0	0	0	0	0	0	47
West Creek,	——	0	0	0	0	0	0	28
		160	30	64	7	18	63	2810

Note.—The ministers' names are in SMALL CAPITALS. Licensed preachers in *italic*. Those marked thus * not present. From the churches marked thus † received no intelligence. A dash —— denotes no settled minister.

MINUTES

OF THE

PHILADELPHIA BAPTIST ASSOCIATION,

HELD, BY SPECIAL APPOINTMENT, AT SOUTHAMPTON, BUCKS COUNTY, PENNSYLVANIA, OCTOBER 29TH AND 30TH,

1793.

[Having been prevented meeting, at the time appointed, in the city of Philadelphia, by a prevailing infectious disdorder, with which God, in his providence, has been pleased to visit that city.]

October 29th.—At three o'clock, P. M., the introductory sermon was preached by the Rev. David Jones, from 1 Cor. xv. 24, 25: "Then cometh the end, when he shall have delivered up the kingdom to God, even the Father; when he shall have put down all rule, and all authority and power. For he must reign, till he hath put all enemies under his feet."

Adjourned to nine o'clock to-morrow morning.

2. October 30th.—Met, agreeably to adjournment. Rev. Oliver Hart was chosen moderator, and the Rev. Burgiss Allison, clerk.

3. Letters from seventeen churches were read.

4. A letter from the Elkhorn, Kentucky Association, was received and read, with their minutes, and Brother David Jones appointed to answer it at his leisure; and transmit the answer by the first good opportunity.

5. Dr. Jones was requested to write to the Danbury Association, in the name of this Association, in reference to their circular letter of last year.

6. Resolved, That the committee appointed in the 19th section of our last year's minutes, still be continued for the purposes therein mentioned.

7. The Association, taking into consideration the awful dispensations of Divine Providence in the epidemical disorder now raging in the city of Philadelphia, together with the great drought in our part of the country, and general declension in vital piety, recommend that Tuesday, the 12th day of November ensuing, be observed as a day of humiliation, fasting, and prayer, throughout our churches; and should it please God to remove any part of those judgments previous to that day, that his mercy therein be remembered with public thanksgiving at the same time.

8. The churches are warned against receiving Joseph Stephens, late pastor of Upper Freehold church, or admitting him to preach amongst them, being an excommunicated person, and holding the erroneous doctrine of universal salvation.

Brother Memminger to preach at four o'clock, P. M.

Adjourned to half-past three o'clock, P. M.

9. Met, agreeably to adjournment.—Brother Fleeson having been appointed to write a circular letter in consequence of Brother Smalley not bringing forward the one he was nominated last Association to write, accordingly wrote one, which, being read, was approved.

10. Brother Smalley was appointed to write the circular letter for the ensuing year, upon the subject on which he was to have written for the present.

11. Mr. Allison requested the messengers to give information to the members of their respective churches, if any more family Bibles should be wanting, that Mr. Collins has yet some of his impression on hand.

12. The Association to meet next year at Philadelphia, on the first Tuesday in October, at three o'clock, P. M.

13. Brother Allison is appointed to preach the introductory sermon; and, in case of failure, Brother M'Laughlin.

14. Brother Allison is also requested to superintend the printing of the minutes, and to disperse the same.

CIRCULAR LETTER.
BY REV THOMAS FLEESON.

The elders and brethren of the several churches belonging to the Philadelphia Baptist Association, met, by special appointment, at Southampton, in the county of Bucks, October 29th and 30th, 1793.

To the churches in union with us, send greeting.

Beloved in the Lord,—In a course of Divine Providence, we were favored to meet at this place, and, blessed be God, our meeting has been comfortable. We trust we have had the presence of the Lord Jesus Christ, the great and exalted head of the church. In all our deliberations we have had a view to the glory of God and the peace and comfort of the church of Christ.

The contagious disorder with which the Lord has been pleased to visit the city, the present great and uncommon drought, the sad decay of vital piety, are circumstances of a very alarming nature,—are sure indications of the displeasure of Almighty God, and call aloud for deep humiliation before the Lord. How necessary is it that we should lay these things seriously to heart; that we should consider the cause of the Lord's displeasure; that we should repent and do our first works; that we should turn to the Lord with all our hearts, with weeping, fasting, and mourning,—rend our hearts, and not our garments, and turn unto the Lord our God, who is gracious and merciful; slow to anger, and of great kindness, and repenteth him of the evil.

The accounts from our churches are such as give pleasure and pain; pleasure, when we consider the peace and unanimity which generally prevail; pain, from the consideration of a too general declension, and the small addition to our churches.

O, dear brethren, be engaged with the Lord, that he would revive his work, that his threatened judgments may be averted, that we may enjoy his presence, that a spirit of grace and supplication may be poured out upon us, and that we may revive as the corn, and grow as the vine.

And now, dear brethren, committing you to God and the word of his grace, which is able to build you up, and to give you an inheritance among all them that are sanctified.

We remain yours in the Lord,

OLIVER HART, Moderator,
BURGISS ALLISON, Clerk.

THE MINISTERS AND MESSENGERS AT THE ASSOCIATION, AND STATE OF THE CHURCHES DURING THE YEAR.

CHURCHES.	MINISTERS AND MESSENGERS.	Baptized.	Received by Letter.	Deceased.	Excom.	Dismis'd.	Restored.	Members.
Pennepek,	Samuel Jones, D. D., Benjamin Dungan, John Holmes,	0	0	2	0	0	0	61
Middletown,	Benjamin Bennet,	17	3	1	0	0	0	142
Piscataqua,†	Reune Runyan,*	0	0	0	0	0	0	141
Cohansie,†	Henry Smalley, A. M.,*	0	0	0	0	0	0	127
Welsh Tract,†	John Boggs,*	0	0	0	0	0	0	114
Great Valley,	David Jones, A. M., Daniel Cornog,	0	1	0	0	1	0	77
Cape May,†	John Stancliff,*	0	0	0	0	0	0	49
Hopewell,	Oliver Hart, A. M., John Blackwell,	3	2	3	0	6	0	163
Brandywine,	Joshua Vaughan,	8	2	1	3	0	0	72
Montgomery,	Charles Humphries, John Harris,	0	0	2	0	0	0	22
Tulpehokin,†	——— ———	0	0	0	0	0	0	0
Kingwood,†	——— ———	0	0	0	0	0	0	76
Haight's Town,†	Peter Wilson, A. M.,*	0	0	0	0	0	0	271
Philadelphia,	Thomas Ustick, A. M.*	0	0	0	0	0	0	124
Southampton,	Arthur Watts, Elias Dungan, William Watts,	0	0	1	0	0	0	54
Knowlton,†	Daniel Vaughan,*	0	0	0	0	0	0	43
Hartford,†	John Davis,*	0	0	0	0	0	0	120
New Britain,	Joshua Jones, Edward Matthew, James Dungan,	0	0	1	0	0	0	26
Salem,†	Isaac Skilman, A. M.,*	0	0	0	0	0	0	62
Dividing Creek,	——— ———	0	0	0	0	0	0	50

CHURCHES.	MINISTERS AND MESSENGERS.	Baptized.	Received by Letter.	Deceased.	Excom.	Dismis'd.	Restored.	Members.
New Mills,	David Gaskill, Benjamin Hedger,	5	3	2	1	1	0	92
Konoloway,†	JOSEPH POWELL,*	0	0	0	0	0	0	0
Coram,†	—— ——	0	0	0	0	0	0	30
Upper Freehold,	Edward Taylor,	0	0	1	2	1	0	72
Pittsgrove,†	—— ——	0	0	0	0	0	0	0
Manahawkin,†	—— ——	0	0	0	0	0	0	0
Vincent,	—— ——	3	0	1	0	0	0	24
Tuckahoe,†	ISAAC BUNNELL,*	0	0	0	0	0	0	46
Cow Marsh,†	JOSEPH FLOOD,	0	0	0	0	2	0	33
London Tract,	THOMAS FLEESON,	0	0	1	0	1	0	35
Hilltown,	JAMES M'LAUGHLIN, Isaac Morris, James Lunn,	0	1	1	0	0	0	101
Lower Smithfield,†	DAVID JAYNE,*	0	0	0	0	0	0	26
Baltimore,†	LEWIS RICHARDS,*	0	0	0	0	0	0	65
Byrn Sion, Duck Creek,	JAMES JONES,*	0	0	0	1	0	0	81
Wilmington,†	THOMAS AINGER,*	0	0	0	0	0	0	52
Jacob's Town,	BURGISS ALLISON, A. M., *Thomas Memminger*, James Cox,	2	0	1	0	2	0	58
Pittstown,†	JAMES FINN,*	0	0	0	0	0	0	134
Marcus Hook,†	ELIPHAZ DAZEY,	0	0	0	0	0	0	18
Rocksberry,	*William White*, John Levering, Michael Conrad,	0	2	1	0	1	0	46
Penn's Manor,	ALEXANDER M'GOWEN, Malachi Richardson,	2	0	2	0	0	0	35
Sideling Hill,†	THOMAS RUNYAN,	0	0	0	0	0	0	47
West Creek,†	—— ——	0	0	0	0	0	0	28
		40	14	21	6	15	0	2817

NOTE.—The ministers' names are in SMALL CAPITALS. Licensed preachers in *italic*. Those marked thus * were not present. From churches marked thus † received no letter. A dash —— denotes no settled minister.

MINUTES

OF THE

PHILADELPHIA BAPTIST ASSOCIATION,

HELD AT PHILADELPHIA, OCTOBER 7TH, 8TH, AND 9TH,

1794.

October 7.—At 3 o'clock, P. M., Rev. Brother Joshua Jones delivered the introductory sermon, from 2d Corinthians ii. 2, "For I determined not to know any thing among you save Jesus Christ, and him crucified."

2. After worship, business was opened with prayer by Brother Oliver Hart.

3. Proceeded to business. Brother William Rogers, D. D., was chosen moderator, and Brother Thomas Memminger, clerk.

4. Letters from twenty-eight churches were read.

5. The business of the day was closed with prayer by the moderator.

Adjourned until nine o'clock to-morrow morning.

October 8.—Met pursuant to adjournment.

6. The business of the day was opened with prayer, by Brother Morgan Edwards.

7. A letter was received and read from the church in Buffalo Valley, Northumberland county, State of Pennsylvania, requesting to be received into this Association. Postponed, no messenger appearing to receive the right-hand of fellowship.

8. Letters were received and read from the Associations of New York, of 1793 and 1794; Vermont, of 1791; Shaftsbury, of 1794; Charleston, of 1792 and 1793; Danbury, of 1793; and Stonington, of 1792 and 1793; and printed minutes, from those of New York, of 1793; Vermont, of 1791 and 1792; Warren, of 1793; Shaftsbury, of 1792, 1793, and 1794; Danbury, of 1793; Charleston, of 1792 and 1793; Middle District, South of James' River, of 1791; and Bethel, of 1792.

9. Brother Vanhorn attended and was received as a messenger from the New York Association; as did Brother Webb, from that of Shaftsbury.

10. The following brethren to write to the corresponding Associations, viz: Samuel Jones, to that of New York; Peter Wilson, to that of Warren; David Loofborrow, to that of Shaftsbury; Isaac Carlisle, to that of Vermont; William White, to that of Danbury; Oliver Hart, at his leisure, to that of Charleston; and Thomas Ustick, to that of Stonington, when convenient.

11. The churches of Cow Marsh, Welsh Tract, Duck Creek, and Wilmington, request the approbation and dismission of this Association to join another.

It is considered and decided that the churches have an undoubted right to depart from this Association, and to join any other they may see fit; but this Association, having been happy in their connection, wish them to continue in union with them as long as (consistently with their own interests) they can; but if they choose to withdraw and join any other, we consent.

12. Resolved, That it be recommended to the different churches in this Association, to institute the chatechising of children in their respective congregations, at stated seasons.

13. Two queries from the church at Philadelphia, viz.:

First, Whether the word *exhibited* would not be preferable to the word *offered*, in question 34th of the Catechism, and in other places where *it* is used in the *same sense?*

Determined, That the word *offered* be expunged, and the words *held forth* be inserted in the place thereof. And,

That a committee, consisting of Brother Samuel Jones, Brother William Rogers, and Brother Thomas Ustick, be appointed to revise the whole of the Catechism, and to recommend such alterations to the next Association as to them may seem proper.

Second, Would it not be advisable for the churches in this connection to make it their invariable practice to transmit a return of the reception of persons by letter, to the churches by whom they were dismissed?

Determined in the affirmative.

14. Resolved, That it be recommended that the minutes of the different Associations in correspondence with this be printed in quarto.

15. A query from the church at Sideling Hill, viz: Shall the evidence of a non-member be taken as valid against a member?

Determined that it be left to every church to judge for themselves in every instance of this nature.

16. Brother William Vanhorn, having been appointed Librarian to this Association, some years past, begs leave to resign.

17. The business of the morning was closed with prayer by Brother Peter Wilson.

Adjourned until three o'clock, P. M.

Three o'clock, P. M.—Met pursuant to adjournment.

18. Business was opened with prayer by Brother William Vanhorn.

19. Letters were received and read from the churches of Balti-

more and Hartford, in Maryland, requesting a dismission from this to the Baltimore Association.

Determined, That their request be granted.

20. The circular letter was read, and Brother Samuel Jones, Brother Oliver Hart, and Brother Thomas Ustick, were appointed a committee to revise the same.

21. Minutes of this Association, from the beginning thereof to the year 1793, inclusive, bound together, were presented to the Association by Brother Morgan Edwards. The unanimous thanks of the Association were directed to be given him for his present.

22. In consequence of information communicated to the Association by Brother William Rogers, it is desired that all donations for the propagation of the Gospel among the Hindoos, in the East Indies, be forwarded to him.

23. Letters written to the New York and Warren Associations were read and approved, and the following brethren appointed as messengers to New York, viz: Samuel Jones, Peter Wilson, and Thomas Memminger.

24. The next Association, by divine permission, to meet in Philadelphia on the first Tuesday in October, Anno Domini, 1795.

25. Brother Peter Wilson to preach the introductory sermon; and, in case of failure, Brother Thomas Ustick.

26. Brother Samuel Jones to write the circular letter.

27. Brother Thomas Ustick is requested to superintend the printing of the minutes, and forward them to the churches.

28. Supplies granted to Great Valley.

29. Supplies to Kingwood, New Jersey.

30. It is earnestly and warmly recommended to the ministering brethren in the neighborhood of Manahawkin, West Creek, and Tuckahoe, to visit those places as often as they conveniently can.

31. The business of the day was closed with prayer by Brother Samuel Jones.

Adjourned until six o'clock to-morrow morning.

Brother Webb preached this evening from Ephesians, ii. 13, "But now, in Christ Jesus, ye who sometimes were afar off, are made nigh by the blood of Christ."

October 9th.—Met pursuant to adjournment.

32. The business of the day was opened with prayer by Brother David Loofborrow.

33. The committee appointed to revise the circular letter, written by Brother Henry Smalley, revised the same, and made report accordingly.

34. Letters written to the Danbury, Vermont, and Shaftsbury Associations, were read and approved. Brother Thomas Memminger was appointed a messenger to the Shaftsbury Association.

35. The business of the Association being gone through, it was closed with a suitable address and prayer by the moderator.

CIRCULAR LETTER.

BY REV. HENRY SMALLEY, A. M.

The elders and messengers of the several churches met in Association, in the city of Philadelphia, October, 1794.

To the churches in union with the Association, send greeting:

Dearly beloved brethren,—According to the order observed in our excellent Confession of faith, the subject from which we shall address you in this circular letter, is the Law of God, commonly called the Moral Law, by some the law of reason and the law of nature, because it is agreeable to the reason and nature of things, and was perfectly understood by our first parents in a state of purity.

False apprehensions of this law, have constituted and spread extensive error and confusion, confirmed men in sin and rebellion against the throne of Jehovah, and eclipsed the glory of gospel grace. It is of great importance, therefore, that we entertain just ideas of the divine law: which law may be defined, "That relation which necessarily exists between the Creator and the creature; and will everlastingly continue necessary to exist, though not independent of the divine will." If this definition be just, the law of God is not arbitrarily imposed on his creatures; it results from their relation to their God and to each other.

Jehovah is our Creator and kind protector, the being of beings, his excellence infinitely transcends all derived excellence; he ought therefore to be loved for what he is in and of himself, as well as for the relation he stands in to his creatures. Nothing can destroy the obligation of rational beings to love their God. Our possessing hearts of enmity against God, is so far from rendering us excusable for not loving and serving him, that it is the very thing, in which our criminality consists. Has the creature a right to hate his God? Surely not. If he has no right to hate, he ought to love. There is no medium in the present case: *We must either bless God, or curse him.* But let us not refer the present question to the partial decisions of men; let us attend to the awful and majestic voice of God, in the ten commands promulgated from Mount Sinai,—which commands, so far as they are moral, are of personal and perpetual obligation; were written in the hearts of our first parents, in their state of innocency, and are written on the heart of every son and daughter of Adam, that has been born again, by the Spirit of the Lord and the power of his grace. This law, we have summarily comprehended by our Lord, in Matt. xxii. 37–39, "Jesus saith unto him, thou shalt love the Lord thy God, with all thy heart, and with all thy soul, and with all thy mind. This is the first and great commandment. And the second is like unto it, Thou shalt love thy neighbor as thyself. On these two commandments hang all the law and the prophets." "Love," says the Apostle, "is the fulfilling of the law."

The law of God refers to the whole man, "Thou shalt love the Lord thy God, *with all thy heart,* and with *all thy soul,* and with *all thy mind.*" The heart is required, the reason is obvious; religion consists in the disposition, and a man may work to eternity,—if his heart is not in the work, it is nothing. "Though I bestow all my goods to feed the poor, and though I give my body to be burned, and have not charity," true love to God and man, "it profiteth me nothing."

This law being founded in reason and righteousness, being the unchangable and everlasting rule of equity; as far as our actions are in agreement with it, they are right; and as far as they deviate from its just requisitions, they are wrong. Christ "came not to destroy the law, but to fulfil." Unbelievers are as much under the curse of the law, as though our Lord had never obeyed it in his own person. See John iii. 18, 36. And those who have a true and living faith in Christ, are as much under the moral law, as a rule of duty, as ever they were. They have received a free and complete pardon of all their sins. "There is no condemnation to those that are in Christ Jesus." But notwithstanding the penalty of the law cannot hurt the believer, he delights in the law of God after the inner man, and shall finally be brought into perfect conformity to its holy dictates. Those who are not conformed to the holy law of God in this world, must forever feel its awful penalty, eternal damnation.

We now proceed to the second grand division of this subject, as made by our Divine Teacher: "Thou shalt love thy neighbor as thyself." If ever there was a period in which this precept required serious attention, it could not require it more than the present, when general discord pervades the nations.

The great Creator has thought fit, that mankind should be united together in society. Mutual love and agreement are necessary to the prosperity of society; and it is as impossible to conceive of a happy community, whose members shall hate each other; as it is to conceive of a material system, where repulsion shall universally take place.

The man who loves others as himself will discover this affection, by promoting the good of his neighbor, in every thing that concerns either his body, his mind, his fortune, or reputation. We show our love to our neighbor by doing him no injury ourselves, and by preventing others from injuring him; by doing him justice in all things, and by promoting his temporal and eternal happiness. Those selfish, narrow-hearted people, who frequently boast that they have done no hurt, are only negatively good, mere cyphers in creation, unworthy the dignified character of loyal benevolent beings; and are wholly unfitted for a place in that more extensive future society, which will consist of beings ennobled by virtue and true benevolence. Love for our neighbor will incline us to do him justice in his property and reputation.

The property received from a parent, who is in duty obliged to provide for his offspring; property acquired by a person's own ingenuity or industry, and property acquired by purchase; these are all lawful, and it is iniquitous for any one to deprive us of such established rights. Whoever loves his neighbor as himself will be as tender of his property, as he wishes others to be of his own; and will be more fearful of breaking in upon another's right, than of losing a part of what he himself possesses. Whoever is raised to a station of power or influence, and takes the advantage of this power to oppress his fellow creatures, shows himself not only unjust but base; for the heart where the law of kindness dwells, contemns every unfair action. And how cruel is it, in such a person, to appropriate to his own use the property of the poor and indigent, who should rather be ready to relieve their wants, when they look up to him in their distress. The withholding of a just debt, all breaches of trust, all undue advantages taken by the trader, in commerce and traffic, are iniquitous, and deserve the severest punishment.

We have already observed, that a man of real goodness will not injure his neighbor's reputation. It is a just remark of an eminent author, that every man has a right to be thought and spoken of agreeably to his real character. Whoever then is the cause why his neighbor is not considered in the light he deserves, grossly violates this sacred rule of duty, nor is he possessed of true benevolence. One of the greatest injuries against our neighbor's reputation, is falsehood in testimony. To open a door to villany, to blast the character of an innocent person, are crimes of the deepest die; and few punishments can be too severe for such as are guilty of them. The voice both of Moses and of Christ, breathes love, peace, and good-will to man; a temper conformed to its dictates, will shudder at the idea of spreading a false report. Even insinuations, by which an innocent character may be blemished, are cruel and impolitic. They are cruel, because they spring from malevolence of heart, and prove too often fatal to the peace and prospects of the unhappy victims; they are irrational, because our own characters are in the hands of others, and our temporal concerns at their disposal.

The malicious causeless defamer, is certainly among the most abandoned characters in the world; neither profit, honor, nor pleasure, can he propose to himself, from the practice of his extraordinary disposition, unless the indulgence of malice be a pleasure; and if so, Satan has no inconsiderable share of happiness. The defamer has been justly compared to the dark assassin, who murders without giving notice of his intention. Here then is a law attended with no inconveniences, which not only leads us to the great duties we owe to our God, but also to the exercise of the first social duties to each other, as well as to practice those which we owe to ourselves.

Human laws are numerous, and too burdensome to the memory, and frequently raise disputes rather than intimate duty. But this worthy maxim is free from all perplexities; the most uninformed mind can scarcely misapprehend it, and the weakest memories are capable of retaining it. This precept lies ready on all occasions; we need but glance, as it were, upon our own minds, where it abides and shines like the polar star, to direct the course of the mariner. This injunction of our divine Redeemer is of vast and comprehensive influence, extending to all ranks and conditions of men, and to all kinds of action and intercourse between them, to matters of charity as well as justice, to negative as well as positive duties, to communities as well as individuals. But the law of God is not recommended to us by its own intrinsic excellence only; how many and how great are the advantages arising from a strict observance of it? The satisfaction it affords a rational mind, is certainly most refined and lasting. From hence arise pleasures that will flourish in the winter of adversity, illuminate death, and exist beyond time. The man who is conformed to the divine law, has the approbation of his own conscience, his great soul ever possesses a continued source of substantial delight. In the near approach of death, peace shall dawn upon his mind, like the radiance of the morning; and as the exiled captive exults with the hopes, that he is returning to his native home, he will look forward with rapture toward the happy country where his heart has fled before him.

To consider the distress and dangers, to which a person who disregards these essential duties is exposed, affords a truly melancholy prospect. At enmity with his God, he cannot be happy in the nature of things; at enmity with his fellow men, they will conspire against him for their mutual defence. Revenge from some baneful corner shall return the injury on the defamer's head,—his character shall bleed by his own arts,—his faith shall be questioned,—his best works misrepresented,—his excellencies, if he have any, be forgotten, and his conduct meet with just and universal abhorrence.

Let us then, dear brethren, contemplate the law, in order to know our obligations to God, and the impossibility of obtaining eternal life, by any performances of our own. This will make us willing to submit to the righteousness of Christ, and enable us to stand with boldness in the great examination day.

By the Association,

WILLIAM ROGERS, Moderator.
THOMAS MEMMINGER, Clerk.

THE MINISTERS AND MESSENGERS AT THE ASSOCIATION, AND THE STATE OF THE CHURCHES FOR THE YEAR.

CHURCHES.	MINISTERS AND MESSENGERS.	Baptized.	Received by Letter.	Dismis'd.	Restored.	Excom.	Deceased.	Members.
Lower Dublin,	Samuel Jones, D. D., John Holmes, Joseph Wright,	1	0	0	0	0	0	62
Middletown,	Benjamin Bennet, John Smock,*	9	1	1	0	4	5	144
Cohansie,	Henry Smalley, A. M., Nathan Shepherd, Jeremiah Brooks,	2	0	1	0	0	6	122
Welsh Tract,	John Boggs,* Ephraim Stoops,* Francis Goteer,	33	0	2	0	1	6	138
Great Valley,	Isaac Abraham, Jonathan Phillips, George Passfield,	0	1	6	0	0	1	71
Cape May,	John Stancliff,*	0	0	0	0	0	0	49
Hopewell,	Oliver Hart, A. M., John Blackwell,* David Stout,	4	0	6	2	2	5	156
Brandywine,	Joshua Vaughan,* John Powell,* Robert M'Coy,* John Vaughan,	8	4	0	0	0	2	82
Montgomery,	Joshua Jones, Charles Humphrey,	0	1	0	1	0	1	21
Kingwood,†		0	0	0	0	0	0	76
Haight's Town,	Peter Wilson, A. M., Peter Groom,	33	0	14	0	2	6	286
Philadelphia,	Thomas Ustick, A. M., William Rogers, D. D., Morgan Edwards, A. M., Hugh Gorley, George Ingolls, John M'Leod, Samuel Davis,*	7	14	6	0	0	17	122
Southampton,	*Thomas Memminger, A. M.* William Watts, William W. Folwell,	8	1	0	0	1	3	59
Knowlton,†	Daniel Vaughan,*	0	0	0	0	0	0	43
Hartford,	John Davis,*	0	0	0	0	0	0	110
New Britain,	Edward Matthew,* Joseph Dungan,	0	0	0	0	0	0	26
Salem,	Isaac Skillman, A. M.,* Ephraim Lloyd,* John Briggs,	9	4	0	1	0	7	69

CHURCHES.	MINISTERS AND MESSENGERS.	Baptized.	Received by Letter.	Dismis'd.	Restored.	Excom.	Deceased.	Members.
Dividing Creek,	GARNER HUNT,* William Mason,* Sylvanus Tubman,* Nathaniel Loring,*	36	1	1	0	3	3	80
New Mills,	*Isaac Carlisle,* *Benjamin Hedger,* David Gaskill,	2	0	2	0	1	1	90
Konoloway,†	JOSEPH POWELL,*	0	0	0	0	0	0	0
Coram,†	—— ——	0	0	0	0	0	0	30
Upper Freehold,	DAVID LOOFBORROW,	0	0	6	0	0	5	61
Pittsgrove,†	—— ——	0	0	0	0	0	0	0
Manahawkin,†	—— ——	0	0	0	0	0	0	0
Vincent,	THOMAS FLEESON,	2	0	0	0	0	2	23
Tuckahoe,†	ISAAC BUNNEL,*	0	0	0	0	0	0	46
Cow Marsh,	JOSEPH FLOOD, Job Meredith,	3	0	0	0	1	2	34
London Tract,	THOMAS FLEESON,	0	3	0	0	0	1	39
Hilltown,	JAMES M'LAUGHLIN, Philip Miller, Griffith Owen,*	1	0	3	0	0	0	99
Lower Smithfield,†	DAVID JAYNE,*	0	0	0	0	0	0	26
Baltimore,	LEWIS RICHARDS,* WILLIAM CLINGAN,* Charles P. Polk,*	3	6	0	1	2	2	69
Bryn Sion, Duck Creek,	JAMES JONES,* JOHN PATTON,* GIDEON FERROL, *James Davis,*	2	0	7	0	4	6	66
Wilmington,	THOMAS AINGER,*	8	2	2	0	1	3	54
Jacob's Town,	BURGISS ALLISON, A. M.,* William Snowden, James Cox,	2	0	0	0	0	1	59
Pittstown,†	JAMES FINN,*	0	0	0	0	0	0	134
Marcus Hook,	ELIPHAZ DAZEY,	2	0	0	0	0	0	20
Rocksberry,	*William White,* John Levering, Charles Nice,	0	0	0	0	0	0	48
Penn's Manor,	ALEXANDER M'GOWAN,	3	0	1	0	0	2	35
Sideling Hill,	THOMAS RUNYAN,*	6	2	5	0	0	1	49
West Creek,	—— ——	5	2	2	0	0	0	34
		189	42	65	5	22	88	2732

NOTE.—The ministers' names are in SMALL CAPITALS. Licenced preachers in *italics*. Those marked thus * were not present. From the churches marked thus † received no intelligence. A dash —— denotes no settled minister.

MINUTES

OF THE

PHILADELPHIA BAPTIST ASSOCIATION,

HELD IN PHILADELPHIA, OCTOBER 6TH, 7TH, AND 8TH,

1795.

October 6th.—At three o'clock, P. M., Rev. Peter Wilson preached the introductory sermon, from 1 John iv. 1, "Beloved, believe not every spirit, but try the spirits whether they be of God."

2. After worship, business was opened with prayer by the Rev. Dr. William Rogers.

3. Proceeded to business. Brother Thomas Ustick was chosen moderator, and Brother Peter Wilson, clerk.

4. Letters were read from twenty-six churches.

5. The business of the day was closed with prayer by the moderator.

Adjourned until to-morrow morning, at nine o'clock.

October 7th.—Met pursuant to adjournment.

6. Business was opened with prayer by Brother Runyan.

7. Received a letter and minutes from the Baltimore Association, newly formed, desiring to hold a correspondence with us. Their letter was presented by our Brother Charles P. Polk, and they were received into fellowship.

8. Rev. John Pitman, from Rhode Island, being present, was invited to take a seat.

9. Received letters and minutes from the Warwick Association for 1793, 1794, and 1795, by the messenger, Rev. Brother Thomas Montanye; from that of Charleston, 1794, and from that of New York, by Rev. Brother Reune Runyan.

10. Appointed the following brethren to write to the corresponding Associations:—Thomas Memminger, to write to the Warwick Association; Reune Runyan, to that of Charleston; Thomas Fleeson, to that of Baltimore; Joshua Jones, to that of New York; Burgiss Allison, to that of Warren; William Folwell, to that of Stonington; and William White, to that of Shaftsbury.

11. Read the circular letter prepared by Samuel Jones, D. D. Our Brethren William Rogers, John Blackwell, and James M'Laughlin, were appointed a committee to revise the same.

12. Distributed the minutes received from different Associations amongst the churches.

13. The committee appointed last year to revise the Catechism,

and make such alterations as they judged necessary, brought their amendments forward. Voted to insert those alterations in our minutes for the inspection of the churches, and they are desired to manifest their approbation, or disapprobation, at our next Association.

14. Query from Cohansie church: Is it not proper, from the consideration of abounding error, infidelity, lukewarmness, and decay of vital piety in the world, and in professors of religion, that a day of humiliation, fasting, and prayer, should be observed in our churches?

Answer: We agree to appoint and recommend Wednesday, the 28th day of October, as a day of fasting and prayer throughout our churches, for the above mentioned reasons, and on account of the late calamitous visitations.

15. Also, agreeably to a query from Philadelphia church, and in conformity to the general concert for prayer, in which many churches have engaged,—

We appoint and recommend the first Tuesday in January, April, July, and October, beginning at two o'clock, P. M., particulary to implore a blessing on the Word, and the general spread of the Gospel.

16. Second query from the Philadelphia church: Whether it might not, at this time, considering the frequency of emigration, be advisable for this Association to insert in their minutes, a request to the transatlantic churches, that they would be particular in their letters of recommendation and dismission of members, to specify whether they intend merely to recommend, or to dismiss; together with the principles and practice of the church so dismissing?

Answered in the affirmative.

17. Query from New Mills: Whether a circular letter published by an Association meeting at Bromsgrove, in England, on the education of children, shall be republished?

Appointed Brethren Isaac Skillman, Henry Smalley, and Samuel Jones, to examine the same, and report thereon.

18. Brother Jenkin Davids concluded by prayer.

Adjourned until three o'clock, P. M.

Met pursuant to adjournment.

19. Brother John Pitman opened the service by prayer.

20. In answer to queries from Cape May, and a request from West Creek churches, we recommend to said churches mutually to call a council.

21. Committed our system of discipline to Dr. Samuel Jones, for revision and amendment. To be brought forward at the next Association.

22. Brother James M'Laughlin closed by prayer.

Adjourned until to-morrow morning, nine o'clock.

Sermon this evening by Brother Thomas Montanye, from Colossians iii. 4, "When Christ, who is our life, shall appear, then shall ye also appear with him in glory."

October 8th.—Met according to adjournment.

23. Brother Peter Wilson opened the Association by prayer.

24. The letters prepared for the Warwick, Baltimore, and Charleston Associations were approved.

25. The committee appointed to examine a piece on the education of children, recommend its publication; together with the Baltimore circular letter, written by the Rev. John Davis.

26. On application for assistance to build a meeting-house in Savannah, Georgia, large enough to admit some hundreds of blacks in the galleries, we recommend to the churches to make subscriptions or collections for the above purpose, and to forward the amount to Mr. Ustick by the 20th of November next; which Mr. Ustick is requested to convey by the first opportunity; together with a letter of condolence to the above-mentioned blacks, and our ardent wishes that Providence may interfere in their favor, at least so far, that their masters may be moved to allow them the free enjoyment of public and private worship.

27. Appointed our Brethren Blackwell, Wilson, Bennet, and M'Gowan, messengers to the New York Association; M'Laughlin, Memminger, and Dazey, to Warwick; Allison, to Warren; Peter Groom, to Shaftsbury; David Rees, to Charleston; and Dazey, Davids, White, Carlisle, and Ustick, to Baltimore.

28. Resolved, That our Brethren Rogers and Ustick, be a committee to revise Edward's materials towards a history of the Baptists in the state of Delaware.

29. Agreed that the churches be advised to make collections for the missionaries to the East Indies, and forward the same to Dr. Rogers.

30. Appointed Brother John Blackwell to write the circular letter for next year. Subject—Christian Liberty, and Liberty of Conscience. Chap. XXI.

31. Brother Thomas Ustick to preach the introductory sermon next year; in case of failure, Brother Isaac Skillman.

32. The Association to meet in the city of Philadelphia on the first Tuesday in October next, by divine permission.

33. Brother Ustick is requested to superintend the printing of the minutes, and forward the same to the churches. Also, the pamphlet on the education of children.

34. The business of the Association was closed with an address and prayer by the moderator.

Sermon in the evening by our Brother Jenkin Davids, from Eph. ii. 8, 9, " For by grace are ye saved."

PROPOSED AMENDMENTS TO THE CATECHISM.

Question. V. May all men make use of the Holy Scriptures?

Answer. All men are not only permitted, but required to read, hear, and seek an understanding of the Holy Scriptures.

Q. VI. What things are chiefly contained in the Holy Scriptures?

A. The Holy Scriptures chiefly contain what man ought to believe concerning God; they also teach what duty God requireth of man in his Law; and in his Gospel how men are reconciled unto God, through a Mediator.

Q. X. What are the decrees of God?

A. The decrees of God are his eternal purposes respecting all events; whereby for his own glory, he worketh all things according to the council of his own will, Eph. i. 11.

Q. XII. What is the work of creation?

A. The work of creation is God's making all things, by the word of his power, in the space of six days, and all very good.

Q. XV.—*A.* Man being created a subject of moral government, God was pleased to give him a positive command for the trial of his obedience, forbidding him to eat of the tree of knowledge of good and evil upon the pain of death.

Q. XIX.—*A.* Adam being made a public head, all mankind, descending from him by ordinary generation, sinned in him, and fell with him in his first transgression.

Q. XXV.—*A.* Add, "and the positive command respecting the forbidden fruit."

Q. XXX.—*A.* Christ's humiliation consisted in his being born, and that in a low condition, made under the law, and in his enduring the penalty of the law as the sinner's substitute and surety; in the miseries of his life, and in the death of the cross, in being buried, and continuing under the power of death for a time.

Q. XXXII. and XXXIII. And in the answer, instead of *purchased*, read *obtained*.

Q. XXXIV.—*A.* For freely offered, read, "freely held forth in the Gospel."

Q. LVII.—*A.* Last line, for instead of to, read, "for his own worship."

Q. LXIV.—Which day of the seven hath God appointed to be the weekly Sabbath?

A. Before the resurrection of Christ, God appointed the seventh day of the week to be the weekly Sabbath; but now the first day of the week is observed, both for rest and worship, in conformity to the example of Christ, and the practice of his holy apostles.

Q. XC. How may we escape the wrath and curse of God due to us for sin?

A. We ought diligently to use the outward means, whereby Christ communicateth to us the benefits of redemption, that we may have faith in Jesus Christ, and repentance unto life; without which it is impossible to escape the wrath and curse of God due to us for sin.

Q. XCI.—*A.* For offered to us, read, "held forth."

Q. XCIII. What are the outward means whereby Christ communicateth to us the benefits of redemption?

A. The outward and ordinary means whereby Christ communicateth to us the benefits of redemption, are the reading, but especially the preaching of the word, which the Spirit of God maketh an effectual means of convincing and converting the sinner, and the ordinances as an additional means of building up believers in holiness and comfort, through faith unto salvation.

Q. XCVI. What is the use of Baptism and the Lord's Supper?

A. Baptism and the Lord's Supper are ordinances of Jesus Christ, and are of use to set forth our faith in Christ, and to increase faith and every grace in us, through the blessing of Christ and the operation of the Spirit.

CIRCULAR LETTER.
BY REV. SAMUEL JONES, D. D.

The Philadelphia Baptist Association, convened at Philadelphia, the 6th, 7th, and 8th of October, 1795.

To the churches they represent, send Christian salutation.

Beloved Brethren,—Through the tender mercy of our God, we have had a comfortable meeting; for which we hope you will join us in thanksgiving.

Referring you to our minutes for information respecting our proceedings at this time, we pass on to the subject, on which, according to our course, we are now to address you. As we always, in our annual epistles, with fervent affection, aim at your instruction and edification, we hope our labor of love will ever be received and attended to with Christian benevolence, and that the effect will be, the building us up in our most holy faith.

The subject of our last address, was the Law—the next in order, in our most excellent Confession of faith, is the Gospel.

Between the Law and Gospel, there is a near connection; but, at the same time, a very material difference. The blending of these together, or treating of them in an injudicious and indistinct manner, has ever been a material source of error in the Christian church. It is, therefore, the more necessary to keep each of them in its proper place; and the rather on account, that a legal spirit is so natural to man, and a legal strain so difficult to be guarded against. Man is so naturally wedded to the Law, that he cannot easily be disengaged from it.

Would you know the difference between the Law and the Gospel? Only observe—the Law denounces wrath; the Gospel publishes peace; the Law convinces of guilt; the Gospel brings an acquittance; the Law pronounces sentence; the Gospel holds out a pardon; the Law requires satisfaction to the last mite; the Gospel discovers, that satisfaction has been made in full; the Law knows nothing of mercy; the Gospel knows nothing else: in the Law, righteousness, justice, and truth, shine gloriously; in the Gospel, love, grace, mercy, pity, condescension, and compassion do also shine, and with much more resplendent glory: commands, prohibitions, conditions, threatenings, penalties, &c., belong to the law; but, in the Gospel, these have no place. In the Gospel we find free grace, free mercy, free pardon; faith and repentance are freely given, and, with them, a new heart, a new nature, new life,—all is new, all is free. The Gospel, as the word signifies, is good message, good news, glad tidings. The language of the angels at the birth of Christ, was, "Behold, we bring you glad tidings of great joy," Luke ii. 10. The angelic prophet Isaiah, in that memorable passage, applied by our blessed Lord to himself and the gospel day, Luke iv. 18, 19, breaks out in the following gospel strain: "The Spirit of the Lord God is upon me, because the Lord has anointed me to preach good tidings unto the meek; he has sent me to bind up the broken-hearted, to proclaim liberty to the captives, and the opening of the prison doors to them that are bound, to proclaim the acceptable year of the Lord, to comfort all that mourn; to appoint unto them that mourn in Zion, to give unto them beauty for ashes, the oil of joy for mourning, the garment of praise for the spirit of heaviness," Isa. lx. 1–3.

The Gospel is sometimes called the Gospel of the grace of God, Acts xx. 24, because it publishes the rich grace and mercy of God in Christ Jesus. Sometimes it is called the Gospel of salvation. Eph. i. 13; Acts xiii. 26, because it brings to light the way of life and salvation provided of God for lost, perishing sinners. Sometimes the Gospel of peace, because it proclaims that glorious peace made by the peace-making blood of Christ; produces peace and tranquillity in distressed minds, makes men to be of a peaceable disposition, directs men to, and leads in the way of peace, and makes meet for eternal peace.

The Gospel brings glad tidings of good things; good things done for us; in that atonement is made for us, our debt paid, a righteousness wrought out, pardon and acceptance procured: good things wrought in us; such as regeneration, meetness for heaven, faith, hope, and every other grace; all the good things of providence and grace that are necessary for our present use during our passage through life; and finally, the good things of heaven itself, even all the glory and happiness of the beatific state. The Gospel, in fine, contains a discovery of all good things for time and eternity, in deliverance from sin and every evil, and the full enjoyment of every bliss and happiness beyond what the tongue of men or angels can express, or the powers of the human mind conceive.

Of the Gospel we farther observe, that it is purely a matter of revelation, and is not discoverable by the light of nature. This revelation was made by slow degrees. On this head a late writer* in our connection expresses himself thus: "The first dawning of the Gospel, and at the same time the first glimmering of hope, appeared to Adam in the promise that was made respecting the seed of the woman, Gen. iii. 15. Here the eternal counsels of the grace of God began to unfold themselves. In the promise made to Abraham, which was afterwards renewed to Isaac and Jacob, the same gospel grace breaks forth with clearer light. What had before been spoken in more general terms of the seed of the woman, is now said in a more particular manner of the seed of Abraham, Gen. xxii. 18. To Jacob the very time of accomplishing the promise was pointed out,

---

* Dr. Jones's Sermon on the Covenant.

Gen. xlix. 10. Moses renders the promise still more manifest, while he points out a character and likeness, Deut. xvii. 15. In the prophets, who were much farther advanced in the dispensation of the promises, approaching to the fullness of time, hastening to the coming of the Messiah, you have his virgin mother, Isa. vii. 5; place of birth, Micah v. 2, and the other circumstances particularly pointed out. Only observe the order and progress of the divine promises, gathering light and strength as they advance. When the first intimation of a Saviour was given, he was to be sought for among all the human race; afterwards we are directed to the particular seed of Abraham; even Isaac and Jacob: of Jacob's numerous sons the tribe of Judah is taken; of the tribe of Judah the family of Jesse; and of Jesse's sons the house of David. Thus, reducing, as it were, to a point, what had at first been delivered but in very general terms.

"These are some of the leading and principal discoveries that were made to the world, of our blessed Saviour before his incarnation. Thus did the promises and prophesies become brighter and brighter, until at last they shone more clear in their full accomplishment, when the sun of righteousness rose, dispelling darkness, and spreading the light of the gospel-day."

This revelation of the Gospel has been made known to such nations, and applications of it made to such individuals of those nations, as it seemed good to the sovereign will and good pleasure of God. "It is not of him that willeth," says the apostle, "nor of him that runneth, but of God that showeth mercy," Rom. ix. 16.

The applications of the Gospel under the influence of the divine Spirit, in the work of conviction and conversion, is absolutely necessary, in order to our receiving saving benefit from it. In this precious work of grace in our hearts, the Law and Gospel, considered as means, go hand in hand, and are often found in the same verse. By the one is the knowledge of sin, by the other the discovery of deliverance. The one worketh despair, the other faith and hope.

Thus, beloved brethren, you see, that the glorious Gospel, in every point of view, is the work of the rich and sovereign grace of God. It was of the sovereign grace and mercy of God, that the glorious plan of redemption was concerted, was published, and was afterwards, as it still is, applied to the elect, with all its saving benefits. O the glorious and blessed Gospel! O the sovereign grace and mercy of God in and through a gracious Redeemer!

From what we have said, various useful observations, by way of inference, might be made; but we shall only mention two: First, that according to the Gospel, the atonement of Christ did not extend to every individual of the human race; and, secondly, that the Gospel contains no conditional offers of salvation.

We mention these, because some in our days seem to favor such notions, and some others, that tend to mar and go a great way towards sullying the glory of the Gospel.

In regard to the first, if atonement was made for all, it was God's intention that it should; that intention must have its full effect; the effect must be that all must and will be saved.

If Christ answered the demands of law and justice for all, and paid the price in full, then there must be guiltless persons in hell for want of being made meet for heaven. Christ has done his part, but the Spirit declines doing his. Why God should appoint satisfaction to be made for all, and afterwards not renew and sanctify all, and bring them to heaven, must be very strange, and utterly inconsistent with the glory and perfections of Him, who does nothing in vain, who never does a part, without doing the whole, who always finishes what he begins.

It is manifest from the holy Scriptures, that Christ made atonement for his people, Isa. liii. 8; Luke i. 68; his sheep, John x. 15, 26, 29; xvii. 9; those that were given him, Heb. ii. 13; who were redeemed from among others, Rev. v. 9.

As to the second, to make salvation conditional, would rob God of his sovereignty, and make his glory to depend on man; while at the same time it would give room for boasting. It would also convert the Gospel of the grace of God into a new law. Is the law of works to be preferred to the covenant of grace? If it be of grace, says the apostle, then is it no more of works, otherwise grace is no more grace. What! make our happiness depend on man? If we will do part, God will do the rest. Alas! what can man do in the business of his salvation first or last, to merit or promote it? Is he altogether dependent on God? Yea, verily, that at every step, in the beginning and progress of the glorious work, he may cry, grace, grace; and whosoever glorieth, let him glory in the Lord.

But these men make a distinction between natural and moral ability. What is the use of this distinction, but to evade, deceive, and confuse? What can natural ability avail towards producing a supernatural effect? The effect can never exceed its cause, any more than a stream can rise higher than its fountain. Now the exercise of any and every evangelical grace is supernatural, is purely of God: but what is born of the flesh is flesh. And besides, if man's natural ability was competent to repent, believe, accept, obey, &c., what good could it do him, since he is never to exert it, unless God induces or influences him thereto; and without which influence, all offers and moral suasion will prove ineffectual. If we speak of repentance, for instance, is not Christ exalted as a Prince and a Saviour to give repentance unto Israel, and remission of sins? If we speak of faith; what faith? natural faith? What can this be better than the faith of devils, who believe and tremble? But if we speak of supernatural and evangelical faith, the Scripture is express. By way of distinction from the other, it is called, the faith of the operation of God, the faith of God's elect, like precious faith with us, that faith which purifies the heart, and worketh by love. And in regard to them, who received him, it is said, to them gave he power. Yea, verily, all the power, influence, and every thing in the business of our salvation is entirely of God alone, and not of us, who are but perfect weakness.

The scheme of divine truth contained in the Holy Scripture, is manifestly this: That man fell from that state of rectitude wherein he was created, and became guilty, polluted, depraved, helpless, &c.; that God in his rich mercy and wisdom, devised a way for the recovery and salvation of such as to him seemed meet, which was doing no injury to others, that were left; that the way of recovery is through the atoning blood of Christ, who glorified the divine perfections in making honorable the law, and bringing in an everlasting righteousness in behalf of and for those that were given him, who in God's own time and way are renewed and sanctified, made holy here and happy hereafter. To this end means are appointed, chiefly the word and the ministration thereof; wherein the state of the sinner by nature, and the way of recovery through rich grace is unfolded; and it pleases God to enlighten the mind; move on the affections, and subdue the will. The sinner is awakened and convicted; he sees his danger; is filled with concern of mind; enquires what he must do to be saved; has repentance unto life given him; is led to see the fulness, freeness, suitableness, and glory of the way of life through a Redeemer; is enabled to lay hold by faith of this hope; is transformed by the renewing of his mind; has the constraining love of God shed abroad in his heart; is humbled and abased in himself, yet triumphs in the mercy and power of God; and thus being filled with holy zeal, he goes on his way rejoicing. He is sensible the Lord of his mere sovereign unconditional grace and mercy began the good work, is now carrying it on, and will complete it in glory, to whom, therefore, without reserve, he ascribes all the praise, and will to all eternity.

It is now, brethren, time that we draw towards a conclusion. We hope you are in a good measure established in these truths, and that they are precious to you. May the Lord bless you, and the Gospel of his grace be among you, and may the time be hastened when it shall be spread in its purity with power and great glory over the whole earth.

Now unto him that is able to keep you from falling, and to present you faultless, before the presence of his glory with exceeding joy; to the only wise God our Saviour, be glory and majesty, dominion and power, both now and ever. Amen.

Thomas Ustick, Moderator.
Peter Wilson, Clerk.

Rev. Morgan Edwards, formerly Pastor of the Philadelphia church, resigned his place in the church militant in the year past. 'Blessed are the dead who die in the Lord."

THE MINISTERS AND MESSENGERS AT THE ASSOCIATION, AND STATE OF THE CHURCHES DURING THE YEAR.

CHURCHES.	MINISTERS AND MESSENGERS.	Baptized.	Received by Letter.	Dismis'd.	Restored.	Excom.	Deceased.	Members.
Lower Dublin,	Samuel Jones, D. D., Benjamin Dungan,	1	1	0	0	0	0	64
Middletown,	Benjamin Bennet, George Hunt,	2	0	3	0	0	2	141
Cohansie,	Henry Smalley, A. M., Nathan Shepherd, David Gilman,	4	1	1	0	0	0	126
Great Valley,	David Jones, A. M.,* Jenkin Davids, Daniel Cornog, Jonathan Philips,	1	1	3	0	0	2	69
Cape May,	John Stancliff,	0	1	0	0	0	3	47
Hopewell,	Oliver Hart, A. M.,* John Blackwell, Jared Saxton,	1	0	3	0	0	4	150
Brandywine,	Joshua Vaughan,* Thomas Davis, John Garret, jr., Thomas Le Telier,	2	1	1	2	0	0	86
Montgomery,	Joshua Jones, Edmund Pennington, Isaac Johnson,	0	0	0	0	0	0	21
Kingwood,	*David Stout,*	0	0	9	0	13	0	57
Haight's Town,	Peter Wilson, A. M., *David Rees,* Nehemiah Dye, John Flock,	12	0	6	0	2	2	288
Philadelphia,	Thomas Ustick, A. M., William Rogers, D. D., *Isaac Carlisle,* Benjamin Thaw, George Ingolls, John M'Leod, Hugh Gorley, Thomas Shields,	3	14	6	0	2	7	124
Southampton,	Thomas Memminger, A. M., Arthur Watts, Elias Yerkes, William Watts,	25	1	2	1	0	2	82
Knowlton,†	Daniel Vaughan,*	0	0	0	0	0	0	43
New Britain,	William White, Edward Matthews,	0	2	0	0	0	0	28
Salem,	Isaac Skillman, A. M., Gamaliel Garrison, Abraham Harris, Jacob Harris,	2	2	0	0	0	5	68
Dividing Creek,	Garner Hunt,	1	0	1	0	2	5	74

MINUTES OF THE PHILADELPHIA ASSOCIATION.

CHURCHES.	MINISTERS AND MESSENGERS.	Baptized.	Received by Letter.	Dismis'd.	Restored.	Excom.	Deceased.	Members.
New Mills,	*Benjamin Hedger*, David Gaskill,	2	1	4	0	0	0	89
Konoloway,	JOSEPH POWELL,* John Cook,	0	0	0	0	0	0	30
Coram,†	—— ——	0	0	0	0	0	0	30
Upper Freehold,†	—— ——	0	0	0	0	0	0	61
Pittsgrove,†	—— ——	0	0	0	0	0	0	0
Manahawkin,†	—— ——	0	0	0	0	0	0	0
Vincent,	—— ——	1	0	2	0	0	0	23
Tuckahoe,†	—— ——	0	0	0	0	0	0	46
London Tract,	THOMAS FLEESON,	0	0	1	0	0	0	38
Hilltown,	JAMES M'LAUGHLIN, Isaac Morris,	0	0	0	0	0	0	99
Lower Smithfield,†	DAVID JAYNE,*	0	0	0	0	0	0	26
Jacob's Town,	BURGISS ALLISON, A. M., William Snowden,	0	0	0	0	0	0	59
Pittstown,†	—— ——	0	0	0	0	0	0	134
Marcus Hook,	ELIPHAZ DAZEY,	0	1	1	0	0	1	19
Rocksberry,	John Levering, Michael Conrad, Nathan Levering,	0	2	2	0	1	0	45
Penn's Manor,	ALEXANDER M'GOWAN, Caleb Jeffers,	0	0	8	0	0	0	27
Sideling Hill,	THOMAS RUNYAN,*	2	0	1	0	0	1	49
West Creek,	PETER GROOM,	1	1	2	0	1	0	33
		60	29	56	3	21	34	2276

NOTE.—The ministers' names are in SMALL CAPITALS. Licensed preachers in *italic*. Those marked thus * not present. From the churches marked thus † received no intelligence. A dash —— denotes no settled minister.

MINUTES

OF THE

PHILADELPHIA BAPTIST ASSOCIATION,

HELD AT PHILADELPHIA, OCTOBER 4TH, 5TH, AND 6TH,

1796.

October 4th.—At three o'clock, P. M., Brother Thomas Ustick preached the introductory sermon, from Rom. i. 15, 16, "So as much as in me is, I am ready to preach the gospel to you that are at Rome also. For I am not ashamed of the gospel of Christ: for it is the power of God unto salvation, to every one that believeth; to the Jew first, and also to the Greek."

2. After sermon business was opened with prayer by Brother Ustick, when Dr. Samuel Jones, was chosen moderator, and Brother Burgiss Allison, clerk.

3. Letters were read from twenty-seven churches.

Business closed with prayer by the moderator.

Adjourned until nine o'clock, to-morrow morning.

Sermon in the evening by Dr. Foster, from 2 Cor. xii. 10, "For when I am weak, then am I strong."

October 5th.—Met pursuant to adjournment.

4. Business was opened with prayer by the moderator.

5. A church newly constituted at Shemokin, having made application to be admitted as a member of this Association, was accordingly received.

6. Brother John Blackwell, having been appointed at the last Association to write the circular letter for the present year, but not having sent it forward; it is requested that at the next Association he will give reasons for such omission.

7. Brother Staughton is requested to write a circular letter to accompany the minutes.

8. Received letters from the following Associations:—Welsh Tract, with a messenger: Charleston, with their minutes; Warwick, with their minutes; New York, with their minutes, by Dr. Foster, as messenger; and Stonington, with their minutes.

9. A copy of the charter for incorporating the Association, was brought forward by Dr. Samuel Jones, and read, and he appointed to proceed with all expedition in obtaining said charter.

10. The committee appointed, in sect. 28th of last year's minutes, to revise and publish Mr. Edward's history of the Delaware Baptists, report, that they have omitted proceeding in the business, on account

of a request from the Delaware Association that it might be postponed in order to rectify some mistakes.

11. A letter being read, from a committee of the New York Association, appointed to confer with us respecting a new edition of the New Testament, wherein the terms of Baptism are proposed to be translated agreeably to their original import; this Association conclude to defer the same until next year for further consideration.

Concluded with prayer, by Dr. William Rogers.

Adjourned until three o'clock, P. M.

Three o'clock, P. M.—Met pursuant to adjournment.

Business opened with prayer by Brother Peter Wilson.

12. Brother Joshua Jones, from Lincoln, in Old England, producing proofs of his having been pastor of a Baptist church there, of the same faith and order with us, was invited to take a seat among us.

13. The proposed amendments to the Catechism were brought under consideration, but for the present set aside.

14. Dr. Samuel Jones, to whom was referred, last year, the revision and amendment of our system of discipline, having given satisfactory reasons why he had not yet brought forward the same, is appointed to go on in the business, and bring forward such amendments at next Association.

15. In answer to the query from Dividing Creek, this Association think it inexpedient to admit Mr. German to administer the ordinances among them, inasmuch as those of his society will not commune with us; and also, as it may be productive of confusion and disorder.

Brother Fleeson to write the letter, and, accompanied by Brother William White, to go as messenger to the Delaware Association; Brethren Rogers and Wilson, as messengers to that of New York; Brother Wilson to write the letter; Brother Memminger to write to that of Warwick; and Brethren White and Groom to go as messengers; Brother Rogers to write to that of Charleston; Brother White, to that of Stonington; and Brother Groom, to Shaftsbury, to which he is also appointed a messenger.

17. A letter from the Warren Association, dated September, 1794, was received and read, and Brother James Ewing appointed to write to them.

Brother Joshua Jones concluded by prayer.

Adjourned until to-morrow morning, nine o'clock.

Sermon in the evening by Brother Skillman, from Isa. xlv. 22, and Eph. ii. 28.

October 6th.—Met pursuant to adjournment.

Opened with prayer by Brother Wilson.

18. Brother Skillman to preach the introductory sermon next year; and in case of failure, Brother Burgiss Allison.

19. Brother Memminger to write the circular letter.

20. Supplies for Dividing Creek.

21. The church at Shemokin request their sister churches to assist them in erecting a meeting-house. The Association, therefore,

recommend it to the churches to make collections for this purpose, and forward the same to Brother Ustick, in Philadelphia, as soon as possible, as the winter season is coming on, and the people are entirely destitute of a suitable place to worship in.

22. The circular letter, written by Brother Staughton, was brought forward, and read with approbation.

23. The brethren appointed to write to our corresponding Associations, brought forward their letters, which were read and approved.

24. Brother Ustick is requested to superintend the printing of the minutes, and to forward them to the respective churches as soon as may be.

25. The business of the Association closed with prayer by the moderator. Sermon in the evening by Brother Staughton.

CIRCULAR LETTER.
BY REV. WILLIAM STAUGHTON.

The ministers and messengers of the Baptist Association, held at Philadelphia.

To the churches they represent, send Christian salutation.

Christian Brethren,—According to the good hand of our God upon us, we are again met in Association. With gratitude to Him who is head over all things to the church, we mention, that the various letters we have received from the churches testify, that among them love and peace prevail, and that in like manner harmony has crowned our recent deliberations.

Accustomed annually to address you, and to derive the theme of our letter from the succession of subjects in our Confession of faith, we expected this year to have set before you the principles and pleasures of Christian liberty and liberty of conscience. Though in this expectation disappointed, we are still desirous of pressing on your minds such reflections as shall be friendly to your advance in knowledge and virtue.

Not more from the present state of religion, than from the pious hints suggested in your letters, our thoughts are turned to the prevalence of infidelity. With that regret and anxiety which every good man must feel when the godly man ceaseth, and when the wicked prevail, we observe crowds of unreflecting youths, pressing on to ruin, fascinated with systems which, though congenial with depravity, are at an infinite remove from holiness and truth. Our eyes, our ears, affect our hearts, while we perceive the sophistry admired which is pointed against the gospel of Christ, and the course of thought and conversation, which tends to the advancement of guilt and confusion, applauded as fashionable and just.

To trace this evil to its proper source we must recur to the original depravity of man, but we perceive a less distant cause in the revolution of empire. Our God sitteth upon the circle of the earth, and guides its affairs as his infinite perfections direct, yet its vicissitudes are usually so connected that one event appears naturally to rise out of another. Europe has for ages been deluged in superstition, and even where the reformation had destroyed its servile fetters, among the professors of religion little of the power of godliness was visible.

We rejoice in the progress of civil liberty, because so intimately related to the liberty with which Christ has made us free; but we perceive that as it moves, papal superstition and protestant insensibility are brought to light. While these are by their advocates termed religion, the infidel, with an air of plausibility, exclaims—all religion is vain.

Permit us, Christian brethren, as those who watch for your souls, to guard your minds against the influence of this prevaling evil. In this unfriendly world, popular sentiments, though evidently erroneous, sometimes produce an unhappy effect on the minds of such as are coming up out of the world. The unavoidable habits of society operating in conjunction with remaining depravity, too frequently give a tone to the thoughts and actions of believers, which is contrary to the simplicity that is in Christ. Brethren, forgive the jealousy we feel, lest they produce this effect among you.

As an antidote to this evil, we affectionately exhort you to labor after an enlarged acquaintance with divine truth. Let the word of Christ dwell in you richly in all wisdom. You have a reason of the hope that is in you, stand prepared, on every proper occasion to give it with meekness and fear. While you implore the teaching of the Spirit of God, search the Scriptures. The religion of Jesus courts the investigation of all, but it has a special claim on the attention of the righteous. Ye are set as a defence of the gospel, the sword of the Spirit, which is the word of God, is put into your hands, be ambitious to use it with a happy dexterity. Prompt and ingenious are the sons of infidelity in disseminating error; and shall the sons of God be inactive and unskilful in the support of truth?—Never do the triumphs of an infidel rise higher than when a man of God stands foiled before him.

But while we urge you to seek an increase of the knowledge of God, and of our Lord Jesus Christ, and, when duty invites, to appear as the advocates of evangelical piety, we beseech you scrupulously to banish a love of vain disputation. Aware of the invincible arguments in favor of the truth as it is in Jesus, and prone to mingle our personal interests with the subject we defend, we are in danger of disputing for the poor reward of victory.

Remember, brethren, the religion we profess is of infinite moment; seriousness ought to attend all our labors to maintain its truth. If you attempt to defend the gospel with infidel wit and heroism, a wound will be received in the house of a friend; but when you appear in its defence with all the weight of eternal concerns on your minds, the circumstance, like the splendor on the countenance of Moses, will make a rebellious people tremble. It is acknowledged that the shafts of satire are sometimes projected with success against vice and error; but they more frequently fall pointless to the ground. The weapon is dangerous, and in the sacred pages little used. Every sentiment has its natural influence. The tendency of infidelity is to produce ridicule and folly, while wisdom and seriousness are the offspring of religion. When we by folly and ridicule attempt to overturn popular errors, we give the wicked an easy triumph, by indulging in ourselves the unhappy influence, at the time we condemn the sentiment. But before a holy savor of truth, as before the incense of the altar in Bethel, the lifted arm of every opposing Jeroboam will be dried up.

But, Brethren, it is not enough that ye maintain the truth by argument: the purity of your walk and conversation will best demonstrate the sincerity and excellency of your faith. Errors have for ages distracted the Christian church; but they have generally originated in the ungodly lives of the professors of religion. The enemies of the cross blend together the gospel of Christ and the lives of its subjects, and, when believers sin, ascribe the iniquity to the gospel itself. At a time like the present, when the adversaries of truth are torturing their invention for new arguments against the cause which ought to be dearer to you than your lives, how ought ye to walk circumspectly, not as fools but as wise, that by well-doing ye may put to silence the ignorance of foolish men.

There is, brethren, an awfulness in piety, before the display of which the most hardened infidel is occasionally confounded. While your conversation is as becometh the gospel of Christ, assure yourselves, that though the ungodly outwardly laugh at and contemn you, they inwardly tremble and approve.

For nearly a century past shame, arising from derision, has been but little realised in the church: we have long sat peaceful and blest as under vines and fig trees. But in the present day, by appearing as the friends of vital and experimental godliness, by determining, assisted by the Holy Spirit, to follow the Lamb of God, whithersoever he goeth, we must expect to have our ideas pitied as mistaken, and our affections derided as enthusiastic. But to suffer for well-doing is an honor; and while we consider shame for the sake of Jesus, not as an evil patiently to be borne, but as a mark of glory of which, like the apostles, we are accounted worthy, like them we shall rejoice in him.

When you enter the sanctuary of the Lord, or retire into your closets, and hold communion with your own hearts, and with the God of your salvation, the hard speeches of the wicked will appear lighter than vanity; and while you reflect, that the natural man knoweth not the things of the Spirit of God, and that base things of the world are chosen, to confound the mighty; for the aversion of the learned and opulent in our day you will as easily account, as for the conduct of the Jews and Greeks, in the days of the apostles, in pronouncing the preaching of the cross a stumbling block and foolishness. As the purity of the gospel is educible from the aversion of wicked men, so the impurity of infidel opinions is demonstrable from their passionate zeal for their diffusion.

From the earliest ages of time the world has had its course. Lust, idolatry, persecution, and superstition, have successively been as mighty streams on which thousands have been borne along to ruin. At present, infidelity prevails; but it is an evil, and every evil, like the frail body of man, has the principle of decay within itself. An infidel exhibits his sentiments, and considers them as a lamp to the nations. His actions testify it is the lamp of the wicked, and heaven declares the lamp of the wicked shall be put out.

While the nations rage, and the earth is moved, ye who love the God of Israel and pray for the prosperity of Zion, like venerable Eli, when the Philistines were contending between Ebenezer and Aphek, may tremble for the Ark of the Lord; but not like him shall ye sink under the distressing information, that the ark is taken—the kingdom of Jesus overthrown. Universal empire and permanent prosperity, are promised to the great Redeemer: of the increase of his dominion and peace there shall be no end. The present spread of infidelity, far from portending the destruction of Christianity, establishes its truths by fulfilling its predicions. The earth is waxing old like a garment, and, like smoke, the heavens will shortly vanish away. All flesh is grass and the grass withereth, but the word of God, which, by the gospel, is preached unto you, shall stand for ever. Banish Christianity from the world, and what remains but guilt and death? But this is a living system, and must prevail till the kingdoms of this world become the kingdoms of our Lord and of his Christ.

When pursuing the interests of Zion, we are fellow workers with God. Do we pray for the coming of the Saviour's kingdom? Martyrs, at the foot of the altar, join our prayers. Do we groan? We groan with the creation, which travails for the redemption of the body of the righteous. Do we expect the period? We expect with Jesus. At the right hand of his Father he sits, henceforth expecting until his enemies be made his footstool.

The God of heaven baffles the designs of Satan, and laughs at the rage of the wicked against his anointed. When persecution was stirred up at Jerusalem, the disciples indeed were scattered; but by their dispersion their sound went out into all lands, and their words unto the end of the world. As persecution was formerly made to promote the Gospel by separating the disciples, in the present age, infidelity appears to answer the same grand design, by uniting them together. The distinctions which till lately destroyed the happiness of different sects of christians, lose their importance, while they prepare to encounter a common enemy. When the tribes of Israel were at peace with surrounding nations, contentions commonly existed among themselves; but, when a foreign foe drew near to battle, the different tribeships were forgotten, while in one great band, as the people of God, they marched to contest and victory.

Amid the important revolutions with which we are daily familiar, let us pray that, standing with our loins girt about, and our lamps burning, we may be prepared for every event, and that, our work on earth being finished, we may enter into the joy of our Lord.

Signed in behalf of the whole,
SAMUEL JONES, Moderator.
BURGISS ALLISON, Clerk.

THE MINISTERS AND MESSENGERS AT THE ASSOCIATION, AND STATE OF THE CHURCHES DURING THE YEAR.

CHURCHES.	MINISTERS AND MESSENGERS.	Baptized.	Received by Letter.	Dismis'd.	Excom.	Deceased.	Members.
Lower Dublin,	SAMUEL JONES, D. D., Benjamin Dungan, Joseph Green, Joseph Evans,	3	7	1	0	2	70
Middletown,	BENJAMIN BENNET,	1	0	0	0	5	140
Cohansie,	HENRY SMALLEY, A, M., David Elwell, Jeremiah Brooks,	0	0	4	1	4	117
Great Valley,	DAVID JONES, A. M., JENKIN DAVIDS, Jonathan Philips, Isaac Abram, Daniel Cornog,	0	0	2	0	4	63
Cape May,†	JOHN STANCLIFF,*	0	0	0	0	0	47
Hopewell,	JAMES EWING, Jared Sexton, David Stout,	0	0	5	1	3	141
Brandywine,	JOSHUA VAUGHAN, John Powell, Robert M'Coy,	1	2	3	1	0	85
Montgomery,	JOSHUA JONES, Charles Humphreys, Isaac Johnston, Silas Hough, Joseph Hubbs, Edward Pennington,	7	1	0	0	0	29
Kingwood,	GARNER HUNT,	2	0	2	0	0	80
Haight's Town,	PETER WILSON, Nehemiah Die, Peter Job, Thomas Appleton,	8	0	14	0	4	277
Philadelphia,	THOMAS USTICK, A. M., WILLIAM ROGERS, D. D., *Isaac Carlisle,* George Ingolls, John M'Leod, Benjamin Thaw, Joseph Keen, Nathaniel Davis,	19	17	2	4	3	151
Southampton,	THOMAS MEMMINGER, A. M., Arthur Watts, Abel Marple, Elias Yerkes, jr.,	6	0	0	0	1	87
Knowlton,†	DANIEL VAUGHAN,*	0	0	0	0	0	43
New Britain,	WILLIAM WHITE, Joseph Matthews, Edward Matthews, Joseph Dungan,	10	0	0	0	0	34

CHURCHES.	MINISTERS AND MESSENGERS.	Baptized.	Received by Letter.	Dismis'd.	Excom.	Deceased.	Members.
Salem,	Isaac Skillman, A. M., John Walker, Joseph Lloyd,	5	2	3	0	2	70
Dividing Creek,	—— ——	0	0	1	0	4	70
New Mills,	*Benjamin Hedger*, David Gaskill,	2	1	3	2	5	82
Konoloway,	Joseph Powell,*	4	0	0	0	0	34
Coram,†	—— ——	0	0	0	0	0	30
Upper Freehold,	—— ——	0	0	0	0	5	52
Pittsgrove,†	—— ——	0	0	0	0	0	0
Manahawkin,†	—— ——	0	0	0	0	0	0
Vincent,	Thomas Fleeson,	0	0	0	0	2	19
Tuckahoe,	Peter Groom,	0	0	0	0	1	25
London Tract,	Thomas Fleeson,	0	0	0	1	0	37
Hilltown,	James M'Laughlin,* Philip Miller, Enos Morris, Joshua Dungan,	6	0	0	0	1	104
Lower Smithfield,†	David Jayne,	0	0	0	0	0	26
Jacob's Town,	Burgiss Allison, A. M., William Staughton, William Snowden,	0	2	0	0	0	61
Pittstown,†	—— ——	0	0	0	0	0	134
Marcus Hook,	Eliphaz Dazey,*	1	0	1	0	0	19
Rocksberry,	John Levering, Michael Conrad, John Walraven,	2	0	0	0	0	47
Penn's Manor,	Alexander M'Gowan,	0	0	1	0	0	26
Sideling Hill,	Thomas Runyan,* John Occoman,	1	0	0	0	0	50
West Creek,	Peter Groom, David Lore,	1	0	0	0	2	32
Shemokin,	John Patten,	34	8	0	0	1	50
		113	40	42	10	49	2332

Note.—The ministers' names are in small capitals. Licensed preachers in *italic*. Those marked thus * were not present. From churches marked thus † received no letter. A dash —— denotes no settled minister.

It hath pleased God, in the year past, to remove from the church militant to the church triumphant, that burning and shining light, the Rev. Oliver Hart, A. M., of Hopewell, New Jersey.

Also, since the rise of the Association, the Rev. Eliphaz Dazey, of Marcus Hook, of respectable memory.

MINUTES

OF THE

PHILADELPHIA BAPTIST ASSOCIATION,

HELD AT LOWER DUBLIN, PHILADELPHIA COUNTY, OCTOBER
3D, 4TH, AND 5TH,

1797.

October 3d.—At three o'clock, P. M., Brother Peter Wilson, in consequence of the non-attendance of the brethren who were appointed last year, was requested to preach the introductory sermon, which he did, from John vii. 46, "Never man spake like this man."

2. After sermon, business was opened with prayer by Brother Samuel Jones, when Brother William Rogers was chosen moderator, and Brother Peter Wilson, clerk.

3. Letters were read from twenty churches.

4. Our Brethren Morgan J. Rhees, William Davis, Jacob Fitz Randolph, and John Evans, lately from Wales, being present, were invited to take a seat with us.

The moderator concluded with prayer.

Adjourned until ten o'clock to-morrow morning.

October 4th.—Met pursuant to adjournment.

Business was opened with prayer by Brother David Jones.

5. A letter and minutes were received from the Warwick Association. Minutes were also received from those of New York, Stonington, and Shaftsbury; but no messengers from either of these Associations.

6. Received a letter from a church at Opeckon Creek, Berkeley county, Virginia, requesting admission among us.

Appointed our Brethren David Jones, Samuel Jones, and Thomas Memminger, a committee to write to the Ketockton Association, and to the church at Opeckon Creek, on the subject.

7. A letter was received from part of the Brandywine church, respecting existing difficulties.

Agreed, That our Brethren, Samuel Jones and John Holmes, from Lower Dublin; David Jones and Daniel Cornog, from Great Valley; and Thomas Fleeson and Josiah Phillips, from Vincent, be a committee to endeavor to accommodate said difficulties, and report thereon to the next Association.

The committee to meet at the upper meeting-house, on Wednesday, November 8th, at nine o'clock, A. M.

8. Read the circular letter. Our Brethren William Staughton and Morgan J. Rhees, together with the writer Brother Thomas Memminger, were appointed a committee to revise the same.

9. Resolved, That those churches which omit sending a messenger, or letter, to this Association for three years successively, shall be dropped from our minutes, and considered as excluded.

10. Brother Ustick having informed us that minutes from several corresponding Associations remain in Philadelphia, in consequence of the calamitous visitation, is requested to distribute them among the churches, when he may return to that now afflicted city.

Brother Alexander M'Gowan concluded with prayer.

Ajourned until one o'clock, P. M.

One o'clock, P. M.—Met pursuant to adjournment.

Brother Benjamin Hedger opened with prayer.

11. The Association recommend it to the churches to observe the first Tuesday in January, April, July, and October, at two o'clock, P. M., to unite in prayer to Almighty God, that he would be pleased to pour out his Spirit on the churches. It is also recommended to observe the third Thursday in the present month, as a day of humiliation and prayer, on account of the manifold sins and iniquities too prevalent among ourselves, and the present calamitous visitation on the city of Philadelphia.

12. Brother Benjamin Bennet is appointed to write to the Warwick Association.

13. The moderator and Brother Ustick are requested to answer the letters from the corresponding Associations, which may have been left in Philadelphia, and designed for this Association.

14. Brother Samuel Jones, to whom was referred the revision and amendment of our system of discipline, brought forward and read the same.

Agreed, That a member be appointed by each church belonging to this Association, to meet on the second Tuesday in December next, at two o'clock, P. M., in the city of Philadelphia, to take into consideration, and make such alterations as unto them may appear proper. And in case any malignant, or contagious disorder should render their meeting in Philadelphia unadvisable, the said committee are to convene in Southampton, Bucks county.

Concluded with prayer by Jacob Fitz Randolph.

Adjourned until ten o'clock to-morrow morning.

Sermon at four o'clock, P. M., by Brother William Staughton, from Acts xvii. 22, 23.

October 5th.—Met pursuant to adjournment.

Opened with prayer by Brother Thomas Fleeson.

16. Brother Samuel Jones, who was appointed last year to proceed with all expedition in obtaining a charter for the incorporation of this Association, having succeeded in the business, brought forward the same, which was read.

The trustees of the said incorporation met this morning, agreeably to the charter, and chose the following officers: Samuel Jones, of Lower Dublin, president, George Ingels, of Philadelphia, treasurer, and William Rogers, of Philadelphia, Secretary.

17. The circular letter being revised by the committee, was produced and unanimously adopted.

18. Brother David Jones is appointed to write the circular letter for the next year.

19. Whereas, the last will and testament of James Honeywell, of Sussex county, New Jersey, appointed as trustees of said will, Benjamin Miller and Isaac Stelle, of New Jersey, together with Samuel Jones, of Lower Dublin, Pennsylvania, and also empowered the Baptist Association of Philadelphia, to fill up all vacancies occasioned by death or otherwise; and, whereas, Benjamin Miller and Isaac Stelle are deceased, this Association taking the matter into consideration, do appoint Gabriel Ogden, and Daniel Pridmore, of Sussex county, New Jersey, to supply those vacancies.

20. Brother Burgiss Allison is appointed to preach the introductory sermon next Association; and, in case of failure, Brother Thomas Memminger.

21. Agreed, That the next Association be held in Philadelphia, the first Tuesday in October next, at three o'clock, P. M. In case that any malignant disorder should then exist in the city, the Association are to meet at New Mills, New Jersey.

22. Brother Peter Wilson is appointed a messenger to the New York Association, and Brother Peter Groom, to that of Shaftsbury. The moderator is requested to give each of them a certificate of their appointment.

23. Brother Thomas Ustick is desired to superintend the printing of the minutes of this Association, and to send them to the several churches in connection with us, and to the corresponding Associations.

24. The moderator concluded the business of this Association by solemn exhortation and prayer.

Sermon at three o'clock, P. M., by Brother William White, from John's Gospel iii. 16.

[NOTE.—The reason why Brother Ustick has not made returns to the Association of the collections for distant churches, ordered into his hands is, that he had not with him the necessary papers and receipts, having no preconception, when he left the city, that the Association would be held elsewhere.]

CIRCULAR LETTER.

BY REV. THOMAS MEMMINGER.

The elders and messengers of the churches belonging to the Philadelphia Baptist Association, met in Association at Lower Dublin, in the county of Philadelphia.

To the churches they represent, send christian salutation:

Dearly beloved,—In the course of his providence, it hath seemed good unto the Lord again to visit the city of Philadelphia with the rod of his chastisement, in sending among the inhabitants a malignant fever; in consequence of which, it has been thought right that this Association should be held in some place free from the disease; from whence we now address you by this our letter.

We rejoice in the Lord that we, as the spared monuments of his mercy, have been permitted to meet each other by the respective messengers of the churches; from whom we have been glad to hear of the general welfare of Zion, and return thanks unto the great head of the church for the unanimity and brotherly love which have existed among us while in Association.

The subjects, upon which you will be addressed by us this year, are the important ones of Christian liberty and liberty of conscience, which come next in order in our Confession of faith.

That there is a liberty, and a glorious liberty too, which is the inheritance and portion of the people of God, is a fact clearly established, not only by the experience of all those who are made alive unto God in Christ, but also by the unerring testimony of the Spirit of truth as given in the word of God, declaring that, he that is called in the Lord, although he be a servant, is the Lord's free man.

The existence of spiritual bondage, as opposed to this liberty, is also clearly ascertained by the same incontrovertible testimony: the sons of men having, because of transgression, even in their first legal representative and head, sold themselves for nought, being brought into bondage unto Satan, and having made themselves the servants of sin, for whosoever committeth sin is the servant of sin.

In this state of bondage mankind are naturally, and their evidence of their being so, is the desperate wickedness of their hearts, inclined to evil as the sparks are to fly upwards, leading them on to the perpetration of all manner of sin and uncleanness with delight and greediness: hence they are brought under bondage to the law, and are under its curse. While thus the wrath of God abideth on them; considered in this point of view they are the slaves of Satan, and remain, unless Jesus deliver them, all their lives long in this servitude, by reason of the fear of death, and the awful prospect of a future state of never-ending punishment. They are also tied to the world, and labor under the guilt of sin. Deplorable state in which men stand! without a deliverance from which the mind shudders at the fearful prospect before them.

But blessed be our God with him there is redemption, that he may be feared; and it hath pleased him to place all power in the hands of Jesus, so that if the Son make us free, we shall be free indeed not only from the guilt and condemnation of sin, but also from the weight and burden of the law, which we are told gendereth to bondage—he bringing them under the gospel, which is the perfect law of life and liberty. For we also were in bondage under the same, until the fulness of the time was come, when God sent forth his Son, made under the law, to redeem them that were under the law, that we might receive the adoption of sons. Wherefore, those that are thus delivered, are no more servants but "sons; and if sons, then heirs of God, through Christ." They are delivered from the condemnation of the law; for " there is now no condemnation to them, which are in Christ Jesus, who walk not after the flesh, but after the Spirit." They are released by him from the dominion of sin and death; "for the law of the Spirit of life, in Christ Jesus, hath made them free from the law of sin and death." From the fear of death, the king of terrors to the sons of men, they are specially released; "forasmuch as the children are partakers of flesh and blood, he also, himself likewise took part of the same; that through death he might destroy him, that had the power of death, that is, the devil; and deliver them who through fear of death, were all their lifetime subject to bondage." From the evil consequences of temporal affliction and distress, which in the children of disobedience work resentment against the good providence of a God of wisdom, they are peculiarly freed; because, by the Spirit of adoption, beholding God as their indulgent father, they know that "all things work together for good to them that love God, to them who are the called according to his purpose."

But, beloved brethren, the glorious liberty of the sons of God as wrought out for them by the blessed Jesus, the deliverer of the captives of sin, extends further than what has been stated unto you. The veil between time and eternity is rent,—for them the everlasting doors of heaven are thrown open: and they who are led by his free Spirit have an access unto the throne of the most high God, and are privileged to go in and out and find pasture. For "now in Christ Jesus, ye who sometimes were far off, are made nigh by the blood of Christ. For he is our peace;" and through him we, both Jews and Gentiles, all that are named of the family in heaven and on earth, all that are called, "have access by one Spirit unto the Father. Now, therefore, ye are no more strangers and foreigners, but fellow citizens with the saints and of the household of God;" and may exercise boldness to enter into the holiest by the blood of Jesus in full assurance of faith.

The service of God is performed, by such as are brought into this precious liberty with perfect pleasure; the love of that God, who hath saved them and redeemed them, casteth out all slavish fear, and with a willing mind and filial affection they delight to do his will.

Such is the glorious liberty which Christ was anointed to proclaim to the captives, such the opening of the prison to them that were bound, such the freedom of which none can deprive you, and from which you cannot be excluded.

But dearly beloved and longed for, our hope and crown of rejoicing, the blessed Captain of our salvation hath thus freed us, that we might manifest to the glory of God, that the liberty in which we stand is not connected with licentiousness, but is continually the attendant of the Spirit of God leading into all truth and righteousness before him: now the Lord is that Spirit: and "where the Spirit of the Lord is there is liberty." For so is the will of God, that with well-doing you may put to silence the ignorance of foolish men, (who charge this doctrine of our liberty as licentious, thinking they spy out that which they know nothing of,) that you as free should not use your liberty for a cloak of maliciousness but as the servants of God. For brethren, ye have been called unto liberty, only use not liberty for an occasion to the flesh.

It is to be regulated by an attention to the whole moral law as the rule of our conduct both toward God and our fellow men: "For whoso looketh into the perfect law of liberty, and continueth therein, he being not a forgetful hearer, but a doer of the work, this man shall be blessed in his deed." Therefore, so speak ye, and so do, as they that shall be judged by the law of liberty, Remembering that of whom a man is overcome, of the same is he brought into bondage; for ye cannot be the freed men of Christ, and the servants of sin, because no man can serve two masters. Christ hath ransomed you for this same purpose; "that you being delivered out of the hands of your enemies, might serve him without fear, in holiness and righteousness before him all the days of your life:" "Knowing this that your old man is crucified with him, that the body of sin might be destroyed, that henceforth we should not serve sin: for he that is dead is freed from sin. For we are become dead to the law by the body of Christ, that we should be married to another, even to him, who is raised from the dead, that we should bring forth fruit unto God."

The all-wise Jehovah has given unto all men an equal freedom and liberty of conscience, the court of which is sacred, and wherein none have a right to tread but the individual himself and the blessed God by his word and Spirit, those only being the judges, who have authority to decide all matters concerning it. The angels of God themselves have no authority to interfere therein, much less any of the sons of men who are creatures of the dust, short sighted beings of a moment; and therefore their commandments, doctrines, or ordinances, unless founded upon, consistent with, and springing out of his word, which alone is truth, are by no means to be considered by you as obligatory; who, having your consciences purged from dead works, are called upon to hearken unto God, rather than unto men, making his word alone your rule and guide in all things.

And now, brethren, we bid you farewell. May that God who hath by his grace placed you in the liberty wherein you stand, enable you to stand fast therein; until you behold the top stone of the building brought forth in Heaven, shouting—Grace! Grace unto it! Amen.

By order of the Association,

WILLIAM ROGERS, Moderator.
PETER WILSON, Clerk.

THE MINISTERS AND MESSENGERS AT THE ASSOCIATION, AND THE STATE OF THE CHURCHES FOR THE YEAR.

CHURCHES.	MINISTERS AND MESSENGERS.	Baptized.	Received by Letter.	Dismis'd.	Excom.	Deceased.	Members.
Lower Dublin,	Samuel Jones, Benjamin Dungan, Jesse Dungan, Joseph Miles,	1	0	0	0	1	70
Middletown,	Benjamin Bennet,	1	0	1	0	2	138
Cohansie,	Henry Smalley,* Joel Shepherd,	2	1	5	1	6	108
Great Valley,	David Jones, Jenkin David,	1	0	1	0	0	64
Cape May,†	John Stancliff,*	0	0	0	0	0	47
Hopewell,	James Ewing,* Nathan Stout, David Stout,	0	0	1	13	5	120
Brandywine,†	Joshua Vaughan,*	0	0	0	0	0	85
Montgomery,	Joshua Jones, Charles Humphrey, Silas Hough, David Davis, Joseph Hubbs,	0	0	1	0	1	27
Kingwood,	Garner Hunt,*	2	0	2	1	2	77
Haight's Town,	Peter Wilson,	11	0	4	1	2	281
Philadelphia,	Thomas Ustick, William Rogers, *Isaac Carlisle*, George Ingolls, Joseph Keen, John M'Leod, Heath Norbury,	3	12	5	3	10	148
Southampton,	Thomas Memminger, Arthur Watts, Thomas Folwell, Elias Yerkes, jr.,	1	0	0	0	1	87
Knowlton,†	Daniel Vaughan,*	0	0	0	0	0	43
New Britain,	William White, John Dungan, Joseph Dungan, Edward Matthew,	3	0	0	0	1	36
Salem,†	Isaac Skillman,*	0	0	0	0	0	70
Dividing Creek,†	—— ——	0	0	0	0	0	70
New Mills,	*Benjamin Hedger*, Jacob Wolston,	13	1	0	0	2	91
Konoloway,†	Joseph Powell,*	0	0	0	0	0	34
Coram,†	—— ——	0	0	0	0	0	30
Upper Freehold,	Andrew Harpending, James Tapscott,	3	1	0	0	1	66
Pittsgrove,†	—— ——	0	0	0	0	0	0

CHURCHES.	MINISTERS AND MESSENGERS.	Baptized.	Received by Letter.	Dismis'd.	Excom.	Deceased.	Members
Manahawkin,†	—— ——	0	0	0	0	0	0
Vincent,†	—— ——	0	0	0	0	0	19
Tuckahoe,	—— ——	1	0	0	0	0	26
London Tract,	THOMAS FLEESON,	0	0	0	0	0	38
Hilltown,	JAMES M'LAUGHLIN, Philip Miller, Isaac Morris,	7	0	0	0	0	110
Lower Smithfield,†	DAVID JAYNE,*	0	0	0	0	0	26
Jacob's Town,	BURGISS ALLISON,* WILLIAM STAUGHTON, William Snowden,	0	0	0	0	1	65
Pittstown,†	—— ——	0	0	0	0	0	134
†Marcus Hook,†	—— ——	0	0	0	0	0	19
Roxbury,	—— —— John Levering, Michael Conrad,	0	0	0	0	0	46
Penn's Manor,	ALEXANDER M'GOWAN, Caleb Jeffers,	1	0	0	0	1	26
Sideling Hill,†	THOMAS RUNYAN,	0	0	0	0	0	50
West Creek,	PETER GROOM,*	0	0	0	2	0	31
Shemokin,	JOHN PATTEN,	0	0	0	0	0	50
		55	15	20	21	36	2332

NOTE.—The ministers' names are in SMALL CAPITALS. Licenced preachers in *italics*. Those marked thus * were not present. From the churches marked thus † received no intelligence. A dash —— denotes no settled minister.

ADDENDA TO 1797.

BAPTIST GRAMMAR SCHOOL—PECUNIARY TRANSFER, &c.

March 29th, 1797.

Whereas, several of the churches belonging to the Philadelphia Baptist Association, about five and thirty years ago, subscribed and collected money, for the purpose of supporting a Grammar school in their connection, that young men, promising for the ministry, might enjoy the benefits of education: Now the subscribers, trustees of said money, considering: That it is inconvenient for them from distant parts to attend to so small a concern; that the trustees of the Association aforesaid have a considerable sum or sums of money in their hands for the very same use; that the said Association trustees could take care of and apply the money now in the care of the subscribers under one trouble, if the same was committed to their care, and that it is troublesome, unnecessary and useless, to have two sets of trustees for the very same purpose:

The subscribers do therefore resolve, vote and determine, that the monies in their care for the use above said, shall be delivered to the trustees of the Association aforesaid, the interest whereof to be applied by said trustees to the original use and design, and no other; and the said Association trustees are hereby desired, authorized, and empowered to receive, sue for, and recover all monies, bonds, notes, book debts, books, papers, or other property whatever pertaining to the subscribers, as trustees as aforesaid, and to give proper receipts and discharges for the same, in as effectual a manner as themselves might or could do.

In witness whereof, they have hereunto set their hands.

SAMUEL JONES, of Lower Dublin.
SILAS HOUGH, of Montgomery.
ARTHUR WATTS,
BENJAMIN BENNET, of Middletown.

[NOTE.—The above act of pecuniary transfer was in my possession, in manuscript, and does not appear ever to have been incorporated with the minutes, nor regarded as belonging properly to the records of the Association; but it belonging now to history, and relating to property for which, I believe, the Association is yet responsible, I have thought best to insert it here.—*Ed.*]

MINUTES

OF THE

PHILADELPHIA BAPTIST ASSOCIATION,

HELD AT NEW MILLS, BURLINGTON COUNTY, NEW JERSEY,
OCTOBER 2D, 3D, AND 4TH,

1798.

October 2d.—At three o'clock, P. M., Brother Burgiss Allison, agreeably to appointment last year, preached the introductory sermon, from 2 Corinthians iv. 5, "For we preach not ourselves, but Christ Jesus the Lord; and ourselves your servants for Jesus' sake."

2. After sermon, business was opened with prayer by Brother William Rogers, when Brother David Jones was chosen moderator, and Brother Burgiss Allison, clerk.

3. Letters from twenty-five churches were read.

Adjourned until ten o'clock to-morrow morning.

October 3d, ten o'clock, A. M.—Met pursuant to adjournment.

4. A newly constituted church at Amwell having addressed us by letter requesting to be admitted into the Association, was accordingly received, by their messengers, John Carr and John Manners.

5. Brother William Burton, from Nova Scotia, being present, was invited to take a seat with us.

6. Letters from the following corresponding Associations, with their minutes, were received: viz., From New York, by Reune Runyan, as their messenger; from Warwick, by their messenger, John Caton; also, from Charleston and Warren.

7. Appointed the following brethren to write to the different Associations: viz., Rogers, to the Charleston; Ustick, to the Warren; Staughton, to the New York; Wilson, to the Shaftsbury; Smalley, to the Warwick; and Fleeson, to the Delaware. And it is further understood, that those who cannot conveniently write during the session of the Association, may write at their leisure, but in time to transmit the letters to the respective Associations prior to their meeting; and present copies to the next Association.

8. The following brethen are appointed as messengers to the different Associations: viz., Wilson, to the New York; White and Groom, to the Shaftsbury and Warwick; and Vaughan, to the Delaware.

9. Brother Ustick brought forward the letter which he had written to the Warren Association, agreeably to the 13th section of last year's minutes, which was approved.

10. The church at Dividing Creek having applied for supplies, our Brethren Skillman, Smalley, Groom, and Stancliff, are requested to supply them at convenient seasons.

11. Received a letter from the church at Opeckon Creek, Berkeley county, Virginia, with reference to their letter mentioned in the 6th section of last year's minutes: and also a statement of their difficulties. The reading of the statement postponed until afternoon.

Adjourned until two o'clock, P. M.

Two o'clock, P. M.—Met pursuant to adjournment.

12. The statement of the church at Opeckon Creek, postponed until this afternoon, being read, it is the opinion of this Association, that the Ketockton Association be again written to on the subject, indicating that if we do not receive from them satisfactory reasons by our next Association, why said church should not be received, we shall admit the church. Brother Samuel Jones was accordingly appointed to write to said Association.

13. The Brethren appointed as a council, in the 7th section of our last year's minutes, to investigate and give advice respecting certain difficulties subsisting in Brandywine church, report:

That they found the church in a disagreeable situation; that party spirit ran high; that they labored after a reconciliation, but were not so happy as to succeed. Nevertheless, hoping that an accommodation may yet be brought about; therefore, appointed another committee, consisting of our Brethren Skillman, Wilson, Ustick, M'Gowan, Smalley, and Carlisle, to attend again upon the above business, on the first Wednesday in November next, at ten o'clock, A. M., and make report at the ensuing Association.

14. The circular letter written by Brother David Jones, was read; and Brethren Samuel Jones, Reune Runyan, Isaac Skillman, William Staughton, and Burgiss Allison, were appointed a committee to revise the same in conjunction with the author.

Adjourned until ten o'clock, to-morrow morning.

October 4th, ten o'clock, A. M.—Met pursuant to adjournment.

15. The committee appointed to revise the circular letter, brought it forward with amendments, which being read, it was approved.

16. The letter to the New York Association, written by Brother Staughton, was read and approved.

17. The committee appointed in the 14th section of last year's minutes, to examine the amendment of the church discipline, report: That having revised, and by a majority approved the same, they ordered it to be printed.

18. Brother Skillman is appointed to write the circular letter for the ensuing year, and left to his own discretion as to the subject.

19. Brother Burton, who is now travelling to make collections from the churches to assist in building a meeting-house in Halifax, Nova Scotia, at the request of the Association, read his credentials,

which were fully satisfactory. We therefore recommend to the churches to assist him in so laudable an object.

20. Brother Memminger is appointed to preach the introductory sermon next year; and, in case of failure, Brother Staughton.

21. Brother Samuel Jones is requested to draw up a map of the relative situations of all the Associations in the Unites States.

22. Brother Ustick is requested to superintend the printing of the minutes.

23. The Association is appointed to meet on the first Tuesday in October, 1799, by divine permission, in Philadelphia; or in case any malignant disorder should prevail in the city, at the Great Valley.

CIRCULAR LETTER.
BY REV. DAVID JONES, A. M.

The messengers of the churches of Christ belonging to the Philadelphia Baptist Association, met at New Mills, in the State of New Jersey.

To their respective churches, send greeting.

Beloved brethren,—We have been once more prevented assembling in the city of Philadelphia by a dreadful visitation from God. Whatever may be the natural cause of this complaint, no doubt SIN is the procuring cause; nor can we reasonably expect a removal of the calamity without a suitable reformation among the inhabitants, for which we ought fervently to pray to God; and who knoweth but he may, in his great mercy, graciously answer our supplications.

The subject to which we shall call your attentions this year is, " Religious worship and the Sabbath day," being Chapter XXII. of our Confession of faith.

That there is an eternal, almighty, unsearchable God, the creator and upholder of all things, the works of creation, as well as divine revelation, do clearly make appear; but the acceptable manner, in which we are to honor and worship him, is made known only by divine revelation, for which we should ever adore our God.

The object of all divine and religious worship, is the Godhead, consisting of Father, Son, and Holy Spirit; and these three personal distinctions are only one and the same Divine Being, from everlasting to everlasting the same one, living, and true God, blessed for evermore.

That He alone is the object of religious worship, is evident from many texts of Holy Scripture, and in particular Matt. iv. 10, " Thou shalt worship the Lord thy God, and him ONLY shalt thou serve."

All religious worship is to be performed in the name of the Lord Jesus Christ, who is the only Mediator between God and men. To call on any other as mediator or intercessor, is contrary to divine revelation, and highly dishonorable to our adorable Redeemer, as well as shameful idolatry. Nor should such idolators ever be esteemed Christians, whatever they may believe, or profess to believe, on other subjects connected with Christianity. Some of the texts of Scripture to which we would refer you, on this subject, are the following, viz., "I am the way, the truth, and the life: no man cometh unto the Father, but by me," John xiv. 6. And in the 13th verse, it is said, "Whatsoever ye shall ask in my name, that will I do, that the Father may be glorified in the Son." "There is one God, and one Mediator between God and men, the man Christ Jesus," 1 Tim. ii. 5; "For through him, we both have access, by one Spirit, unto the Father," Eph. ii. 18.

And whereas, by reason of the fall, all men are depraved, blind, and insensible of their spiritual wants, it is necessary to have the assistance of the holy Spirit to prepare our hearts, and strengthen our souls to give glory and honor to God suitable to the divine nature. Our faith on this subject is founded on the following texts, with many others: viz., "And I will pour upon the house of David, and upon the inhabitants of Jerusalem, the spirit of grace and of supplications," Zach. xii. 10; "Likewise the Spirit also helpeth our infirmities: for we know not what we should pray for as we ought; but the Spirit itself maketh intercession for us," Rom. viii. 26. Many other passages of Scripture might be mentioned to the same purpose; but this subject is generally acknowledged by all who are worthy of the name of Christians. At the same time, we may confess with deep humility and sorrow of heart, that God has in a great measure suspended the powerful operations of his Holy Spirit in our churches. Oh that it were with us as in years past! All our preaching, and all your hearing, will be to little purpose, without the gracious operations of the Holy Spirit.

We now proceed to observe a few things with respect to the time of performing religious worship. We are taught that God is a Spirit, and must be worshipped in spirit and in truth, and that we should pray without ceasing; yet it is necessary to have, in the churches, fixed times for public worship. And it is to be wished that all Christians were unanimous on this subject; but there is little hope of this being the case, till we drop all traditions and traditional modes of speech; for these things will cause many mistakes.

The compilers of our Confession of faith were desirous to use the same language with other Christians, as far as was thought consistent with a good conscience; and it may be, on this subject, they conformed more than can be supported by the Holy Scriptures, or any arguments justly drawn from them. Should we express ourselves in a manner different from them, we are in hopes it will give no offence to any of our brethren; and we are rather persuaded the manner in which we shall treat this subject, will be generally acceptable, if the arguments are calmly considered.

We shall inquire into two points relative to the subject.

I. Whether the fourth command was moral or ceremonial?

II. By what authority Christians observe the first day of the week as a day of worship?

I. It is not pretended that the word moral is used either in the Old or New Testament. By it, we understand those obligations, which in their nature are unalterable, and binding on all men; and by ceremonial, we are to understand such commands as were types or shadows of spiritual things, which might be abolished by the will of the legislator.

Having premised these things, we proceed to show that the fourth command was not moral, notwithstanding it is sometimes placed with moral commands; but this is not always the case.

There is in the nature of things no reason why one day should be appropriated to religious worship more than another, for God is the same every day, and is to be worshipped in spirit and in truth. The observance of one day more than another was instituted for certain reasons, and was binding on those to whom the will of God was made known; but not on the Gentiles, who were never charged with a breach of the Sabbath. The word Sabbath signifies rest; and two reasons are given in Scripture why God enjoined it on the Jews. The first is that God finished the works of creation in six days, and rested the seventh, Ex. xx. 11. The second reason is the deliverance of Israel from their bondage in Egypt. When Moses repeated the law in Deut. v. 15, he said, "And remember that thou wast a servant in the land of Egypt, and that the Lord thy God brought thee out thence, through a mighty hand, and by a stretched out arm; therefore, the Lord thy God commanded thee to keep the Sabbath day." The Sabbath is repeatedly mentioned as a sign between God and the children of Israel throughout their generations, and seems limited to them.

For want of room, we must omit many arguments; but it may suffice to say that a ceremonial command is an institution of God to bring to mind some events past, or to come. Such was the passover, and such was the Jewish Sabbath. It brought to mind the finishing of the creation in six days, and God's resting the seventh, as well as the deliverance of the children of Israel from their bondage in Egypt; and it alludes to that rest which a soul enjoys when enabled to believe in Christ.

The answer of our blessed Lord to the Pharisees, accusing his disciples of breaking the Sabbath, plainly proves that he considered the Sabbath as a ceremonial command. We shall transcribe the passage and make a few remarks. "And he said unto them, Have ye never read what David did, when he had need, and was an hungred, he, and they that were with him? How he went into the house of God in the days of Abiathar, the high priest, and did eat the shew bread, which is not lawful to eat, but for the priests, and gave also to them that were with him? And he said unto them, The Sabbath was made for man, and not man for the Sabbath; therefore, the Son of man is Lord also of the Sabbath," Mark ii. 25, 26, 27, 28. This passage affords an unanswerable proof in what light Christ considered the Sabbath; for had the Sabbath been a moral command, there would have been no propriety in quoting the breach of a ceremonial command as a parallel case.

II. We proceed to show by what authority we keep the first day of the week, as a day of Christian worship.

We would premise that the duties of the Gospel differ in many respects from the law of Moses; for the law says, "Do this and thou shalt live;" but the Gospel says, "Live, and as a child of God and joint heir with Christ, do this, for his yoke is easy and his burden is light."

We do not say that there is any express command in the New Testament positively making it a duty to worship on the first day of the week; yet from the examples of the disciples, we have reason to believe that the disciples met by the authority of Christ; for some of his last words to his apostles were a solemn injunction, to do as he commanded, which are these: "Teaching them to observe all things whatsoever I have commanded you," Matt. xxviii. 20. If we admit that the apostles were faithful, of which we can have no doubt, we must believe that their practice was conformable to the command of Christ; we would, therefore, refer you to their example, recorded in John xx. 19 and 26, "Then the same day, at evening, being the first day of the week, when the doors were shut where the disciples were assembled, for fear of the Jews, came Jesus, and stood in the midst, and saith unto them, Peace be unto you." "And after eight days, again his disciples were within, and Thomas with them. Then came Jesus, the doors being shut, and stood in the midst, and said, Peace be unto you." And in Acts xx. 7, "And upon the first day of the week, when the disciples came together to break bread, Paul preached unto them." The historian mentions it as the practice of the church at Troas, and hence we find it as the known and established order of Christian churches in Galatia and Corinth, as appears from 1 Cor. xvi. 1, 2. And in John's time, it seems to have obtained the name of the Lord's day, Rev. i. 10.

We must close this epistle in a few words respecting the manner in which this day of worship ought to be observed.

1. Let us avoid all worldly business as far as possible, that we may with singleness of heart wait upon God in all the appointed means of grace. In order to obtain this end, we should use our best endeavors to dismiss all our worldly affairs on the seventh day of the week, that we may be prepared for divine worship.

2. We should spend the morning of the Lord's day in prayer or reading the holy Scriptures, or other good books composed by the servants of Jesus Christ; and never allow small excuses to prevent our meeting with the disciples of Christ for divine worship. None can tell how much is lost by omissions of duty. It is good to wait on the Lord, for he walks in the midst of the golden candlesticks, and sits as a refiner or purifier of his people. From the apostle's words, in Heb. x. 25, it seems some were faulty in his day, and forsook the assembling together, a sure sign of backsliding of heart. Think not the duties of the day ended when you have attended public worship; but make a good improvement of time, for it is very precious. Therefore, redeem the time by doubling your diligence.

Be not conformed to the vain customs of the present age, in paying or receiving unprofitable visits on the Lord's day, for this will tend to destroy the power of religion.

From the above arguments, we may justly infer, that the religious observance of the Lord's day for divine worship, is warranted by the examples of the apostles and churches in their days. Consequently, we have sufficient grounds to believe that it was by the authority of our Lord and Saviour Jesus Christ, who is the head of his church and lawgiver to the body.

And now, dear brethren, we commend you to God and the word of his grace, and remain in the Gospel of Christ.

By order of the Association,

DAVID JONES, Moderator.
BURGISS ALLISON, Clerk.

THE MINISTERS AND MESSENGERS AT THE ASSOCIATION, AND STATE OF THE CHURCHES DURING THE YEAR.

CHURCHES.	MINISTERS AND MESSENGERS.	Baptized.	Received by Letter.	Dismis'd.	Excom.	Deceased.	Members.
Lower Dublin,	Samuel Jones, Benjamin Dungan,	0	5	0	0	1	74
Middletown,†	Benjamin Bennet,*	0	0	0	0	0	138
Cohansie,	Henry Smalley, Isaac Wheaton,	0	0	0	0	3	105
Great Valley,	David Jones,	1	0	1	0	1	63
Cape May,†	John Stancliff,*	0	0	0	0	0	47
Hopewell,	James Ewing, Paul Hill, Abraham Servis,	17	1	9	1	0	128
Brandywine,	Joshua Vaughan, William Simeson, Thomas Davis,	0	0	1	1	0	84
Montgomery,	Joshua Jones,* Charles Humphrey, Silas Hough,	0	1	0	0	0	28
Kingwood,	Garner Hunt, John Robinson,	6	0	10	1	1	68
Haight's Town,	Peter Wilson, Thomas Dye, Peter Job, John Blakeley,	12	2	1	0	4	290
Philadelphia,	Thomas Ustick, William Rogers, *Isaac Carlisle*, George Ingolls, John M'Leod, Benjamin Thaw, George Allen, (No return.)	0	0	0	0	0	148
Southampton,	Thomas Folwell,	2	1	0	0	1	89
Knowlton,†	Daniel Vaughan,*	0	0	0	0	0	43

CHURCHES.	MINISTERS AND MESSENGERS.	Baptized.	Received by Letter.	Dismis'd.	Excom.	Deceased.	Members.
New Britain,	William White, Edward Matthew,	0	1	0	0	1	36
Salem,	Isaac Skillman, John Walker, Sylvanus Shepherd,	17	1	1	2	4	82
Dividing Creek,	—— ——	0	0	0	0	5	55
New Mills,	Alexander M'Gowan, *Benjamin Hedger*, Henry Chambers, Jacob Woolston, Samuel Jones, Job Rogers,	13	1	1	1	1	102
Konoloway,	Joseph Powell,* Abednego Stephens,	6	1	0	0	1	40
Coram,†		0	0	0	0	0	30
Upper Freehold,	Andrew Harpending, James Tapscott, David Burcalo,*	7	0	0	0	1	72
Pittsgrove,†	—— ——	0	0	0	0	0	0
Manahawkin,†	—— ——	0	0	0	0	0	0
Vincent,	—— ——	0	1	1	0	1	23
Tuckahoe,	—— ——	2	0	0	0	0	29
London Tract,	Thomas Fleeson,	0	0	0	0	0	39
Hilltown,	James M'Laughlin,* Philip Miller,	2	2	1	0	1	111
Lower Smithfield,†	David Jayne,*	0	0	0	0	0	26
Jacob's Town,	Burgiss Allison, William Staughton, William Snowden,	2	2	8	0	1	60
Pittstown,†	—— ——	0	0	0	0	0	134
Markus Hook,†	—— ——	0	0	0	0	0	19
Roxbury,	—— ——	2	1	0	0	0	49
Penn's Manor,	Caleb Jeffers,	0	0	6	1	1	18
Sideling Hill,†	Thomas Runyan,*	0	0	0	0	0	50
West Creek,	Peter Groom, Lemuel Edwards,	8	0	0	0	1	38
Shemokin,†	John Patten,*	0	0	0	0	0	50
Amwell,	John Carr, John Manners,	0	0	0	0	0	16
		97	20	40	7	29	2394

Note.—The ministers' names are in SMALL CAPITALS. Licensed preachers in *italic*. Those marked thus * were not present. From churches marked thus † received no letter. A dash —— denotes no settled minister.

⁎ A particular return of the collections for distant churches is necessarily deferred until next Association, when it is expected the business will be concluded.

MINUTES

OF THE

PHILADELPHIA BAPTIST ASSOCIATION,

HELD AT THE GREAT VALLEY, CHESTER COUNTY, PENNSYLVANIA,
OCTOBER 1ST, 2D, AND 3D,

1799.

October 1st.—At three o'clock, P. M., Brother Thomas Memminger being prevented by indisposition, Brother William Staughton, agreeably to appointment last year, preached the introductory sermon, from Psalm xlviii. 12, 13, "Walk about Zion and go round about her, tell the towers thereof, and mark well her bulwarks, consider her palaces, that ye may tell it to the generations following."

2. After sermon, business was opened with prayer by Brother David Jones, when Brother Burgiss Allison was chosen moderator, and Brother William Staughton, clerk.

3. Letters from twenty-nine churches were read.

4. Brother Isaac Skillman, who was appointed to write the circular letter, being removed by death, Brother Samuel Jones is requested to prepare one.

After prayer by the moderator, adjourned till nine o'clock to-morrow morning.

October 2d, nine o'clock, A. M.—Met pursuant to adjournment.

Brother David Jones prayed.

5. Letters from the following corresponding Associations, with their minutes, were received:—From New York, by their messenger, Rev. William Vanhorn; from Warwick, by Rev. John Williams; from Delaware, by Brother Jesse Walraven, and from Charleston.

6. Appointed the following brethren to write to the different Associations:—Staughton, to Charleston; Ellis, to Warren; Ustick, to New York; Wilson, to Shaftsbury; Ewing, to Warwick; Hunt, to the Delaware; and to produce the letters to-morrow.

7. The following brethren are appointed messengers to the Associations:—M'Gowan, M'Laughlin, and Ewing, to New York; Vaughan, to Delaware; and Harpending, to Shaftsbury.

8. The church at Salem having applied for assistance, we will endeavor to supply them.

9. The church at Manahawkin may expect supplies.

10. Supplies also granted to Pittsgrove.

11. To Tuckahoe.

12. To Dividing Creek.

NOTE.—It is particularly recommended by the Association, that such churches as are destitute of Pastors, do endeavor regularly to support divine worship. Their widowed state bespeaks the necessity for prayer, and the promises of the Lord of the harvest encourage it. In most churches there are brethren who can with acceptableness to a congregation read sermons; and the support of unity and intercourse among the brethren, as well as the duty of publicly venerating the Lord's day in the midst of an infidel world, loudly call for these holy services.

13. The brethren appointed as a committee to give advice relative to existing difficulties in Brandywine church, reported the course of conduct they had recommended to that church, which was fully approved.

Brother Samuel Jones concluded in prayer.

Adjourned for an hour—one o'clock.

Two o'clock, P. M.—Met pursuant to adjournment.

14. Agreeably to the request of the committee, the church at Brandywine reported their proceedings consequent on the committee's advice; on which the Association directed, That its opinion be transmitted to the complaining parties, in writing, which was accordingly done.

Brother William Rogers prayed. Adjourned till ten o'clock tomorrow morning.

Sermon at four o'clock by Brother William Vanhorn, from Col. ii. 10, "And ye are complete in him, which is the head of all principality and power."

October 3d, 10 o'clock, A. M.—Met pursuant to adjournment.

15. The case of the church at Opeckon Creek being taken up by the Association, and a letter from the Ketockton Association, and another from the church at Opeckon Creek, on the subject, being read, it is the opinion of this Association that the subject be dismissed, and that Brother Samuel Jones be appointed to write, both to the Ketockton Association and to said church, our reasons for this measure.

16. The letters to the different Associations were read and approved.

17. The circular letter, produced by Brother Samuel Jones, was read and approved.

18. The church at Sidling Hill requesting dismission to a nearer Association, it was granted.

19. Brother Staughton is appointed to write the circular letter for the ensuing year, and left to his own discretion as to the subject.

20. Brother Samuel Jones and Brother Staughton are appointed to prepare a map of the situation of the churches in this Associa-

tion, and to inform themselves of the probable expense attending its engraving.

21. Apprehensive that many advantages may result from a general conference, composed of one or more members from each Association, to be held every one, two, or three years, as may seem most subservient to the general interests of our Lord's kingdom; this Association respectfully invites the different Associations in the United States to favor them with their views on the subject.

22. Brother Ustick is requested to forward to each Association in the United States a copy of our minutes, on account of the above request.

23. The four following days, viz., the first Tuesday in January, April, July, and October, are recommended as days of humiliation and prayer, that we may humble ourselves under the hand of God, and seek his forgiveness and favor; and that he would be pleased to pour out his Spirit upon his churches.

24. This Association, desirous of spreading ecclesiastic information, recommend "Crosby's History of the English Baptists" to our churches and sister Associations, as a valuable work; and hope that, should our Brother Ustick be disposed to publish it, he will meet with universal encouragement.

25. Brother Ustick reports that the moneys raised for the Savannah African church were:

From the church at Middletown,	$22 00
From the church at Montgomery.	13 50
From other churches in smaller sums,	36 34½
	$71 84½

Which was remitted in the following manner, viz.

Cash sent by Mr. Michaels,	$10 00
Paid by Rev. Mr. Furman,	30 00
An order on Mr. John Hamilton, for	31 89
	$71 89

26. Collections received for Shemokin church, viz., from the church at

Montgomery,	$4 56½	Paid Mr. Daniel Rhees,	$55 27
Philadelphia,	40 05	Paid to Rev. Mr. Patten,	4 75
Penepek,	5 03		
Hopewell,	5 62½		
Hilltown,	4 75		
	$60 02		$60 02

27. Brother Samuel Jones is appointed to preach the Association sermon next year; and in case of failure, Brother William Rogers.

28. Brother Ustick is requested to superintend the printing of the minutes.

29. The Association is appointed to meet, on the first Tuesday in October, 1800, at two o'clock, P. M., at Philadelphia; but in case of the return of the fever there, to be held at Cohansie.

CIRCULAR LETTER.
BY REV. SAMUEL JONES, D. D.

The elders and messengers of the several Baptist churches, pertaining to the Philadelphia Baptist Association, convened at the Great Valley, on Tuesday, October 1st, 1799.

To the several churches to whom they relate send Christian salutation.

Beloved Brethren,—While we lament the distress in which our metropolis is involved, which prevented our meeting there, yet we have the pleasure to observe that we have had a pretty general representation from the churches in our connection, and a comfortable opportunity, for which we desire to be thankful.

You will see by the returns from the churches, that although it be a dark and declining day, yet the Lord has not left us without the manifestation of his power and grace, but has granted some quickening and refreshing showers of divine influence in divers places, both in our bounds and those of our sister Associations.

Being disappointed in addressing you at this time, from the pen of that great man we last year appointed to that service, you can expect but a few general hints, imperfectly penned, in the midst of the hurry of business.

Dr. SKILLMAN is no more! He has been removed, we trust, from his labors in the church militant to that rest which remaineth for the people of God, and though we feel and lament the loss we sustain by this heavenly visitation, yet we desire to be resigned to the divine will, in a comfortable assurance that our loss is his gain.

When we take a view, brethren, of the number of churches destitute of those to go in and out before them, and break unto them the bread of life, and at the same time that there are so few likely to come forward in the ministry, while so many are removed from their posts on Zion's walls; we think it a time, when we should feel with solemn weight on our minds, the force of our blessed Lord's injunction when he said, "Pray ye the Lord of the harvest, that he would send forth many laborers into his harvest," and we wish it to be more effectually impressed on each of our hearts. Yes, brethren, we beseech you all to attend seriously to this weighty consideration.

When we consider the unbounded mercies of God, the rich displays of his goodness and grace in the various dispensations of his hand, both in a spiritual and temporal way, we have the highest reason to praise and adore his holy name. May the streams of his bounty lead us to him who is the fountain of all good, may they lead us to unfeigned repentance, that shall be attended with reformation of life, and influence us to walk worthy of the high vocation wherewith we are called. How desirable to experience the shedding abroad of the constraining love of God in our hearts. Then shall we love as brethren, then shall we be moved to diligence in the use and improvement of the privileges, means and opportunities we enjoy, whereby we may grow in grace, and abound in holy zeal. How indispensable to cause our light to shine before men, that they seeing our good works may glorify our Father who is in heaven. Yes, brethren, let us, by our demeanor and deportment in life, recommend to others the holy religion we profess, as it were stamp it with the seal of reality and truth, and cause the beholders to observe, that we have been with Jesus and learned of him. Is it not of serious concern, that when the preacher explains the principles of pure and undefiled religion, in regard to their native tendency to holiness and purity of life; the very professors of that religion should by their unworthy conduct, caution the hearers not to believe the preacher, and as it were testify that there was not a word of truth in what he says?

Permit us, brethren, before we close, to beseech you to bear in mind those who labor among you in word and doctrine. We beseech and intreat you to pray for them; that a door of utterance may be given unto them abundantly, and that the power of God may rest on their labors; and withal make conscience of contributing towards their comfortable support as God has prospered you. Finally, Brethren, farewell.

"Now the God of peace, that brought again from the dead our Lord Jesus, that great Shepherd of the sheep, through the blood of the everlasting covenant, make you perfect in every good work, to do his will, working in you that which is well pleasing in his sight, through Jesus Christ, to whom be glory for ever and ever. Amen."

BURGISS ALLISON, Moderator.
WILLIAM STAUGHTON, Clerk.

NOTE.—Crosby's History will be comprised in 4 volumes octavo, neatly bound and lettered, at six dollars, unless it should be thought more eligible to abridge the work. The sister Associations are requested to send their advice and subscriptions to the meeting of this Association in October next, or to T. Ustick, previously.

THE MINISTERS AND MESSENGERS AT THE ASSOCIATION, AND STATE OF THE CHURCHES DURING THE YEAR.

CHURCHES.	MINISTERS AND MESSENGERS.	Baptized.	Received by Letter.	Dismis'd.	Restored.	Excom.	Deceased.	Members.
Lower Dublin,	Samuel Jones, Thomas Holmes,	0	1	0	0	0	0	75
Middletown,	Benjamin Bennett,*	0	0	4	0	0	4	132
Cohansie,	Henry Smalley,* David Shepherd,	3	0	0	0	1	8	99
Great Valley,	David Jones, John Boggs, Daniel Cornog, Isaac Abraham, James Abraham, Jonathan Philips, Enoch Jones, David George, Isaac Bewla,	2	0	2	0	0	2	61
Cape May,†	John Stancliff,*	0	0	0	0	0	0	47
Hopewell,	James Ewing, John Blackwell,* David Stout, Joseph Ott,	55	0	1	1	0	4	179
Brandywine,	Joshua Vaughan,* William Simonson, John Garret, jr., Thomas Davis, Thomas Stroud,	0	1	0	0	0	0	85
Montgomery,	Joshua Jones, Charles Humphreys,	0	1	0	0	0	1	28
Kingwood,	Garner Hunt,	4	0	0	0	0	1	70
Haight's Town,	Peter Wilson, John Mawford,	38	1	3	0	1	3	322
Philadelphia,	Thomas Ustick, William Rogers, *Isaac Carlisle*, George Ingolls, John M'Leod, Hugh Gorley, Joseph Keen,* Benjamin Thaw,*	0	0	0	0	0	0	126
Southampton,	Arthur Watts, Abel Marple, Thomas Folwell,*	0	0	0	0	0	2	87
Knowlton,	—— ——	0	0	0	0	0	0	17
New Britain,	William White,* Edward Matthews, William James, Ephraim Thomas,	21	1	0	0	0	3	54
Salem,	Benjamin Thompson Henry Mulford,	0	2	0	0	0	5	79

CHURCHES.	MINISTERS AND MESSENGERS.	Baptized.	Received by Letter.	Dismiss'd.	Restored.	Excom.	Deceased.	Members.
Dividing Creek,	—— ——	0	0	2	0	0	3	60
New Mills,	{ Alexander M'Gowan, Levi Wilson,	11	0	0	0	1	3	109
Kolonoway,†	Joseph Powell,*	0	0	0	0	0	0	40
Coram,	—— ——	0	0	0	0	0	0	30
Upper Freehold,	Andrew Harpending,	4	3	0	0	1	1	79
Pittsgrove,	—— ——	0	0	0	0	0	0	12
Manahawkin,†	—— ——	0	0	0	0	0	0	0
Vincent,	{ Josiah Philips, Enos Miles, Thomas Lloyd,	6	1	0	0	0	0	30
Tuckahoe,	—— ——	0	0	0	0	0	0	26
London Tract,	Thomas Fleeson,	0	0	0	0	0	0	38
Hilltown,	{ James M'Laughlin, Philip Miller, Isaac Morris, Thomas Matthias,	15	0	0	0	1	4	120
Lower Smithfield,†	David Jayne,*	0	0	0	0	0	0	26
Jacob's Town,	{ Burgiss Allison, William Staughton,	2	0	0	0	0	0	62
Pittstown,*	—— ——	0	0	0	0	0	0	134
Marcus Hook,	{ *John Ellis*, George Mustin, George White,	0	2	3	1	2	1	17
Roxbury,	{ John Levering, Anthony Levering, Cornelius Holgate,*	0	0	0	0	0	3	46
Penn's Manor,†	—— ——	0	0	0	0	0	0	18
Sideling Hill,	{ Thomas Runyan, John Ockerman,	0	0	1	0	0	1	48
West Creek,	{ Peter Groom, Lemuel Edwards, James Edwards,	7	2	0	0	1	2	43
Shemoken,	John Patten,	46	8	3	0	0	0	101
Amwell,	{ —— —— William Merrell,	10	3	0	0	0	0	29
		224	26	19	2	8	51	2529

Note.—The ministers' names are in SMALL CAPITALS. Licensed preachers in *italic*. Those marked thus * not present. From the churches marked thus † received no intelligence. A dash —— denotes no settled minister.

MINUTES

OF THE

PHILADELPHIA BAPTIST ASSOCIATION,

HELD AT PHILADELPHIA, OCTOBER 7TH, 8TH, AND 9TH,

1800.

October 7th.—At three o'clock, P. M., Brother Samuel Jones, agreeably to appointment last year, preached the introductory sermon, from Acts xx. 23, "I kept nothing back that was profitable unto you."

2. After sermon, business was opened with prayer by Brother Burgiss Allison, when Brother Samuel Jones was chosen moderator, and Brother Peter Wilson, clerk.

3. Letters from twenty-four churches were read. Prayer by Brother Wilson.

Adjourned till nine o'clock to-morrow morning.

Sermon this evening by Brother John Stanford, from Acts vi. 4, "But we will give ourselves continually unto prayer."

October 8th, nine o'clock, A. M.—Met according to adjournment. Brother David Jones prayed.

4. Brethren Jonathan Jerman, Thomas Jones, and Joseph Flood, being present, were invited to take a seat with us.

5. Received a letter and minutes from the Warwick Association, by their messengers John Stanford and Thomas Montanye; letter and minutes from the Delaware Association, by their messenger John Boggs, jr.; letters and minutes from the New York and Charleston Associations. Also, minutes from the Shaftsbury, Middle District, Neuse, Dover, Flat River, Goshen, Roanoke District, Kehuke, and Culpepper Associations.

6. Brethren Ewing, Staughton, and Stanford, are appointed as a committee to examine the printed letters from the different Associations, and report thereon.

7. Read the circular letter to the churches, and appointed Brethren David Jones, Allison, and M'Laughlin, together with the author, to examine the same and report thereon.

8. Appointed the following brethren to write to the different Associations:—David Jones, to the Warwick; Horatio G. Jones, to the Delaware; White, to New York; and Staughton, to Charleston.

9. The following brethren are appointed messengers to the Associations:—M'Laughlin, to Warwick; Vaughan and Horatio G. Jones, to Delaware; and White and Wilson, to New York.

10. No communications having been lately received from the following churches, the brethren whose names are annexed to them, are appointed and do agree to write unto, or visit them.

Samuel Jones, to visit Knowlton; Ustick, to write to Coram.

M'Laughlin and White, to visit Lower Smithfield, on the third Lord's day in November, and Pittstown the Monday evening following, enquire of them relative to their faith and practice, and report thereon to the next Association.

David Jones, to write to Konoloway, relative to a resolution of the Association to drop off such churches' names out of our minutes, who neglect to write for three years in succession.

Brother M'Laughlin prayed.

Adjourned till three o'clock, P. M.

Three o'clock, P. M.—Met pursuant to adjournment. Brother Hunt prayed.

11. Conscious that the interposing Providence of God hath preserved the city of Philadelphia, during the present season, from the malignant fever, and caused the earth to bring forth her fruits more abundantly than for some years past, the Association set apart, and recommend, Thursday the 13th of November next, to be observed as a day of thanksgiving by all the churches in our connection.

12. The committee appointed to examine the printed letters from the different Associations, reported thereon.

Brother Rogers prayed.

Adjourned till half after six o'clock to-morrow morning.

Sermon this evening by Brother Montanye, from Col. i. 18, "And he is the head of the body."

October 9th, half after six o'clock, A. M.—Met pursuant to adjournment. Brother Ewing prayed.

13. The Association having received approving resolutions from three of their sister Associations, respecting the general conference, as recommended by the 21st article of our last year's minutes, beg leave to call the attention of the other Associations to this important subject, and solicit from them, severally, their views as to the time when, and place where, the first general conference ought to assemble.

This Association also recommend, that the different messengers from those Associations who may meet with us by divine permission, next year, be authorised to confer with a committee to be appointed by our body, on this subject, in digesting a plan relative to the general conference, and to do whatever may have a tendency to accelerate this beneficial design.

Brethren William Rogers, Thomas Ustick, Burgiss Allison, William Staughton, and Peter Wilson, are appointed a committee by this Association to receive and answer all communications from the different Associations in the United States appertaining to the business, in order that we may bring the whole to a conclusion.

14. The letters to the different Associations were read and approved. The committee appointed to examine the circular letter to the churches, report that they approve of the same.

Brother Hedger prayed.

Adjourned till half after ten o'clock, A. M.

Met pursuant to adjournment.

15. The Association recommend to the churches, that collections be immediately made and forwarded to Brother Ustick, for the instruction and assistance of Thomas Jones, a young man lately from Wales of promising gifts; and that Brother Ustick pay forty dollars to Thomas Jones, if as much be received; if more, to retain the same to be at the future disposal of the Association.

16. A query having been received from the church at Philadelphia on the subject:—

Resolved, That it be particularly urged on our churches, that, as stewards of God, and influenced by a strong desire to spread the cause of our blessed Redeemer, they endeavor to raise, as early as possible, and to maintain a fund for the assistance of such ministers as may be called to supply destitute churches, or otherwise publish the gospel in their connection: and as there are flattering prospects at the church of Manahawkin, which has been recently visited with much success, they earnestly entreat that some collections may be immediately forwarded to brother Rogers, for the desirable purpose of affording them ministerial aid.

17. The four following days, viz., the first Tuesday in January, April, July, and October, are recommended as days of humiliation and prayer.

18. Whereas, the church of Philadelphia have presented a query, on the propriety of forming a plan for establishing a missionary society: This Association, taking the matter into consideration, think it would be most advisable to invite the general committee of Virginia and different Associations on the continent, to unite with us in laying a plan for forming a missionary society, and establishing a fund for its support, and for employing missionaries among the natives of our continent.

19. The Association conceive, that the regular business of the Association is to take into consideration those matters which are introduced by the churches; yet, that the Association consider themselves at liberty to take up any matter of consequence introduced by any individual member.

20. It is recommended to our churches, that a sermon be annually preached among them, and after it a collection be made, the amount to be forwarded to the Association at their subsequent meeting, in order to augment the fund for the education of such pious young men as appear promising for usefulness in the ministry of the gospel.

21. The committee appointed to prepare a map of the situation

of the churches in this Association, and to inform themselves of the probable expense attending its engraving, presented a map; and report, that the expense will be about one hundred dollars. It is, therefore, recommended that each church send, by its messengers, at the next meeting, four dollars, to complete the designs.

22. The Association, understanding that objections lie against the character of Andrew Harpending, desire the Shaftsbury Association to inquire into the grounds of those reports.

23. Brother Ewing to write the circular letter for next year.

24. Brother William Rogers is appointed to preach the Association sermon next year; in case of failure, Brother John Boggs.

25. Brother Ustick is requested to superintend the printing of the minutes.

26. The Association is appointed to meet on the first Tuesday in October, 1801, at two o'clock, P. M., at Philadelphia; and in case of the return of the fever there, to be held at Hopewell.

27. The moderator concluded by prayer.

CIRCULAR LETTER.

BY REV. WILLIAM STAUGHTON.

The ministers and messengers of the Philadelphia Association, to the churches they represent, send Christian salutation.

Beloved Brethren,—Having once more been permitted to meet in Association, to consult the interests of the Redeemer's kingdom, not as having dominion over your faith, but as helpers of your joy, we once more affectionately address you.

It affords us the highest pleasure to find from your letters, that peace, like a river, flows among you; that additions have been made to many of our churches; and that your adherence to the faith of the gospel remains unshaken. We trust you will continue to abound in the work of the Lord, assured that in your holy profession, you have followed no cunningly devised fable, and that in prospect of the invisible world you know whom you have believed. To assist you in repelling every temptation to abandon your profession, and in surmounting the obstacles which may lie in your path to glory and virtue, in an age when thousands are treating the doctrines we maintain as unintelligible, and the duties we practice as irrational, permit us to bring to your view, some of the proofs of the divine origin of that gospel, which has been preached unto you, which also ye have received and wherein ye stand.

The evidences which address the understandings of all men, are the performance of miracles and the accomplishment of prophecy; but there is an evidence too little regarded, which particularly addresses itself to the consciences of believers,—equally convincing with any of the rest, and perhaps, in point of perspicuity and usefulness, superior to them all. It consists in that consciousness, which every Christian in his measure possesses, that he is born of incorruptible seed, which is well expressed by the beloved disciple, where he says, "He that believeth on the Son of God hath the witness in himself."

We know not any occasion on which this evidence can be more seasonably illustrated and enforced, than when writing to such as have tasted that the Lord is gracious.

We wish not, brethren, to direct your thoughts to any fancied internal light, any capricious impulses, which may be supposed to supersede the necessity of scriptural instruction: we refer to those operations of sovereign grace, which include the regeneration and sanctifying of the heart, strong consolation in trouble, and lively hopes in death.

As He who formed the mind is the author and finisher of our faith, we are not surprised that there is a visible harmony between the natural faculties and relative circumstances of the one, and the divine excellencies of the other. An understanding deeply penetrating is the privilege of few, and still fewer are blest with the external means which swell its capacity and assist its researches. " Ye see your calling, brethren, how that not many wise men after the flesh, not many mighty, not many noble, are called." If the proofs of the gospel were to be derived only from the investigation of ancient histories, the collating of original manuscripts, the acquisition of several languages, or the pursuit of deep metaphysical reasonings, by far the greater part of mankind must remain invincibly ignorant of its heavenly nature. But God, of his infinite wisdom and goodness, has made provision for the poor: He has let fall into the bosom of the Christian, who has both to pray and to toil for the daily bread of himself and family, a key which can open every door of the doubting castle. The evidence we are contemplating is so plain, that the wayfaring man, though a fool, need not err; so rational, that the attempts of the enemy to gainsay or resist are impertinent and abortive; and so universal, that babes, young men, and fathers in Christ, may alike enjoy its power.

We possess, naturally, that intimacy with ourselves which renders the perception of the exercise of our senses, affections, and understandings, obvious to us all. Should a philosopher tell you that the morning sun can shed no lustre on the hills—that there is no noise in the thunders of summer—that there are no such passions as joy and grief—that a human being is not able to reason, or if he be, that he cannot distinguish the operations of his mind—you would reject his assertions, convinced that if you know not these things, you know nothing; convinced that these are to be classed among those self-evident facts which do not properly admit of proof, because nothing in their support can be adduced plainer than themselves. In like manner, should an infidel assert, that there is no glory in the person of Jesus, no terrors in the law of God to the transgressor, no joy in the Holy Ghost, no brokenness of heart for sin, that there exists no such power of discernment as that which Paul ascribes to him that is spiritual; the believer having no internal sense of moral truth, perceives clearly that such declarations are false.

Permit us, brethren, to illustrate the nature of this evidence more fully. Does the infidel declare that the Bible is an imposition on the credulity of mankind? Your experience can answer: "Unless the law of God had been our delight, we had perished in our afflictions." Have you heard him assert that Christ was an impostor? You know he is mistaken; for Christ is formed in you the hope of glory. More blind than the Jewish ruler, does he ridicule the doctrine of the regeneration of the heart? You know what it means, and from its influence argue its origin. Once you loved the world; now you place it beneath your feet. Once you saw no loveliness in religion; now her ways are pleasantness. Pious persons you once hated; now they are your beloved associates, and for the very reason which formerly commanded your aversion, because they bear the image of the heavenly. Effects like these are irresistible proofs that you have passed from death unto life. It is in vain that an infidel contend, that it is absurd to suppose that God would pardon sin by so strange a means as the death of his Son; the Christian has felt the efficacy of the blood of Christ on his conscience. It is of no avail, his deriding the idea of an infernal agent; you know you have such an enemy, and are not ignorant of his devices. Let the foes of piety, if they please, term our religion wild and visionary; we have felt its soothing power, when our bodies have been tortured with pain, when our friends have been removed from our embraces, when the waters of complicated affliction have overwhelmed us.

This inward conviction assisted the primitive Christians to hold fast the faithful word. While the unbelieving Jews and Greeks were requiring a sign and seeking after wisdom, the disciples beheld, in a crucified Saviour, the power and the wisdom of God. No opposition could induce them to be ashamed of a system, which is the power of God unto salvation to every one that believeth.

In the days of our Lord when Philip could not immediately answer Nathaniel's objection to the Messiahship of Jesus, satisfied that he had found him of whom Moses in the law and the prophets did write, he requested Nathaniel to come and see. We may give the same invitation, both to the friends and enemies of Christianity. Come and see, how swearers become praying persons—how the unclean become chaste—how Sabbath breakers become devout—how he that stole, steals no more, but rather labors, working with his hands the thing which is good. Come and see how the churlish become liberal and the inebriated sober; see right hands cut off, and right eyes plucked out, rather than the whole body should be cast into hell. Come and "see how a Christian can die," and whether you behold him surrounded with weeping friends on his couch in the chamber, or with exulting enemies at the stake amid the flames, you may hear him singing with surprise and joy, "O death where is thy sting? Come, Lord Jesus, come quickly!"

We are sensible, brethren, that infidels may reject this evidence as unfounded; but, while we ask them to assign some other adequate cause, if they can, for the important changes we have named, we beg of you to remember, that "the natural man receiveth not the things of the Spirit of God: for they are foolishness unto him: neither can he know them, because they are spiritually discerned."

This change of heart and conduct, this inward witness, you need not be told is not of your own producing. God, who is rich in mercy, hath quickened us together with Christ. Neither moral suasion nor gentile philosophy, could have accomplished it. It could have been effected neither by the providences of God, nor by the ministry of the Gospel itself, separate from the power of the Holy Ghost. Indeed, the opposition made to it by our depravity, the world and the tempter, prove it a work essentially different from their nature and influence.

Paul, when standing on the stairs in Jerusalem, when speaking for himself before Agrippa, and when writing to the Galatian churches, demonstrates the truth of the Gospel, and his commission to proclaim it, from the history of his conversion. We wish you, brethren, ever to exercise that wisdom which dwells with prudence; but, we would recommend to you on proper occasions, even in the presence of infidels, to relate the story of your conversion to God. Some, like the Jews, may deride you; many, like Agrippa, may be almost persuaded to become Christians; while others, by the blessing of God, may, like the Galatians, be made not almost, but altogether disciples of Jesus Christ.

It is frequently observed respecting prophecy, that it is a growing evidence; the same is true as to the witness within. The more you grow in grace and the knowledge of Christ, the stronger will be your faith; purity and stability are the companions of each other.

Suffer us then, dear brethren, to exhort you to every good word and work. Enable your ministers, while they behold your faith, your patience and charity, to say, "Ye are our epistles written in our hearts, known and read of all men." Dwell much in your meditations on the redemption of the Son of God, Christ; increasing in love to him who first loved you and to your brethren in the Lord. Let grace and truth govern all your actions. Pray for and pursue the prosperity and peace of Jerusalem. Mortify the deeds of the body. Mind not the world nor the things of the world. Let your conversation be in heaven. In short, labor to attain to such a progress in knowledge and purity, as shall compel a wicked world to exclaim with the damsel of Philippi, "These men are the servants of the most high God."

Though the evidence we have been explaining brightens with our advance in the divine life, yet we hope none of you will write bitter things against yourselves, because the knowledge or joys of your brethren may be greater than yours. While we expect you to give all diligence to make your calling and election sure, we wish you to remember, that the evidence lies in the fact itself. Fire is as truly in the smoking flax as in the great volcano; the small dust of the balance is as really a part of the creation as the mountain of Libanus.

A careful investigation of the work of grace on the heart, will enable each of you to say before Jehovah, with a great divine* of the last century, " I see no doctrine so pure and heavenly, as bearing the image and superscription of God; nor any so fully confirmed and delivered by the attestation of thy own omnipotency; nor any which so purely pleads thy cause; calls the soul from self and vanity; condemns its sin; purifies it, and leads it directly unto thee. Thou hast mercifully given me the witness in myself! not an unreasonable persuasion in my mind, but that renewed nature, those holy and heavenly desires and delights, which sure can come from none but thee. And O! how much more have I perceived it in many of thy servants than in myself. Thou hast cast my lot among the souls that Christ hath healed; I have daily conversed with such whom he hath raised from the dead. I have seen the power of thy Gospel upon sinners. All the love that ever I perceived kindled towards thee, and all the true obedience I ever saw performed to thee, hath been effected by the word of Jesus Christ. And if confidence in Christ be yet deceit, must I not say that thou hast deceived me, who I know canst neither be deceived, or by any falsehood or seduction deceive?"

You will perceive with the pious Watts, that this is a powerful witness, and ever ready to baffle the most learned sophisms and the boldest temptations: it lies so near, that it is a present shield against every arrow from the camp of infidelity. It is an argument drawn from sense and vital experience, and effectually answers all the subtle cavils of false reasonings. The quibbles of logic against the experience of the Christian, are but as darts of stubble against the scales of a leviathan.

That you may enjoy this earnest of the Spirit, this unction from the Holy one, more and more, is the hearty prayer of, beloved brethren, your servants, for Christ's sake.

Signed in behalf of the whole,

SAMUEL JONES, Moderator.
PETER WILSON, Clerk.

---

*Richard Baxter.

THE MINISTERS AND MESSENGERS AT THE ASSOCIATION, AND STATE OF THE CHURCHES DURING THE YEAR.

CHURCHES.	MINISTERS AND MESSENGERS.	Baptized.	Received by Letter.	Dismis'd.	Excom.	Restored.	Deceased.	Members.
Lower Dublin,	Samuel Jones, Joseph Wright, Jesse Dungan,	0	0	0	0	0	1	74
Middletown,	Benjamin Bennet,	8	3	1	0	0	2	140
Cohansie,	Henry Smalley, Jeremiah Brooks, Isaac Wheaton,	7	0	0	0	0	5	101
Great Valley,	David Jones, John Boggs, *Horatio G. Jones*, Daniel Cornog, Isaac Abraham, David George,	4	0	0	0	0	0	65
Cape May,†	John Stancliff,*	0	0	0	0	0	0	0
Hopewell,	James Ewing, William Salyer, Moses Quick,	30	1	7	0	0	3	200
Brandywine,	Joshua Vaughan, William Simpson, John Garrett, jr., William Griffith,	1	0	0	2	1	1	84
Montgomery,	Joshua Jones, Charles Humphrey, Joseph Lunn, Silas Hough,	30	0	0	0	0	1	57
Kingwood,	Garner Hunt, Jonathan Robinson, John Heath,	4	0	0	0	0	1	73
Haight's Town,	Peter Wilson, Thomas Dye, John Morford,	19	1	6	0	0	4	332
Philadelphia,	Thomas Ustick, William Rogers, *Isaac Carlisle*, George Ingolls, John M'Leod, Joseph Keen, Samuel Oakford, John Peckworth, Hugh Gorley, Benjamin Thaw,	15	12	5	1	0	2	145
Southampton,	Jeremiah Dungan, Elias Yerkes, Peter Sowerman,	0	0	0	2	0	1	84
Knowlton,	—— ——	0	0	0	0	0	0	17
New Britain,	William White, Abel Matthew, Isaac Oakford, John Dungan,	40	3	1	0	0	1	96

MINUTES OF THE PHILADELPHIA ASSOCIATION. 357

CHURCHES.	MINISTERS AND MESSENGERS.	Baptized.	Received by Letter.	Dismis'd.	Excom.	Restored.	Deceased.	Members.
Salem,	Benjamin Thompson, Henry Mulford,	0	0	0	1	0	3	75
Dividing Creek,	Jonadab Shepherd,	0	1	0	0	0	3	58
New Mills,	ALEXANDER M'GOWAN, *Benjamin Hedger,* Jesse Cox,	15	0	2	0	0	3	119
Konoloway,†	JOSEPH POWELL,*	0	0	0	0	0	0	40
Coram,†	———— ————	0	0	0	0	0	0	30
Upper Freehold,†	———— ————	0	0	0	0	0	0	79
Pittsgrove,†	———— ————	0	0	0	0	0	0	12
Manahawkin,	———— ————	0	0	0	0	0	0	5
Vincent,	Josiah Philips, Æneas Miles,	5	1	2	0	0	0	34
Tuckahoe,†	———— ————	0	0	0	0	0	0	26
London Tract,	Samuel Carlisle,	0	0	1	0	0	0	37
Hilltown,	JAMES M'LAUGHLIN, Isaac Morris, Abel Jones, Thomas Matthias,	39	1	6	1	0	2	151
Lower Smithfield,†		0	0	0	0	0	0	26
Jacob's Town,	BURGISS ALLISON, WILLIAM STAUGHTON, James Cox,*	0	0	1	0	0	0	61
Pittstown,†	———— ————	0	0	0	0	0	0	134
Marcus Hook,	*John Ellis,* George Mustin,	0	0	0	0	0	0	17
Roxbury,	THOMAS FLEESON, John Levering, Titus Yerkes,	7	1	2	0	0	0	52
Penn's Manor,†	———— ————	0	0	0	0	0	0	18
West Creek,†	PETER GROOM,*	0	0	0	0	0	0	43
Shemokin,	JOHN PATTEN,	0	0	0	4	0	1	96
Amwell,	William Merrell, John Runyan,	16	0	0	0	0	0	45
		240	24	34	11	1	34	2626

NOTE.—The ministers' names are in SMALL CAPITALS. Licenced preachers in *italics*. Those marked thus * were not present. From the churches marked thus † received no intelligence. A dash ———— denotes no settled minister.

MINUTES

OF THE

PHILADELPHIA BAPTIST ASSOCIATION,

HELD AT PHILADELPHIA, OCTOBER 6TH, 7TH, AND 8TH,

1801.

October 6th.—At three o'clock, P. M., Brother William Rogers, agreeably to appointment last year, preached the introductory sermon, from Psalm lxxxiv. 4, "Blessed are they that dwell in thy house; they will be still praising thee."

2. After sermon, business was opened with prayer by Brother Samuel Jones, when Brother James Ewing was chosen moderator, and Brother William Staughton, clerk.

3. Letters from twenty-seven churches were read.

4. Application being made by a newly constituted church in Burlington for admission into this Association, they were cheerfully received.

5. Read the circular letter to the churches and appointed Brethren Rogers, Wilson, M'Laughlin, Allison, and Vanhorn to examine it, and report respecting it to the Association.

Brother M'Laughlin concluded by prayer.

Adjourned till half after eight o'clock to-morrow morning.

October 7th, half past eight o'clock, A. M.—Met pursuant to adjournment. Brother White prayed.

6. Brethren John Morgan, from England, John Ellis, and Jethro Johnson, being present, were invited to seats with us.

7. Received, from the Charleston Association, a letter and minutes; from the Warwick Association, a letter and minutes; from the Delaware, a letter and minutes, by their messenger, John Boggs, jun.; from New York, a letter and minutes, by their messenger, William Vanhorn; from the Stonington, Warren, and Shaftsbury Associations, minutes, with the printed corresponding letters.

Received also a letter from the Miami Association soliciting correspondence with us; on which we cheerfully entered.

8. Our Brethren Samuel Jones and Garner Hunt were appointed a committee to inspect the minutes and corresponding letters from different Associations, and report them to-morrow.

9. Appointed Brother Staughton to write to the Charleston Association; Brother Montanye, to the Warwick; Brother Ellis, to the

Delaware; Brother Horatio G. Jones, to the New York; Brother White, to the Miami; Brother Smalley, to the Warren; Brother Boggs, jun., to the Shaftsbury; and Brother Hough, to the Stonington.

10. Appointed messengers to the following Associations:—To the Delaware, Brethren Joshua Vaughan and Jethro Johnson; to the New York, Brethren Burgiss Allison, Samuel Jones, and Thomas Ustick; and to the Warwick, Brethren William White and Thomas B. Montanye.

11. Monies were sent to Brother Ustick, agreeably to the 15th minute of our last Association, from

Lower Dublin,	$6 07
Great Valley,	4 00
Philadelphia,	10 00
Vincent,	4 00
Height's Town,	3 00
	$27 07

Paid as directed, to Brother T. G. Jones.

12. Monies received by Brother Rogers, for the purpose expressed in the 16th minute of our last Association, from

Philadelphia,	$29 00
Lower Dublin,	8 20
Haight's Town,	5 00
Great Valley,	4 00
	$46 20

Which were by him applied as directed.

13. Monies were received towards the education fund from the following churches.

Lower Dublin,	$14 02
Hopewell,	15 52
Burlington,	15 00
Haight's Town,	12 00
Jacob's Town,	3 00
	$59 54

14. Several churches and individuals presented sums for the defraying of the expense attendant on the engraving of the proposed map; but as the amount was inadequate for the purpose, and as it was understood from several messengers that more money might be obtained, we recommend it to our churches, and to such individuals as may be disposed to send their subscriptions next year; but it is considered that the plate is to be the property of the Association, and the impressions to be disposed of at the lowest rate possible.

15. It is recommended that a portion of the first Tuesday in January, April, July, and October, be devoted to prayer for the diffusion of the gospel.

16. The remaining members of the Manahawkin church having some doubts on their minds, because of the fewness of their numbers, whether they exist as a church or no:—it is the sense of this Asso-

ciation, that the church still exists; and while they rejoice in that prosperity which has lately attended the preaching of the gospel among them, they exhort them to proceed to the reception of members and the election of officers.

Brother Fleeson concluded with prayer.

Adjourned till three o'clock, P. M.

Three o'clock, P. M.—Met pursuant to adjournment. Brother Boggs, sen., prayed.

17. Query from the church at Great Valley: Is it consistent with the independence of the churches, for the Association to admit any charges and publish them to the world, against a minister or member, without first referring to the church, to which he stands related?

Answer. This depends on circumstances: in some cases it is consistent, in others, not so.

18. Appointed a committee to attend to certain business, relative to the Dividing Creek church, agreeably to that church's request. This committee to consist of Samuel Jones, John Boggs, sen., Alexander M'Gowan, Henry Smalley, and Jonathan Bowen.

19. Supplies appointed for Manahawkin.

20. Supplies for Upper Freehold.

Brother Peter Groom prayed.

Adjourned to ten o'clock, A. M., to-morrow morning.

Sermon this evening by Brother Vanhorn, from Matt. vii. 28, 29, "And it came to pass, when Jesus had ended these sayings, the people were astonished at his doctrine; for he taught them as one having authority and not as the scribes."

October 8th.—Met according to adjournment. Brother Samuel Jones prayed,

21. The committee appointed to attend to certain business relative to the Dividing Creek church, report:—

That it referred to a variety of circumstances concerning Brother Peter Wilson, Brother John Rutter, and the said church: That Brother Rutter, since his becoming a Baptist, has been blameless, excepting as to his entering on the ministry, with regard to which the Dividing Creek church, through wrong influence, have been too precipitate:— That they are inclined to justify Brother Wilson altogether. That matters past ought to be buried; and that Brother Rutter be viewed as of good character.

22. The 13th of our last minutes, which respects the general conference, to be continued.

23. The committee appointed to examine the circular letter produced it, and it was unanimously approved.

24. Letters were read by our Brother Rogers, received by him from Brother Carey, at Serampore, in the East Indies, and from Dr. Hawes of England, respecting promising appearances among the Hottentots.

This Association exult in every prospect of the success of the gospel, and wish the missionaries God speed.

Brother Ustick prayed.

Adjourned to three o'clock, P. M.

Three o'clock, P. M.—Met according to adjournment. Brother Vaughan prayed.

25. The letters to the different Associations were read.

26. Brother Montanye was appointed to write to the church at Manahawkin.

27. The 18th minute of our last Association, which respects the stablishment of a missionary society, continued.

28. The following brethren are requested, when convenient, to visit the church at Lower Smithfield:—William White, James M'Laughlin, Isaac Carlisle, John Ellis, T. B. Montanye, G. Hunt, and such other of our brethren as can make it convenient. Brother Vaughan will supply the first Lord's day in December.

29. Brother Montanye to write the circular letter for next year.

30. The 16th minute of our last Association, relative to collections for the church at Manahawkin, to be continued.

31. The 20th minute of our last, which respects the annual sermon for the education fund, it is hoped will be still regarded.

32. Brother Boggs being about to remove from the precincts of this Association, Brother Smalley is appointed to preach the sermon next year; in case of failure, Brother M'Laughlin.

33. This Association, impressed with a sense of the numerous and laborious services of our venerable Brother Samuel Jones, with respect to the pecuniary and other affairs of the Association, while they solicit his future aids, beg his acceptance of their most affectionate and grateful acknowledgments.

34. Brother Ustick is requested to superintend the printing of the minutes.

35. The Association is appointed to meet on the first Tuesday in October, 1802, at two o'clock, P. M., at Philadelphia; but in case of the fever being there, to be held at Hopewell, New Jersey.

The moderator concluded with prayer.

Sermon this evening by Brother M'Laughlin, from Heb. ii. 3, "How shall we escape if we neglect so great salvation; which at the first began to be spoken by the Lord, and was confirmed unto us by them that heard him."

At a meeting of the trustees, October, 1800—

Resolved, That T. Ustick be appointed librarian to take charge of the books belonging to the Association, and make report of their condition.

B. ALLISON, Secretary.

Such as have in possession any of the books belonging to the Association, are requested to forward them to

THOMAS USTICK, Librarian.

CIRCULAR LETTER.

BY REV. JAMES EWING.

The Philadelphia Baptist Association convened in Philadelphia, October 6th, 7th, and 8th, 1801.

To the several churches thereunto belonging, sendeth Christian salutation.

Beloved brethren,—Under the smiles of an indulgent Providence, we have been once more so favored as to meet in this city, unawed by the angel of death. The interview has been comfortable, and our deliberations have been in peace.

Custom will lead you to expect an address from us in our collective capacity. We comply with the expectation; "not as having dominion over your faith, but as helpers of your joy."

We have entered upon a new century; and while it is yet the morning of it, let us take a view of some of the works of God in the last.

Ninety-four years have rolled on since the first meeting of this Association, the first in America, and then composed of only five churches; but viewing the present state of our connexion in this country, we perceive it to be as the thousands of Israel, embracing numerous Associations, composed of, at least twelve hundred churches, including more than a hundred thousand members.

The circumstances of our brethren in this country, prior to the Revolution, in several of the then colonies, were much the same as those of our brethren in Europe, at that time and since. Civil establishments of religion, the natural foes of civil and religious freedom and of the progress of truth, were only partial here; yet where they had a being, persecution of our brethren was the consequence, the establishment in Britain having considerable influence in those colonies where no such establishment actually existed, owing to the power of the British king in this country, who is the head of the established church, and who, as such, accordingly bestowed his favors.

But Jehovah changed the times, and so overruled the matter, that the then colonies not only became sovereign independent States, but have taken a national form under the federal constitution. The constitutions, and generally the laws of the individual States, and that of the United States, declaring and guarantying full religious freedom, we are not only released from that yoke of bondage which the witnesses for Christ have borne almost in every age and nation since the commencement of the Christian era; but we see the effects of this freedom in the increase of our connexion, which, since the Revolution, is comparable to an accelerated motion.

The display of the sovereignty of God in this progress of gospel truth is great, teaching us that Christ's kingdom needs no support from union with the governments of this world; that the more distinctly the line is drawn between them the better. Indeed, all attempts to unite them are in direct contempt of Christ's authority as

"Head over all things to the church;" directly destroy her glory, and effectually impede the general progress of truth. During the space of nearly fourteen hundred years, have men and devils attempted the church's destruction by such a union. The existence of civil establishments of religion in Europe, humanly speaking, presents an insurmountable barrier to the spiritual reign of Christ in that quarter; for while they remain, we see no way in which the pure gospel and unadulterated ordinances of Christ can have general countenance.

The course of Divine Providence induces the idea, that Zion's defence is opening another field for the displays of his grace. And, perhaps, while he pours out the vials of his wrath on those nations which have given their power to the beast; for the destruction of the monster produced by the union of church and state, in order that he may be "King over all the earth," he will show his gracious power, and "make the place of his feet glorious," where this part of antichristian tyranny has no existence.

Ever mindful of his promise, God, in the latter part of the last century, brought to the knowledge of those nations where the gospel was, large and populous parts of the world, which in former times were unknown; and, also, disposed the minds of his people in Europe to send the gospel there, in a way as unexpected.

The generality of the denominations of professed Christians having originally derived their various forms of ecclesiastical government, from attempts to mould the church after the model of the polity of the nation into which they were intended individually to be incorporated, and the civil support of which they sought and needed; having departed from the simplicity of the divine constitution, which knows no other aid but that of its divine head; their frame admitting of worldly grandeur and prosperity, as well as support and defence; and naturally leading them to court a civil establishment, made them unfriendly to each other; but, in a manner, as unexpected as unexampled, God weakened their mutual jealousies, and they have united in sending to, and, at a vast expense, supporting missions in those distant regions; and in that respect appear to have dropt their particular pursuits of temporal power and aggrandizement, which, as well as union, was necessary to their success in the work.

Many endeavors to christianize the heathen have proved abortive, owing to collateral attempts of the society which sent the missionaries to gain political power or exaltation thereby. But the order of our churches having never been derived from the wisdom or policy of man; not being framed according to the model of any body politic, we cannot, in any consistency therewith, have such views in sending or supporting the gospel where it is not; and so humanly speaking, are more likely to be successful in it. This consideration, over and above those commonly urged, calls upon us as a people, to exert ourselves in the great and important work.

Connected with this view of the subject, the success of the brethren of our denomination, in England, ought to arrest our attention. They have sent, and, with such pecuniary aids as the Lord stirred up others to afford them, have supported a mission in the idolatrous and far distant country of Hindostan, where the inhabitants, by their customs, appear to be more strongly fortified against the introduction of Christianity among them than perhaps in any other heathen land. Yet not only many of the people, but in some instances their Brahmans, lend a patient ear to the doctrines of the cross. The gospel by Matthew, printed in the language of that country, has reached America; and probably the whole of the Bible is by this time distributing among the blinded Hindoos in their native tongue by the extraordinary efforts of that mission.

The success of the missionary sent to the western Indians by our sister Association of New York; and the disposition to hear the gospel manifested by whole nations of them, when met in council, satisfied that neither he nor those who sent him, sought any temporal aggrandizement by, or emolument from them, claims our particular notice; it may operate as a stimulus upon us to be found in like exertions, hoping the Lord is about to come in his kingdom.

In comparing our happy circumstances with those of our brethren in past ages, or at present in other countries, we view ourselves as surrounded with calls to adore the Divine Sovereignty that has brought us into existence now, rather than four hundred years ago, and here rather than in Europe. And although we pretend not to know with certainty when "the earth shall be full of the knowledge of the Lord," yet the events of Divine Providence within the last twenty-five or thirty years are incentives to adore the "Head over all things to the church," that He, ever mindful of his purpose, is at least beginning, to bring about predicted events in ways declarative of his wisdom and care, securing the glory to himself by using unexpected means.

How safe is his church in his hand! How immovable! when unconnected with national governments, she rests alone on him as her firm foundation.

The time in which we live, the late providential occurrences, and the general appearance of things call loudly upon us as a people for particular exertions in duties arising from our circumstances. While in times of persecution, a decided testimony for the Gospel and Laws of Christ, and patience in suffering are required;—so now, besides that testimony, to cleanse our hands from seeking worldly honor, as connected with the affairs, offices or prosperity of the church of Christ, and to exert ourselves in sending the gospel where the Lord may farther open a door for it among the heathen, may be mentioned as some of those duties that providence demands from us.

We hope better things of you, than to suppose that you are negligent in prayer for the coming of Christ's kingdom; yet we cannot but conclude, from solid grounds, that together with importunity at the throne of grace, pecuniary exertions for the diffusion of the gospel are particularly necessary.

We also hope, that not only the Lord will incline you to make such exertions; but that you will look up to him as the disposer of all events, that he may both raise up persons endowed with missionary qualifications, and open "a great door and effectual" of gospel usefulness before them.

It is probable that difficulties will present themselves to you as individuals, in the prospects of usefulness in this way, as "that all you can do will be ineffectual; but be not discouraged. Let each one act conscientiously, according to the magnitude of the object, and the ability God has given, leaving it in his hand, and we shall have a solid hope that a blessing will follow; for it is common for the Lord to blast the blooming expectations of his people, and succeed those attempts made according to his will which promise less. Nor need we expect that Satan will refrain from attempting, by every method in his power, to impede any thing that may be thought of, or done to disturb or destroy the empire he has so long maintained among them. But to be the humble instruments in the Lord's hand, of sending that gospel, and those pure ordinances which European civil establishments of religion almost shut out or naturally hinder the progress of, to those poor heathen whose hearts the Lord has opened or may open,—to be thus the means of benefit to one poor soul, will unspeakably overpay all the exertions you may use, or expense that may accrue.

And finally, dear brethren, we exhort you to walk circumspectly. A time of such outward peace and prosperity is a time of peculiar trial. We are in danger of sinking into remissness in secret devotion, and thus becoming exposed to every temptation; of becoming worldly minded, and, by eagerly pursuing the accumulation of wealth, giving the lie to our profession of love to Christ, his people and laws; of conforming to the world in their customs and insipid conversation, and thereby encouraging infidelity. What can strengthen and encourage the infidel more than the worldly conduct and conversation of professors, and especially of those who exhibit a testimony for purity of doctrine, worship and discipline, according to the will of Christ?

But we have professed simply to follow him in these things, and as, on the one hand, we ought to do it as our privilege, our happy employment; so on the other, the world will busily compare our conduct with our profession. We earnestly beseech you to be beforehand with them in the comparison, and steadily consider whether your common conduct be according to the divine pattern you have professed and engaged to imitate. And seeing we are compassed about with crowds of spectators, some of them professed christians, some professed deists, and some who appear to care for none of those things, "let us lay aside every weight, and the sin which doth so easily beset us, and let us run with patience the race that is set before us, looking unto Jesus," as our pattern, glorying to tread in his footsteps; and as our support, knowing that we cannot make any progress in our professed subjection to him or for his glory, without assistance from him; but which he has promised, and will assuredly give to those who trust in him.

"Now the God of peace, that brought again from the dead our Lord Jesus, that great shepherd of the sheep, through the blood of the everlasting covenant, make you perfect in every good work, to do his will, working in you that which is well pleasing in his sight, through Jesus Christ: to whom be glory, for ever and ever. Amen."

By the Association,

JAMES EWING, Moderator.
WILLIAM STAUGHTON, Clerk.

THE MINISTERS AND MESSENGERS AT THE ASSOCIATION, AND STATE OF THE CHURCHES DURING THE YEAR.

CHURCHES.	MINISTERS AND MESSENGERS.	Baptized.	Received by Letter.	Dismis'd.	Restored.	Excom.	Deceased.	Members.
Lower Dublin,	Samuel Jones, John Holmes, Thomas Holmes,	0	1	0	0	0	0	75
Middletown,†	Benjamin Bennet,*	0	0	0	0	0	0	140
Cohansie,	Henry Smalley, Jonathan Bowen, David Gillman,	0	0	0	0	0	5	96
Great Valley,	David Jones,* John Boggs, *Horatio G. Jones,* *Thomas G. Jones,* Isaac Eaton, Daniel Cornog, Isaac Abraham,	0	4	2	0	0	2	65
Cape May,	John Stancliff,*	0	0	0	0	0	4	39
Hopewell,	James Ewing, John Blackwell, Levi Stout, Benjamin Stout,	33	3	9	0	1	4	222
Brandywine,	Joshua Vaughan, John Garret, Robert Frame, John Powell, William Griffith,	1	3	1	0	0	1	86
Montgomery,	Joshua Jones,* Peter Evans, Thomas Davis, Daniel Morgan, Silas Hough,	7	1	0	0	0	1	64
Kingwood,	Garner Hunt, Isaac Blue,	7	4	3	0	0	0	81
Haight's Town,	Peter Wilson, Peter Job,	8	1	9	0	0	3	329
Philadelphia,	Thomas Ustick, William Rogers, *Isaac Carlisle,* George Ingolls, Jeseph Keen, John Peckworth, Samuel Oakford,	7	11	4	0	6	3	150
Southampton,	Thomas B. Montanye, William Watts, Elias Yerkes, Abel Marple,	0	4	2	0	0	0	86
Knowlton,†	—— ——	0	0	0	0	0	0	17
New Britain,	William Waite, Benjamin Matthew, Edward Matthew, Isaac James, Erasmus Thomas,	2	2	6	0	0	1	93

CHURCHES.	MINISTERS AND MESSENGERS.	Baptized.	Received by Lett'r	Dismis'd.	Restored.	Excom.	Deceased.	Members.
Salem,	Joseph Lloyd, Erasmus Hogbin,	3	0	0	0	1	3	74
Dividing Creek,	*John Rutter,* William Mason, Amos Bradford,	0	0	0	0	0	1	56
New Mills,	ALEXANDER M'GOWAN, *Benjamin Hedger,* Jesse Cox,	23	0	6	1	1	2	135
Konoloway,	JOSEPH POWELL,*	27	3	1	0	0	4	65
Coram,†		0	0	0	0	0	0	40
Upper Freehold,	— —	0	1	0	0	0	1	79
Pittsgrove,†		0	0	0	0	0	0	12
Manahawkin,	— —	0	0	0	0	0	1	4
Vincent,	Æneas Miles,	1	0	2	0	1	1	32
Tuckahoe,	Elias Smith,	2	0	0	0	0	1	27
London Tract,†		0	0	0	0	0	0	26
Hilltown,	JAMES M'LAUGHLIN, Robert Shannon, John Mathias, Joseph Mathias,	3	0	2	0	1	0	151
Lower Smithfield,†		0	0	0	0	0	0	26
Jacob's Town,	BURGISS ALLISON, James Cox, Richard Sexton, Joseph Sexton,	0	0	8	0	0	1	52
Pittstown,†		0	0	0	0	0	0	134
Marcus Hook,	Richard Riley,	0	0	3	0	0	0	14
Ridge, in the township of Roxbury,	THOMAS FLEESON, John Levering, Jonathan Yerkes,	0	1	0	0	0	0	53
Penn's Manor,†		0	0	0	0	0	0	18
West Creek,	PETER GROOM, Joseph Chester,	5	0	0	0	3	0	46
Shemokin,†	JOHN PATTEN,*	0	0	0	0	0	0	96
Amwell,	Samuel Hunt, William Merrell,	10	0	0	0	0	0	55
Burlington,	WILLIAM STAUGHTON, Joseph Barber, William Collins,	4	0	0	0	0	0	18
		143	39	58	1	14	39	2756

NOTE.—The ministers' names are in SMALL CAPITALS. Licensed preachers in *italic*. Those marked thus * not present. From the churches marked thus † received no intelligence. A dash ——— denotes no settled minister.

MINUTES

OF THE

PHILADELPHIA BAPTIST ASSOCIATION,

HELD BY SPECIAL APPOINTMENT, AT HOPEWELL, NEW JERSEY,
OCTOBER 5TH, 6TH, AND 7TH,

1802.

October 5th.—At two o'clock, P. M., Brother Henry Smalley, agreeably to appointment last year, preached the introductory sermon, from Isa. ix. 6, "And the government shall be upon his shoulder."

2. After sermon, business was opened with prayer by Brother Ewing, when Dr. Hezekiah Smith, who was present as messenger from the Warren Association, was chosen moderator, and Brother Burgiss Allison, clerk.

3. Our ministering brethren present, viz., Benjamin Coles, of Oyster Bay, Long Island, W. Collier, of New York, and Peter Smith, of Miami,, were invited to seats with us.

4. Letters from twenty-six churches were read.

Prayer by the moderator.

Adjourned till half past eight o'clock to-morrow morning.

October 6th, half past eight o'clock, A. M.—Met according to adjournment. Prayer by Brother Wilson.

5. After finishing reading the letters from the churches belonging to the Association, a letter was read from the church at Mount Holly, requesting admission into our body; which was cheerfully granted.

6. Application also being made by a newly constituted church at Dover, in York county, in Pennsylvania, for admission into this Association, it was received.

7. Received letters from the following Associations: viz., Warwick, by their messenger John Palmer, with their minutes; Delaware, by their messenger John Boggs, jun.; New York, by their messengers Reune Runyan, Charles Lahat, and Lebbeus Lathrop, with their minutes; Warren, by their messenger Dr. Hezekiah Smith. Received also a copy of the minutes of the Miami Association, by Brother Peter Smith.

8. Appointed Brethren S. Jones, Staughton, and White, a committee to inspect the minutes and letters from the corresponding Associations, and report to-morrow.

9. The following brethren were appointed to write to the corresponding Associations: viz., Brother Ustick, to Charleston; Brother Montanye, to Warwick; Brother White, to Delaware; Brother

Staughton, to New York; Brother Wilson, to Stonington; Brother Smalley, to Warren; Brother Boggs, to Shaftsbury; and Brother Ewing, to Miami.

10. Appointed messengers to the following Associations:—To Warwick, Brethren Montanye and White; Delaware, Brother Vaughan; New York, Brethren Montanye, D. Jones, Wilson, and White; Warren, Brother Hezekiah Smith; Miami, Brother Peter Smith.

11. After reading the circular letter, Brethren Samuel Jones, David Jones, William Staughton, with Brother Montanye, the author, were appointed a committee to revise the same, and make report.

12. The following sums were contributed, viz.,

FOR THE EDUCATION FUND.		FOR THE CHURCH AT MANAHAWKIN.	
From Lower Dublin,	$10 00	From Haight's Town,	$5 00
Haight's Town,	12 00	Southampton,	4 00
Southampton,	8 00	Salem,	4 00
Salem,	15 00		
Jacob's Town,	5 00		
Burlington,	15 11		
Total,	$65 11	Total,	$13 00

13. It is recommended that the first Tuesday in January, April, July, and October, be observed as days of prayer, for the effusion of the Divine Spirit; and it is earnestly requested, that particular attention be paid to it.

14. Brother White is appointed to write the circular letter for the ensuing year.

15. A general conference not being likely to be accomplished, a plan was laid before the Association, designed to answer all the purposes, and the following committee appointed to examine the same, and report, viz., Brethren S. Jones, R. Runyan, W. Rogers, and T. Montanye.—Brother S. Jones, concluded by prayer.

Adjourned to two o'clock.

Two o'clock, P. M.—Met according to adjournment. Brother Rogers prayed.

16. Supplies granted to Manahawkin, Upper Freehold, and Dover, York county, Pennsylvania.

17. It is recommended to the churches belonging to this Association, to appoint a day, to have a discourse delivered in each of them, upon the subject of a mission for propagating the gospel in destitute places; to make a collection for a fund to defray the necessary expenses of the missionaries, and to forward the money to Brother Rogers, between this and the first of April ensuing.

It is agreed that a committee be now appointed to form a plan for a missionary society, and present the same at the next Association, and that Brethren S. Jones, B. Allison, W. Rogers, T. Ustick, and W. Staughton, be the committee.

18. The churches are requested to recollect, that an annual sermon is recommended to be preached, for the purpose of collecting money for the education fund, to be transmitted to the Association.

19. The committee to examine the "plan for a committee of cor

respondence," reported, and the plan was adopted as amended; and the following brethren are appointed as a committee to carry the same into execution: viz., S. Jones, B. Allison, W. Rogers, T. Ustick, W. Staughton, W. White, T. Montanye, J. Peckworth, Silas Hough, M. D., G. Ingles, T. Holmes, J. M'Leod, J. Holmes, and W. M'Gee. The plan is as follows:—

PLAN OF THE COMMITTEE OF CORRESPONDENCE.

I. That a general committee be appointed by the Philadelphia Association, for the purpose of corresponding with all the Baptist Associations, churches, and ministers, on the continent of North America.

II. That this committee be selected out of those ministers and private brethren who may reside in the city and vicinity of Philadelphia. Their number may consist of ten or fifteen, including a President, Vice President, Treasurer, and two Secretaries; two-thirds of whom may make a quorum for business.

III. That this committee open a correspondence with the several Associations, requesting an accurate account of its origin, constitution, numbers, increase, decrease, declensions, revivals, ministers, ordinations, &c.

IV. That this committee of correspondence meet once in the year, or as often as circumstances may require, whether in the city of Philadelphia, or in towns adjacent, for the purpose of examining the communications which may have been made, and to adjust the same as they may deem necessary.

V. That the committee publish once in the year, or in two years, as to them may appear necessary, a pamphlet, containing the most interesting and important intelligence, and that such periodical publication do not exceed in price one-half dollar.

VI. After the expence for printing, &c., be discharged, the overplus, if any, to be appropriated to the relief of ministers' widows and orphans; for the improvement of young ministers, or other laudable purposes, as to the committee may seem good.

20. The delegates of this Association do engage, on the part of themselves and the churches they represent, to pay at, or before, the next Association, the sum of two dollars for each church, for the purpose of defraying the expenses which may be incurred by a correspondence with the different parts of the Union, agreeably to the plan which this Association has adopted.

Brother Staughton concluded by prayer.

Adjourned to eight o'clock to-morrow morning.

Sermon in the evening by Brother Hezekiah Smith, from Heb. xiii. 20, 21, "Now the God of peace, that brought again from the dead our Lord Jesus, that great Shepherd of the sheep, through the blood of the everlasting covenant; make you perfect in every good work, to do his will, working in you that which is well-pleasing in his sight, through Jesus Christ: to whom be glory for ever and ever. Amen."

October 7th, eight o'clock, A. M.—Met according to adjournment.
21. Letters to corresponding Associations were read and approved.
22. According to information from Kentucky, the following are the numbers of communicants in the Baptist churches belonging to the respective Associations in that State.

In the Elkhorn Association,	- -	5,310	communicants.
" Green River "	- about -	800	"
" Salem "	- -	2,023	"
" Bracken "	- - -	753	"
" Tates' Creek "	- -	1,802	"
" S. Kentucky "	- - -	1,384	"
Total,	- - - -	12,072	

Allowing six Baptists in a congregation, to one communicant, which is a very moderate allowance, the number of Baptists in Kentucky will amount to 72,426.

It is supposed that throughout the whole of the United States, the societies of Baptists amount to 700,000 persons and upwards.

23. The brethren appointed to inspect the minutes and letters made their report.

24. The following brethren are appointed as a committee to prepare, and bring forward to the next Association, a set of rules for conducting the business of this Association; viz., S. Jones, W. Rogers, T. Ustick, W. Staughton, G. Ingles, and J. M'Leod.

25. The Association to meet next year on the first Tuesday in October, in Philadelphia; but should the epidemic then prevail in the city, to meet at Cohansie. In which case the clerk will give notice in the public prints.

Service to begin at three o'clock, P. M.

26. Brother M'Laughlin to preach the introductory discourse; and, in case of failure, Brother Ewing.

Sermon this evening by Brother Staughton, from Acts iii. 26, " Unto you first, God, having raised up his Son Jesus, sent him to bless you, in turning away every one of you from his iniquities."

CIRCULAR LETTER.
BY REV. T. B. MONTANYE.

The elders and messengers of the Philadelphia Association,
To the churches they represent send Christian salutation.

Beloved brethren,—We were highly pleased, and much gratified, in the enjoyment of such a general representation of the churches, and the kind reception we met by our sister church at Hopewell, while the cause of our convening in this place gave us pain. Philadelphia being once more visited by trying dispensations of Providence, her situation demands our united cry, that God would turn away this calamity from her, and her inhabitants to himself.

Anxious for your increase in knowledge, and to be instrumental in advancing the kingdom of our Lord the Messiah, we have chosen as the subject of this our epistle—The Baptism of the Holy Ghost. In making this choice at the present time, the following reasons have guided our pen:

1. That though this point has been often mentioned, we think seldom clearly explained; and for want of a right idea of it, the glory of the Gospel lessened.

2. It has, almost universally, been so blended with the work of regeneration and sanctification, that it is commonly called the inward baptism, and the only necessary preparative for heaven; whereas, it was never inculcated in this light in the Gospel, and we think ought not to be considered as constituting any part of the office work of the Divine Spirit in renewing the heart.

3. That haply we may be of use to some of our respected friends, by showing them, that, though they may be regenerated, and enjoy the highest consolation in the sweet incomes of the Holy Comforter, and the most sensible communion with Christ; yet, as all this does not constitute the baptism of the Holy Spirit, nor is designed by it in the sacred Scriptures, it follows of consequence, that, rejecting the water baptism, they have no baptism whatever, and ought cheerfully to submit to that prescribed in the example of Jesus Christ.

4. It being extremely absurd to hold one point of the Christian religion under the denomination of another, especially when there is no well founded evidence of its present existence.

To render this subject plain, and the truth of it familiar, we call your attention to the following considerations:

The term baptism of the Holy Ghost, is only to be found in the New Testament, and was first taught by the harbinger of Jesus Christ, Matt. iii. 11, "He shall baptize you with the Holy Ghost and with fire;" confining it wholly to the office work of the Saviour, in executing the trust committed to him by the Father; and so in Acts ii. 33, "Therefore, being by the right hand of God exalted, and having received of the Father the promise of the Holy Ghost, he hath shed forth this which ye now see and hear," which evinced the power of Christ, and confirmed the divine mission of John.

The subject itself is the fulfilment of prophecy and the accomplishment of the promise made by Jesus Christ to his disciples, Joel ii. 28, and recorded Acts ii, from the 16th to the 22d verse, "And it shall come to pass in the last days," saith God, "I will pour out of my Spirit upon all flesh, and your sons and your daughters shall prophesy," &c.; also in Luke xxiv. 49, "And, behold, I send the promise of my Father upon you: but tarry ye in the city of Jerusalem, until ye be endued with power from on high;" which promise is again mentioned by Luke, in Acts i. 4, 5, as the ground on which the apostles went to Jerusalem, and there in holy concert joined in prayer and supplication for the accomplishment of such qualifying aid, to promulge the knowledge of their exalted Redeemer.

The nature of this baptism, most clearly evinces it to be distinct, and materially different from that of regeneration. The one a still small voice, saying, "This is the way;" the other, that of "a rushing mighty wind." One invisible, "A white stone, and a new name given, which no man knew save he that had received it;" the other, to be seen, "Cloven tongues of fire sat on them." One internal, filling the heart with secret consolation, joy and pleasure; the other external, "The whole house where they were sitting."

This renders the term baptism proper, because they were immersed in the fountain of the Spirit, and thereby made partakers of such extraordinary and miraculous influence, as in regeneration and conversion were never promised.

The design of this baptism, is another important argument in favor of this idea. To qualify otherwise ignorant and unlearned men, to cope with all the greatness of this world, and to meet the wisdom of men, in all their formidable attacks, putting them to silence. To establish the greatest doctrines in the councils of heaven, or among men, God and man dwelling in one Christ; and that Jesus of Nazareth, crucified by the envious and treacherous Jews, was he; and, though the master was exalted, the disciple could effect, in his name, visible evidence of his Godhead, and by signs and miracles, as well as Scripture prophecy, prove him to be the Messiah promised to the fathers.

To establish the gospel dispensation, by the instrumentality of a few illiterate persons, raised up in the land of Judea, (who declared that the whole economy made known to the ancient fathers, the costly grandeur of the temple and the expence of its worship, was fulfilled, and all its glory exceeded, in him who expired on the accursed tree,) needed the power of omnipotence, to make its way against the formidable force raised in opposition. Another reason was to assure the apostles, primitive Christians, and all subsequent believers, that Jesus Christ was the Son of God, and only Saviour of Jews and Gentiles. For which reason, the Holy Ghost, in his miraculous gifts of speaking with divers tongues, fell on the Gentiles in a visible form, as upon the apostles on the day of Pentecost, Acts xi. 15, 16, "The Holy Ghost fell on them, as on us at the beginning;" which extraordinary gifts served to confirm Peter that he was doing right, in hearkening to the vision he had seen; and to satisfy the church of the divine right of all nations in common to partake of salvation by the cross of Jesus Christ.

The subjects of this baptism differ essentially from those of regeneration. The work of grace is upon the hearts of the unregenerated, bringing them from a state of moral death to life, from darkness to light, and from the power of sin, and service of Satan, to the liberty of the gospel, and the enjoyment of fellowship with God. Whereas, the baptism of the Holy Ghost was upon the apostles; who, having experienced the work of grace upon their souls, and being thereby made partakers of all that is peculiar to regeneration, could not be regenerated by the descent of the sacred Spirit, which being a work only once in the divine life, could not be effected again. As an assurance of this fact, they are declared to have "their names written in heaven," and Jesus Christ had manifested the Father to them, (John xvii. 6,) and "that they had known surely Christ came from God, and had believed on the Son of God," (verse 8.) "Flesh and blood had not revealed it unto them, but the Father in heaven." They are called by every near and dear appellation, that could express the love of God to them. And as for Cornelius, he had intercourse with God, and was acquainted with the power of renewing grace, as the cause of sending for Peter. As for the twelve on whom Paul laid his hands, none can doubt of their previous interest in Christ; for they are said to have believed. To render this point more clear, not only regeneration is not the baptism of the Holy Ghost, nor yet the receiving of the sacred Spirit; this is most clearly manifested in the case of the disciples, who, after the resurrection of Christ, were visited by him, and he breathed on them and they received the Holy Ghost, (John xx. 22,) no doubt as much, if not more, than believers in common; and yet, notwithstanding, they are ordered to tarry at Jerusalem until baptised of the sacred Spirit. All which join to show, that whatever any Christian may have gained in the experience of grace, he has no right to the term, baptised by the Spirit, unless such a person professing this miraculous attainment, for no other is called the baptism of the Holy Ghost, prove it by signs and wonders, as did the primitive Christians.

The effects which followed this baptism: Casting out devils; Paul dispossessed the damsel that had a spirit of divination, commanding the spirit, in the name of Jesus Christ, to come out of her, and it did; and also of others, by the power and in the name of Christ; speaking with new tongues—not such as all others were ignorant of, but such as they had never learned or understood before; taking up serpents without injury—so Paul had a viper fastened on his hand, which he shook off, and to the amazement of the beholders, received no harm, but their united testimony that he was more than mortal; drinking deadly poison, without hurt; laying hands on the sick, and they recover; the father of Plubius was healed of a fever and the bloody flux; the lame man from his mother's womb made whole, and the shadow of Peter effected the cure of many; (Acts v. 15, 16;) others were healed by handkerchiefs and aprons taken from the body of Paul: (Acts xix. 12:) all of which were then necessary for the confirmation of the gospel, and the establishment of Christianity in the world.

Here it is proper to remove some apparent difficulties, which are a means of puzzling the minds of many. First, What baptism the apostle denominates one baptism? We answer, The instituted appointment of Jesus Christ, which he authorised after his resurrection, which remains a standing ordinance in the church, and which Peter, when filled with the Holy Ghost, enjoined on Cornelius and the rest of the believing Gentiles, even after they were baptised with the Holy Spirit; though the baptism of the Spirit was never an essential prerequisite to water baptism; but a striking evidence to the Jews of the salvation of the Gentiles, and confirmation of the existence of grace in the heart; as only such were the subjects of his miraculous operations.

The next we meet is in 1 Corinthians xii. 13: "For by one Spirit are we all baptised into one body, whether Jews or Gentiles, and have been all made to drink into one Spirit." By attending to the chapter, you will at once perceive that the scope of it is upon the extraordinary work of the Spirit, and indeed miracles are named in verse 10, and divers tongues, which, as we have shown, were given to the Gentiles as well as the Jews. The former stood now, under the gospel dispensation, on an equal ground with the latter, and had come into the fellowship of the saints by the same miraculous evidence from heaven; and to us there seems no absurdity in saying that the same Spirit influences all nations to yield an obedience to the instituted appointments of Jesus Christ, and so come into the union of the body the church. As for sundry other Scriptures, such as Rom. vi. 3, 4., Col. ii. 12, 1 Peter, 3, 21, Gal. iii. 27, they have an evident relation to water baptism, and are no way connected with, nor yet refer to, the work of grace in the heart.

The narrow limits of a letter call us to a close. We must, therefore, leave you to gather further instruction from the few inferences deducible from the whole.

1. That though regeneration and sanctification be essential to the character of a Christian; yet neither of them constitute the baptism of the Holy Ghost.

2. However much you may enjoy of the Spirit, as the Spirit of life, light, and love; you have no Scripture grounds to call this inward baptism, and so the one baptism, and thereby live in the neglect of the appointments of Jesus Christ.

3. That as the baptism of the Holy Ghost was given for the confirmation of the gospel dispensation, it has effected its design; the sacred prophecy is fulfilled, and it has ceased.

4. That as the extraordinary work, and no other, is known in the gospel as the baptism of the Holy Ghost, and that took place after faith in Christ, or regeneration, we have no right to call regeneration baptism.

5. Though we are the hopeful subjects of divine grace, and live in the smiles of heaven; it is both our duty and privilege to submit to the appointments of Jesus Christ, as laid down in his word.

And now, dear brethren, you may perceive, that our intention is not to deny any of the blessed operations of the holy Ghost upon the human mind; but to distinguish between truth and error. While we write these things to you, we hope that God may give you and us more of his Spirit, that we may live unto Him, who has died for us. And as churches, we would exhort you to live in the Spirit, and grieve not the holy Spirit of God, whereby ye are sealed until the day of redemption. In the mean time, pray for us, that as instrumental of your joy, you and we may honor our profession by holy living, in the smiles of God's gracious Spirit.

Signed by order of the Association.

HEZEKIAH SMITH, Moderator.
BURGISS ALLISON, Clerk.

MINUTES OF THE PHILADELPHIA ASSOCIATION. 377

THE MINISTERS AND MESSENGERS AT THE ASSOCIATION, AND STATE OF THE CHURCHES DURING THE YEAR.

CHURCHES.	MINISTERS AND MESSENGERS.	Baptized.	Received by Letter.	Dismis'd.	Excom.	Restored.	Deceased.	Members.
Lower Dublin,	Samuel Jones, John Holmes, Thomas Holmes,	0	0	0	0	0	2	73
Middletown,	Benjamin Bennet,* J. Stillwell, Samuel Ogburn, Jacob Conover,	6	0	0	4	1	0	139
Cohansie,	Henry Smalley, Samuel B. Harris, Joseph B. Cook,	54	3	2	1	0	0	149
Great Valley,	David Jones, James Abraham,	0	0	0	0	0	3	62
Cape May,†	Jonathan Garman,*	7	0	0	0	0	1	40
Hopewell,	James Ewing, John Blackwell, James Stout, James Hunt, Andrew Stout, Hezekia Stout, Nathan Drake,	9	0	9	1	0	1	222
Brandywine,	Joshua Vaughan,*	5	0	0	0	0	2	89
Montgomery,	Joshua Jones,* Charles Humphrey, Silas Hough, John Hartel, jr.,	7	0	0	1	0	0	69
Kingwood,	Garner Hunt, David Stout, Daniel Bray, Isaac Blue,	3	1	2	0	0	1	81
Haight's Town,	Peter Wilson, John Flock, John Jones, Amos Hart, John Walling,	32	0	17	2	1	4	339
Philadelphia,	Thomas Ustick, William Rogers, *John Peckworth,* George Ingolls, John M'Leod,	23	10	8	5	0	3	167
Southampton,	Thomas B. Montanye, Thomas Folwell, Jeremiah Dungan,	4	2	0	0	0	1	91
Knowlton,†		0	0	0	0	0	0	17
New Britain,	William White, Edward Matthew, George Sigfried,	1	0	0	1	0	0	96
Salem,	Horatio G. Jones,* Benjamin Thompson, Henry Mulford,	25	2	0	0	2	4	99

CHURCHES.	MINISTERS AND MESSENGERS.	Baptized.	Received by Letter.	Dismis'd.	Excom.	Restored.	Deceased.	Members.
Dividing Creek,	JOHN RUTTER,*	4	0	0	1	0	1	58
New Mills,	{ ALEXANDER M'GOWAN, *Benjamin Hedger*,	22	1	58	1	0	3	96
Kolonoway,†	JOSEPH POWELL,*	0	0	0	0	0	0	65
Upper Freehold,	*John Morgan*,	11	5	1	0	0	0	75
Pittsgrove,	—— ——	0	0	0	0	0	0	124
Manahawkin,	{ Edward Jennings,	4	20	0	0	0	1	27
Vincent,	—— ——	2	0	0	0	0	1	33
Tuckahoe,†	—— ——	0	0	0	0	0	0	27
London Tract,†	—— ——	0	0	0	0	0	0	26
Hilltown,	{ JAMES M'LAUGHLIN, Philip Miller, John Mathias, W. H. Roland,	1	0	0	2	0	4	146
Jacob's Town,	{ BURGISS ALLISON, William Snowden, Asher Cox, James Cox,	5	2	1	0	0	0	57
Marcus Hook,	—— ——	4	1	0	0	0	0	19
Roxbury,	THOMAS FLEESON,*	2	0	2	0	0	0	52
Amwell,	{ Nicholas Ott, John Teurny,	4	0	0	0	0	1	58
Burlington,	{ WILLIAM STAUGHTON, Isaac Gifford, Elijah Condon,	12	3	0	0	0	1	32
Mount Holly,	{ Jesse Cox, George Allen, Edward Thomas,	0	0	0	0	0	0	52
Dover, York county,	—— ——	0	0	0	0	0	0	15
		247	50	100	19	4	34	2695

NOTE.—The ministers' names are in SMALL CAPITALS. Licensed preachers in *italic*. Those marked thus * were not present. From churches marked thus † received no letter. A dash —— denotes no settled minister.

The Rev. JOHN STANCLIFF, of Cape May, died on the 19th of January, 1802.

MINUTES

OF THE

PHILADELPHIA BAPTIST ASSOCIATION,

HELD BY SPECIAL APPOINTMENT, AT COHANSIE, NEW JERSEY,
OCTOBER 4TH, 5TH, AND 6TH,

1803.

October 4th.—At three o'clock, P. M., Brother James M'Laughlin being prevented by affliction in his family, from attending, Brother James Ewing preached the introductory sermon, from Matt. xxiii. 8, "One is your Master, even Christ; and all ye are brethren."

2. After sermon, business was opened with prayer by Brother Allison, when Brother Samuel Jones was chosen moderator, and Brother William Staughton, clerk.

3. Letters from twenty-nine churches were read.

Adjourned to nine o'clock, to-morrow morning. Brother Rogers concluded by prayer.

October 6th, nine o'clock, A. M.—Met according to adjournment. Prayer by the moderator.

5. After reading the letters from the churches belonging to the Association, a letter was read from the second Philadelphia church, and another from the second Hopewell church, requesting admission into our body; which was cheerfully granted.

6. Our Brother Jacob Bishop, being present, was invited to a seat with us.

7. Received letters from the following Associations: viz., Warwick, by their messenger Benjamin Montanye, with their minutes; Charleston, with their minutes; from Middle District Association, with their minutes only; from New York, the corresponding letters, with their minutes; from Delaware, a letter by Thomas G. Jones, with a copy of their minutes.

8. Having obtained a parcel of minutes through the medium of Brother Herrick, from the Rensellaer Association, this Association rejoicing in their prosperity, are desirous of commencing a correspondence with them.

9. Learning from a minute in the Delaware Association, that Joseph Flood has not only preached the plurality of wives, but actually put the pernicious doctrine into practice, we join with our sister Asso-

ciation in cautioning the churches against him as an excommunicated person.

10. London Tract and Conolaway churches having requested dismission from us, the former to the Delaware, the latter to the Baltimore Association, this Association agrees to their dismission.

11. The following brethren are appointed to write to the corresponding Associations; Brother Montanye, to the Warren; Brother Allison, to the Charleston; Brother Ellis, to the New York; Brother Hough, to the Warwick; and Brother Vaughan, to the Delaware.

12. The New York and the Warwick Associations having unitedly requested that three of ten brethren whom they have named, be appointed as a council to assist in the adjustment of some difficulties subsisting between them; this Association appoints Brethren Samuel Jones, David Jones, and Burgiss Allison; and in case of the sickness or death of either of these, Brethren Wilson and Ewing.

Brother Rogers prayed.

Adjourned to half past two o'clock.

Half past two o'clock, P. M.—Met according to adjournment. Brother Staughton prayed.

13. Query from the first Church of Philadelphia: "Is it in order to have a moderator appointed in our Association, who is not a member of one of the churches belonging to it, and a delegate at the same time to the Association from the church so belonging?"

Answer: This Association is not of opinion that it is, strictly speaking, out of order to have a moderator appointed, who is not a member of any of the churches which compose this body; yet, in addition to other considerations, his being unacquainted with the course of our business, and his inability, by reason of absence, to discharge some duties which among us devolve on the moderator in the interval of our meetings, render such a choice improper.

14. Collected for the education fund:

Lower Dublin,	$10 35
Haight's Town,	10 00
Southampton,	8 00
Salem,	15 00
Burgiss Allison,	2 00
Burlington,	12 56
	$57 91

15. Appointed a committee, consisting of Brethren George Ingles, John Holmes, and William Magee, to enquire into the expenses which have attended such of our brethren as have visited destitute churches for the two years past.

16. After reading the circular letter, Brethren David Jones, W. Staughton, M. A. M'Gowan, H. Smalley, and B. Allison were appointed a committee, together with the author, to revise it for publication.

17. Supplies for Sculltown, Upper Freehold, Manahawkin, Hopewell, Frankford, Philadelphia, and Dover.

Adjourned till eleven o'clock to-morrow morning.

Sermon in the evening by Brother B. Montanye, from 1 John iii. 5, "And ye know that he was manifested to take away our sins."

October 7th, eleven o'clock, A. M.—Met according to adjournment.

18. A letter was read from Brethren Bryan, Vanhorn, and Lahatt, requesting the aid of our funds for the improvement of Thomas Brown, a member of the church at Newark, he being a young man of very promising gifts for the ministry. The moderator is requested to write to the brethren on the subject.

19. Resolved, That the studies of any young man who may apply to this Association for assistance in his learning, shall be directed in such a way as the Association then sitting shall think proper: the extent of the term of his studies is not to exceed one year.

Brother Smalley prayed.

Adjourned to half past two o'clock.

Half past two o'clock, P. M.—Met according to adjournment. Brother Vaughan prayed.

20. The letters to the corresponding Associations were read. Brethren Peckworth and Vaughan were appointed messengers to the Delaware Association; Brethren Montanye and Allison, to the Warwick; Brother Montanye, with the committee, to the New York.

21. The plan of a missionary society was read, and with some alteration approved and recommended. It is also recommended that sermons be preached for the education and mission funds.

22. It is hoped the quarterly days of prayer will be continued through the churches.

23. Report of the corresponding committee was received.

At a meeting of the committee of correspondence at Lower Dublin, September 20, 1803,—

Resolved, That the recording secretary be directed to copy from the minutes, a statement of the intelligence that has been received to be presented to the Association.

The committee accordingly report, that they have received,

I. A view of the rise and progress of the churches composing the Otsego Association, in the west part of New York State, by A. Hosmer and John Lawton, forwarded to Brother Ustick by John Lawton.

II. A letter from Andrew Brown, a member of the Rensellaerville Association in the west of New York State, dated Berne, August 8th, 1803, and with it the minutes of the Association from 1799 to 1802, inclusive.

III. A short history of the Baptist churches in Wayne and Luzerne counties, Pennsylvania, forwarded July 8th, 1803, by Samuel Stanton, of Mount Pleasant, to Brother Rogers.

IV. A communication from the Roanoke District Association, forwarded by their committee, August 1st, 1803, to Brother Ustick, in which they furnish us with a short history of their rise and progress, and mention their intention of forwarding annual accounts.

V. A letter from Benjamin Watkins, of Powhattan county, Virginia, forwarded to Brother Rogers, in which he gives a short account of the Middle District Association. He has also sent several of the minutes for 1802 and 1803.—A true extract.

WILLIAM STAUGHTON, Recording Secretary.

The committee adjourned to the 26th of April, 1804; to meet at Philadelphia, at 3 o'clock, P. M.

24. Brother Benjamin Thaw, of Philadelphia, was appointed to supply the vacancy, in the corresponding committee, occasioned by the decease of Brother Thomas Ustick.

25. Brother Staughton is appointed librarian to the Association, in the place of our late Brother Ustick, to whom it is requested that the books may be forwarded, in order to the making out a regular catalogue of the whole.

26. Brother M'Laughlin to preach the Association sermon next year; in case of failure, Brother T. B. Montanye.—Brother Allison is appointed to write the circular letter.

27. Brother Staughton is requested to superintend the printing of the minutes.

28. The Association is to meet next year, on the first Tuesday in October, in Philadelphia; and in case of the disease in the city, at New Britain.

The Association closed with an address and prayer by the moderator.

Sermon this evening by Brother T. B. Montanye, from Jer. xxxi. 9.

This Association recommends to the churches the edition of the Bible now publishing by Mr. Matthew Carey, Philadelphia, as worthy their patronage.

CIRCULAR LETTER.
BY REV. WILLIAM WHITE.

The elders and messengers of the Philadelphia Baptist Association, To the churches they represent, send Christian salutation.

Beloved brethren,—As it has been our custom to address you annually in an epistolary way; in conforming therewith this year, we have deemed it expedient to continue an investigation of the office-work of the Holy Ghost. In our last year's epistle, relation is had to the work of the Spirit in qualifying the apostles to discharge the great duties entrusted to them; but we shall confine ourselves to that part which relates to preparing those that were given to Christ to redeem, for the fruition of happiness in the presence of God. When we speak of the Holy Ghost, we mean the third person in the divine essence, to whom many significant titles are applied, the consideration of which, will probably be edifying. He is called the Holy Spirit, Psalm li. 11, and Eph. i. 13; intimating thereby, that such is the purity of his nature, being purity in the abstract, that there is an absolute necessity that those who would enjoy the fellowship of the Spirit, Phil. ii. 1, should be holy, not using the members of the body, which is the temple of the Holy Ghost, 1 Cor. vi. 19, in the service of sin. He is also called the Spirit of holiness, Rom. iv. 1, because he implants a principle of holiness in all the elect; and forasmuch as there is not any thing amiable or lovely in God's dear children, but what is the fruit of the Spirit, Gal. v. 22. Eternity is ascribed to him, and, therefore, he is called the eternal Spirit, Heb. ix. 14, to show that he is not God by office, or in a figurative sense only; but that, as he possesses eternity, one of the attributes of the divine nature, he is truly and properly God. He is called the Spirit of grace, Heb. x. 29, because the holy Scriptures, given by inspiration of the Spirit of God, make known all the gracious designs of Jehovah towards his people; and because he implants gracious affections, and applies the blessings of grace to the subjects of it. He is called the Comforter, John xiv. 16, by reason of that support which pious men derive from him, when under affliction. He is styled the Spirit of promise, Eph. i. 13, with relation to his bringing the promises to our view, applying them to us, so as exactly to suit our particular cases, and enabling us to take consolation from them: or, because the marvellous descent of the Spirit on the day of Pentecost was the fruit of promise, as well as the indwelling and aid of the holy Spirit to believers, to whom it is promised, that he shall abide with them forever, John xiv. 16. He is called the Spirit of the Lord, 2 Cor. iii. 17, and the Spirit of Christ, Rom. viii. 9, denoting that he comes in consequence of covenant stipulations, for which cause Christ is said to receive gifts for men, Psalm lxviii. 18, and to shed forth the Spirit, Acts ii. 32, and to send the Comforter to abide with the disciples, John xvi. 7; and lastly, he is called the Spirit of glory, because he gives a foretaste of it—assures us of our right to it—and prepares us for the complete enjoyment of it.

In treating further on this subject, we shall show, 1st, That the children of the Lord only, are made partakers of the Holy Spirit in its operations on their hearts. And 2dly, What is effected by the Holy Ghost in such. Many well meaning persons have certainly handled this subject very injudiciously: and we are convinced, if they would but for a moment consider, they must see into what difficulties they are involved; and that if they have a system of doctrine at all, they must systematically become Armenians, as it is impossible to hold the precious doctrines of grace upon such ground. It is not uncommon for many, from whom we might have expected better things, after treating upon some of the sublime doctrines of the gospel, in applying their subject and addressing impenitent and unrenewed sinners, to tell them God's most holy Spirit has been striving with them from their infancy up, and that hitherto his attempts have been unsuccessful. If such doctrine is according to godliness, brethren, you will readily discover that the sinner, and not the Spirit of God, is omnipotent; and that from henceforth, instead of saying confidently, that the dead shall hear his voice and live, John v. 25, we must always add, provided men will condescend to let the Holy Spirit work, since then, and not till then, shall they be quickened or made alive. Such doctrine, is evidently in direct opposition to the Scriptures of truth; for the sinner, prior to regeneration, is always represented as passive, and therefore is declared to be dead, Eph. ii. 1, and is said to be born; to be begotten. As the creature begotten, cannot be said to be active prior to his existence, or be the instrument of its own existence, these expressions fully show, that it does not depend upon the favorable reception the divine Spirit meets with, that the work of grace is effected in the soul. The work of the Spirit is called a creation, Ps. li. 10, 2 Cor. v. 17, in allusion to an almighty agent giving existence to the system of nature, both with respect to matter and form. As there was no pre-existing matter to form the present material world, and consequently infinite power was necessarily engaged in producing it, these phrases evidently show, that the sinner is not an effectual agent to hinder the work, and that nothing can possibly frustrate that grace which creates the soul in Christ Jesus to good works. In addition to what has been said it will be sufficient to observe, that the language of holy writ is absolute: "They shall be my people," 2 Cor. vi. 16; "they shall be willing," Psalm cx. 3; "which were born, not of the will of the flesh," John i. 13; "all that the Father giveth me shall come," John vi. 37; "the dead shall hear my voice," John v. 25.

Some urge the strivings of the Spirit, as essential to constituting a judicial right in God to punish the finally impenitent. This may suit well enough for those that believe in general redemption and universal provision; but how it suits with the Calvinistic scheme, (which we believe to be founded on the word of God,) we cannot comprehend. Such doctrine is one of the greatest insults that can be offered to the Divine Being. It supposes that the infinite Jehovah, intends no good to the sinner, but on the contrary has determined to make him miserable; not having sufficient reason to make him so, and knowing that he has no power nor inclination to receive Christ and his benefits, yea, that God himself does not intend that he shall, he will make him some insincere offers of salvation, and afford him, what some persons call, common operations of the Spirit, which he knows will be entirely ineffectual; and, after this pretence of trying to save him, very gravely tells him, that for his not letting the Spirit convert him, he must be miserable to all eternity. It would be hard to say worse of the great God, than what is said of him in the above sentiment; for, therein he is charged with hypocrisy and cruelty—hypocrisy, for his only making pretence to commisserate the case of the sinner and afford him relief; and of cruelty, since, on such principles, men are not punished as offenders, but simply as creatures. It makes God proceed therein, not as the moral governor of the world, but upon the ground of arbitrary or despotic authority. You will readily perceive, brethren, that it is not merely the want of faith and repentance, that is the procuring cause of the sinner's destruction, but a want of moral rectitude, of coming up to the requirements of the divine law; and, therefore, there is no need that God should seek an occasion against him, forasmuch as there is sufficient reason that he should punish men, even if no Saviour had been provided. As for common operations of the Spirit and days of grace, these are links of the same chain, and are necessary to help the legal preacher along: but though they may be necessary to the system of the Armenian, they are equally unscriptural. As to the first, there is no mention made of them in any part of the sacred oracles—they have existed only in the fancies of men; and the latter opinion, which that much abused scripture, Luke xix. 42, is used to support, is far from being substantiated thereby. The text in question, had respect simply to the treatment of Christ as the promised Messiah; for the rejection of whom, after his mission had been attested by so many miracles, the city of Jerusalem was doomed to a dreadful overthrow, and the Jewish commonwealth wholly ruined: but the text has no relation whatever to the day of their salvation being past; for it is manifest, that many of those very persons, of whom it has been said that their day of grace was past, were afterwards converted under the preaching of Peter. See Acts ii.

But let us inquire further, upon what the abettors of this doctrine build their theory. It is certain, that these sentiments have been chiefly gathered from observing a kind of legal exercise, which more or less exists in the hearts of unregenerated persons who sit under the gospel, and especially if the ministry be powerful and alarming; and also from some passages of holy writ, which have been amazingly misunderstood.

As to the first, it may be properly called the workings of natural conscience; such is the evidence which divine truth brings with it to the mind, searching the hearts of the children of men, bringing to light their enmity against God, and their immoral conduct generally. Hence, sinners, merely by the light of reason, perceiving that God's holy law condemns them, and that the penalty of it is no less than eternal misery, are at times very uneasy. Paul says, "the Gentiles which have not the law are a law unto themselves," and that "their thoughts accuse or excuse each other, their conscience in the mean time bearing witness." By way of inference, he adds, " which show the work of the law written in their heart," Rom. ii. 15. Here the apostle plainly accounts for the above-mentioned feelings of unregenerate persons, which he intimates do not come from the immediate operations of the Holy Ghost, but from the law, some faint traces of which continue in the mind: and that it is conscience, and not the Spirit of God, which bears testimony to their actions, the result of which is, that their thoughts accuse or excuse one another. Is it any wonder, therefore, that persons sitting under a gospel ministry, hearing the word and beholding the ordinances, and enjoying withal a pious education and the godly example of religious parents, (for it is unregenerate persons of that class who feel most uneasy,) should sometimes, when under some qualms of conscience, enter upon some legal duties? The same matter is forcibly illustrated in the case of Felix, Acts xxiv. 25. It is said, Paul "reasoned," (not a word about the strivings of the Spirit;) that the subjects were "righteousness, temperance, and judgment," (very suitable indeed to alarm a rapacious, rioting, and wicked governor;) that he, as is usual with such, trembled at the thought of a day of retribution: and the whole of this is attributed to Paul, and not to the Spirit. It has been a prevailing opinion, that these feelings are peculiar to youth; but then it must be remembered, that it is only in such (as has been before observed) as enjoy religious instruction. And as for others, however young, they appear to be as insensible as those in mature age who live carelessly. It may be again remarked, that such as have lived all the early part of their lives without religious instruction, when, in the course of divine Providence, they are cast under a powerful ministry, become as much disturbed, at times, as persons do in youth. From all which we may infer, that these feelings are not from the Spirit of the Lord, working in persons in early life, and trying to make them Christians, who, not being able to effect it, at length, when old, leaves them as persons out of the reach of mercy—and, as some tell us, because their day of grace is past; for we find that many, very many of that description of persons, are afterwards converted to God, and live sober and religious lives.

Those texts which have been understood as countenancing the striving of the Spirit in all men, we shall consider so far as the bounds of a letter will admit. We are frequently reminded of John xvi. 8, as a text in point, to prove the doctrine; but, by consulting the context, it will appear, that the apostles were the subjects of the promise, and that it did not relate to the workings of gracious affections in them by the Spirit, (for these they enjoyed before,) but the effusion of the Holy Ghost, which they were to wait for in Jerusalem, that they might "be endued with power from on high," Luke xxiv. 49. By "the world," is primarily intended the Jewish nation, a vast multitude of whom were then at Jerusalem keeping the feast; by the fulfilment of Christ's promise, in the outpouring of the Spirit, they were reproved for, or convinced of sin, not only in putting Christ to death, but of not believing on him, as the Messiah—of righteousness, either his personal rectitude, being no impostor, or more especially that it was he who was the subject of Daniel's prophecy, of whom it was foretold that he should "bring in everlasting righteousness," Dan. ix. 24; and of judgment, because, by the outpouring of the Spirit, complete evidence was given that he was really risen from the dead, and consequently thereby giving assurance of his coming to sit in judgment on them, Acts xvii. 31.

Nor can Heb. vi. 4, be brought to prove the doctrine. As the being made partakers of the Holy Ghost there intends, not his regenerating influences, but merely gifts, or ministerial abilities. Such was the case with Balaam and Judas. Christ says, "Rejoice not that the devils are subject to you; but rather rejoice because your names are written in heaven," Luke x. 20. When St. Paul says, that "the manifestation of the Spirit is given to every man to profit withal," 1 Cor. xii. 7, he has respect to gifts, and not to grace; for by the "every man," is meant the gifted persons in the church of Corinth; and his design is to show, that although their gifts differed widely, yet they were given by the same Spirit for the edification of the church, and would be profitable to the body.

But it may be objected, that the holy Spirit is said to "strive with man," Gen. vi. 3; to be resisted, Acts vii. 51; and vexed, Isa. lxiii. 10. We have no inclination to deny that the Spirit may strive, be resisted, and vexed in a certain sense; but not in the sense in which the words are commonly used. It is manifest that the Spirit in the apostles and prophets is intended, when said to strive, to be vexed, and resisted by the impenitent. As to the first, the Spirit in Noah was intended; and in this sense it is the apostle Peter affirms, (1 Pet. iii. 19,) that Christ preached to those antediluvians who are now in prison, because that his Spirit was in Noah as a preacher of righteousness, and they were strove with in the ministry of the word. When it is said that the children of Israel vexed his holy Spirit, as in the above text, it is also added, which he put in him (Moses), by whose right hand they were led. And it is also plain, that the same thing is intended in the Acts. For Stephen, in charging the Jews with resisting the Holy Ghost, observes, they did as their fathers had done before them, who persecuted and slew the prophets which showed the coming of the Just One, of whom (says he) you have been the betrayers, and murderers, thereby resisting and rejecting the testimony of the Holy Ghost as they did. A parallel passage with those mentioned is Zech. vii. 12, "Yea, they made their hearts as an adamant stone, lest they should hear the law, and the words which the Lord of hosts hath sent in his Spirit by the former prophets."

We have now, brethren, briefly noticed the principal places in holy writ, which have been supposed to countenance the strivings of the Spirit in all men: and taking it for granted that what has been said is sufficient, we shall now proceed to show some Scripture arguments, to prove that the Holy Ghost is given to the elect only.

By the good work begun in the people of God, (Phil. i. 6,) most unquestionably must be meant, the operations of the Spirit of the Lord in their souls. But if so, how can we be assured that it will be performed until the day of Christ, if, according to the abovementioned sentiment, this work does not always prove victorious—is not always completed—yea, is absolutely relinquished and the subjects of it suffered to perish eternally? Surely, upon this hypothesis, the apostle's reasoning is very inconclusive, and the argument advanced with a design to encourage, must have had quite a contrary effect for they would reply, How can this be, when you constantly assure us that this work may be, and often is, frustrated? All evangelical obedience, being the fruit arising from the holy Spirit, is made the evidence of adoption; "For as many as are led by the Spirit of God are the sons of God," Rom. viii. 14. But in case men may possess the divine Spirit, and yet be lost, then the evidence of adoption is vague and uncertain; and it follows, that the having of this Spirit in his influence is no evidence at all, and the reasoning impertinent. The apostle to the Galatians speaks of receiving the Spirit by the hearing of faith (or the gospel which is so called), Gal. iii. 2; but if God ordinarily uses the gospel, through which to communicate the gifts and graces of the Spirit, then every man has not the Spirit, forasmuch as the gospel is withheld from many nations of the earth. In the epistle to the Romans, the having of the Spirit is made the criterion of belonging to Christ, Rom. viii. 9, "If any man have not the Spirit of Christ he is none of his." But if every man has the Spirit, it is no criterion at all, or else every man is a Christian, an adopted child of God; but the apostle, making it a test by which to try our standing, supposes clearly that some have not the Spirit of Christ, and therefore are not his. The same apostle to the church of Corinth, (1 Cor. ii. 14, 15,) draws a line of distinction between the natural and spiritual man; but if all have the Spirit, there can be no distinction; in vain does he talk of a spirit of discernment in divine things, wherein they differ from other men; and he must surely have been mistaken, when he said the things of the Spirit of God are foolishness to such; but if we understand him as making a clear distinction between the believer and unbeliever—the one having the Spirit of God and the other not—then there is a beauty in his reasoning, and not else. But, brethren, it is of no use to multiply quotations in a case so plain; we shall therefore only make an observation or two on the following passages, and leave them to your meditations. Paul to the Thes. iv. 8, says, "Who also hath given unto us his holy Spirit." John, in his first epistle says, "Hereby we know that he abideth in us, by the Spirit which he hath given us," (ch. iii. 24,) "Hereby know we that we dwell in him and he in us, because he hath given us of his Spirit," (ch. iv. 13.) You will remark, brethren, that the above are addressed to the churches of Christ and consequently to all believers composing them, and not to men of the world at all. Now, when he says, he hath given it us, it is clearly implied, that he has not given it to others; and as our bodies are temples of the Holy Ghost, and we know, by the indwelling of the Spirit, our union to Christ; therefore, let us never part with this precious test of an interest in the favor of God. But to crown all, and to show with certainty, putting the matter beyond all doubt, that every man has not the Spirit of the Lord, in Jude 19, it is expressly said, "These be they who separate themselves, sensual, having not the Spirit."

We come to show what is effected by the Holy Ghost in the elect, all of whom are effectually called to the knowledge of God and finally saved. All the elect are called the mystical body of Christ, of which he is the Head; and it is not only said that the church (complete) is the fulness of him that filleth all things; but it is also affirmed, that there is a fulness in him, Col. i. 19, out of which all his people receive grace for grace. Therefore, provision has been made in Christ for all that were given to him; and as they are justified by his blood and saved from wrath through him, so also, by the holy Ghost which Christ sheds forth, they are completely emancipated from the tyranny of the prince of darkness, and made meet for the inheritance among the saints in light.

The first work, in order, effected by the holy Spirit, is regeneration, which consists in an infusion of spiritual life into the soul. In this work, the creature is wholly passive; so that, instead of doing any thing of a preparatory nature, in order to invite the Spirit to undertake and effect it, men, on the contrary, are represented as "dead in trespasses and sins," Eph. ii. 1, as having hearts full of "enmity against God," Rom. viii. 7. From this principle, thus implanted, flow all those holy affections, such as faith, hope, love, and humility, which are usually denominated graces of the Spirit, because they originate from him and are all of grace. Notwithstanding the spiritual man, thus begotten, is perfect with relation to parts, he is not so in stature; for those graces become more vigorous under divine cultivation, which we shall have occasion to notice hereafter. This work is instantaneous; some examples of which we find in the New Testament, as in Paul's conversion, that of the jailor, and of the three thousand under Peter's sermon. Conversion and regeneration are distinct from each other, and by no means the same thing, and the former is an effect of the latter; the former being brought about through the gospel preached as means, whereas the latter is immediately from the Spirit of God, without any instrument whatever. The divine Spirit does, by the word, effectually convince of sin, causing the regenerate soul to loathe it—makes known the amazing depths of misery into which it has been plunged by the fall—gives a discovery of divine justice as demanding the punishment of the guilty; and it is in consequence of these views, that so much alarm is created, and such dreadful apprehensions of divine wrath are felt. It is peculiarly the office-work of the Spirit to discover the Lord Jesus, in all his glory and fulness, to such; "He shall take of mine and show it unto you," John xvi. 14; "No man can call Jesus Lord, but by the Holy Ghost," 1 Cor. xii. 3. So that regenerated sinners, beholding the plenitude of grace that is in Christ, and made sensible of their extreme need of him, by discovering more and more their spiritual poverty and weakness, being thus taught of the Spirit, they come to Jesus, John vi. 45. A soul deeply convinced of sin, and viewing the divine perfections, would not have courage sufficient to approach unto God, were it not for the gracious promises in the word to the weary and heavy laden; but in vain does the convinced sinner essay to take hold upon the promise, until the Spirit of promise (Eph. i. 13) make an application of them to him. How desirable is it to experience a manifestation of divine favor, and to enjoy those raptures which Jehovah sees meet to bestow on many of his people when first initiated into gospel liberty! The apostle says, "the love of God is shed abroad in our hearts by the Holy Ghost which is given to us," Rom. v. 5. Many are the powerful temptations that assault us, so that by reason of contending passions for victory over us, and the prince of darkness presenting sin in its most alluring form, we feel our weakness and frequently despair of making head against them. But behold, we are "strengthened with might by his Spirit in the inner man," Eph. iii. 16. Yea, when our way seems hedged up on every side, so that there seems no way to escape, and error, like a flood, carries all before it. Yet, says the prophet, "the Spirit of the Lord shall lift up a standard against the enemy," Isa. lix. 19. Mixing with the world and being necessarily engaged in temporal concerns, we often get into a lukewarm state and experience spiritual languor and the consequence, a loss of the sensible presence of God. But the divine Spirit disengages us from time-things, dissipates our coldness, invigorates our souls, and, after showing us that it is easier to lose than to regain those divine joys, transports us with a view of the unchangeable love of God. Having lost a spirit of prayer, so that the heavens seem as brass above, and the earth as iron beneath us, at the same time a preached gospel making no impression, and the holy Scriptures seeming like a sealed book, this divine Spirit " helps our infirmities with groanings which cannot be uttered," Rom. viii. 26 : and giving efficacy to the word preached and read, we can once more take delight in public and secret devotions. It is by the agency of the Spirit our perception of divine things is enlarged. It is truly desirable that we should not be always children tossed to and fro by the sleight of men, but on the contrary become acquainted with the mysteries of the gospel —be built up in our most holy faith and become firmly established thererein: these favors are conferred by that Spirit which leads into all truth, John xvi. 13. An assurance of faith comes from the divine Spirit. Upon this assurance our comfort much depends, and as there are different degrees of it, and each degree his work, we ought to remember with thankfulness that " the Spirit bears witness with our spirits that we are the children of God."

Lastly: The work of sanctification must be carried on in us, in conformity with which the apostle prays, (1 Thess. v. 23,) that the believers of the church of Thessalonica might be sanctified wholly in "spirit and soul and body," and " be preserved blameless unto the coming of our Lord Jesus Christ." This work consisteth in the mortifying of our inbred corruptions, so that our sinful affections become more and more weakened, and we are set apart, (as the signification of the term is,) to the service of God. Therefore, as this work progresses, sin loses its dominion over us, (Rom. vi. 14,) and we are made conformable to the death of Christ, (Phil. iii. 10,) the " old man is crucified with him, that the body of sin might be destroyed, that henceforth we should not serve sin," (Rom. vi. 6,) and " changed into the image of the Lord from glory to glory, even as by the Spirit of the Lord," 2 Cor. iii. 18. The instrument used in sanctification is the divine word, which has a transforming effect: "Sanctify them through the truth: thy word is truth," John xvii. 17; " That he might sanctify and cleanse it (the church) with the washing of water, by the word," Eph. v. 26: the preaching and reading of which, under the influence of the divine Spirit, furnishes such powerful motives to obedience, and to forsaking of sin,—setting the one in so abhorrent a point of view, and the other in such an amiable light, that the soul falls in love with and embraces the service of God, and flees from sin as the most deadly evil. Hence it is that the word has different effects, as awaking our fears, exciting our hopes, abounding with threatenings, promises, warnings, reproofs, expostulations, exhortations, tender and pathetic addresses, lively descriptions of the glory of the person and offices of Christ, and of the joys of the heavenly world; all which, set home upon the heart by the divine Spirit, produce fruit unto holiness and the end everlasting life. How comfortable must the reflection be to the Christian, that all the changes he meets with in this world, whether in spiritual or temporal things, are closely connected with his sanctification! To this we must attribute sickness and pain, poverty and disgrace, personal and relative afflictions, severe temptations, spiritual desertion, trials which faith and patience meet with; and, what seems most of all astonishing, that even their very backslidings, by being made the instruments of their correction, are made use of by the divine Spirit, who brings light out of darkness, order out of confusion, and causes "all things to work together for good to them that love God," (Rom. viii. 28.) This work of sanctification is not, like regeneration, instantaneous; nor is it perfect during life, but more or less of the body of sin still remains; but so as that it does not reign over us, but disturbs our peace, and creates in us much self-abhorrence. But the crowning work of all is the sealing of the Spirit, by which we "are sealed to the day of redemption," Eph. iv. 30. This consists in the enjoyment of a calm and tranquil mind, waiting with composure for our great change, and giving evidence to others with ourselves, that we have "a house not made with hands eternal in the heavens," and having a longing desire to be at home with the Lord.

And now, dear brethren, having treated on the office-work of the Spirit, and merely touched on the most important points, to help your meditations, we close this epistle, by earnestly intreating you to labor after a greater sense of your need of his influences, and not to grieve, by an unholy life, this sanctifying and sealing Spirit. And that you may, under his influence, become exemplary for purity of doctrine, zeal in his service, and uprightness in your lives, is the sincere prayer of your brethren who represent you in this our associate capacity.

Signed in behalf of the whole.

SAMUEL JONES, Moderator.
WILLIAM STAUGHTON, Clerk.

THE MINISTERS AND MESSENGERS AT THE ASSOCIATION, AND STATE OF THE CHURCHES DURING THE YEAR.

CHURCHES.	MINISTERS AND MESSENGERS.	Baptized.	Received by Letter.	Dismis'd.	Excom.	Restored.	Deceased.	Members.
Lower Dublin,	Samuel Jones, John Holmes, T. Holmes,	0	1	2	0	0	0	72
Middletown,†	Benjamin Bennet,*	0	0	0	0	0	0	139
Cohansie,	Henry Smalley, Jonathan Bowen, David Gillman, James Shepherd, David Plats, Nathan Shepherd, Jeremiah Brooks, Joel Shepherd, Eldad Cooke, David Shepherd, John Elmer,	25	0	0	1	2	5	170
Great Valley,	David Jones,	0	0	2	0	0	0	60
Cape May,†	Jonathan German, Christopher Smith,.	12	1	0	0	2	4	51
Hopewell,	James Ewing, James Hunt,	4	0	29	3	0	1	193
Brandywine,	Joshua Vaughan,	16	0	1	1	0	0	104
Montgomery,	Silas Hough, Daniel Harrar,	10	0	0	0	0	2	77
Kingwood,	Garner A. Hunt, David Stout,	5	0	0	0	0	2	84
Haight's Town,	Peter Wilson, John Jones,	46	3	7	0	0	4	377
Philadelphia, 1st church,	William Rogers, John Peckworth, George Ingolls, John M'Leod, Heath Norberry,	35	15	31	1	0	4	181
Southampton,	Thomas B. Montanye, William Magee, William Watts,	4	2	4	0	0	0	93
Knowlton,†	——— ———	0	0	0	0	0	0	17
New Britain,	William White,	0	0	0	2	0	0	95
Salem,	Horatio G. Jones, Joseph Lloyd, William Walker,	26	0	3	1	0	3	118
Dividing Creek,	Jonadab Shepherd, Hosea Shepherd,	0	0	0	0	0	0	58
New Mills,	Alexander M'Gowan,	10	1	0	0	0	0	107
Upper Freehold,	——— ———	2	0	2	0	0	0	75
Pittsgrove,	Josiah Nichols, Stanford Mayhew,	7	0	0	2	0	1	20

CHURCHES.	MINISTERS AND MESSENGERS.	Baptized.	Received by Letter.	Dismiss'd.	Excom.	Restored.	Deceased.	Members.
Manahawkin,	—— ——	9	0	0	0	0	0	33
Vincent,	—— ——	5	0	0	0	0	0	38
Tuckahoe,	George Knoll,	1	0	2	0	0	0	28
Hilltown,	James M'Laughlin,* John Matthias, sr., John Matthias, jr.,	3	0	3	0	0	5	141
Jacob's Town,	Burgiss Allison,	2	1	0	0	0	0	60
Marcus Hook,	—— ——	0	0	0	0	0	0	19
Roxbury,	Thomas Fleeson,*	1	0	0	1	0	1	51
West Creek,	Peter Groom,	1	0	0	0	1	1	48
Shemokin,†	John Patten,*	0	0	0	0	0	0	96
Amwell,	—— ——	8	1	1	1	0	0	65
Burlington,	William Staughton, John Fisher,	18	3	0	0	0	1	52
Mount Holly,	Jesse Cox,	26	1	2	0	0	1	76
Dover, York county,	—— ——	4	1	0	0	0	2	22
Philadelphia, 2d church,	John Ellis, Cornelius Trimmull,	25	5	0	0	0	0	50
Hopewell, 2d church,	Daniel Drake,	0	0	0	0	0	0	28
		305	35	89	13	5	37	2898

Note.—The ministers' names are in SMALL CAPITALS. Licensed preachers in *italic*. Those marked thus * not present. From the churches marked thus † received no intelligence. A dash —— denotes no settled minister.

Among the number of our deceased this year, we have the affliction to class our venerable and beloved Brethren Joshua Jones, of the church at Montgomery, and Thomas Ustick, of Philadelphia. The former slept in Jesus, December 26, 1802, aged 82, after being engaged in his Master's service about 50 years; the latter, April 18, 1803, in his 50th year, and after laboring 30 years in the same glorious cause. "Blessed are the dead who die in the Lord!"

The Rev. John Boggs, sen., late of our Association, finished his course this year, in the 63d year of his age, and in the 27th of his ministry.

MINUTES

OF THE

PHILADELPHIA BAPTIST ASSOCIATION,

HELD, BY APPOINTMENT, AT PHILADELPHIA, OCTOBER 2D, 3D, AND 4TH,

1804.

October 2d.—At three o'clock, P. M., Brother James M'Laughlin preached the introductory sermon, from Heb. i. 13, "But to which of the angels said he at any time, sit on my right hand, until I make thine enemies thy footstool."

2. After sermon, business was opened with prayer by Brother Samuel Jones, when Brother William White was chosen moderator, and Brother Silas Hough, clerk.

3. Letters from thirty-two churches were read.

Brother Daniel Dodge prayed.

Adjourned until nine o'clock to-morrow morning.

October 3d, nine o'clock, A. M.—Met pursuant to adjournment. The moderator prayed.

4. Brethren Thomas G. Jones and Isaac Eaton being present, were invited to seats with us.

The church, constituted in the year past at Blockley in Philadelphia county, applied for admission into this Association, which was freely granted, after they had given full satisfaction as to their faith and practice.

6. Received corresponding letters and minutes from the following Associations, viz. :—from the Warwick, letter and minutes, by their messenger Luke Davis; from the Delaware, letter and minutes, by their messenger Daniel Dodge; from the New York, letter and minutes, by their messengers William Vanhorn and Peter Bryant; from the Charleston, letter and minutes; from Danbury, letter and minutes; from the Miami, a letter but no minutes; and from the Shaftsbury, letters and minutes for the years 1803 and 1804.

7. After reading the circular letter, Brethren Samuel Jones, Thomas B. Montanye, and Henry Smalley, together with Burgiss Allison, the author, were appointed a committee to revise it.

Brother Bryant prayed.

Adjourned to three o'clock.

Three o'clock, P. M.—Met pursuant to adjournment. Brother Carlise prayed.

8. The following brethren are appointed to write to the corresponding Associations:—Joseph Mathias, to the Delaware; Isaac Eaton, to the New York; Carlile, to the Shaftsbury; Peckworth, to the Charleston; Hedger, to the Warren; Zebulon Holmes, to the Warwick; Samuel B. Harris, to the Danbury; and Allison, to the Miami.

9. Appointed messengers to our corresponding Associations. Brethren J. M'Laughlin, Joshua Vaughan, and John Peckworth, to the Delaware; Peter Wilson, James M'Laughlin, and John Rutter, to the New York.

10. Query from the first Philadelphia church: "Should not the supplies for our destitute churches, and our messengers to our sister Associations, with all other committees which may be appointed by the Association, make report to the Association succeeding, that the Association may ascertain whether or not their engagements have been complied with?"

To this query the Association answer in the affirmative.

11. Brethren M'Laughlin and H. G. Jones are appointed a committee to examine the letters and minutes of the corresponding Associations, and make report of such facts as particularly concern us.

12. Collected for the education fund:

At Lower Dublin,	$12 73
Cohansie,	10 00
Brandywine,	2 18
Montgomery,	4 00
Haight's Town,	6 00
First Philadelphia,	23 96
Southampton,	10 50
Salem,	15 00
	$84 37

13. This Association, aware of the great benefits arising from a regular contribution of the churches to the education fund, do hereby most affectionately recommend its continuance.

14. Collected for the mission fund:

At Cohansie,	$6 00
First Hopewell,	7 27
Montgomery,	6 00
Haight's Town,	4 00
First Philadelphia,	57 30
New Britain,	4 00
Salem,	12 50
Hilltown,	4 00
Roxbury,	20 21
	$121 28

The circular letter, being approved by the committee, was adopted by the Association.

16. Resolved, That the future collections for the education fund,

be applied to discharge the debts contracted by borrowing from that fund, for the prosecution of the suit against the executors of Silas Hart, late of Virginia, deceased.

17. The query from the Great Valley is laid over till next Association, when it shall be taken up, provided that church sees proper to renew it.

Brother Luke Davis prayed.

Adjourned to eleven o'clock to-morrow morning.

Sermon this evening by Brother Vanhorn, from 2 Cor. v. 20, "Now then we are ambassadors from Christ, as though God did beseech you by us: we pray you in Christ's stead, be ye reconciled to God."

October 4th, eleven o'clock, A. M.—Met pursuant to adjournment.

18. Supplies for Frankford, Manahawkin, Hill Town, Upper Freehold, and Pittsgrove.

19. The corresponding letters were read and approved.

Brother Vanhorn prayed.

Adjourned to three o'clock.

Three o'clock, P. M.—Met pursuant to adjournment. Brother Wilson prayed.

20. Brother Hough is appointed to write the circular letter for next year.

21. Brother Thomas B. Montanye is appointed to preach the introductory sermon; and in case of failure, Brother Horatio G. Jones.

22. It is recommended that the quarterly prayer meetings be continued as heretofore, excepting the day in October. Instead of meeting on the first Tuesday in October, we recommend the Friday preceding; but the other days to be observed as formerly recommended.

23. Brother Samuel B. Harris, who has been licensed to preach by the Baptist church at Cohansie, made application to the Association for assistance from the education fund, to help him in his learning. It is therefore agreed, that Brother Samuel B. Harris shall have the interest of the fund for two years, to assist him in his education.

24. Agreed, that Mr. Stephen C. Ustick print the minutes; and that Brother Allison be requested to superintend the printing, and, in conjunction with the printer, to distribute them to the churches and corresponding Associations.

The Association is appointed to meet, on the first Tuesday in October, 1805, in Philadelphia; but, in case of any malignant disorder prevailing in that city, at New Britain, at three o'clock, P. M.

Closed with prayer by the moderator.

Sermon this evening by Brother D. Dodge, from Rom. i. 16, "For I am not ashamed of the gospel of Christ."

CIRCULAR LETTER.

BY REV. BURGISS ALLISON.

The elders and messengers of the Philadelphia Baptist Association, To the churches they represent, send Christian salutation.

Dearly beloved in the Lord,—It is with gratitude to the Supreme Head of the church, through whose superintending providence we have been favored with another interview in an associated capacity, that we have the happiness in announcing to you the general harmony which has subsisted among us during our deliberations.

For information respecting the prosperity of Zion, in the enlargement of her borders, by additions to our churches within the last year, we refer you to our minutes hereto annexed.

From year to year you have been addressed upon subjects of the highest importance by our letters; and as we feel no less anxious now than formerly to promote the spiritual welfare of the churches with whom we are connected, in particular, as well as the interest of the Redeemer's kingdom in general, we have been solicitous to select a subject which has been less frequently discussed, though not less important than many others upon which you have been addressed in the course of our epistolary correspondence with you. We know that no means can become effectual without the blessing of God; but, with the benign influence of his grace, the smallest effort will be crowned with success. Important are the doctrines of grace with which it behoves you to be acquainted; various are the divine truths necessary to be exhibited to the Christian's view, and many are the duties requisite to be inculcated and warmly recommended to practice. As occasion and circumstances occur, and as the unerring Spirit of wisdom directs, we should press one and another of those doctrines and duties upon your notice, that we may stir up your pure minds by way of remembrance.

The subject to which we would invite your serious attention at this time, is Prayer. That we may be the more fully able to perform this incumbent duty with acceptance to God, and comfort to ourselves, and that we way learn rightly to appreciate its exalted worth, and blessed effects, we shall endeavor to consider,

First, the nature of prayer.
Secondly, the seasons for prayer.
Thirdly, the importance of prayer, and
Lastly, the incentives to prayer.

In defining the NATURE OF PRAYER, taken in a religious point of view, we would call it an intercourse between God and man, or an address from the needy creature to the independent and bountiful Creator, Preserver, and Redeemer, respecting what the creature hath either received, or whatever he may need for time or eternity—for grace or glory.

As prayer is addressed to the Omniscient Jehovah, who is the searcher of hearts and trier of reins, (Psalm vii. 9; Jer. xi. 28;) who looketh not at the outside appearance, but at the heart, (1 Sam. xvi. 7;) so it is the language of the heart which is to be addressed to God in prayer. Nevertheless, prayer is not always to be confined to the secret elevation of the soul in ejaculations; but our mental exercises are to be at proper seasons expressed in an audible language: and that language should be framed with propriety, decorum, and reverence. Propriety of language should be adopted, both as it regards the dignity of the Being addressed, and the comprehension of those who unite in this duty, when one becomes a mouth for the rest.

But let it be remembered, that a prayer, composed of the best form of words and most elegant diction, which is not accompanied by true internal devotion, is less acceptable to a prayer-hearing God, than the humble groan or fervent desire of a broken and contrite heart, though expressed in language the most plain and unadorned. Hence our Lord accuseth the hypocritical Pharisees, "This people draweth nigh unto me with their mouths, and honoreth me with their lips, but their heart is far from me," Matt. xv. 8. Let no one, then, be discouraged from attempting the performance of this duty, from a conscious deficiency in point of diction, or apprehension of inability to express himself in appropriate language: for if that humble address of the publican, "God be merciful to me a sinner," is put up in sincerity, it will ascend to heaven as an incense of sweeter savour than the boasted perfection of the Pharisee, decorated in all the flowers of rhetoric. Propriety of language, however, is commendable, and is what we should endeavor to attain, especially in imitating the example given us in God's word, where the aspirations of his people are recorded, and furnish us with a specimen of that style of address which doubtless meets the divine approbation; the Holy Ghost having inspired it, and influenced the writers thereof to leave it on record for our imitation.

Although we address God in specific language, we do not infer from hence that he is unacquainted with our wants: on the contrary, he knoweth what we need before we ask; yea, he is perfectly acquainted with each particular of our address, before it is conceived in our minds or uttered with our lips; yet he saith he will be sought unto by the house of Israel for all these things. He whose eyes are over the whole earth, and who is omnipotent as well as omniscient, can assuredly supply all the wants of his people unasked, and bestow his benefits unsought: but this is not the method of his grace. He hath annexed a blessing to even the means of attaining the end sought: for we should not be in a suitable disposition for receiving his favors, were we not in a praying frame and temper of mind: and hence we experience a sweetness in performing the duty.

Our address should be performed also with DECORUM. In order to attend to a due decorum in our addresses to God, it is proper that some attention should be paid to the order thereof. That which has been more generally adopted by many eminently pious children of God, in something like the following, viz: *Adoration, Confession, Petition,* and *Thanksgiving.*

Prayer, literally speaking, is undoubtedly confined to petition; ut as we have considered it, in a theological and scriptural view, to be an intercourse between the Creator and creature, or an address from man to God in a general sense, it may with propriety comprise the parts assigned to it. In our addresses to God, adoration is unquestionably the most suitable exordium. With what profound reverence, with what humble adoration should a worm of the earth approach the great I AM; should a being of yesterday, whose foundation is in the dust, draw near the eternal Jehovah, the exalted majesty of heaven!

Let us, then, approach him with expressions of admiration and reverential awe: with acknowledgments of his uncreated excellencies and boundless perfections. By such reflections and such acknowledged sentiments of the attributes and perfections of the ever-blessed God, we shall acquire a reverence of sentiment, a solemnity of mind and humility of soul, more suited to the character which we justly sustain of guilty and self-condemned criminals, at the footstool of an offended Judge, ready to make a confession of our guilt. It is true, the omniscient Jehovah is fully acquainted with our most secret sins before we acknowledge them; for he knoweth our out-going and our in-coming, our up-rising, and our down-sitting; he compasseth our path about, and is fully acquainted with all our ways: none can conceal his offences under the cover of night or a mantle of secrecy, for darkness and light are both alike to him. Yet a soul under a sense of guilt, and conscious of the aggravation of his transgressions, feels a relief in unbosoming himself to his God, and in pouring out his soul in confession of his iniquities. Such ingenuous and unreserved acknowledgments are also acceptable to God,—as Prov. xxviii. 13, Psalm xxxii. 5,—besides which passages, there are many examples in the sacred Scriptures of the confession of God's people, recorded for our sakes, both as an argument in favor of the propriety and necessity of this part of our address, and as an incitement to our imitation. Confession may not only be said to include self-accusation of guilt, but also an acknowledgment of our helpless and needy condition; each of which paves the way to a deprecation of divine displeasure on account of sin, and to an earnest request for a supply of needful blessings; both comprised in that part denominated petition.

Under what we call petition, may properly be included deprecation of the anger of God against our sins, and punishment as the just demerit thereof, inasmuch as this is included in our petition for mercy. Hence a soul approaching God in prayer, after a humble confession, will earnestly plead for the pardon of his sins, so offensive to God, and which appear so heinous in his own eyes, and will supplicate a deliverance from that punishment which he knows they have justly merited. As all the miseries, to which in this life we are liable, are the consequences of sin, so in deprecating sin with its effects, we shall pray to be delivered from the reigning power, and even inheritance of sin; the darkness of our minds and the temptations of Satan.

Added to these are other petitions for mercies and benefits which we know we need from his hand, in which are included the comforts and blessings pertaining to this life, all which should be requested with becoming deference to the divine will. Blessings of a spiritual nature, as the sanctifying influence of his Spirit to fit us for the enjoyment of God in glory, are such as the knowledge and feelings of the Christian will dictate to him. Some are in the habit of particularizing, and entering into the minutiæ of every want, every circumstance, and every concern; but such extreme minuteness does not seem necessary, nor is it enjoined in the word of God.

Although we do not deem it indispensable at all times to follow verbatim, that form which our Lord gave his disciples, provided we include in our addresses the substance of it; yet we think it exhibits so much of the nature of prayer, as to inform us, that neither a particular enumeration of every want, or petition of every desire is requisite; and that the protraction of our prayer to an immoderate length, is not sanctioned by that comprehensive, concise form. Our Lord, indeed, expressly condemns the Pharisees for their long prayers, and mistaken supposition that they would be heard for their much speaking. We would, however, be delicate on this subject, and avoid the other extreme, lest we quench the Spirit by a suppression of holy desires, where the spirit of prayer is poured out in an extraordinary manner.

With all our wants, all our deficiencies, which so amply furnish us with matter for petition, we have also received much from the Lord's hand, for which we are bound to be thankful: so that the surplusage of our enjoyments is far above our sufferings. We shall, therefore, consider thanksgiving as a necessary part of our address to God.

When we reflect upon God as the self-sufficient and self-dependent Jehovah, who needeth not the services or praises of his creatures to make him happy: that no essential glory can be added to him who is glorious in holiness and fearful in praises, who is the very abstract of perfection and essence of glory; it would seem as though the ascriptions of praise from our polluted lips were an indignity offered to the High and Holy One: but that we may not be discouraged from engaging in this important duty, we are exhorted in God's word to praise him, and to render thanksgiving to his great and holy name, Psalm ciii. 1, 2: as also in various other passages.

Although we cannot add to the essential glory of God, it is our indispensable duty, declaratively to glorify him. By such exercises we excite each other to those sentiments of gratitude, acknowledgment of our obligations, and grateful sensibilities for favors received, as will burst forth in pathetic expressions of thankfulness. There is no Christian, but who, upon the least reflection, or under the exercise of gracious affections, must ever glow with gratitude to the Omniscient and Bountiful Giver of every good and perfect gift, for the loving-kindness and tender mercies wherewith he hath crowned our lives, both in the dispensations of his grace toward us, in mercies unsought by us, early provided in the covenant of grace, and in answers to our petitions.

Although in the preceding remarks we have in general considered prayer as addressed to the most high God; yet it may not be improper to treat more particularly the OBJECT of prayer.

The only and proper object of prayer is God the Father, Son, and Spirit, the ever adorable Trinity.

The mode of address which is more generally adopted in the Scriptures, is to the Father, through the Son, and by the aid of the Spirit. We know that in our sinful condemned state, as outcasts from God, we cannot approach him as an absolute God: that there is no medium of access but one, and that is through the mediation of our Lord Jesus Christ. Our Lord says, expressly, "no man can come unto the Father but by me." He hath opened the way to the throne of grace, in which we may approach with humble boldness and our prayers ascend as an acceptable sacrifice, perfumed with the incense of the New Testament Altar. But it doth not appear, that all our addresses are to be confined to the Father personally, as we are furnished with examples of personal addresses to the Son. There have been some, who strenuously opposed the propriety of making our addresses to any but the Father in particular; but if the martyr Stephen, when filled with the Holy Ghost, when he saw the heavens opened and Jesus standing at the right hand of God, could call upon our Lord, saying, "Lord Jesus receive my Spirit," we ought not to be scrupulous, or fearful of following such an illustrious example. That in the primitive church it was customary to call on the name of the Lord Jesus, we learn from Acts ix. 14; chap. iv. 24; chap. xxix. 30; Rev. xxii. 20.

From the many instances afforded in the holy Scriptures of prayer offered to the second Person in the adorable Trinity, we infer that the Spirit, the third Person, the same in essence with the Father and the Son, equal in power and glory, and equally concerned in the work of Redemption, is an object of religious worship: and that occasional invocations of the divine Paraclete are admissible. If in our doxologies we offer distinct adoration to the holy Spirit, we may with the same propriety offer to him occasional petitions. In following, however, our sacred guide, the word of God, we shall be led to imitate the examples therein, of more generally addressing the Father, for the sake of the Son, through the influence of the Spirit, and thus worship the Triune God.

In farther illustrating the nature of prayer, we may consider the qualifications requisite in the petitioner to enable him to pray with profit.

By qualifications, we do not mean inherent qualities or personal merit, to entitle us to an answer to our prayers, since all our answers must come through the merit of Christ alone; but such qualifications as are imparted by the Holy Spirit:—A knowledge of God and ourselves—a knowledge of God in Christ reconciling the world unto himself—a knowledge of God, as willing to receive and hear all that come to him by Christ—a knowledge of God as one who is mighty to save, even to the uttermost—a knowledge of ourselves, as poor, sinful, hell-deserving creatures—of ourselves as needy, helpless and dependent creatures.

Another requisite qualification is a trust in God, through faith in our Lord Jesus Christ. Again, "And this is the confidence that we have in him, that, if we ask any thing according to his will, he heareth us,"&c., 1 John v. 14, 15. This trust must be grounded on the promises contained in the word, and encouragement given therein.

Another excellent qualification is the spirit of prayer, by which, we not only mean a readiness of conception and aptness of expression in prayer, but also those gracious aids of the Spirit, by which we are enabled to approach God in a becoming manner, and with comfort to our own souls. "The Spirit helpeth our infirmities, for we know not how to pray as we ought; but the Spirit itself maketh intercession for us with groanings which cannot be uttered," Rom. viii. 26.

Prayer, to be acceptable to God, must be made with submission to his will, *i. e.* according to his word. In our petitions for a supply of our many wants, especially in such things as are of a temporal nature, we ought not to be peremptory, as we know not what will be for our advantage, as it is said, "Ye ask and ye receive not, because ye ask amiss." As God is infinitely wise and knows what will promote our real good, we should always ask with submission to his holy will. In such things as tend to his own glory, we may be more importunate, as they are always according to his will: which comprehends whatsoever is contained in his promises, and expressed in his requirements. We cannot be too earnest in our supplications, for a greater abhorrence of sin, for a more ardent love to God, a more fervent desire after holiness, and a growing conformity to his image: far more of a submissive acquiescence in all the dispensations of his providence, and a firm reliance on his word.

Secondly: Having touched upon some of the important points connected with the nature of prayer, we proceed to consider the SEASONS OF PRAYER.

Although we are exhorted to "pray without ceasing," yet we conceive there are some seasons more peculiarly adapted to this duty.

The first which we shall notice, are public seasons, in the great congregation, or when people are assembled for public worship, (Zach. viii. 20, 21; Luke xxiv. 53.) At such seasons all are not to pray audibly, or express their feelings indiscriminately; for this would produce confusion and tumult: but the minister, whose duty it is to officiate on the occasion, should be a mouth for the people to God, with whom they may join mentally. For the minister to address the throne of grace previous to his commencing his discourse, is both a duty and a privilege, as it respects not only himself, but the people also: that he may receive assistance, and a blessing attend the word,—which part of worship has a tendency to promote a solemnity of mind in the audience, and to fit them to hear the word with profit. Nor is it less a duty to subjoin an address at the conclusion of the discourse.

Another season for prayer is when the church of Christ is convened, or in an assembly of the saints in social worship, (Acts i. 14; chap. ii. 42.) In such societies it appears a duty for the different male members to exercise their gifts in prayer alternately, as this tends greatly to promote a growth in grace, and improvement in the gift of prayer, and to discover to the church such gifts as may be likely to become useful in the ministry.

Domestic worship, or family prayer, is likewise a duty which ought to be performed in the families of all such as have professed to put on Christ. Many arguments might be adduced to enforce this duty; but suffice it to say, that the good example and salutary influence of such a practice, should be a sufficient inducement. Every Christian to whom the Lord hath given children, has, no doubt, a fervent desire that they should be brought to a saving acquaintance with the truth as it is in Christ Jesus. What influence their example may have in an uniform attendance on the duties of family worship they cannot tell, but have great reason to hope for a happy result: as the first soul exercises of many young people have had their rise under the influence of domestic devotion.

Public prayer, however, is not to be considered as a substitute for private or closet devotion: this is an important part of the Christian's exercise, "But thou, when thou prayest, enter into thy closet; and when thou hast shut thy door, pray to thy Father which is in secret, and thy Father which seeth in secret will reward thee openly," Matt. vi. 6. Here the Christian can unrestrainedly pour out his soul before his God; here he can confess his sins, and plead for forgiveness through the merits of Christ. This, indeed, is a great and precious privilege, but such devotions should in reality be in secret, agreeably to our Lord's directions; to enter into the closet and shut the door; not to go on the house top, or in an exposed apartment; not to elevate the voice in such manner as to become audible to the neighborhood, as this savors too much of hypocrisy, and the practice of the Pharisees which our Lord condemns.

Those seasons for prayer which the examples in the Scripture more particularly sanction, and which the nature of the duty seems to point out, are, on the Lord's day, and other stated periods of worship; in the performance of domestic prayer, the morning and the evening seem proper, to which David also adds the noon, "In the evening and morning and noon will I pray and call aloud, and he shall hear my voice," Psalm lv. 17. The evening calls for thankfulness for protection through the day, and supplication for support through the night. The morning again renews our obligations for protecting providence through the silent watches, while nature demands the refreshment of sleep for our bodies, whilst our senses are locked up, and the vigilant eye closed in darkness. When we consider our proneness to neglect, and forgetfulness of our duties, the advantage of having stated periods for the performance of them, that thus impressed, our memories may not let them slip, is obvious to every reflecting mind.

But our stated periods for public devotion or private retirement for prayer, ought not to interfere with occasional duties. There are many occurrences, many exercises or peculiar circumstances, which may call for our special application at the throne of grace. Besides the actual retirement to our closets, that there we may in more humble position, or energetic effusions, pour out our desires before God, we also enjoy the privilege of frequently raising our souls to God in secret ejaculations, even whilst engaged in our common occupations or secular concerns, and whilst surrounded by our fellow-creatures; without their notice or observation.

The IMPORTANCE of PRAYER, which we proposed also to consider, will appear from various considerations, amongst which, that of our great need is worthy of attention. We are in a moral sense, poor and blind, and naked, and destitute. Grace hath provided a rich store of every thing requisite to supply our deficiencies; and prayer is the instrument by which we may obtain the needful supply. We are hungry, and prayer supplies the heavenly manna as food for the soul: we are sick, and prayer administers the never-failing restorative, prepared and furnished by the best of physicians. Its consequence will be enhanced in our apprehension, when by faith we behold the inexhaustible store of sacred treasure deposited in Christ for us, notwithstanding our utter unworthiness, and abject debasement by reason of sin. Again, prayer is the most effectual means of delivering the Christian from darkness of mind and deadness in the exercise of duties. Though the dejected child of God approaches the throne of grace with scarcely a sensible evidence of his right so to do, and almost without a desire of so doing, he frequently becomes animated with a participation of divine love, and a spirit of prayer, whilst thus lowly bowing at the footstool of divine mercy; so that before he is aware, his soul is made like to the chariot of Aminadab. Indeed, the gracious soul never goes quite empty away, though insensible of any additional supplies, or actual blessing derived from his late intercourse with God.

We derive another argument in favor of the importance of prayer, from the blessing frequently attendant on the united prayers of God's people, in times of declension in vital piety, and a general deadness in religion. When the people of God say to each other, "O come, let us worship and bow down, let us kneel before the Lord our Maker," Psalm xcv. 6; when we see them forming concert in prayer, and uniting in the petition for a revival, a revival generally follows. Hence our Lord says, "Where two or three of you shall agree touching any thing; and ye shall ask it, I will do it."

Lastly, In speaking of the INCENTIVES to PRAYER, or encouragement to the performance of this duty, we would observe, that this part of the subject has in a great measure been anticipated in the preceding observations, as many incentives to prayer have been comprised therein; but we would bring to your recollection a few more, and particularly some, which are comprised in various passages of holy writ, which exhibit the blessed effects of prayer in the answers returned, and hold out encouragement to the performance thereof.

Our Lord, in speaking of the intercourse between God and his people, in order to strengthen our confidence and encourage us to expect returns to our petitions, calls our attention to the endearing relation subsisting between a father and son, and towards the natural result of a petition offered by filial affection to paternal regard: "If," says he, "a son shall ask bread of any of you that is a father, will he give him a stone? or if he ask a fish, will he give him a serpent?"—and draws that heart-cheering inference from it, that if we, who are sinful creatures, are influenced by parental feelings to administer good to our children, much more shall our heavenly Father, who is all perfection and goodness, make bountiful returns to his beloved children. Hence we may approach as children to a father, who is both ready and able to help, and who is the powerful and bountiful rewarder of all such as diligently seek him. The believer may always derive encouragement from the constant success which attends the prayer offered up in faith, (1 John v. 14, 15; Rom. x. 12; John ix. 31.) Also, from the promises which God hath given of hearing and returning answers of peace, (Ps. cxlv. 18, 19;) that he will hear them, (Isaiah xlv. 11–19;) that he will answer them, (Matt. vii. 7, 8.) As he hears our prayers, so he directs all things by his providence, that they shall eventually accomplish his will in returning answers to them. If immediate answers are withheld, it is only for a little season, until in the course of providence they may be given in a way more suited to our case, and more for his own glory. The various examples on record of the successful prayers of God's ancient people, afford ample encouragement, as Abraham, (Gen. xx. 17;) Isaac, (Gen. xxv. 21;) Jacob, (Gen. xxxii. 9–12, 24–26; and xxxiii. 4;) of Moses, (Exod. xxxii. 11–14;) David, (2 Sam. vii. 17–29;) Solomon, (1 Kings iii. 5–13;) Hezekiah, (2 Chron. xxxii. 24;) Daniel, (Dan. ii. 17–19;) of Peter, (Acts xii. 5;) Paul, (Acts xx. 36;) the apostles united, (Acts i. 14, and ii. 42;) besides a multitude more.

Seeing, therefore, we have such a cloud of witnesses, let us take heed that we let not this duty slip, or omit it on any account. Should no other argument be offered, this one alone is sufficient, that God has made it our duty to pray, by his command: to which also we shall add, that he has made it our privilege, by the pleasure which he takes in accepting our offerings. We are informed that the prayers of the saints ascended up to the throne of God as a sweet incense, holy and acceptable. The odours which were contained in the golden vials of the elders, were the prayers of the saints, (Rev. v. 8.) Also, the incense that ascended from the golden censer of the angel, was offered up with the prayers of all the saints.

That the God of all grace may endue you with the grace and spirit of prayer, by the instrumentality of which, you may enjoy much of his presence and live more to his glory, is the prayer of yours in the Lord. Amen.

WILLIAM WHITE, Moderator.
SILAS HOUGH, Clerk.

THE MINISTERS AND MESSENGERS AT THE ASSOCIATION, AND STATE OF THE CHURCHES DURING THE YEAR.

CHURCHES.	MINISTERS AND MESSENGERS.	Baptized.	Received by Letter.	Dismis'd.	Excom.	Restored.	Deceased.	Members.
Lower Dublin,	Samuel Jones, Thomas Holmes, Jesse Dungan, Joseph Wright, John Keen,	22	1	0	0	0	0	95
Middletown,	Benjamin Bennet, John Smock, John Bowne,	10	0	2	0	0	4	143
Cohansie,	Henry Smalley, Samuel B. Harris, Jeremiah Brooks,	11	1	3	1	0	0	178
Great Valley,	David Jones,* Isaac Abrams, Jonathan Phillips, Michael M'Clure,	6	0	0	0	0	1	65
Cape May,	Jonathan German,*	1	0	0	0	0	4	47
Hopewell, 1st Church,	James Ewing,* David Stout, Richard Stout, Lewis Labaw,	3	0	17	2	0	4	173
Brandywine,	Joshua Vaughan,* Robert M'Coy, William Griffith,	8	4	4	0	0	0	112
Montgomery,	Silas Hough, Charles Humphrey, Joseph Lunn, William Collom,	3	0	0	0	0	1	79
Kingwood,	Garner A. Hunt, Daniel Bray,	9	0	1	0	0	0	92
Hight's Town,	Peter Wilson, Amos Reeder, John Welling,	33	2	9	1	0	5	398
Philadelphia, 1st church,	Willam Rogers, John Peckworth, Thomas Billings, Hugh Gorley, John Bradley, George Ingolls, John M'Leod, Joseph Keen, Benjamin Thaw,	6	2	10	0	0	2	177

CHURCHES.	MINISTERS AND MESSENGERS.	Baptized.	Received by Letter.	Dismis'd.	Excom.	Restored.	Deceased.	Members.
Southampton,	Thomas B. Montanye, Arthur Watts, William Magee, Abel Marple, Peter Sowerman,	15	1	4	0	0	1	103
Knowlton,†	—— ——	0	0	0	0	0	0	17
New Britain,	Edward Matthew, Isaac James, Erasmus Thomas,	1	1	2	0	0	6	89
Salem,	Horatio G. Jones, Sylvanus Shepherd, Joseph Harker,	18	5	3	0	0	7	131
Dividing Creek,	David Stout,*	0	1	0	0	0	3	56
New Mills,	Alexander M'Gowan, *Isaac Carlisle*, *Benjamin Hedger*,	10	3	1	0	0	1	118
Upper Freehold,	—— ——	7	0	0	0	0	0	82
Pittsgrove,†	—— ——	0	0	0	0	0	0	20
Manahawkin,	Samuel Gray, Amos Southard,	1	0	0	1	0	2	31
Vincent,	—— ——	1	0	1	0	0	0	36
Tuckahoe,†	—— ——	0	0	0	0	0	0	28
Hilltown,	James M'Laughlin, Isaac Morris, Robert Shannon, Joseph Mathias,	0	0	4	1	0	4	132
Jacob's Town,	Burgiss Allison, William Snowden,*	3	0	0	0	0	1	62
Marcus Hook,	—— ——	6	0	2	0	0	0	22
Roxbury,	Thomas Fleeson, John Levering, Titus Yerkes, Tilman Culp,	3	1	1	0	0	0	54
West Creek,	Peter Groom,*	1	0	0	0	0	1	48
Shemokin,	John Patten,*	5	1	4	1	1	3	93
Amwell,	John Carr, Levi Stout,	3	0	3	0	0	0	68
Burlington,	William Staughton,* Thomas Potts, William Boswell, John Fisher, Matthew Randall, Zebulon Holmes,	12	4	1	1	0	2	63
Mount Holly,	Jesse Cox, John Pipit, Joseph Evans,	22	0	3	0	0	1	92

CHURCHES.	MINISTERS AND MESSENGERS.	Baptized.	Received by Letter.	Dismis'd.	Excom.	Restored.	Deceased.	Members.
Dover, York co., Pa.	—— ——	5	0	0	0	0	0	27
Philadelphia, 2d church,	WILLIAM WHITE, John Ellis, Isaac Johnson, Thomas Timmings, Cornelius Trimmul, Philip Halzel, William Magee, Adam Corfield,	25	8	2	0	0	0	81
Hopewell, 2d church,	James Hill, Levi Knowles,	23	0	0	0	0	0	51
Blockley,	JOHN RUTTER, Heath Norbury, Amos Penager,	0	0	0	0	0	0	16
		273	35	77	8	1	53	3079

NOTE.—The ministers' names are in SMALL CAPITALS. Licenced preachers in *italics*. Those marked thus * were not present. From the churches marked thus † received no intelligence. A dash —— denotes no settled minister.

We have to announce the mournful intelligence of the death of our much esteemed and reverend fathers in the gospel, JOHN GANO and JOSEPH POWELL, since our last Association.

MINUTES

OF THE

PHILADELPHIA BAPTIST ASSOCIATION,

HELD IN NEW BRITAIN, BUCKS COUNTY, PENNSYLVANIA,
OCTOBER 1ST, 2D, 3D, AND 4TH,

1805.

October 1.—At three o'clock, P. M., Brother Thomas B. Montanye preached the introductory sermon, from 1 Cor. iv. 2, "It is required in stewards, that a man be found faithful."

2. After sermon, business was opened with prayer by Brother William White, when Brother Thomas B. Montanye was chosen moderator, and Brother William Staughton, clerk.

3. Letters from thirty-four churches were read.

Brother Samuel Jones prayed.

Adjourned until half past eight o'clock to-morrow morning.

October 2d, half past eight o'clock, A. M.—Met pursuant to adjournment. Brother David Jones prayed.

4. Brethren James M'Laughlin, David Cooper, from Natchez, Samuel B. Harris, and William Inglesby, deacon of the Baptist church at Charleston, South Carolina, being present, were invited to a seat with us.

5. The newly-constituted church at Squam, in Dover township, Monmouth county, New Jersey, applying for admission into our body, was acordingly received.

6. Received corresponding letters and minutes from the following Associations: viz., from Charleston, a letter and minutes; from New York, minutes and corresponding letter, by their messenger, William Vanhorn; from Warwick, a letter and minutes, by their messenger John Stanford; from Warren, minutes and corresponding letter; from Miami, a letter and copy of their minutes; from Redstone, a letter and their minutes; from Delaware, a letter and minutes, by their messenger Daniel Dodge.

Brother Vanhorn prayed.

Adjourned to three o'clock.

Three o'clock, P. M.—Met pursuant to adjournment. Brother James M'Laughlin prayed.

7. The circular letter was read, when Brethren Vanhorn and Dodge were appointed a committee, in conjunction with the author to revise it.

8. The following brethren were appointed to write to the corresponding Associations:—Brother William Rogers, to the Charleston; Allison, to the Delaware; Ewing, to the New York; Stanford, to the Shaftsbury; Wilson, to the Warren; Horatio G. Jones, to the Warwick; Bennet, to the Danbury; David Cooper, to the Miami; and Staughton, to the Redstone.

9. The following query, received from the Great Valley church last year, was considered: "Was the baptism of the Holy Ghost external or internal?

Answer: This Association believes it was purely external, though attended with some internal effects. For a statement of their sentiments on the subject, they refer to their circular letter published in 1802.

10. Resolved, That this Association cannot take up a question that relates to an individual member of any church without interfering with the independence of such church.

11. Resolved, That whereas, there is some difference of sentiment with respect to a certain individual between the churches of Middletown and Hightstown, this Association recommends the two churches, by mutual delegates, of such a number as they shall think proper, to call a council, at an early period, to whom they may submit their documents, and who, it is hoped, may promote the felicity and harmony of both churches: the result of which the Association wishes to receive the next year.

The moderator prayed.

Adjourned to ten o'clock to-morrow morning.

Sermons were delivered this evening, by Brother Stanford, at New Britain, Brother Wilson, at Hill Town, Brother Dodge, at Montgomery, and Brother Staughton, at Doylestown.

October 3d.—Met pursuant to adjournment. Brother Samuel Jones prayed.

12. Letters to the corresponding Associations were read and approved. The following brethren were appointed our messengers:— To the Delaware Association, Joshua Vaughan, Horatio G. Jones, Silas Hough, and John Rutter; to the New York, William White and Peter Wilson; to the Warren, Peter Wilson; to the Warwick, Thomas B. Montanye.

Brother Rogers prayed.

Adjourned to three o'clock.

Three o'clock, P. M.—Met pursuant to adjournment. Brother Ewing prayed.

13. The circular letter, revised by the committee, was adopted by the Association.

14. Resolved, That for the purpose of a speedy termination of the difficulty referred to, in the 11th article of these minutes, with the approbation of the delegates of the Middletown and Hightstown churches, this Association takes the liberty of recommending as the council referred to, the following brethren:—James M'Laughlin, Thomas B. Montanye, James Ewing, Samuel Jones, Burgiss Allison,

William Vanhorn, William Staughton;—and that the time and place of their meeting be Friday, the 25th instant, at eleven o'clock, at Bordentown, New Jersey.

Brother Staughton prayed.

Adjourned to eight o'clock to-morrow morning.

Brother Vanhorn preached this evening at New Britain, and Brother Carlile at Hill Town.

October 4th, eight o'clock, A. M.—Met pursuant to adjournment. Brother Rogers prayed.

15. Two queries were proposed from the first church in Philadelphia.

First. Is it consistent with the divine word, and the desirable harmony of our churches, that any church encourage and practice the reception of individuals into membership, who live in the vicinity of another sister church?

Secondly. If not, what measures ought the aggrieved church, under such circumstances, to pursue?

Agreed, That, for want of time, and with the approbation of the delegates from the church of Philadelphia, the queries be laid over for the consideration of this Association next year.

16. It is recommended that the quarterly prayer-meeting be continued, excepting the first Tuesday in October, instead of which, the Association recommends the Friday preceding.

17. This Association having sympathized with the destitute state of our churches, and considered the utter impropriety of the expense falling on a few of our ministers, agree, that as many of our churches had contributed for the laudable end, the collections of all the churches should have been deposited for the purpose the Association then sitting determined.

18. The report from the corresponding committee, drafted by the recording secretary, was reported, read, adopted, and is as follows:

REPORT OF THE SECRETARY TO THE ASSOCIATION,

Agreeably to the Resolution of the Corresponding Committee, at their meeting, June 11th, 1805.

At the meeting, April 26th, 1804, Brother Rogers, the corresponding secretary, reported as follows:

That Charleston, Warren, Danbury, New York, and Warwick Associations, have generally adopted our recommendation, for the appointing of committees to correspond or confer with us, and have forwarded their minutes expressive of the same.

Letters were also communicated and read by him, from our Brethren Smilie, Holcombe, Furman, and Backus; severally giving pleasing information, as it respects the growth of religion and the advancement of the Baptist interest.

The minutes of the Charleston, Warren, and Danbury Associations for 1803, and those of Savannah for the present year, were delivered by the corresponding secretary to the president of the committees, and also the first number of the Massachusetts Baptist Missionary Magazine.

By particular request, recent letters received by the corresponding secretary, from our Brother Carey in India, and Dr. Fuller of England, relating to the concerns and progress of the Bengal mission, were read and gave peculiar satisfaction.

At the meeting of September 18th, 1804, letters and papers were communicated and read by the corresponding secretary, from the Rev. Mr. Hersey, Fayette county, Pennsylvania, dated July 7th, 1804; Samuel Stanton, Wayne county, May 1st, 1804; Rev. Mr. Caton, Orange county, New York, May 30th, 1804; with a statement of the Baptist churches in Wayne and Luzerne counties, Pennsylvania, dated June 9th, 1803; also, a narrative of a convention of Baptist churches held in Chemung, Tioga county, New York, from November 10th, 1796, to October 26th, 1803: all of which letters and papers were deposited in the hands of the president, agreeably to a resolution of this committee, at their meeting of September 20th, 1803.

At the meeting of June 11th, 1805, the following letters and communications were received and read by the corresponding secretary:— From our Brother John Morgan, a letter announcing the formation of a church at Ebenezer, Loudon county, Virginia; a letter from Brother Vanhorn, of Scotch Plains, New Jersey, giving an account of the baptism and death of Mrs. Elizabeth Hampton, whose experience and history were unusually interesting; also a letter from Brother Holcombe of Savannah, written at the request of the general committee of Georgia Baptists, and accompanied with the minutes of said committee, which met at Kioke, in Columbia county, 1804.

Intelligence was received from Brother Rogers, relative to the prosperous situation of the mission at Serampore, and of the work of God in New England, New York, and South Carolina particularly; information was received of the adoption of the faith of our society relative to baptism, by the Rev. Daniel Merrill of Sedgwick, New Hampshire, (formerly a pædobaptist minister,) and a large body of the society over which he presided.

WILLIAM STAUGHTON, Recording Secretary.

19. It is desired that the collection fund be continued and appropriated as recommended last year.

20. The following sums were collected:—

FOR THE EDUCATION FUND.		FOR THE MISSION* FUND.	
From Lower Dublin,	$11 91	From Middletown,	$6 00
Middletown,	12 00	Cohansie,	5 00
Cohansie,	5 00	Hight's Town,	5 00
Hight's Town,	5 00	Philadelphia,	30 03
Southampton,	9 00	Salem,	6 93
Salem,	6 93		
Pittsgrove,	3 31		
	$53 15		$52 96

*The Mission Society will meet, with divine leave, the 18th of December 1805, at the First Church, in Philadelphia, at three o'clock, P. M.

21. The following Brethren, Isaac Carlile, John P. Peckworth, and John M'Leod, who have been appointed to examine the letters from our sister Associations, report that they see no particular business referred to in them, that requires the attention of this Association.

22. It is recommended that collections be made, or subscriptions increased, or both be attended to, for the use of the mission society, as much as can conveniently be done.

23. Supplies were appointed for the following destitute churches: Upper Freehold, Pittsgrove, Manahawkin, Dover, First Hopewell, Frankford, and Squan.

As several of our brethren, who are present, cannot immediately fix upon any particular times for supplying the above churches, and some of our brethren who are absent, we believe are disposed to serve them, it is affectionately recommended to the said ministering brethren to visit the said churches, at such seasons, as are not already provided for.

24. Resolved, That a committee, consisting of Brethren Rogers, Peckworth, Ingles, and M'Leod, in conjunction with the librarian, Brother Staughton, are requested to use their exertions for obtaining intelligence respecting the books belonging to the Association, and that the churches be requested to assist the operations of the committee.

25. Brother Rogers is appointed to write the circular letter for next year.

26. Brother Horatio G. Jones is appointed to preach the introductory sermon; and in case of failure, Brother David Jones.

27. The Association is appointed to meet on the first Tuesday in October, 1806, in the first Baptist church, in Philadelphia, at three o'clock, P. M.; and in case of any malignant disorder prevailing in that city, at Nottingham meeting-house, Hightstown church, New Jersey.

28. Resolved, That the Association recommend to the churches, the consideration of the propriety of altering the time of our usual meeting in October.

29. Agreed, That Brother Stephen C. Ustick print the minutes, and that Brother Staughton be requested to superintend the printing, and to distribute them to the churches and corresponding Associations.

CIRCULAR LETTER.
BY REV. SILAS HOUGH.

The elders and messengers of the Philadelphia Baptist Association, sitting at New Britain, the 1st, 2d, 3d, and 4th of October, 1805.

To the churches they represent, send greeting.

Beloved Brethren,—In conformity to our usual custom of annually addressing you on some important religious subject, which may serve to promote your doctrinal knowledge, as well as to excite you to the practice of every Christian virtue; we shall call your attention, at this time, to the important object of Brotherly Love.

Though every suitable respect is to be paid to all men, yet there is a peculiar affection due to every believer, which is called brotherly love, and which Peter enforces in his exhortation to "Love the brotherhood," 1 Peter ii. 17. This, as one of the relative duties which Christians owe to each other, stands pre-eminent in the word of God. From the repeated exhortations to this duty, and the variety of forms in which it is enforced in the Bible, we believe the inference, of its being of the first magnitude, is not inconclusive. Moses gives the sum of all moral precepts in the ten commandments; and Christ comprehends them all in two. The first and principal one is, "Thou shalt love the Lord thy God, with all thy heart, soul and mind." The second is like and subordinate unto it, "Thou shalt love thy neighbor as thyself." And then he declares that "on these two commandments hang all the law and the prophets," Matt. xxii. 37–39. Hence we see the propriety of Paul's declaration, that "love is the fulfiling of the law," Rom. xiii. 10. For every duty required of us is to be performed from a principle of love to God, as the exciting cause, and in obedience to his revealed will, as the rule of all our actions; therefore, this is called "THE FIRST AND GREAT COMMANDMENT."

The first table of the law, containing our more immediate duty to God, is here, by our Saviour, comprehended in this one sentence, "Thou shalt love the Lord thy God with all thy heart, soul, and mind." The second table, which contains our duty to our neighbor is also comprised in this single sentence, "Thou shalt love thy neighbor as thyself." Hence we are authorized to conclude, that, though all our duties are to be performed from a principle of love to God; yet, love to the brethren, abstractedly considered, is the source from which arise all the other relative duties we owe unto them. For as love to God is that active principle which constrains us to delight in his worship—which makes the "ways of wisdom to be ways of pleasantness, and all her paths peace;" so love to man is that principle of action, which compels us not only to fly from the thought of doing him an injury, but prompts us to give relief when in distress, and render him happy. "Love worketh no ill to his neighbor: therefore, love is the fulfiling of the law," Rom. xiii. 10. This is what James calls the Royal Law. "If ye fulfil the royal law according to the Scriptures, Thou shalt love thy neighbor as thyself, ye do well," James ii. 8. And granting we are to take this command in an unlimited sense, to extend to every individual of the human race; yet we still contend for the proposition before advanced, that there is a peculiar affection due to the children of God. The apostolic advice on this subject runs thus, "As we have opportunity, let us do good unto all men, especially to them who are of the household of faith," Gal. vi. 10. We are to love all men, *as men;* though some, by their abominable practices, forfeit their respect, and bring upon themselves merited contempt. But Christians are to be loved, as the adopted children of God, and for his image which they bear.

The obligations we are under to love God and his children are inseparable. It is therefore folly in the extreme for any one to deceive himself under an idea that he loves God, when at the same time he has no disposition to love, and do good to his people. For says John, "This commandment have we from him, that he who loveth God, love his brother also." And, if a man say, "I love God, and hateth his brother, he is a liar," 1 John iv. 20, 21. From this, and similar language used in the Scriptures, it is evident, that brotherly love is an indispensable duty upon all the followers of the Lamb.

Brotherly love is not only an incumbent duty upon all believers, but it is a very comfortable evidence of their gracious state; for says the apostle, "We know that we have passed from death unto life, because we love the brethren: he that loveth not his brother abideth in death," 1 John iii. 14. From this passage it appears evident that all Christians, from the circumstance of their loving the brethren, may draw the comfortable and assured conclusion, that they have passed from spiritual death to spiritual life, or in other words, that they are regenerated or born of God, and made heirs of eternal glory. As an evidence of gracious affections, it is not common for this to stand alone; but is generally attended with other distinguishing marks whereby a person may judge of his gracious state. But we still think that there are seasons when almost every other mark is lost, and when this is the Christian's principle, if not only support. And we believe it to be abundantly sufficient to preserve him from sinking in despair.

We will review the delightful passage. Figure to yourselves a person just made acquainted with his dreadful situation as a sinner—condemned by the law of God—a load of guilt upon his soul—ready, in his own apprehension, to drop into endless misery—but waiting, with an anxiety bordering on despair, to receive some comfort from the word of God, querying with the beloved disciple as he delivers these words, in the following manner, "We know," says John,—'what,' says the disconsolate sinner, 'do you know?' "That we have passed from death unto life." O! happy saint! do you certainly know that this is your situation? A knowledge this, worth ten thousand worlds! would to God that I had but the smallest gleam of hope, that such a blessing belonged to me! But let me ask, 'How do you know it?' "Because we love the brethren." O! beloved of the Lord! do you say that this is a certain sign of such an important event as that of having passed from death unto life? Yes; the Holy Ghost instructs me to assert it for the benefit of his people; and you may rest assured that he who truly loves his brother hath been delivered from death, and hath a right to all the blessings of the covenant of grace. And to check the presumption of hypocrites, I am further instructed, by the same authority, to declare that "he that loveth not his brother abideth in death."

Brotherly love is not only an evidence to ourselves that we are born of God, but also to others: For says Christ, "By this shall all men know that ye are my disciples, if ye have love one to another," John xiii. 35. It is only when Christians are wearing Christ's livery, and completely equipped with the gospel armor, that they appear "fair as the moon, clear as the sun, and terrible as an army with banners," Cant. vi. 10. It is only those whose general conversation is such as becometh the gospel, that appear respectable to the eyes of mankind. For the path of the Christian is so plainly pointed out in the word of God, that even the wicked world can readily discern the least deviation in their steps. And when professors allow themselves to fall in with the vain and sinful customs of the world, and especially when they are contentious, and give themselves up to backsliding and evil-speaking, one of another, they become a stumbling-block to young converts, and a laughing-stock to infidels. Let us, therefore, be exceeding careful, in all our conduct, to "give none occasion to the adversary to speak reproachfully," 1 Tim. v. 14.

As every thing that is valuable may be counterfeited—and as there may be danger of the love we profess to have for the brethren being spurious, (and therefore no certain mark of our sonship,) we will describe the nature and effects of brotherly love, that you may be able to determine what degree of consolation you may draw from it.

With respect to its nature. It is a holy love—of the same kind that is in God himself: for it is a grace communicated from him, therefore must be the same in kind, though not in degree. Here we will just observe, that the love of God is the display of his attribute of goodness which delights in the happiness of its object. And though God is good to all his creatures, "making his sun to rise on the evil and on the good, and sending rain on the just and on the unjust," (Matt. v. 45;) yet his approving, everlasting, and unchangeable love is only placed upon his elect ones. These, as sanctified, and especially as having the perfect righteousness of Christ imputed unto them, Jehovah beholds with complacency, and delights to do them good. Of this he has given the highest proof, in the gift of his Son—and, with him, he will freely give them all things that will be to their advantage, Rom. viii. 32. "The Lord will give grace and glory: no good thing will he withhold from them that walk uprightly," Psalm lxxxiv. 11. And brotherly love, having a divine origin, must be an holy affection—and, like that of Jehovah, will fix upon suitable objects, and delight to promote their happiness.

Our love to God will be manifested by our obedience, (John xiv. 15,) and our love to his people, by our exertions to do them good. It is in vain to say we love them, and at the same time be in the habit of spreading, and perhaps magnifying, their faults. Had we that "fervent charity among ourselves," to which we are exhorted by Peter, it would "cover the multitude of sins," 1 Peter iv. 8. It is incongruous to suppose we love them, if, having the means, we withhold relief when they need it. Or as John expresses it, "whoso hath this worlds good, and seeth his brother have need, and shutteth up his bowels of compassion from him, how dwelleth the love of God in him?" 1 John iii. 17. Dear brethren, "let us not love in word, neither in tongue, but in deed and in truth." Let us evidence our love, by feeding the hungry, clothing the naked, visiting the sick, and cheerfully rendering them all the service in our power. In this way, let us manifest to the world that our professions are not mere empty sound; and give them reason to say, like the heathen in former days, "See how these Christians love one another."

There are many important duties that Christians owe to each other, the source of which is love. And where this is active, those will be performed. Some of them are of a negative kind, and are essential to the peace and prosperity of the church. Such are the exhortations to avoid all unprofitable debates, envying, backbiting, tattling, and busying ourselves in other people's matters. If we possess this active principle, instead of being guilty of these, we shall be found in the practice of those positive duties enjoined upon us. Such as relieving the distressed—bearing with one another—praying with and for one another—promoting peace and harmony—watching over each other—and where any are wandering out of the way, endeavoring, in the spirit of meekness, to restore such—and by every other means in our power, advancing the interest of the Redeemer's kingdom, and promoting the happiness of its subjects.

Dear brethren, if you are found faithful in the cheerful performance of these duties, you are in possession of one bright evidence that you are the children of God, and heirs of eternal glory, in their pilgrimage towards their future inheritance, "standing fast in one spirit, with one mind affectionately striving together for the faith of the gospel," (Phil. i. 27;) and uniting against their common enemies. "Behold, how good and how pleasant it is for brethren to dwell together in unity," Psalm cxxxii. 1.

This precious grace will extend itself to all who bear the divine image. It knows no bounds till it meets with unworthy objects. For as he who truly loves God, loves him as possessing all the perfections of Deity; so will he love all those who bear the marks of being born of God, of all nations, languages and denominations whatever. And those who live nearest to the Lord in all holy conversation, together with a zealous attachment to the pure principles of religion, will be most loved by all the true followers of Christ.

We shall close with the apostolic exhortation, "Add to your faith, virtue, knowlege, temperance, patience, godliness, brotherly kindness, and charity. For if these things be in you and abound, they make you that ye shall be neither barren nor unfruitful in the knowledge of our Lord Jesus Christ," 2 Peter i. 5–8. "Finally, brethren farewell: be perfect, be of good comfort, be of one mind, live in peace; and the God of love and peace shall be with you," 2 Cor. xiii. 11. Amen.

THOMAS B. MONTANYE, Moderator.
WILLIAM STAUGHTON, Clerk.

THE MINISTERS AND MESSENGERS AT THE ASSOCIATION, AND STATE OF THE CHURCHES DURING THE YEAR.

CHURCHES.	MINISTERS AND MESSENGERS.	Baptized.	Received by Letter.	Dismis'd.	Excom.	Restored.	Deceased.	Members.
Lower Dublin,	Samuel Jones, Thomas Holmes, Jesse Dungan, Joseph Wright, Abednego Whilton,	24	1	1	0	0	3	116
Middletown,	Benjamin Bennet, John Stillwell, Jacob Conover,	4	0	0	1	0	2	144
Cohansie,	Henry Smalley,* Jeremiah Brooks,	6	3	3	0	0	2	182
Great Valley,	David Jones, Horatio G. Jones, Isaac Buley,	0	2	2	0	0	0	65
Cape May,	Jonathan Garman,*	0	0	0	0	0	1	46
Hopewell, 1st church,	James Ewing, Nathan Stout, Jesse Stout,	0	3	17	2	0	0	157
Brandywine,	Joshua Vaughan, John Petit,	5	0	2	0	0	0	115
Montgomery,	Silas Hough, Charles Humphrey, Joseph Lunn, Thomas Davis, John Harris,	1	1	2	1	1	0	79
Kingwood,	Garner A. Hunt,* Thomas Lequear, Thomas Robertson,	24	0	0	0	0	3	113
Hight's Town,	Peter Wilson, Thomas Allen,	37	3	74	2	1	11	352
Philadelphia, 1st church,	William Staughton, William Rogers, John P. Peckworth, *Thomas Billings,** George Engles, John M'Leod, Joseph Keen,	10	14	5	2	1	5	190
Southampton,	Thomas B. Montanye, Nathan Marple, Nathan Banes, George Shelmire, Peter Sauerman, Barnard Vanhorne,	21	1	1	1	0	2	121
Knowlton,†	——— ———	0	0	0	0	0	0	17
Salem,	John Walker, Joseph Lloyd,	5	0	10	1	0	2	123

MINUTES OF THE PHILADELPHIA ASSOCIATION. 419

CHURCHES.	MINISTERS AND MESSENGERS.	Baptized.	Received by Letter.	Dismis'd.	Excom.	Restored.	Deceased.	Members.
New Britain,	Edward Matthew, Benjamin Matthew, Ephraim Thomas, William James, Abiah James, John Hines,	0	0	1	2	0	1	85
Dividing Creek,	DAVID STOUT,	4	0	0	0	0	0	60
New Mills,	ALEXANDER M'GOWAN, ISAAC CARLISLE,	6	1	0	0	0	2	123
Upper Freehold,	——— ———	5	1	1	0	0	1	86
Pittsgrove,	——— ———	1	1	1	0	0	0	21
Manahawkin,	Samuel Gray,	44	2	3	0	1	0	74
Vincent,	Enos Miles,	3	1	1	0	0	1	38
Tuckahoe,†	——— ———	0	0	0	0	0	0	28
Hilltown,	Joseph Matthias, Philip Miller, Ashbel Jones, John Davis, Thomas Lunn, Lewis Bitting,	0	0	3	0	0	1	127
Jacob's Town,	BURGISS ALLISON,	2	0	2	0	0	1	61
Marcus Hook,†	——— ———	0	0	0	0	0	0	22
Roxbury,	THOMAS FLEESON, John Levering, Nathan Levering, jr.,	2	0	1	4	0	0	50
West Creek,	PETER GROOM,*	0	0	0	0	0	1	53
Shemokin,	JOHN PATTEN,*	0	0	3	1	0	0	89
Amwell,	Samuel Hunt, Aaron Stout,	10	0	0	2	0	0	76
Burlington,	William Boswell,* Joseph Shepherd, George Allen, Stephen C. Ustick, Matthew Randall,	14	3	2	0	1	0	79
Mount Holly,	Jesse Cox, Joseph Evans, William Rogers,	44	2	2	4	0	2	130
Dover, York county,	Moses Davis,	1	0	4	0	0	2	21
Philadelphia, 2d church,	WILLIAM WHITE, Isaac Johnson, Adam Corfield, Richard Proudfoot, Thomas Altimus,	34	5	3	6	0	0	111

CHURCHES.	MINISTERS AND MESSENGERS.	Baptized.	Received by Letter.	Dismis'd.	Excom.	Restored.	Deceased.	Members.
Hopewell, 2d church,	James Hill, Daniel Drake,	1	5	2	1	0	0	54
Blockley,	JOHN RUTTER, Heath Norbury, Amos Penager,	16	1	0	1	1	0	33
Squan,	Samuel Haven,	0	0	0	0	0	0	38
		324	50	146	41	6	43	3279

NOTE.—The ministers' names are in SMALL CAPITALS. Licensed preachers in *italic*. Those marked thus * were not present. From churches marked thus † received no letter. A dash —— denotes no settled minister.

⁎ Six persons have been baptised and added to the Welsh church, at Lower Dublin, during the year.

MINUTES

OF THE

PHILADELPHIA BAPTIST ASSOCIATION,

HELD, BY APPOINTMENT, AT PHILADELPHIA, OCTOBER
7TH, 8TH, 9TH, AND 10TH,

1806.

October 7th.—At three o'clock, P. M., Brother Horatio G. Jones preached the introductory sermon, from Matt. xxviii. 20, "Lo I am with you alway, even to the end of the world."

2. After sermon, business was opened with prayer by Brother T. B. Montanye, when Brother Henry Smalley was chosen moderator, and Brother William Staughton, clerk.

3. Letters from thirty-six churches were read.

Brother Rogers prayed.

Adjourned till nine o'clock to-morrow morning.

October 8th, nine o'clock, A. M.—Met agreeably to adjournment. Brother Carlile prayed.

4. Ministering brethren of sister Associations and churches, of good standing in their respective churches, who were present, were invited to a seat with us.

5. The newly constituted church at Evesham, and another new church at Trenton and Lamberton, applying for admission into our body, were accordingly received.

6. Received corresponding letters and minutes from the following Associations:—From Charleston, a letter and minutes; from New York, minutes and corresponding letter, by their messengers William Parkinson and John Ellis; from Warren, minutes and corresponding letter; from Miami, letters and copies of their minutes for 1805 and 1806; from Redstone Association, minutes; from Delaware, minutes and a letter, by their messengers Gideon Ferrell and Daniel Dodge; from Shaftsbury, their minutes and corresponding letter.

7. Received a letter from Brother Stephen Gano, of Providence, with proposals for a small work, entitled, "Biographical Sketches of the late Rev. John Gano, written principally by himself." This Association, retaining an affectionate remembrance of that worthy servant of Jesus, recommend the work to the purchase of the brethren.

8. The following brethren were appointed to write to the corresponding Associations:—Allison, to the Charleston; Montanye, to the

New York; Hough, to the Warwick, ; Rogers, to the Warren; Hunt, to the Miami; Ustick, to the Redstone; Sheppard, to the Delaware; Samuel Jones, to the Shaftsbury.

Brother Ferrell prayed.

Adjourned to three o'clock, P. M.

Three o'clock, P. M.—Met pursuant to adjournment. Brother S. Jones prayed.

9. Appointed our Brethren Samuel Jones, William White, and Thomas B. Montanye, a committee to examine the minutes of the different corresponding Associations, and report if there be any business upon them, to which it may be proper this Association should attend.

10. The circular letter, drawn up by our Brother Rogers, was read, and our Brethren David Jones, Staughton and Allison, in conjunction with the writer, were appointed a committee to revise it.

11. This Association heard the report of the committee, who were appointed on the subject of a difficulty between the churches of Middletown and Hightstown, and are happy to find that the difficulty which had respect to John Cooper, is removed.

12. The church at Hightstown having found that the conduct of said Cooper (late of Nova Scotia, now of Middletown) has been notoriously censurable, have excommunicated him. The churches will govern themselves accordingly.

13. The following brethren were appointed messengers to our sister Associations:—To New York, Brethren Thomas B. Montanye and Henry Smalley; to Warren, Brethren William Rogers and Peter Wilson; to Delaware, Brethren William White, Isaac Carlile, and Joshua Vaughan.

Brother David Jones prayed.

Adjourned till to-morrow morning at 10 o'clock.

Sermon this evening by Brother Parkinson, from Rom. ix. 22–24, and by Brother Ferrell, from Jer. xxiii. 29.

October 9th, 10 o'clock.—Met pursuant to adjournment. Brother Samuel Jones prayed.

14. On reconsidering the queries sent to the Association by the first church of Philadelphia last year, they agree to withdraw them, substituting the following query in their stead:

"Would it not be advisable to appoint a committee to examine and see if there be not rules in the new system of discipline which are discordant with the old, and which might be so connected as to render them both harmonious?"

Agreed that it be postponed for consideration until the next Association.

15. It is recommended that the quarterly prayer meetings be continued, excepting the first Tuesday in October, instead of which the Association recommends the Thursday preceding.

16. It is recommended that collections be made, or subscriptions increased, or both be attended to, for the use of the mission society, as much as can conveniently be done.

17. The Association recommends that collections be made in all the churches in which they have not been made, and repeated, if found convenient, in the churches in which they have already been made, for assisting our brethren in Serampore in the translation of the Scriptures into the several languages of India, and that the moneys be transmitted, by or before the next Association, to our Brother Rogers, to be by him deposited in the hands of Robert Ralston, Esq., to whom gratitude is due for his disinterested and obliging attention to the reception of moneys, and their transmission to India.

18. Appointed supplies for Pittsgrove, Manahawkin, and Dover. Brother Wilson prayed.

Adjourned to three o'clock, P. M.

Three o'clock, P. M.—Met agreeably to adjournment. Brother Allison prayed.

Continued the appointing of supplies, for Frankford and Squan.

The ministering brethren in Philadelphia, engage to supply the Frankford brethren as often as they can.

As several of the ministering brethren who are present, cannot immediately fix upon any particular times for the supplying of the above-named churches, and some who are absent, we believe, are disposed to serve them, it is affectionately recommended to the brethren that they visit the churches named above, as often as they conveniently can.

Supplies were also appointed for Trenton and Lamberton.

19. The circular letter presented by the committee was adopted by the Association.

20. Resolved, That our Brethren Samuel Jones and T. B. Montanye, with the librarian, William Staughton, be a committee to make out a list of the books belonging to this Association, and that the persons holding the books send certificates of what books they possess as soon as they may be able.

21. Brother William Staughton is appointed to write the circular letter for next year, and the subject recommended is an answer to the inquiry,—"What are the qualifications of a Gospel Minister?"

22. Brother Samuel Jones is appointed to preach the Association sermon of next year, which is intended to be a century one—a hundred years having passed since we were first formed. In case of failure, Brother White will deliver a sermon on any subject he may approve.

23. Query from the first church in Philadelphia: What is the smallest number of members necessary for forming a gospel church?

Answer: On this head different sentiments are entertained. Some have supposed two or three are sufficient, others have imagined five, some ten, and others twelve, because it would seem that the church at Ephesus was formed of twelve men, Acts xix. 7. The Association is of opinion, however, that much depends on the probability of the persons living permanently together who may be about to be constituted. It appears desirable that there be in a new settlement, where removals are frequent, at least seven, and that of these two or three be males.

24. Query: Whether can an orthodox Baptist church receive a person who has been baptized by a Tunker Universalist, without baptizing him again? The person has renounced Universalist principles.

Answer. Yes.

Brother M'Gowan prayed.

Adjourned till nine o'clock to-morrow morning.

Sermon by Brother Montanye, from John x. 28; by Brother Dodge, Acts viii. 5; by Brother Parkinson, Matt. viii. 2.

October 11th.—Met pursuant to adjournment. Brother Peter Smith, of the Miami Association, prayed.

25. The letters appointed to be written to the sister Associations were read, and, after some amendments, adopted.

26. Voted a revision of the rules for conducting business in this Association; and that Brethren Samuel Jones, Rogers, and Staughton, be a committee for the purpose, who are requested to produce them the next Association.

27. The committee appointed on the memorial of six members of the first Baptist church of Philadelphia, report that in their opinion, said memorial ought not to be taken up by this Association.

The Association concurred with the report.

28. Brother Rogers submitted to the Association, "Proposals for continuing by subscription, the Massachusetts Baptist Missionary Magazine, published for the benefit of the society." This Association recommend the work to the churches, and for their information observe that eight numbers are already published, and that it comes out quarterly, at twelve and a half cents each number. Our Brethren W. Rogers and Peter Wilson, are appointed agents for this work, within the bounds of this Association.

29. This Association recommend to Dr. Samuel Jones the abridgment of Robinson's History of Baptism, so as to reduce it to the size of a dollar volume; but, that every sentiment in it, contrary to our received evangelical doctrines, be totally expunged.

30. The following sums were collected:—

FOR THE EDUCATION FUND.		FOR THE MISSION FUND.	
From Lower Dublin,	$9 50	From Great Valley,	$19 17
Cohansie,	10 00	Montgomery,	7 62
Hight's Town,	5 00	New Britain,	5 63
Salem,	8 00	Southampton,	9 00
Middletown,	3 00	Hilltown,	8 20
First Hopewell,	4 00	Roxbury,	10 15
		Hight's Town,	5 00
		Trenton and Lamberton,	5 00
		Salem,	8 00
		Philadelphia,	32 94
	$39 50		$110 71

31. The Association is appointed to meet in 1807, in the first Baptist

Church, Philadelphia, and in case of any malignant disease prevailing in that city, at Trenton and Lamberton meeting-house.

32. Our Brother S. C. Ustick is appointed to print the minutes and letters, and our brethren at Philadelphia, Rogers, White, Peckworth, and Staughton, are requested to superintend their distribution.

Brother Staughton concluded by prayer.

REPORT OF THE CORRESPONDING COMMITTEE.

At their meeting, January 29th, 1806, the following communications were produced and read by the corresponding secretary.

1. A letter from Brother Asahel Morse, of Stratfield, Fairfield township, Connecticut, mentioning the death of Elder Stephen Royce, and the prosperity of the churches within the vicinity of his residence, together with a copy of the Danbury Association minutes.

2. A letter from Thomas G. Jones, stating the origin, constitution, and present state of the churches, Warren and Sharon, which lie North West of the Ohio river, and belong to the Redstone Association: with several other articles of interesting information.

3. A communication from some of the brethren of the Sarepta Association, who mention their high approbation of the plan the committee has adopted: They state that there are four Associations in Georgia—the Hephzibah, the Savannah, the Georgia, and the Sarepta—and express their hope to be able to transmit other communications shortly.

4. A letter from our Brother Bradley, of Newport, Rhode Island, addressed to Mr. John Dayton, of Philadelphia, mentioning the existence of a revival in the church with which he is connected.

At their meeting, October 10th, 1806, a communication was read by Brother William Rogers, corresponding secretary, from the Bethel Baptist Association, South Carolina, containing a large and interesting account of its rise. It was formed November, 1789, and consisted of only ten churches, but so increased, that in August, 1800, fourteen churches were dismissed from their body to form the Broad River Association; and, in the year 1802, nine churches were dismissed to assist in forming what is called the Saluda Association. In the years 1802 and 1803, a great revival took place among them. In 1805, the number of churches was forty-nine—of ministers, fifty, and of members, 4092.

The committee feel a sense of gratitude to the Bethel Association, for their pious, affectionate, and instructive communication, made by Brother David Lilly, and hope to hear further from them.

A true extract from the minutes.

WILLIAM STAUGHTON, Recording Secretary.

Brethren Ferrell and Matthias preached this evening.

CIRCULAR LETTER.

BY REV. WILLIAM ROGERS.

The ministers and messengers of the Philadelphia Baptist Association.

To the churches they represent, send Christian salutation.

Beloved brethren,—Having been permitted, once more, to assemble together, in our metropolis, without any interruption from pestilential disease, we would offer our thanks to Almighty God; and having received and heard your affectionate communications, our hearts rejoice in your joy and sympathize in your griefs.

Accustomed to address you annually, in a letter of Christian love, we proceed with pleasure to the task, and fervently pray that by this service your bosoms may be strengthened and refreshed in the Lord. At the present season, when a new era appears to have sprung up in the Christian church, when the servants of God, both in the Old World and in the New, dissatisfied with exhibiting the glories of the Redeemer in the vicinity of their own habitations, stand prepared to bear the lamp of the Lord's Anointed amid the glooms of the deserts and into the regions where the human frame is almost stiffened with cold or scorched with sunshine;—at a season too when distinguished success follows such pious endeavors, and when we are loudly called upon to come "to the help of the Lord, to the help of the Lord against the mighty," we feel desirous of addressing you on the important subject of Christian missions.

We will endeavor, by divine assistance, to exhibit—

I. The principles on which they proceed.

II. The extent to which they have been carried, and

III. The encouragements we possess for future exertions.

I. In inquiring into the principles which have given birth to missionary toils, we are struck with the difference between them and those principles which actuate the world. Distant climes are not traced that wealth may be gotten, reputation and ease secured—that curiosity may be indulged, or the blood of thousands wantonly shed. The servant of Christ goes forth prepared to suffer, with his Lord, poverty and reproach; perils from his countrymen and perils from the heathen. The awfulness of his message and the responsibility of his office elevate him above the vanities of curiosity, and on the banners which he plants are inscribed, "Peace on earth and good will towards men."

The following principles have given rise to Christian missions, and sway the conduct of faithful missionaries:

1. A deep conviction of the fallen state of the human race.

Once indeed man was in honor, but now he is in disgrace. "Wo unto us that we have sinned."—In our common father we have all sunk in the abyss of original defection, and are all actual offenders against a righteous God. Many have endeavored to extenuate the offences of the heathen world. Idolaters have been represented as the untaught children of nature, whom the Supreme being would rather pity than punish; but such are not the representations of the holy Scriptures, the oracles of divine truth. That they who have sinned without the law, will be judged without the law, is admitted; but it is expressly declared, that "the wrath of God is revealed from heaven against all ungodliness and unrighteousness of men." That such as "change the glory of the uncorruptible God into an image" are "without excuse." And that "the judgment of God is," that "they who commit such things are worthy of death." Who will dare to oppose his judgment to the judgment of infinite wisdom and righteousness? Or, who can be inactive when he hears the Bible proclaim "Indignation and wrath, tribulation and anguish, upon every soul of man that doeth evil, to the Jew first and also to the Gentile?"

2. Another principle influencing to holy labor is—the total inability of the sons and daughters of men to deliver themselves.

The Jews on our earth, amounting to, at least, seven millions of its inhabitants, are still resting in the Mosaic law, a law which Christ has abolished, and which, were it now in force, could not effect their salvation, it being impossible for the blood of bulls and goats to take away sin. The Mahometans, whose number is full one hundred and thirty millions, found their hopes of paradise on zeal for the Koran, veneration for Mahomet, pilgrimages to Mecca, and the persecution of heretics; but alas, what can these do for a sinner's salvation, if, as we are persuaded, the Koran is false, Mahomet an impostor, the pilgrimage folly, and the persecution iniquitous?—The heathen, amounting to about four hundred and twenty millions, place their expectations of life eternal, in the adoration of the heavenly bodies, or of idols, which having eyes see not. They hope for salvation because they worship and wash in rivers, or because they torture and abuse their bodies in a variety of ways at which reason shudders and humanity weeps. Spits run through their tongues, threads passed through the sides, hooks fastened in their backs, the burning of women on the funeral piles of their husbands, and the crushing to death of men under the wheels of the carriages of their gods, are among the numberless devices invented by them to take away sin.— Of the remaining inhabitants of our earth, consisting of one hundred millions of Roman Catholics, forty-four millions of Protestants, and thirty millions of the Greek and Armenian churches, how many are found depending on future happiness on penances, dispensations and unscriptural rights and ceremonies. Do and live was the law given to man in innocence. Do and live is the favorite maxim of our fallen race; whereas all our doings are polluted, and the word of God expressly declares, "that by the deeds of the law no flesh living shall be justified."

3. Another principle is, that there is in Christ all that fulness of salvation that poor and miserable sinners stand in need of.

Jesus Christ is the glorious Mediator between God and man: his blood can atone and his righteousness can justify. His Holy Spirit can change the stoutest heart, arrest the deepest prejudices, beget in the breast where sin has abounded the most fervent desires after perfect holiness, and transform the most infatuated idolator, or the most abandoned profligate, into a child of wisdom and an exemplary saint. The faithful missionary knows that Christ Jesus the Lord is appointed of the Father, and is exalted by his own merit, to be a hiding place from the storm and a covert from the tempest, and that there is "no other name under heaven given among men whereby we can be saved."—An experimental sense, therefore, of the glory and the worth of the Redeemer, inspires the wish that all the ends of the earth may come and serve him.

4. It animates the heart farther to learn that this way of salvation shall be known in all the earth.

The sacred page is replete with prophecies to this effect. A few may serve as a specimen of many. "It shall come to pass, in the last days, that the mountain of the Lord's house shall be established in the top of the mountains and shall be exalted above the hills, and all nations shall flow unto it," Isa. ii. 2. "For the earth shall be full of the knowledge of the Lord as the waters cover the sea," Isa. xi. 9. "Living waters shall go out from Jerusalem,"—like an ocean breaking forth on each side,—"half of them towards the former sea, and half of them towards the hinder sea: in summer and winter shall it be. And the Lord shall be King over all the earth; in that day shall there be one Lord, and his name one," Zech. xiv. 8, 9. "Afterward he measured a thousand; and it was a river that I could not pass over: for the waters were risen, waters to swim in, a river that could not be passed over," Ezek. xlvii. 5. The progress of Christ's kingdom will be gradual, like the growth of the mustard tree or the operation of leaven, but at last it will be victorious. The stone which has already smitten the image is becoming a great mountain and must fill the earth.

5. We will mention but one missionary principle more, namely,—That the means by which, instrumentally, the great work is to be effected, is the ministration of the Divine Word.

We would not be understood as supposing that this is the only means. Whenever salvation goes forth as a lamp that burneth, it will be in answer to the prayers of Zion, and as it extends, private Christians will, in their several circles, be instructors too: "Every man shall teach his neighbor and every man his brother until all shall know the Lord." The King of kings may also render famines, earthquakes, pestilence, wars, or revolutions of empires, channels of peculiar instruction; but, it is at least presumable, that under the indefatigable labors of Zion's missionaries, his kingdom will come. Earthen vessels will bear the celestial treasure. The commission of Christ directs his ministers to "go out into all the world." "Many shall run to and fro and knowledge shall be increased." Israel anciently was often recovered from the backslidings by the holy prophets. The light of the reformation came forth and spread, while eminent men of God were bearing their testimony. Then may we not hope, and ardently expect, that the glory of the latter day will be visible, when the precious sound of evangelical ministers has gone out into all lands and "their words unto the ends of the world?"

II. Influenced by these important considerations, and urged on by the love of immortal souls, many of the servants of IMMANUEL have gone forth, and are now employed in various and distant climes.

To give you, dear brethren, a full statement of the extent and success of their labors would, were it even in our power, be transgressing the bounds prescribed for our annual epistle. We will, however, in as brief a manner as possible, mention a few facts for your information and encouragement.

The commission of our Lord, as before observed, directed the apostles to go and teach "all nations," and, in Mark xvi. 20, we read that they went forth and preached "EVERY WHERE." They were not stationed ministers, but ITINERATING missionaries. From the testimony of Eusebius and others, it appears that Peter visited Pontus, Galatia, and the places adjacent; that Andrew directed his course into Scythia, John into Lesser Asia, Philip into Media and Armenia, Bartholomew into Arabia, Matthew into Persia, Thomas into Judea, Jude into Syria, Simon the Canaanite into Lybia and Egypt, and Matthias into Capadocia; while Paul, as a seraph, flew almost everywhere to win souls to Jesus Christ.

The first age of Christianity was eminently an age of missions. But after the decease of the apostles, the seed they had sown was left to spring up,—corruptions gradually entered the church,—the man of sin began at length to be revealed, and desire for the salvation of men was lost in the pursuit of ecclesiastical usurpation, pomp, and revenue.

It is however, a very remarkable circumstance, that in modern missions Papal Rome has led the way.—" When the Roman Pontiffs," says Moshiem, "saw their ambition checked by the progress of the Reformation, which deprived them of a great part of their spiritual dominion in Europe, they turned their lordly views towards the other parts of the globe." The society, which in the year 1540, took the denomination of Jesuits, or the company of Jesus, were by the Pope chiefly employed, at first in India, Japan and China, after which they spared no pains in propagating their erroneous sentiments in the West Indies and on the continent of America.

In the year 1556, Protestants began to feel for the nations involved in paganism. Fourteen missionaries were sent from Geneva to America. The Swedes also exerted their zeal for the conversion of the superstitious Laplanders, and both the English and the Dutch carried with them into their increasing foreign settlements the doctrines of the reformation.

Early in the last century the Moravians began to organize and exert themselves in the missionary cause. Their spheres of action have gradually increased; besides their missions in six of the West India islands, they have settlements in Greenland, Upper Canada, and South America; their missionaries are employed also at the Cape of Good Hope, on the coast of Labrador, and in the Russian part of Asia. The zeal, the afflictions, and the success of these United Brethren have been great.

Patronized by Christians in Scotland and in America, Elliott, Brainerd, Edwards, and others labored among the aborigines of our country; but it was not till about the year 1790, that the great missionary spirit, which now exists, began to diffuse itself.

On the minds of our Brother Carey and of several of the brethren of the Northamptonshire Baptist Association in England, the case of the benighted pagans lay with weight. Prayer meetings for the spread of the gospel were established, and a pamphlet was composed and published by Brother Carey, stating and enforcing the obligations of Christians to exert themselves for the conversion of the heathen. The holy flame spread, until in the year 1792, the Baptist missionary society was formed. Bengal was determined upon as the seat of the mission, and our Brethren Carey and Thomas were first sent thither. A mission house has been purchased and a church constituted at Serampore, near Calcutta. Many of the natives have been added to the Lord, and some of them have died triumphing in redeeming love. Though the mission has suffered loss in the removal of several of the missionaries by death, yet the loss has been repaired by the accession of others. Ten or twelve brethren with their wives were, by the latest accounts, engaged there in advancing a Redeemer's interest. Several natives, and some of them Brahmans, are also preachers of a glorious gospel. A new church has lately been formed at Dinagepore, under the care of Brother Fernandez, and the constitution of two or three more churches was in contemplation when our brethren last wrote us. Twenty-seven persons were baptized last year, and fifteen more were under hopeful impressions. The whole word of God is translated into the Bengalee, and the second edition of the New Testament is in the press. Nearly the whole of the New and some parts of the Old Testament are translated into Mahratta, Orissa, Hindostanee, and Persian languages, and the good work is still proceeding. The gains that are drawn by our Brother Carey from the College of Fort William, in which he is the oriental professor, and those by our Brother Marshman from the school, and by our Brother Ward from the press, are cordially devoted, as are the gains of all the brethren, to the advancement of the cause of Jesus. Oh that the Lord may abundantly recompense their self-denial, and gloriously prosper their arduous and pious effort!

By the same society an attempt was made to establish a mission at Sierra Leone, in Africa. Two brethren were sent thither, but the sickness of the one and the imprudent political interference of the other, terminated the favorable expectations which were indulged of a settlement on that coast.

The piety, the engagedness, and the activity, which were so visible among the members of the Baptist churches, operated on other evangelical societies to such a commendable degree as to produce anxious desires to be employed in the same way.

Hence, in the year 1795, two hundred ministers of different denominations assembled in London and formed "the London Missionary Society." Large sums have been collected, and this numerous society is zealously alive in causing the name of the Lord Jesus to be made known far and wide. Its first efforts were directed toward the islands in the South Seas. They have since sent missionaries to the Cape of Good Hope, Canada, Newfoundland, and India. It is generally believed that there are under their patronage about one hundred missionaries.

Several societies of a similar kind have arisen of late in Scotland, and other parts of Europe, and in the United States.

Aided by our Baptist friends, and especially by the New York convention, our Brother Holmes has labored among the Indians of the Six Nations, among whom, to the praise of illustrious grace, great inquiries have been made respecting the way to heaven.

At the last Association in New York, a Baptist mission society was established there.

The Dutch Reformed Church have also sent missionaries on the frontiers of our country and into Upper Canada.

The Methodists likewise, amidst great opposition and persecution, are persevering in maintaining a public ministry among the negroes and others in the West Indies.

The Massachusetts Baptist Mission Society, which was formed in May, 1802, have, in manifold instances, found the blessings of the Lord following their Christian and benevolent exertions. The magazine published by them quarterly, the profits of which are appropriated for the furtherance of the cause of God and of truth, is fraught with desirable information on this interesting subject.

The Philadelphia Baptist Missionary Society, of which several of us are members, though of recent formation, has not been left to struggle in vain. Brother T. G. Jones, who is our missionary in the eastern parts of the State of Ohio, has already made a communication of agreeable tidings. In order to baptize believers in Jesus, he has led them into waters where this holy ordinance was never administered before, and on a late tour he constituted a new Baptist church near the town of Lisbon. Numbers listened eagerly to the preaching of the cross, and in the work his heart appears to be much enlarged.

The general assembly of the Presbyterian church in the United States has of late become a missionary body. During the three years previous to 1802, seven or eight missionaries were annually employed, and since then have increased to fifteen or twenty. The principal spheres of their exertions are among the settlers on the frontiers of the country, the blacks and a few of the Indian tribes.

The Charleston Baptist Association of South Carolina, at their last session, received favorable accounts from their missionary, Brother John Rooker, relative to his ministration among the Catawba

Indians. They have engaged him to continue with them, and are about establishing a school for the instruction of their youth.

Of the Congregational Mission Societies of Connecticut, Massachusetts, and New Hampshire, we would now give brief statements, with pleasure, were it not for the circumscribed limits of our annual letter. We wish them every one success, so far as truth is maintained, in the name of the Lord God of Sabaoth!

III. And now, beloved brethren, from the unvarnished accounts we have given you, though by far too short, permit us with all seriousness to intreat you to judge of the signs of the times. Have we not almost superabounding encouragements for future exertions?—The sky looks red and we think rain may be expected. Oh for showers of righteousness to bless the plains below!

Prophecy, as it relates to time, is no rule of action. It has been the pleasure of the Holy Ghost so to involve in mystery the numbers, according to which the time when "these things shall be" is to arrive, as that the profoundest theologians, the ablest servants of Jesus have been, and still are, divided in their interpretations of the same. But if the time, the set time to favor Zion may be known by her children taking pleasure in her stones, we cannot but ardently hope that it is at hand.

The best interpreter of prophecy is its fulfilment. It is an excellent remark of Sir Isaac Newton, that "The folly of interpreters has been to foretell times and things by prophecy, as if God designed to make them prophets. The design of God was much otherwise. He gave the revelations of John and the prophecies of the Old Testament, not to gratify men's curiosity by enabling them to foreknow things, but that after they were fulfilled, they might be interpreted by the event; and his own providence, not the interpreter's, be manifested thereby to the world." Such seems to be the meaning of the answer of the "man clothed in linen, who was upon the waters of the river," to Daniel (Ch. xii. 9.) The prophet was eager to know what and what manner of time the prophecy he had heard referred to: the reply was, "Go thy way, Daniel, for the words are closed up and sealed till the time of the end." The keys of time, as the great, Poole observes, "hang only at the girdle of Christ."

The object of missionary societies, beloved brethren, is great. greater indeed than the Reformation itself. *That* aimed at the overthrow of the beast; *this* at the destruction of the dragon, from whom the beast derived its power: "For this purpose was the Son of God manifested, that he might destroy the works of the devil." The Almighty Conqueror is on his way. In numbers of our churches, in various parts of our Union, the preaching of the cross is evidently the power of God. The uttermost parts of the earth have also furnished us with songs!—O may the season soon come when

"Europe and Asia shall resound,
   With Africa, his fame;
And thou! America, in songs
   Redeeming love proclaim."

O that we all may be truly active in the Saviour's cause. "There is the same difference between diligence and neglect or idleness, as between a garden curiously kept, and the sluggard's field. The one is clothed with beauty, the other with deformity." That the eternal God may be glorified, immortal souls saved, civil society benefited, savage cruelties superseded, and millennial days introduced, are among the many objects contemplated by the industrious sons and daughters of grace. They cannot sleep as do others!—If Macarius did penance for only killing a gnat; if the least misconduct require purification, as was the case with the Jews when they touched things unclean, what must, on reflection, be the suffering of those professing Christians, who, owing to their indifference or sloth, cannot be represented—to put the most favorable construction on their demeanor— as SAVING MUCH PEOPLE ALIVE! What purifications, what interpositions of mercy will they stand in need of, who, while thousands around them are full of energy in order to promote the universal spread of the gospel of peace, are themselves indulging in sleep! "O our souls, come not ye into their secret; unto their assemblies," let each one of us say, "mine honor, be not thou united." The industrious bee, by his sedulity in summer, lives on honey all the winter, while the drone is not only cast out, but beaten and punished. Dear brethren, imitate the industrious bee ; feast on the luxuries of well-doing. Oh be much in prayer. Our Lord teaches us before we ask for daily bread, to petition for the coming of his kingdom. May we be watchful against sin and Satan, circumspect in our deportment, patient in suffering, fervent in spirit, active in duty, and joyful in hope. That the God of peace may sanctify you wholly, is the prayer of yours, in a dear Redeemer,

HENRY SMALLEY, Moderator.
WILLIAM STAUGHTON, Clerk.

It has been the pleasure of the Supreme Head of the church to remove from us, this year, our beloved Brother JAMES EWING. "Blessed are the dead that die in the Lord."

THE MINISTERS AND MESSENGERS AT THE ASSOCIATION, AND STATE OF THE CHURCHES DURING THE YEAR.

CHURCHES.	MINISTERS AND MESSENGERS.	Baptized.	Received by Letter.	Dismiss'd.	Excom.	Restored.	Deceased.	Members.
Lower Dublin,	Samuel Jones, Benjamin Dungan, Thomas Holmes, Jesse Dungan, Abednego T. Whitton, Joseph Wright,	10	12	3	0	1	2	124
Middletown,	Benjamin Bennet, Jehu Patterson,	2	0	1	1	0	4	140
Cohansie,	Henry Smalley, Jeremiah Brooks, Nathan Shepherd, James Shepherd,	17	2	3	1	0	2	195
Great Valley,	David Jones, Horatio G. Jones, Isaac Abraham, Michael M'Cleas, David George,	2	0	2	0	0	3	64
Cape May,	Jonathan Garman,*	1	0	2	1	0	2	42
Hopewell, 1st church,	David Stout, Abraham Servis, Jesse Stout,	2	0	2	2	1	5	150
Brandywine,	Joshua Vaughan, Thomas Baldwin, Thomas Hickman, John Powell, William Griffith,	9	4	3	0	0	3	122
Montgomery,	Silas Hough, Charles Humphrey, Joseph Lunn, William Johnson, William Collom,	3	3	0	0	0	0	85
Kingwood,	Garner A. Hunt, Daniel Bray,	5	0	0	0	0	3	115
Hight's Town,	Peter Wilson,	28	1	50	1	0	2	328
Philadelphia, 1st church,	William Staughton, William Rogers, John P. Peckworth, *Thomas Billings,* George Ingolls, Joseph Keen, Hugh Gorley, Sampson Davis, Jared Sexton, Levi Garret, Benjamin Thaw, John M'Leod,	61	20	4	2	0	3	262
Dividing Creek,	David Stout, Jonadab Shepherd,	1	0	2	0	0	1	58

MINUTES OF THE PHILADELPHIA ASSOCIATION. 435

CHURCHES.	MINISTERS AND MESSENGERS.	Baptized.	Received by Letter.	Dismis'd.	Excom.	Restored.	Deceased.	Members.
Southampton,	Thomas B. Montanye, Elias Yerkes, William Maghee, John Folwell,	3	3	0	0	0	0	127
Knowlton,†		0	0	0	0	0	0	17
New Britain,	Edward Matthews, Ephraim Thomas, William James,	1	0	3	0	0	1	82
Salem,	Thomas Brown, John Walker, Joseph Lloyd,	4	1	12	3	0	4	109
New Mills,	Isaac Carlisle, Benjamin Hedger, Lemuel Howell,*	4	0	7	2	0	4	114
Upper Freehold,		12	1	0	0	0	1	97
Pittsgrove,		1	0	2	0	0	1	19
Manahawkin,	Edward Jennings, Samuel Gray,	2	0	6	0	0	1	69
Vincent,	James Thomas,	8	0	0	0	0	1	46
Tuckahoe,	Elias Smith, Thomas Doughty,	1	0	1	0	1	0	29
Hilltown,	Joseph Matthias, Philip Miller, John Matthias,	0	1	3	0	1	3	123
Jacob's Town,	Burgiss Allison,	0	0	1	0	0	0	60
Marcus Hook,		0	1	1	0	0	2	20
Roxbury,	Thomas Fleeson, John Levering, Anthony Levering, John Walraven,	5	1	0	0	0	0	55
West Creek,	Peter Groom,*	6	1	0	0	0	2	52
Shemokin,	John Patten,* John Hill,	3	0	0	1	0	0	91
Amwell,	James M'Laughlin, Nathaniel Higgins,	1	1	0	0	0	1	77
Burlington,	William Boswell, Joseph Shepherd, Thomas Potts, Stephen C. Ustick, Matthew Randall,	7	0	3	1	0	0	82
Mount Holly,	William Rogers,	11	2	55	1	0	0	55
Dover, York co., Pa.	William Layard,	0	0	0	0	0	0	21

CHURCHES.	MINISTERS AND MESSENGERS.	Baptized.	Received by Letter.	Dismis'd.	Excom.	Restored.	Deceased.	Members.
Philadelphia, 2d church,	William White, Thomas Timmings, Isaac Johnson, Adam Corfield, Thomas Gilbert, James Wiley,	52	8	6	1	1	2	163
Hopewell, 2d church,	——— ——— Levi Knowles,	1	2	2	1	0	0	54
Blockley,	Heath Norberry, William Sheldrake, George C. Lentner,	0	0	0	2	0	0	31
Squan,†		0	0	0	0	0	0	38
Evesham,	Alexander M'Gowan, Joseph Evans, Job Lippincott, Amos Sharp,	0	0	0	0	0	0	64
Trenton and Lamberton,	Amos Raeder, John Sunderland,	0	0	0	0	0	0	46
		263	64	174	20	5	53	3456

Note.—The ministers' names are in SMALL CAPITALS. Licensed preachers in *italic*. Those marked thus * not present. From the churches marked thus † received no intelligence. A dash ——— denotes no settled minister.

MINUTES

OF THE

PHILADELPHIA BAPTIST ASSOCIATION,

HELD BY APPOINTMENT AT PHILADELPHIA, OCTOBER 6TH, 7TH, AND 8TH,

1807.

October 6th.—At three o'clock, P. M., Brother Samuel Jones preached the introductory sermon, from Isa. liv. 2, 3, "Enlarge the place of thy tent, and let them stretch forth the curtains of thine habitations: spare not, lengthen thy cords, and strengthen thy stakes; for thou shalt break forth on the right hand and on the left; and thy seed shall inherit the Gentiles, and make the desolate cities to be inhabited."*

2. After sermon, business was opened with prayer, when Brother William Staughton was chosen moderator, and Brother William White, clerk.

3. Letters from thirty-four churches were read.

Adjourned to nine o'clock to-morrow morning.

Brother Runyan prayed.

Sermon this evening by Brother Lebeus Lathrop, from Hebrews xiii. 5.

October 7th, nine o'clock, A. M.—Met agreeably to adjournment. Brother M'Gowan prayed.

4. Ministering brethren of sister Associations, and of good standing in their respective churches, who were present, were invited to a seat.

5. The newly constituted church of Frankford, applied for admission into this body, and were accordingly received.

6. Received corresponding letters and minutes from the following Associations, viz:—From Charleston, a letter and minutes; from New York, minutes and corresponding letters, by their messengers, Brethren Reune Runyan and Jacob F. Randolph; from Warren, minutes and letters for 1806 and 1807; from the Redstone Association, a letter and minutes; from the Warwick Association, a letter and minutes, presented by their messenger, Lebeus Lathrop; from the Delaware, a letter and minutes, by their messenger Daniel Dodge; from the Shaftsbury, a letter and minutes; from the Stonington, their circular, corresponding letter, and minutes.

---

* The Sermon will be found at the end of the volume.—ED.

7. The following brethren were appointed to write to the corresponding Associations:—To Charleston, Brother Samuel Jones; New York, Silas Hough; Warren, Burgiss Allison; Redstone, Horatio G. Jones; Miami, David Jones; Delaware, Daniel Sharp; Shaftsbury, John Boggs; Stonington, Thomas B. Montanye; Chemung, Peter Wilson; Warwick, William Staughton.

8. Appointed messengers to the following Associations:—To New York, William Staughton, John P. Peckworth, and Peter Wilson; to the Warren, Thomas B. Montanye, Burgiss Allison, and William White; to the Redstone, John Patton; to the Delaware, James M'Laughlin and Joshua Vaughan; to the Chemung, David Jones.

9. Brethren Peckworth, M'Laughlin, and Matthias, were appointed to examine the minutes of the several corresponding Associations, to report to this body such things therein as particularly have respect to us.

10. The circular letter drawn up by our Brother Staughton, was read, and our Brethren Samuel Jones, and Thomas B. Montanye, in conjunction with the writer, were appointed a committee to revise it.

Adjourned till three o'clock, P. M.

Brother Fleeson prayed.

Three o'clock, P. M.—Met pursuant to adjournment. Brother David Jones prayed.

11. In answer to the query from the first church in Philadelphia: "Would it not be advisable to appoint a committee to examine and see if there be not rules in the new system of discipline which are discordant with the old, and which might be so connected as to render them both harmonious?"

Resolved, That it is not expedient.

12. It is recommended that the quarterly prayer meetings be continued, excepting the first Tuesday in October, instead of which the Association recommends the Thursday preceding.

13. It is again recommended to the churches respectively of this body, that collections be made, or subscriptions raised, to support the domestic mission.

14. This Association again repeats their recommendation to the churches, that collections be made, and repeated, if convenient, to assist the Serampore mission in the translation of the Scriptures.

15. Appointed supplies: for Dover, Freehold, Frankford, Kingwood, West Creek and Tuckahoe, Trenton and Manahawkin.

16. Query from the first church in Philadelphia: "Would it not correspond with the design of the original donors, relieve the Association of much solicitude, and tend more to the profit of the churches, if the Association library were to be distributed equitably among them? And if so, would it not be expedient to advise the churches, or private members, to transmit to the city, at or before the next meeting of the Association, whatsoever books they may possess, or can find, by their delegates, that such distribution may be made?"

To which the anwer was in the affimative; and the churches and brethren who have books in their possession, are earnestly requested to forward them accordingly to Brother Staughton, who will, on account of this Association, defray the expenses accruing on their removal.

Adjourned till eleven o'clock to-morrow morning.

Brother Wilson prayed.

Sermon this evening by Brother Reune Runyan, from Mark iii. 3.

October 8th, eleven o'clock, A. M.—Met agreeably to adjournment. Brother Allison prayed.

17. The circular letter presented by the committee, was by the Association adopted without amendment.

18. Brother Montanye is appointed to write the circular letter for the next year.

19. Brother William White is appointed to preach the Association sermon of next year; in case of failure, Brother Thomas Brown.

20. Query from the church of Blockley: Is it consistent for an excommunicated minister to perform the solemnities of marriage between persons? Can such marriages be viewed by us, as a people, as strictly legal.

This Association are of opinion that, with an excommunicated minister we have no more to do, except as it may relate to the announcing of such excommunication; the law or any society he may join, must become the judge of his conduct; for ourselves, we cannot countenance such marriages.

21. The thanks of this Association are presented by this body to our aged Brother Samuel Jones, for his laborious Association discourse. They request the favor of a copy for publication.

22. The churches in our connection are cautioned against impostors, several of whom, we understand, are now going about; and we solicit sister Associations to give us every information in their power relative to persons of such character, and we will do the same as they may come under our notice.

23. The churches in our connection are notified that John Rutter, late pastor of Blockley church, has been excommunicated; they will therefore not countenance him as a preacher.

Adjourned till three o'clock, P. M.

Brother Montanye prayed.

Met agreeably to adjournment. Brother Jarman prayed.

24. Understanding that Mr. W. W. Woodward, of Philadelphia, has issued proposals for the publication of Dr. Gill's "Exposition of the Old and New Testaments," this Association resolves to support the publishing of the work to the utmost; they also recommend to each church to subscribe for a copy of this incomparable work for the use of their minister, and urge on all their sister Associations to aid in the accomplishment of this desirable object.

25. This Association recommend a neat, correct, cheap, and original edition of Watts' Psalms and Hymns, just published, with a view to accommodate the Baptist churches, by Mr. Dobson of this city. They may be had of our Brother John Bradley, No. 78 Market

street. They also inform the churches that a third edition of the book of Hymns, done by appointment of the Association, has been published, and may be had of Mr. Woodward, or Mr. Dobson, Philadelphia.

26. The letters appointed to be written to our sister Associations were read and adopted.

27. The Association affectionately recommend to the churches with whom they stand connected, to make their letters to the Association as short as may be, confining them chiefly to facts, as the reading of many lengthy letters consumes much of their time.

28. This Association is appointed to meet the first Tuesday in October, 1808, in the first Baptist church, Philadelphia, and in case of any malignant disease in the city, at Trenton and Lamberton meeting house.

29. Our Brother Stephen C. Ustick, is appointed to print the minutes and letter; and our brethren William Staughton and William White to superintend their distribution.

Concluded with prayer, by Brother Hough.

Sermon this evening by Brother Dodge, from Hebrews xii. 2, and by Brother M'Laughlin, from Hebrews xi. 6.

CIRCULAR LETTER.

BY REV. WILLIAM STAUGHTON.

The ministers and messengers of the Philadelphia Baptist Association,

To the churches they severally represent, send Christian salutation.

Beloved Brethren,—At our last annual meeting, the inquiry was proposed, as the subject of the present letter, "WHAT ARE THE QUALIFICATIONS OF A GOSPEL MINISTER?" The question is an important one, inasmuch as, on a proper reply, depend not only the ability of a candidate for the office of the ministry to examine himself, and of the church with which he is connected to judge of his talents, but also the discriminating between those who are in truth "ministers of Christ and stewards of the mysteries of God," and those who are such only in name.

As there are some things which are regarded as qualifications, which in reality are not, and others that are supposed to disqualify, but from which no discouragement ought to be drawn, a few distinctions must be made.

We need not prove to you that mere morality of character, powers of eloquence, or heirships to livings are insufficient: a heathen or an infidel may possess them all. But it may be necessary to state that,

1. A persuasion in the mind of the subject himself is no genuine proof. We acknowledge that whom the Lord calls he inclines, but desire and talent are different things. Most young Christians, brought up from the horrible pit and taught the excellency of Jesus, feel ardent to proclaim his character to thousands. This anxiety for

the salvation of sinners is lovely as a fruit of the work of God in the heart. It designates the saint but not the preacher.

2. The confident decisions of friends and relatives are not always to be trusted. These, the youth who is impatient to ascend the pulpit, commonly regards as sufficiently confirming the propriety of his own impressions. He is not aware that natural affection usurps the seat of sober judgment. Many a fond parent, like the mother of the sons of Zebedee, has wished a child exalted in the service of Christ, without observing the mixture in the motives which govern the heart. To long earnestly that a son or a friend may glorify God in the work of the ministry is an effect of grace, while the sentiment we form of his ability may be nothing but nature.

3. Success is no satisfactory proof that a preacher is qualified of God. Many whose after-conduct has proved them, like Simon the sorcerer, to be "in the gall of bitterness," have been useful in a high degree. They have urged their success as a test of their call. But it should be remembered the blessing respects the doctrine, not the preacher. God has said, "My word that goeth forth out of my mouth shall not return unto me void!" This glorious word, therefore, may be quick and powerful though its preacher be held in the bonds of iniquity.

There are, besides these, some things which are often supposed to disqualify, but do not.

1. A deep persuasion of our entire unworthiness. When we reflect on the high honor done by the Lord to his faithful ministers, and connect with it, in our meditation, our own guilt and impurity, we may well recede and exclaim, "Lord, what am I, or what my father's house!" To appear an ambassador of Christ and to stand in His stead in the midst of the great congregation; to be employed in the hands of his Spirit in training up the children of God for mansions in their Father's house, are exercises in which the mightiest angel in heaven might glory. But if only the worthy are to serve in the sanctuary, where shall they be found? Paul, who came not behind the chief of the apostles, with relation to his preaching the unsearchable riches of Christ, terms himself "less than the least of all saints." His services in the cause of his Lord were attended "with all humility of mind, and with many tears and temptations." Self-abasement will aid rather than hinder in the work of God. It will trample under foot the serpent-pride, and cast the crown at the feet of Jesus.

2. Great fear and trembling of spirit, in prospect of the service, should not lead to the conclusion that requisite qualifications are not possessed. When we reflect on the solemnity of the work, and on the awful responsibility of the minister of God, we may wonder the dread of soul is no greater. "Son of man, (said the Lord to Ezekiel,) I have made thee a watchman,—hear the word of my mouth. When I say to the wicked, Thou shalt surely die, and thou givest him not warning, the wicked man shall die in his iniquity, but his blood will I require at thy hand." One of the fathers terms the sentence

thunderbolts and not words. The sincere minister of Christ perhaps cannot be found, who has not trembled at the address. But impressions such as these have been common to the most eminent of God's servants. It was in the dread of his spirit that Moses said, "O my Lord, send I pray thee by the hand of him whom thou wilt send." Jehovah encouraged Jeremiah when he cried, "Oh Lord God, I cannot speak: for I am a child," by saying, "Be not afraid." "I was with you," said Paul to the Corinthians, "in weakness and in fear, and in much trembling." Holy fear is useful and not injurious, when it leads to greater faithfulness in the ministry, and to a more entire reliance on the Lord for his assistance.

3. The neglect, or even the contempt of many who profess the name of Christ, does not prove that we ought not to gird up the loins for the labors of a steward. Different measures of talent are given to different elders, all designed for the perfecting of the saints. "One star differeth from another star in glory." But he who contemns a Christian minister possessing two talents, because he equals not another possessing ten, should fear lest he see it and be angry, who hath said, "whoso despiseth you despiseth me." The heart of man is easily vanquished by prejudice, and still easier by pride. Not all the eloquence and zeal, and purity and usefulness, of an apostle were sufficient to restrain his adversaries from saying, "his bodily presence is weak and his speech contemptible."

4. The discovery of no immediate or great success, should not lead any of God's servants to conclude he has never been called to his Master's work. Self-examination may be proper, whether truth has been exhibited in all its parts, or whether the heart may not be too vain "to bear" the glory of much usefulness. But we know that though Isaiah found occasion to exclaim, "Who hath believed our report," he continued still to prophesy. Few, in comparison of the multitude of his hearers, appear to have been converted under the teachings of our Lord, yet he still remained the minister of the circumcision. If we have as yet toiled and rowed and caught nothing, who can tell, but that the next endeavor may bring the greatest success? Whatever be the result, like the disciples we should say, "At thy word we will let down the net." A minister is no adequate judge of the degree of his usefulness. Seed may have been sown and harvests be rising where he suspected all was barrenness. We have sometimes discovered more of the usefulness of a minister after his decease than before. The lamp has burned when the pitcher was broken.

The qualifications requisite for a gospel minister may be divided into two classes, the essential, without which he cannot properly bear the name, and the contributory, or those which tend to assist, adorn, and complete the holy character.

The essential qualifications appear to be these four, godliness, knowledge, readiness of communication, and a divine call.

1. Godliness is requisite. Under the term we include holiness of heart, and purity of life.

An unconverted man is a wicked man; but unto the wicked God

saith, "What hast thou to do to declare my statutes, or that thou shouldst take my covenant into thy mouth: seeing thou hatest instruction, and castest my words behind thee." (Psalm l. 15, 16.) In the epistle to Timothy and Titus, where the qualifications of a bishop are distinctly stated, it is required that he be "holy," and a "lover of good men." He must hold the "mystery of the faith in a pure conscience." The apostles gave themselves unto prayer. Timothy is addressed as "a man of God," and Barnabas described as being "a good man and full of the Holy Ghost and of faith." David in his 34th Psalm, first relates his gracious experience, and then adds, "come, ye childen, hearken unto me, I will teach you the fear of the Lord." Describing the state of his disciples, our divine Prophet said, "ye are clean," and it was after Peter's avowal of his love to Jesus, that he received the injunctions, "feed my sheep, feed my lambs." What indeed can be expected from an unconverted ministry? How shall an ungodly preacher illustrate the excellency of the divine character which his heart abhors, or the glories of a law he loves to violate? How shall he describe the distress of an awakened sinner which he never felt, or the extacy of one who has received pardon through the blood of Christ, while he lies himself under sentence of condemnation? If he refer to the temptations and conflicts, the fears and consolations of the true believer, he proceeds with such awkward irregularity as compels the afflicted good man to cry out, "the legs of the lame are not equal, so is a parable in the mouth of fools." The lip must be touched with a coal from the altar, and iniquity purged, before the prophet receives the commission, "Go tell this people, hear ye." "It pleased God," says the apostle Paul, "to call me by his grace, and to reveal his Son in me, that I might preach him," Gal. i. 15, 16.

But "the root of the matter" is not all,—the verdure and fruit of a holy conversation are required also. The bishop must be visible in domestic life. He must be "the husband of one wife," polygamy being as contrary to the course of nature as to the laws of God. He must be "one that ruleth well his own house, having his children in subjection with all gravity." For if a man know not how to rule his own house, how shall he take care of the church of God? Paul collects the virtues that should adorn the personal character of an ambassador of God into one bright constellation. He must be vigilant, sober, of good behavior, given to hospitality, and not to wine: not ready to strike, or attached to filthy lucre, but moderate; not given to contention, not a lover of money, not self-willed, but sober, just, holy, and temperate,—blameless in all things as the steward of God. He must take heed to himself, to his flock, and to his doctrine. Hence,

2. Knowledge is requisite. The new man is renewed in knowledge; but spiritual understanding is progressive, and in this it is required that a minister of the word abound. "The heart of the wise teacheth his mouth." "The priest's lips should keep knowledge, and they should seek the law at his mouth; for he is the messenger of th⸺

Lord of hosts." As if God had said, should the Bible be not at hand, the mouth of the priest will supply its absence. An ignorant person can no more feed the church of God with knowledge and understanding, than can a shepherd his flock by leading them through a desert, which has only here and there a shrub. John must first eat the book and then prophecy.

To ascertain the precise degree of spiritual information that is necessary in a candidate for the ministry, is scarcely practicable. It seems, however, requisite that he should possess general views of the plan of salvation, of the doctrines of grace, and of the "law of the house of the Lord." It appears also proper that a church solemnly exhort a young licentiate brother, to give attendance to reading, to exhortation, and doctrine: to meditate on these things that his profiting may appear to all.

When we are taught that a bishop must not be "a novice," we are not from the term to infer that he cannot sustain the character while young. Timothy's youth, Paul instructed no man to despise. The term "novice" has allusion to a plant newly set. Dr. Doddridge renders the word "one newly converted." Of the time requisite for the plant to take root and flourish, for the young convert to acquire a competent acquaintance with evangelical doctrines and duties, proficiency in the divine life is so different in different individuals, you, brethren, observing the characters, will be best able to judge. The conversations of aged saints, contribute much to the information of the young. Apollos was an eloquent man, and mighty in the Scriptures, but Priscilla and Aquila taught him the way of the Lord more perfectly.

3. An aptness to teach is requisite. It consists in a readiness to communicate "the good treasures of the heart" to others. "The well spring of wisdom is a flowing brook." Many of the servants of the Lord are "filled with the knowledge of his will in all wisdom and spiritual understanding," but they cannot bring to light the intelligence they enjoy. They are shut up as with a wall, and cannot come forth. Now the qualification we speak of is like a passage through the wall; it is called "a door of utterance to speak the mystery of Christ." "We were willing," says the apostle, "to have imparted unto you, not the gospel of God only, but our own souls also, because ye were dear unto us." It includes an ardent love for the souls of men, holy diligence, a fullness of ideas, a vigorous memory, and a flowing elocution.

4. There must be a divine call. No man must take to himself the honor, unless called of God as was Aaron. How can they preach except they be sent? Christ displays his sovereignty in calling to office whomsoever he pleases. His call is delivered not by visiting angels: it is not heard from the flame of a bush, or from the lightning and clouds of a trembling mountain; nor is it an audible address from our Lord Jesus Christ. To be so called in this last sense was one of the signs of an apostle, but is not to be applied to the vocation of ministers now. It is the still voice of God in the soul, saying,

"Occupy till I come." The subject feels a necessity laid upon him: a dispensation of the gospel committed unto him. The souls of men appear of greater value than he had before conceived,—already he begins to travail in birth. He thirsts to be engaged in the work, as a hart for the waterbrook. He would rather be a preacher of Christ than master of all the mines in the world. This secret fire begins in the end to break forth. In his countenance, in his converse, in his prayer, in his exhortations, his exercises discover themselves. At length they engage the attention of the church of God.

The churches of old were accustomed to watch the openings of the ministerial character, and as if desirous of encouraging the candidate and of imitating their own attention to the utmost, the saying appears to have prevailed among them, "If a man desire the office of a bishop, he desireth a good thing." It was by a public act of the church at Jerusalem that Matthias was chosen to the ministry, from which Judas by transgression fell, and from the best testimony that we can obtain from ecclesiastical history, such appears to have been the way in which the election of ministers took place in the churches, until aspiring prelates arrogated to themselves the privilege which belonged to the faithful at large.

The process a church, in the fear of God, observes in the call of a member to the ministry being stated so fully in the discipline of our churches, it is unnecessary to enlarge on it in the present letter.

Besides these leading and essential qualifications, there are several that are contributory to the improvement of the minister of God. These may be referred to two objects—the furniture of the mind and the affections of the heart. We acknowledge with gratitude and joy that every able minister of the New Testament is made such of God and not of men. We acknowledge that it has been common for God in all ages, to execute his purposes by instruments which should secure honor to his great name. He raised up Gideon from the threshing-floor, and David from the sheepfold. The wealthy and the learned were not called to be the apostles of our Lord, but fishermen, publicans, and tent-makers. Many among the most useful of the ministers of Christ in the present day, have received instruction only at the Master's feet. The celebrated Dr. Samuel Johnson, notwithstanding his ardor for classic learning, confesses, that, "compared with the conversion of sinners, eloquence and erudition are less than nothing." The ablest preacher is but an earthen vessel, and the feeblest bears heavenly treasure. We are sensible that an ostentation of learning, may be food for a weak or aspiring mind; nevertheless, as knowledge of almost every kind may be useful to a gospel minister; as in the Bible we have only a translation, behind the veil of which many a beauty is concealed; as we have no reason to expect that extraordinary assistance which the apostles enjoyed; and as education places a minister of the gospel on equal ground with a learned adversary, to seek an acquaintance with language, history, and other similar studies, where it can be accomplished, is praiseworthy.

An increase in all the gracious affections of the heart well becomes a minister of Christ. To none with more propriety than to him may it be said, "Keep thy heart with all diligence, for out of it are the issues of life."

How beauteous do the feet of that minister appear who approaches his flock clothed with humility! If he must be greatest, he will acquire the elevation by becoming the servant of all! How charming the voice that returns not evil for evil nor railing for railing, but, contrariwise, blessing! Being defamed, said Paul, we entreat, being reviled, we bless, being persecuted, we suffer it. How surpassing the heroes of the world is that man of God seen, who, brandishing the armor of righteousness on the right hand and on the left, prefers bonds and imprisonments, and derision and death, rather than the work of his God should be done deceitfully! How valuable that prudence which never forgets, that "to every thing there is a season, and a time to every purpose under the sun!" Of the Messiah, the Father said, "My servant shall deal prudently, and shall be extolled very high." How amiable that sympathy, which, forgetful of its subject, enters the circles of friendship or the chambers of sickness, and looking round, rejoices with them that rejoice, and weeps with them that weep! And O, how lovely that evangelical piety, which, when all is done, falls at the feet of Jesus, and prompts the cry, "God be merciful to me a sinner!"

The original Bunyan has in a few touches admirably drawn the picture of a faithful preacher. The interpreter introduces his Christian into a room, where he saw the picture of a very grave person hang up against the wall, and this was the fashion of it:

"It had eyes lifted up to heaven, the best of books in his hand, the law of truth was written upon its lips, the world was behind his back, it stood as if it pleaded with men, and a crown of gold did hang over its head."

Contemplating the qualifications of a minister of the gospel, you must perceive that their nature is important and solemn. Dear Brethren, pray for your ministers. O, when it is well with you, pray, pray for them. Did you perceive half the toils, or half the afflictions which fill the hands and press down the hearts of your ministers, you would, and we hope you do, remember them always in your prayers. Let your prayers also ascend that more laborers may be thrust into the great harvest field.

Our intercourse with each other in association, has been pleasant, and the tidings from the churches generally encouraging. Permit us to exhort you to abound more and more in the work of the Lord, forasmuch as you know that your labor is not in vain in the Lord.

We remain, beloved brethren, your servants for Christ's sake.

Signed in behalf and by order of the whole,

WILLIAM STAUGHTON, Moderator.
WILLIAM WHITE, Clerk.

THE MINISTERS AND MESSENGERS AT THE ASSOCIATION, AND STATE OF THE CHURCHES DURING THE YEAR.

CHURCHES.	MINISTERS AND MESSENGERS.	Baptized.	Received by Letter.	Dismis'd.	Excom.	Restored.	Deceased.	Members.
Lower Dublin,	Samuel Jones, Thomas Holmes, Jesse Dungan, John Thaw, Abednego T. Whitton, John Richardson,	17	0	3	0	0	0	138
Middletown,	Benjamin Bennet,	0	0	0	0	0	5	135
Cohansie,	Henry Smalley,* William Stelling,* David Gilman, Joel Shepherd, Daniel J. Swinney,	11	0	5	1	0	2	198
Great Valley,	David Jones, Horatio G. Jones, Jonathan Phillips, Isaac Abrams, Phineas Phillips,	2	2	0	0	0	1	67
Cape May,	Jonathan Garman.	8	0	0	0	0	0	50
Hopewell, 1st church,	John Boggs, David Stout, Richard Stout,	8	4	11	2	0	1	148
Brandywine,	Joshua Vaughan, Robert M'Coy, Thomas Baldwin, John Smith, William Griffith,	18	0	2	0	0	3	135
Montgomery,	Silas Hough, Charles Humphrey, Joseph Lun,	0	0	0	0	0	2	83
Kingwood,	Thomas Davis, Edward West, Thomas Robertson,	2	0	2	1	0	2	112
Hight's Town,	Peter Wilson, Andrew Perrine, John Jones,	11	0	6	3	0	2	328
Philadelphia, 1st church,	William Staughton, William Rogers,* John P. Peckworth, Thomas Billings, George Ingolls, George Mustin, Joseph Keen, Benjamin Thaw, Jared Sexton, Hugh Gourley, John M'Leod, Tilman Culp, J. M'Leod, jr.,	38	21	7	5	1	3	307

MINUTES OF THE PHILADELPHIA ASSOCIATION.

CHURCHES.	MINISTERS AND MESSENGERS.	Baptized.	Received by Letter.	Dismis'd.	Excom.	Restored.	Deceased.	Members.
Southampton,	Thomas B. Montanye, William Watts, Abel Marple, John Shelmire, Nathan Banes, James Dungan,	2	4	0	0	0	2	133
Knowlton,†		0	0	0	0	0	0	17
New Britain,	Edward Matthew, Joshua Riale,	4	1	1	0	0	3	83
Salem,	Thomas Brown, Joseph Lloyd, Henry Mulford, Benjamin Thompson,	11	1	6	0	0	3	113
Dividing Creek,†		0	0	0	0	0	0	58
New Mills,	Isaac Carlile,* *Benjamin Hedger*, Lemuel Howell,	3	3	5	1	0	3	111
Upper Freehold,†		0	0	0	0	0	0	97
Pittsgrove,†		0	0	0	0	0	0	19
Manahawkin,	Thomas Edman,	0	0	4	3	0	1	61
Vincent,	Levi John, Robert Phipps,	7	0	0	0	0	0	53
Tuckahoe,†		0	0	0	0	0	0	26
Frankford,	Joseph Mathias, Philip Miller, Isaac Morris, Griffith Owen,	4	0	1	0	1	1	126
Jacob's Town,	Burgiss Allison, Asher Cox,	6	0	0	0	0	3	63
Marcus Hook,		0	3	2	0	0	0	21
Roxbury,	Thomas Fleeson, John Levering, Cornelius Holgate, James Patterson, Charles Levering, Nathan Levering,	1	0	0	0	0	0	56
West Creek,	Joseph Pricket,	6	2	1	0	0	1	58
Shemokin,	John Patten, Charles Saxton,	5	2	1	1	0	0	92
Amwell,	James M'Laughlin, John Carr, William Merrell,	2	0	2	1	0	0	76
Hopewell, 2d church,	William Salyer, Joseph Boss,	3	0	2	0	0	0	55

CHURCHES.	MINISTERS AND MESSENGERS.	Baptized.	Received by Letter.	Dismis'd.	Excom.	Restored.	Deceased.	Members.
Burlington,	William Boswell, Joseph Sheppard, Stephen C. Ustick, Matthew Randall, Joseph Barber, George Allen,	12	0	2	1	0	1	90
Mount Holly,	Jesse Cox, William Rogers,* Edward Thomas,	0	0	2	0	0	0	83
Dover, York co., Pa.	Moses Davis,	2	0	0	1	0	0	22
Philadelphia, 2d church,	WILLIAM WHITE, Samuel Harris,* Isaac Johnson, Thomas Timings, Adam Corfield, James Wiley, Philip Halzel, Jacob Keen,	42	10	32	1	0	1	181
Blockley,	Amos Penegar, W. Sheldrake, G. Helmbold,	3	0	2 0	1	1	0	34
Squan,	Samuel Haven,	4	2	0	3	0	1	45
Evesham,	ALEXANDER M'GOWAN, Joseph Evans, George Sparks, Eli Evans,	12	4	0	0	0	0	80
Trenton and Lamberton,	Amos Reader, John Coleman,	7	3	5	0	0	1	48
Frankford,	James Clark, John P. Skelton, John Dainty,	0	0	0	0	0	0	30
		251	62	102	25	3	42	3632

NOTE.—The ministers' names are in SMALL CAPITALS. Licensed preachers in *italic*. Those marked thus * were not present. From churches marked thus † received no letter. A dash —— denotes no settled minister.

We announce to the churches the afflictive tidings, that our beloved brother PETER GROOM, has been this year removed by death.—"Blessed are the dead who die in the Lord."

A CENTURY SERMON.

DELIVERED IN PHILADELPHIA,

AT THE OPENING OF THE

PHILADELPHIA BAPTIST ASSOCIATION,

OCTOBER 6TH, 1807.

BY SAMUEL JONES, D.D.

PASTOR OF THE BAPTIST CHURCH IN LOWER DUBLIN, PENNSYLVANIA.

PHILADELPHIA:
PUBLISHED AT THE REQUEST OF THE ASSOCIATION.
1807.

EDITOR'S PREFACE.

AMONG the transactions which were recorded by the delegates at the ninety-ninth session of the venerable body, whose minutes we herewith present to the public, item twenty-second reads as follows:—"Brother Samuel Jones is appointed to preach the Association Sermon of next year, which is intended to be a *Century one*, a hundred years having passed since we were first formed."

In editing the following discourse, as well as the foregoing minutes, I have strictly observed the instructions of the Committee, that imposed upon me the pleasant, yet arduous duty of superintending the work through the press, which instructions were: "To preserve, as far as possible, the ancient style of composition, as found in the original minutes."

That the work now given to the world may do good, and awaken a becoming degree of gratitude to God, in the church, for the lives and labors of the men whose names and deliberations it transmits to our own and future ages, is the sincere desire of one who, in relation to the procuring of the materials and publishing this work, "has done what he could."

A. D. G.

A CENTURY SERMON.

Enlarge the place of thy tents, and let them stretch forth the curtains of thine habitations: spare not, lengthen thy cords, and strengthen thy stakes; for thou shalt break forth on the right hand and on the left.—Isaiah, liv. 2, 3.

I HAVE had it on my mind, that it would be proper for me, before I proceed, to confess openly that I am not going to preach but to read. You may therefore perhaps have remarked, that in addressing the throne of grace I have not dared to ask for assistance in this part of the service. I must however observe, that I think reading is admissible on particular occasions, especially such as the present, when the chief of what is to be said is to be historical; yet such historical facts as have some relation to religion.

After saying this much I need not now be at any pains to conceal my notes.

I had some thoughts of committing the whole to memory, but I did not like it very well, because I should seem to act the part of a school-boy, or, what would be worse, to play the hypocrite, by pretending to do what I did not. I shall only add in this way, that for the present I shall omit the notes, to preserve the thread of discourse. I will now enter on the subject before us.

Enlarge the place of thy tent, and let them stretch forth the curtains of thine habitations: spare not, lengthen thy cords, and strengthen thy stakes; for thou shalt break forth on the right hand and on the left.

These are the words of the elegant and sublime Isaiah, who, on account of the clearness of the discoveries made to him of the gospel day, obtained the name of the evangelical prophet. Indeed in some places his predictions have the air of a history, rather than a prophecy. (See chap. vii. 14; ix. 6, 7; l. 6; liii. *passim.*)

The passage before us refers to the implantation of the gospel among the Gentiles. It began to be accomplished in the days of the Apostles, and has been fulfilling in all ages of the Christian church to this day, and will continue so to be to the commencement of the millenium. "Their sound," says the Apostle, "went into all the earth, and their words unto the end of the world." Rom. x. 18.

But we are now to speak more particularly of the work of the Lord, and the spread of religion in our Society during the last century, and especially within the bounds of this Association: to show that there has been a fulfillment of the prophecy in the text among us; that we have "enlarged the places of our tent, and stretched forth the curtains of our habitations: have lengthened our cords, and strengthened our stakes, because we have broke forth, on the right hand, and on the left."

We shall now, then, apply ourselves, in the first place, to take into view what relates to our body, within the time under consideration.

This Association originated in what they called general, and sometimes yearly meetings. These meetings were instituted so early as 1688, and met alternatively in May and September, at Lower Dublin, Philadelphia, Salem, Cohansie, Chester, and Burlington; at which places there were members, though no church or churches constituted, except Lower Dublin and Cohansie. At these meetings their labor was chiefly confined to the ministry of the word, and the administration of gospel ordinances. But in the year 1707 they seem to have taken more properly the form of an Association; for then they had delegates from several churches, and attended to their general concerns. We therefore date our beginning as an Association from that time, though we might with but little impropriety, extend it back some years.

They were at this time but a feeble band, though a band

of faithful brothers; consisting of but five churches. The church at Lower Dublin, Piscataqua, Middletown, Cohansie, and Welsh-Tract. There were at that time but these five in North America, except Massachusetts and Rhode Island.*

Here it may not be amiss to take some notice of the first ministers in succession in each of the constituent churches, as a brief memorial of those venerable fathers, who were the instruments of propagating the gospel in these parts of the new world.

The church of Lower Dublin had for their first minister, Rev. Elias Keach, son of the memorable Benjamin Keach of London. He, returning to England in 1692, was succeeded by the noted John Watts, who departed this life in 1702, in the midst of his days and growing usefulness, the fortieth year of his age, and twelfth of his ministry. So was the will of God. After him they had Samuel Jones, Evan Morgan, and Joseph Wood; and in the year 1712, came over sea, by invitation, Abel Morgan, who had been pastor of a church at Blaene Gwent, in South Wales. He is said to have been indefatigable and abundantly useful in his ministry. He supplied Lower Dublin and Philadelphia, besides visiting other places. He wrote and published the first Welsh Concordance of the Holy Scriptures, that was ever published in that language. This good man was called home to reap the fruit of his labor, and much lamented, in the year 1722.

Piscataqua, had Thomas Killingsworth, Mr. Drake, Henry Loval, and Benjamin Stelle, sr.

Middletown, had James Aston, James Brown, Elias Keach, Thomas Killingsworth, John Burrows, and the incomparable Abel Morgan.

Cohansie, had Thomas Killingsworth, Timothy Brooks, William Boucher and Nathaniel Jenkins.

---

*When the first church in Newport, Rhode Island was one hundred years old, in 1738, Mr. John Callender, their minister, delivered and published a sermon on the occasion. It principally relates to the civil and religious affairs of that province, in connection with the other New England provinces.

The last of the five was the church of the Welsh-Tract, who had for their first minister Thomas Griffith. He came to this country from Wales with the church, for they were constituted there, and was very useful among them to the day of his death, which came to pass in the year 1725. He was succeeded by Elisha Thomas and Enoch Morgan. Besides the above, this church was blessed with four others at the same time, that were men of first rate abilities. Jenkin Jones, who became minister of Lower Dublin, and then of Philadelphia; Owen Thomas, who settled at Vincent in Chester county; David Davis, who succeeded Enoch Morgan at the Welsh Tract; and above all the great Abel Morgan, who moved to Middletown. These were men of shining talents, with whom we have had few, if any since, that will bear a comparison.

I will take the liberty to mention as the contemporary of the above, the late Rev. Benjamin Griffith, of Montgomery, who, though he was not of one of the constituent churches, nor distinguished for ministerial abilities, yet was eminent in council, and perhaps more so for the use of his pen.

Under the appointment of the Association he wrote our first discipline; and then, a brief account of the first seventeen churches in our connection, which he entered in the Association book, together with their most material transactions to the year 1758.

I will add in this way, that a junior class came forward in the churches, who were in a pretty high degree eminent in their day: as John Davis, of Harford, in Maryland, yet living, aged 86; Robert Kelsay, of Cohansie; Peter Peterson Vanhorn, of Lower Dublin; Isaac Eaton, of Hopewell; Mr. Walton, of Morristown; Isaac Stelle, jr., of Piscataqua; Benjamin Miller, of Scott's-Plains; and John Gano, of New York. These were burning and shining lights, especially the three last. May the God of Elijah grant that a double portion of their spirit may rest on all, that stand as watchmen on Zion's walls.

We have mentioned that our number of churches at first was but five. As the country increased in population, our number, through the blessing of God on the faithful and zealous ministry of the word, has increased to 38, comprehending 3556 communicants. But we should doubtless be more than treble that number, if we had not detached churches on all sides, to form five or six other Associations,* that may be denominated our daughters, while some of them, again, have dismissed churches to form still other Associations, that stand as it were in the relation of grand daughters.

Now if we suppose, that there are three hearers in a congregation for every communicant in the church, it will give us above 10,000 hearers; and as there does not half the number in the family, on an average, attend public worship, on account of age, infirmities, &c., it will follow, that the population within our bounds must be above 20,000, and above 80,000, taking in the detachments.

Thus have we spread to the North and South, to the East and West, and have seen the text abundantly verified among us. Doubtless it is the Lord's doings, and to him be all the glory.

It may now be proper to extend our views to our brethren in other parts of the Union: for the work of the Lord was far from being confined to our bounds. He, who gave the word, attended it also with power, and great was the company of those who published it.

But here we are at a loss for want of information. Had there been attention paid to the circular address of your committee of correspondence, appointed five years ago; it might be in our power to lay before you a correct statement, of what would be both agreeable, entertaining, and useful: as it is, we are left to wander in the dark by the aid of uncertain conjecture.

---

*Ketockton, Redstone, Baltimore, Delaware, New York, and Warwick.

To form the Redstone Association, I think we dismissed no churches; but several of our ministers settled in those parts, and were instrumental in forming it.

Mr. Asplund mentioned in the above address, to his immortal honor, has given us, at a great expense of labor, a particular account of our state and number, at that time, in the United States, which he collected in his travels from characters on the spot, who were competent to give him correct information. But this was done seventeen years ago. Great changes have taken place since. We shall however make use of his calculation for our ground work, and build thereon by a reasonable allowance for those changes.

It appears from him, that the number of members, or communicants, belonging to our society in the several States at that time, was 65,233. If we add for the Menonists, Dunkers, and Universalists,* the moderate sum of 4767, we shall have the round number of 70,000.

This was their number seventeen years ago. What may it be now? As we have good reason to think there are in some of the States more than three communicants for every one there was seventeen years ago, one would think we might very safely, for all the States, double the number that there were then: but we will only add three-fourths, which must be allowed to be very moderate. This will give us 122,500, for the present number of communicants throughout the United States.

Now as the number of communicants in a church are to the number of hearers in a congregation nearly as one to three; multiplying the aforesaid number of communicants by three, we shall have 367,500 for the present number of hearers.

This must be below the mark. For there were seventeen years ago, above seventy churches, that had but from eight to twenty communicants each, who, beyond all doubt, had of hearers not only three times their respective numbers of communicants, but more than ten times. This may serve to show we do not wish to exaggerate.

And farther, as we observed awhile ago, since on account of age and infirmity, &c., there does not half a family, on

---

* Who then baptised by immersion only.—ED.

an average, attend public worship, by multiplying the last number by two we shall have 735,000 for our present population, which is about one-eighth part of the whole population in the Union.

It ought to be remembered, that we have not brought into the account the multitudes, that are fully convinced in favor of our religious principles and practice, and are ready to burst the bands of the prejudice of education, their connections, &c., which are doubtless very binding and strong. But when the small still voice of the Spirit of God shall follow the light of knowledge they have received, and whisper in the ear of conscience, and in the mean time the constraining love of God shall be shed abroad in their hearts, we may expect to receive them with joy.

It may also not be amiss to observe, that this remarkable increase, of which we have been speaking, has been chiefly within the last fifty years, and much greater in those States, where oppression for conscience sake has been most severe, except the State of New York.

In Virginia, I think, there was not one church of our denomination in the year 1760; in 1790, only thirty years after, there were two hundred and two. In Massachusetts previous to 1755, there were, as far as I can find, but seven churches, now there are one hundred and ninety-four.*

In the State of New York, there are now I imagine, one hundred and fifty churches; previous to 1770 there were but very few.

It is with pleasure I observe, that oppression on account of religion has in Virginia totally ceased; and in Massachusetts also has greatly abated.

When the first Congress met in this city, I was one of

---

*Rev. John Callender, in his afore-cited centurial discourse for Rhode Island, p. 58, mentions from bishop Sanderson, that the Rev. Archbishop Whitgift, and the learned Hooker, men of great judgment and fame in their times, did long since foresee and declare their fear, that if ever Puritanism should prevail, it would soon draw in Anabaptism after it. That Anabaptism had its rise from the same principles the Puritans held, especially that one principle, that the Scripture was the only and all sufficient rule of faith and practice, so as nothing might lawfully be done, without express warrant, either from some command or example therein contained.

the committee under the appointment of your body, that, in company with the late Rev. Isaac Backus,* of Massachusetts, met the delegates in Congress from that State, in yonder State House, to see if we could not obtain some security for that liberty, for which we were then fighting and bleeding by their side. It seemed unreasonable to us, that we should be called upon to stand up with them in defence of liberty, if, after all, it was to be liberty for one party to oppress another.

But our endeavors availed us nothing. One of them told us, that if we meant to effect a change in their measures, respecting religion, we might as well attempt to change the course of the sun in the heavens.

Should any be ready to inquire, if we are so numerous as just now mentioned, and of course entitled to about twenty seats in the general legislature, how comes it to pass, that we seldom have more than three, four, or five? This is easily accounted for by observing, that being scattered and dispersed among those of other societies, and every were in the minority, we cannot have a chance to rise, if we had the ambition. To which may be added, that as we are generally of the middle class, agreeable to Augur's prayer, and, as the Apostle observes, "not many mighty, not many noble are called," these considerations will fully account for the fact. But if we cannot obtain seats for ourselves, we can however give them to others. For doubtless, casting our weight into the political scale must have an effect in turning the beam. This, it is thought, has actually been the case within a few years past.

Perhaps some, in accounting for this circumstance, will be ready to mention the want of information among us. Be it so. There may be something in it. But suppose I should suggest a more probable reason.

Having been persecuted and oppressed, suffered imprison-

---

* This great and good man was dismissed from his labor below to wear a crown of glory above on the 20th of November, 1806, in the 83d year of his age, and 60th of his ministry.

ment and alienation of property; it is but reasonable to expect, we should be very jealous of our religious liberty, which indeed is the case: and it has been thought by many that the rights of conscience are safer, in the hands of those who care but little for religion of any kind, than in the hands of zealots, devoted to the interest of a particular sect.*

Let it not be said, that this zeal for religious liberty cannot take place, where persecution has not been felt. For the report of it is gone every where, and although it has not every where excited alarm, yet it has sympathy. And then the thing itself is so horrible: to invade the rights of the Deity, to compel people to obey man rather than God, to do what they verily believe they ought not, and to pay for what they never had, nor wish to have; every feeling of the moral sense, to go no farther, rises against it.

It has been often said, that all parties will persecute when they have the power. This may be admitted as a general rule; but I am bold to aver that the Baptists are an exception. They have had the power in Rhode Island,† if

---

* An historian observes, that the worst of men made the best emperors for heretics. In regard to the correctness of this maxim, the writer has not the least doubt. Nevertheless, as it may seem strange to some pious minds, that the wicked should be set up on high, and preferred to the religious, he begs them to consider,—

First, That by those, who care but little about religion, is not meant the profane, nor those who are professed enemies to revelation, who, it is expected, will never be raised to dignified stations by the people in this country.

Secondly, That there may not be clear evidence, that a zealot has any real religion, though he bears the name.

Thirdly, Suppose he should have real religion, and be elevated to the first office in the Union, what security can the people have, that he will be possessed of such firmness of mind, as to direct his own councils, and escape the influence of religionists, or clergy, with whom he will be encompassed, and who have never been thought to be over-favorable to equal rights and free inquiry in matters of religion.

In unison is the observation of the historian, "The worst of men made the best emperors for heretics"—*i. e.*—for dissenters from the ruling party. *Rob. Eccles. Researches, p.* 74.

† Rev. John Callender, in his aforesaid discourse, (p. 103,) speaking of Rhode Island, has these words: "Liberty of conscience was the basis of this colony. Our fathers thought it just and necessary, to allow each other mutually to worship God as their consciences were respectfully persuaded; they thought no man had power over the Spirit of God, and that the duty of the magistrate was to leave every one to follow the light of his conscience. They were willing to exhibit to the world an instance, that liberty of conscience was consistent

not in Portland: but not a single instance can be produced of their abuse of that power any where.*

Hoping you will excuse these few political observations, I will now go on to what may be more agreeable.

We would not be understood to suppose, that the work of the Lord has been confined to our society. We occupy but a small part of the Lord's vineyard: and we rejoice, that there are so many others engaged with us in spreading and promoting the kingdom of our Lord and Saviour.

About the middle of the century a glorious revival took place and spread through the States, wherein that eminent servant of the Lord, the Rev. George Whitefield, bore a conspicuous part. He was the blessed instrument in the hand of the Lord, both in commencing and spreading that wonderful work.

This revival had a happy effect, not only in bringing many thousands out of the kingdom of Satan into the kingdom of God's dear Son, but also in being the means of introducing into the ministry many pious and zealous dispensers of the word, especially among Presbyterians in the Middle States, and the Congregationalists in the Eastern States. Without detracting from the merit of those who have appeared since in the ministry, we must be allowed to give a decided preference to the eminent characters that sprung up in the great day of God's power, the names of many of whom are had in precious remembrance to this day, as the Tenants, Edwards, Burr, Davis, Findley, Treat, Beaty, Hunter, Bostwick, Rogers, Rowland, and a long list of others, whose names have not come to our knowledge.†

There have been many, and some of them very consider-

---

with the public peace, and the flourishing of a civil commonwealth, as well as that christianity can subsist without compulsion." And he might have added, that it could subsist a great deal better without than with it.

* When the Quakers in Pennsylvania did something like persecuting the Keithians, Holme, a Baptist Judge or Justice, on the bench, opposed it.—*Vide Mr. Edward's Matt. Vol.* 1st, p. 56.

† It is not here meant that those referred to, were greater than those now on the ministerial stage for natural powers of mind, much less for literary improvement, but for powerful evangelical preaching.

able revivals and seasons of the refreshment since the above, and that in many, or rather in all the States, particularly in Virginia, the Carolinas, Kentucky, &c., of which we have not room to speak at large, and shall only observe that there have been within those three or four years, and even now are, considerable revivals in Taunton, Norton, Aurelius, Providence, Addison, Columbia, Stuben, Upper Canada, Marlborough, St. Andrew's, Hamilton, Suffield, Bristol, Colchester, Wardsborough, Windham, Winhall, Straton, Wilmington, Granville, Lyme, Philadelphia, Lower Dublin, Southampton, and in many places in Virginia, the Carolinas, Georgia, &c., wherein multitudes have been baptised. Rev. Henry Taler, in Virginia, baptised above 400 in little better than one year, 135 in one day. Glory to God for those refreshing showers of grace.

About forty years ago the Methodist society took root among us, under the labors of Messrs. Pilmore, Boardman, and many others, who, for the time, by their diligence and zeal, have certainly been very successful, at least as to respectability of numbers, and a very considerable reformation of manners, and there is reason to hope, that a real work of grace has taken place among them to a considerable extent.

The many other religious societies are also progressing in numbers, weight and influence; serving we hope, our common Lord and Master, according to the light they have received; on whom, as on all, may the Lord shine, to give the light of the knowledge of his glory in the face of Jesus Christ.

What shall we say of the missionary spirit, that has for some years, and more especially of late, prevailed in many places, and among different societies, with a view to spread the knowledge of the gospel and the way of salvation among the heathen in various parts, as well as among Christians in places destitute of the means. Whether the latter does not merit the greater attention we pass over, only observing, that it is thought it has been attended with more success and far less expense.*

Time would fail us to cross the Atlantic and recount the displays of divine power and grace among them, within the period we are speaking of, especially in Great Britain, that favored isle,—so highly favored particularly for the knowledge of divine things, promoted among them by the ministry of the word, and by writing. Whether, with reference to the last, they are not now rather stationary, since that great luminary Doctor Gill has finished his course, we leave. Be that as it may, it would seem that knowledge, civil and religious liberty, and with them religion itself are tending westward. With the sun they rose in the East, after a course of ages crossed the Atlantic, and it is likely will progress westward until they reach the Pacific Ocean, civilizing and making happy this western hemisphere in their course.

We mentioned awhile ago the names of some in the ministry, that were eminent in their day for talents, piety and usefulness, who now rest from their labors, and "their works do follow them."

At this time also there are not a few among us in the sacred office, of distinguished worth, not so much for their literary acquirements, as for what is of infinitely more value in promoting pure undefiled religion before God—namely, true piety, ardent zeal, ministerial gifts, and indefatigable diligence, and faithfulness in saving the souls of men and promoting the kingdom of our Redeemer.†

---

*The Massachusetts Baptist Missionary Magazine, published quarterly, and which merits high encomium and support, gives us very pleasing intelligence of the success of missionaries east of Penobscot river, in Nova Scotia, back parts of the State of New York, Upper Canada, &c.

One of their missionaries, Rev. Isaac Case, in a short time baptised 205, and constituted six churches.

† The Baptists, as a society, have never considered the higher branches of learning as essential to the gospel ministry, and there is no doubt but the sentiment is perfectly correct. They have, nevertheless, held education in high esteem, as a handmaid to grace, and have always had not a few among them, that ranked pretty high for literary improvement and extensive reading.

In the year 1756, the late Rev. Isaac Eaton, M. A., of Hopewell, in New

Some are Boanerges, sons of thunder, qualified to lay the axe at the root of the trees; to awaken, alarm, and strip sinners of their carnal hopes and self-dependence: while others are sons of consolation, fitted to apply the healing balm of gospel grace, and mercy; to excite faith in the merits and mediation of Christ, and lead the subject of grace to rejoice in hope; fitted to build up, comfort, establish and edify the faithful, leading them on as a peculiar people zealous of good works; while all have a measure of all gifts, as God has distributed to all by the same Spirit. Of these there are a few, especially Southward and Eastward* of us, the force of whose natural genius has raised them far above the common level, whose names, for obvious reasons, we for the present suppress, and

<blockquote>Hail the sons of glory when they set.</blockquote>

Thus when we look back, as from an eminence, on what

Jersey, opened a Grammar School under the patronage of the Philadelphia Baptist Association.

In the fall of 1763, the writer of these sheets, on request, repaired to Newport, in Rhode Island, and new-modelled a rough draft they had of a charter of incorporation for a college, which soon after obtained Legislative sanction. The summer following the institution went into operation under the Rev. James Manning, President, at Warren, at which place the first commencement was held in 1769. Two years after, an elegant edifice was erected at Providence, and the institution flourished under its worthy President, the late renowned Dr. Manning, as it did since his death under President Maxy, and does now under President Mercer. At the commencement of last September, twenty-nine were admitted to the degree of Bachelor of Arts. It is now called Brown's University, in honor of the generous Nicholas Brown, merchant, of that place.

The writer kept a boarding school between twenty-nine and thirty years, at Lower Dublin, in which many were educated, that are now useful in the different learned professions.

One of them, the Rev. Dr. Allison, kept a large Academy under his sole direction, at Bordentown, in New Jersey, from whence issued many useful characters.

The Philadelphia Baptist Association have a fund for the education of young men promising for the gospel ministry, as have also the Charleston Association.

The Baptists, in Georgia, have in contemplation to erect a College in that State, on Mount Enon, at the distance of 140 miles from the Atlantic, in latitude 33 north, on an elevation of 200 feet perpendicular, accommodated with salubrious air, and two fine springs that issue out of rocks on the north and west sides.

The business is in some forwardness, as unsolicited donations already amount to about five thousand dollars. This account of Enon College bears date of December, 1806.

* Of these my good and intimate friend, the late Doctor Samuel Stillman, of Boston, was one, to whose memory, memorable as it was, Doctor Baldwin, in the funeral discourse, has done such ample justice. It would be well, if on such occasions, truth was always so strictly attended to.

has taken place within a small compass, in the course of the last century, in promoting the kingdom of the Messiah in the world, we see a glorious accomplishment of the prophecy in the text, and if we look forward, a still more glorious prospect lies before us.

Before another century will revolve, before another opportunity will offer, of delivering another discourse on the like occasion with the present, we hope and expect, that the latter day of glory, the spiritual reign of Christ, will commence, in comparison of which, what we have seen, however glorious, can be but a prelude, a faint shadow.

We have indeed lately seen a whole church with its ministry,* as it were a whole town, turn from will-worship to the apostolic practice, in a manner with one consent. This was great and remarkable, I confess, for our day and time. But how much greater and more glorious will it be, when superstition and false coloring of Scripture shall cease, when the Lord Jesus thall destroy every species of antichrist with the spirit of his mouth and the brightness of his coming, when his ancient people the Jews shall be brought in, together with the fullness of the gentile world; in one word, when a nation shall be born in a day. Should it enter the mind of any that this is a figurative expression, we grant it may be so: but then if it be, it is such an one as denotes something very great and glorious indeed; nor is there room to doubt, but the power of God is able to bring that saying to pass literally. May the Lord hasten and accomplish his holy purposes to the praise of his glory.

The glorious day spoken of will be the time of the *Lord's reformation.* The reformation, which has been so much gloried in was but a poor piece of business, although it has been attended with valuable consequences. The reformers shook off the Papal yoke, but in the main retained its principles and spirit. They did not establish the right of

---

* This refers to the Rev. Daniel Merril, of Maine. That of N. Dodge, at Lebanon, in Connecticut, is not very dissimilar.

free inquiry, liberty of conscience, and the word of God as the only rule of faith and practice: but, on the other hand, opposed, restrained and suppressed every attempt to promote a thorough reformation. They were influenced by worldly motives, connected religion with worldly establishments, were the abettors of tyranny and oppression, and even of persecution by fire and the sword. But we look for a far different reformation. The Lord will come, and will not tarry. Let us wait for him.

Having thus, my brethren, laid before you our original state, and the progress made within our compass, and then extended our views to our brethren in the Union; and having said a few words in regard to the state of religion among other societies, it may now be time to draw towards a conclusion. But, before I close, I shall take the liberty to say a few words with reference to the nature of our subject.

Some may say, that we have talked too much about our numbers, and that it looks rather like boasting. I would inquire of such, whether it would not be more candid in them, to consider it as exulting in the riches of divine grace and goodness. If, however, we may not speak of the great things God has done for us, without being charged with boasting, then let us determine with the Apostle, that no man shall stop us of this boasting. In the Lord we will triumph, and in his salvation.

That our subject, however, is dry, and does not admit of much fervor and devotion is readily granted. It does not call for that pathos which the common subjects of the sacred desk, not only allow, but often require.

To speak of the deplorable state of man under the wrath of God, and the sentence of condemnation; to display the unsearchable riches of the grace and love of God in the way of recovery and salvation through Jesus Christ; to describe the work of the Spirit in taking the things of Christ and showing them unto us, his work of conversion and sanctification; to paint the awful process in the great day, and finally the irrecoverable perdition of the ungodly, and the glory and felicity of the righteous; these are subjects that will admit, and even call for animation. Here the preacher may well glow with ardor, and the hearer feel an interest. These subjects, when accompanied with divine power, will melt the affections, bow the will, and mend the heart.

But if our subject does not rise to the height of those now mentioned, it is nevertheless well worth while, to devote one hour, once in an hundred years at least, to review the ways and doings of God with his church and people, in accomplishing the purposes and decrees of his grace and goodness.

Such contemplation may be of advantage to us, not only for present satisfaction, but because it tends to call forth into exercise the best powers and faculties of the soul, and to excite to action the graces of the Spirit there implanted.

Here we are led to exult and triumph in his power and goodness. In this contemplation our gratitude, thanksgiving and praise, those heavenly exercises, will be most powerfully moved. From what has been done in the accomplishment of his promises, we are led to hope for the fulfillment of those that remain, we are led to a steadfast confidence in him, who has said, " And lo, I am with you always, to the end of the world;" and that no weapon formed against Zion shall prosper.

Every device of man to unite the church and the world must come to naught. For the Redeemer has said, " My kingdom is not of this world." Human schemes and policy will not long avail. The church will shortly come up out of the wilderness.

In the spirit of true piety and ardent affection it is fit we should therefore join in the general chorus of the redeemed throng through all ages, saying, " Come Lord Jesus, come quickly."

Let us then unite with one heart and voice in ascribing " honor and glory, praise and power, might, majesty and dominion to him that sitteth on the throne, and to the Lamb forever and ever." Amen.

Index.

Adoption, Circular Letter on, 218; import of the word, 219; origin, 219; distinguished from justification, 220; and from regeneration, 220; much gained by it, 221; a high privilege, 221; God's revelation as a Father, 222; present privileges arising from the state, 223; the future still greater, 224; relative duties great, 224.
Allison, Rev. B., assisted in his education, 142, 155; Circular Letters by, 248, 397.
Alloway's Creek, Church at, received, 72.
Amwell, Church at, received, 333.
Apocrypha, its publication disapproved of, 248.
Apostles Paul and Barnabas, preachers before ordination, 51.
Appeal to Association admitted, 25; impropriety of the term, 105.
Ardent Spirits, disuse of, recommended, 239.
Ashfield, persecution of Baptists at, 115.
Asplund, Mr., his work on denominational Statistics, 458.
Association, formation and regulations of 25, 97; proposals to change its meetings, 40; character of its Churches 54; Essay on power and duty of, 60; change as to the Sermons, 79; intercourse with similar bodies, 97; Records of, copied, 142, 206; by whom and where to be kept, 82; proposed division of, 143; Century Sermon to, 451.
Associations in the United States and Vermont, tabular view of, 269.
Assurance of Faith, as essential to baptism, 70.
Assurance, Circular Letter on, 284; importance of the doctrine of, 284; degrees in, 284; attainable in the present life, 285; privileges of believers in common, 285; inculcated on Christians, 286; not the faith of reliance, 287; may be counterfeited, 287; great utility of, 288.

B.

Backus, Rev. J., vote of thanks to, for his history, 206.
Baltimore, Church at, received, 72.
Baltimore Association, correspondence with, 305.

Baptism, not to be administered by an unbaptized person, 33, 238; nor by an unordained Minister, 49, 60, 104, 229, 282; nor to persons of other Churches, 43; by a minister of the Church of England valid, 95; and by a Tunker or Universalist, 424; prerequisite to communion, 42; treatise on, proposed, 54; query on examination of candidates for, 89; is assurance of faith essential to, 70; may married persons, separated from each other, be admitted to, 229.
Baptism of the Holy Ghost, Circular Letter on, 372; prevalent mistakes concerning, 373; term only in the New Testament, 373; nature of it, 373; design of it, 374; effects which followed it, 375; difficulties removed, 375; inferences from the subject, 376.
Bateman's Precincts, Church at, received, 77; advice to, 109; conduct of, approved, 124.
Benedict, J., sufferings of, 163.
Bethlehem, early history of the Church at, 20.
Bible, Aitkin's edition of, recommended, 180; Collins' edition of, recommended, 247, 255, 270; and Matthew Carey's edition, 382.
Bishop and Elder, synonymous words, 382.
Blackwell, Rev. J., Address by, 119.
Blockley, Church at, received, 354.
Boggs, Rev. J., death of, 393.
Bonham, Mr. Malachi, ordained, 20.
Books, advertisement of, 132.
Booth, Rev. A., republication of, on baptism, 238; letter from, 270; decision on, 282.
Brandywine, early history of the Church at, 18; advice given to, 27, 131, 342; state of, 324, 334.
Branson, Rev. Daniel, disowned, 173.
Brotherly Love, Circular Letter on, 413; due to Christians, 414; commanded by Christ 414; origin of other duties to them, 414; love to God and his people inseperable, 414; is an evidence of regeneration, 414; holy in its nature, 416; manifested by obedience, 416; and is universal in its operations, 417.
Brown University, see Rhode Island.
Burlington, Church at, received, 358.

Burrows, John, arrival of, 12.
Butcher, Mr. W., ordained, 14.
Butler, Mr. Simon, acknowledgment of wrong-doing, 48.

C.

Calamities of the times, prayer on account of, 155, 159.
Callender, Rev. John, Century Sermon, 455, *note;* extract from, 461, *note.*
Cape May, early history of the Church at, 16; advice to, 254.
Carey, Rev. Dr., letters from, 360, 412.
Carman, Mr. James, ordination of, 21.
Catechising, duty of, 141, 297.
Catechism, whether to be reprinted, 39, 83, 163; alterations in, 297, 307, 317.
Century Sermon, by Rev. Dr. Jones, 451.
Charleston Association, correspondence with, 135, 140, 148, 169, 205, 217, 218, 227, 236, 254, 271, 283, 296, 297, 305, 316, 341, 348, 358, 379, 394, 409, 421, 436.
Charter, committee appointed to obtain, 271; object secured, 325.
Christ the Mediator, Circular Letter on, 181: office of, 182; difference between God and man, 182; inability of man, 182; God could not pardon as a simple act of mercy, 182; appointment of Christ to the office, 182; his own voluntary act, 183; fully qualified for, 184; the two natures were united in him, 185; relations sustained by Christ as head, surety, advocate, prophet, priest, and king of his people, 186; what Christ has done as Mediator, 187; effects of his mediation towards God, the divine law, and man, in giving peace, pardon, justification, adoption, renewing liberty of access to God, and eternal life, 189.
Christ, query as to his being an object of prayer, 200, 206, 216.
Christian liberty, and liberty of conscience, Circular Letter on, 326; nature of spiritual bondage, 327; redemption effected by Jesus, 327; introduction by it to high privileges, 328; objects accomplished by it, 328; to be regulated by the law of God, 329; freedom of conscience equal right of all men, 329.
Church, query on the number of members to form a, 423.
Churches, admonitions to the, 55, 57, 59, 64, 66, 67, 69, 70, 72, 73, 75, 76, 78, 80, 83, 97; general letter to, proposals to change the character of, 136; members of allowed to be present at the Association, 107; statistics of, 85, 88, 93, 94, 96, 98, 100, 103, 106, 110, 111, 117, 122, 127, 133, 138, 146, 152, 157, 179, 192, 197, 203, 215, 225, 234, 243, 251, 267, 278, 289, 294, 303, 314, 322, 330, 339, 346, 356, 367, 377, 392, 406, 418, 434, 447.
Cohansie, early history of the Church at, 14; advice given to, 31, 42, 89, 305.
Committee on grievances appointed, 141; query on reports of committees being duly presented, 395.
Communion with the unbaptized censured, 200; query on members separately communing, 206, 218; on transient communion of Churches, 54; query on communion with a man and wife, the sister of his first wife, 74.
Conference of Association proposed, 343, 349.
Confession of Faith, appealed to, 27, 29, 37; proposal to reprint, 46; resolution to reprint, 94.
Congaree Association, letter from, 128.
Connecticut, persecution in, 108.
Cooper, Rev. John, disowned, 422.
Coram, Church at, received, 94; advice to, 148.
Correspondence, plan of, a committee of, 371; reports of, 381, 411, 425.
Council, jurisdiction of, 284.
Covenant of God with man, Circular Letter on, 175; first and subsequent promises, 175; nature of a covenant, 176; Abrahamic and Christian covenants distinguished, 176; between the persons of the Deity, 177; terms of, 177; administration of the subject, 178.
Cranberry, early history of the Church at, 21.
Craner, Thomas, proposal to reprint his Manual, 193.
Crosby's History of the Baptists, proposal to reprint, 343.
Curtis, Mr. Thomas, ordination of, 20, 49.

D.

Danbury Association, correspondence with, 254, 271, 281, 283, 292, 296, 297, 394.
Darrah, Mr. J., assisted in his education, 155.
Dawson, Mr. Henry, conduct of, 105, 108, 124, 129.
David, Mr. B., assisted in his education, 119.
Davis, Mr. John, ordained, 16; testimonial given to, 77.
Davis, William, improper conduct of, 35.
Dazey, Rev. E., death of, 323.
Deacons, query as to ordination of, 52.
Decree, doctrine of God's, Circular Letter on, 150; right of God to decree, 150; in harmony with the free agency of man, 150; special objects of, 150; difficulties removed, 151; caution in reference to, 152.

INDEX.   471

Delaware Association, correspondence with, 341, 348, 358, 369, 379, 394, 409, 421, 437; history of Baptists in, proposed, 307, 316.
Denominational proceedings to be recorded, 54.
Destitute Churches, expense of visiting, 380.
Discipline, Book of, prepared, 48; revision of, read, 325; printed, 334; query on harmonizing two systems of, 422, 438; how to be conducted towards a member dissatisfied, 102.
Disease, spiritual, remedy for, 64.
Dismissions, not to be granted when residence is not removed, 29, 36, 37.
Dissatisfied brethren, how to be treated, 44, 45.
Divided Churches in England, how to be treated, 28.
Divinity, new system of, discouraged, 256.
Dividing Creek, Church at, received, 81; advice given to, 317, 360.
Disbanded Churches, duty of members of, 119.
Dover, Church at, received, 369.
Drake, Mr., ordained, 13.
Duties of Churches, Circular Letter on, 160; importance of steadfastness, 160; consideration of Christ, 161; attendance on public worship, 161; motives to the discharge of duty, 161.

E.

Eaton, Mr. Isaac, ordained, 18.
Eaton, Mr. Joseph, ordained, 20; his acknowledgment of wrong, 47.
Effectual calling, Circular Letter on, 201; an act of sovereign grace, 201; its subjects, 202; its tendencies, 203.
Edwards, Rev. Morgan, death of, 313.
Elder, Ruling, query on ordination of, 102.
Election, query on the denial of, 68.
Elkhorn Association, correspondence with, 292.
Emigrants, Letters of dismission of, 306.
Evangelist, choice of, 119, 130.
Evans, John, arrival of, 19.
Evesham, Church at, received, 421.
Ewing, Rev. James, Circular Letter by, 362; death of, 433.
Excommunicated members, proper conduct, 59.
Excommunication, query on public, 89, 101; whether to be extended to persons of good morals, 228.

F.

Fairfax, Church at, received, 72.
Fairfield, Church at, received, 140.

Faith, saving, Circular Letter on, 240; the gift of God, 240; properties of, 241; receives the whole truth, 241; not dead, 241; cleaves to Christ, 242, exhortation to attain it, 242.
Fall of man, Circular Letter on, 170; change in the state of our first parents, 171; results of Adam's sin, 171; practical improvement of, 171.
Family worship, query on the neglect of, 109.
Fasting and Prayer, Circular Letter on, 167; nature of fasting, 167; occasions of, 167; necessity for, 168.
Fast days kept at Lower Dublin, 11; Great Valley, 16; Hopewell, 17; Montgomery, 19; Morristown, 22; Oyster Bay, 23; Tulpohokin, 24; recommended, 28, 33, 71, 73, 74, 76, 77, 79, 81, 83, 87, 142, 149, 155, 159, 170, 292, 306, 325, 346, 371.
Fees, refused by the Recorder of Philadelphia, 86.
Fleeson, Rev. Thomas, Circular Letter by, 293.
Flood, Rev. Joseph, disowned, 379.
Foreknowledge of God, query on, 58.
Fore-ordination of God, query on, 82.
Foster, Rev. Benjamin, Circular Letter by, 261.
Frankford, Church at, received, 437.
Freedom of Man's will, Circular Letter on, 194; importance of the subject, 194; extent of Providence, 195; God not the author of sin, 195; nature of actions, 196; free agency of man, 196; important practical uses of the doctrine, 197.
Fuller, Rev. Dr., Letter from, 412.
Fund for the Association, proposal for, 65, 97; commenced, 101; for itinerancy, 159; expenditure of, 411

G.

Gano, Rev. John, account of his travels, 135; Circular Letter by, 201; death of, 408; biography of, 421.
Georgia Association, correspondence with, 217.
Gier, Mr. T., assisted in his education, 131.
Gilbert, Rev. Curtis, death of, 289.
Gill, Dr. J., proposal to reprint his Exposition, 228; and his Nature of the Church, 282; Exposition recommended, 439.
God, being and perfection of, Circular Letter on, 143; proof of his unity, 144; Trinity in the Godhead, 144; Christ, 145; eternal generation of, 145; improvement of the doctrine, 145; foreknowledge of, query, 58; his fore-ordination, 87.

INDEX.

Good Works, Circular Letter on, 261; nature of, 261; have reference to God, 262; not the foundation of justification, 263; or election, 263; always performed by Christians, 263; to be persevered in, 264; motives to, 264; happy influence of, 265; exhortations to, 265.

Goshen, Church at, received, 108; advice given to, 119; messengers sent to, 180.

Gospel, the, Circular Letter on, 309; distinction from the law, 309; manifestation of grace, 310; tidings of good, 310; matter of revelation, 310; given but in part, 311; application of it, 311; extent of the atonement, 311; salvation not conditional, 312; inability of man to believe it, 312; scheme of truth developed in it, 313; *Divine origin of*, Circular Letter on, 351; external evidences important, internal evidence yet stronger, 351; such as regeneration, sanctification and support in trouble, 352; Christian's reply to infidels, 353; influence of such evidence on primitive Christians, 353; change effected by Divine power, 354; exhortation to corresponding duties, 354; extract from Baxter, 355.

Grammar School, established, 74; recommended, 76, 77; transfer of funds of, 332.

Great Valley, early history of Church at, 16; advice given to, 29, 35, 40, 44, 89.

Griffiths, Rev. A., Pastoral Letter by, 110, 119.

Griffiths, Mr. Benjamin, ordination of, 20; appointed to collect statistics, 54, 60; Pastoral Address by, 98; Essay on Associations, 60; author of the first book of Discipline, 456.

Groom, Rev. Peter, death of, 449.

H.

Halifax, N. S., new meeting-house at, to be collected for, 334.

Hammond, Rev. N., received, 94; death of, 148.

Harris, Rev. J., Letter from, 121.

Harris, Mr. Samuel B., assisted in his education, 396.

Hart, Rev. O., Circular Letter by, 181; death of, 323.

Haweis, Rev. Dr., Letter from, 360.

Heaton, Mr. S., relieved, 74.

High Hills, Letter from Association at, 155.

Hollis, Thomas, Esq., of London, regard for young ministers, 27; correspondence with, 28, 30; gift of books by, 81; how to be used, 82.

Holy Spirit, work of, Circular Letter on, 382; children of God partake of his influence, 383; errors respecting, 383; strivings of the Spirit, work of conscience, 385; text erroneously applied, 386; work in the hearts of Christians completed, 387; nature of. 388: regeneration, 389; to make Christ known, 389; sanctification, 390; query on, 410.

Hopewell, early history of the Church at, 17; advice given to, 102; second Church at, received, 57.

Horse Neck, Church at, received, 57; advice given to, 58.

Hough, Rev. S., Circular Letter by, 413.

Hymn Book, preparation of, recommended, 239; third edition of, 440.

I.

Infidelity, Circular Letter on, 318; origin, 318; evil of its influence, 319; antidotes to the evil, 319; enlarged acquaintance with truth, 319; avoidance of disputation, 319; importance of religion, 319; consistency of conduct, 320; experimental religion, 320; let all Christians unite in this work, 321.

Itinerancy, ministers employed in, 283; fund for support of, 159, 350.

J.

Jacobstown, Letter from, 237.

James, Mr. John, arrival of, 19.

Jenkins, Mr. J., arrival of, 12.

Jones, Rev. D., Missionary to the Indians, 124; Circular Letters by, 239, 335.

———, Rev. Joshua, Circular Letter by, 284; death of, 393.

———, Mr. Samuel, ordination of, 11; Pastoral Address by, 87; Circular Letters by, 143, 160, 164, 175, 194, 257, 309; thanks of Association to, 361, 439; journey to Rhode Island. 465.

———, Rev. Thomas, death of, 237.

———, Mr. Thomas, assisted in his education, 350.

Justification, Circular Letter on. 207; distinguished into eternal and declarative, 207; author, 207; works excluded, 208; unconditional, 208; grace of God its moving cause, 209; Jesus its procuring cause, 209; imputation, 209; by medium of faith, 210; persons interested — pardoned sinners, 210; blessings resulting from it are great — deliverance from sin, 211; enjoyment of peace with God, 211; our acceptance, blessed now and forever, 212; inferences — futility of self-dependence 212; necessity of prizing the

INDEX. 473

righteousness of the Gospel, 212; security of standing in Christ, 213; tends to holiness, 213; honors the Christian, 214; must be firmly maintained, 214.

K.

Keach, Rev. Benjamin, proposal to reprint his book on the Parables, 119.
———, Rev. Elias, Confession of Faith by, 13.
Kelsay, Rev. R., Circular Letter by, 156; account of sermon by, 237.
Kentucky, information from, 217; number of Baptists in, 372.
Kingwood, advice to the Church at, 68, 70, 81, 130, 200.
Konoloway, Church at, received, 94; their building case commended, 97.

L.

Laying on hands, prerequisite to administration of ordinances, 30; on the baptized, query, 194.
Leaton, Rev. W., irregular conduct of, 70.
Leland, Rev. John, Letter from, 227,
Letters of recommendation, 25; to the Association, how they should be written; to the Churches, 29, 31, 33, 34, 36, 38, 39, 41, 43, 45, 47, 50, 54.
Library, commencement of, 82; proceedings relating to, 173, 180, 200, 205; librarians appointed, 361, 382; distribution of, 438.
Little River Association, Letter from, 135.
London, correspondence with Baptist Board in, 83, 84.
Lovall, Henry, ordination of, 13.
Lower Dublin, early history of the Church at, 11, 455; advice to, 228.
Lower Smithfield, Church at, received, 199.
Lyon's Farms, Church at, received, 107.

M.

M'Lean, Rev. D., erroneous preaching of, 227.
Manahawkin, Church at, received, 116; advice to, 359.
Manning, Rev. Dr., death of, 272.
Marcus Hook, Church at, received, 246.
Marriage—may a Christian marry an unbeliever, 27, 329; a woman marry her sister's husband, 274; a man marry his first wife's sister, 102; a woman marry her husband's nephew, 270, 282; may it be celebrated by an excommunicated minister, 439.
Massachusetts Baptist Missionary Magazine recommended, 424.
Medfield, Letter and Messenger from Association at, 140.

Memminger, Rev. Thomas, Circular Letter by, 326.
Merrill, Rev. D., baptism of, 412.
Miami Association, correspondence with, 359, 394, 409, 421.
Middletown, early history of Church at, 13; advice given to, 29, 35.
Mill Creek, Church at, received, 72.
Miller, Mr. Benjamin, ordination of, 22.
Minister, qualification of a Gospel, Circular Letter on, 440; morality no proof, 440; nor eloquence, 440; nor persuasion in the mind, 440; nor decision of friends, 441; nor is a man disqualified by a sense of unworthiness, 441; nor by trembling of spirit, 441; nor by neglect of many, 442; nor by want of immediate success, 442; essential qualifications are, godliness, 442; knowledge, 443; aptness to teach, 444; a Divine call, 444; Churches should look out suitable men, 445; Bunyan's picture of a minister, 446; importance of examination of ministerial character, 27; query on the restoration of a minister, 254.
Ministers, former character of many, 121; of other denominations, how to be treated, 35; propriety of publishing charges against, 360; scarcity of, 344; young, to be looked out for, 27, 32, 33, 42; education of, 27, 110, 246, 350, 381.
Minutes, first printed by order of the Association, 107; set of, presented to the Association, 298.
Missions, Christian, Circular Letter on, 426; principles on which they proceed, 426; the means by which the work is to be effected is the Divine Word, 426; extent to which missions have been carried, 429; by apostles, 429; Catholics, 429; Protestants, 429; Moravians, 429; Christians in Scotland and America, 430; Baptists in England, 430; Pedobaptists in England, 431; in the United States, 431; encouragement to missions, 432; fund for support of, 298, 307; sermons for, recommended, 370.
Missionary Society, proposal for a, 350, 370, 381.
Moderator, query as to the, 380.
Montanye, Rev. T. B., Circular Letter by, 372.
Montgomery, early history of Church at, 19; advice given to, 28, 47, 49; state of Church at, 56; advice to, 58; Ministers appointed to visit, 38.
Moral law, Circular Letter on, 299; love to God reasonable, 299; standard of right, 300; love to man essential to social prosperity, 300; due regard to property secured, 300; and to reputa-

tion, 301; easily retained in the memory, 301; results of disregarding it, 302.
Morgan, Rev. A., Letter to Kingwood, 130; Circular Letter by, 136, 150, 167, 170.
———, Mr. Evan, ordination of, 11.
Morris, Rev. Robert, disowned, 173.
Morristown, early history of the Church at, 22.
Mount Bethel, Church at, received, 104.
Mount Holly, Church at, received, 369.

N.

New Britain, Church at, received, 72.
New England, persecution in, 141.
New Jersey, proposal to print the history of Baptists in, 206, 218, 248, 255.
New Mills, Church at, received, 91; advice to, 104.
Newport, R. I., correspondence with, 125.
New Divinity, advice on the, 256.
New Testament, proposal from the New York Association, to revise, 317.
Newtown, Church at, received, 75; advice to, 194.
New York, Church at, received, 89; Letter from, 123; second Church applied, 123, 129; received, 135; advice to, 270, 282; Association appointed at, 131; held at, 135; new Association at, correspondence with, 281, 296, 297, 298, 305, 333, 341, 358, 369, 379, 394, 409, 421, 437.
Niagara, proposal to visit, 283.
Nova Scotia, application from, for preaching, 229.

O.

Officers of the Church, queries, is their membership forfeited with office? 27; whether to be ordained when removed from one office to another? 39.
Opekon, Church at, received, 71.
Ordination, a prerequisite to the administration of ordinances, 30, 49.
Organ, used in public worship, 86.
Oyster Bay, early history of the Church at, 23; advice given to, 82, 129.

P.

Pastoral Address, by Rev. P. P. Vanhorne, 83, 132; S. Jones, 87; I. Stelle, 90, 114; by ———, 92, 125; John Sutton, 95, 105; A. Griffiths, 98, 110, 119; James Sutton, 102; Messrs. Griffiths, Blackwell, and Vanhorne, 119; Messrs. Rogers and Vanhorne, 132.
Pennepeck, advice to the Church at, 56, 59.
Perseverance of the Saints, Circular Letter on, 272; its character, 273; secured by the eternal love of God, 274; union of Divine decrees and grace, 274; by the nature of the divine life, 275; obstructions removed, 275; means are well established, 275; all things overruled to promote it, 276; secures the performance of duty, 276; improvement of doctrine, 277.
Philadelphia, Church at, received, 12, 21; and Pennepeck, advice to, 26; case of meeting-house recommended, 32; advice given to, 65; second Church at, proposed, 108; applied to unite, 113; received, 118; new Church at, received, 379.
Philips' Patent, Church at, received, 112; second Church at, received, 124.
Pigskill, messengers sent to, 130.
Piscataqua, early history of Church at, 13; advice given to, 31, 43; messengers sent to, 32.
Pittsgrove, Church at, received, 116; advice given to, 254.
Pittstown, Church at, received, 228; advice given to, 283.
Polygamist, query on communion with a, 58.
Potts, Mr. Joshua, ordination of, 21.
Powell, Rev. Joseph, death of, 408.
Prayer, Circular Letter on, 397; adoration, 397; confession, 397; petition, 397; deprecation, 397; Lord's prayer, 400; thanksgiving, 400; object of prayer, 401; qualifications, 401; seasons for it, 402; importance of prayer, 404; proved from our spiritual poverty, 404; blessings attendant on it, 404; incentives to prayer, 404; endearing relations in which God stands to us, 405; the promises, 405; successful prayers, 405; exhortation to the duty, 408; concert of, recommended, 306, 359.
Preaching, its lawfulness before ordination, 50.
Presbyterians of New England, privileges of, 115.
Primitive Churches, book on, disowned, 141.
Providence, Divine, Circular Letter on, 164; nature of, 165; mystery of, 165; practical improvement of, 166.

Q.

Quekuky, Association, Letter from, 128.

R.

Ralston, Robert, Esq., kindness of, to the Baptist Missionaries, 423.
Redstone Association, correspondence with, 409, 437.
Religious Worship and the Sabbath day, Circular Letter on, 335; God the ob-

ject of worship, 335; to be performed in the name of Christ, 335; and by the assistance of the Holy Spirit, 336; nature of the fourth commandment, 336; time of worship appointed by Jehovah, 337; change of the Sabbath, 337; way in which the day should be observed, 338.
Repentance unto life, Circular Letter on, 248; definition of, 249; its author, 249; connexion with salvation, 250; and with sanctification, 250.
Review of eighteenth century, Circular Letter on, 362; commencement of Association, 362; events of Revolution, 362; opening prospects, 363; origin of missions, 363; missions from England, 364; to western Indians, 364; duties of the times, 365.
Rhode Island, Baptist College in, 91; support recommended, 91, 99, 101, 109; letter from Charleston on, 135; supported, 142; resolutions of Warren Association respecting adopted, 181.
Ridge, Church at, received, 246.
Rippon, Rev. Dr., Letter from, 236.
Robinson's History of Baptism, proposal to abridge, 424.
Rogers, Rev. W., Circular Letters by, 207, 426.
Rocksberry, early history of Church at, 23; Church at, received, 70.
Ruling Elders, how to be chosen, 29; query on ordination of, 102.
Rutter, Rev. John, disowned, 439.

S.

Sabbath, query as to the change of, 27.
Salisbury Association, correspondence with, 236.
Sanctification, Circular Letter on, 231; signification of the term, 231; necessity of, arising from the fall of man, 231; without it we cannot honor God, 232; was the design of Christ's incarnation, 232; its effects appear in hatred to sin, separation from the law, 232; importance of considering it, 232.
Savannah, new meeting-house for the blacks contributed to, 307.
Scotch Plains, early history of the Church at, 22; received, 57.
Scribe of Association first chosen, 57.
Scriptures, and the Holy Spirit, query on, 82; Circular Letter on, 137; authority of, 137; importance of a proper use of, 137; translations of, in India, encouraged, 423.
Seagrave, Mr. A., disowned, 247.
Selby, Mr. Thomas, arrival of, 12; disturbance created by, 26.
Sermon, by Rev. M. Edwards, refusal to print, 128; Century, by Rev. Dr. Jones, 451; preface to, 452; reasons for writing, 453; sketch of the Churches, 455; character of ministry, 456; increase of the denomination, 457; Mr. Apslund's statistics, 458; effort to obtain freedom, 459; general characteristics of the Baptists, 460; triumph of freedom in Rhode Island, 461; revival under Whitefield, 462; origin of missionary spirit, 462; Baptists in Great Britain, 464; regard of Baptists for education, 464; approaching reformation, 466; improvement of the review, 467.
Seventh-day Baptists, how to be treated, 31.
Shaftesbury Association, correspondence with, 236, 254, 270, 281, 283, 296, 297, 340, 394, 421, 437.
Shemokin, Church at, received, 316; assisted in building meeting-house, 317, 343.
Sideling Hill, application of the Church at, for admission, 279; received, 281; advice to, 297.
Skillman, Mr. J., ordination of, 124; death of, 340.
Slavery, abolition of, recommended, 247; restraint of, desired, 307.
Smalley, Rev. H., Circular Letter by, 299.
Small matters, not to be subjects of contention, 37.
Smiths' Creek, Church at, received, 86; advice to, 95.
Smith, Mr. P., education of, assisted, 131.
Southampton, early history of Church at, 20.
South Carolina Association, correspondence with, 123, 125.
Squam, Church at, received, 409.
Stancliff, Rev. J., death of, 378.
Stamford, messengers to, 130; Church at, received, 135; advice to, 156.
Staughton, Rev. W., Circular Letters by, 318, 351, 440.
Staten Island, contributions for Church at, 238.
Statistics, Rev. B. Morgan appointed to collect, 54, 60; of Churches. (See Churches.)
Stelle, Mr. Benjamin, ordination of, 13.
———, Rev. I., Pastoral Addresses by, 90, 105, 114.
Stennett, Rev. Dr., correspondence with, 114.
Stephens, Rev. Joseph, disowned, 293.
Stonington Association, correspondence with, 236, 270, 296, 297.
Stout, Mr. David, assisted in his education, 271.
Stratfield, separation at, on washing the disciples' feet, 104.

Sutton, Rev. A., death of, 271.
———, Mr. David, ordination of, 86.
———, Rev. Isaac, Pastoral Address by, 102.
———, Rev. John, Pastoral Address by, 95.

T.

Temperance, recommendation of, 239.
Testimony of wives to be received, 283; query on, of non-members, 297.
Thanksgiving, day of, proposed, 193, 349.
Thomas, Mr. David, ordination of, 86.
———, Rev. John, death of, 271.
Thompson, Mr. Charles, assisted in his education, 101, 104.
Trenton and Lamberton, Church at, received, 421.
Tulpohokin, early history of Church at, 23.

U.

Unbaptized persons, not to be communed with, 200.
United States, estimated number of Baptists in, 372.
Universal salvation, doctrine of, opposed by the churches, 173; persons to be excluded for believing, 237; Circular Letter on, 257; nature of the system, 257; no scripture in favor of it, 258; injurious tendency of, 260.
Ustick, Mr. Thomas, assisted in his education, 109; Circular Letter by, 218; death of, 393.

V.

Vanhorne, Mr. P. P., ordained, 12; Pastoral Addresses by, 83, 119; Circular Letter by, 231.

Vanhorne, Rev. W., Circular Letter by, 272.
———, Mr., Jr., assisted in his education, 114.
Vermont Association, correspondence with, 254, 296, 297.
Vincent, Church at, received, 116.
Virginia, formation of Association in, 95; correspondence with, 97, 102, 103, 104, 108, 115, 118, 123, 125, 227; union of Baptists in, 227, 233.

W.

Walton, Rev. J., death of, 115.
———, Mr. S., assisted in his education, 246, 254.
Warren Association, correspondence with, 102, 104, 108, 114, 118, 123, 125, 128, 148, 167, 173, 174, 181, 199, 205, 217, 218, 227, 236, 254, 281, 283, 298, 333, 341, 369, 409, 421, 437; persecution at, 108, 114, 128.
Warwick Association, correspondence with, 281, 305, 324, 333, 341, 348, 358, 369, 378, 394, 409, 437.
Washing of feet, queries on, 119, 130, 283.
Watts, Rev. Dr., Psalms and Hymns, Dobson's edition of, 439.
West Creek, Church at, received, 281.
Welsh Tract, early history of Church at, 15, 456; Association, correspondence with, 316.
White, Rev. W., Circular Letter by, 382.
Wilmington, recommended assistance to, for the removal of their debt, 288.
Winchester, Rev. Elhanan, disowned, 174.
Women, query, whether they may vote in the Churches, 53.
Wood, Mr. Joseph, ordination of, 12.
Worship, how to be maintained without a minister, 27, 31, 35.
Worth, Rev. William, disowned, 247.

THE END.

Appendices

APPENDIX 1 - LIST OF DOCTRINAL SERMONS

In 1759 it was "Agreed and concluded upon, that one of our ministering brethren yearly, and from year to year, who is esteemed qualified in some competent measure, is to preach, at the opening of the Association, upon one of the fundamental articles of the Christian faith, and his subject to be given him by the Association the year before."

Page 79
Minutes of The Philadelphia Baptist Association From A.D. 1707 to A.D. 1807 &c.
(Philadelphia: American Baptist Publication Society, 1851).

DATE	PREACHER & ALTERNATIVE:	SUBJECT:	PAGE:
1760	Isaac Taylor - Abel Morgan	The Being and Attributes of God	79
1761	Abel Morgan - Benjamin Griffith	The Divinity & Authority of the Holy Scriptures	81
1762	Benjamin Griffith - Morgan Edwards	Doctrine of the Trinity	83
1763	Morgan Edwards - David Davis	The State of Man Before and After The Fall	89
1764	John Gano - Samuel Jones	The Recovery of Man	90
1765	Samuel Jones - Isaac Stelle	Effectual Calling	92
1766	Isaac Stelle - Peter Vanhorne	The Incarnation of the Son of God	95
1767	Peter Vanhorne - Benjamin Miller	Final Perseverance	99
1768	Benjamin Miller - John Davis	Imputed Righteousness	102

APPENDIX 2 - LIST OF CIRCULAR LETTERS

"The Association of ministers and elders, from the several Baptist churches, met at Philadelphia, October 12th, 1773, thought it expedient that some plan of the general letter to the churches, some what different from the usual mode of addressing them, should be considered and fixed upon, and nominated Brother Abel Morgan to present a specimen at the next Association; who, considering the case, proposes as follows:

I. That the contents of the general letter shall consist of observations and improvements of some particular article of faith, contained in our Confession, beginning with the first, and so on in order, unless occasion require the contrary; the manner and improvement, whether explanatory, confirmatory, consolatory, or by questions and answers, to be concluded by the writer. Also, that a brother be nominated beforehand, to prepare against the next meeting.

II. Let diligent care be used to caution the churches against innovation in doctrine and practice, and to watch against errors, and avoid them wherever they rise, and by whomsoever they may be propagated.

III. That suitable endeavors be made as heretofore, to resolve cases and questions proposed by the churches, to the best of our knowledge, according to the Scripture.

IV. That all seasonable counsel and advice be given to the churches; and, as occasion may require, let them be pressed with fervency and convincing arguments.

V. That records be kept of all the copies of letters sent from, and received by, the Association."

Page 135-136
Minutes of The Philadelphia Baptist Association From A.D. 1707 to A.D. 1807 &c.
(Philadelphia: American Baptist Publication Society, 1851).

DATE	**PREACHER**	**SUBJECT:**	**PAGE:**
1774	Abel Morgan	The Scriptures	136
1774	Samuel Jones	The Trinity	143
1775	Abel Morgan	God's Decree	150
1776	Robert Kelsay	General Exhortations	156
1778	Samuel Jones	General Exhortations	160
1779	Samuel Jones	Divine Providence	164
1779	Abel Morgan	Fasting and Prayer	167
1780	Abel Morgan	Fall of Man	170
1781	Samuel Jones	God's Covenant	175
1782	Oliver Hart	Christ the Mediator	181
1783	Samuel Jones	The Freedom of Man's Will	194

(CONTINUED: APPENDIX 2 - LIST OF CIRCULAR LETTERS)

DATE	PREACHER	SUBJECT:	PAGE:
1784	John Gano	Effectual Calling	201
1785	William Rogers	Justification	207
1786	Thomas Ustick	Adoption	218
1787	Peter Vanhorne	Sanctification	230
1788	David Jones	Saving Faith	239
1789	Burgiss Allison	Repentance unto Life and Salvation	248
1790	Samuel Jones	Universal Salvation	257
1790	Benjamin Foster	Good Works	261
1791	William Vanhorne	Perseverance of the Saints of Grace	272
1792	Joshua Jones	The Assurance of Grace and Salvation	284
1793	Thomas Fleeson	General Exhortations	293
1794	Henry Smalley	The Law of God - the Moral Law	299
1795	Samuel Jones	The Gospel	309
1796	William Staughton	The Prevalence of Infidelity	318
1797	Thomas Memminger	Christian Liberty and Liberty of Conscience	326
1798	David Jones	Religious Worship and the Sabbath Day	335
1799	Samuel Jones	General Exhortations	344
1800	William Staughton	Proofs of the Divine Origin of the Gospel Witness Within	351
1801	James Ewing	Exhortations to Missionary Activities	362
1802	Thomas B. Montanye	The Baptism of the Holy Ghost	372
1803	William White	The Office-Work of the Holy Spirit	382
1804	Burgiss Allison	Prayer	397
1805	Silas Hough	Brotherly Love	413
1806	William Rogers	Christian Missions	426
1807	William Staughton	What are the Qualifications of a Gospel Minister?	440
1807	Samuel Jones	A Century Sermon	451

THE BAPTIST STANDARD BEARER, INC.
A non-profit, tax-exempt corporation
committed to the Publication & Preservation
of The Baptist Heritage.

SAMPLE TITLES FOR PUBLICATIONS AVAILABLE IN OUR VARIOUS SERIES:

THE BAPTIST *COMMENTARY* SERIES
Sample of authors/works in or near republication:
John Gill - *Exposition of the Old & New Testaments (9 & 18 Vol. Sets)*
   (Volumes from the 18 vol. set can be purchased individually)

THE BAPTIST *FAITH* SERIES:
Sample of authors/works in or near republication:
Abraham Booth - *The Reign of Grace*
Abraham Booth - *Paedobaptism Examined (3 Vols.)*
John Gill - *A Complete Body of Doctrinal Divinity*

THE BAPTIST *HISTORY* SERIES:
Sample of authors/works in or near republication:
Thomas Armitage - *A History of the Baptists (2 Vols.)*
Isaac Backus - *History of the New England Baptists (2 Vols.)*
William Cathcart - *The Baptist Encyclopaedia (3 Vols.)*
J. M. Cramp - *Baptist History*

THE BAPTIST *DISTINCTIVES* SERIES:
Sample of authors/works in or near republication:
Alexander Carson - *Ecclesiastical Polity of the New Testament Churches*
E.C. Dargan - *Ecclesiology: A Study of the Churches*
J. M. Frost - *Paedobaptism: Is It From Heaven?*
R. B. C. Howell - *The Evils of Infant Baptism*

THE *DISSENT & NONCONFORMITY* SERIES:
Sample of authors/works in or near republication:
Champlin Burrage - *The Early English Dissenters (2 Vols.)*
Franklin H. Littell - *The Anabaptist View of the Church*
Albert H. Newman - *History of Anti-Paedobaptism*
Walter Wilson - *History & Antiquities of the Dissenting Churches (4 Vols.)*

For a complete list of current authors/titles, visit our internet site at
www.standardbearer.com or write us at:

The Baptist Standard Bearer, Inc.
No. 1 Iron Oaks Drive • Paris, Arkansas 72855

Telephone: (501) 963-3831   Fax: (501) 963-8083
E-mail: baptist@arkansas.net
Internet: http://www.standardbearer.com

Specialists in Baptist Reprints and Rare Books

Thou hast given a *standard* to them that fear thee; that it may be displayed because of the truth. -- Psalm 60:4

www.ingramcontent.com/pod-product-compliance
Lightning Source LLC
Chambersburg PA
CBHW021825220426
43663CB00005B/129